THE ART OF VERBAL WARFARE

THE ART OF VERBAL WARFARE

RIK SMITS

REAKTION BOOKS

Published by
REAKTION BOOKS LTD
Unit 32, Waterside
44–48 Wharf Road
London N1 7UX, UK
www.reaktionbooks.co.uk

First published 2022
Copyright © Rik Smits 2022

Printed and bound in Great Britain by Bell & Bain, Glasgow

A catalogue record for this book is available from the British Library

ISBN 978 1 78914 594 6

'Talk, I suppose, is a way of defending and attacking,
but I don't need
to defend myself. I don't want to attack you.'

'How kind!'

CONTENTS

PREFACE

This is a book about how people shape and warp their own lives as well as those of others by means of language. It explores the rough and tumble of swearing, cursing, name-calling, quarrelling and rage, and delves into the manoeuverings of intimidation, invective and propaganda. It considers bullying, insults and ridicule as well as impropriety and sexual innuendo, blood-dripping war songs and the now accusatory, now exculpatory lamentations of the blues. But it also looks at how feelings of belonging, intimacy and love are achieved and maintained through what we whisper and write. It is as much about the more exotic aspects of the structure of human language as about its magic, about humour and satire, off-colour and sometimes appalling jokes and good clean fun. So ultimately, this is a story about us and what makes us tick.

Or should I say 'made us tick'? For during the years I've been writing it, people seem to have changed, and not for the better. Loudmouth louts and liars set the tone on and increasingly also off the Internet, which has become all-powerful and not at all the welcoming, creative utopia it was once thought to grow into. Disinterested fact finding and careful research have been discredited by well-intentioned zealots and malevolent manipulators alike, as has the mere idea of objectivity. Open debate is increasingly being stifled by ideologically motivated de-platforming and a callous cancel-culture. Cancelling people, now there's a concept the implications of which are too horrific to even contemplate.

Worse, the forces of intimidation and violence have already brought back censorship in our free, enlightened post-modern world.

I had intended, for good reasons, to show a *Charlie Hebdo* cover by cartoonist Riss in the chapter on satire and propaganda. Nothing blasphemous, just a silly cartoon mocking the stodgy orthodoxy that constrains the lives and freedoms of many Muslims living in the Western world. However, in their own words, 'the publishers weren't convinced by the inclusion of one specific cartoon which might have provoked anti-muslim tension without making any substantial contribution to the argument of the book.'

To me, it just added to the relevance and urgency of what I was doing. For the only strategy for reasonable people – who, lest we forget, still comprise a vast majority – to counter the gathering forces of intimidation, disinformation and deceit begins with recognizing and understanding their ways and means, as well as the workings of our own minds.

On the bright side, much has remained more or less the same. A few truly new developments like social media and big data do present fundamental challenges we'll have to work hard to learn to master, while there is no guarantee that we ever shall. Otherwise, however, much of what we find ourselves confronted with is largely a matter of scale. World-wide trial by media, including apparently novel phenomena like revenge porn, is little more than a modern equivalent of the equally lethal trial by gossip that ruined lives in earlier, more isolated communities. Likewise, anonymous threats, curses, hate speech and most other verbal violence have been with us since the beginning of time.

That said, what keeps you here? Get thee to Chapter One!

1

VERBAL BLOODY WARFARE

'Large scotch,' he ordered. 'No bloody ice.'

This is how, in his autobiographical *The Pigeon Tunnel* (2016), John le Carré pictures the man who inspired him to invent Alec Leamas, the hero of his famous spy novel *The Spy Who Came In from the Cold* (1963). Just those five words, spoken in an airport bar, conjured up a whole person in the mind of the writer. Or rather, the deftly interposed 'bloody' did. By itself, it signalled so much more than the man's wish to ingest a shot of whisky. It spoke of his state of mind and warned both the bartender and the then fledgling author on the next stool not to strike up a conversation with him lightly. It was a one-word psychological report.

It was also a terse example of verbal warfare, the art of using language as a deterrent, to defend your turf, to get your way and make others do your bidding, and as our best means to annoy and deride others, to jeer and to express emotions – even positive ones. Although you won't find anything about most of it in any grammar or coursebook, verbal warfare is ubiquitous and of all times, ranging from simple swearing to highly sophisticated trickery, emotional blackmail and political manipulation. It is a fundamental feature of everybody's life: understanding in good time what someone else is trying to do to you or make you do can make a considerable difference. Ray Charles could not have been more wrong when he sang 'Bricks and stones may break my bones, but talk don't bother me.' Talk can wound, and it often does. Words can mislead, sting and do great damage. In the mouth of a shrewd verbal warrior, words can launch a thousand ships and cajole whole nations into marching willingly towards their own destruction.

Perhaps the most poignant proof of this in history was provided on 18 February 1943 by Nazi-Secretary of Propaganda Joseph

Goebbels in a notorious speech at the Sportpalast in Berlin. By then, things had become very different from the heady early days of the Second World War, when nothing in the world seemed able to slow down the Nazi conquest, let alone stop it. Now, more than three long years into the war, Allied bombers were over Germany every night and the heavily bruised African expeditionary army under General Erwin Rommel was floundering in the Libyan desert. At Stalingrad in Russia, more than half a million German troops had just been lost with nothing to show for it. Even worse, that disaster had quashed all Nazi hopes of availing themselves of the indispensable oilfields of Baku. Doubts and, in the long run, despair lay on the doorstep of the Third Reich, and Reichspropagandaminister Goebbels knew he had to act boldly if he was to nip dissent in the bud.

So that's what he did. In an intoxicating performance centred on the many perfidious things the 'Engländer' said about Germans, he put ten questions to the crowd of loyal partisans and Nazi officials that filled the Sportpalast. Most were typical wartime exhortations to loyalty and devotion to the Reich and its leaders, but number four was different: 'I ask you: do you want total war? And if need be, do you want it more total and radical than we can even imagine it today?' Like the other questions, this one was met by a thunderously cheered 'yes', which duly impressed the real audience Goebbels had in mind: the millions of Germans who were listening in on the radio. What the crowd at the venue saw, but those listeners could not, was the gigantic billboard that ran high along the balcony railing of the Sportpalast, which said: 'TOTALER KRIEG – KÜRZESTER KRIEG' (TOTAL WAR – SHORTEST WAR), and Goebbels did not let on. That way, the horrendous prospect of total war became at once both inevitable and acceptable to the whole German nation in a matter of minutes.

This is propaganda at its most sinister. The other truly pernicious form of verbal warfare is its converse: censorship. Propaganda and censorship are typical weapons of nasty authoritarian regimes, used for the express purpose of misleading, confusing and oppressing people. It is not a coincidence that they were mainstays of all three great genocidal regimes of the twentieth century: Nazism, Soviet-communism and Maoism. But let not that fool us into thinking that propaganda and censorship are the prerogative of criminal regimes alone. Censorship thrives in every non-democratic organization,

Josef Goebbels's speech at the Sportpalast, Berlin, 18 February 1943, photograph by Ernst Schwahn.

such as corporations, semi-public institutions and the civil service everywhere, as well as in families, tribes, clans and cabals. Even democratically organized associations, societies and nations suffer from it in myriad ways. People are routinely bound to secrecy by ritual oath, by the threat of excommunication, by contract, by judicial gagging order, by state security and other laws, or by sheer intimidation. And propaganda of every grade and shape is equally widespread.

Other forms of verbal warfare include libel, slander and insults, from ethnic and racial slurs to blasphemy, each of which, depending on one's whereabouts, can have serious legal consequences, up to and including long-term incarceration or even death. Specifically among Muslims and Hindus, purported cases of blasphemy are regularly used to whip up a lethal frenzy among the populace – notorious Western victims are Salman Rushdie, the Dutch cinéaste Theo van Gogh, the Danish cartoonist Kurt Westergaard and the editorial staff of the French satirical shock-magazine *Charlie Hebdo*.

Strangely, other far more innocuous ways of waging verbal war are much more likely to incur general opprobrium than these. They are what the BBC calls 'strong language', priests and pedagogues 'profanity', and normal people 'swearing', 'cussing' or 'foul-mouthing'. It is the only kind of verbal warfare that has inspired strictly enforced codes of conduct such as the Motion Picture Production Code which stifled Hollywood from 1930 until 1968, and the only kind that all over the world has given rise to associations striving to root out what they consider inappropriate language as zealously as nineteenth-century American temperance societies waged war on alcohol. It has also been the only kind to inspire self-appointed watchdogs of propriety such as the legendary Mary Whitehouse of Nuneaton, England.

In October 1922, when the BBC was the first national broadcasting organization in the world to be incorporated, Whitehouse was twelve years old. It is fair to say that her adult life ran exactly parallel to the spectacular growth and heyday of modern broadcast media: radio and television. She died in 2001 on the brink of the next revolution: the rise of social media and, a few years later, the birth of the smartphone. In a sense, Whitehouse was the broadcast era.

First film, then radio and last but by no means least television did for twentieth-century society what social media are doing to us today: they informed and shocked by exposing to the general public an avalanche of subjects, practices and ideas that had formerly remained under wraps through taboo or the restraints imposed by good manners, or did not travel beyond the intimate circle of personal friends and acquaintances. They shattered the bubbles everybody was living in. Religious, economic and class barriers did not go away, but for the first time they became transparent. The people at large could not wait to satisfy their curiosity about just about everything and everyone outside their own familiar habitat. And, of course, to gorge themselves on the excesses, the transgressions and the scandals of the rich and famous.

Naturally, the new media were immediately seized upon by those who felt they had something to say that dearly needed to be heard: missionary zealots, social reformers, politicians, educators, artists, would-be revolutionaries and fighters for every cause imaginable. People from all walks of life who probably didn't agree on anything but had one thing in common: they strongly felt that something must change. They were rattling the cages of accepted morality, ideology and class.

It is hardly surprising that many had difficulty coming to terms with the openness, the unfamiliar thoughts and attitudes and the new shameless celebrity cult that barged into their lives. The broadcasters staked out their fresh turf with gusto and eagerly explored crossing the boundaries of what was morally and socially acceptable – but from 1964 onwards they found Mary Whitehouse and her following in their way. Whitehouse was a true reactionary who would have nothing of Bob Dylan's 'the times they are a'changing'. She was a staunchly traditional, conservative Christian who balked at what she saw as the depravity and iniquity of the early 1960s and the then budding sexual revolution.

In 1965 Whitehouse founded the National Viewers' and Listeners' Association, a vehicle for criticizing not the shifting public morale itself but what she saw as the excessive portrayal of it on television, meaning bad language and images of a violent or sexual nature. Although this attitude of 'I don't care what festers underneath, as long as I and others don't have to see it' made her the butt of much ridicule, the number of those who secretly supported her was quite large and her influence, although mostly indirect, remains considerable to this day (witness the BBC's often somewhat-squeamish warnings against 'violence', 'strong language' and 'sexual content' requiring 'parental guidance').

It is understandable that Whitehouse and similar-minded individuals and groups in other countries targeted the messenger – the broadcast media and the words and images they sent into the living room – rather than the evils behind it all. Conventional lower-middle-class people everywhere define themselves as decent people, far removed from the unsavoury goings-on that are typical of the riff-raff. Conventional middle-class and upper-middle-class folk consider themselves responsible upstanding citizens, way above the ill-mannered and ill-educated working class and worse. In turn, conventional elitist people define themselves as refined and well-bred personalities, miles above the banalities of hoi polloi. So each class identifies itself not so much by some special achievement or talent as by its restraint. The difference between U and non-U at any level is that U people shudder at a lot that is perfectly acceptable to non-U people. One's social standing is defined by what is not openly acceptable in one's peer group. One of these things was, and to some extent still is, speaking with a regional accent. Another was, and is, swearing.

In England, what would happen once the modern mass media seriously began to make their mark on mainstream society was famously foreshadowed in 1914, at the London opening night of George Bernard Shaw's *Pygmalion*. In the play a Professor Henry Higgins, loosely based on the then renowned phonetician Henry Sweet – actually a grumpy sourpuss who did nothing to live up to his name – takes it upon himself to turn a cockney flower of the gutter called Eliza Doolittle into a sophisticated socialite, just as the mythical sculptor Pygmalion of classical Greece chiselled away at his ideal marble woman. Most importantly, Eliza must learn to speak impeccable King's English. 'Yes, you squashed cabbage-leaf, you disgrace to the noble architecture of these columns, you incarnate insult to the English language! I could pass you off as the Queen of Sheba!', Higgins yells at the poor girl in the colonnade of the Covent Garden theatre. Shaw's real theme is the changes that are becoming noticeable in a society that is slowly wresting itself from the stifling fetters of Victorian morality, the first tiny cracks appearing in the rock-solid class barriers. Those changes are most readily noticeable in what is considered acceptable vocabulary among educated middle-class people. 'I have got accustomed to hear you talking about men as rotters, and calling everything filthy and beastly; though I do think it horrible and unladylike,' Shaw has Mrs Eynsford Hill, a social climber keeping up appearances who is visiting the Higginses, say to her daughter Clara, who immediately retorts by calling her mother old-fashioned and out of touch. But just before this small altercation, the really scandalous thing has happened: the successfully house-trained Eliza, also present, is asked by Clara's brother Freddy if, going home, she will be walking through the park. 'Walk! Not bloody likely,' she answers, reverting to her broad lower-class cockney. 'I am going in a taxi.' At the mention of 'bloody', the audience gasps, flabbergasted at the impropriety of the thing – as Shaw knew it would, for this is literally what the script said:

LIZA: Walk! Not bloody likely. [Sensation.] I am going in a taxi.

Shaw was not to be disappointed. Eliza's 'bloody' caused such sensation among civilized, literate people in Britain that 'bloody' came to be known and referred to as the Shavian Adjective for a while.

To us, such prissiness seems positively droll, and it cannot have been altogether disingenuous either, since by the time *Pygmalion* opened in London the play had already run in Vienna, Berlin and New York, in a German translation with Eliza's 'not bloody likely' rendered as the equally improper *'verdammt unwarscheinlich'*, 'damned unlikely'. In view of Shaw's artistic prestige, chances are that at least some in the audience had a pretty good idea of what they were in for.

Although some commotion about Shaw's unusual choice of words was to be expected, even the rest of the English-speaking world wondered at the peculiar bloody-phobia those Brits displayed. In 1929, fifteen years and a world war after *Pygmalion*, the American literary critic I. J. Semper wrote: 'The American is frankly puzzled by the attitude of the refined Englishman to this word, and inquiry generally elicits the information that the word is frightfully vulgar, not because of any hidden meaning attached to it, but because it is used by frightfully vulgar people.'[1] Certainly the Australians had no qualms about using it, which is why, when the First World War brought an army of Antipodeans to the European front and its cities, the Shavian Adjective quickly changed its guise to become the Great Australian Adjective.

Whatever it was that made the better circles of Great Britain particularly squeamish about poor innocuous *bloody*, the point remains the same: among cultured people, swearing was absolutely not

---

How 'bloody' came to be the 'Great Australian Adjective'

When the highly respectable Melbourne professor Edward E. Morris compiled *Austral English: A Dictionary of Australasian Words, Phrases and Usages* (London, 1898), he piously omitted the already highly popular word 'bloody'. His students took exception to that, and when in 1899 Morris was awarded the first doctorate of letters of the University of Melbourne, where he had set up and run the modern languages department, they put on a burlesque show featuring a bogus doctor toting an enormous tome entitled *The Great Australian Adjective*. That same year, one W. T. Goodie published the following poem with the same title in the *Sydney Bulletin*:

The sunburnt bloody stockman stood,
And, in a dismal bloody mood,
Apostrophized his bloody duddy:
'The bloody nag's no bloody good,
He couldn't earn his bloody food –
A regular bloody brumby*, bloody!'

He jumped across the bloody horse
And cantered off, of bloody course!
The roads were bad and bloody muddy;
Said he: 'Well, spare me bloody days
The bloody Government's bloody ways
Are screamin' bloody funny, bloody!

He rode up hill, down bloody dale,
The wind it blew a bloody gale.
The creek was high and bloody floody.
Said he: 'The bloody horse must swim,
The same for bloody me and him,
is something bloody sickenin', bloody!'

He plunged into the bloody creek,
The bloody horse was bloody weak,
The stockman's face a bloody study!
And though the bloody horse was drowned
The bloody rider reached the ground
Ejaculating 'Bloody? bloody!'

* Wild horse

done. This does not mean that, as a people, the British had ever been averse to swearing or using foul language. On the contrary, during the Hundred Years War, the medieval English were commonly referred to by the French and Joan of Arc herself as *'les godams'*, not because they were goddamned English, but because of their lavish use of the term. In the early twentieth century swearing and foul-mouthing were as rife among the English as ever before. Nor did those prissy post-Victorians show unusual consideration towards others; witness the callous way Higgins dresses down his 'squashed cabbage-leaf' without causing 'sensation'. What did matter was that decent people refrained from uttering certain taboo words. That raises the question as to why this was so important in Shaw's day as well as when Whitehouse crusaded against rude and lascivious TV-talk, and why it remains a matter of importance today. Looking at it from Semper's perspective: what makes people who swear and use taboo terms 'frightfully vulgar'?

@#$%!

IN 1651 THE ENGLISH PHILOSOPHER Thomas Hobbes took a long, hard look at his maligned land, torn limb from limb by civil strife and wholesale bloodshed, and formed a pretty dismal opinion of mankind. Man's most fundamental drive, he concluded, is self-interest. Everybody strives towards a secure, comfortable life for himself, if need be at the expense of others. As a consequence everybody mistrusts their neighbours, and is desperate for a chance to put one over on them. This sorry state, Hobbes said, is man's natural condition, the result of which is a war of all against all that makes life 'solitary, poore, nasty, brutish, and short'.[2] Conditions could improve only if people surrendered their rights and freedom to a stern all-powerful authority keeping order and meting out justice. He named it Leviathan, after the ancient mythical sea monster.

Hobbes was not the only one to take a dim view of man's character, nor would he be the last. The *homo economicus* that economists long believed in and to a considerable extent still do is an equally bleak idea. This 'economical man' supposedly acts exclusively on the basis of rational choices motivated by self-interest. He – or she – is a miserly cheapskate who is in it only for the money. Over the years, however, it has become apparent that people more often than not spend their money based on considerations that are far from rational or even selfish, and that Hobbes was wrong about what makes us tick as well.

Instead of cold-hearted, self-centred self-preservation machines, people are like any gregarious or group species. We are inclined both to further our own interests and to cooperate with others. This means that we normally don't go around stealing from members of our own group, or rob or even kill them just to get our hands on their belongings. But we aren't disinterested altruistic angels either. It is the human condition to be eternally torn between the

Scylla of cooperative altruism that benefits the group (including ourselves) and the Charybdis of unmitigated personal desire and covetousness.

Because of that cooperative streak in us, we have no need for Hobbes's oppressive Leviathan to maintain viable social relations. Instead, we need only keep on signalling our good intentions to our family, friends and all others we have dealings with in everyday life, in order to make it clear that we are not those rogues who simply follow their greedy or hostile instincts and are out to harm others. To do this, we use two strategies.

One is to go out of our way to keep out of everybody else's way. Think deference, think 'ladies first', 'excuse me?' and 'after you'. Think also of how strangers act when they first meet, going through greeting rituals, offering chairs and tea and so on – the modest refusal 'Oh, don't trouble yourself on my account,' countered by the inevitable 'No no, it's no trouble at all.' Cultures differ widely in the precise

U.S. president Lyndon B. Johnson, all smiles, intimidating future Supreme Court associate justice Abe Fortas by invading his personal space, and probably saying something jocularly nasty to him, July 1965.

forms of such introductory pussyfooting, with westerners and northerners generally cutting to the chase rather faster than orientals and southerners, but all cultures have these rituals.

The other is to make a show of not doing certain relatively innocent things that come to us quite naturally but may be unsettling to others on account of their inherently taboo character. Once more, differences between cultures abound, but think of farting, belching, picking your nose, public nudity, public snogging or other indiscreet sexual activity, and laughing and screaming at people. Plus, of course, threatening, belittling or ridiculing people, and swearing. The goal of such restraint is to avoid any undue presumption of intimacy and anything that might betray improper feelings of superiority towards the other, thus granting them room to move and sufficient confidence to let their guard down. It is the abstract counterpart of respecting someone's personal space, that sacred square metre or so around their body that only intimate friends may enter without it proving intimidating.

The pivotal notion here is face, which is a person's own understanding of how others see them. Face depends on a multitude of factors, which may, depending on the culture you're in, include wealth, academic and artistic prestige, marital status and number of children, age, intelligence, wit, celebrity or notoriety, your job, your political power, your family's place in the social pecking order, your position within that family, or even having a rich and powerful husband or a trophy wife. And, of course, looks! In Biedermeier Germany young middle-class men, once settled, set to work on excessive beer bellies, which were considered a sign of prosperity and solidity and so enhanced their face. In nineteenth-century Germany a *Schmiß*, a fencing scar on the face from a *Mensur*, a student duel, did the same for academics and military cadets. It proved that they were courageous red-blooded men. At that time a Western woman's face profited from having alabaster skin. It meant that she did not have to work in the fields for a living, an important point in times when some 95 per cent of the world's population depended on tilling soil or herding cattle for a living. Nowadays, a nice tan is preferred, symbolizing not only health and youth but that the woman in question has time on her hands to lounge in the sun. Last but not least, men literally enhance their faces with martial moustaches, the scraggy beard of the true believer or, since Roman times, the clean-shaven cheeks of civilized citizenship, whereas women across the world literally put on face by using make-up.

There is obviously a lot one can do to create, preserve and enhance face, but eventually everything depends on what others make of you. Face is the mainstay of self-confidence (even if you claim that you don't care what others think of you), and if it's threatened, you react accordingly by clamming up or becoming mistrustful, angry and, above all, uncooperative. Loss of face lets Hobbes raise his ugly head.

Together, deference and face-preserving restraint constitute the core of what is called politeness, a phenomenon that is wonderfully successful at greasing the cogwheels of human interaction, minimizing uncertainty and inspiring mutual trust. Politeness begins and ends with respecting the other's face. It is not egalitarian; a government minister going native on a lowly doorman succeeds only in putting both in an awkward position, as does a worker chumming up to his CEO. Instead, people engaging in polite conversation stick to their social roles and shirk anything that might upset their partners. Typical subjects to avoid in polite conversation are politics, religion and money. Such topics draw attention to class differences and are all too likely to stir up negative emotions such as aggression, uncertainty and embarrassment. Likewise, one avoids using taboo words and expressions related to frightening or combustible phenomena such as sickness, bodily effluvia and sex.

One of the good things about being polite is that it gives people meeting for the first time a chance to size each other up without putting any noses out of joint, and allows them to generate mutual trust, upon which a relationship can be built. The downside is that polite conversation tends to be bland and uninformative, if not downright boring.

Over time, in any culture, many of the elements of polite interaction become codified and ritualized in a sprawling set of systems of rules called etiquette, a term that originally referred to the complex system of ceremonial observances that from the late sixteenth century onwards dominated the day-to-day private life of the kings of France and their family and entourage. For many, etiquette has a bad reputation as a cumbersome and opaque system of seemingly arbitrary dos and don'ts, full of pitfalls. Actually, etiquette, like politeness itself, took shape to facilitate social interaction and allay feelings of insecurity, especially between strangers. Having a standardized, shared set of rules of behaviour in more or less formal situations is a good thing. This is easiest to see in the extreme case of diplomacy.

Diplomatic encounters can be highly flammable and stakes can be high, up to and including the outbreak of full-scale war. So they are dangerous and must be conducted with great care. Often the people involved don't know each other and neither trust nor like each other. Often, also, diplomats are bearers of unwelcome, disappointing news. Moreover, it is not unusual for them to have to champion causes and set demands and conditions they don't personally agree with or believe in. Inevitably, then, there is a lot of second-guessing, reading between the lines and double entendre going on in diplomatic circles, even in the best of cases. In these circumstances, etiquette does a lot to reduce uncertainty about what the other side is doing and implying. The diplomatic world is one where adherence to form, protocol and etiquette is paramount. Really worrying would be an intentional breach of etiquette; it would constitute a clear signal of unwillingness to cooperate – of hostility, even.

At the other extreme of the spectrum are lovers and newly-weds, who wish to share as much as possible, even their most intimate secrets. Between ardent lovers, sheer affection obviates the need for formal politeness or etiquette. There is just no etiquette to nibbling someone's toes or sucking their genitals. The day-to-day goings-on within an ordinary modern Western family are almost as carefree and informal. Most parents and children know each other intimately and treat each other very casually, almost as equals. But even within these families certain points of polite behaviour and etiquette hold, such as in table manners, in requiring the kids to say 'Yes, mum' and 'No, dad' instead of just a gruff 'Yes' or 'No'. To a large extent this derives from the parental effort to socialize children and the desire for a pleasant, untrammelled family life. But it also fits in with the parents' sense of decorum and social standing. And there's the rub.

Etiquette smooths and eases social interaction between people who share their society's codes of conduct. But these codes must be learned; they are not given as part of our biological inheritance. This makes etiquette a weapon as well, suitable for use in the struggle to distinguish oneself from lesser folk and assert one's social standing. Shared knowledge is a very effective means for keeping ranks closed and shutting out others. And so a means to assist in connecting to and keeping in contact with others half turned into a tool for the opposite: separating U from non-U people and impressing the latter. In his *Mémoires* the French king Louis XIV put it this way: 'Since the people we reign over lack real insight, they tend to judge by appearances and usually apportion their respect and obedience according to precedence and rank.'[3] And etiquette was the way to express who was what for all to see. It led to evermore complex rules and rituals, dusted with arcane, often arbitrary niceties, first at and around the court, but soon also among society at large, trickling down through the class system.

Far from disappearing with the French upper classes during the French Revolution, the grip of etiquette on European society became evermore stifling, culminating in the oppressively calcified society of the Victorian age. Similar developments, although not at exactly the same time, took place in cultures such as China and Japan. It took the emancipation of the working classes through socialism and two world wars to break the suffocating grip of etiquette on society, and new technology and widely disseminated increasing prosperity did the rest.

This is not to say that etiquette has lost its relevance. Etiquette as codified politeness still helps to regulate what goes on in the workplace, in theatres and restaurants, at functions and even at home. And it still functions to mark class distinctions, albeit to a far lesser degree than it did in Victorian times. People are just too insecure to be able to dispense with preserving face, and etiquette is eminently cut out for the job of keeping that intact. In fact, the new digital media seem to have caused the emergence of a whole new area of etiquette, namely sexual play. Now that pornography has moved from being hush-hush hard-to-obtain to just a mouse-click away at any time, anywhere, it seems that young insecure girls have come to think that the correct way to give their partner a blow job is to pull the same faces and produce the same noises as porn actresses typically do, *including* looking up as if into a camera. It is a sobering thought that the whole emancipatory process of liberation and relaxation of norms, mores and etiquette that got under way in the nineteenth century and culminated in the sexual revolution of the 1960s and '70s has ultimately resulted in the emergence of a new bedroom etiquette based on the crass ceremonies of the average porn video.

Returning to Semper's question, it is now clear what makes people who swear so frightfully vulgar. It is not that they swear per se. Rather, the likes of Semper live by certain standards of politeness and etiquette, which people who swear fail to comply with, out of habit or on purpose, as an act of verbal warfare. Verbal warfare is everything that flies in the face of cooperative politeness, from insult to manipulation, from emotional outcry to insidious falsehood and blatant untruth, and from denial of the obvious to the repression of free thought and speech. And swearing is its cudgel. It is its least sophisticated instrument, but it can be bloody effective.

2

FIRE AND BRIMSTONE

Hayduke, under the hair and sunburned hide, appeared to be
blushing. His grin was awkward. 'Well, shit,' he said. 'Fuck, I don't
know, I guess . . . well, shit, if I can't swear I can't talk.' A pause.
'Can't hardly think if I can't swear.'
'That's exactly what I thought,' said Bonnie. 'You're a verbal
cripple. You use obscenities as a crutch.'

The ecological activist Bonnie Abzug, a protagonist of Edward
Abbey's adventure novel *The Monkey Wrench Gang* (1975), was
not alone in considering swearing and using obscenities a sign
of a lack of sophistication and inability to put thoughts and feelings
into appropriate words. Nearly four centuries earlier, Shakespeare
had Hamlet lament in sheer frustration: 'What an ass am I . . ./ That I,
the son of a dear father murder'd,/ Prompted to my revenge by heaven
and hell,/ Must, like a whore, unpack my heart with words,/ And fall
a-cursing, like a very drab,/ A scullion!' (*Hamlet*, II.2). The prince's
frustration is twofold: he can revenge himself only with words, and
in doing so is reduced to swearing, the weapon of 'a very drab, a
scullion', in contemporary terms a despicable lowlife, a deplorable.

Hamlet was right about one thing: for the time being, he lacked
the power to do anything about the murder of his father except hurl
hollow words. But other than that he was wrong. Swearing and hurling obscenities may be the preferred weapons of the coward, but not
necessarily of people as low down the social ladder as 'a very drab,/
A scullion'. On the contrary, those at the bottom of the social ladder
have always been reputed to be more prone to physical violence
than princes, and quite likely they were more feisty than princes
in Shakespeare's rougher age as well. Princes are taught to exercise
greater restraint. As with physical violence, so with verbal fire and
brimstone. Swearing is a means of expressing great anger and deep
frustration, regardless of one's station in society. It is only appropriate
that language so used transgresses the limits of normal conversation

and decency, for it expresses emotions that transgress those same limits. True verbal aggression is first and foremost an effective warning that the swearer may no longer act rationally and is on the brink of becoming physically violent. In this regard it functions in the same way as the hissing of a cat or the threatening growl and bared teeth of a dog. It also serves as a useful lightning rod for funnelling off aggressive energy. Let a truly exasperated man rant, and before long he'll most likely run out of steam.

On the other hand, loud, shocking, threatening and intimidating verbal abuse is highly unsettling because it directly reflects our instinctive, primeval urges. It brings out the Hobbesian beast in us, which is not a pretty sight and precisely what civil behaviour is supposed to mask. This is why under any circumstances, even under great pressure, swearing is frowned upon by decent, civilized people.

Whereas Hamlet was at least half right, Abbey's Bonnie Abzug is completely wrong, first in calling Hayduke a verbal cripple. Hayduke appears to be as capable of expressing himself as the next man; he is just in the habit of interspersing what he says with swear words. But look closely at the quotation, and you'll see that all his swear words are in slots where we might also put a procrastinating 'eh':

'Well, eh,' he said. 'Eh, I don't know, I guess . . . well, eh, if I can't swear I can't talk.'

So Hayduke, a former green beret, might actually be right in claiming that he can hardly think or talk if he can't swear. The swear words he employs to this end are fillers exactly like 'eh', giving him time to mull things over. And actually, he is doing something rather nifty: he is filling the 'eh' slots in his sentences with a running commentary on his state of mind. Although there might be, there is not even a hint of anger or any other negative emotion in Hayduke's speech quoted above; all that his swear words signal is a perfectly normal state of slight arousal from the effort of thinking and conversing with Bonnie. It would seem that emotionally charged words just seep into the 'eh' slots in his sentences. If his level of arousal rises, either to the positive or negative, it won't be the words he uses that change, but his tone of voice. 'Shii-it, did you *fucking see* that?' may equally well signal exasperation as admiration, but never equanimity.

Le Carré's neighbour at the airport bar in Chapter One did something rather different when he ordered his 'large scotch, no bloody ice'. His 'bloody' signalled a measure of irritation or preoccupation, and it was not in a low-current 'eh' slot. Instead, he used an adjective, a very common strategy in English for signalling irritation, stress and frustration. Yet the drinker did not mean that there was something wrong with the ice at the bar, nor did he in all probability want to inform the bartender that he did not like the taste of ice. Rather, from where the drinker sat, there was something 'bloody' about the whole situation. He *felt* 'bloody'.

This is the kind of swearing that is typical of people who are preoccupied with something, angry or battling some kind of adversity. It is the car mechanic in a tight spot, arm outstretched from underneath the bonnet, commanding 'Give me the fucking number ten spanner!' It is the fed-up parent at dinner barking to their son 'Put that bloody phone away already!' But as before, the emotions signalled need not be negative. Someone saying 'And you know what? He turns up in a bleedin' *minicab*!' about the Moldavian prime minister visiting Downing Street expresses mainly amused astonishment, and 'You'll never guess what's happened: I've won the fucking lottery!!!' radiates surprise and delight.

All these instances of swearing are expressions of one's current emotional state, from minimal arousal to outright exhilaration. What is called cathartic swearing is a bit different. Cathartic swearing is the way we tend to respond to unexpected strong jolts, such as touching a hot stove, hitting your thumb instead of the nail or dropping your smartphone into the toilet bowl. At moments like this, either a primeval shriek or shout escapes us, or a swear word or two. Instead of 'Aaargh!' or good old 'Ouch!' we might yell 'Shit!', 'Bloody hell!' or 'Jesus!' Cathartic swearing occurs with sudden emotions such as being startled, shock and surprise, but not mere anger, which builds up much more slowly. Once more, the emotions can be negative or positive, as when someone unexpectedly finds a brother presumed dead standing on the doorstep and only manages to stammer: 'F-fuck!'

@#$%!

ONE OF THE MOST intriguing aspects of swearing, and cathartic swearing in particular – the kind we least control – is this: why is it that obviously negative and taboo terms are so often used to express positive emotions? It is not for lack of suitable positive terms. Exclamations such as 'Fantastic!', 'Terrific!', 'Hooray!', 'Great!', 'Nifty!', 'Cool!' and 'Huge, man!' are clearly and exclusively positive. Nobody in their right mind would vent an equally heartfelt as inadvertent 'Fantastic' on painfully stubbing his toe or witnessing a car slam into a pedestrian. 'Wow!' and 'Awesome!', even 'Hallelujah!', are clearly neutral with a positive twist. They come out frequently in the rush of joy caused by realizing one has won a prize or when casting eyes on the most adorable girl or the juiciest hunk on Earth for the first time. They are often the equivalent of an admiring, impressed wolf whistle. But they escape many of us just as easily on seeing a boxer downing his opponent, or when watching American army choppers blaring Wagner while they strafe rice fields dotted with Vietnamese farmers in *Apocalypse Now*. They are used to express joy, but also admiration, shock and awe. They signify thrills, but not truly negative ones. They are fit for stylized horrors such as boxing and Hollywood violence, not actual slaughter. Someone gasping 'Awesome' or 'Fucking brilliant' on witnessing a truck ploughing through a pavement full of Christmas shoppers obviously has a screw loose. (Either that, or he is a teenage boy attempting to preserve his cool among his peers.)

In fact, while cases abound of negative terms such as 'bloody', 'shit' and 'fuck' being used to express positive and semi-positive emotions and thrills, I have only ever come upon a single case of a positive term being used to express something resembling a negative emotion. This happened when an amateur football player, running at breakneck speed to keep the ball from going out while an adversary tried to wrest control over it from him, vented his concentration, physical exertion and fear of losing the ball by means of a loud, long drawn-out 'Motheeeeeeeeeeeer!' The real question, then, is why negative emotional terms seem perfectly capable of expressing positive emotions while, sarcasm excepted, the opposite is not true. So far, nobody has offered an unequivocal explanation, so let's have a go ourselves. To do so, we must first take a closer look at what emotions, positive and negative, actually are.

The fundamental principle governing any organism is homeostasis, which basically means keeping your act together. All organisms try to stay alive, to which end they strive to maintain their integrity with respect to the world outside and a healthy equilibrium within. At heart, life is an inveterate dullard, conservative and risk-averse.

From its point of view any occasional imbalance, even any sensation at all constitutes an unwelcome disturbance of the precious peace and quiet. In a sense, life prefers to play dead.

Only some of the simplest creatures actually achieve this oblivious ideal of *dolce far niente*. They are monocellular spongers whose only activity, if we can call it that, is to absorb the nutrients they float around in. Throughout their lives they enjoy homeostasis, unless they are dividing in order to keep the species going. The downside is that they are completely dependent upon a stable, all-inclusive environment to cater to their every need. They have no strategies, no skills, no defences. If their internal balance is disturbed in any way, say by a shortage of nutrients or fluids to float in, they die.

As soon as organisms increase in complexity, they develop more specific needs, which means that they have to adopt a more active stance with respect to their survival. They develop urges and drives that make them get up and search for specific foods and look for partners to ensure the continued existence of their species. Hunger, thirst and sexual arousal are self-generated disturbances of the internal balance, bouts of discomfort that serve a greater good.

But this is only half the story. A powerful sex drive is a good thing, as is a reliable hunger signal. But there have to be braking systems as well. It is all very well for Sloane Rangers to shop till they drop, but a burst gut from overeating, oedema from over-ingesting water or bruised private parts or, heaven forbid, a heart attack from indulging in a never-ending sexual frenzy is in nobody's interest. This is where positive emotions come in: the feeling of satisfaction after a hearty meal, which is more than just the absence of hunger; the contentedly mellow, sadly short-lived condition following orgasm, which also differs from a state of mere non-arousal.

Such emotive pairs of drive and fulfilment are mostly regulated by hormones. Take hunger. First the lining of the empty stomach starts secreting ghrelin, which makes you feel hungry. Then, eating not only stops the secretion of ghrelin, but causes depleted fat cells to be replenished. These fat cells signal their happiness by releasing another hormone, leptin, which makes you feel satiated. Likewise, testosterone and oestrogen make men and women feel horny, whereupon engaging in satisfactory sexual activity triggers the release of hormones such as oxytocin and endorphins, which cause a sense of general well-being and satisfaction.

Hormone-regulated emotions such as these are slow, and may take minutes, hours or even days to build up before they are quenched. The release is fast by comparison; satiation sets in even before one finishes eating. What may linger is the feeling that you have overdone it, 'stuffed' yourself, which need not be unpleasant in itself, but is not the same. In sex, not long after orgasm everything is back to normal, and lovers go about their business as if nothing happened. What lingers is just a memory, which can be very pleasant but, again, is not the same.

Many common emotions aren't like that at all. They strike as fast as lightning and abate relatively slowly. The archetype is fright, which takes over when something unexpected and possibly untoward happens. It is that involuntary hair-raising stiffening of the body accompanied by instantaneous goose pimples and often some kind of uncontrolled shriek, which may take the form of a curse. Fright is an unspecified call to arms from the senses to the brain, an electrochemical signal relayed through the nerves in a matter of milliseconds. The brain then decides what to do: is there a real threat? If so, how can it best be met? We all know what the brain decides when someone makes you jump for no good reason, by accident or as a prank. Your brain gets angry – 'You sod!' – or annoyed – 'Oh, for God's sake, William!' – and will stay that way or return to normal, depending on your general disposition at the time.

Most quick emotions are negative; they are danger signals requiring an immediate response. Their source is sensory: a sudden sound, something you see or feel, or even smell – 'Oh God, the spuds!' Fright, by definition, lasts only as long as it takes the brain to man battle stations (which includes ordering the secretion of the stress hormone cortisol) and decide on fight or flight. From there on, we use more specific names for what has overcome us: fear, panic, horror, revulsion, rage and whatnot. And, of course, shock – the temporary inability to react at all – which may be a remnant of an earlier freezing response, or just the consequence of momentary emotional overload. In its mild form shock may not amount to more than someone stammering 'What the . . .?' and halting for a second or two, but it may also leave a person seriously out of whack for hours or days.

Lest we forget, there exists at least one positive quick emotion: elation. This is the emotion that prompts gasps and cries of 'Ooooh!' from the audience at a spectacular fireworks display, or from a six-year-old on his birthday setting eyes on the bicycle he has so ardently been wishing for. It may give rise to exclusively positive exclamations such as 'Yippeeee!', 'Fantastic', 'Terrific' and 'Cool, mum', but may occasionally elicit a heartfelt 'Jesus Christ!', 'Bloody hell!' or 'Holy shit!' as well.

By and large, all these emotions are the province of relatively old parts of the brain, our reptilian brain, so to speak. Swimming pools and saunas show us that the much younger neo-cortex, which is, among other things, the seat of consciousness and structured thinking, takes a back seat here. When you are sitting on the edge of an outdoor pool in spring or the cold tub in a sauna, you are eminently aware of the cold sensation that awaits you. Yet when you jump in, your body reacts every bit as surprised as it always does, with stifled breath and goose pimples galore. Similarly, when children are dared to touch something really icky, such as a slimy toad, a hairy spider or a dead animal, they may take minutes of full concentration to force themselves to do it, putting their finger ever closer to the revolting target, only to startle and shriek on finally making contact, as if they had never seen it coming: 'Ieeeeeeeeeeeeeeeeeee!'

Another sign of the tenuous connection between these quick emotions and consciousness is the fact that we can deliberately anticipate them by mimicking the experience. If you know something is probably going to hurt, you may find yourself uttering some kind of 'Ouch!' expression way before the pain actually hits you. If you have to do something truly revolting, such as cleaning up somebody's vomit, a decaying mouse carcass or a dog turd on your doorstep, you may find yourself showing all the outward signs of revulsion before you actually come into contact with anything. These anticipatory actions aim to mitigate the shock of the eventual experience, to prepare you for what's coming. You may even do some swearing: 'Oooh shit . . . ooh shit.' But it never really works. The jolt to your brain on impact is almost as bad as when the sensation comes as a surprise. It may help, however, to keep better control of your body when the shit actually hits the fan – or you hit the shit, as the case may be.

All this is very different from slow emotions. You can relish the anticipation of a good meal, even without being hungry yet. Likewise, you can dream of the steamy sex that may be in store for you if you play your cards right tonight. But you typically don't do all that by making the appropriate noises. There is no contented throaty nyam-nyam-growling involved, nor any kissing sounds or panting. At best the prospect of a meal might elicit something like 'Yummy, can't wait for those bangers!', or we might lick our lips. As for sex, people usually do their best not to let on about their plans and desires at all, and especially avoid licking those lecherous lips.

On the other hand, slow emotions can be repressed or ignored. We have a considerable measure of control over them. People can fast or keep to a rigorous regimen for long stretches of time, and Roman Catholic clergy are supposed to sublimate their sexual urges throughout life. Some slow emotions, such as sexual arousal, will spontaneously abate even without release. Once more, quick emotions are different. Although the British stiff upper lip may suggest otherwise, quick emotions are as keenly felt by stiff-upper-lippers as by anyone else. The fright is there; their restraint just helps them to regain control so fast that they can by and large suppress the secondary reaction. They dampen their natural behavioural *response* to an emotive electrochemical signal, but the signal itself and the fight-or-flight decision process it triggers in the brain remain unchanged.

So slow and quick emotions seem to differ in almost every respect: the former are induced by hormones, build up gradually, have a relatively short release period ending in a normal condition, and can to some extent be suppressed or ignored. Quick ones are electrochemically induced, can be anticipated by mimicking them, strike in a flash and then give rise to an enduring state of distress, false alarms apart. Also, the majority of slow emotions seem positive in nature, working from the inside towards homeostasis, whereas most quick emotions are negative and cause temporary disruption of homeostasis in order to deal with external threats. However, there is one thing that binds them: when they become a reality, both slow and fast emotions are usually accompanied by snorts, grunts or shrieks, or by cathartic swearing.

The root of this vociferousness lies with the limbic system, a complex of old brain structures that, among other things, handles emotions and sensations such as smell and pain. It also includes what is called the rage circuit, which can make its owner explode into blind and chaotic violence. If your cat shrieks and claws at you when you step on its tail, that's the rage circuit unleashed. It functions as a last-resort tactic, a desperate manoeuvre in what is experienced as suddenly life-threatening circumstances. From an evolutionary point of view such a device makes excellent sense: if you unexpectedly find yourself backed into a corner and about to become breakfast, all you can do is dazzle and damage your assailant as best you can, hopefully confusing him sufficiently for you to have a chance to make off to safety.

However terrifying it may make a creature look, the rage response is not normal aggressive behaviour, which serves to ward off an attacker, chase away a rival or catch prey. First and foremost it is a signal, a message meant to impress and confuse a perceived enemy when overpowered or taken by surprise. This makes it an extreme example of the ancient animal communication system that is still active within us – extreme in that it takes signalling a step further, into actual no-holds-barred aggressive action.

Animal communication systems, including our own, must not be confused with human language. Although both are used for communicative purposes, they are so different that they would seem to be almost completely unrelated. Animal systems typically comprise a very limited number of signals, at most a few dozen, each with its own specific and immutable meaning. The signals are for the most part innate; they need not and indeed cannot be learned. Animal systems are also invariably closed, meaning that no new signals can be added to the system during life. Even though certain songbirds learn the details of their largely innate songs from their parents, vervet monkeys must learn the precise meanings of their three alarm calls and there do seem to be group accents in certain species: no bird will ever come up with a completely new, really different song, nor will a singing whale ever come up with the Marseillaise or be-bop-a-loo-lah. By contrast, the average human individual's lexicon contains 30,000 words easily, and there is no fixed link between the sound pattern of a word and its meaning. To give an example, the spoken form *masa* means tortilla dough in Middle America, mass, mash or crowd in Dutch and table in Turkish. Conversely, a house is called *maison* in French, *ev* in Turkish and *bahay* in Tagalog. Not a single word of any human language is innately given, so they must be learned one by one, a never-ending task that begins in infancy. Human language is an open system; new words are invented or imported from other languages daily and often find their way into the long-term shared lexicon of a language.

Next, the signs of animal systems are isolates, meaning they cannot be combined to create new, more articulate messages. None of the claims that have been made to the contrary has ever been substantiated. As a consequence the number of expressions in any animal communication system is no greater than the number of signals it contains. The only meaningful variation concerns the intensity of a signal, as in bee dancing, where the enthusiasm of the dancer is directly proportional to the value of the reported find. In these respects, too, human language is the exact opposite. People typically combine the basic signals of their languages into larger units called phrases and sentences, thereby creating completely novel messages. Owing to the properties of the rules for doing so, our language faculty allows us to create a literally infinite number of different messages.

There are many more deep differences between language and animal communication systems, but the really important one here is multimodality. The signals of animal communication systems are multimodal, which means that they can be carried by any means available. Many animals mark their territories by scent; countless kinds of insect signal 'not edible' through the colours and patterning of their carapace; and Californian ground squirrels threaten rattlesnakes by raising the temperature of their tails a degree or two, which the snakes can sense. In addition, many signals are quite complex amalgams of different types of cue. An angry cat will simultaneously hiss *and* bare its teeth *and* put up its back *and* raise the hair on its tail. A very scared dog will crouch down or even roll on to its back *and* whimper *and* nervously wag its tail *and* exude the stench of fear, all inextricably bundled up into one holistic message: 'I'm yours, I acknowledge your anger, have mercy on me.' Take parts of the amalgam away, and other animals have trouble understanding the signal.

At first glance, the expressions of human languages do not seem to be all that different, for we use several modalities as well. Our messages are usually transferred by sound, but may also reach their destination along a visual path, as in reading or in sign language, which involves gestures and postures as carriers of meaning. Even touch can be marshalled, as Braille or the exceptional Helen Keller show. Born in Alabama in 1880, Keller had gone both blind and deaf before she turned two. Her governess, the tireless Anne Sullivan, found a way into her isolated mind by spelling out words in Keller's palms by means of finger tapping, more or less like Morse code. Keller caught on to what Sullivan was doing at about the age of seven, and she went on to have a remarkable career as an intellectual celebrity, mastering Braille as well as lip-reading with her fingers on the way. She even acquired some sign language and learned to speak, although her speech, which she could not monitor, remained difficult to understand. Despite this wide range of modalities, Keller communicated in the same way all people do: once a conduit had been chosen, be it gesturing, speech or finger tapping, she held on to that single modality at least for as long as a single complete utterance, just like the rest of us. Nobody ever switches from speaking to writing in mid-sentence, for instance. Unlike animal signs, there exist no words that can be expressed only by a combination of sound and gesture, or a gesture and writing.[1]

And yet it is precisely here – and only here – that the worlds of animal communication systems and human language touch. Many if not most of the signals in the communication systems of at least mammals, the class of animal we ourselves belong to, involve a sound. These sounds are not random. They are structured and well defined. It follows that somewhere in a dog's brain, the precise motor instructions for producing a correct bark, growl, yelp or whimper must be stored. In addition, dogs know exactly when a bark is in order, or a growl, a whimper or a yelp, just as adult vervets, which have a repertoire of different warning cries for airborne, tree-borne and terrestrial threats, know full well when to use which call. In short, an inventory of all sound patterns, plus information about which complex signals they are part of and to which sensory inputs and emotions they are linked, must be part and parcel of each animal's communication system.

Such an inventory looks a lot like a simple version of the mental lexicon of human languages, which at minimum comprises an inventory of the sound patterns of words, each accompanied by the motor instructions for producing them, plus information about their grammatical category (noun, verb and so on) and peculiarities, their precise forms, and their meaning and connotations. It seems not unlikely, then, that in the course of the evolutionary development of early *Homo sapiens* into 'us', the existing inventory of animal signals served as a seed upon which the lexicon of what was to become human language could grow, more or less as a grain of sand in an oyster can be the seed upon which a pearl can develop. This is not to say that the animal inventory simply expanded into our mental lexicon. For one thing, the original animal inventory is obviously

Twenty-one ways to say 'ouch'					
Arabic	*uwsh*	Indonesian	*aduh*	Russian	*oy*
Chichewa	*phula*	Italian	*ahia*	Spanish	*ay*
Chinese	*āiyō*	Japanese	*itai*	Tamil	*accō*
Dutch	*au*	Kirgizian	*uç*	Thai	*xúy*
French	*aie*	Korean	*aya*	Turkish	*ah*
Greek	*och*	Mongol	*tiim ee*	Xhosa	*i-ouch*
Hungarian	*jaj*	Punjabi	*ā'uṭa*	Yoruba	*orch*

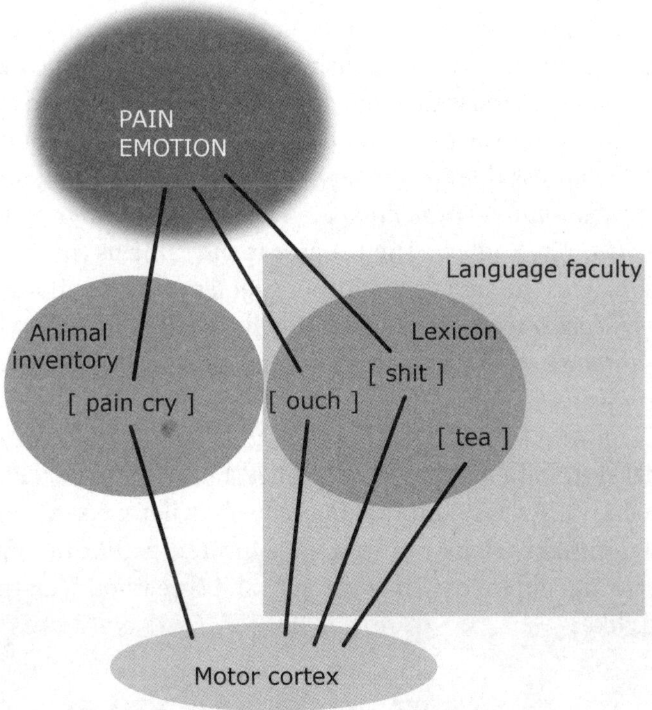

Why our animal pain cries, conventionalized cries like 'ouch' and associated words
like 'shit' occur in cathartic swearing, and a neutral term like 'tea' does not.
It looks like the animal inventory can reach the motor instructions for producing
'ouch' and 'shit' through their association with quick, overwhelmingly negative
emotions, and thus produce all three cathartic signals.

still there, next to and independent of the lexicon. For another, the sound patterns in the animal inventory remain largely given, but not those of the words that fill the human lexicon. It does mean, however, that both the animal inventory and the human lexicon in us are most likely structured on the same basic principles and might to some extent be transparent to each other.

If this is indeed what happened, it would be no surprise if the two systems rub off on each other in those areas where they share properties. And the one thing words and animal signals have in common is a sound pattern.

To some extent, then, the sound patterns of animal signals might be subjected to rules and processes that, strictly speaking, should operate only on real words. And this actually happens. Many animal signals, but not all, have been phonetically bent and honed to fit the limited subset of all possible speech sounds that a particular language uses. Thus the standard 'I'm suddenly in pain' signal is usually pronounced *ouch* in English, *aua* in German and *au* in Dutch. Only when the pain is extreme do these conventionalized forms give way to the primeval animal pain shriek. Likewise, the sound people make to express their joy at seeing or eating something delicious is rendered as *mmmm* or *nomnom* in Dutch, and as *mmmm, yummy* or *nyam nyam* in English. The process is the same as that which conventionalizes the signals that other species produce. The same cock crows *cocorico* according to the French, *kükelekü* in the Netherlands, *cock-a-doodle-do* if it's up to an English person and *ha-ii-ha-e* if you ask a Navajo.

Given this connection between our language faculty and the animal system in us, we would expect there to be a certain amount of creep both ways, and that is precisely what we see. On the one hand, animal shrieks can to a very limited extent be marshalled to serve in sentences. Thus we get 'She screamed "Aaargh!"' and things like:

where you say the words and then do the (animal) bewilderment gesture-with-grimace. The possibilities are real, but they are highly restricted. Animal signals, whether oral or visual, can only be cited, they can't really be integrated into a normal sentence.

On the other hand, animal signals may replace their original sounds with their conventionalized form, and even by a sound pattern borrowed from a fully fledged word in the lexicon, as long as that word is emotionally sufficiently compatible. So instead of the animal system blurting out 'Aargh!', we may hear ourselves exclaim 'Ouch!', 'Damn!', 'Fuck!' or 'Drat!', or even 'Jesus bloody Christ!' And there we have it: cathartic swearing.

All this points to what I'll call the Cathartic Swearing Hypothesis: the existence of something like a pathway linking certain elements of the lexicon of a human language to the inventory of animal signals. Whatever this hypothetical pathway may turn out to be, we would expect that it mainly links sound patterns of emotionally charged words and set phrases to animal signals, because these signals are virtually all directly linked to emotions. Since the emotions involved are mostly quick, negative emotions, the bulk of the links will be to emotionally negatively charged words. And so it is that negative terms frequently crop up in the context of positive emotions, whereas positive terms show up only rarely in emotionally negative contexts.

But wait: what about someone snarling 'Oh, great!' on knocking over a glass of milk? That's sarcasm, an intellectual ploy that will not occur if someone is truly taken unawares. Or not immediately, at least. For instance, if you spill hot tea into a colleague's lap, you're likely to hear something like 'Aaargh! Oh, great, now look what you've done,' or 'Shit! Oh, great, now . . . !' Only the 'Aaargh!' and 'Shit!' parts are cathartic here.

@#$%!

OUR CATHARTIC SWEARING Hypothesis helps to explain a couple of other things as well. One is why habitual swearers such as Hayduke always fill their sentences with negative and taboo terms such as 'fuck' and 'shit'. Why don't they, even when they are perfectly happy, ever spontaneously say things like:

> 'Well, terrific,' he said. 'Hallelujah, I don't know, I guess . . .
> well, fantastic, if I can't swear I can't talk.'

Tourette's syndrome

An ill-understood phenomenon is Tourette's syndrome, which is unjustly famous for coprolalia, the involuntary uttering of obscenities, swear words, and insulting words and phrases. In reality, to qualify as a patient one must be affected by some combination of a broad array of motor tics, at least one of which is vocal. Tics are a typical breakthrough phenomenon, disrupting whatever physical activity a person is engaged in and as such not part of any normal activity. Rather they seem to reflect some maladjustment of the electrochemical inhibitors in the brain that dampen involuntary and spurious motor activity.

Tourette's syndrome is fairly common, occurring in about 1 per cent of the population. It usually presents itself in childhood, reaching its apogee in adolescence. After that, symptoms tend to wane. In many people the symptoms are so mild that they are unaware their condition even has a name and are never diagnosed. Extreme cases, on the other hand, can put quite a strain on a patient's daily life.

The prevailing myth is that Tourette's is characterized by the irrepressible and highly embarrassing urge to utter obscenities or swear words. Although such cases do occur, they are quite rare. More than 90 per cent of Tourette's patients never utter anything untoward. In fact, the words or phrases a patient will get stuck on seem completely random, even including such bizarre and unexplainable things as 'cup of coffee!'

Actually, this would be no surprise if it is indeed the animal system that is doing the filling, spurred on directly from the limbic system. Once more, most of the sound patterns in the inventory are linked to negative emotions, so the sound patterns borrowed from the human lexicon that will come out will generally be those of negatively charged words.

The other thing is an intriguing phenomenon among people suffering from Broca's aphasia. Aphasia is a cover term for a broad range of language disorders brought on by accidents and strokes that destroy part of the brain structures involved in producing utterances or processing incoming language. These structures are by and large located in the left hemisphere of the brain, in areas close to the temple and the ear. Since there is no telling where exactly a stroke or accident will strike or how extensive the damage will be, no two patients are exactly the same. Some lose all capability to speak and understand, and others manage to make a quasi-complete recovery, but most end up somewhere between those two extremes. Among the endless variations, two identifiable groups stand out. One consists of people who have serious trouble understanding language, but are still capable of fluent, albeit meaningless, speech. This syndrome is called Wernicke's aphasia, after the nineteenth-century German neurologist Carl Wernicke, who first identified part of the left temporal lobe, an area just behind the left ear, as the one typically affected in such cases.

The other group suffers from Broca's aphasia, a syndrome named after the French physician Paul Broca, who in 1861 announced his discovery of a brain area just in front of and a little above the left ear that was crucial to the production of human language but did not affect comprehension. Disregarding any other brain functions affected by their particular trauma, people with damage to Broca's area typically have trouble finding words and using the grammatical glue for combining them into neat sentences. In short: they know what they want to say, but have trouble getting it out. They speak slowly and haltingly, if at all, and in a telegrammatic style. It is their bane that the impatient world of carefree people often mistakes them for mentally disabled on account of it.

The strange thing about Broca patients is that even people who have lost their powers of speech completely can often still swear to some extent. This means that someone may not be able to tell you what he sees when shown a picture of a turd or a cowpat, but may blurt out 'Shit!' or 'Dammit!' in exasperation at his own inability. How is it possible that they cannot say a word they obviously *can* say? This conundrum is immediately solved by the Cathartic Swearing Hypothesis. If a person cannot say a word any more, the normal pathways from the lexicon through the language faculty to the motor cortex have obviously been blocked or cut off at some point. But the animal system and its inventory may be unaffected, so that grunts and cries and other animal signals will come out normally. So will the sound patterns of swear words and taboo words associated with an animal signal through the emotional centres of the brain. And they will do so only as isolated, emotionally driven signals.

@#$%!

WHEN PEOPLE TALK about swearing, they may refer to several very different types of utterance. English has become a murky language in this respect, for at its core, the verb 'swear' of course refers to the act of taking an oath. Indeed, right up to the nineteenth century, that was all it referred to. Only then did its meaning begin to broaden, and by the end of the century it encompassed almost any kind of expression, any utterance that people might take exception to. Nevertheless, there is not nor ever was anything wrong with taking an oath, although there is no real evidence that such moral pressure actually 'works' other than the American psychologist Dan Ariely's famous experiment of 2008. There, he found that people who were reminded of the Ten Commandments before playing some game were more honest than others who had not been so cautioned. Unfortunately, when researchers replicated the experiment in 2018, they found no effect at all.

Regardless, oaths have been an important tool of courts and other authorities throughout history and remain so today. Putting people under oath is standard practice when we want to pressure witnesses into telling the truth, however inconvenient it may be. Also, oaths are quite the thing if we want to make people such as doctors, lawyers and, lately, bankers follow certain rules and honour particular principles and professional standards. We use oaths to bind members of parliament, government ministers, policemen, soldiers and army officers to putting the interests of their country before their own. In many countries an oath of allegiance is part of the process of naturalization, and in some countries such an oath is obligatorily renewed every day by all pupils in all schools. From this perspective making people take an oath is a kind of verbal warfare, but there is nothing untoward in it.

In fact, it is remarkable how seriously people still take swearing an oath. It helps, of course, that penalties for perjury – lying under oath in court or before a government committee – are generally quite heavy. Similarly, failing to honour a professional oath may result in being struck off the register of certified professionals, which is no small matter either. On the other hand, oaths seem more than a little old-fashioned. Wouldn't a tailor-made legal contract in most cases be more sensible in this literate day and age? Perhaps so, but for some reason people don't seem to feel that way. They prefer the mystical magic of the oath.

For most of human history, oaths were by and large the only guarantee that people would honour their promises, deliver goods ordered and paid for in advance, or render services or care. Until the rise of capitalism and the nation state in the eighteenth century, oaths were also fundamental to the political power structure, which depended largely on patronage, personal loyalty and pledges of allegiance between landed nobles. Once again, face was the pivotal element. If someone went back on his word, he would lose face because he would be shown up as a cheat and a liar. In the absence of effective law enforcement, insurance, written records and reliable, accessible legal procedures, oaths mattered a great deal.

For the threat of loss of face to work, it was important for oaths to be witnessed by respected people. But having those around wasn't always feasible or even desirable. Many deals were, and are, confidential or downright secret. Nobody likes to advertise the fact that they are going to transport a large sum of money, gold, cocaine or other valuables. And, like Lancelot, illicit lovers certainly can do without an audience when they pledge themselves to their Guineveres. You are equally ill-advised to brag about your solemn vow to get back at that underhanded slimy swine of a colleague who dropped you in it to anyone but your most trusted friends. In such cases, calling on some imaginary holy or venerable entity as a witness can add the necessary weight to one's promise – whether straight, as in 'As God is my witness, I'll make the bastard's life hell for doing that to me,' or more indirectly, as in 'By Jove' or even 'By the prophet's beard,' and ultimately 'By everything I hold dear.' The point is that calling on a magical higher power such as God or Jove as a witness puts the credibility and reliability of that higher power in the balance. If the swearer fails to fulfil his pledge, that higher power loses face and the renegate will incur its wrath.

But what about the prophet's beard and 'everything I hold dear'? Those are notions that cannot lose face, so why do people swear by them? These are really cases of swearing *on* something, as they do in courtrooms, where people swear on the Bible or some other holy writ. What is sworn on is almost invariably something sacred, which would be desecrated by reneging on the oath. That, in turn, would offend the supernatural being connected with it, and its congregation. Otherwise, it's something dear to you and highly valued, which would be demeaned if you broke your vow. Perjuring yourself

Performative speech acts: free, bound and cloaked

A performative act of speech creates a new fact by saying something: saying equals doing. Excepting cloaked performatives, all performatives involve the use of a specific verb, such as:

I welcome you to . . .; I'm Robinson, I'll call you Friday; I bet my hat that . . .; You are invited to . . ./I invite you to . . .; I acknowledge/agree/ask/ assure/beg/bequeath/confess/declare/demand/deny/forbid/implore/insist/ promise/recommend/urge/warn/. . .

Bound performatives usually or necessarily occur in a ritual context:

This is to confirm that . . . (written, usually on official stationery)

I swear to/that . . . (often accompanied by holy books, hands on heart, two fingers in the air and so on)

Sold! (with a handshake or slap, or a knock of an auctioneer's hammer)

I pronounce you man and wife (can be adorned by endless pomp and circumstance or not at all, as in a cheap Las Vegas love chapel)

I hereby pronounce/proclaim Amelia Earhart officially dead (in context of press conference, coroner's office or being written on official stationery)

I nominate Bamako for the 2032 Olympics (same)

I name this ship *Titanic* (in context of ship's launching)

I hereby sentence you to three years' imprisonment (in court context)

I baptise you . . . (sprinkling water on or submerging the person to be baptized)

With this ring I thee wed . . . (in combination with ring ritual)

I bless you, in the name of . . . (combined with ritual gestures such as the cross with thumb and forefinger)

Cloaked performatives

Rarely, a performative does not contain a specific performatively used verb. A famous example is Winston Churchill's declaration of war to Japan of 8 December 1941, which contains nothing so direct as the word *declare*, but merely informs the Japanese ambassador to the Court of St James's that 'a state of war exists between our two countries.' Later Churchill commented that 'When you have to kill a man it costs nothing to be polite.'

on the Bible is not unlike putting a dent in your neighbour's car: if they find out, they won't take kindly to it. Perjury on something dear and valuable to you amounts to an act of wanton vandalism, so *you* lose face.

It is therefore usually wise to allow whoever must take an oath to choose their own higher power, sacred or beloved object or concept. A Muslim or Hindu will not feel bound all that much to an oath by Jove or on the Bible, nor will people who don't believe in any supernatural powers. They will just feel uneasy about the whole thing.

Oaths belong to a very peculiar class of events in human life called performatives. Although probably as old as human language itself, they weren't identified as a special phenomenon until about 1950, by the American philosopher John Langshaw Austin. Normally, what people say does one of three things. First, it may simply describe some aspect of a situation real or imagined. 'An empty car pulled up outside number 10, Downing Street' is an example, as are 'I feel dizzy,' 'This is my mother' (and you point to her) and 'I give you ten seconds to answer my question.' Second, there are orders, such as 'Fire!', 'Have a seat' and 'Pass the salt, please,' which serve to get people to do something. Third, there are requests for information, such as 'Have you seen my umbrella?', 'Which is your favourite colour?' or 'Would you pass me the salt please?' (the positive answer to that last one is usually given in the form of actually passing the salt; it's an order disguised as a request for information). All these cases are the same in one respect: they involve something outside language. Knowledge is shared or requested about a state of affairs or someone's state of mind, or an activity is required of the addressee. Not so with performatives. They are pure acts of language – verbal rituals, in fact – that construct new facts. The act of taking an oath is in saying so, as are the acts of naming and betting. Conversely, there is no oath, name or bet until someone says there is. Similarly, when haggling, a sale becomes final only once the buyer or seller says 'Sold!'

The power of oaths essentially relies on the sincere intentions of the swearer and, in relevant cases, the pretence remaining intact that the supernatural power called on will indeed intervene when an oath is not kept, irrespective of the fact that they only ever do so in myths and urban legends. This is why even today taking an oath lightly or, worse, in jest is so frowned on by many. It is how the word *swearing* got its bad reputation in English. Oaths and flippancy simply don't mix. Expressions such as *so help me God, heaven forgive me, God strike me down* and *the Devil get me if . . .* are widely considered inappropriate except when something really serious is at stake, not to speak of *on my life, on my mother's grave* or the preposterously hysterical *on the lives of my children.*

@#$%!

FOR SOME, especially devout subscribers to one of the monotheistic religions, swearing means first and foremost profanity, the use of a holy name for other than sacral purposes. Among them, there are those who consider all use of such names sinful, even such innocent expressions as *God forbid* and *thank heavens.* Others have no qualms in this respect, and terms such as *good God, Jesus* and *jeez* mean nothing to them. They may take exception, however, to another phenomenon the English notion of swearing may refer to: cursing. The essence of cursing is wishing ill on someone, pure and simple. It is a magical ritual act motivated by spite, jealousy or any other form of ill will.

Cursing is in at least two ways the counterpart of taking an oath. Whereas swearing an oath is about taking on a moral obligation and therefore essentially positive, even when it's done insincerely or cavalierly, cursing is essentially negative. Second, an oath binds the person uttering it, whereas a curse puts someone else in a bind, not the speaker. In two other respects, however, oaths and curses are alike: they are both performative, and in their canonical forms they rely on the laws of magic and religion, explicitly or implicitly invoking the help of supernatural powers.

About 2,500 years ago the citizens of the Greek isle of Teos inscribed on two pillars at the entrance of their harbour: 'He who hinders importation of grain, let him perish.' Such a curse was not just a ritual expression of frustration, but a pledge to all pirates and other interlopers: don't interfere with our business, for we will come after you and kill you. But the good people of Teos were mere amateurs at the art of cursing compared to the Roman Catholic Church, which produced highly complex all-purpose curses, to be levelled at any enemy. The greatest example of this is the famous and hatefully vicious Curse of Bishop Ernulphus of Rochester, an otherwise gentle eleventh-century English cleric:

May the heavens and earth, and all the holy things remaining therein, curse them. May they be cursed wherever they may be, in their house or in their field, or in the highway, the path, the wood, the water or the church. May they be cursed in living, in dying. May they be cursed in eating and drinking, in being hungry, in being thirsty, in fasting, in sleeping, in slumbering, in walking, in standing, in sitting, in lying, in working, in resting, in pissing, in shitting and in bloodletting!

That's how it goes halfway through its approximately 750 words. 'Our armies swore terribly in Flanders,' Laurence Sterne has Uncle Toby remark to this volley in *Tristram Shandy* (1759–67), 'but nothing to this. For my own part, I could not have the heart to curse a dog so.'

As do all cultures, gypsies have their own style of cursing. A typical example is: 'May you wander over the face of the Earth forever, never sleep twice in the same bed, never drink water twice from the same well and never cross the same river twice in a year.' This may seem strange, coming from a nomadic people, but the real theme is of course excommunication, expulsion from the fold. Especially among an isolated people, this is a harsh punishment. It renders one an un-person, welcome nowhere and nowhere at home. By a cruel coincidence – or is it? – the same idea of people who do not belong is echoed in Adolf Hitler's damning speech of 10 November 1933 against the 'footloose international clique' – by which he meant the Jews, although he did not actually name them – 'who are at home everywhere and nowhere' and whom *das Volk*, 'the people', cannot keep up with, because it is tied to the land, its country and the provisions of *die Nation*, 'the state'.

Most such direct curses against someone or something are deadly serious. Save for the obvious hyperbole and lurid embellishments one truly wants the damage, the pain and the loss of life that are wished for to befall the target, if not literally, then figuratively. In this sense these are unadulterated magic spells. But that is not true of the vast majority of curse-like expressions.

Malevolent wishes are quite close to classical curses, but of a more modern aspect. In English, many of them derive from older Christian religious curses, such as *(God) damn you,* hence *Fuck you!* and *Devil may care,* but this is an accident of the language. *Arnatatakh!,* 'I wish you'd bleed to death,' an inflamed Armenian may yell at someone he has an axe to grind with – giving a new edge to that hackneyed phrase. Or *Boyet takhem!*, 'I wish you were buried full size.' *Krijg de kolere!*, 'May you contract cholera,' is a common curse from the Dutch, who may also wish *tyfus* (typhoid fever), *pest* (plague), *pokken* (pox) or even *pestpokken* (plague-pox), *tering* (consumption), *het heen en weer* (the to-and-fro) or *een dikke* (a fat one) upon you. Strangely, even though *kanker* (cancer) is widely used in slurs, especially among the young, the Dutch do not normally wish that particular affliction upon anybody, except in the rather contrived *Krijg de grafkanker achter je hart*, 'May you contract grave-cancer behind your heart.' Unlike Dutch, English does not wish illnesses on people any more, although it certainly did in the past. 'A pox of this gout! or, a gout of this pox! For the one or the other plays the rogue with my great toe,' Shakespeare has Falstaff say, in bitter jest, in *Henry iv, Part 2*.

None of these is to be taken literally. *Damn you* and even *God damn you* are frequently used by completely unreligious people, just like *Devil may care*, which expresses only the speaker's complete indifference about its target. Likewise, *fuck you* is not an order to go and fuck somebody or get fucked by somebody. Instead, it signifies that the addressee has displeased the speaker and will henceforth be ignored. Many an Armenian would be horrified if the one he'd hurled *Arnatatakh* at actually did as he'd been told, and no Dutchman wishing the *tering* on someone actually wants them to start coughing up blood. In fact, most Dutchmen haven't the foggiest idea what *tering* means any more, nor do they have direct knowledge of any of the other scourges of humanity that are popular in swearing, all of which are a thing of the past and extremely rare in the well-appointed world of the Low Countries. And of course Falstaff and his *auctor intellectualis* knew full well that afflictions cannot become ill. Truth or aptitude is immaterial; they are all expressions of general displeasure.

The same is true of malediction, a kind of indirect curse. Maledictions are symbolic violent assaults on a person or institution. *Tofu no kado ni atame o butsuketehinde shimae!*, a displeased Japanese may counsel, 'Go and knock your head on a lump of tofu and die!' This is a mild malediction, for tofu is comfortably mushy. Things get a bit hairier when malediction takes the form of a threat, as in *Omanko ni buta no ashi o tsukkonde okuba gata-gata iwasete yaru!*, 'I'll stick a pig's leg up your cunt until your back teeth rattle!'

Rather less personal are expressions such as the Russian *Idí v žópu*, which literally means 'Go up my arse', but is the equivalent of 'Kiss my arse', Hebrew *Kus imxa* and Arabic *Kus ommak*, both meaning 'your mother's cunt'. In a tenth-century German-Latin phrase book for French travellers to the German-speaking world, we find the useful expression *Vndes ars in tine naso – Canis culum in tuo naso*, 'a dog's arse up your nose'. Usually, such exclamations have little to do with the shortcomings of the person being spoken to. Rather, they are general expressions that convey disbelief of, disagreement with or disappointment about what has just happened or been said. They may even be little more than comments on the situation as a whole, or on one's own state of mind, just as 'no bloody ice' was. The French *putain* (whore), *merde* (shit) and *putain de merde* (shit-whore) are in this class, as are the English *shit* and *fuck* and the Spanish *joder!* (fuck). Catalan sports a lurid series of exclamations involving things that are holy in the eyes of the Roman Catholic Church, such as *mecàgum Déus de Déus*, 'I shit on the God of gods,' *mecàgum la puta Madre de Dèu*, 'I shit on the mother of God, that whore,' and – somewhat less rude – *Ostres!* (oysters), a euphemism for the Host. As do most cultures, Catalonia has a few examples to offer that border on real works of art, such as *mecàgum Déu, en la creu i en el fuster que la feu (i en el fill de puta que va plantar el pi)*, 'I shit on God and the Cross and the carpenter who made it (and on the son of a whore who planted the pine).'

Swearing and cursing don't by any means cover the vast territory of verbal abuse. Slurs and insults have their own vocabulary of offensive and taboo terms, which we will have more to say about later on. First, however, we should take a closer look at the world of magic, the art of playing the presumed supernatural forces that underlie oaths, curses, religion and a considerable part of our understanding of the world.

Egyptian curse at the end of many contracts (if you don't honour it), c. 800 BC, 23rd Dynasty, stating: 'A donkey shall copulate with him, a donkey shall copulate with his wife, his wife shall copulate with his child.'

3

I PUT A SPELL ON YOU

'Are you Rima?'
'I'm done with names. Names are nothing but collars men tie round
your neck to drag you where they like.'
Alasdair Gray, *Lanark: A Life in Four Books* (1981)

In the more enlightened parts of today's world, the word 'magic' is more likely to evoke images of the adventures of Harry Potter or the sleight of hand of the vaudeville theatre than feelings of insecurity, danger and doom. Nevertheless, magic and sorcery are alive and kicking. In Africa, the rhinoceros is all but extinct because of the magical, primarily libidinous powers that people in eastern Asia attribute to its horn – which, by the way, isn't even a horn but a tightly tangled mass of hair. For similar reasons, tigers in the wild have been reduced to a sad few. And it doesn't stop with animals. In Congo's Kasaï region, the insurgent Kamuina Nsapu militia has been recruiting child soldiers since 2016 and sends young girls into battle in straw skirts that they're told they can catch enemy bullets in. The militia sells boys rings that enable them to 'jump' to other places, make them invisible or enable them to hypnotize government forces. In order to empower the kids, it makes them drink human blood and potions with mashed human skulls. In Tanzania, hundreds of women accused of being witches are murdered each year. And all over central Africa albino children are being persecuted as witches, sometimes even butchered and processed to make powders and potions to which all sorts of medicinal powers are ascribed – positive and negative.

Let's not be deceived into thinking that the most developed, technologically and educationally advanced parts of the globe – roughly the Western world – have freed themselves from believing in supernatural powers, in sorcery and magic, just because 'magic' is primarily associated with entertainment there. Nor do twenty-first-century Westerners stop at innocent clichés about horseshoes, black cats and walking under ladders. Just look at the enormous dietary industry, the countless people who willingly pay a small fortune to follow schemes and buy stuff that some self-proclaimed guru says will help them lose weight. More often than not such diets have no scientific basis to speak of, and many are outright bogus. The greatest example of this in recent history is the way the French amateur dietician Michel Montignac enthralled millions of spoiled and overfed Western Europeans in the 1990s. Achieving your ideal girth, he claimed, had little to do with the number of calories you ate in a day. The ingenious title of his best-selling book, published in 1987, was *Eat Yourself Slim . . . and Stay Slim!* It was not how much you ate that mattered, but what you ate and when. The important thing was never to combine fat and carbohydrates, and to avoid 'fast' carbohydrates altogether. For many, Montignac's diet initially worked, because avoiding fast carbohydrates drastically reduced the total number of calories they ingested; it meant goodbye to French fries, white bread, most fatty and salty snacks, soft drinks and so on. The rest was speculation at best, or complete gobbledygook.

As with running a kosher kitchen, keeping fat and carbohydrates on separate plates in separate meals is no mean task. It meant hard work for those who jumped on to the Montignac bandwagon, and maximized the chances that they would make mistakes or fall off now and again. And, as the success of such institutions as the Roman Catholic Church has taught us, there is no better way to strengthen the faith than to impose all kinds of discomforting restrictions and complicated, time-consuming rituals on believers, and no better way to inspire feelings of guilt in them for not being able to comply with all those requirements. Instigating feelings of guilt and insecurity is half of how the Holy Mother Church has succeeded in keeping its flocks together for the best part of two millennia.

The other half of Rome's strategy was to offer its guilt-ridden sinners a way out of their predicament by means of absolution after confession or through buying indulgences, the practice that so infuriated Martin Luther five hundred years ago. These reprieves made sinners not only thankful towards the Church, but tributary to it. Montignac offered his own kind of reprieve, an enormous array of high-priced Montignac-proof prepared dishes and ingredients for meals, sweets and condiments. It earned him a fortune, but not much else. In 2010 he died of prostate cancer at the age of 65.

The point about the Montignac story is not that people are gullible and will clutch at any straw in order to achieve that seemingly unattainable ideal of a taut, slim body. It is that they do so without asking any questions themselves, and do not listen to others who do ask critical questions and sometimes even provide reliable answers. Montignac's claims were debunked right from the start, but that did not stop the extraordinary excitement about his diet or the phenomenal growth of his following. People deliberately behaved irrationally. They wanted to believe, not to know. They preferred hoping for the glorious ideal to striving rationally for the less glamourous attainable.

The hype around the Montignac diet is an exceptionally good example of modern magical thinking, because the people who could afford the diet were mostly intelligent, educated and holding good jobs. It showed that magical thinking is not particular to the unenlightened and the illiterate. The world of slimming is far from the only example of modern middle-class magical thinking. Horoscopes and astrology are as popular as ever, and feng shui and all kinds of alternative medicine have been on the rise in recent years. The police still occasionally consult clairvoyants in hopeless missing-person cases, and the popularity of spiritual leaders from George Steiner to Bhagwan, or mystical cults such as Scientology or the Avatars, shows no sign of waning.

Of course, if you ask believers in astrology or mysterious spiritual healing practices whether they believe in sorcery and witchcraft, most of them will categorically say no. That is only to be expected, because those nowadays mainly folkloristic activities are not what magical thinking is really about. Ultimately, magical thinking is about two things only. One is a form of wishful thinking that makes us disregard Occam's razor, the other is an inability to accept coincidence as being just that.

Occam's razor, named after the fourteenth-century monk William of Ockham, is the popular name for the most basic requirement of all rational thought and scientific inquiry. Like all medieval scholars, Ockham formulated his idea in Latin:

Pluralitas non est ponenda sine necessitate

which translates as 'Do not suppose anything more than you really have to.' What he meant was that one should always try to explain a phenomenon or solve a problem by the simplest, best-understood means available. Hence the razor image: at each stage, you should cut away everything from your reasoning that does not really need to be there. If your briefcase is not in its usual place in the morning, you don't immediately call the police; you look in the other room first. If the car won't start, you check the fuel and the battery before you start dismantling the engine. If your daughter is late home from school, you don't immediately suppose she's been abducted by aliens; you first call her friends.

Occam's razor is the exact opposite of what magical thinkers and, in their wake, conspiracy theorists do. Instead of looking methodically for a rational explanation for a phenomenon, avoiding rash suppositions, the magical thinker or conspiracy theorist simply attributes its occurrence to some unseen force. The pernicious twist is that the believers who first propose the existence of a supernatural force or dark and malevolent cabal to explain a phenomenon then see the occurrence of that same phenomenon as proof that said dark force actually exists.

Here's how it works. Suppose you have been feeling unusually morose for a while. It's nothing dramatic, not bad enough to get professional help, but you can't get rid of those depressing ruminations. So when a friend tells you enthusiastically about how feng shui brightened up her life, you listen. She tells you that your whole house is wrongly arranged, so 'of course' you don't feel happy. Thankful that there finally seems to be a reason for your discomfort, you set about studying the rules of feng shui and rearranging your house accordingly. This takes your mind off whatever was bothering you and gives you a sense of purpose, so you start feeling better. After a few weeks, your hear yourself telling your friends that feng shui really works, and that you're living proof.

The second cause of the continued popularity of magical thought is our irrepressible propensity for discerning patterns everywhere. This is a very human trait, part and parcel of our hereditary endowment; all people are subject to it and it is impossible to shut it off. You just cannot help seeing faces in clouds, camels in the cracks in the ceiling or a Dalmatian in what is no more than a sprinkle of black dots on a white background. It is what makes us appreciate drawings and paintings, but it is not limited to the visual. We also tend to see connections between events, even if they are as unrelated as black spots on white paper and a Dalmatian dog. If two things happen, we are naturally inclined to consider one to be the cause of the other. This can take quite bizarre forms. A soccer player puts on polka-dotted boxer shorts one day, scores three goals and is convinced that he will score again next week only if he is wearing those very same shorts. Who has not been caught in the rain thinking it would not have rained had you only thought to bring your umbrella? Who has not felt that buses are always just pulling away when you come running to catch them? Even the least paranoiac among us find it hard to accept pure coincidence. And if coincidence is not an option, there must be something behind events, some unknown, unseen force orchestrating things. Something supernatural.

A special case of this wariness of coincidence is our inability to accept the unexplained, and especially unexplained disasters that befall us. In time, we all get to deal with 'our share' of illness and infirmity, accidents, wars, crime and stupid bad luck. But the life-long smoker who develops lung cancer can find at least a modicum of comfort in the idea that his plight is a punishment for bad behaviour. The cancer can be seen as a more or less predictable consequence of his own actions. But of all cars in a car park, why should *yours* be the one to get broken into? Why should *your* bicycle be the one that is stolen, *your* town the one to become flooded in that rainstorm? Why should *your* child be born with a disability, *your* brother develop cystic fibrosis, *your* country be struck by hunger or deadly pestilence? The true but least acceptable answer to such questions is 'Dunno, shit happens.' If there is no sense to the disaster, your suffering is meaningless too. So we invent a reason for what happens to us, some unseen power, a mover that we can blame for our misfortune or that we can think had reason to punish us.

This is what we do and what we have been doing since the beginning of time. Especially at the beginning of time, since so very little was known about the world then, and so many things were mysterious. What with there being no medicine to speak of, hardly any effective means of storing and preserving food, and only the simplest of weapons to keep human and animal predators away, living was a high-risk occupation in a dangerous, often hostile environment.

@#$%!

THERE ARE DIFFERENT WAYS of dealing with a world you barely understand, depending on your idea of where the powers reside that rule it. One way of looking at things is to attribute powers to objects and phenomena themselves, on the basis of their appearance. According to James G. Frazer, author of *The Golden Bough* (1890), this is one of the two great 'laws' underlying magic: the Law of Similarity. The idea is that if something looks, smells, feels or in some other way closely resembles something else, it *is* essentially the same thing. That is what's behind driving needles or nails into the head of an effigy or doll with the aim of giving the person that the puppet is supposed to represent a headache, or into its belly to bring on the runs, appendicitis or other abdominal discomforts.

Similar thinking lurks behind cannibalism. People do not consume each other lightly, so cannibalism is pretty rare. But, the odd psychopath aside, where it does occur, the idea is invariably that by eating parts of a slain enemy or deceased relative you ingest their mental powers and add them to your own. Ironically, eating the brains of their family did not give the women and children of the Fore, a people of the New Guinea highlands, courage or cunning at all. Instead, it gave them kuru, a lethal prion disease akin to Creutzfeldt–Jakob disease, the major symptoms of which are tremors, impaired equilibrium, incontinence, behavioural problems and early dementia.

Somewhat closer to home, similarity is also the logic behind many supposed aphrodisiacs. Oysters are thought to enhance potency, simply because they look and smell like female genitalia, or so it is said. The same goes for figs – if you fail to see the likeness, take a fresh one and cut it in half from top to bottom. Masculine variants are the asparagus and the leek, vanilla pods and chillies.

Oysters, figs, asparagus and leeks look like sex organs, so they are sex organs, and if you ingest them, you ingest undiluted sexual power. For obvious reasons, Frazer calls magical rituals and ideas that, like these, are based on the Law of Similarity imitative or homeopathic. This too is ironic in a way, for although homeopathy as a form of medicine is indeed an instance of application of the Law of Similarity, it is at the same time an example of the kind of magic that rests on the second great law of magic, the Law of Contact.

This law says that if two things once formed a whole and were then separated, the properties of that whole still reside in both.

A well-known example is the idea that someone can be hurt – or healed, for that matter – by doing something to a hair or nail clipping that belonged to them. Although man and hair have taken leave of each other, they are still magically in contact as if they constituted a single organism. Likewise, the placenta and umbilical cord can be used to affect their 'owner'. Such ideas go far, and the two things involved need not have started out as one. It is enough for them to have been brought into contact at some point. Thus, writes the Roman general and scholarly jack of all trades Pliny, if a man regrets having wounded another, he need only spit on the hand with which he inflicted the wound for it to heal swiftly and smoothly. Some time during the thirteenth century Roger Bacon noted that 'it is constantly received and avouched that the anointing of the weapon that maketh the wound will heal the wound itself.' The *doctor mirabilis*, an awe-inspiring scholar, had some doubts as to whether this was actually true, but nevertheless added that the ointment should be 'made of diverse ingredients, whereof the strangest and hardest to come by are the moss upon the skull of a dead man unburied, and the fats of a boar and a bear killed in the act of generation'.[1] Healing a wound made by a weapon had certainly become a lot harder over the millennium that separated Bacon from Pliny.

One step beyond is the widespread belief that one can hurt someone by hurting their footprints. Frazer relates how the Aboriginal people of southeastern Australian used to stick sharp pieces of quartz or bone fragments into footprints in the sand in order to lame the person who had made them. Apparently, by pressing his feet into the sand, a man created an unbreakable bond between himself and the depression he had made – essentially a hole, an absence, at best a shape.

This brings us to the rarefied, almost ethereal world of homeopathic medicine, an innovation from the Romantic era by the German physician Samuel Hahnemann. The perfectly healthy Hahnemann experienced how chewing the bark of the cinchona plant, then a relatively new and uniquely effective cure for malaria, did precisely the opposite for him. His body began to show the symptoms that were typical of malaria. But next to the shivers and cold sweats, the experiment also gave Hahnemann his eureka moment, and he made the age-old idea that *similia similibus curentur*, 'like is cured by like', the cornerstone of his medical philosophy. According to him, illnesses

The modern life of the Law of Contact

The Law of Contact explains a lot of modern tourism as well as much of the economics of the art world. People travel from all over the world to gaze on the very toilet bowl Elvis Presley died on, or stand on the very balcony where Martin Luther King Jr was shot dead. Nothing makes you feel closer to Caesar and the whole history of the Roman Empire than to stand inside the remains of the Curia in Rome looking at the benches those senators once sat on. Artefacts such as a letter written by John Lennon or a hat said to have been worn by Napoleon can be auctioned off for vast amounts of money.

Something similar holds for our reverence for 'the real thing'. These days, copies of famous paintings are almost better than the originals. Yet copies sell for a few quid, whereas a real Rembrandt, Monet or Hockney is priceless, even if it's faded or torn. On top of this, many originals have been so heavily touched up, repaired or remounted that there is not much left that is truly original. Nevertheless, such 'real' paintings have the lure of having been in true contact with the demigod who produced them, and copies don't.

should be countered by administering agents that were known to cause the very symptoms the patient displayed. In Hahnemann's universe of bloodletting and other medical hocus-pocus, his idea of deploying specific drugs to fight specific ailments was certainly a commendable advance. Nevertheless, for want of rational, fact-based arguments, his homeopathic philosophy was first and foremost a clear case of magic according to the Law of Similarity. But that is only half the story. Hahnemann knew well enough that simply administering debilitating concoctions to the sick would benefit no one, so he added the idea of 'potentization', of diluting the active substance step by step in distilled water or alcohol until it had almost or completely vanished from the solution. With Hahnemann, all modern homeopaths believe that diluting away the noxious substance gets rid of its negative effects, while its healing power is somehow absorbed in the remaining dilutant. And that, in turn, is a paradigm case of contagious magic, an instance of the Law of Contact. Like the footprint of the Aborigine, the water or alcohol retained a bond with the agent that had been diluted away, a memory of it, so to speak.

@#$%!

ALL THE EXAMPLES ABOVE, and many more like them, are instances of straight magic, where the magician tries to influence people, objects, materials and phenomena directly, without recourse to a third supernatural party. But this is not always so. Regardless of what we may believe, we cannot help feeling that we are a person who inhabits and directs our body. A soul, if you will, that is inherently bound to the body, but not identical to it. Similarly, the potential that lies dormant in a stream, a weapon or any other object or natural phenomenon might be seen as something supernatural connected with, but not identical to, it. So, for example, instead of calling directly on a dry source to start flowing again, an appeal would be made to the spirit of the well, the supernatural force that controlled it. This is the beginning of an almost inevitable process of anthropomorphization, and ultimately of personalization.

Anthropomorphization is what people inevitably do with everything they strike up a conversation with. Whether it is a source in a primordial forest at the dawn of humanity, a horse or dog you own, or the personal computer on your desk: as soon as we begin to talk to something, we start treating it as if it were not only sentient, but capable of understanding and obeying us. In short, we treat it as if it were a human being itself. The reason is that we are simply unable to fathom what it must be like to be something fundamentally different from ourselves. To see how strong this effect is, try to imagine yourself to be a brick in a wall. What do you see and sense? Do you see the people passing on the pavement in front of you? The trees in the park across the street? Do you imagine yourself lazily thinking about how snugly you lie there, embedded between strong neighbours, with nothing to do other than just be there? That is precisely where you go wrong, for a brick does not see, it does not think and it has no perception of snugness or anything else. Bricks are dead matter, and we cannot deal with that. We just project ourselves, our liveliness, sentience and human perspective onto the brick. At least in this sense each one of us is involuntarily and inescapably infinitely more self-centred and self-absorbed than poor Narcissus ever was.

So long as there were no supernatural powers involved in magical interaction between a person and other people, objects or phenomena, everybody could be their own magician. But once the idea took root of supernatural powers *mediating* between a person and the behaviour of other entities, it cannot have taken long before the first shamans came on the scene, people who claimed to be able to converse with those unseen powers. These weren't in all probability tricksters who preyed on the gullibility of their fellow men, but honest people who actually believed in their gift. Some people do not find it all that difficult to put themselves in a trance by readily available means such as chanting or spinning or reciting mantras, and in that way to transcend the boundaries of the here and now. A famous, if often misrepresented, example from today's world is the Haitian *danse-lwa*, the fit of possession experienced by those attendants at certain festive voodoo rituals who have been entered by a *lwa*, one of many powerful spirits. The afflicted lose control of themselves, behaving wildly as if very drunk. They imitate behaviour that is characteristic of the particular *lwa* that has taken possession of them: those under the spell of Dambala will start writhing like snakes; victims of Gédé make lewd gestures and belch out curses and obscenities; and if Legba is the master, the person becomes violently aggressive. Afterwards, when the *lwa* has left them, they don't remember a thing about what has happened. Ecstatic trances similar to such 'fits of possession' are not uncommon during some Methodist and related religious services in the rural south of the United States. And drugs, which have always been readily available everywhere in plants and mushrooms, are especially easy instruments for opening the doors of perception. Nowadays small pills and flashing lights help thunderously loud music to put many of the thousands of ravers at the immensely popular large-scale dance events into a trance-like state. It is not an accident that the archetypal party drug is called ecstasy or XTC.

Third, it is not all that uncommon to hallucinate, especially among older people with deteriorating vision. An estimated 10–40 per cent of the elderly with impaired vision – estimates are rough because many people are too ashamed or afraid to admit to 'seeing things' – suffer from Charles Bonnet syndrome, an affliction characterized by extremely clear and realistic visual hallucinations. They may see brightly coloured dinky toys careening around the floor, a deer prancing across the sofa or Donald Duck waving to them from a tree in front of their house. They even may see long-dead friends or strangers having a cup of tea in their kitchen. There is also an aural variant, where hearing-impaired people start hearing voices. Just as sufferers of Charles Bonnet are aware that what they see are just hallucinations, these people are fully aware that those voices aren't real. Although hearing such voices is probably even more common than Charles Bonnet syndrome, its true incidence remains a mystery, because, still more than experiencing visual hallucinations, 'hearing voices' is a popular hallmark of dangerous madness and psychosis. Many sufferers therefore prefer to keep their affliction to themselves. Today we know that the images and voices are generated spontaneously by the brain itself. They are annoying but essentially innocent. But in a world dominated by lack of understanding and magic, they could easily be mistaken for manifestations of supernatural powers.

Those early shamans were also the first intellectuals to walk on the face of the Earth. They were the first people who specialized in dealing with the spiritual side of things and how the world worked. And, being specialists, on whose access to and grip on the supernatural all others depended, they gained considerable power.

The idea that the behaviour of things in nature was not just of itself, but in some sense directed by a supernatural force that was not quite identical with those things, took magic out of the hands of ordinary people and created a caste of specialists who could mediate between humans and these supernatural forces, a caste who could harness and control them. But by and by those supernatural forces became evermore anthropomorphic, and ultimately personal. This has happened everywhere where there are people, perhaps driven by the memories of dead ancestors. If their personality, their supernatural spirit still hung around somewhere after it had clearly left the deceased body, as was believed ubiquitously as far as we know, those spirits were very personal entities. People had spoken to them when they still inhabited their mortal bodies, had *known* them intimately. One's relationship with, and understanding of, such spirits is very different from that with impersonal, somewhat amorphous and abstract forces.

By personalization, supernatural forces are recreated in human image. It turns them into what we call gods, demigods, spirits and mythical creatures such as elves, naiads, fairies, genies, satyrs and the rest, all the way down to the almost completely humanized selkies of the Faroe Islands, the seal-skinned mermaids who, if caught, can live among the people and have children with them. With personalization, the relationships between people, the mediating shamans and the supernatural changed too. Quite unlike an abstract force, a personal god is endowed with a will, a temper, and goals and plans. They can be jealous, magnanimous, irritable or insincere. Personal gods can have it in for specific people, or have a soft spot for someone, something not given to impersonal 'forces'. Whereas abstract forces can be harnessed and controlled or deflected only by means of magic, one can try to propitiate a god. With a god you can make a deal, and you can buy his or her favour through sacrifices, pledges and prayers. In short, a god can be served, and this is when, as Frazer first proposed, magic turns into religion and magicians turn into priests. Magic is about forcing and controlling the behaviour of things, people, events and supernatural forces by supernatural means. Religion, on the other hand, is about serving and placating the supernatural, hoping, of course, that the deity will reward your service.

From a sceptical, strictly rationalist point of view this may come as a shock, but both magic and religion actually work. That is something most of the stauncher modern atheists find extremely annoying, so they prefer to ignore it. It is nonetheless true, with one restriction. Of course there is no way in which magic spells or walking seven times around city walls chanting to the Lord is going to make one bit of difference to the physical world. Nor will spinning prayer mills, bowing towards Mecca or intoning the Lord's Prayer. The rationalists are right about that. But whereas our physical world, Mother Earth, is more or less spherical, our mental world is circular: God exists in the eyes of those who believe he exists, but not for an atheist. Religious rituals mean something to believers; to non-believers they are superstition or folklore, of touristic interest at best. Similarly, the demands and prohibitions set by a religion and the threats and promises of magic carry real weight for those who think they do so. And they will act accordingly in the real world. Because of this, ideas that are completely flawed from a rationalist, sceptical, areligious point of view can still make their mark on the physical world and have real and often dire consequences for other people. History, with all that has been perpetrated in the name of gods from Astarte to Allah and Jehovah, is blood-dripping testimony.

Perhaps the most decisive incident ever recorded of religion changing the course of the real world is the battle fought in 312 CE at the Ponte Milvio – a still-existing bridge across the River Tiber, then a few miles to the north of the city of Rome – between the rival Roman emperors Constantine and Maxentius. The odds were on Maxentius, who commanded the bigger army. But Constantine told his troops on the morning of the battle that he had had a vision, and a voice had told him '*in hoc signo vinces*', 'in this sign you will win.' According to Constantine's biographer the Palestinian scholar Eusebius of Caesarea, who claims to have been told the story by Constantine himself, that sign was a fiery cross in the sky. To his worried troops, who found themselves in a pinch and could use all the support they might get, this supposedly supernatural intervention was just what the doctor ordered. They eagerly chalked crosses on their shields, fought for all they were worth and came out victorious.

Contrary to Christian propaganda, Constantine, who was now the undisputed ruler of what was left of the Roman empire, did not convert to Christianity after the battle. But he did put a definitive stop to the discrimination and occasional persecution of Christians – and the rest is history.

Whatever Constantine really did or did not experience is immaterial. What counts is the brilliant if perhaps opportunistic use he made of mass-psychology and the power of mere words, on a par with the surge of inspiration that made Martin Luther King Jr turn a rather flat performance at the end of black America's March on Washington on 28 August 1963 into the resounding 'I have a dream' speech that shook the world. There were a fair number of Christians among Constantine's troops, as he well knew. By this time, Christianity had become quite strongly entrenched in Graeco-Roman society. But it was still officially considered fishy and somewhat subversive, which may have had a lot to do with its exclusive monotheism and corresponding deprecatory attitude to all who didn't see things in quite the same way. Christians did well not to advertise their convictions too loudly, lest they trigger another pogrom. To the Christians in his army, Constantine's act must have meant acknowledgement and liberation at once, both powerful incentives. To the pagan rest, the idea that some deity had explicitly put himself behind them must have come as something of a relief as well. Their army might be outnumbered, but at least they were not alone.

Examples of equally earth-shattering effects of magic and sorcery have never been found, at least not in recorded history. By the time the first writing systems were invented, in Sumer some 5,000 years ago, the development of religion out of primordial magic had already taken place. On account of its servile nature, religion suited

Magic, religion and monotheism

In the competition between magic and religion the latter has had the upper hand right from the beginning, if only on account of the close ties between religious officials and secular authorities, who in some cases merged into one, with the king himself as the god of choice. That said, it took a long time for a clear distinction between religion and magic to develop, and when it did it was only a by-product of much larger developments. In the old polytheistic worlds, there wasn't much that separated gods from ancestor spirits, jinxes or countless other supernatural forces. The main difference was that believers in a god or goddess had someone to support, serve, admire and consider their champion, more or less as today's club fans do, whereas believers in magic, who thought in terms of controlling the supernatural (and fate, and other people), did not.

Members of a polytheist society will consider the deity of their choice to be the best, strongest, most powerful god of all, or he wouldn't be their god. But there is room for people with different preferences, or for different kinds of worship to coexist. Even where king and god fell together, or where the state enforced the service to one preferred deity, there would be unhindered cults of ancestor spirits and house gods.

That all changed where monotheism reared its head. In a monotheistic society there can be but one god, and no competitors or even colleagues of any kind are to be tolerated. As it says in Exodus 20:5, 'for I, the Lord your God, am a jealous God,' and in 22:20, 'Whoever sacrifices to any god other than the Lord must be destroyed.' Not only that, but magic is also doomed (Exodus 22:18): 'Do not allow a sorceress to live.' With the rise of monotheism, religion embarked on a course of bloody, brutal intolerance that the world is still suffering from today.

the needs of secular authorities much better than magic. Kings and priests were created, as it were, to complement each other, and they have been in profitable collusion since long before Hammurabi, the first ruler of a well-organized state known by name. God, king and country form an ironclad trinity to be *served*, and from that point of view the unruly magicians, sorcerers and witches who claim to be able to control the supernatural instead of serving it are unwelcome interlopers. They are subversive hecklers who pose a threat to the stability and security of the state. As a consequence, magic on a grand scale was largely driven underground perhaps even before the wheel was invented, a few centuries before writing first arrived on the scene in the Middle East.

On a much smaller scale, all sorts of magic continued to be a part of people's lives and of religion to this day. Many folk charms are attempts to make something happen or go away without any appeal to a mediating supernatural power. An example is this English charm for getting rid of warts. First rub the wart with a bean pod, then bury the pod beneath an ash tree while saying: 'As this beanshell rots away, so my wart shall soon decay.' The following Dutch charm against warts, which is still doing the rounds, calls upon the moon to help. When the moon is full, go out at night. Then rub your hands three times while looking at the moon without blinking, and say:

Volle maan, kijk mij aan *en jaag mijn wratten naar de maan.*	Full moon, look me in the eye and chase my warts away (lit. 'to the moon').

When they cut themselves, German peasants used to call upon the maiden Hille, a figure identified by the nineteenth-century philologist and folklorist Jacob Grimm as the Valkyrie Hilda, who could make blood flow and curdle:

Sprach Jungfrau Hille, *Blut stand stille.*	When the maiden Hille speaks, then the blood no longer leaks.

Christianity has incorporated many magical ideas and rituals. Saints, for instance, used to have all the trappings of Graeco-Roman gods and demigods, if we can believe the word of William Tyndale, the man who translated the Bible into English and was strangled and burned at the stake for it by the Catholic Inquisition in the Flemish town of Vilvoorde in 1536. 'That we worship saints for fear, lest they should be displeased and angry with us, and plague us or hurt us (as who is not afraid of St Laurence? Who dare deny St Anthony a fleece of wool, for fear of his terrible fire, or lest he send the pox among our sheep?), is heathen image-service,' he noted. Nowadays saints are perceived more as benevolent spirits, who can be called upon to assist, protect or procure things for people. St Anthony of Padua (not the same as Tyndale's Anthony the Great) can be recruited to

Erzsébet Báthory's magic curse

The curse below is attributed to the Hungarian Countess Erzsébet Báthory (1560–1614), better known as Countess Dracula. Purportedly, the exceedingly beautiful and vain Báthory tortured and killed scores of adolescent girls in order to bathe in their blood to keep her looks. She was caught in the act and arrested by her son-in-law Imre Megyery and Count György Thurzó, Palatine of Hungary, who also acted as accuser at her trial in 1611. Mozes Cziráky was a court notary who compiled more than thirty witness statements. Despite the curse, harm did come to Báthory: she was never formally sentenced, but bricked into a windowless room nonetheless, where she died four years later.

Isten, segíts! Isten, segíts, te felhőcske! Isten segíts, felhőcske! Adj, Isten, adj, Isten, egészséget Báthory Erzsébetnek. Küldj, küldj, te felhőcske, kilencvenkilenc macskát, ezt parancsolom neked, ki a macskák főura vagy, hogy parancsolj azoknak, és őket egybegyűjtse!, bárhol legyenek is, akár hegyeken túl, akár vizeken túl a tengereken túl, hogy jöjjön ez a kilencvenkilenc macska, és menjenek szerte, és Mátyás király szívét harapják és a palatínus uram szívét, és a vörös Megyery szívét is egyék meg, valamint Cziráky Mózes szívét is, nehogy Báthory Erzsébetnek bántalma legyen! Szentháromság, végezd így el!	God, help! God help thee too, cloudlet! God help thee, cloudlet! Give, God, give, God, Erszébet Báthory good health. Then send, cloudlet, send ninety-nine cats, I bid thee, for thou art master of cats, to go there and order them to assemble, wherever they are, even beyond the mountains, beyond the waters and the seas beyond those, to come, these 99 cats, and then swiftly go and bite the heart of King Matthias, and the heart of Mr Palatine, as well as the heart of Mozes Cziráky, and let them also tear asunder the heart of Megyery the Red, so that no harm will come to Erzsébet Báthory! Holy Trinity, do this!

lead you to things you've lost – or even a suitable man to marry. The Dutch do this by saying:

Sint Antonius, lieve vrind, maak dat ik mijn . . . vind.	St Anthony, darling friend, make me find my . . .

St Barbara protects miners, armourers, firemen and those suffering from burns, and St Matthew cares for accountants. If you don't succeed in getting pregnant, you can always enlist the help of the Holy Virgin Mary (who better to turn to when in need of miraculous conception?), her mother, St Anne, or St Elisabeth. There is even a saint whose brief encompasses newly-weds as a separate category, St Dorothy of Caesarea (brewers, florists, fruiterers and gardeners also welcome; will protect against false accusations). Even the Fon people of Benin in West Africa, with their wide variety of dedicated spirits, cannot match this extremely fine-grained division of labour.

But that is not all the magic the Mother Church has to offer. It also has guardian angels, very much like pagan protective personal spirits. And ultimately there is the Devil himself, evil incarnate and 100 per cent magic. Beelzebub is not to be placated, served or sacrificed to. He is not to be honoured. He is a force to be battled, fought off, exorcized and ultimately subdued. Lucifer is the prince of sorcerers and witches, the supreme magician and the eternal loser, always coming in second. When push comes to shove, the Devil looks a lot like an allegorical representation of what happened in the real world when religion arose out of magic and teamed up with those who wielded secular power to kick magic from Olympus, forcing it henceforth to eke out a marginal existence as a darker, lesser force.

@#$%!

THE POWER OF BOTH RELIGION and magic resides primarily in rituals, secrecy and words. Keeping a secret, or at least making others believe that he is keeping one, gives the sorcerer, the shaman and the priest an edge over other people. It is no accident that two of the central concerns of the Reformation were to make the Bible available in the vernacular and to stop conducting services in Latin, so that the average churchgoer might judge for himself what his religion was all about, and take a more active part in its practice and development. Taking away so much of the mystery, the Roman Catholic clergy feared, would strip it of most of its power over the flock. Even a simple village parson could, if need be, settle nasty disputes to his advantage and defuse awkward questions just by pulling a grave face and mumbling some random Latin-sounding words such as *Gabeas lactatum – omnia ad retis*. Who would gladly give up so multifunctional a tool and source of authority?

Whereas the reformists uniformly took to the vernacular, the Roman Catholic Church hung on to the magical impenetrability of Latin until the second half of the twentieth century. Citizens of the city of Maastricht on the River Meuse, a crumb in the deepest pocket of the Roman Catholic part of the predominantly Protestant kingdom of the Netherlands, still love to tell visitors how the nineteenth-century industrialist Petrus Regout, fervently hated for the appalling conditions in his earthenware mills, once explained to the local bishop over a glass of wine how the people of the city could best be taken advantage of: 'You keep them ignorant, and I'll keep them poor.'

A similar ploy is common among doctors, some of whom still have a tendency to talk in jargon full of pig Latin. The profession even developed the legendary doctor's handwriting, penmanship aimed at keeping from the patient what was on the prescription. This partly served the rational goal of preventing patients from going shopping for themselves, but awe-inspiring mystification was just as important. Certainly things have become better over the past few decades, especially among the GPs of Western Europe, where much of the mumbo jumbo has gone the way of the white coat. But deep down the modern medicine man still has not entirely shed his shamanist feathers.

The incomprehensible formulas the doctor uses closely resemble the secret spells of the witch doctor and the sorcerer. Like the Roman Catholic Church, other religions and the world of magic – including the medical profession, which used to be 80 per cent magic anyway – have always set great store by secret knowledge and cryptic texts. Ultra-Orthodox Haredi Jews and the Eastern European Traditionalists and their forebears have been studying the Jewish holy texts full-time for thousands of years now, without ever coming to a uniform, generally accepted interpretation. Failing to do so is precisely the point: reaching consensus would take away the mysticism and the mystery, leaving only a mundane set of moral guidelines and rules of behaviour. The holy texts of Islam, particularly the Quran, the word of God as He had the archangel Gabriel dictate it to the Prophet and his minions during the course of the first half of the seventh century, are extremely vague and often defy confident interpretation. This is partly because of the existence of different variants, partly because of the unvocalized Arabic script, which allows for considerable differences of opinion concerning the 'true' wording, and partly because of the rambling nature of the texts themselves. The result is enormous mystical prestige, and a cornucopia of mysterious and endlessly malleable formulas that, in common with much of the Christian Bible, can be deployed to justify, condemn, prescribe or proscribe virtually anything.

Whereas Jews, Christians and Muslims are deeply convinced that there exists a 'correct' interpretation of their holy texts, and make great efforts to discover it, the South Asian religions of Hinduism, Buddhism, Jainism and Sikhism view their mantras in a completely different way. Mantras are essentially poems, valued at least as much for their rhythmic and melodious qualities as for their meaning. Some are so old that said meaning is lost in the mists of time; others may never have had a literal meaning at all. Others yet, such as the mono-syllabic archetypical mantra *Om*, have so many different meanings that it is useless to try to isolate a 'real' meaning. It would be sense-less, too, because meaning in the usual sense is not what mantras are about. Their precise role and function vary from religion to religion, but essentially they are a means for the chanter or the audience to achieve an altered state of mind of some sort. Heightened sensitivity is one, or loss of self, enhanced concentration or mystical fulfil-ment and elation, as can be observed in the bands of Hare Krishnas who roam the streets of big cities across the world, chanting their four-line mantra:

> *Hare krshna, hare krshna*
> *Krshna krshna, hare hare*
> *Hare rama, hare rama*
> *Rama rama, hare hare.*

Often, but not always, endless repetition is part of the process, and often, but again not always, mantras must be chanted out loud.

The South Asian religions are not alone in their recognition of the psychological effects of the melody, sound and rhythm of words and sentences quite apart from their meaning, if any. All the great reli-gions of the world have elements of community singing, collective prayer and priests chanting melodious, sometimes incomprehens-ible formulas. So does magic. Spells in all cultures, from all corners of the world, contain words chosen for their sounds alone. Quite often, these are words that imitate sounds associated with whatever the spell is supposed to secure, invoke or guard against. As Derek and Julia Parker put it in their *The Power of Magic* (1992):

> Pronouncing a spell to make a fishing boat successful, for instance, a tribal magician will use the names of various kinds of buoyant woods which float especially well; and other words which mimic the sounds made by the waves and winds. Similarly, a spell for successful hunting will use words which imitate the sound of running animals or wounded or dying beasts.[2]

Spells intended to harm and hurt may contain so-called words of power, nonsense words concocted just for their supposedly unpleasant and ominous sound, such as *atalsloym* or *charusihoa*. Perhaps the best-known example of a spell whose direct meaning is doubled by its sonorous qualities is in Shakespeare's tragedy *Macbeth*. After winning a decisive battle against an invading army from Norway, this Scottish general is told by three witches that he will be king of Scotland. The prediction is borne out the very next day, when, on the instigation of his ambitious wife, Macbeth kills his rightful king before sunrise, usurps the throne in the morning and starts liquidating the competition. Then, his conscience beginning to trouble him a bit, he rides out to search for the witches and ask them for guidance. He finds the hags on the moors, busy preparing some filthy poisonous potion while chanting this bleak refrain:

> *Double, double toil and trouble;*
> *Fire burn, and cauldron bubble.*

It's bubbly, black and altogether baleful with all those low, dark, round vowels. The bard makes clever use of our instinctive association of dark sounds, low-pitched voices and to some extent lax vowels with things that are big, burly and drab. High tweeting sounds and voices, on the other hand, like tense vowels, are commonly associated with smaller, weaker, more benevolent phenomena. That's only natural. In the real world, mice squeak, sparrows tweet and cats meow, but bears growl, eagles – according to the Bible – cry 'Woe, woe' in a great voice and lions roar.

People have always made use of these instinctive associations to scare, dumbfound or impress other people. War drums are an example, and the braying of the great war horns of the Roman legions is said to have made many a fearless barbarian turn and run. Steam locomotives had a shrieking flute to warn trespassers off the track, but huge ocean steamers bray deeper than St George's dragon, partly because deep sounds travel far in all directions, and partly because they befit the sheer size of the ships. During the first years of her career, the soon-to-be British prime minister Margaret Thatcher diligently trained her voice to become deeper, knowing that a lower pitch would increase her authority. The screeching, relatively high-pitched bagpipes that so admirably helped the British to establish their empire are only an apparent exception. Their strength is not pitch, but the eerily unreal, wailing, magical quality of the noise they produce, so unlike anything that walks the Earth. Just imagine yourself waiting with nothing but your spear and shield for a fight to the death to commence, when suddenly a line of giants in bear hats looms up out of the morning fog under the nerve-rending racket of bagpipes.

Higher pitch is what we use to get intimate with others and gain their confidence. The almost complete opposite of the witches' refrain, as regards the mood it is supposed to conjure up, is the way the teenybopper idol Brian Hyland in 1960 extolled the virtues of an

Itsy bitsy teenie weenie yellow polka dot bikini

Almost everything is tense here, the vowels pronounced with the tongue high in the mouth. It all adds to the sense of a sunny, joyfully relaxed beach and the both endearing and exciting frailty of the bashful beauty who has come out in her new skimpy attire for the first time. Another case in point is so-called motherese, the special tone of voice and vocabulary we all tend to use to address infants, or even puppies. We speak at an extremely high pitch, using all kinds of nonsense words, and greatly exaggerate the dynamics of the melody of our sentences, somewhat like this:

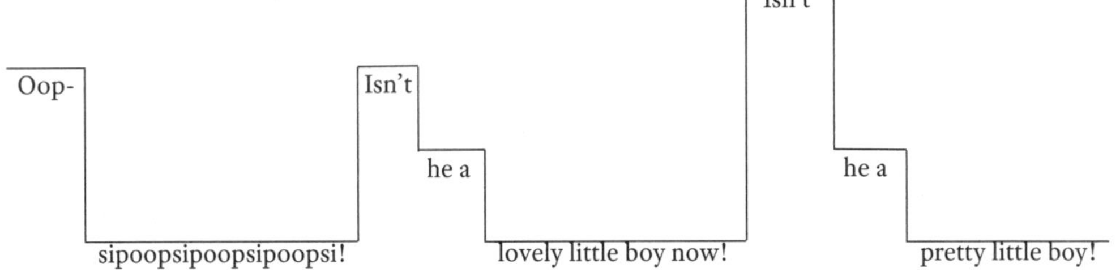

Notice that we do this only when talking to the infant itself. The moment we turn to somebody else in the room, we switch to normal mode. We also stop using motherese shortly after a child begins mumbling its own first real words – only its mother may carry on using it for a while in play, as a token of their special intimacy.

@#$%!

WITH THE INVENTION of writing, priests and sorcerers alike acquired a wonderful new source of power. Writing was invented independently several times over the course of world history. The New World, living up to its name, came last, when in what is now Mexico first the Olmec people and after them the Maya developed hieroglyphic scripts during the last millennium BCE. Long before that, sometime around 3200 BCE, the Sumerians who inhabited the fertile mudflats of Mesopotamia had developed cuneiform, a syllabic writing system that became the mother of just about all the alphabetic writing systems in existence today. At roughly the same time the hieroglyphic system – pictogrammatic at first, later developing into a mixture of alphabetic and formulaic signs – was invented in the Nile delta, although it is unclear whether this was a truly independent invention, or whether its emergence was sparked by ideas imported from Mesopotamia. It is also likely, although not certain, that in about 1200 BCE the Chinese invented their writing system completely on their own. That system, still in use today, differs deeply from all other systems, consisting of a great wealth of often quite complex characters that generally represent monosyllabic words. Out of it the syllabic systems of Japanese and Korean were developed.

Bookkeeping is what originally drove the invention of writing. It all started with signs for numbers to take stock of supplies and keep track of levies. Writing was a tool in the hands of the powerful and well-to-do from the very beginning; poor people have no use for accounts, since they can take stock of their belongings in the blink of an eye. Even in the days when only very few people were capable of reading or writing, everyone realized the enormous power that lay in those diminutive scrawls in clay or on papyrus or vellum. In a world full of the supernatural, reading alone must have seemed at least as wondrous to the uninitiated as a priest reading the entrails of a sheep or a diviner telling the future from the flight of a bird. On top of all that, it was a bidirectional form of 'magic'. Anyone literate could not only quite literally 'read the signs', he could send messages back to wherever those signs had come from. Readers and writers could pass their secret messages between themselves without even bothering to keep the coding from illiterate people. Just think of the sheer power bestowed on the literati: if they wanted to, they could have a messenger convey his own death sentence without the poor man ever suspecting a thing. Writing considerably deepened the chasm between illiterate ordinary people and those who claimed to have access to the supernatural: the witch doctors, the soothsayers, the sorcerers and above all the priests. It also strengthened the position of the last with respect to their secular masters, the kings and chieftains who now depended on the loyalty of their literate servants for both their livelihood and their information.

Of course, the whole point of the art of reading and writing is to record things so that they won't be forgotten, and to convey thoughts and information across distances in space and time. What a person writes down is usually meant to be read by another, if not others in general. Throughout history, the profitability of literacy to both the individual and society as a whole has increased with the percentage of people being able to read and write. That fact does not sit well with the secrecy and the exclusion of the uninitiated that have always been so desirable from the point of view of those who wish to exploit their literacy as a source of power and awe. Writing is a code by nature, but at the same time, it is necessarily a weak one. It won't have taken long for people who preferred their writings to remain secret to code the code itself, either by manipulating the relationship between symbols and their meaning or simply by inventing a jealously guarded secret alphabet.

Nowadays, the professional business of codes and ciphers has become the exclusive domain of mathematicians and computer scientists. Before that, codes could be surprisingly simple yet effective.

Most of us have dabbled in making codes at school. A popular one consists of simply replacing each letter of a message with its immediate predecessor or successor in the alphabet. 'Shifting one down' is how Stanley Kubrick and Arthur C. Clarke came to name the computer in their film *2001: A Space Odyssey* (1968) HAL – a play on the name of the dominant computer hardware company of the time, IBM. More than 2,000 years ago, replacing letters by their alphabetic successors was what Julius Caesar did to keep his enemies in the dark about his intentions. In fact, until quite recently all professional ciphers were variations, sometimes extremely convoluted ones, on this same theme of substitution. Everything depended on a secret key, a mechanical procedure known only to the sender and the receiver. The sender applied the key to his message to generate the coded version, which the receiver could turn back into its readable form by reversing the procedure. Even the famous Enigma coding machine used by the German forces during the Second World War was based on this principle. Still it took all the intelligence, energy and electronic technology the British and, to a lesser extent, the Americans could muster to crack just a few of its coded messages.

The world of magic never cared much for the bone-dry discipline of ciphers that depended on keys, perhaps because of a deep disdain for rationalism and its strict logic. And yet, it too had to record its secrets, spells, charms, rituals and recipes lest they be forgotten or imperfectly remembered, which would render them ineffectual. This was done in books that are nowadays called grimoires, some of which date back to the early Middle Ages or beyond. One of the oldest and best known, first compiled around the year 500, is *The Chaldean Oracles of Zoroaster*, of which only fragmentary texts have survived. An extremely old specimen that did survive intact is a little 1,300-year-old parchment from Egypt. It is written in Coptic and contains, among other things, spells for love and success, exorcisms and a ritual cure for leptospirosis, or Weil's disease, a potentially lethal infectious disease that is still endemic to the Nile region and affects more than 7 million people worldwide each year.

The term 'grimoire' itself is much younger. It was coined in France during the nineteenth century as an intentional corruption of *grammaire*, the French word for grammar, and has found its way into ordinary French to denote an unreadable book or incomprehensible text. This is apt: magic spells often do not follow the rules of ordinary language use, since magicians prefer mystification over clarity and add lots of words, either pre-existing or made up for the occasion, for their associative strength or their sonorous qualities rather than their meaning. More importantly, grimoires were often literally unreadable because they were written in some secret script.

There are quite a few writing systems to which magical qualities were traditionally attributed. Strangely, the most notorious one, the runic script, is not one of them. Runic script, in its most common form called Futhark, after the first six letters (F, U, Th, A, R, K) of the runic alphabet, did always have mystical overtones. This was partly because certain letters were associated with Nordic deities and partly because runes never became an ordinary communicative tool, unlike the Latin alphabet that is used in the Western world today. Instead, apart from short notes and messages for trade purposes, it was primarily used for inscriptions on memorial stones and on swords, combs and other personal belongings, and for compiling calendars and the like. All these uses are highly charged with symbolic and mystical meaning. Runes belonged primarily to the Germanic world, but have been found as far away from there

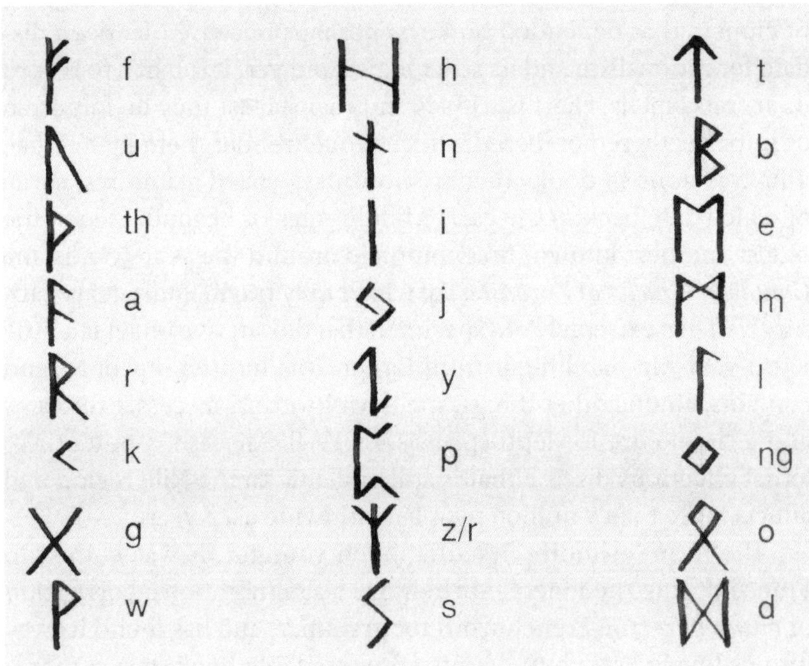

The Runic alphabet, or Futhark.

Dutch National Socialist Movement (NSB) cap from the Second World War era (*left*)
and the Ukrainian Azov Battalion insignia over the text 'Eastern Brotherhood' (*right*),
both sporting the Wolfsangel.

as Russia, the Balkans and Turkey. They date back to the second
century, and although the Christianization of Europe did much to
marginalize the 'heathen' runic script, it remained in use for mainly
decorative purposes in the remoter parts of Scandinavia until the
early twentieth century.

The association of runes with dark mysticism, with magic and
evil, and eventually with Nazi culture and mythology is down to the
Austrian writer, occultist and self-styled noble Guido von List. List,
who played an important part in developing the racist-occult Aryan
philosophy of *Blut und Boden*, 'blood and earth', in 1902, claimed
that the 'true' rune system had been revealed to him in a vision. He
stated that this was the symbol system of the original Aryans and
introduced two new symbols that had never before been part of any
runic alphabet. One of these was the *Wolfsangel*, 'wolf's hook', both
an actual tool for catching and killing wolves and an ancient magical
symbol of the Germanic world, frequently encountered in heraldry
and in architectural decoration. The *Wolfsangel* was subsequently
adopted by several ss and Wehrmacht divisions and by the Dutch
National Socialist movement. Other runes too, such as *odal* in the
German puppet state of Croatia, were adopted by fascist groups.
After the Second World War the symbols remained popular among
extreme right-wing and neo-Nazi groups, up to and including the
Ukrainian free corps Azov Battalion, which acquired quite a reputation when it took on the pro-Russian separatists in the Donbass

Modern font for the Enochian alphabet.

region of eastern Ukraine in 2014. Ever since List runes have been somewhat disreputable, but for all the wrong reasons.

Scripts expressly developed and intended for the secret codification of magical texts and spells include the Theban alphabet, which maps straightforwardly onto the modern Latin alphabet, and Celestial Writing, Malachim and a script called 'Passing the River', all mapping on to the Hebrew alphabet. A special case is so-called Enochian, which is not just an alphabet but a mysterious angelic language, instrumental in a system of Enochian magic.

Enochian was revealed to the prominent sixteenth-century English scholar, astrologer and occultist John Dee. These days, the combination of scientific inquiry and magic, or even strong religious ideas, seems odd, but in Dee's time there was hardly a distinction between science and alchemy, astronomy and astrology, medicine and sorcery, philosophy of nature and religion. Dee – who taught as a young man at the Sorbonne in Paris and went on to become an adviser to Queen Elizabeth I – claimed that angels had dictated to him, through his assistant, the scryer and spiritual medium Edward Kelley, the celestial language God had used when creating the world. This was purportedly the original language spoken by Adam and Eve and their offspring, knowledge of which had been lost when its last speaker,

Enoch, Noah's great-grandfather, had died. Apart from the Enochian alphabet everything is mostly a mystery, since the angels left much of what they told Kelley and Dee untranslated. In this respect the angels were less obliging than the archangel Gabriel when he dictated the Quran to Muhammad a thousand years before, or the angel Moroni in 1827, when he lent Joseph Smith the original gold plates inscribed with the text of the *Book of Mormon* for translation into English.

@#$%!

LINGUISTS AND OTHERS have tried unsuccessfully to determine whether or not Enochian reflected an actual language and, if so, whether it was just obfuscated English or Latin, or a language in its own right. Some noticed that Enochian had certain features that do not occur in natural languages, but were reminiscent of a phenomenon that is not really language, but closely related to it: glossolalia, also known as 'speaking in tongues'. Glossolalia, which derives from the classical Greek words γλῶσσα, meaning 'tongue' or 'language', and λαλέω, 'to babble', refers to a kind of more or less spontaneous, often dramatic outburst of ecstatic babbling or vocalizing common among Pentecostal and Charismatic Christian congregations, but also occurring among the Inuit and the Saami of northern Scandinavia, in voodoo and in several shamanic cultures. It is a kind of frantic trance that is also reported to occur with mental illnesses such as schizophrenia, but it is far more common in religious contexts. The common feature is temporary lack of control, which in religious contexts is caused by self-induced hysteria.

As it turns out, what people blurt out during such fits are not expressions in some mysterious celestial or diabolical language. Rather, their utterances are strings of unrelated syllables: sounds that are lengthened, bent and warped, but generally remain in keeping with the phonological laws and restrictions of the speaker's native language. A French glossolalist will sound somewhat French, an Englishman a tad British and a Cantonese will have a Chinese ring to his utterances. Nevertheless, people have always been quick to read all kinds of deeper meaning into these ramblings: messages from 'the other side', from God, from the Devil, and in voodoo from a *lwa*, a spirit.

Glossolalia was also a feature of early Christendom, and even of the fledgling sect led by Jesus himself. At the end of the Gospel according to Mark (16:17–18), Christ instructs the Apostles to go into the world to spread the faith before ascending to heaven, adding:

> And these signs will accompany those who believe: in my name they will drive out demons; they will speak in new tongues; they will pick up snakes with their hands; and when they drink deadly poison, it will not hurt them at all; they will place their hands on sick people, and they will get well.

From the magically laden context, it is clear that by 'new tongues' the Lord does not mean Iberic, Egyptian or Urdu. This is a mage talking, and what he is referring to are miraculous events, involving 'tongues' yet unheard – in short, glossolalic rants.

This goes to show that even in those days, glossolalia was not a new or unknown phenomenon. On the contrary, it became so popular among early Christians that the Apostle Paul deemed it necessary to discuss it at length in his first letter to the Corinthians. Paul is obviously aware of the danger that enthusiastic but unruly Christian cells like the one in Corinth will forget what being a Christian is really about and turn their gatherings into raves not unlike the dance festivals of today, where people lose themselves and their inhibitions in a noise- and drugs-induced trance. He is well aware that glossolalia is too alluring and too powerfully addictive for him to be able to put a stop to the practice, so he does not simply forbid the Corinthians to indulge in it. He only warns them not to get carried away, as a concerned parent would:

> For anyone who speaks in a tongue does not speak to people but to God. Indeed, no one understands them; they utter mysteries by the Spirit. But the one who prophesies speaks to people for their strengthening, encouraging and comfort . . . I would like every one of you to speak in tongues, but I would rather have you prophesy. The one who prophesies is greater than the one who speaks in tongues, unless someone interprets. (1 Corinthians 14:2–5)

Paul is on a roll here, really hammering it in, but taking good care not to antagonize the Corinthians:

Unless you speak intelligible words with your tongue, how will anyone know what you are saying? You will just be speaking into the air. Undoubtedly there are all sorts of languages in the world, yet none of them is without meaning. If then I do not grasp the meaning of what someone is saying, I am a foreigner to the speaker, and the speaker is a foreigner to me. So it is with you . . . For this reason the one who speaks in a tongue should pray that they may interpret what they say. For if I pray in a tongue, my spirit prays, but my mind is unfruitful. So what shall I do? I will pray with my spirit, but I will also pray with my understanding; I will sing with my spirit, but I will also sing with my understanding. (1 Corinthians 14:9–15)

A few verses later (14:18–19) comes the clincher:

I thank God that I speak in tongues more than all of you. But in the church I would rather speak five intelligible words to instruct others than ten thousand words in a tongue.

Most people know about glossolalia through a different biblical story, the account in Acts 2:4 that details what happened at Whitsun after the Resurrection. As the Apostles were sitting together somewhere in Jerusalem there was suddenly a loud rustling sound, like a strong wind blowing through trees. As people came running to see what the weird sound was, tongues of fire appeared on the Apostles' heads, and they began speaking in every language one could think of. Everyone who was there was addressed in his own native tongue, or so the story goes. This is of course a complete reversal of straight glossolalia: the Apostles did not blurt out incomprehensible gibberish, but talked lucidly and eminently clearly in languages they had never learned how to speak. A miracle!

A miracle indeed, just not exactly this miracle. For although glossolalia is well established and broadly attested, there are no reliable accounts at all of xenolalia, as such speaking coherently in unlearned languages is called, let alone of speaking several different languages at once. It is also not exactly what the Bible says happened. The Good Book states that 'All of them were filled with the Holy Spirit and began to speak in other tongues as the Spirit enabled them,' and goes on to explain:

> Now there were staying in Jerusalem God-fearing Jews from every nation under heaven. When they heard this sound, a crowd came together in bewilderment, because each one heard their own language being spoken. Utterly amazed, they asked: 'Aren't all these who are speaking Galileans? Then how is it that each of us hears them in our native language? Parthians, Medes and Elamites; residents of Mesopotamia, Judea and Cappadocia, Pontus and Asia, Phrygia and Pamphylia, Egypt and the parts of Libya near Cyrene; visitors from Rome (both Jews and converts to Judaism); Cretans and Arabs – we hear them declaring the wonders of God in our own tongues!' Amazed and perplexed, they asked one another, 'What does this mean?'
>
> Some, however, made fun of them and said, 'They have had too much wine.'
>
> Then Peter stood up with the Eleven, raised his voice and addressed the crowd: 'Fellow Jews and all of you who live in Jerusalem, let me explain this to you; listen carefully to what I say. These people are not drunk, as you suppose. It's only nine in the morning! No, this is what was spoken by the prophet Joel: "In the last days, God says, I will pour out my Spirit on all people. Your sons and daughters will prophesy, your young men will see visions, your old men will dream dreams."' (Acts 2:5–17)

The key words here are 'all people'. These, according to Peter, are the last days, for the Messiah has come. So this must be when the Spirit is being poured out on all people, not just the Apostles. It happens again a few days later, when the Holy Spirit falls upon all who are listening to one of Peter's speeches:

> While Peter was still speaking these words, the Holy Spirit came on all who heard the message. The circumcised believers who had come with Peter were astonished that the gift of the Holy Spirit had been poured out even on Gentiles. For they heard them speaking in tongues and praising God. (Acts 10:44–6)

Around this time, then, God was in the habit of pouring out the spirit on all people, believers and non-believers alike, just as Joel had predicted. And we may take it on Peter's authority that this was the case at Whitsun as well, which means that not only the Apostles but everyone present was under the influence. So the miracle may not be about what the Apostles were saying – provided they said anything intelligible, since not a syllable is recorded in the Bible – but about what the audience perceived. The miracle is in their heads, their minds. After all, it is hard to see how, even with the help of God, one man can hold forth in numerous languages *simultaneously*, and still be heard by every individual in a multilingual crowd of perfectly normal, sane and un-intoxicated listeners, to speak only his particular language. What happened that day seems like a case of collective self-delusion or hysteria, a phenomenon not all that rare in closed and inspired communities to this day – be they religious congregations, sects or boarding-school classes.

In fact, the story in Acts 2 need not reflect anything miraculous at all. There is a perfectly reasonable explanation for what happened that day in Jerusalem, as well as for why those events took place only then. First, notice that Peter himself has no trouble at all addressing everybody simultaneously at the gathering. As the theologian Robert Zerhusen has pointed out, this is quite understandable. The audience on Whitsunday consisted of 'God-fearing Jews from every nation under heaven'. These Jews were on the streets of central Jerusalem for a good religious reason: they had come to the city to celebrate Pentecost. They were religious tourists, not unlike the modern visitors to the festival of Avignon or the sports fans from all corners of the world who jam the streets of each city that the Olympics are held in. In those days, all Palestinian Jews including the Apostles, and the majority of those who had come from further away, were native speakers of one of two languages. Westerners spoke Greek, easterners Aramaic. It is not difficult for twelve men to address a crowd in two languages in such a way that everybody present may pick out an Apostle using *his* particular native tongue, and let us not forget that there were no public-address systems, so if a sizable crowd were to be addressed, a speaker needed repeaters who relayed what was said to those standing further away. People were used to picking up a speech from some repeater close by within the crowd, while watching the speaker on his dais. But why, then, were these languages called 'other languages', and why are the Apostles ridiculed as having had too much wine? This is where Hebrew comes in. Although classical Hebrew had ceased to be used as the vernacular, it was still the language of choice for religious purposes, and Pentecost is a religious feast. In this context, Jews would expect speakers on religious matters to speak proper Hebrew at Pentecost. For the Apostles to express themselves in the 'other languages', to wit Greek and Aramaic, would have been considered bad form. Who were these louts, who hadn't the wherewithal to behave themselves properly? Drunken vagrants, perhaps?

@#$%!

AS WITH WORDS, so with numbers. Numbers have had a strong magical appeal since time immemorial. Before the invention of written number symbols, there was no arithmetic, only counting. The only way to keep track of things and the amounts in which they occurred was by tallying: a notch or scratch for a unit and another for the next. This was practical only as long as numbers were small, but it was sufficient for people to develop an understanding of the moon cycle and the way the seasons worked – by counting full moons, for instance – or to grasp the cyclic character of the mystery of menstruation, which has intrigued mankind, it would seem, for as long as it has existed. At the Ignatievka Cave near Chelyabinsk in the southern Ural Mountains of Russia, a red-ochre human figure was found in 1980 with 28 spots between its legs. The work has been carbon-dated to about 6000 BCE, way before the invention of any kind of writing. Elsewhere, archaeologists have found even older traces of red ochre that could be interpreted as 28 lines running down from a natural fold in the rock, shaped somewhat like a woman's crotch. These are without doubt the oldest testimonies to a sense of numbers ever to have been discovered, and they clearly show that numbers were connected to mysteries and the incomprehensible from the very beginning. Counting is a first step on the way to predictability, which in turn offers the perspective of control. In an otherwise uncertain, ill-understood world, even a modicum of predictability or control is a precious commodity.

It wasn't until written number symbols and their names were invented, however, that people came to fully recognize the immense power that lay hidden in them. The basic difference between the scratches used in tallying and real number symbols is that numbers are not mere representations of units – one scratch stands for one bushel of wheat, two scratches for two bushels, and so on

– but represent an abstract idea, a concept that cannot be matched to objects or observable phenomena directly. 'Five' and its Latin, Chinese or Hindi written symbols 5, 五 and ৭ may refer to a stack of five bushels of wheat, of course, but there is no object or phenomenon in the world that equals 'fivehood'. So here was something really, fundamentally new: there was a deeper unobservable quality to number symbols.

Number names and their symbols soon proved to open the gates of a conceptual realm of immeasurable richness and power. Number symbols could refer to quantities, but might also be viewed as units, abstract entities whose only representation in the physical world was the symbol for writing them. Thus began arithmetic, which not only tamed and domesticated even the largest numbers imaginable, but also unlocked a fully predictable, absolutely reliable world of numbers and rules. This hierarchical system exists and functions irrespective of the kinds of entity its numbers are used to refer to. Whether it is bushels in a barn, children in the village or steps to get to the next town, three and three invariably equal six and ten times ten is always a hundred. And, while arithmetic does not depend on anything in the material world, the material world obeys the rules of arithmetic to the letter.

Soon there turned out to exist laws and regularities of all kinds between numbers themselves, and mathematics was born, the inquiry into the characteristics of numbers and the relations between them. Mathematics proved an eternally flowing source of wonder and amazement, yielding many of the insights that allowed humanity to shape and change the world, but also complete mysteries, games and phenomena that are merely odd and funny, or aesthetically pleasing. Around 530 BCE one of the first serious thinkers of the classical world, Pythagoras of Samos, set up an influential philosophical society in Croton, a Greek colony in southern Italy, devoted to the study of nature, society and religion. No eyewitness account of what went on there has come down to us, but according to Plato and other, still later classical writers, Pythagoras and his disciples were among the first to take up mathematics as a subject in its own right, and discovered many numerical regularities involving natural phenomena. Today, every thirteen-year-old in the developed world is still taught Pythagoras' theorem, describing the proportional relationships between the edges of right-angled triangles. This theorem is the bedrock of essential skills such as surveying and architecture, and although the proportionality expressed by the theorem was already known in India and Mesopotamia long before Pythagoras was born, it seems fair to credit his school with giving it concrete shape. Pythagoras' school also seems to have discovered how musical notes, overtones and scales were related, as well as the rudiments of the laws of musical harmony. Furthermore they recognized, or theorized, that the movements of the celestial bodies must also be governed by mathematical laws. In fact, they got so carried away with their discoveries that they proposed that the whole world and indeed the whole universe was governed by numbers – that numbers were 'the real thing', the essence from which the whole physical world was derived.

In those days, when there was no distinction between science, mysticism, religion and magic, mystical powers of all sorts were readily imputed to numbers. Much of that survives today. Millions of people all over the world believe in lucky and unlucky numbers. Although there is no conceivable reason for any number to be lucky or unlucky, these beliefs are not only widespread but also extremely persistent – with real consequences. In much of the Western world, the number thirteen has had a bad reputation since the days of the Roman Republic and before. Especially in the English-speaking world, high-rises and big hotels tend to skip the number when counting floors or numbering rooms. Likewise, airline companies skip thirteen as a row number. The Iranians have also always mistrusted thirteen, which counted as unlucky in Zoroastrianism. Even after

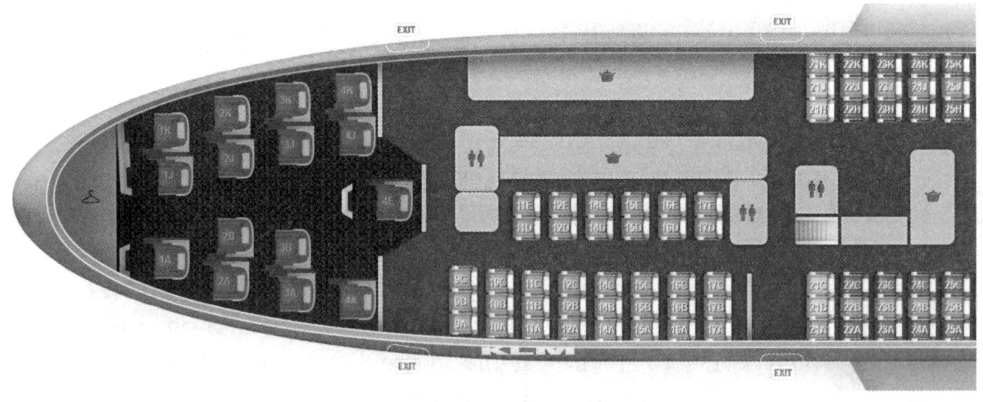

Seating plan of a KLM Boeing 747-400. Note the lack of a row 13.

the Islamic Revolution of 1979 they did not give up the tradition of Sizdah Be-dar, the thirteenth day. According to Iranian folklore, the thirteenth day of the new year is one when evil spirits may strike, so Iranian families get out of town and out of the way of the unruly spirits on that day to spend it picnicking in the countryside.

In the Far East, the number eight is considered perfect and lucky, partly because in languages such as Chinese, it sounds more or less like words meaning prosperity and wealth. People in China, Taiwan and Korea will spend impressive sums of money on securing a car registration or telephone number containing as many eights as possible. Even the authorities are sensitive to this. Before the 623-metre-high (2,044 ft) Shanghai Tower was constructed, the highest building in Pudong, the newly developed business centre of Shanghai, was the Jin Mao tower, which had 88 floors for double good fortune. And it was no accident that the opening ceremony of the 2008 Summer Olympics in Beijing began at eight minutes and eight seconds past eight on the eighth of August, the eighth month of the year, in 2008.

In the Christian world, the number 888 enjoys some notoriety as the Jesus number. It is a result of applying the Gematria, a numerological system the Hebrews of antiquity adopted from the Assyro-Babylonians, to the Greek version of Christ's name, Ιησούς (*Iesous*). Like Latin and Greek, the languages of the Middle East used letters as number symbols, which gave people the idea that words and numbers were somehow mystically related. In the Gematria, which the Jews later developed into the Kabbalah, the letters in the name Ιησούς stand for the numbers 10, 8, 200, 70, 400 and 200 respectively, adding up to 888. Much better known than the Jesus number is the biblical number 666, mentioned in Revelation 13:18 as the 'number of the Beast' – the Antichrist. It is presented as a puzzle to be solved: 'This calls for wisdom. Let the person who has insight calculate the number of the beast, for it is the number of a man. That number is 666.' Unfortunately – or should we say fortunately, for all things occult must remain shrouded in mystery by definition – so far nobody has been able to come up with a numerologically sufficiently credible name, although many still believe that the Roman emperor Nero was meant.

And yet, 666 is avoided by many people and frowned upon by even more. In 1986, when the Greek government was rumoured to be about to introduce new identity cards with numbers beginning

666, thousands of Athenians rallied to protest in front of the parliament building in Syntagma Square. Another example is the former American president Ronald Reagan, a great believer in the occult. After his presidency he moved back to California, to a house on 666 St Cloude Drive, Los Angeles, and immediately had the number changed to 668. Reagan was far from the only modern politician to dabble in numerology and astrology. Like him, for instance, both the former French president François Mitterrand and Neelie Kroes, European Commissioner for Competition and for the Digital Agenda from 2004 to 2014, used to consult astrologers.

@#$%!

WATER IN THE FORM of springs, wells, ponds and streams has always held magical appeal. It is clear, yet dark. It seems to offer a passage to the underworld, but we cannot get through. It is both indispensable to life and dangerous, for it can devour and kill you. It gurgles and bubbles and hisses as if speaking and seems full of life, yet has no shape. Small wonder that belief in water nymphs, naiads and spirits was and in many parts of the world still is widespread, as is the belief in an underworld with its own deities, associated with the mysteries of fertility and growth as well as death and decay. Until quite recently, farmers in rural Italy cursed their enemies by casting a spell over a stone in their hand, which was then hurled into a pond or stream to petition the supernatural powers inhabiting it. Even today the idea of enlisting the services of supernatural powers that reside in water and below the earth's surface still echoes through the Western world in the form of wishing wells. And don't forget love locks, which are typically hung on bridges – almost never viaducts or overpasses.

How long ago such magical cursing rituals developed and how common they have been through the ages must remain a mystery, because they leave no trace. Still, we can safely assume that they are very old and very widespread indeed, judging from the ubiquity of traces of similar written magic. Curses inscribed on tablets and stones were common to the classical world and the Middle East from early on and have been found in considerable numbers in ancient waterways, springs and ponds – or what's left of them – and sometimes even in graves. When the world was young, the art of writing still new and hardly anybody literate, writing must have counted as very powerful 'medicine'.

It was the Romans who carried the art of these written curses to exceptional heights and gave them the name *defixiones*, 'binding spells'. At first glance, *defixiones* look a bit like the practice of sticking pins or hammering nails into a doll representing the object of one's anger in an attempt to make that person suffer or even die. Actually they are very different. Torturing dolls or footprints is based on the Law of Similarity, as we have seen. But proper *defixio*, although it was occasionally accompanied by a figurine in a little coffin or with needles stuck through it, is primarily based on the Law of Contact. Next to writing, it usually involves something intimately belonging to the person to be cursed, such as a few strands of hair or nail parings.

The idea was to write a curse or spell on a thinly hammered-out sheet of lead, fold it up around the material taken from the target, drive a pin or nail through the package and throw it into a spring, pond or stream, so that it would reach deities of the underworld, who were called upon to effect the spell. These spells, mostly curses, could be quite elaborate, as is this one, found in the vicinity of Rome:

> Malchio, (son or slave) of Nikon: his eyes, hands, fingers, arms, nails, hair, head, feet, thigh, belly, buttocks, navel, chest, nipples, neck, mouth, cheeks, teeth, lips, chin, eyes, forehead, eyebrows, shoulder blades, shoulders, sinews, guts, marrow, belly, cock, leg, trade, income, health, I do curse (bind) in this tablet.[3]

In this case, as in many others, the curser resorted to using stone or clay, although lead was easy to hammer out, inscribe and fold as well as cheap and readily available. It is easy to picture the man scratching away at his tablet, burning with indignation and spite, and intent on letting not even the least significant part of damned Malchio get away. Romans loved cursing each other this way, throwing binding spells at each other for the flimsiest reasons, like so:

> O, Proserpina, I ask, entreat and implore thee to punish the person, whoever he be, who has borrowed or stolen or abstracted from my wardrobe six shirts and two linen cloaks.[4]

Besides personal hatred and spite, binding spells were sometimes also used to light the fire of love in a hoped-for amorous companion,

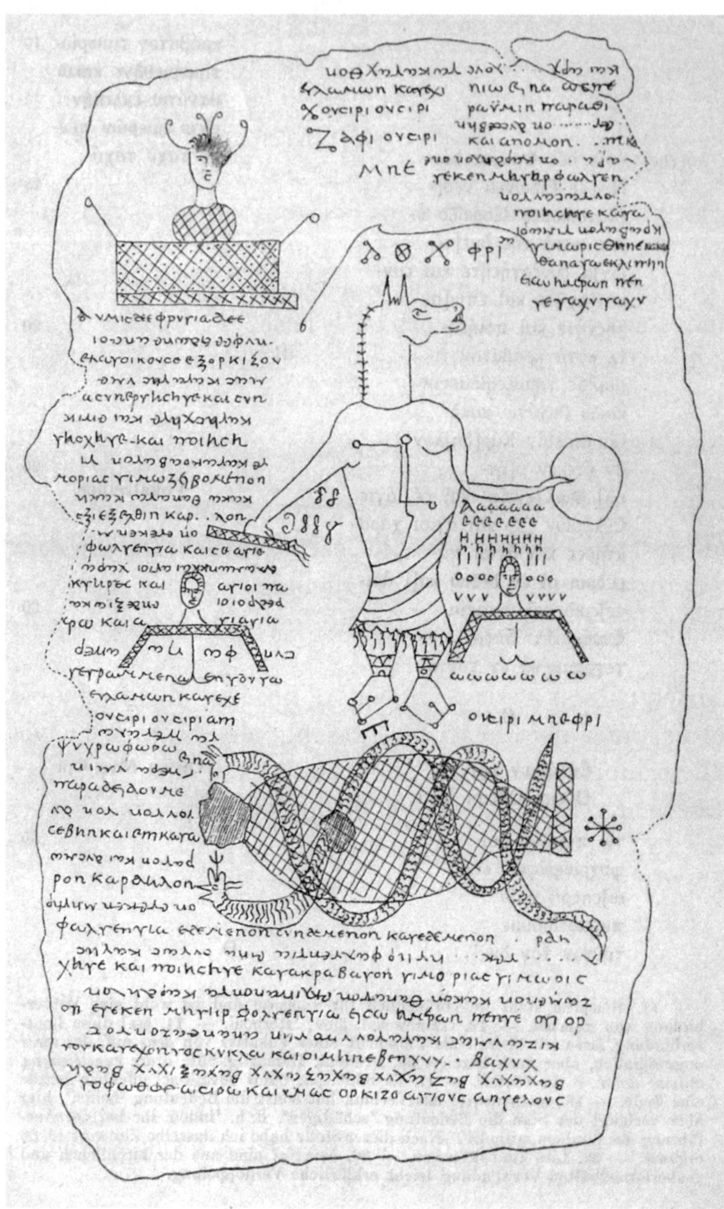

Drawing of a defixive lead plaque, c. AD 400, found in the Vigna Marini alongside the Appian Way in Rome, motivated by sports rivalry. It shows how the idea of binding must be taken quite literally. At the bottom is the dead and mummified accursed rival jockey, swathed in cloth and smothered by two snakes for good measure. The figure with the horse's head in the middle is presumed to be a spirit connected to the circus. At the top, Osiris emerges from his tomb to do his work, binding strings sprouting from his head and coffin.

The Curse of Babylon

Something very like the Roman *defixio* is found in the Old Testament, in Jeremiah 51:61–4. God has told the prophet Jeremiah at great length how he will destroy Babylon, the greatest power in the world, for conquering Jerusalem, razing the temple and abducting the population. When the Judean king goes on a trip to the city to cheer up the exiled community, Jeremiah hands his chief chamberlain a scroll with God's rant against the city, and instructs him as follows: 'When you get to Babylon, see that you read all these words aloud. Then say, "Lord, you have said you will destroy this place, so that neither people nor animals will live in it; it will be desolate forever." When you finish reading this scroll, tie a stone to it and throw it into the Euphrates. Then say, "So will Babylon sink to rise no more because of the disaster I will bring on her. And her people will fall."'

or inspired by rivalry, particularly in the world of horse racing, another Roman obsession. The horses of rival teams were cursed to break their legs or create havoc by rearing. Such *defixiones* have been found fastened to starting gates or other structures in the circus, raising the suspicion that it wasn't always the person throwing the curse who put it in its place, but a professional with contacts in the right places. In fact, over time there emerged a whole industry of professional spell writers who composed spells on demand and even kept stocks of prefab spells in which only the name of the target was left blank. These professionals also knew their way around the *voces mysticae*, 'mystical expressions', that in time came to dominate *defixiones*. These were unintelligible words and apparently meaningless series of letters that were supposed to represent the 'true' names and titles of deities and other powers in supernatural language, in order better to reach them.

Strictly speaking, all this was illegal almost from the city's beginning. Table seven of the Twelve Tables, Rome's first written body of law, put up in the Forum in 449 BCE, branded 'incantations and magic' to make crops fail or people ill a capital offence, on a par with poisoning. Judging from the number of curses found, nobody took much heed. Still, flippancy did not sit well with the usually rather stuffy Roman authorities, who found the practice socially disruptive and tried unsuccessfully to ban it again during the last years of the Republic. The real mystery here is, of course, how the authorities became convinced of the social undesirability of *defixiones* if the curses were indeed thrown into water or, failing that, buried, only to be found more than 2,000 years later by diligent archaeologists. Either they must all have been at it themselves as well, or people took care to make it known to others, perhaps their intended victims, that a curse had been laid upon someone.

In spite of all the efforts by religious and secular authorities to root out this kind of magic, written curse tablets remained popular for many centuries and were still used in Greece until shortly before the First World War. Equally unsuccessful were efforts to stamp out the use of two other kinds of magically tainted words and expressions: taboo terms and obscenities.

4

THE QUEEN'S CUNT

What could be offensive about the Queen's cunt? It is an essential feature of her anatomy, one that is shared by half the people on Earth and highly appreciated, even revered, if you will, by most of the other half. In fact, humanity would not exist without it, so one might say that the Queen's cunt has a lot going for it. And yet, the mere mention of it made you feel uneasy just now, just as Gustave Courbet's painting *L'Origine du monde*, 'The origin of mankind' (1866), never fails to stir up feelings of unease in viewers. Like the painting, naming the royal vagina is confrontational, very uncomfortably 'in your face'.

Why should that be so? The easy answer is, of course, that the term *cunt* is taboo. Not only that, the Queen herself is in some sense taboo as well: mentioning the Queen's cunt constitutes a double transgression. But that doesn't really explain anything except that 'taboo' can mean both unmentionable and untouchable. To find out what it is that renders a word taboo, meaning improper, dirty or obscene, we must first establish where the taboo resides.

Clearly, it is not in the sounds of the word itself. There are only a few verbal expressions that are obscene on account of how they sound alone. The raspberry is one, as is the guttural 'bleh' that resembles vomiting and expresses disgust, but on the whole such onomatopoeic obscenities are rare – they are not even real words. Also, in a handful of cases similarity between the sound patterns of an emotionally neutral word and a taboo one has led to the former being marginalized or replaced. In English, *coney* (rhymes with *honey*) has given way to *rabbit* and in America *ass* and *cock* have been supplanted by *donkey* and *rooster* on account of their similarity to *cunt* (which also appears as *cunny*), *arse* and *cock* meaning penis, respectively. But again, such cases are very rare, except perhaps among extreme prudes.

Sporadically, sound-pattern clashes occur in multilingual environments. One such case is the English word 'such', which sounds almost identical to the phrase for *wet cunt* in Nootka, an indigenous language spoken on Vancouver Island, British Columbia. Speakers of Nootka feel squeamish every time they have to use *such* in their English, and tend to avoid it. Similarly, Thai people feel uncomfortable saying English *yet* and *key*, which are rather too close to their own *jéd*, to copulate, and *khîi*, shit. In the eleventh century the Arab lexicographer Mahmūd al-Kāšgari recorded that the Oğuz, the people now known as the Turkish, would skip verses containing the Arabic conjunction *ʔam*, 'or', when reciting the Quran because it sounded like Turkish *am*, cunt. In fact, the same was true of any Arabic word containing the syllables *am*, *sik* (Turkish for prick) or *tılak* (Turkish for clitoris, literally 'little tongue'). In the Netherlands every school class titters when it is first taught the English verb *cut*, virtually identical to Dutch *kut*, cunt, and the noun *bill*, which means 'buttock' to them. Some years ago Dutch tourists in London were surprised and amused by the huge blue signs blaring LUL, short for London Underground Limited, at the entrance to every tube station. Dutch *lul* is the direct equivalent of English *prick* and *dickhead* rolled into one. Imagine how a headline such as 'Budget Cuts – LUL Drivers to Pay Bill' would strike them.

The converse of this phenomenon exists as well. Sometimes people will avoid using perfectly innocent words in their own language if there are speakers around in whose language they resemble taboo words. In the presence of English-speaking white people, those of the Creek Nations in North America will avoid using words such as *fákki*, 'soil', *fakkinú:la*, 'brick', and *apíssi*, 'fat, obese'. Thai students in the United States do the same with *fàg*, 'bean pod', *fág*, 'pumpkin', *phríg*, 'chilli pepper' and *khán*, 'to squeeze out'.

Awkward as such inconveniences may be, these are no more than rare and random linguistic traffic accidents. In no way do they point to a phonetic source for the negative appraisal of multitudes of words in every language you can think of. It is quite safe to say that, generally, there is no connection between the sound pattern of a word and its appreciation.

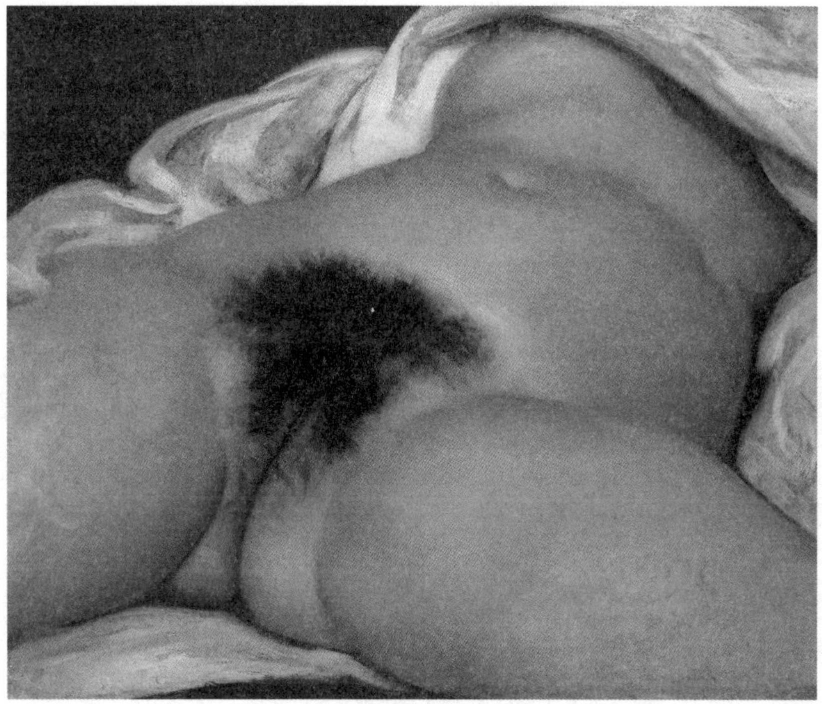

Gustave Courbet, *L'Origine du monde*, 1866, oil on canvas.

If taboo-ness does not reside in the sound pattern of a word, then perhaps we should look the other way, at the actual thing a word refers to. Here we seem to fare somewhat better. It does indeed look as though certain physical objects are in some sense taboo by and of themselves. Prime examples are excrement and bodily fluids. People generally have an aversion to shit, vomit, urine, pus, snot, spit, blood and semen – even, and sometimes especially, their own. While it is true that over the past four or five centuries our aversion to these substances has increased enormously and the taboos about some of them have deepened accordingly, they were never appreciated as completely unproblematic. Nobody in their right mind ever began munching a sandwich next to a pool of reeking human barf if they could avoid it. We feel similar revulsion towards dead bodies, sick and deformed creatures, rats, mice and large insects in close proximity, and all animals that move fast, come near us and behave unpredictably, such as moths and bats. This makes perfect evolutionary sense: excrement, all those fluids and unsound bodies are associated with sickness, danger and death, and if something comes close and you cannot control it, it is best avoided.

Swedish public transport fun for English speakers: the sign says 'final station'.

It is reasonable to assume that the taboo character of objects and substances rubs off on the terms referring to them. The same probably holds for actions involving them, so that activities such as fucking and shitting, as well as the verbs referring to them, are taboo because they involve taboo body parts and substances. Even so, biologically inspired taboos are a partial explanation at best. It is true that most terms for excrement and body fluids are felt to be taboo to varying degrees, as are terms for dead, sick and deformed creatures. But quite generally, the names of other disagreeable animals and of equally horrifying, rotting or stinking matter are not, unless the animal forms a real threat. Moreover, a great many taboo words do not refer to anything in the physical world at all, including a lot of rather unacceptable slurs. The *motherfucker*, *slut*, *pederast*, *scumbag* and *brown-noser* are figments of the imagination alone. They do not reference objects or actions; they are human judgements on other humans.

Also, most of the things that are referred to by taboo words have many names that differ widely in acceptability. A *cunt* is the same thing as a *pussy*, a *clam*, a *quim*, a *slit* and a *vagina*, and has more than a thousand other names in English alone, up to and including the enigmatically ominous *down there*. Most of these synonyms are definitely not part of civilized conversation, but in specific spheres they serve a purpose. Safely among themselves, women may discuss the details and condition of their intimate anatomy in any terms, depending on their own attitudes, how well they know and trust each other, and to what extent they are prepared to let others into their private lives. When consulting their doctor, however, these same women in all probability revert to the stodgy *vagina* and perhaps even *down there*. Doctors are never to be made light of. Your very presence in the consulting room is proof that something may be amiss, and your doctor is the magician with access to healing spells, potions and rituals. Even if your GP is the nicest, most sympathetic GP in the world, you are still the beggar and he or she the benefactor, with power over pain, misery, life and death. So yes, people feel the need for a little distance.

As the table 'Shades of shit in English' shows, the differences in acceptability between words for the same thing cannot be ranked on a simple scale from good to bad. Rather, synonyms tend to belong to specific, occasionally overlapping spheres of life and experience. In the table, only the first 7 out of a total of 43 (there are still more, by the way) are rated according to their acceptability alone. Within categories, there is a surprising lack of difference in acceptability, and the words are freely interchangeable – bar other considerations,

Shades of shit in English	
Taboo	shit
Mildly dysphemistic	crap, turd
Mildly euphemistic	(bodily) waste, faecal matter, filth, muck
Formal	faeces, excrement, excreta, defecation, ordure
With children	poop, poo, poo-poo, doo-doo, doody, caca, job, whoopsies, jobbies, cack, business, number two, BM
Of nappies	soil, dirt, load
Medical	stool, bowel movement
Animal, large units	pat, chip, pie, mess
Animal, small units	droppings
Animal, scientific	scat, coprolite, dung
Animal, agricultural	manure, guano
Human, agricultural	night soil, humanure, bio solids

(adapted from Steven Pinker, *The Stuff of Thought: Language as a Window into Human Nature* (2007))

such as the fact that *pat*, *pie* and *chip* refer to the excreta of specific animal species only (a cow does not produce *chips*, nor does a horse drop *pies*).

All these synonyms for shit exude a faint odour of unease, owing to the icky substance they ultimately refer to. But apart from that, they are perfectly appropriate within the bounds of their particular environment. *Stool* and *vagina* are part and parcel of the medical universe, as natural as *poop* in the nursery and *shit* and *slits* and *cunts* in a locker room full of zitty wannabe football heroes or among a troupe of aggressively drugged-out hooligans. It is the environment that determines what is and is not appropriate, and taboo words are taboo only if they are used or heard outside the spheres to which they belong.

So there we have it, finally: taboo language is language out of place, just as rubbish and debris are matter out of place, pests animals out of place and weeds plants out of place. Outside, sand and earth are the indispensable matter supporting our lives, but within the confines of our houses – our sphere, not theirs – they count as dust and dirt. There is nothing wrong with dandelions and clover in a meadow, but in a carefully maintained lawn they are considered weeds to be exterminated. Similarly, rats and mice are fine in the wild and in cages, but become pests when they trespass on our quarters and barns, and precious toys on the floor become junk to be cleared away as soon as their little owners turn their backs and start doing something else.

It is the same with inherently taboo substances such as excrement and other stuff that oozes from the body. Nobody gives a toss about them as long as they stay in their proper place: out of sight, safely under the skin. To a naive observer, say a Martian scouting our planet, it would be very puzzling indeed that the mere suggestion of a smear of shit on a shoe or even a toilet bowl gives the shudders to people who are wholly indifferent to the fact that they carry a pound of the same substance around inside themselves every day. Or that they willingly, even ecstatically, exchange bodily fluids such as semen and saliva (fondly calling it 'making love' and 'kissing'), but primly avoid stepping in a gob of spit on the pavement. Some people react strongly to blood, sometimes to the point of panicking, throwing up or fainting, but only when it is outside the body. The pulse of blood coursing through their veins does not affect them in any way, nor

**"I said, 'Eat your fucking vegetables, you
scum-sucking pig.' What did you think I said?"**

does the telling reddish complexion in others that can result from
embarrassment, exertion or hypertension.

Just as blood is all right as long as it stays where it belongs, inside
the network of veins and arteries in the body, almost any term is all
right in the context of an appropriate sphere. Some of these spheres
are obvious to everyone and created by circumstance. The doctor's
consulting room is a good example. It is a kind of hideaway where a
patient must feel safe enough to let his guard down and, quite literally, expose himself and be vulnerable. This calls for a certain level of
intimacy between patient and doctor. On the other hand, it is a place
where important, even life-threatening issues are at stake, where the
balance of power is skewed enormously in favour of the doctor. Such
imbalance calls for restraint and formality in order to keep emotions
from getting out of hand. These two conflicting requirements are
important reasons for the typical comportment of doctors, including
the friendly, avuncular tone of voice, the white coat, the persistent
use of pig Latin, and the typical vocabulary of expressly neutral
words such as *vagina* and *stool* for taboo notions and formal terms
for serious afflictions. No doctor worth her salt will inform you that
you suffer from the runs or have contracted a dose of the clap; she'll
call it diarrhoea and gonorrhoea.

Another easily recognizable sphere is the public arena, where relative strangers cross paths. It includes newspapers, broadcast media
and all kinds of public and semi-public venue. Almost anything is

appropriate here, as long as it's not too emotionally laden, either positively or negatively. Both carefree banter and serious commitment to a point of view are welcomed, but strongly emotional displays of either anger or elation, disrespect or adulation are not. Overly positive behaviour, such as dancing in the street or joyous shouting, is not frowned upon as much as unsettling displays of anger or aggression are, but only as long as it is not so extreme that it becomes threatening in its own right. As a consequence, in public virtually all words for taboo subjects are usually out of place. Cunts and shit are just as inappropriate in public places, from the greengrocer's to the House of Commons, as are vaginas and poo-poo or stool. In 2016 the American president Donald Trump caused a considerable stir by stating about women that, as a powerful person, 'you can do anything to them, grab 'em by the pussy.' But even this unrivalled vulgarian had not risked those words in public. He said them when he mistakenly thought he was safely among sycophants who wished and needed to be impressed; in the video of the event, you can actually hear one giggling in the background.[1]

Certain spheres are so stressful that they have strong and strange effects on what language is deemed appropriate. One, perhaps the most extreme, is the lift, where perfect strangers are forced to invade each other's personal space. This appears to be such a breach of the social laws governing intimacy that virtually nothing is appropriate any more and people clam up. To a slightly lesser degree the same applies to overcrowded trains, buses and subways.

Another example is offered by combat conditions in the military. It would seem that in the face of fire and brimstone, rough-edged language props up morale and helps to keep fear and panic at bay. In this sense, 'real men' are just afraid men who hang on to sanity by the skin of their teeth – and a volley of swearing and cursing. It's verbal testosterone. On the other hand, in basic military training, drill sergeants shell their quarries with extremely intimidating and demeaning parlance, in order to break the spirit of restive recruits and at the same time inoculate them against the effects of fear and horror that the future holds in store for them. An excellent example is the performance of former drill sergeant R. Lee Ermey in Stanley Kubrick's classical Vietnam War film *Full Metal Jacket* (1987).

Despite the stark hygiene, the impersonal plastic attire and everybody's best intentions, a hospital operating theatre essentially remains a chamber of horrors. Everything there flies in the face of our deepest and oldest instincts, all our sensory alarm bells ring like mad, but there is no escape. Underneath the calm professionalism nerves twang like the strings of an ill-tuned guitar, or they would if surgeons, assistants and nurses did not muster all their mental powers to control their instincts. One of the ways they cope is by creating a sphere that is as incongruous as their own brain stem considers their conscious behaviour. They joke, they dehumanize, they use vulgar terminology and they swear. This is not disrespect but self-defence. Fighting shock with shock is yet another application of the Law of Similarity that governs magic. Ridiculing reality helps us to stay on top of things. It plays down the unbearable frightfulness of the situation, and helps to fight the very natural urge to hide in a corner and cry. Interns are probably the worst at this, since they haven't been subjected to the numbing effect of routine yet, and still inhabit the student's frame of mind where irreverence is paramount. So a patient badly bleeding from multiple lacerations may callously be referred to as a *road map* and a badly burned one as a *crispy critter*. And when despite all efforts of the medical staff a patient dies, he's an *ungrateful patient*.

Soldiers, doctors and nurses all work in sometimes wildly overtaxing circumstances and ward off the urge to flee by creating a forced sphere of jocularity and rough camaraderie. Camaraderie is not friendship; it is a form of intimacy among relative strangers. It develops everywhere people are thrown together not by choice, but by circumstances beyond their control, and have a common 'enemy' in the authorities that hold sway over them: school classes, students in universities, office workers, supermarket staff, tourists on a group trip, hospital patients, prison inmates and so on. Some professions, such as soldiers and medical professionals, face an additional enemy. Doctors must attempt to ward off the never-ending mental onslaught of pain, blood and death, and soldiers must curb their fear of enemy fire and their own revulsion at maiming and killing others. Something similar holds for the police, who are confronted with accidents, violent crime and disgruntled, often aggressive civilians every day of the week. And let's not forget firefighters, who must deal with the dangers of flames and fumes, and take on the risk that comes with rescuing others from burning and collapsing buildings. Such fearsome shared emotional experience engenders strong solidarity based on the idea that 'we' are special and poorly understood by 'the rest'. A special case, for lack of the truly gruesome experiences shared by the groups just mentioned, is that of the student society. Next to being subjected to the demands of school and parents, their main enemy is the fortress of adult society that they must storm and make their own. These bonds are strong and can render groups extremely hard to manage.

Group solidarity is expressed as conformism and camaraderie, with two effects. With respect to the world at large, both set the group apart from all others. They separate 'us' from 'them', the outsiders who are often called 'civilians'. Within the group they bolster solidarity and a sense of belonging. This is achieved by means of initiations, rites of passage, secret handshakes and other rituals, dress codes and a special group language. Part of this last is pure jargon, which serves both to facilitate professional in-group communication and to keep nosy outsiders in the dark. Its other use is to create a collective sense of daring and even guilt, and this is where taboo terms come in: by engaging in taboo language and off-colour jokes, the group members share a guilty secret, which is a great way to create intimacy. The element of secrecy or semi-secrecy is essential and present on different levels in all groups, from the irreverent nicknames teens in school use for their teachers to the rustic humour of the police nick and the barracks. People who blow the whistle on unacceptable language and humour in a group break the group code of secrecy and are invariably ostracized.

So far, we have seen taboo language shape spheres that existed anyway. But it is also employed to create and define temporary and local spheres of intimacy. An obvious example is the sphere of personal intimacy between spouses, which changes according to circumstances. At home among themselves, people are wont to address their significant other by an affectionate nickname such as *darling, angel, baby, honey bun, duck* or any of a thousand sometimes sentimental, sometimes silly or downright embarrassing others. If they have visitors, they may continue to do so, although many don't or at least tone it down. After all, they are in their own home, just about the strongest and most intimate sphere imaginable. Out in public, they will also keep using their intimate terms of endearment as long as no one seems to be listening. This way they create a mobile sphere of intimacy to take with them, more or less like sharing an umbrella. However, it is decidedly odd if in a conversation with anyone but the

<table>
<tr><td colspan="2" align="center">The Language of Love</td></tr>
<tr><td colspan="2">

What do people call their loved ones in private? Ubiquitous classics are variations of 'love', 'darling' and 'treasure', but names of animals and sweet things are also common. Even excrement isn't wasted on lovers, as well as a whole junk shop of rather peculiar verbal bric-a-brac. And, like the Dutch, the Italians wallow in diminutives. Here is a tiny selection of common pet names. Of course, they all mean 'darling', but if they have a different vanilla meaning, it is given in quotation marks.

</td></tr>
<tr><td>Dutch</td><td>

lief(je), *liefste* '(be)love(d)'; *schat* 'treasure'; *schattebout*; **animals** *aap(je)* 'monkey'; *beer(tje)* 'bear'; *hangbuikzwijntje* 'Vietnamese pot-bellied swine'; *kippetje* 'chicken'; *kuikentje* 'chick'; *poes(je)* 'kitten, pussycat'; *tijger* 'tiger'; **sweets** *drop(pie)* 'liquorice'; *kersje* 'cherry'; *lekkertje* 'sweetie'; *perzikje* 'peach'; *snoepje* 'sweet'; *suikerbeestje* 'fondant animal'; **other** *foefje* 'pussy'; *honnepon*; *kanjer* 'big/great one'; *kleintje* 'little one'; *kuttemefrutje* 'cunty-frunty'; *lekkerbekje* 'deep-fried fish-fillet'; *m'n allesie* 'my everythingy'; *mop(pie)*; *poekie*; *pop(je)* 'doll'; *poep(ie)* 'turd'; *poepertje* 'shithole, shit(s)ter'; *poepescheet(je)* 'turdyfart'; *pukkeltje* 'little pimple'; *scheet(je)* 'fart'.

</td></tr>
<tr><td>French</td><td>

amour 'love'; *bébé* 'baby'; *trésor* 'treasure'; **animals** *bichette* 'baby deer'; *biquette* 'baby goat'; *câlinours* 'snuggle bear'; *canard* 'duck'; *chaton* 'kitten'; *crevette* 'shrimp'; *gazelle* 'gazelle'; *p'tit grenouille* 'little frog'; *loulou* 'Keeshond dog'; *loup* 'wolf'; *louve* 'she-wolf'; *minet* 'kitten'; *puce, pupuce* 'flea'; *serpent à lunettes* 'cobra'; *tourterelle* 'turtle dove'; **sweets** *chamallow* 'marshmallow'; *mon chou* 'my puff'; *chouchou(te)*; *guimauve* 'marshmallow'; *pain d'épices* 'gingerbread'; **other** *beau bazou* 'beautiful jalopy'; *câlinette* 'snuggles'; *choupette* 'cowlick'; *ma couille* 'my testicle'; *coussinette* 'little pillow'; *gros poilu* 'big and hairy one'; *homme des cavernes* 'cave man'; *loupiotte* 'kid, little light'; *lutin* 'rascal'; *poupoune* 'baby doll'; *Schtroumpfette* 'Baby Smurf'.

</td></tr>
<tr><td>German</td><td>

Liebling 'darling'; *Schatz* 'treasure'; **animals** *Bär* 'bear'; *Hase* 'hare'; *Kätzchen* 'puss, kitten'; *Maus* 'mouse'; *Spatz* 'sparrow'; *Schnecke* 'snail'; *Tiger* 'tiger'; *Schnucki/Schnuckelchen/Schnuckiputzi* 'sheep, lamb'; **sweets** *Süßi/Süße(r)* 'sweety'; **other** *Sonnenschein* 'sunshine'; *Töffel* 'slipper, klutz'; *Schnuffel* 'snuggle bunny'; *Puschel* 'pom-pom'; *Knallerchen* 'hit, success'; *Krümelmonster* 'crumb monster'; *Knutschkugel* 'snog-ball'.

</td></tr>
</table>

Italian	*amore* 'love'; *tesor(in)o/a* 'treasure'; **animals** *bestiaccia* 'beast'; *cerbiatto* 'deer'; *cocinella* 'ladybird'; *farfallina* 'butterfly'; *gattina* 'puss'; *maialino/a* 'piggy'; *marmottina* 'marmot'; *orsetto* 'little bear'; *paperina* 'ducky'; *passerotto* 'sparrow'; *pulcino/a* 'chick'; *topino* 'mouse'; **sweets** *biscottino* 'biscuit'; *ciliegina* 'cherry'; *cioccolatino* 'chocolate'; *nocciolino* 'nut'; *piselletta* 'pea'; *zuccherino* 'sugar'; **other** *caccolina* 'little bogey'; *cucciolotto/a* 'snuggles'; *formaggino* 'cheese'; *merendina* 'snack'; *panzarotto* 'fritter'; *patato/a* 'spud'; *polpetta* 'meatball'; *principessa* 'princess'; *puzzona* 'big stinkster'; *stellina* 'little star'; *tato/a* 'baby'.
Turkish	*aşkım* 'my love'; *giğerparem, bebeğim* 'my darling'; *sevgilim* 'my beloved'; **animals** *bülbül seslim* 'my nightingale's voice'; *kuzucuğum* 'my little lamb'; **sweets** *çokolatalı kekim* 'my chocolate cake'; *frambuazlı pastam* 'my raspberry cake'; *fıstığım* 'my pistachio'; *şekerim* 'my sugar'; *tatlım* 'my sweet (dessert)', 'sweety-pie'; **other** *benim gönlümün sahibi* 'ruler of my heart'; *bir tanım* 'my only one'; *canım* 'my soul'; *gözümün nuru* 'light of my eyes'; *güneşim* 'my sunshine'; *hayatım* 'my life'; *iki göz-üm* 'both my eyes'; *meleğim* 'my angel'; *selvi boylum* 'my lanky one' (*selvi* = cypress); *yakışıklım* 'my handsome one'; *güzelim* 'my lovely/beautiful'.

most intimate friends, say at a party, someone keeps addressing their partner as 'pet'. Incongruous, even, since the high intimacy of 'pet' clashes with the less intimate sphere of the party flock. At a party, people are supposed to open up to others on more or less equal footing and mingle. Maintaining a bubble of intimacy shuts people out.

Perhaps the most intriguing temporary sphere is talking dirty in the bedroom. For quite a few people, raunchy talk such as 'come here, let me squeeze those balls now, I'll make 'em fill up to bursting, yes, grab my cunt, I'm dripping for you, run those fingers along my slit, you bastard, God, I'm so horny' is a terrific turn-on. An important part of the fun is no doubt the unsurpassable intimacy that such shameless behaviour not only is a sign of, but actually creates. The terms used are typically extreme, graphic variants that carry as much emotional weight as possible and cannot be used except in the most intimate company. Also, saying those very private things out loud or whispering them in your partner's ear is risky, as you let down all your defences. This way, you create an exhilaratingly fragile sphere, one your partner can turn into embarrassing disappointment with one wrong word. It's a sphere with a tinge of exhibitionism, not unlike 'doing it' in a place where people might walk in on you, for what if anybody overheard? This holds for both partners, since the hearer is the equally vulnerable, equally 'guilty' accomplice – they share an embarrassing secret. But that is not all. Saying taboo things out loud and hearing them said is titillating in any case, and may tickle your fancy even more strongly if you're already in a state of arousal. For the speaker, but really for both partners in this highly intimate conspiracy, there is the added thrill of mastering taboos. For mentioning the names of things is a form of exerting power over them.

Most importantly, perhaps, talking dirty enhances the abandonment that is crucial to reaching and experiencing sexual satisfaction. Of course, this is all temporary make-believe that lasts no longer than it takes for us to satisfy our sexual urges, after which the hormonal storm dies down. From then on and in all other contexts, talking dirty strikes us as rather silly. As does the whole sex thing, actually, which without arousal boils down to people engaging in curious poses and a lot of rather unsightly heavy breathing.

Incongruity between spheres is not necessarily infelicitous, though. It can be exploited on purpose to create distance or set hierarchical boundaries. The same couple who refrain from calling each other 'sweetheart' and 'honey' in the presence of equals may expressly do so when, for example, checking into a hotel: 'Have you got my passport, sweetheart?' 'Yes hon.' Such a show of intimacy expressly shuts out the desk clerk and reaffirms the fantasy that the customer is king and the desk clerk a negligible underling. We can take this one step further by calling the desk clerk 'love', 'darling' or, worse, 'pumpkin'. That is a verbal invasion of their personal space that borders on intimidation, but it usually works, for it is very hard to protest when someone is 'only being nice to you'. Similarly, shop assistants, barbers and beauticians usually create a general public sphere when they speak to customers – you're on their turf and it's in their interest to meet all customers at least halfway. But people doing repairs in someone else's house are not even visitors, they are simply passers-by in the other people's world. They may stress this by showing typically workmanlike behaviour and speech, thus maintaining a clear dividing line between the world of the occupants of the house and their own. The message they send by keeping to a sphere of their own (and most likely having a blaring radio man its battlements) is 'we'll ignore you and please ignore us, except for coffee.'

@#$%!

TABOO IS NOT an absolute quality; it's gradual and there are different kinds. Verbally, the ultimate taboo is complete silence on a subject. This sometimes occurs in families where a dead sibling or child, or a severely disabled one hidden away in an institution, a wife who ran off with someone in the motor trade, or a seriously delinquent banged-up uncle is never mentioned or even hinted at any more. The irony is that such a total blackout tends to make the presence of the absence felt all the more keenly. Many a novelist has based a successful career on describing the damage this kind of taboo can do to a family.

Only slightly less severely taboo are things that are so terrifying that people don't dare 'touch' them by mentioning them directly or in full. Thus, fifty years ago, when cancer was all but untreatable and patients and their families often weren't even told what was what, many referred to it only as 'C' or 'it'. The Devil is also best not mentioned by name, lest you raise his interest. In areas where they constitute a real threat, the same taboo holds with respect to the names of dangerous animals such as tigers, sharks and crocodiles. 'Speak of the wolf, and it comes running into the house,' they say in Ukraine, and the bear is generally referred to only indirectly as *honey eater* or by some other circumspect description in most Slavic languages. Similarly, having sex is frequently euphemistically referred to as 'doing it'. So much so, in fact, that 'do it' and 'be at it' have become fully fledged but relatively taboo-free synonyms of fucking. People who have fallen from grace and shameful things or events often end up as 'you know who' and 'you know what' or, of course, our famous 'down there'. Nowadays, notions experienced by some as painful, such as 'negro', 'fucking' and 'autism', get disguised as the 'n-word', 'f-word' and 'a-word', respectively.

A naming taboo of considerable severity is found among the Yurok and Karok, indigenous tribes of northern California. Among them, it is strictly not done to mention to someone the name of any of their dead relatives, until that name is once again given to a newborn child. Transgressing this taboo is a serious matter that must be compensated for. Legend has it that, long ago, an angry man gravely insulted a group of people passing in a canoe by merely yelling 'your deceased relatives!' at them, and had to make up for his insolence by paying them $20, a shotgun and a string of shell-money.

Dead or disgraced relatives are only a few of the people whose names must not be mentioned. Many societies, particularly in the southern hemisphere, practise some form of *hlonipha*, a system where certain names and terms are avoided, usually involving the in-laws. Depending on the language in question, the taboo terms are either eschewed completely or deformed in some way. Among the Nguni, a group of South African bantu peoples including the Ndebele, Swazi, Xhosa and Zulu, a woman must not pronounce the name of her father-in-law, or even any of the syllables in that name, especially not in his presence, so she must bend over backwards to choose words that do not contain those syllables. Complicated as it sounds, it is not a very severe taboo, since inadvertent slip-ups can be remedied by spitting on the ground.

Hlonipha systems and the Yurok ban on dead relatives' names may seem exotic, but they are really just elaborate variants of a both deep-seated and multifaceted universal taboo concerning names. Naming is a creative act, related but not identical to performatives. Giving someone or something a name does not create the item named, as performatives do, but it does bestow it with identity. Shopping excepted, when coming into contact with strangers, giving your name is an indispensable first token of good faith and good intentions everywhere. It is the verbal analogue of the medieval knight's open visor. Declining to give your name is a sure sign that something is amiss, an indication of bad intentions. So is giving a false name. This is not just a symbolic matter; it is a very real issue, as shown by the modern phenomenon of digital identity theft as well as by the very first recorded case of using a false identity, the ruse Ulysses uses in book 9 of the *Odyssey* to escape the wrath of the one-eyed giant Polyphemus. Trapped with his ship's crew inside Polyphemus' cave, Ulysses introduces himself to the murderous behemoth as Outis. At night, when Ulysses' men have blinded Polyphemus by driving a stake through his one eye when he is asleep, his roars of pain rouse other giants living nearby, who come to the rescue asking what is bothering their neighbour so much. The desperate Polyphemus screams through the closed door of his cave: 'Outis is bothering me! Outis is attacking me!' *Outis* meaning 'no one' in Greek, the other giants conclude that their services are not needed and return home. This is somewhat less naive, or stupid, if you will, than it would seem. We still call a person of no consequence a nobody or even a non-entity. Without a name, you don't matter or even exist.

Names are intimate and important things. Your name is, in a very real sense, who you are – not a label, but your identity. It is bestowed on you by others and is your passport to the society you are born into. In Western societies, and many others, names are given at or shortly after birth, but this is not always the case. In some cultures where infant mortality is still high, children are named only after they have proven viable, in some cases not until they have made it through their first few years. Until then, they literally don't count.

Naming a ship or child also asserts ownership and authority, as does the custom in many cultures for women to adopt their spouse's surname upon marriage. Throughout history, victorious conquerors have asserted ownership of cities they have taken and nullified the claims of those they have vanquished by renaming them. Thus, the old Javan city of Jacatra became Batavia as soon as the Dutch took hold of it in 1619, and was promptly renamed Jakarta when the colonial regime was ousted in 1949. For similar reasons, the growing self-confidence of China and India has made them insist on the rest of the world giving up traditional names such as Peking, Bombay and Calcutta in favour of Beijing, Mumbai and Kolkata.

In circles where naming conventions aren't set in stone, naming a child is often a task fraught with sensitivity, with grandparents and other relatives vying for pride of place. In the field of human communications, there are few things people are more allergic to than seeing their name misspelled or hearing it mispronounced.

For all these reasons, giving your name, something we do almost every day without thinking, is no small matter. In a way your interlocutor 'gets' your name, and with it, by virtue of the old magical Law of Contact, he gains a measure of power over you. Telemarketers and other modern-day pedlars use that power to their advantage. They can exert considerable pressure on people they talk to on the phone simply by mentioning their name at every turn:

Salesperson: Good morning Mr Brown, how are you doing?
Brown: . . .
Salesperson: That's great, Mr Brown. Have you heard of Communal United Network Telerama, Mr Brown?
Brown: . . .
Salesperson: Ah, you haven't. Well, Mr Brown, as it happens, we can make you an exceptional offer, Mr Brown, one that

will surely brighten up your day, Mr Brown. [slight pause]
Mr Brown, what would you say if . . .

And so on and so forth, until the victim becomes so nervous and confused that he folds and agrees to take out a subscription he never wanted or needed.

If people feel that giving their name to someone gives her power over them, it is no surprise that some names are jealously guarded and must not be known or spoken. Hidden names are even a theme in folk culture, as in the Faustian German fairy tale of Rumpelstilzchen. Rumpelstilzchen is an imp who strikes a bargain with a miller's daughter to make her queen in exchange for her first-born child, unless she can guess his name. He loses the deal when, at the last moment, the princess discovers him dancing around his isolated hovel singing *Ach, wie gut, dass niemand weiß, dass ich Rumpelstilzchen heiß!* – 'Oh, how good that no one knows I'm called Rumpelstilzchen!' It is an extremely old story, some say no less than four thousand years old, with parallels in many cultures. *Rumpelstiltskin*, as the imp is called in English, is *Repelsteeltje* in the Netherlands and *Myrmidon* in France. He can be found as *Gilitrutt* in Iceland, *Khlamushka* in Russia and *Joaidane* ('blabbermouth') in the Arab world, and in various guises also in Eastern Europe and South America. Even faraway Japan has a version, called *Daiku to Oniroku*, 'the carpenter and the ogre'.

Nowadays, the only name that is seriously taboo in Japan is that of the emperor, who is still referred to only as *Tennō Heika*, his Majesty the Emperor, and sometimes as *Kinjō Heika*, the Current Emperor. However, the taboo used to encompass many more highly important figures, and was adhered to so strictly that not even historians know the proper identity of many a historical figure. From time to time, pronouncing or writing the names of emperors in full was strictly taboo in imperial China as well. It was considered proof of serious disrespect, for which people could be fined or even executed, as happened in 1777, during the Qing dynasty, to the scholar and bureaucrat Wang Xihou and his family. Wang's fault was to have included Emperor Qiánlóng's full name in a book he wrote, when he should have left out at least one stroke of each character, preferably the last one drawn. Or, alternatively, he should have used different, synonymous characters.

Somewhat closer to home, according to Egyptian mythology, the goddess Isis succeeded in putting her son Horus, the falcon god who symbolizes the pharaohs, on the Egyptian throne, which had until then been occupied by the sun god Ra, by wresting his 'true name' from him and thus gaining absolute power over him – what that name was, she never revealed. And then, of course, there is the well-known Jewish taboo about speaking the real name of the Lord. Only the high priest could do so in the discreet isolation of the temple of Jerusalem, and only once a year, on the Day of Atonement. This was not something ordained from above, by the way, but a custom that took root during the fifth century BCE, after the Jews had returned from exile in Babylon, rebuilt the temple and begun expanding and revising much of the Bible. It was an innovation, part of the new reality of the Jewish state.

Jewish people avoided the name of God out of fear of mispronouncing it, so essentially in awe and deference. This is not entirely unlike the custom among older Italians, who, when things go haywire again in their country, until recently were wont to whisper *se fosse ancora Lui*, 'if only He were still around,' meaning Mussolini, the man who was said to make the trains run on time, but whose name cannot be mentioned. In recent years the same deferential *Lui* has been heard with reference to Silvio Berlusconi, Italy's great man of the 1990s and the first decade of this century.

By and large, authoritarian name taboos are on the wane and with a few exceptions have become quite weak, although it seems that the superstition is still going strong that naming something bad or dangerous out loud – an illness, the Devil, an animal – in a sense conjures it up. Still less significant transgressions of verbal taboos are the ways in which Westerners can vent impatience, irritation or frustration by using terms that are just one step too graphic, too direct to fit the current sphere. Something like 'I'm sorry, but if you ask me the man is a complete arsehole, a twat and a bloody waste of space' is typical of fairly refined or formal spheres where arseholes and twats and wastes of space are definitely not *de rigueur*. It is typically accompanied by an apology such as *excuse me, but, please don't hold it against me* or even *pardon my French*, which mirrors the French *excusez le mot*. The Dutch use *neem me niet kwalijk, maar*, the equivalent of 'excuse me, but', or excuse themselves by introducing their transgression by *ik zeg het maar gewoon op z'n Hollands*, 'I'll just put it in plain Dutch.' This is what you do when you want to call a spade a bloody great shovel in circumstances that require polite behaviour.

@#$%!

SPHERES CAN BE EPHEMERAL, such as the short-lived super-intimacy aroused lovers conjure up by whispering obscenities in each other's ears, and the sphere of mutual denial that obtains only as long as we are shut in a lift with strangers; it vanishes the moment we or the others step out. Other spheres exist and are carefully maintained for generations. One of those is the public arena, where the rules of interaction and communication tend to change only very, very slowly. Other highly permanent and carefully maintained spheres are those which serve to define and distinguish social groups, of which there are two kinds. One is social class, the other is vocational or defined by some shared interest. They are the sources of euphemisms, jargon and slang.

Wherever people form groups of a more or less permanent kind, they will develop a special vocabulary, specific to the interests or activities that bind them. Such vocabularies are called jargon, and they serve primarily to facilitate communication between members of the group without regard to outsiders. Everyone in the judicial chain and the police knows what DUI and GBH are, while most law-abiding citizens don't, unless they've picked up sufficient police and judiciary jargon from watching films and television series. Doctors and above all lawyers are notorious for their impenetrable professional language, but they in turn have no inkling what a *paardenlul*, a 'horse's dick', is. (It is Dutch bricklayers' jargon for an exceptionally long brick.) If rock musicians complain that the lead guitar is *jerking off*, they mean that he is indulging in endless solos at the cost of the other members of the band, and if a ship's officer tells a crew member to *belay that order*, he wants the sailor not to tie a rope around it, but to stop carrying it out. Behind the counter at Domino's Pizza, anchovies used to be known as *smellies* or *guppies* and green peppers as *lizards*, and a pizza with 'everything on it' was aptly called a *garbage can*. Jargon often contains a measure of jocular vulgarity, but that is not essential. What is essential is in-group efficiency and clarity. To those working within the Domino's sphere, yelling 'two *bitch pies*' or 'two PMS' is a lot clearer than 'two pizzas with pepperoni, mushrooms and sausage'.

What's what when talking about language	
Language	According to some, a language is a dialect with a flag and a fleet, and intuitively, that's not a bad definition. However, most of the approximately 5,000 extant languages aren't associated with any national identity, and within virtually every nation more than one language is spoken. We'll say that a language is the set of linguistic rules (grammar) and words (vocabulary) shared by any group of people who claim to understand each other: a language community.
Dialect	Any variant of a language that is characteristic of a relatively large region or social group, including the variant considered standard by the community. Dialects may differ from each other in pronunciation and vocabulary as well as, to a limited extent, grammar.
Patois	A smaller-scale dialect, usually rural and held in low esteem.
Jargon	A particular vocabulary used by groups of people who share a profession, hobby or some other interest, facilitating efficient communication between group members.
Slang	A particular vocabulary used by groups of people to distinguish and shield themselves from the rest of society.

There isn't a clear-cut boundary between jargon and slang – far from it. But there is a deep difference in purpose and functionality between the two. Whereas jargon exists to facilitate communication within a group and keep things clear, slang is expressly designed and used to keep outsiders out by confusing them. It works like a club jacket, which reaffirms the in-group solidarity and stigmatizes its wearer in the eyes of the world at large. Slang is typical of groups who feel they are not part of mainstream society and want to distance themselves from it, who consider themselves, broadly speaking, not middle class. Traditionally, it has been associated with marginal groups such as tinkers, gypsies, travelling salesmen and criminals. However, social and political activists are typical slang users as well, as are adolescents.

Slang has probably existed as long as there have been marginal groups. In England, at any rate, slang dictionaries go back to the sixteenth century. This is hardly surprising, because in a world without proper policing, what 'thieves and scoundrels' were discussing was a matter of interest to everyone. Whereas slang dictionaries (mostly bad ones) are two-a-penny, dictionaries of jargon don't exist as such. They are simply technical dictionaries dedicated to a specific profession or subject.

One more fundamental difference between jargon and slang is that jargon is efficient and generally fairly stable, whereas slang is neither. In France, a type of slang very popular among the young is Verlan, named from *français à l'envers*, 'backwards French'. The core idea of Verlan is to invert the order of syllables in an existing word to form a new one. Although its rules are quite simple, Verlan is not efficient, since all the trouble of rehashing words yields nothing more than alternative word forms with meaning and associations identical to the originals they derive from. Worse than Verlan, one of the most cumbersome kinds of slang is cockney rhyming slang, in which a word is replaced by a phrase that rhymes with it, or its first word. Thus, a *butcher's* or *butcher's hook* is the rhyming-slang alternative for a look, and a tramp is called a *wet 'n' damp*. Such a system is completely impenetrable unless you learn by heart which random rhymes have been adopted, word for bloody word.

Of course, slang does not always involve inventive mechanisms. Much, if not most, amounts to no more than a set of synonyms for perfectly normal notions. Often, these are somewhat garbled loan words from a low-prestige minority language; in other cases they are selected on account of some kind of semantic association. The term *slammer* for the more mainstream *gaol* is an obvious example, as is the moniker *ho*, derived from *whore* for *girl* or *woman* in rap and hip-hop circles.

Although inefficient, slang of any kind can be quite effective and inscrutable to outsiders. Among the early population of the penal colony Australia, a slang called Flash was so widely used that it all but replaced mainstream English. As a consequence, the deportees often had no way of expressing themselves other than in Flash. According to the navy chronicler Watkin Tench in his *Complete Account of the Settlement at Port Jackson* (1793), it became so bad that the courts of his day had to employ interpreters when hearing convicts as witnesses or defendants.

Verlan is all about sound, so the results on paper can be somewhat surprising. But the rules are quite simple:

1. Invert the order of syllables, not forgetting the silent e-sound that is not always spelled;
2. Drop any final vowels;
3. If the result ends in a cluster of two or more consonants that normally do not occur at the end of French words, drop the last one; repeat if necessary.

Racaille [ra-kai] (1) → *caillera*
Femme [fem-meu] (1) → [*meu-fã*] (2) → *meuf*
Arabe [a-ra-beu] (1) → [*beu-ra-a*] (2) → [*beu-ra*] (2) → *beur*
Flic [fli-keu] (1) → [*keu-fli*] (2) → [*keu-fl*] (3) → *keuf*

Rhyming slang, purportedly having originated in mid-nineteenth-century London, works as follows:

1. Replace a word with an arbitrary phrase of at least two words that rhymes with it;
2. Optionally drop everything except the first word of the phrase, to make things really opaque.

telephone (1) → dog-and-bone (2) → **dog**
gravy (1) → army and navy (2) → **army**
hair (1) → Fred Astaire (2) → **Fred**
back (1) → Cilla Black (1960s singer) (2) → **Cilla** ('Gawd, me Cilla's playing up again!')

Sometimes, the rhyming phrase has a meaning that might be associated with the 'slanged' word:

wife (1) → trouble and strife (2) → **trouble**
flowers (1) → **early hours** (on account of the early hours florists keep to buy their stock for the day)

The inefficiency of slang is essential, because that serves its two most important characteristics: exclusiveness and inscrutability. Using the right slang terms is like flashing your membership card at both fellow slang users and outsiders. But doing it to the latter invites a problem: outsiders absorb, store and reproduce what they hear, sometimes in an attempt to join the club, sometimes just because that is what people do. As a consequence slang terms tend to lose their discriminating value. Verlan terms such as *beur* (inverted *Arabe*, someone of North African descent), *meuf* (*femme*, girl, woman) and *keuf* (*flic*, police officer) have even made it into the prestigious Larousse dictionary. For this reason slang is inherently unstable, needing continual replenishment with new inventions to retain exclusivity. The fastest turnover seems to occur among teenagers and students, youngsters engaged in carving out an identity for themselves through membership of peer groups with strict norms concerning clothing and accessories, music and slang. Research has shown that at one university in the United States, over a period of just fifteen years 90 per cent of student slang expressions had disappeared or been replaced. If you think about it, this is only natural, since all adolescents are in the business of shaping their personality by distancing themselves from the authorities that undisputedly governed their early lives: parents, teachers and also older youngsters, who are always bigger, stronger and more worldly than they are. So, year after year, yesteryear's slang is already obsolete.

Being first and foremost a defence mechanism against the more powerful and fortunate, slang is mostly thought to be particular to socially weak and marginal groups – criminals, vagrants, paupers, the lunatic fringes, adolescents – and therefore necessarily vulgar. Although this is to some extent true, slang does occur among the high and mighty as well, and it does not have to be vulgar. Rhyming slang, for example, is a nineteenth-century working-class invention associated with the London underworld, but most of its rhymes are perfectly innocuous. What could be wrong with calling the *mind* a *Chinese blind* or saying that you're getting *Benny'd up*, meaning you'll take your *Benny Hills*, more commonly known as pills (and not to be confused with the chiefly American *bennies*, contraband Benzedrine tablets), apart from it being somewhat silly?

Upper-class slang partly consists of deliberately using outdated terms such as *icebox* instead of *fridge*, signalling that your family enjoyed the luxury of cooling before electric cooling was even invented. You use the *loo* and never the plebeian *toilet*. You know what the word 'plebeian' means and use it, along with a host of other references to classical Latin and Greek. You let go the occasional 'Alas, poor Yorick' and 'I smell a rat!' You season your words with a sprinkling of French and other foreign terms with a certain *je ne sais quoi* or even *panache*. And, of course, never say *pardon*, say *what*.

Upper-class slang works in just the same way as any other slang except for one thing: it uses some expressly rustic terminology (*bog, what?!*) to let its users distinguish themselves from what they perceive as social inferiors and bolster their authority, whereas other slang is normally used to wriggle away from under the oppressive gaze of social superiors and authorities. This is an effect of how class systems work. Top dogs have no superiors, a fact they can advertise by flaunting the rules everyone else obeys.

In pre-modern times, class membership was determined largely by descent – patricians versus plebeians, nobility versus commoners, free men versus serfs and slaves – and vocation. There were classes of traders, knights, artisans, priests, farmers, lawyers and so on, and China had its class of civil servants. Many of these classes were highly stable, with membership being passed on from father to son. Nowadays, vocation has all but vanished as a determinant of class, excepting royalty, landed gentry, clergy, the occasional posh lawyer family and the ongoing plight of the Indian Dalits, the casteless who are still largely limited to menial jobs such as cleaning and unskilled labour. In the modern world, members of a social class usually have little in common except their membership itself, which they either inherited from their parents or fought hard to secure; the latter are the social climbers. There is no apparent rational reason why people would set store by belonging to a class, but the mere fact that all over the world those who thought they could do away with the phenomenon have failed dramatically shows that we do. In any culture, the urge to identify with like-minded people and to distinguish oneself positively from 'them' is as irrational as it is heartfelt, so it is most likely part of our biological constitution. Group membership is clearly important, then, yet it is not the be-all and end-all that adherents of modern identity politics take it to be. Reducing identity to group membership not only mistakenly snubs important other factors involved in shaping one's identity, but is also highly polarizing and deeply divisive.

Class has to do with dominance, but not so much with sheer power or a crude pecking order. To see this, look at how people think of their own class compared to others. Such comparisons are to an overwhelming degree negative. Primarily, people don't identify a class by what its members do, but by what they do not do. We, all of us, consider ourselves superior to others in terms of restraint: 'we' don't shit in the street, piss in the garden, fart or pick our noses in public, spit on the pavement, eat with our fingers, wear shorts and sandals to work, and so on and so forth. Such civilized behaviour is all about repressing and canalizing our instinctive animal urges and drives. The same mechanism by which we distinguish ourselves from the animal world also establishes distinctions among ourselves. It differs from politeness in that civilized behaviour serves to define oneself, whereas politeness serves to facilitate others.

This civilization process, as the sociologist Norbert Elias called it, could and did only begin once we had acquired the ability to reflect upon ourselves, which came to pass some time before the invention of agriculture, roughly 14,000 years ago.[2] The new selfawareness allowed our distant forebears to monitor and judge their own behaviour and hence to control it much better than before. This in turn allowed them to deal with the pressures of living in closely knit groups larger than the 100 to 150 individuals characteristic of the hunter-gatherer groups that had roamed the Earth before. The new larger and sedentary agricultural groups allowed for specialization, which sparked an avalanche of cultural and technical innovation that has been gaining momentum ever since. And with it came the birth of vocational classes.

Patrimony, group loyalty and vocation remained the bedrock of society until the late Middle Ages, when in Europe an evermore confident class of city-dwelling merchants inspired a growing appreciation of money and personal merit. With it, the importance of the individual and his responsibilities increased as well, both in secular and religious matters. As a consequence, the weight of vocational classes and the guild system that went with it began to dwindle, while the importance of civil behaviour as a distinguishing factor for class membership grew. Ever so slowly, the social balance began to shift from *what* you were towards *who* you were. Europe found itself making the transition from the Middle Ages to the Early Modern Age and everybody except the countless penniless paupers and outcasts began striving for a place somewhere up the newly forming social ladder.

During the primarily communitarianist, group-orientated Middle Ages there had been little regard for privacy, which was in very short supply anyway. Most dwellings consisted of a single room used by the whole family for living, eating and sleeping in. Even the wealthy and powerful used to sleep and have sex in the same room as servants and others. At inns, travellers would share beds with complete strangers. But this happy-go-lucky attitude was now slowly beginning to change. In devising new codes of behavioural restraint, people naturally looked first to behaviour linked to things that were inherently more or less taboo anyway: bodily effluvia. English court regulations from the sixteenth century state that 'One should not, like rustics who have not been to court or lived among refined and honourable people, relieve oneself without shame or reserve in front of ladies, or before the doors and windows of court chambers or other rooms.' And in 1530 the great humanist Erasmus of Rotterdam in *De civilitate morum puerilium* (On Civility in Boys), warned that 'it is impolite to greet someone who is urinating or defecating.'[3] Obviously it was still quite normal in his day to come upon people who were 'busy', but modesty already required that they be ignored, a first step towards the present taboo.

As with behaviour, so with language. During the Middle Ages, people did not care much about the status of what we now consider dirty words or taboo terms. For instance, Geoffrey Chaucer's *Canterbury Tales* are chock-full of scenes that we consider bawdy and obscene, phrased in like terminology, which Chaucer's fourteenth-century readership thought merely funny. An early fifteenth-century English medical treatise states blandly that 'in women the neck of the bladder is short and made fast to the cunt,' and explains the functions of the two holes in a man's *yard*, then a colloquial term for the penis. What people did regard as inappropriate language in those days was profanity and blasphemy.

As class consciousness kept forming, those who set their aim higher began to refrain from using the colloquial terms for more and more things that carried an inherent taboo, and in the long run even for things that were merely vaguely associated with such notions. That way, many formerly neutral terms acquired an aura of vulgarity – a term that itself originally just meant 'of the people', but now evolved to mean 'of uncivilized people'. In time each class developed its own quite complex verbal sphere, in which any terms that fell into disgrace had been replaced by euphemisms, literally Greek for 'good-speech'.

'Apt speech' would in fact be a better term, for euphemisms are not 'better' than other terms; they are just word forms that people think better suited to their social class and its sphere.

Euphemisms are invariably somewhat vaguer, more equivocal or less well-known terms, which is natural if your aim is to distance yourself from the populace and their coarsely direct parlance. There are several ways to create them. One is to widen the meaning of an existing word that refers to something related to cover the meaning of the word to be replaced; in this way *bathroom*, a place to wash oneself, came to cover the loo as well. So did, in England, the French term *garderobe*, in a time when, among the well-to-do, chamber pots disguised in a piece of furniture were often placed close to the wardrobe. For similar reasons *closet*, which originally referred to a small study, came to refer to the most private cubicle in a house.

Another way is to invent new, intentionally vague terms, such as *restroom* and *powder room* for toilet, or *fiddlesticks* for bullshit. Alternatively, people invent fantasy words that fit a particular sphere, such as the nursery terms *doo-doo* and *number two* for shit, and *sleep with*, *make love* and *do it*, but also *shag, bonk, fiddle, make whoopee* and a multitude of others for coitus. Also quite effective is adopting a term from a jargon that your own group is not too familiar with, or from a different language, such as *coitus, vagina, penis, faeces, copulate* and *fornicate* from Latin or medical jargon, and *toilet*, which English incorporated from French in the early twentieth century. This strategy works because we are simply unaware of many of the connotations, including undesirable ones, that such borrowed words might have in their home language. Here, ignorance is indeed bliss. Lastly, we can dress up unwanted words to look or – better – sound like something else. This is popular with expletives, such as *darn!* for *damn!*, *jeepers!* for *Jesus!*, *golly!* for *God!* and *chips!* for *shit!*

The civilizing, refining process that had ushered in the modern age reached its apogee in the stifling, strictly segregated European class societies of the eighteenth century, at the end of which the French Revolution, with its egalitarian ideas, took the wind out of their sails. The British, who ultimately came victorious out of the ensuing Napoleonic turmoil, had hardly been affected by revolutionary thought and the reforms that had swept the continent, and continued for a while along the old path, towards the extreme niceties and affectations of the Victorian age, when among cultured people almost anything became taboo, including words such as *leg* and *breast*, even when they referred to innocent chicken meat.

More than a century since then, the provisional result is a highly intricate system of different terms and expressions for the same thing or idea, each of which suits one or more particular spheres: the *shit* of the locker room turns into *stool* in the doctor's office, *poo-poo* in the nursery and *dung* in gardens and meadows. What is natural and appropriate depends entirely on the occasion or, better, on the sphere that fits the occasion. There are no intrinsically correct or preferred terms that always work, a fact of life that greatly complicates the task of learning a second language really well. To see this, consider the equivalent expressions *take a leak* and *urinate*. Every dictionary will tell you that the former is informal and the latter neutral or technical. Yet there is quite a range of functions, even classy ones, where 'Excuse me a moment, I have to take a leak' won't raise eyebrows. 'Excuse me a moment, I have to urinate' is never acceptable, however, the reason being that *take a leak* is less direct. *Urinate* conjures up too concrete an image of piss, which is precisely what we do not wish to be brought to mind at a party.

And this, finally, is what is so unsettling about the Queen's cunt. Of course, the whole system of hereditary monarchy is premised on the supposition that the Queen not only has a cunt, but puts it to good use and produces an heir. But she is also an icon, symbolizing all that is valuable, desirable and great about her country. She is, and must be, untouchable, so nobody except perhaps a staunch anti-monarchist wants to be confronted with her all too human, taboo sides: her spit, her shit and her clit. Emotionally, a Queen is a lot like a mother to everyone. Every teenager knows full well what her parents are or at least have been up to in their bedroom, or she would not be there. But no child wants to have its nose rubbed in the fact. To children the very idea is gross, icky: 'Euw!' This is precisely the point Courbet was making back in 1866. Like his *Origine du monde*, the Queen's cunt is simply too much information.

5

TAKING THEM DOWN
A PEG OR TWO

Coulter shoved through the bracken to the path and started
walking down it. After a few yards he turned and shouted,
'Ye bugger! Ye damned bugger!'
'Ye bloody damned bugger!' shouted Thaw.
'Ye fuckin' bloody damned bugger!' yelled Coulter,
and disappeared from sight among the trees.
ALASDAIR GRAY, *Lanark: A Life in Four Books* (1981)

When, in Alasdair Gray's novel *Lanark*, this altercation between two ten-year-old boys takes place somewhere on the west coast of Scotland, the adult world has waded halfway through the Second World War. But the boys neither know nor care, having been evacuated from bombed and sooty Glasgow to a remote, rural world of their own. Chances are that neither of them knows what a bugger is either, much less what fucking involves. But that doesn't worry the boys. To them the words *bugger*, *damned*, *bloody* and *fucking* are just so many stones to hurl at each other.

What the boys engage in is an archetypal shouting match: two disenchanted parties flinging random abuse at one another, the way enraged chimps in a zoo throw shit, sticks and stones at the public. Those chimps don't take accurate aim; they can't, in fact. They just kick up as much fuss as they can. Their purpose is not to prey on the audience or to take them out as dangerous enemies, but rather to impress, intimidate and humiliate them. It is King Kong beating his chest.

The chimps' tactic works fine in nature, but not at the zoo. To us, visitors, it is clear that the animals are powerless, a fact that renders their posturing rather more ridiculous than threatening – and we laugh. People who allow themselves to be drawn into a shouting match in public suffer a similar fate: passers-by will gather round and watch with amused interest how the combatants verbally box each other's ears until they run out of steam. Only when it seems to come to real blows are bystanders at all likely to intervene.

Slanging in all its variants differs from the kinds of swearing we saw before in that slurs and imprecations are, ironic use excepted, invariably negative. Its function is twofold. On the one hand it serves to express one's temporary displeasure with somebody. This is what's going on between Coulter and Thaw, who are in fact on the way to becoming friends. On the other hand slurs and imprecations can be used to hurt, disparage and ridicule a person, organization or institution that one thinks fundamentally flawed. Only then does it really gets personal.

If the emphasis is primarily on showing displeasure, what is actually said hardly matters as long as the terms used are labelled sufficiently dangerous: they must in some sense count as rude, taboo or derogatory. Nobody yelling *you bugger, you bastard, you son of a bitch!* or *hijo de puta!* ('son of a whore') at someone else, or – as they do on the tiny atoll Ulithi in the Carolines – *homa waswu's*, 'sister-fucker', really believes that he is informing anyone about a shameful family secret. He neither thinks nor cares about the parentage of the object of his wrath. Nor does the German who barks *du Sau!* ('you pig') at someone, or the Yoruba speaker shouting *ọmọ ajá!* ('child of a dog'), think for a moment that the object of their annoyance is a domestic animal or was born to one. Rather, the meaning of dog, bitch, pig and whore in such expressions is reduced to its inherent negative aspect, and then generalized to 'something despicable'. This is how the boys Coulter and Thaw could throw abuse at each other – and *hurt* each other – without either of them knowing the meaning of the terms they used; all they needed to know was that things like buggers and fuckers are fishy to a degree way above average, as are properties such as damned and bloody.

As the balance shifts from expressing displeasure at someone else's actions or opinions towards finding fault with their physique, character or personality, slurs grow more picturesque. Still, most of them do not reflect actual qualities, personality traits or physical or mental shortcomings of the target. *Me:qsece:hkêw*, 'has anal hair', is a somewhat bizarre imprecation among the Menominee, a Native American tribe in Wisconsin. Who would know about something like that? And if they did, would they want others to know that they knew? The Argentines have their *pendejo de mierda*, 'pubic hair of shit', which means something like snot-nose or little shit. The Dutch routinely sling things like *eikel* ('glans'), *klootzak* ('scrotum'), *zak hooi* ('sack of hay'), *zak tabak* ('sack of tobacco') and the fully farcical *klotebibber* ('balls-shiver') at men, and *rotwijf* ('rotten hag'), *klotewijf* ('testicle hag'), *kutwijf* ('cunt-hag'), *kuttekop* ('cunt-head'), *doos* ('box') and *muts* ('knit cap') at women, all merely meaning obnoxious or worthless person. Farsi *tūlih sag*, 'puppy', means something like 'pleb', and is easily used about or against people whose actual provenance or social status is both unknown and immaterial. Mandarin *wú-tóu chāng-yíng*, 'headless fly', is an equivalent of idiot, which we use against people who do something stupid, regardless of their actual IQ.

If Ronald Reagan has been immortalized as the Great Communicator, Karl Marx can most certainly lay claim to the title Great Imprecator. This inveterate *Schimpfer* called his own friends and allies names such as *Deutsche Hunde* ('German dogs'), *Esel* ('asses'), *Viecher* ('beasts') or *Knoten* ('louts'), all clearly hyperbolic. Even the accusatory 'homo', highly popular nowadays among teenage boys and in locker rooms all over the Western world, can mean anything from a relatively meaningless slur on a par with *prick*, *dickhead* or *jerk* to a threat that you are going to be written off as a sissy, but seldom reflects a real suspicion that the victim is in fact homosexual.

Using terminology that is neither here nor there or unmistakeably over the top is a practical solution with targets whom you don't know anything about. It is the kind of abuse you can yell at some suicidal oaf stepping right in front of your car on a busy intersection. It is, however, also a tactic that can be deployed when one wishes to lash out at someone but not personally devastate them. There are many situations in which you definitely want to avoid hitting the bullseye, for fear of making a lifelong enemy. The thing is that the truth is often too much to stomach. This is why the Ulithi will call anyone *löl lïpich*, 'bastard', unless they know the target actually is one. Likewise, nineteenth-century English upper-class gentlemen would call each other anything from *cad* to *cur* or even *cunt* to their face, but never *bastard*. There were just too many extramaritally sired chums around.

Many of these low-intensity, figurative imprecations are fully ritualized set phrases. In English, hurling *son of a bitch* at someone is fairly innocuous, just part of the vanilla repertoire. But calling a woman a *daughter of a bitch* is a different kettle of fish, illustrating that innovations and variations are taken literally. At the very opposite end of the spectrum is a small group of slurs such as *four-eyes*, *bandy-legs* and *fatso* that can be used only against people who actually do show these characteristics. Yelling *fatso* at someone slender or *four-eyes* at someone not wearing spectacles is merely incongruous, and won't be understood by either the target or others around. Such insults can only be used literally. If they are deployed, they sting deeply, because they typically hit an obvious weak spot of the target. Literally used slurs are salt rubbed into an open wound.

In between this small group of exclusively literal slurs and the fully ritualized figurative ones like *son of a bitch* is a vast and dynamic array of terms that can be used either literally or figuratively to varying degrees. How hard they hit depends on the one hand on their intrinsic rudeness and taboo-ness, and on the other on how literally they are being used. Take *bastard*. By and large, in quite a few cultures this is a fairly mild term if used figuratively. It can even have semi-positive overtones, as in the slightly envious *clever bastard* and the affectionately condescending *poor bastard*. But if it is intentionally levelled against someone whom we know actually is a bastard in the technical, literal sense, it assumes a much more vicious character. Similarly, a hyperbolic *cripple* against someone accidently tripping over a rug may not be the apogee of subtleness, but it is a comment on a slip-up rather than on one's person, so it does not sting that badly. Using it against someone who actually suffers from a locomotive deficiency is quite a different matter. A Japanese father may affectionately, if somewhat gruffly, call his pretty daughter *busu*, 'ugly', but would get into trouble if he targeted someone who was actually physiognomically challenged. A hyperbolical *retard* can still be heard within male groups coveting an unpolished image, but even then it is positively rude. If the target is actually developmentally disabled, however, it is nowadays completely unacceptable.

Interestingly, terms that are used literally need not be literal themselves. Creativity, often crass and bizarre, runs rife. *Butterfingers*, for instance, refers to someone who is clumsy, not someone with fat or greasy fingers. And *fuckface* is quite inexplicably levelled against people acting or looking revoltingly ugly, for who would actually be sexually aroused by a fuckface? They probably would prefer the more obvious, squarely distasteful *office dickwipe*. Nobody in Britain has any idea whence came the term *nonce* for a sex offender, especially one who is into children, back in the 1970s, but everyone knows it is not a term to use lightly. Like *four-eyes* it can be used literally only, unlike *pervert*, which can be used in flippant jocularity.

As the allegedly highly intelligent but not all that suave Elon Musk learned so painfully in July 2018, it is not always easy to separate the wheat from the chaff here. A rescue diver accused Musk of abusing the plight of a Thai youth soccer team trapped inside a flooded cave for his own public relations, causing the incensed entrepreneur to brand the man a *paedophile* on Twitter. This kicked up such a storm of disgust that Musk realized that, unlike *pervert*, *paedophile* is taken strictly literally, deleted his tweet and grudgingly apologized in public.

@#$%!

IT REMAINS A MATTER for debate whether Dostoevsky was right when, in his short story 'Notes from the Underground', he claimed that verbal abuse was the main thing distinguishing mankind from the other animals. But we can be certain about one thing: people all over the world keep at it with impressive enthusiasm and creativity. New slurs are made up as easily as new words, and rude and taboo terms will pop up even where there is absolutely no negative emotion to be found.

Some common slurs echo long-forgotten politics. *Dunce*, for instance, began its career as a derogatory term for the followers of John Duns Scotus, a thirteenth-century Scottish theologian and philosopher on a par with William of Ockham and Thomas Aquinas. During the English Reformation, the Duns Scotians fell out with sixteenth-century Protestant humanism and were derided as stupid, old-fashioned reactionaries: dunces. Equally medieval and even more colourful is *bugger*, which derives via French *bougre* from *Bulgar*. Medieval Bulgaria adhered to Eastern Orthodoxy, and as a consequence Bulgars were considered heretics in the West. They were thrown in with early reformist Christian groups that originated in Asia Minor, and then spread through Bulgaria into Eastern Europe and further west. Most prominent among these were the Cathars, who around 1200 settled in the Languedoc region of France and gained such popularity that they scared the Pope out of his wits. So impressed was undivided Catholic Western Europe with them that eight centuries later the Germanic words for heretic are still derivatives of 'Cathar': *Ketzer* in German, *ketter* in Dutch and *kjetter* in Norwegian, *kättare* in Swedish and *kaetter* in Danish. Part of the relentless and successful efforts by the Catholic authorities to exterminate the Cathars was a smear campaign accusing them of being out-of-place 'Bulgar' interlopers who sacrificed babies and practised 'unnatural' sex, which in England came to be known as buggery.

Something similar, although less vicious, gave rise to the modern Greek term μπάιρον (*báyron*) for a gentle, elegant and well-bred homosexual. It echoes the fame of that greatest of all nineteenth-century Hellenophiles, Lord Byron, whose sexual inclinations were obviously not lost on the Greeks.

Another area infused with graphic and rustic terms are toponyms, the names of geographical phenomena. Early American settlers seem to have enjoyed the occasional toponymic prank, giving hills and mountains names such as Nellies Nipple in California, Bald Peter in Oregon, Coon Butt in Tennessee, Wee Wee Hill in Indiana and Squaw Tit, of which there were two, in Arizona, one of which was duly renamed Squaw Butte to avoid confusion. Other saucy names are Whorehouse Meadows in Oregon, and in North Carolina the wonderfully evocative Smackass Gap and French Broad, a river. Germans live happily in Vegesack ('screw scrotum'), Hodenhagen ('testicle woods'), Geilenkirchen ('horny churches') or Außernbrünst ('outside-lust'). In Macedonia, there are landmarks called Pučigăs ('stick-out-ass') and Prdeškov Rit ('farter's hill'), and wells bearing names such as Bričen Kurec ('shaven prick') and Pičkina Vada ('cunt water'). Some Finns have friends and family in Karhunperse ('bear's arse') or Isomulkku ('big dick'). Others swim in Peräsuolijoki, the

Not everybody agreed with Castrillo Matajudíos ('Camp Kill the Jews') changing its name back to the original Castrillo Mota de Judíos ('Camp Jew-Hill') in 2015.

'rectum river', or enjoy fishing in one of several small lakes called Paskolampi ('shitpond') or one named Pahakala ('evil fish').

A toponym of a rather different kind is the Spanish hamlet that was until recently called Castrillo Matajudíos, 'Camp Kill the Jews'. Apparently, this community of nowadays some fifty inhabitants had originally been called Castrillo Mota de Judíos, 'Camp Jew-Hill', but had changed its name in 1627 in compliance with the expulsion order the Catholic monarchs Ferdinand II of Aragon and Isabella of Castile had issued against the Jewish population of Spain. This seems unlikely, since the expulsion order – which was real enough and had been quickly effectuated, dated back to 1492, some 135 years earlier. Rather, it would seem the inhabitants changed the name to keep on the right side of the Inquisition in one of its campaigns against the *conversos*, Jews who had converted to Christianity to avoid expulsion. It was not until 2015 that the name raised sufficient protest for the authorities to change it back to its original form.

This is not the only case of its kind. The easternmost Mexican town on the Texas border is called Matamoros, kill the blacks, the Africans. Far from being a hamlet, it had close to half a million inhabitants.

Even food – to most of us a source of joy and deep satisfaction – is not immune to our quirky and dirty imagination. Hence, the French call a torpedo-shaped loaf a *bâtard*, 'bastard', perhaps because its shape is between the straight *baguette*, 'stick, baton, knitting needle', and the more or less oval traditional *pain de campagne*, 'country loaf'. Italians like to dine on *pasta puttanesca*, 'whores' pasta' (with tomatoes, anchovy and capers – some add tuna) or, when in Turin, munch a *bagascia*, 'whore', which is a deep-fried bun slit open and filled with olive paste or cheese, prosciutto crudo, salami and so on. When in Holland, order a *berenlul*, 'bear's prick', at any snack bar and they'll promptly serve you a deep-fried dark-brown sausage of equally doubtful culinary value as good old soapy British bangers.

Some of these decidedly odd names are the result of history going awry. Gorno Dupeni and Dolno Dupeni, 'upper arse' and 'lower arse', are tiny villages in Macedonia whose names are based on an old word, *dup(k)a*, meaning 'hole', which by and by came to mean 'arse'. The village of Podmočani, 'under-pissed, piss-soaked', allegedly got its name centuries ago after it had been flooded by the Turks. In time, the archaic verb *moči* meaning 'to soak', on which the name was formed, dropped from usage, and people began to mistake the middle part of the name for the modern word *moča*, 'piss'.

Others, such as Geilenkirchen, a German border town close to the Netherlands and Flanders, may have resulted from simple corruption. In Flemish, the town is called Geelkerken, 'yellow church', and in the regional dialect the name was long pronounced 'yellekercken', now 'Gelekerken'. This 'yelle' or 'gele', meaning yellow, was then misheard by speakers of standard high German, so to speak, and misspelled as *geil(e)*, which also happens to be the word for 'horny'.

Otherwise, ooh-la-la names of places, foods and other objects mostly look like attempts at wry humour, steeped in irony with a twist of hyperbole. Squaw's Tit speaks for itself, as do the Dutch *berenlul* we have already encountered, and *patatje ongesteld*, 'monthlies fries', which refers to French fries topped with mayonnaise and tomato ketchup. The ten or so Finnish 'shitponds' are relatively diminutive, on average measuring less than 3 hectares (8 ac): they're shitty excuses for a lake. The idea behind the *bagascia*, the 'whore' the people of Turin like to eat, might well be that it's a bun that does not care what it's stuffed with. The Macedonian moniker *Pičkina Krasta*, 'cunt mange', for a piece of wasteland might just be a scathing appraisal of its agricultural qualities.

@#$%!

Just as ubiquitous as the urge to take the other down a peg or two are the themes on which slurs are based. There are two basic categories: personal shortcomings and social shortcomings, which pertain to groups of people. Next to physical or mental imperfections that one cannot do anything about, there are also behavioural personal shortcomings.

Undeniable physical imperfections are a very popular target among bullies, all the more poignant if the accusation is true, if only in the eyes of the target. A jarring example is the pubescent girl who began wearing heavy eyeliner to hide her abnormally bulging eyes after someone had called her 'frog-eyes', only to discover years later that there was actually nothing to hide. The Dinga, one of the peoples of Southern Sudan, use a peculiar array of slurs that leave little to the imagination and play on women's worst uncertainties. The stuck-up bitch who refuses to dance with a teenage boy is likely to be blasted with *mabial atea-teal mabial me nsiem,* 'you have breasts as long as an eel.' Others are accused of having to make do with two peas on a plate: *mabial agpi-agpi ke mabial nganswang,* 'you have very short breasts like those of a porcupine.' And young women who come into conflict with an older woman are likely to shout angrily *mabial inear-inear,* 'your tits are emaciated,' at them. Of course the Western world shares the Dingas' obsession with women's breasts, and Westerners do comment on the shape, size and condition of the female bosom, but not in quite the same way. They usually gossip about breasts behind their owners' backs. In their books, telling a woman – any woman – to her face that she has drooping breasts is just about as churlish as one can get. Nevertheless, the Dinga slurs don't seem to be intended to create lifelong enemies; rather they seem little more than expressions of temporary disenchantment. The difference is, cultural standards of beauty aside, that among the Dinga breasts are – or at least were, until recently – traditionally uncovered. Therefore, they are less taboo and slurs about them are less heavily charged. This is also behind other Dinga imprecations that sound unusual to Western ears, such as *mukwom umpwal,* 'swollen navel', which means glutton.

Slurs involving abnormal belly buttons are quite common among the languages of central Africa and, one would expect, equatorial regions elsewhere, but non-existent in those parts of the world where the navel is generally covered by clothing. Physical slurs usually target imperfections one can actually *perceive.* Examples are *fatty, four-eyes, freckles, Casper* (for a very pale person, after Casper the friendly ghost, a cartoon character), *bandy-legs, midget* and *ginger* or *carrot top* for redheads. Bald people suffer from *baldy* or *chrome dome* or, in Dutch, *vleespet,* 'flesh cap'. *Moyashi,* 'bean sprout', is a Japanese word for a very thin person, and so is *gari,* an onomatopoeic for the sound of scratching or biting. On this same note, the Dutch contribute *gratenpakhuis,* 'fish bone warehouse', for very thin people.

Age is another physical vulnerability. Being too young and inexperienced makes one a *runt,* a *greenhorn* or, in Mandarin, a *rǔ-còu wèi-gān,* literally 'milk stink not dry'. Being relatively old earns you titles such as *fogey, fuddy-duddy, biddy, crank* and *fossil* in English, *lǎo-bú-sě,* 'old but not dead yet', and *cán-hūa bài-lǐu,* 'faded flowers', in Mandarin and *carcamán,* 'unseaworthy vessel', in Argentinian Spanish.

Mental abnormalities are ascribed to people for almost any reason you can think of. A lack of skill, knowledge or savvy will earn you a disdainful *wú-zhē*, 'no knowledge; ignoramus', in China. Germans prefer *Esel*, 'ass', and in Bavaria, for women, *Gretl*, a girl's name, in such cases, or in Switzerland *Hün*, 'hen'. In the Netherlands, you're liable to be called a *rund*, 'bovine', or an *achterlijke gladiool*, 'retarded gladiolus'. Russians might call you *mudák*, a word for 'simpleton' that derives from *mudó*, 'penis'. They might even warn *ne suj (sun') huj v čaj!*, 'don't hang your prick in the tea,' reportedly a bizarre play on the name of an ancient Chinese philosopher Sun' Hui Chai, meaning don't do anything stupid. There's a nearly endless stock of slurs attributing lack of intelligence or sanity, ranging from *airhead, fool, oaf, loopy* and *nincompoop* through *halfwit, fuckwit, moron* and *shit for brains* to the downright offensive *mongol*. If you're too clever, on the other hand, you are bound to be branded a *smart-arse, professor, egghead, whizz, wise guy* or *nerd*. Men of the Greek underworld have a particularly nifty way of telling someone that they don't value his opinions much. While the other is speaking to them, they look down at their own groin saying *akous, Apostoli?*, 'Do you hear, Apostolis?' The meaning is clear: you're so uninteresting or stupid, you should be talking to my dick.

Excepting ethnic and racial slurs, imprecations that refer to traits or character flaws that are not directly associated with intelligence or sanity are few and far between.

Personal behavioural eccentricities in some way affect the lives of others, and our mutual vexations have given rise to an endless variety of imprecations on this score. Self-explanatory examples are *loud-mouth, bully, coward, liar, swindler* and *slob*. If you can't, won't or don't dare go along with what the group you are a member of plans to do, you are a *homo*, a *sissy*, a *wet blanket* or a *party pooper*. Unreliable and untrustworthy people are *fraudsters* and *cheats* or, in China, *xié-mén wài dàu*, 'lopsided door, illegitimate path', and in Iran *aghrab zir ghālih*, 'scorpion under the rug'. People who bend over backwards to keep on the right side of someone else are called *brown-nosers* or, in Afrikaans, *gatkruipers*, 'arse crouchers', in Russia *žopoliz*, 'arse licker' and in Iran *mă-pì-jīn*, 'horse fart spirit'. A man who transgresses the limits of heterosexual propriety is a *philanderer* in English, a *júbočnik*, 'skirter', in Russian and a *rokkenjager*, 'skirt chaser', in Dutch. The Menominee call him *ke:mena:qsow*, 'has illicit love-affairs', or *ke: menewê:w*, 'strokes women on the sly'. Traditionally a sexually oblig-ing woman is a *slut* or in Mandarin *rén jìn kě-fū*, 'anyone can be her

How to call someone an idiot					
Afrikaans; South African English	*bobbejaan* (lit. baboon)	Hungarian	*hülye*	Samoan	*valea*
Dutch	*halve gare* (lit. half-baked)	Indonesian	*(orang) bodoh*	Spanish	*rayado* (lit. striped); *zonzo*
Finnish	*idiootti, typerys*	Irish	*leath-cheann*	Swahili	*punguani*
French	*abruti* (lit. dazed)	Italian	*imbecille*	Turkish	*salak*
German	*Vollidiot*	Japanese	*aho, baka, bakayarō*	Vietnamese	*kẻngốc*
Greek	*ilithios* (lit. dazed), *anoètos*	Korean	*baegchi*	Welsh	*hurtyn*
Haitian creole	*enbesil*	Russian	*idiot*	First World War Army English	*cunt*

Originally, in classical Greek, ιδιότης (*idiotes*) referred to someone who did not partake in the social and political duties of the *polis*, the Greek city state — hence someone antisocial, unwise and ignorant.

husband'. If she is not forthcoming men are wont to call her a *stuck-up bitch* or, in Dutch, *stijve trut*, 'stiff biddy, stiff cunt'.

A special case is homosexuality. Homosexuals constitute a stable and ubiquitous minority in human societies around which has always hung a whiff of impropriety. In part at least, this may well have been because of the fact that, like adultery and incest, homosexuality upsets the normative heterosexual applecart. It thereby threatens the order of the traditional family, on the stability of which the livelihood and prosperity of all family members depended throughout most of human history, and in most parts of the world still do. Another reason might be insecurity among men about their own feelings and their position in the social pecking order, especially during adolescence and early adulthood – the fighting age, so to speak. In some sense, going for other men puts a man on a par with women, whose status was, and in many parts of the world still is, hardly if at all better than that of a slave. This would also explain why the traditional panic about homosexuality is much greater among men than among women, who mainly seem to worry about the fate of a possibly homosexual son.

In the few societies that seemed to embrace homosexual relationships between men (women never counted), the practice was strictly limited. In classical Greek society it was all right for adult free men to openly covet other men, but that was it. For actual erotic contact, an *erastes*, an interested man, must find an *eromenos*, a free teen boy whom he might entertain and take to his bed until the boy began to grow pubic or facial hair. Also, there should be no penetration. Sexual contact between a man and his *eromenos* consisted of kissing and caressing, and ultimately *diomerizein*, 'doing the thing between the thighs'. This was what is now called intercrural sex, where the *erastes* rubs his member between the thighs of the *eromenos*. It's close to the real thing, but, as Bill Clinton might say, no cigar.

Of course, this kind of *pederasty* (from *pais, ped-*, 'child', and *erastes*) was the official standard. Reality between free men and boys may have been somewhat messier. And the devil may know what went on between free citizens and slaves of either sex, although the Latin graffito *Cosmus Equitiaes magnus cinaedus et fellator est suris apertis*, 'Cosmus, slave of Equitias, is a great queer and cocksucker with his legs wide open', found in Pompeii, gives us some idea. But the classical ideal does illustrate one of the few cultural laws that seem to be really universal, with the recent partial exception of only the richest, best-organized and freest postmodern societies: the hierarchy of sexual partnership. Right at the top are dominant heterosexual males, hunting for partners among womanhood. To varying extents teenage boys may be substituted for women, from the Greek *eromenos* to modern rent boys, even in cultures where 'real' homosexuality is considered a serious crime, such as the Islamic world. Sexual relations between adult men are usually considered out of bounds, with special disdain for the one on the receiving end, either orally or, still worse, anally, like poor Cosmus. So heterosexuality trumps homosexuality and dominance trumps submission. In classical Greece, being called a *kinaidos*, the one who lends his body to the pleasure of others, was just about the worst humiliation conceivable. These days, the Greeks use the word *pústis*, which is about as nice as English *cocksucker* and its Russian equivalent from the Gulag *xuesós*, Turkish *İbne*, the Arabic *xawal* and the Farsi slur *kūnī*, 'arse', all referring to a passive homosexual.

In a television interview in 1975, the linguist James McCawley remarked that there seem to be no derogatory terms specifically referring to dominant homosexuals. As he put it, next to the cocksucker, there is no such term as 'cocksuckee'. He attributed this lack

How homosexuals became gay

Gay, related to the French *gai*, dates back to Middle English and long meant exuberantly cheerful, full of mirth, light-hearted and pleasure-seeking. Hence, it also took on overtones of superficiality and airy off-handedness. In Puritan seventeenth-century England, it came to be applied to men and women of loose morals, but it still had nothing to do with homosexuality – a condition the Puritans would probably have denied existed. The transfer to homosexuality in men took place only in about 1900. Then nothing much happened until the arrival of AIDS in about 1980, which paradoxically gave an enormous boost to the emancipation of homosexuals in the Western world. During the 1980s the traditional opposition between *heterosexual* (right) and *homosexual* (wrong) was replaced by the pair *straight* (normal) and *gay* (also acceptable). At the same time, homosexuality turned from a 'mere' sexual orientation into something much bigger: a lifestyle and something of an ideology. From this time on not only people were gay, but bars, festivals, some literature and films. At many universities, there are even gay studies. Of course, none of these can be homosexual in nature; they merely subscribe to the gay lifestyle and ideology, or take them as their subject of inquiry. In radical emancipatory circles, as Reinhold Aman noted, the pair *straight-gays* has since given way to the oppositional pair *homophobic* (wrong, abnormal) and *gay* (right, normal). In the process, *gay* won the world but lost its innocence. Calling someone or something *gay* carries a big load these days.

to the inherent macho character of verbal abuse: it simply wouldn't do to deride the dominant, active partner in a male-to-male relationship. But he was wrong. Most probably a form such as 'cocksuckee' does not exist because it is a very passive term, completely unfit for the purpose of characterizing, either negatively or otherwise, the one who calls the shots. But McCawley was more generally wrong as well. At best, he had stumbled on a quirk of English, for derogatory terms for active homosexuals do at least exist elsewhere. The German *Spinatstecher*, 'spinach miner', is hardly a compliment, nor are Dutch *rugridder*, 'backside knight', *bruinwerker*, 'brown-labourer', and *darmtoerist*, 'gut-tourist', and perhaps Georgian *bičebis moqvaruli*, 'lover of boys', Turkish *kulampara*, 'bugger', or even English *bugger* itself, and lurid slurs such as *ass-burglar*.

Sex by all accounts being the most controversial behaviour engaged in by mankind, it is hardly surprising that many languages are full of sex-based general-purpose slurs and imprecations. Obvious examples in English are the *motherfucker*, the *(cock)sucker*, the *son of a bitch*, the *prick* and the *cunt*. Other languages have parallels to English *fuck*: Dutch *kut!*, 'cunt', and Spanish *joder!*, 'fuck', and *puta madre!*, 'whore Madonna', which as *de putra madre* may also serve as an adjective meaning something like 'super', 'tremendous' or 'as hell'. Farsi plays on just about any kind of illicit sexual activity imaginable in the expression *bābāt bi kūnit*, 'your dad is in your arse', which is a general-purpose slur used by and against men and women alike. If you hear *ebí koróvu*, 'go fuck a cow', in Russia, they are merely telling you to get lost. And there is always what the Poles and Ukrainians refer to as the Russian curse and in Yiddish is called the Russian blessing: *ēb tvojú mat*, 'fuck your mother', also used as the English use 'bloody': *Peredáj, ēb tvojú mat', sol!*, 'Pass the bloody salt!'

Still, some languages seem to be largely devoid of sexual slurring, preferring excrement, animals, illnesses or religious terms instead. Somewhere halfway between things sexual and the world of excrements is the extremely rude Spanish expression *me cago en la leche de tu madre*, 'I shit in your mother's milk', meaning something like 'fuck off'. Something similar is true of the Dutch *kankerlul*, 'cancer prick', and *strontzak*, 'shit scrotum', mixing sex organs with illness and excrement but just meaning 'obnoxious person'. The place of *fuck!* in English is taken by *merde!*, 'shit', *putain!*, 'whore', and even *putain de merde!*, 'shit-whore', in France, *vaffanculo!*, 'go and do it in your arse', in Italian, *Scheisse!*, 'shit', in German and *kut!*, 'cunt', or varieties of *god(ver)domme!*, 'God damn', in Dutch.

@#$%!

SOCIAL SLURS DIFFER from personal slurs in that they target groups of people, or individuals as incarnated instances of a group. Most of these groups are abstract concepts rather than actual societies one consciously signs up with. They can be defined along social, economic, cultural, intellectual, political, ethnic and racial lines, but definitions are always simplified, stereotypical and prejudicial. So are the derogatory terms that come with them, from the semi-neutral *hipsters* through the old-fashioned *commies* and *capitalists*, and monikers such as *pigs* and *the filth* for the police, to Hillary Clinton's fateful invention in 2016 of the *deplorables* and worse, such as *dago*, *Nazi* and *nigger*. As Clinton's *deplorables* illustrate, it is not unusual for a group to spring to life just because someone coins a defining slur for it. Also, people don't belong to just one group, but include themselves or are included by others in many different groups, even several groups of roughly the same kind or groups that would seem to be incompatible. 'Us', as opposed to 'them', can be quite a complicated notion, as the following example shows.

In February 1941, as razzias to round up the Jews of Nazi-occupied Europe for deportation were getting under way, one of these sparked a large protest in the Netherlands in the form of a strike, under the slogan *Blijf met je rotpoten van onze rotjoden af*, 'Keep your filthy paws off our filthy Jews.' The actual wording may be apocryphal – nobody seems to have noted it down at the time – but that does not lessen the veracity of the sentiment expressed, nor its instructive value as to what it really means to be human. The human race being a gregarious species, the natural propensity of many Dutch to be loyal to and protect members of their own group against onslaughts from outsiders even extended to those who were by many considered to be on the margins of their society. As everywhere else in Europe, Jewish people in the Netherlands were often regarded with a wary eye, as somewhat obsequious, somewhat unfathomable people, not to be entirely trusted. For a good impression of the utterly thoughtless normality of such attitudes back then, read Graham Greene's thriller *Stamboul Train* (1932; also published as *Orient Express*). As it was, the strike didn't do much good, since there was simply no stopping the unfolding Nazi murder-machine. But it did show the potential of group solidarity.

Inextricably linked to this human penchant for closing ranks against a common enemy is a deep disdain for 'them', meaning all those who are not 'us'. Unlike other animals, people don't just distinguish between their group and the rest of the world, but attach a value judgement to the distinction: 'we' are also the best, the most worthy, the cream of the crop. And, above all, 'we' are *normal*. 'We' set the norm for others to follow. Everyone who disagrees with 'us' or does things differently is necessarily in the wrong. How could it be otherwise? If our ideas, our practices weren't the best, we wouldn't entertain them, would we?

It is this perfectly airtight and circular logic that has caused an endless stream of slurs and disparaging jokes against the neighbours. Townspeople speak of country folk as *yokels* or *hicks*, or, in the case of Scottish Lowlanders targeting Highlanders, *teuchter*, who, as the comedian Billy Connolly noted, are amazed when they leave their dank glens for the city and for the first time clap eyes on a 'house wi' whééls' – the thing which 'we', who know better of course, call a bus. Americans from the urbanized coastal regions of the United States dismiss the rest as *fly-over people*, and the denizens of the island of Manhattan sneer about the *bridge-and-tunnel-people* inhabiting the other four boroughs of New York City. More than 150 years after the end of the American Civil War, one half of the country still disparages the other half as either *Yankees* or *rednecks*.

Interestingly, in the late 1970s a survey among American students suggested that people were more aware of disparaging names for their own group than of those applying to others. Specifically, southern participants were better acquainted with the derogatory terms *redneck* and *cracker* than northerners were.[1] This might partly explain why disparaging group names often sting so badly. It is not so much the verbal onslaught by others, but your own insecurity that is to blame. Group membership, especially membership of a non-dominant group such as (in the United States) the descendants of the old Confederacy, is a vulnerability. It is like a badly healing wound waiting to be broken open by another, a wound that faintly keeps throbbing and itching even when no one has actually scratched it.

In many cases group disparagement amounts to no more than ritual, jocular and fairly good-natured banter. Traditionally,

Canadians make fun of the Newfies of Newfoundland, and the Swiss of the Appenzeller, who inhabit one of the smaller and most conservative cantons of the country. The Poles ridicule the citizens of the city of Chelm and the Italians those of Cuneo. The Swedes joke about (and actually discriminate against) the Saami of Lapland and Germans have their fictional Schildbürger. And so it goes on, the world over. Almost every people seems to have a favourite stupid and gullible dupe.

However, social slurs are not always so innocent. They can even be a serious political instrument. During the Cold War era, the East German authorities issued officially approved terminology for speakers and writers to use when referring to Britain and its people. This included *paralytic sycophants, carrion-eating servile imitators, effete betrayers of humanity, conceited dandies, gang of women-murderers, arch-cowards and collaborators, degenerate rabble, parasitic traditionalists* and *playboy soldiers*. On the other hand, the West was quite fond of its own anti-communist rhetoric, with *commies* who were *pinko rats*, and dire warnings against the *Ivans* and *red* and *yellow menaces*. Nowadays, terms such as *elite, leftists, right-wing extremists, fascists* and *Nazis* are frequently heard as serious disparaging epithets, plus, of course, *racists, sexists, homophobes* and *Islamists* or plain *Muslims*. Just calling someone any of those relieves you from the duty of considering what they say. They are *fascists, populists* or *left-wing scum*, with whom there is no reasoning.

Most social slurs are comments on the choices one makes in life, and directed at groups one becomes a member of as a consequence. People can get rich and become, in the eyes of certain others, a *class traitor, capitalist* or *plutocrat*, or attain stardom and enter the ranks of the *happy few* or the *glitterati*. Or they can lose their fortunes and end up as *paupers, trash* or, in the southern United States, *crackers*.

Social slurs differ from personal slurs in more ways than one. Irony apart, personal slights such as *jerk, asshole* and *bitch* and their equivalents in other languages always mean more or less the same thing: obnoxious, unsatisfactory person. Most social epithets, on the other hand, have quite different meanings and associations, depending on the position of their user. Among communists, *capitalist* is a very negative handle, whereas to the average American it is not. Likewise, *intellectuals* and *intelligentsia* may both be used in admiration of the collective of highly educated, erudite and inspiringly intelligent thinkers about society and whatnot, and as disparaging handles for a privileged class of educated people helping to suppress the *proletariat*, which is now a moniker for the honest, hardworking people, now a slight referring to a despicable class of uncouth layabouts. *Liberal* and *socialist*, both as nouns and as adjectives, mean so many different things across so many different cultures, and even within cultures, that the terms cause lots of confusion and misunderstanding.

One consequence of this is that social slurs can be appropriated by the targeted group as a *nom de guerre*, a proud moniker. Usually, this works only within the group. Examples are derogatory terms for homosexuals such as *queer* and *dyke* and the Dutch *flikker*, 'queer', and also *nigger* and *negro*. All these retain their negative character, but are consciously used among like-minded people as a positive identifier. Such terms are shared by and bind the members of the group, who consider them their property, free for them to use but not for others. Simply put, some black people have no qualms about calling each other *nigger*, but deny all others the right to do so. Sometimes such appropriated terms are adopted by society at large as well, and thereby lose their negative load. *Yankee*, for example, originated as a disdainful British term for Dutch pirates and was then used by British soldiers as a disparaging name for what they considered to be rough-hewn riff-raff: the American colonists. In time, the colonists appropriated both the term and the colonies, and before long *Yankee* became a fairly neutral name for northeastern Americans. Of course, during the American Civil War it once again acquired a very negative meaning in Confederate circles.

Today's proud Tories are another example. Initially *tory* was a corruption of the Irish *thórai*, 'outlaw, brigand', scathingly applied to the few scattered bands of Royalist Irish who kept resisting the roundheads (another social slur) of Oliver Cromwell's New Model Army when it overran Ireland in 1649. The nickname was quickly transferred to the Royalist faction in the English Civil War in general. It stuck and was later used against and adopted by a variety of political groups in Britain who shared a lack of aversion to Roman Catholics, and it ended up as the accepted nickname for those who favour conservative, traditionalist policies.

Something similar happened in about 1650 with the Religious Society of Friends, a movement aiming to restore what they thought

> ## How the Germans came to be called 'Huns'
>
> During the first half of the twentieth century and especially during the First World War, the Germans were commonly referred to by the English-speaking world as 'Huns', associating them with Attila's murderous fifth-century savages. It was a serious slur, of course, expressing disgust and disdain. But it was not invented as such. In fact, the Germans acquired their *nom de guerre* in a way that is the exact mirror image of what normally happens. On 27 July 1900, in the city of Bremerhaven, Kaiser Wilhelm II gave a send-off to troops embarking for China to suppress the Boxer Rebellion. In his speech, he urged the men to be ruthless and take no prisoners. 'Whoever falls into your hands is forfeited,' he impressed upon them. 'Just as a thousand years ago the Huns under their King Etzel [Attila] made themselves such a name that they appear formidable and legendary even today', they were to put the fear of God into the Chinese 'for a thousand years'. German diplomats realized the danger that lurked in Wilhelm's display of revoltingly bloodthirsty enthusiasm, and the reference to Attila and his men was carefully redacted from the official version of the speech – but to no avail. The kaiser's speech had already caused something of a stir and the disparaging nickname *Hun* stuck with the English.

was the pure, vigorous original form of Christianity. In those days of bitter religious strife, their claim that the official church was superfluous since God was everywhere and anyone could conduct a service did not sit well with the authorities, nor did their unorthodox and exuberant style of worship, which included shaking and quaking. Inevitably, their mover and shaker at the time, a man called George Fox, ended up before the courts and in prison more than once. At one of his trials, in 1650, the judge ordered the unruly Fox to tremble and quake before the might of the court, whereupon Fox retorted that the court should 'quake before the word of the Lord'. At this, the incensed judge ranted 'What? Are you some kind of *quaker*?', and threw him in prison for blasphemy. But Fox's followers immediately adopted the term, and nowadays hardly anyone realizes that 'Quakers' is not the society's actual name.

Tory, communist, Ted, hipster, punk(er) and *Catholic* are all allegiances, ways of life or beliefs people can choose to subscribe to or not, at least in theory. Tories and communists can switch allegiance, most Teddy boys, punkers and hipsters turn into burnt-out, boring bourgeois midlifers at some point, and a Catholic can renounce their faith and become a Protestant, a Pentecostal missionary or even a pagan. This is not to say that it is always easy to do so. Especially if religion is involved, social control can be merciless and peer pressure enormous; witness the fate of apostate Muslims or Amish. To them, leaving their faith means saying goodbye to family and friends as well. In addition, apostate Muslims must also reckon with real repercussions at the hands of their former fellow faithful. Even Christians in northwestern Europe, the least religious region on Earth, had a hard time breaking away from their churches until roughly 1965. Likewise, poverty and even being rich are hardly a matter of choice for most people. If you are born on the wrong side of the tracks, it is extremely hard to get wealthy. But it's not impossible. Likewise, people born with a silver spoon in their mouth are highly likely to lead a privileged life, but some do succeed in squandering their entire fortune and join the ranks of the *riff-raff*.

However, there are three types of social slight that target conditions one cannot choose at all. One is sexual orientation and gender. The other two are ethnicity and race. Nowadays, these three areas have the highest personal and socio-political impact of all social slurs. Welcome to the wonderful world of really vicious and dangerous verbal abuse.

@#$%!

UNLIKE PERSONAL SEXUAL SLURS, social sexual slurs do not play on the uncertainties that plague most people. Personally, for instance, women are regularly targeted for their looks and physical beauty – or lack thereof – and men for insufficient physical prowess or lack of dominant behaviour. Socially, sexual slurs are against minorities and ideological subgroups. Thus in the early twentieth century feminist women who fought against the second-rate position of the female sex in modern Western society, particularly the fact that they were still denied suffrage, were derisively branded *suffragettes* until Emmeline Pankhurst and her comrades in arms appropriated the term. Half a century later, women who rose against the persisting discriminatory practices against their sex founded Women's Lib and took up the old nineteenth-century moniker *feminists* once again. Their actions and demands proved so controversial that their chosen nickname was pinched and turned into a slur in the mouth of conservative forces. Successively, feminism radicalized and became mixed up with muddy identity politics, adding further strength and increased popularity to the negative understanding of the term. So it goes.

The most conspicuous sexual minority is of course homosexuals, and nowadays especially the vociferous, ideologically inspired 'gay community' among them. This is reflected in the number of widely known negative terms for homosexuals and homosexual behaviour. English alone has a long list of terms for homosexual men, including *ass-peddler, boy-lover, bugger, fag(got), fairy, fruit(er), gay, nancy, pansy, ponce, poof(ter), queen, sod, sodomite, stud* and, in the United States, *turk*, none of which need be explained to the average eighteen-year-old. Lesbians have always attracted much less attention. *Femme, butch, dyke* and perhaps the highly contemptuous *carpet muncher* are just about the only terms to be used with any frequency. Homosexual practice in its least prestigious form has also long been present in popular imprecations such as *up yours* or, in Cuba, *Vete por ahí a que te den por el culo*, 'Go where you'll get it up the arse.' Or, wordless, in giving someone the finger.

Although sexual slurs can be quite unpleasant and gender issues are very *en vogue*, it is racist slurs that are generally considered the apogee of offence these days, for two reasons. One is the fact that in the 1930s the German Nazi regime founded its short-lived Thousand Year Reich on the concepts of racial hierarchy and racial purity, and in doing so ended up creating an unprecedented and, it is to be hoped, unique industrial extermination machine murdering millions and millions of people, in addition to ruining the lives of countless others and laying waste to an entire continent. The other is the bitter and extremely protracted aftermath of the abolition of slavery in the United States, keeping relations between black and white in America tense as a bowstring even more than 150 years later.

In fact, together with the plantation economies of the New World colonies of the eighteenth century, it was the Enlightenment that laid the cornerstones of racial theory and racist thinking. By and large, slavery, slave trading and serfdom had been around for as long as anyone could remember, and until the early Middle Ages they were a fixture of virtually all societies. Slavery and serfdom were matters of bad luck or God's will – of being born in bondage, of giving up your freedom out of poverty and want, of being captured in a war or raid, or of losing one's freedom to make good on a debt. It could happen to anyone. Then, slowly, region by region, city by city, more or less successful bans began to be issued in Europe on the importation of slaves from certain regions, the sale of slaves to non-Christians, the slavery of Christians and so on. By the time Christopher Columbus, funded by the Catholic monarchs Ferdinand and Isabella of Spain, put out to sea in search of India in 1492 and found America instead, slavery had been all but abolished across Western Europe. What's more, in 1493, after Columbus's return, Ferdinand and Isabella decreed that no native American should be enslaved, provided they were not cannibals or hostile to the Spanish invaders. This to the great chagrin of their protégé, who had counted on a nice profit on the almost six hundred indigenous people he had captured and brought back to Spain. Instead, he and others were forced to send them back where they came from. In doing so, however, the *Reyes Católicos* laid the groundwork for the infamous transatlantic slave trade, since the newly developing colonies in the West Indies and what was to become the southern United States still depended on forced labour for the exploitation and expansion of the plantations that were their lifeblood. For more than three centuries a highly lucrative cooperation existed between black and Arab Africans harvesting slaves from the African interior and herding them to trade posts on the west coast, and European and American slave traders who took them off their hands there and transported them on across the Atlantic for sale in the markets of the New World.

Although slavery had been ubiquitous throughout most of human history, racism as we know it – the sustained and systematic disparagement of and discrimination against a people merely on account of their skin colour and physiognomy – was as good as non-existent. From a European point of view, Chinese people were just different, as were Africans and Arabs. Provided they did not interfere with European interests, that was it. When in 193 CE Septimius Severus, a Roman general of African extraction, became Rome's first black emperor, nobody raised an eyebrow the way the Americans did when Barack Obama came to power in 2008. All that mattered was that he was a Roman citizen with sufficiently many legions behind him. In these respects Africans, Arabs and Indians probably did not differ much from Europeans. For most of their history, Native Americans had no idea other people existed, and the Chinese have always considered everybody else to be *quantité négligeable*.

According to the Dutch-Canadian cultural historian Devin Vartija, things began to change when in the course of the eighteenth century the traditional bedrock of historical and philosophical thought, the Bible, started showing cracks. Bit by bit evidence turned up to suggest that the world and all that was in it had not been created over the course of a week in October of the year 4004 BCE after all, as the Irish bishop James Ussher had calculated in the seventeenth century, but had evolved into its present shape over a much longer period, perhaps even millions of years. Evidence for this included fossil remains of what seemed to be 'primitive' forms of existing species. This suggested that nature was not immutable, the way God had crafted it, but that plants and animals had changed gradually over time from something else into what they looked like now, people included. As a consequence, there had to be different stages of development, which might even coexist at the same time in different places. In time, the somewhat naive idea took root that Europeans, Africans, Native Americans and Chinese represented different stages of development of a single species, humankind. That the Europeans and maybe the Chinese were technologically more advanced, running ahead of the rest, was only natural: they lived in colder, more demanding climates than the Africans, the Middle Easterners and most of the Native Americans Europeans knew about at the time. As a consequence, they had been forced to work harder. Thinkers such as Jean-Jacques Rousseau even looked upon the tropical black African with a mixture of jealousy and admiration as the pristine 'noble savage', unspoiled by the Europeans' craving for wealth and power.

Meanwhile, the Enlightenment also brought new ideas about the position of ordinary human beings in society, culminating in 1789 in the French revolutionary *Déclaration des droits de l'homme et du citoyen* (Declaration of the Rights of Man and of the Citizen). This raised a serious problem for the authorities and economic elites of the slavery-based economies of the New World. For how could slavery be condoned if the very first article of the declaration stated plainly that all men are born free, with equal rights, and remain so? The only solution was to formally deny slaves – meaning black Africans in the Americas – their human status. This was a particularly pernicious move since it meant that black Africans no longer represented a stage in the cultural development of humankind. Instead, they were seen as subhumans, fundamentally different and fundamentally flawed.

If you really thought it through, the thinking went, such 'creatures' could hardly be expected to fend for themselves in the sophisticated world of the American whites. Naive, childlike and simple, negroes were not equipped to maintain such a standard of living, and required firm guidance. From this point of view, the plantation owners felt they were doing their black Africans a good turn by providing them with the sheltered, segregated and strictly regulated life of a slave.

From the end of the eighteenth century onwards, then, black Africans in the Americas and to some extent elsewhere counted as *Untermenschen*, as the Nazis would much later call the races they thought inferior and therefore without rights. Modern racism had been born, and with it the notion of white supremacy, which

White on black and black on white in Brazil

With the exception of Nigeria, Brazil has the largest population of black African descent in the world. Although there has been far less segregation there after the abolition of slavery than in the United States, African Brazilians are still the underdog, as is shown in their verbal jousting.

White on black	Black on white
Branca para casar, preta para trabalhar, mulatta para amar – 'A white woman to marry, a black one to work and a mulatto for love	*No escuro, tanto vale la rainha como a negra na cozinha* – 'In the dark, the queen is no more than the kitchen negress'
Do branco o salão, do negro o fogão – 'To the white man the salon, the kitchen for the black man	*O trabalha é do negro e a fama é do branco* – 'The black man gets the work, the white man the glory'
Negro quando não caga na entrada, caga na saida – 'If a black man does not shit at the entrance, he shits at the exit	*Papel higiênico também é branco* – 'Toilet paper is white too'
Negro ensaboado, tempo perdido, sabão esperdiçado – 'Washing a black man is a waste of time and soap	*Carne de branco também fede* – 'White flesh stinks too'

persisted in the Americas, but most virulently in the United States, after slavery as an institution was abolished in the nineteenth century.

If the slaveholders' racism was largely a simple matter of discriminating against, belittling and exploiting people of black African descent, the Nazis made rather more of a muddle of it. To them, racial theory was a branch of science that was to bring about two things. One was a clear hierarchy of individual people and of populations. This was a matter of grave import, because national socialism, their brand of fascist ideology, is first and foremost grounded in the authoritarian concept of power. In fascism, everything begins and ends with the social pecking order: who has the right to boss whom around, and who is obliged to simply and unquestioningly obey. Within Nazi Germany, social power relations were largely regulated through the Nazi party NSDAP and by the SS, essentially a paramilitary society for the sufficiently Aryan civilian elite that everyone who aspired to a position of some authority had better try to become a member of. Unlike its later armed branch the Waffen SS, the Allgemeine SS was not a truly military institution, but it did use uniforms and a military hierarchy of ranks, which did a lot to clarify and order things in a society where everything was a matter of pulling rank. Beyond the German borders, the Nazis wished to ascertain whom they could respect and to what degree, and who should be written off as expendable or worse. More to the point, they wanted to furnish themselves with justifications for their own supposed superiority and their prejudicial disdain for certain other peoples.

The other goal of Nazi racist theory was racial purity. Romantic nineteenth-century thinkers and scholars had conjured up a myth about a pristine but long-lost race of noble and gallant steppe warriors on horseback, fair-haired, blue-eyed, strapping lads who spoke Proto-Indo-European, the matriarch of virtually all modern European languages. Thanks to ill-founded suppositions and some sinuous reasoning, these Aryans, as they were called, miraculously turned out to be the direct ancestors of the German people, making the latter at least *primus inter pares* among Europeans. This half-baked creation myth was mixed with another Romantic idea, namely that a *Volk*, a people, was defined by a shared mythology, language and ethnicity, plus a territory to which it was mystically bound. This is why the Nazis referred to themselves as the Aryan race and why they set such great store by *Lebensraum im Osten*, 'living space in the East': The mythical

Aryans had supposedly roamed the steppes of roughly present-day Ukraine, a territory that by the mystical bond between *Blut und Boden*, 'blood and earth', therefore belonged to the German people.

In short, Nazi theory held that the Aryan Germans were a *Herrenvolk*, a 'people of leaders', destined to dominate others. Other 'races' were inferior to varying degrees, some so undesirable as to be fit for extermination. But there was a problem. The true hierarchy among the races had been obfuscated by intermingling and inter-breeding, so the Nazis set out to restore the proper order and purify and reinvigorate their Aryan race. They took this quite literally, as if it were a matter of dog-breeding. As early as 1935, for instance, the ss launched the Lebensborn programme, centred on a string of maternity homes for ss wives, homes that were also used for raising and indoctrinating suitably Aryan children born to single mothers and, later, children born from liaisons between German soldiers and women from occupied countries, as well as, mainly in Eastern Europe, children who had been kidnapped by simply being ripped from their mothers' arms.

As far as purification was concerned, there was at least a sem-blance of brutal rationality to what the Nazis were doing. They were actually trying to breed a race as the world usually understands the term: a subtype of an existing creature, defined by a set of primar-ily external physical characteristics such as, in the case at hand, the colour of skin, eyes and hair, and – as far as could be predicted in infants – a tall, athletic body. To that end they selected children, weeding out any who were deficient in any way, and stimulated prime ss members to start families with women of the desired Aryan aspect. However, racial theory could not provide the desired yardstick for ranking peoples or races. Consider dogs again. Individual dogs can conform to a higher or lower degree to a set of racial requirements, ranking them qualitatively within a breed. But between breeds, there is no hierarchy. A spaniel isn't better or worse than an Alsatian or a chihuahua; it's just different. As with any other dog breed, it is better suited to some circumstances, environments and tasks than to others. Racial distinctions among humans are no different. They roughly reflect basic properties of the climates and natural environ-ments people have been living in for aeons, plus certain apparently random physical characteristics such as a flat nose here, monolid eyes there, a lanky or squat build and profuse or scant facial hair.

What the Nazis were unwittingly using as their yardstick was in fact ethnicity, a more complex, more culturally orientated notion. Ethnicity is rooted in tribal thinking, a particularly dangerous kind of depreciating all those who are not 'us'. Essentially, a tribe is like a widely extended family, kept together by blood ties and a common culture, and actively protecting both its cultural capital and its other assets, such as territory or grazing and hunting rights, from interlopers, competitors and raiders. Intermingling and interbreeding with neighbouring tribes is strictly regulated, and all outsiders are first and foremost regarded as untrustworthy enemies. This is most probably how the ancient hunter-gatherers who came before us viewed the world, as well as the last remaining isolated tribes in Amazonia, the Sentinel Islands and New Guinea, who are extremely wary of external contact. Generally, however, as contact with the world outside became more frequent and isolation waned, the range and scope of social interaction grew and tribal cultures began to merge somewhat into larger, regional entities. With that, tribal limitations lost some of their importance and the prominence of blood ties dwindled. But the fundamental mistrust of the stranger remained alive, as did the idea of belonging to an abstract kind of family with a common history, a common language and culture, and even certain typical physical characteristics – the Greek nose, the combination of black hair and pale skin common among Celtic people and so on. People's identity did not just change, it became layered, and still more layered when over time states grew stronger and better organized and people began to identify with a nation – a culture with an effective administration and a clearly delimited territory – as well.

Long before then, in a time when most people lived in an illiterate world of faraway kings and caliphs and local hetmen, and had never even heard of states or nations, large-scale organized religions had already driven out and replaced many of the older locally worshipped deities. Christianity, Hinduism, Buddhism, Confucianism and Islam became yet another layer contributing to the group identity of huge numbers of people belonging to great numbers of different tribes and realms, which need not share much else, either physically or culturally. Migration and occupation, and sometimes even the deportation of whole populations, complicated matters further, adding nostalgia and split or conflicting loyalties to the mix. Nowadays, almost everybody's socio-cultural and socio-political identity is built from

Amazon impressively tall, athletic woman (mythological race of female warriors); **Assassin** political or religious murderer, from a Muslim sect renowned for their fanaticism and murderous skills in the days of the Crusades (Persia); **Bohemian** vagabond, artistic person (Bohemia, Czech Republic); **Bugger** sodomite, homosexual (from Bulgar); **Canadian bacon** uncircumcised penis (gay slang); **Cannibal** man-eater (corruption of Carib); **Cretin** oaf, from old Swiss French term *crestin*, 'Christian', used to denote deformed and deranged people; **Cuban pumps** heavy boots (gay slang); **Cyprian** prostitute (Cyprus); **Dutch courage** courage induced by drinking alcohol; **Dutch uncle** someone who berates or gives stern but benevolent advice; **Dutch widow** prostitute; **Dutchman** uncultured, dull person; **French (love)** fellatio; **French letter** condom; **French screwdriver** hammer; **German silver** sham silver, an alloy of copper, nickel and zinc; **Go Dutch** share the cost of a dinner, commit suicide; **Greek** gibberish, anal sex; **Gyp** swindler (gypsy); **Hessian** unruly person or child; mercenary (Hessen, Germany); **Hottentots** buttocks; **Hun** German; **Indian coffee** coffee made from old grounds; **Indian giver** one who gives only to take away; **Irish banjo** shovel; **Irish draperies** pendulous breasts; **Irish shave** defecation; **Jew** swindler; **Jewish penicillin** chicken soup; **Laconic** terse, succinct (Laconia/Sparta, Greece); **Lesbian** homosexual woman (Lesbos, Greece); **Lilliputian** petty, narrow-minded person (from Jonathan Swift's *Gulliver's Travels*, 1726); **Lombard** moneylender, usurer (Lombardy, Italy); **Mandarin** influential bureaucrat or intellectual (Chinese imperial civil servant); **Mexican credit card** syphon for stealing petrol; **Mexican foxtrot** toothache, the runs; **Mogul** dominant person, from Farsi *mughul*, 'Indian Muslim'; **Pariah** outcast (an old term for casteless Indians); **Patagonian** very tall person, giant (Patagonia, Argentina); **Philistine** insensitive anti-intellectual materialist (biblical Palestine); **Pygmy** very small person (Equatorial Africa); **Scotchman** penny-pincher; **Slave** after the Slavic peoples of Eastern Europe, reduced to servile status around the year 1000; **Sodomite** homosexual (biblical Sodom); **Spanish athlete** braggart; **Swede** blunderer, large ungainly man; **Swedish fiddle** accordion; **Swiss** mercenary; **Swiss admiral** person pretending to be important; **Sybarite** debauchee, roisterer (Sybaris, a Greek town in Italy); **Take French lessons** contract a sexually transmitted disease; **Tell a French

> **joke** lick anus; **Vandal** intentionally destructive person (Vandals, a people who ravaged Europe and sacked Rome in 455 CE); **Welsher** one who defaults on a bet (formerly swindler); **Yahoo** rude, noisy or violent person (an imaginary species in *Gulliver's Travels*); **Zealot** fanatical religious or political missionary (a Jewish sect striving for world theocracy, crushed by the Romans in 70 CE).

a bewildering amalgam of overlapping and sometimes hardly compatible elements. It is not uncommon to find a dyed-in-the-wool American who claims she is a sixth-generation Pole or Italian (even if she has never seen the country in question) and then again a Catholic and, oh yes, of course, a Hoosier if she is from Indiana. Likewise, a Germany-born son of a Turkish immigrant in Munich may identify himself with equal ease as a Münchener, a Bavarian, a German, a Turk and a Muslim – and, oh yes, a European. Some of those who see themselves as Mancunians, Scousers or Geordies, Englanders and Brits, may call themselves Pashtu, Pakistani and Muslim as well, thus placing themselves in the same basket as most citizens of Peshawar, thousands of miles away, just beyond the Khyber Pass. Social identity can be a confusing concept.

When people are defining or explaining their own identity, they freely choose from the multitude of elements at their disposal. But when they look upon others, they make sense of things by simplification, generalization and stereotyping. They tend to reduce the other to a single, preferably exotic, characteristic, often something the 'others' in question would never have thought of themselves. In keeping with people's basic mistrust of strangers, such sweeping generalizations are usually intended to be derogatory. 'Typical' foods are popular. To Americans, the French became *frogs* because they eat them, and Italians *spaghetti eaters* or *meatballs*. A Quebequois was dubbed a *pea souper*, a French immigrant *Jean potage*, a Korean an *egg roll*, a Jewish person a *matzo*, an Irishman a *spud* or *potato head*, a German a *kraut* (a reference to sauerkraut) and people from the West Indies, in particular those who inhabit Key West, *conches*, after the edible *Strombus* seashell also known as Triton's horn.

First names provide familiar examples, too. An old one is the offensive term *dago* for Spaniards, probably a corruption of the common Spanish personal name Diego. Similarly, take *Heinz* or *Fritz* for Germans, or the *Ivans*, who were the great enemy of the West during the Cold War. Two positive exceptions come to mind, both exclusively concerning the military. One is the nickname *Tommy* for British soldiers, which dates back to the eighteenth century and has nothing to do, by the way, with the *Tommy gun* they toted, which was named after its manufacturer, Thompson. The term gained great popularity during the First World War among the German troops, and in the Second in the occupied countries the *Tommies* came to liberate. The other is the more than three-hundred-year-old moniker *Jantjes*, 'Johnnies', for Dutch navy personnel.

Language and behaviour are easy targets as well. Americans would call people of Latin American or Spanish extraction *spics*, possibly a reference to the clumsy way they would say 'No speak English' when they came into contact with Americans. Italians were reduced to *wops,* a corruption of the Neapolitan *guapo*, 'handsome', echoing Jacob Barclay's characterization of Italians as insincere charmers in his *English Dictionary* of 1774. Poles use the term *Niemiec* for Germans, from *niemy*, 'mute', and *nie mieć*, 'have not'. To them, Germans are people without a language, as all foreigners and particularly the dreaded Persians were to the ancient Greeks, who called them *barbaroi*, 'barbarians', on account of the horrid, incomprehensible 'barwrawraw' they thought passed for a language among them. Those Greeks had a point: even today, if you want party background noises in a film scene or on the stage, just tell the extras to keep murmuring 'bawrawraw' and the effect will be quite convincing. As for behaviour, few people realize that the Nemene Indians were given their much better-known name, *Comanche,* by some other tribe. It means 'those who attack us all the time'. Another case in point is the nowadays deprecated name *Eskimo*. This ethnic moniker was coined not by the ice-dwelling people themselves, but by the Menominee Indians. In their language, *aske:pow* means 'eats raw things', which of course is, or at any rate used to be, true enough.

The converse – turning the name of a feared or despised people into a stereotypical slur, either seriously or in jest – occurs as well. Arabs use the uncomplimentary term *firangi* for all white people, a corruption of *français* that originated in nineteenth-century Egypt. Italians will complain that a heavy smoker *fuma come un Turco*, 'smokes like a Turk', as do the French. The Dutch used to say *hij ziet eruit als een Turk*, 'he looks like a Turk', about someone looking dirty and dishevelled. In keeping with the stereotype that East Asians can't hold liquor very well, the Dutch may also call someone who is drunk as a lord (a class slur!) *zo zat als een Maleier*, 'as drunk as a Malayan'. Ethnic prejudice also shows in the Spanish expression *irse a la Francesa*, 'leaving the French way', meaning to slink away unnoticed, which the French call *filer à l'anglaise* and the English *taking Irish leave*. In Hungary, spraying oneself with deodorant or cologne instead of washing is called a *szovjet zuhany*, 'a Soviet shower', which is known in Sweden as a *Turkdush* ('Turkish shower'), in Poland as a *Rosyjski prysznic*, 'Russian shower', and in the United States as a 'Mexican' or 'Polish shower'. The targets differ, but the sentiment is always the same.

The classical Mexican term *gringo* for someone non-Hispanic is probably a corruption of 'Greek', meaning someone who does not speak Spanish. This use is somewhat similar to that in the English expression *It's all Greek to me*. The Germans use *Kanaken*, actually a Hawaiian word for 'man', as a vituperatively denigrating term for non-Western immigrants, especially Turks and people from the Middle East. The French used to call big-city criminals *Apaches*. Still older are slurs such as *Janissary* and *Cossack* for mercenaries, *Cretan* for liars and lazybones, and 'solecism' for a grammatical or

The Russian perspective on humanity

Derogatory ethnic and racial nicknames; literal meanings in square brackets

араб *aráp* [Arab] black person, thief; Ахмедка *axmétka* [little Ahmed] Tatar; баб *bab* [old woman] Tatar; бульба *búl'ba* [potato (Polish)] potato-eater, i.e. White Russian; елдач *eldáš* [derivative of *eldá*, prick] Kazakh; искаглазый *uzkoglázye* [slant-eyes] Chinese; лягушатник *ljagúšatnik* [frog man] French; макака *makáka* [monkey] Japanese; макароник *makarónnik* [maccheroni man] Italian; малшик *malšýk* [homosexual] Armenian; митар *mýtar'* [old Bulgarian word for tax collector] Jew; просим пана *próšem pána* [excuse me, sir] Pole; унтерменш *úntermenš* member of an inferior race; фазан *fazán* [pheasant] Chinese (on account of the colourful attire of the old imperial officials); Фрици *frítzi* [Fritz] German; хуй Голландский *xuy gollándskij* [Dutch prick] jerk, obnoxious person; цыган *cygán* [gypsy] Hungarian, Romanian; чернозадняя *černozádnij* [black arse] inhabitant of the Turkic southern republics; черномазь *černomázyj* [black grease] black person; чопорный сыновья *čópornye synov'yá* [proper sons] prim and proper boys – British; шмул *šmul* Jew; эфиоп *èfióp* [Ethiopian] dunce.

social gaffe, a long-forgotten reference to the people of Soloi, a Greek colony in the island of Sicily, who were notorious for the corrupted Attic Greek they spoke. To the British, the French always seemed past masters between the sheets, which gave rise to *French letter* for a condom, *French pox* for syphilis and *French* for rude language, as in *Pardon my French*. The Dutch, who vied with the English for dominance of the seas and naval trade for more than a century, were rewarded for their stubbornness with, among other expressions, *Dutch courage*, which is the kind inspired by heavy drinking, *Dutch wife* for a body-length cushion for use in the tropics instead of a blanket (but nowadays also used for an inflatable doll), and *Dutch uncle* for a harsh critic or stern mentor.

Ethnic simplifications work wonders when it comes to putting down people, especially since they don't just dehumanize but also de-individualize. It is much more difficult to harm your neighbour Mr Jennings or Jack the milkman than to fight the despicable *taigs*, as Catholics in Northern Ireland are still called by Protestant loyalists who strive to drive out those *Popeheads*, *Fenians* and *papists*. Southerners in the United States had fewer qualms about hunting down a few *coons* than about chasing black people, and it is much easier to hate and shoddily treat *chinks*, *zips*, *Polacks*, *wetbacks*, *hebes* and *kikes* than it is to discriminate against East Asians, Vietnamese, Poles, illegal Mexican immigrants or Jewish people, not to mention people with a name and a face. Likewise, during the Vietnamese War American soldiers, rather than going for Viet Cong insurgents, let *Charlie* have it, an abstract faceless foe coined from the abbreviation vc, 'Victor Charlie' in military radio parlance. Similarly, the allies of the two world wars fought *the Hun*, *Krauts* or *Jerries*, the *boches* if they spoke French, *moffen* if their language happened to be Dutch, and the *Şvabo* if they were Yugoslavian partisans. The Poles called the German invaders *szkop*, an old word for a castrated ram.

As these examples show, ethnic vilification is where verbal abuse meets and facilitates organized violence. It would be a mistake, however, to think that this is simply a matter of identifying people by sometimes half flippant, sometimes deeply derogatory terms or nicknames. It takes sustained, conscious and systematic effort to whip up tension sufficiently for violence to erupt, but the results can be truly horrifying. A prime example is what happened in April 1994 in Rwanda, a small East African country traditionally torn by bloody

In October 2014, 'Kill All Taigs' (Taigs meaning Roman Catholics) graffiti appeared within one day of Catholics moving into new so-called interface homes in Belfast, Northern Ireland.

ethnic strife between the three indigenous tribes, Hutu, Tutsi and Twa, of which the Hutus were the largest by far. The Hutu radio station Radio Télévision Libre des Mille Collines (RTLM) had already been fuelling and fanning mounting political tension in the country for many months, casting everything in an ethnic mould. When finally on 6 April the president's aeroplane was shot down with him, a Hutu, in it, RTLM immediately and openly called upon all Hutus to go out and kill all Tutsis and those Hutus who supposedly sided with them. The very same day wholesale slaughter began, a frenzy that lasted for more than three months and cost the lives of anywhere between 500,000 and a million Tutsis, Twa and moderate Hutus.

Around the same time wars in the former Yugoslavia were entering their most bloody phase. Yugoslavia, a central European communist state that was not a member of the Warsaw Pact, had begun to disintegrate after the death of its leader, Josip Broz, better known as Marshal Tito, in 1980. After the demise of the Soviet Union, the rickety conglomerate of half a dozen small states finally fell apart and almost everybody went for each other's throats. The wars that ensued were cruel and hard to understand. Of course there were old gripes and jealousies among the peoples of the former confederation, especially between the domineering Serbs and all the rest.

There was indeed a long history of ethnic and religious animosity, but nothing to warrant the rampant hate and bloodshed that tore the region to pieces for almost half a decade. To drive people who had lived peacefully together since the end of the Second World War, and had meanwhile turned their country from a war-torn backwater into a fairly prosperous industrial and touristic nation, to throwing in their trowels and waiters' towels and starting to shoot and execute each other, took the dark oratory talents of Slobodan Milošević and Radovan Karadžić. The former was a second-rate apparatchik who while Yugoslavia was disintegrating rose to become leader of the Serbian Communist party in 1987. At one time he had also been the patient of one Dr Karadžić, a curiously flamboyant quack psychiatrist-cum-poet, megalomaniac serial liar and fantasist who had taken it upon himself to lead the Serbian minority in Bosnia to a glorious future by ridding Bosnia of its Muslim majority. Both men began pushing a strongly nationalist great-Serbian agenda. Karadžić simply fanned the smouldering embers of old ethnic strife among the Bosnians until the state erupted into flames, but back in Belgrade, Milošević had to dig deeper to find kindling for his campaign for a Serb-dominated Yugoslavia. In June 1989 he found it in the unacceptable, unavenged humiliation the Serbs had suffered at the hands of the Ottomans after the loss of the Battle of Kosovo in 1389. In 1389! Six hundred years later his hyper-nationalist commemorative speech about an ancient half-mythical battle lost against a now irrelevant foe (Ottoman rule in Serbia ended in 1817) sufficed to put Milošević in the Serbian presidential palace and bring 3 million people out into the streets in support of his hopeless agenda – and persuaded them to go to war for it against their former compatriots. As for Karadžić, let the following lines from his poem '*Podne*' (Noon) testify to the corrupting power of his inky imagination:

> A strong and strapping wolf
> Bit off half the morning*
> And in his heart he took it
> Up into the hills, into the wild.
> After that, everything wept.

* 'Half the morning': a reference to the crescent moon that symbolizes Islam.

6

THE TROUBLE WITH TWITTER: WHY SOCIAL MEDIA ARE HARD TO HANDLE

So far, the most important new techno-cultural development of the twenty-first century has been the advent of social media. It is hard to realize that as late as 2004 the world had not yet heard of Facebook or Twitter or any other social networking site. Now these networks have billions of accounts, and politicians rely on Twitter to manipulate their constituencies and the press. Quite a few even conduct some form of political and diplomatic discourse there. Yet, there are deep worries about the kind of behaviour social media seem to trigger in both their owners and their users.

The owners of these platforms have by now turned out to be in it only for the money, and have proved to be prepared to go to great lengths to maximize and protect their revenues. They are, or have become, not nice people. One very important means to achieve their goal is the sale of data they collect about their users and their interests and predilections – that is how users pay for these ostensibly free services. The other is good old censorship. Advertisers, the other big providers of income for the platform owners, are extremely sensitive about the environments with which their brand names are associated – at least, that is what the network owners think – so anything that might scare them off must rigorously be resected like an incensed appendix. To different degrees they have all contributed to the demise of social media's beautiful promise of limitless opportunities for human contact and friendship, unfettered self-expression and worldwide dissemination and availability of thoughts and ideas, creating what old-fashioned hippies used to call 'love and understanding'. Instead, they have turned it into a cynical campaign of manipulative intrusion into innocent civilians' privacy of a depth and size hitherto unheard of. On the one hand, networks are busily wringing every detail from us about our private urges, feelings and interests, packaging us and selling us out to the highest bidder. On the other they try to suppress the products of those urges, feelings and interests as soon as they touch on mundane stereotypical taboos (such as nudity) or on what governments and other authorities consider sensitive subjects. It is telling that both Facebook and Twitter have developed elaborate protocols censoring taboo contributions from users and punishing those who break their rules, but have done nothing to create a fair and above all practical way of honouring the requirements of intellectual ownership. The potential of the technology that is being developed to monitor people and mine their minds – the infamous 'algorithms' – goes way beyond what even the most repressive surveillance states of recent history, such as the former German Democratic Republic, better known as East Germany, could dream of. Think, for instance, of the way China has been developing the stiflingly oppressive concept of social credit.

Equally unfortunate, it would seem, is the way users go about handling the technological wonders they've been handed. Instead of forging bonds of friendship with others, satisfying their curiosity and improving their knowledge of the world, they create constant

---

Pre-Internet trolls and anonymous threats

It would be a mistake to think that the Internet has caused the storms of anonymous threats and slander that so beset social media, although it has intensified things a lot. Victims of such abuse have certainly become more open about it than before, but it was always there, as chaplain Prendergast tells us in Evelyn Waugh's novel *Decline and Fall* (1928):

There was a time when I used to get five or six letters a day, not counting circulars. My mother used to file them for me to answer – one heap of charity appeals, another for personal letters, another for marriages and funerals, another for baptisms and churchings and another for anonymous abuse. I wonder why it is the clergy always get so many letters of that sort, sometimes from quite educated people. I remember my father had great trouble in that way once, and he was forced to call in the police because they became so threatening. And, do you know, it was the curate's wife who had sent them – such a quiet little woman.

Typical example of how things go wrong on Twitter. First, SILENT MAJORITY abuses a Trump tweet to push his own totally unrelated cause. Then Spudmonkey explains that his idea holds no water and boom, SILENT MAJORITY starts ranting.

pandemonium. An open sewer, a lunatic asylum run by the patients, a slanderers' paradise and a fount of filth and fake photos, filched films and horrific hoaxes – these are but a few of the disparaging ways in which sensible people have been referring to social media. It's true, platforms such as Twitter and Facebook do seem to be full of hoaxes, many of them planted there on purpose. And they have indeed increased the flow of disparaging and hateful rants and imprecations against all and sundry from a mere trickle to a turbulent torrent of seething venom. A timeline is often a sorry sight. Even worse, it would seem that owning a social-media account awakens the bully in many people, provoking an irrepressible urge to yell abuse at folks and threaten them, often disturbingly viciously. This puts further pressure on network-owning companies and authorities alike to 'do something' about the unpleasant bedlam well-meaning people frequently find themselves caught up in, leading to yet more repression and censorship, to the detriment of the idea of a free Internet serving creativity and the unfettered flow of ideas and information.

Much of the blame for this has been laid at the doorstep of the platforms, for allowing people to use their services anonymously. But while it is undoubtedly true that anonymity helps many a frustrated or tipsy user fire broadsides they would never dare let loose if their audience knew who they really were, it is an illusion to think that merely requiring people to fly their true colours would make a significant difference. The point is that one doesn't know 99.9999999 per cent of the adult world population from Adam whatever they're called, and these are the people you electronically brush shoulders with on the busy streets of social media. In all other circumstances, people have a pretty clear idea of whom it is they enter into a conversation with. This is evidently true for encounters in the flesh, but it also holds in virtually all other circumstances. On the telephone, people always identify themselves right at the start as someone you know already, or they introduce themselves so that you can form a psychological picture of them as a person. When you read an article in a newspaper or magazine, there is a byline, and if not, your interlocutor is the paper itself. As the French say, *le journal, c'est un monsieur*, 'the paper is a gentleman,' and it has a clear personality. If you read a book, you enter into a conversation of sorts with its author, which explains why there is almost always a photo and some inconsequential biographical information about the writer on or inside the cover; 'Rabindranath Scribbler lives in Athens with his wife and two children' is not an invitation to go and look him up, it just rounds him out as a character. When listening to the radio, you also know who's who. DJs and programme hosts take great care to identify themselves and introduce studio guests, and if you missed their introduction you spend half your time not listening but wondering: who is this?

Television, lastly, is no different, but social media are. Many of the interactions there are fleeting encounters between people who know nothing about each other and don't much care. Therefore, it hardly matters whether people call themselves Sutrisno, Adèle Pelletier, Kofi M'bele or Killum666, and whether those are their actual names or not. To your psyche they remain empty and unreal, which makes it difficult to enter into a structured conversation with them and to treat them with the same care and respect as you would actual people.

Although most people nevertheless do behave themselves when using social media and primarily just go about their interests within their own circle of friends and acquaintances, the problem of psychological emptiness is real. And it is greatly exacerbated by the presence of a troublesome minority, an unsavoury cocktail of one part intentionally disruptive trolls and hecklers spreading misinformation, negativity and fear, one part fanatical zealots, one part habitually disgruntled individuals and one part ordinary people who can't handle disagreement, misunderstanding or being corrected. This is something we probably just have to learn to live with: stupid, stubborn and malicious people will not go away, nor will fanatics. However, the awkward fit between the architecture of social media and the way people go about communicating with each other contributes at least as much to our lack of control over what we do in social media, and here, at least, some improvement might be possible. To see this, we must take a closer look at what actually happens when people communicate by means of language.

@#$%!

ONE OF THE MOST POWERFUL characteristics of human language is its ability to fully function through a single channel, unlike animal communication systems. Once we have learned to speak a language, to read and write or to use sign language, we don't need to see someone to converse with them, hear the writer's voice when reading, or consult subtitles when we see someone signing, nor do we need to touch or smell them. This enables us to use the telephone and radio, and to read and write, each of them ways of conversing with people at a distance, either geographically or in time. By phone and letter or email we can talk to colleagues, friends and relatives who are thousands of miles away, and in writing Egyptian pharaohs and Sumerian kings speak to us directly across thousands of years. But this immense advantage comes at a price: loss of context.

The most natural way for people to communicate is through face-to-face conversation, in either a spoken language or sign language, where what they say is coloured, amended and adorned by body language such as supportive gestures, facial expressions, nods, winks and grunts, and whatever other clues the setting provides. Listeners always simultaneously respond in kind. Even the simplest conversation involves an incessant to-and-fro of such secondary information between participants. As a result, it is fairly easy for all involved to keep the conversation on track and appreciate what people mean, how they feel about themselves, their interlocutors and the topic of conversation, and how serious and sincere they are about any of those. And when in doubt or confused, you can simply ask for clarification, raise an objection or express your agreement or displeasure with the way things are going. In all other settings, some of this wealth of linguistic and non-linguistic clues and ploys is lost.

On first consideration, television and film seem closest to a normal conversation, but in fact they are not. They allow viewers to keep all the visual and auditory context, but rob them of even the slightest chance of influencing the way things are going. There is no feedback; television and film are not interactive. Television viewers and cinema-goers are reduced to passivity even more strongly than the audience in a theatre, who can at least applaud, boo and whistle, and throw rotten eggs, tomatoes or their knickers at the performers. In fact, it is the telephone that comes closest to a normal conversation. It dispenses with all visual clues, but fully retains the much more important interactive character of a conversation. The hearer compensates for the lack of visual secondary information with expressions such as 'yes', 'hm-hm', 'huh?' and 'you don't say!', and simply asks for clarification if something is insufficiently clear: 'what do you mean?', 'are you serious?', 'didn't you find that odd?' and so on. Radio, useful as it is, robs listeners both of all visual information and of their active involvement in the conversation. But poorest of all is reading and writing. Not only does it deny us everything the radio takes away, it also does away with all the auditory information. Gone is the melody of sentences. Gone is the stress that marks something as important, and gone are the tone of voice and its volume, the pauses, hesitations and false starts, and that hardly audible but ever so meaningful chuckle or sigh. All that remains is a rough and schematic representation of the speech sounds the writer would have used had they been speaking instead.

Nonetheless, the extreme poverty of written language has its merits. It makes writing a very effective and efficient means of structuring, storing and retaining neutral, factual information. This is why people who think hard about some problem always resort to taking notes, and why schools and science necessarily rely on books, papers and notepads. By the same token writing is pretty hopeless when it comes to communicating emotions. In fact, the better part of literary fiction is an ongoing struggle by authors of both prose and poetry to find ways to do just that. Writers of all kinds make up for the austerity of their medium by choosing their words carefully and honing their sentences much more meticulously than people do when they speak. Whether they are creating a book, compiling a report or writing an article, memo, blog, postcard or email, writers need to take their time; theirs is a slow and painstaking business.

At the same time, the exceptionally low speed of the writing process – on average people produce fewer than ten words per minute on paper – is one of the things that make writing well so difficult. Our short-term memory is not equipped to retain the exact linguistic details of a phrase or sentence for more than the second or two it would take to utter or process them in a direct conversation. As a consequence, writers inevitably lose track of the sentence under construction, forcing them to check back and recapitulate time and time again. The texts resulting from these cumbersome labours are read at speeds thirty to fifty times higher, or more. That is one reason why written language always feels more formal and less spontaneous than spoken conversation.

In a direct conversation, speakers and listeners process language at the same speed. One might think that the limiting factor here is the speed at which the many muscles of the tongue, mouth and throat can be marshalled into the right positions to produce the next speech sound, but that would be a mistake. More often than not, people who speak extraordinarily fast are told to slow down, because their interlocutors can't follow. Auctioneers at work are among the fastest talkers, some producing as many as four hundred words per minute in English, but they aren't much fun to listen to and can function at those speeds only because of the strictly regulated, highly formulaic character of the performance. Their listeners hardly listen in the normal sense of the word; they just wait attentively for certain familiar cues. This suggests that as speech gets faster, the brain soon begins to have trouble processing, interpreting and storing the incoming speech signals in time. On the other hand, with training, so-called speed talkers can produce speech flawlessly at even higher speeds than the fastest auctioneers – some rappers specialize in it. But if they do, what they produce differs greatly from normal, spontaneous speech. They typically recite set phrases, things such as well-known nursery rhymes or thoroughly rehearsed lyrics. Unlike ordinary sentences such chunks of language are not constructed on the spur of the moment, but off-the-shelf ready-mades drawn from memory.

One reason for this is that if they did try to rattle off normal, unpredictable sentences at such speeds, nobody would be able to follow or even to decide whether what they heard was actually real language. Another reason might well be that our brains are simply incapable of coming up with sufficient new stuff to say at such tremendous rates. Even the most agile mind needs some time to pre-pare a thought and turn it into enough of a precise linguistic structure that it can be converted into instructions to the lungs, the vocal cords and all the rest of the speech apparatus.

The highest processing speeds are found in reading. On aver-age proficient readers process something like 250 to 300 words per minute in a language such as English, but depending on factors such as the familiarity and complexity of the subject, the style of the writer, the purpose for which one reads a text, its presentation on the page or screen and time pressure, people can attain much, much higher speeds. One of the things that enable people to read faster than they can listen is the permanence of written text. If a reader realizes he has missed a point or can't recall something that went before, he can check back immediately. Listeners cannot do that, since all they retain and store in memory is a general, integrated interpretation of what they are told. The words themselves seldom make it past the cramped space of short-term memory. To appreciate how cramped that is, consider that in dictation even phrases of five or six words must be repeated and repeated again to make sure that everybody gets the right words in the right order. Yet nobody has any trouble remembering what the dictated text meant.

This difference has important effects. Speaking is always a work in progress. People don't first cast a complete, fully fledged thought into a complete sentence 'with everything on it', and then start speak-ing. Instead, they cast off immediately, tentatively hacking their way through ideas and shaping their thoughts and choosing their words as they speak. More often than not, they reshuffle and amend their own thoughts or change plans halfway through a sentence, causing it to derail or be cut short and replaced by a new one. Some of the time they do so spontaneously, and sometimes because of linguistic and non-linguistic feedback from their interlocutor. Also, speaking is such a complex and challenging task that people routinely make all kinds of mistakes in getting their message out, such as mixing up words and sounds, stumbling over their own tongues or accidentally retrieving the wrong term from memory. As a result, it is perfectly normal for a guest in an entertainment programme to say to the host things like:

Yeah, yeah, that's a good point, good question, I actu . . . you know, when I came up here, just now, driving up here on the M43, you know . . . with the heat and the sleeter on and my effing feet freezing off . . . ooh, the horror of it, and I was thinking, eh, now don't laugh, I'm being SERIOUS here! ha-ha, well, like I said, I was asking myself if you'd – IF I got here, you know, IF I got here at all – if you'd let me, eh – ah, no, I was afraid that . . . thought you wouldn't. So no, let's talk about something else.

Written out it looks chaotic, but it is actually quite natural and there is method to the madness. This is the way our minds work – the way language and conversation work. In fact, we are so used to such seemingly haphazard input that we immediately notice when someone is delivering a speech from paper and so avoiding many of these so-called performance errors. Moreover, highly trained and talented speakers excepted, we tend to find their presentation stiff, unnatural and most likely boring.

Just as speakers immediately jump in at the deep end, listeners don't wait passively for what people have to say to them. They start guessing right away where speakers might be going, thinking along with them and filling in as best they can what is still to come. That is why and how listeners, if speakers hesitate or seem likely to be making a point the listener already knows or agrees with, are quite good at (and inclined to) finish the occasional sentence for them. The bottom line is that in direct conversation both speakers and listeners just wing it, and there's no going back. This is very different from reading and writing. People would never accept the sort of chaotic jumble they produce in direct conversation on paper. Performance errors, from derailing sentences to unnecessary repetition and spelling mistakes, are seriously frowned upon, not least because they hamper the reading process. Writers must prepare their messages meticulously, even simple ones, for alongside hindering the reading process, mistakes are considered proof of stupidity or a lack of education as well as insufficient application and consideration for the reader. For these reasons writers are not in a position to wing it. Readers can, and do, go back to re-read and find fault.

Next to speed and interactivity, permanence is the third main factor differentiating between modes of linguistic communication. As we have seen, writing or recording language liberates information

The main factors determining the traditional modes of human communication by means of language			
mode	approximate speed range/words per minute*	interactive	permanent
direct conversation telephone		yes	no
theatre	100–300	marginally	
television, film, video radio, sound recording			
reading	up to 600		
writing	< 10	no	yes

* These are rough estimates. What matters is the scale of the differences.

from the fetters of the here and now. Messages, conversations and complete scenes can be stored for any length of time, and then, cultural changes aside, retrieved as fresh as when they were taken down. By means of reading and writing in particular, utterances acquire an existence of their own, independent of any speaker. This independent existence gives extra importance and weight to anything 'in black and white', as we all know from experience. Unlike remembered speech, which relies on fallible and quirky memory, written text is guaranteed not to change spontaneously over time. Since it is not very easily tampered with either, writing has acquired an aura of truth and even objectivity. Written text is generally accepted as proof as well – nothing beats having it in black and white. A contract in black and white is proof of a deal and of the reality of the obligations mentioned in it, and a signature in black and white is proof of a person's commitment to it. The signature is the single truly magical element in writing. Signatures are binding spells, mainly differing from their classical predecessors in that they bind the signer. As with most magic, it is the ritual act that is decisive, not its contents. Hence

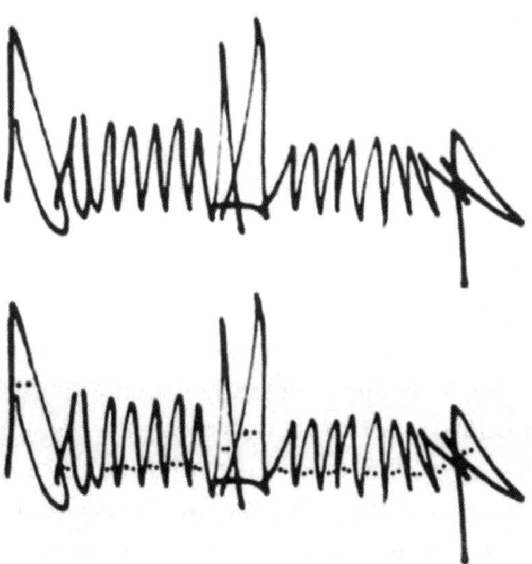

Quality Twitter humour does exist: 'Trump's signature looks like a Klan rally', unattributed, 2018.

a signature need not be readable, and illiterate people can 'sign' with a simple cross.

@#$%!

BY NOW, IT SHOULD BE somewhat clearer why we are so bad at keeping control of ourselves and those we converse with on social media. The natural order of things is that if communication is interactive it is not permanent, and the converse. Media such as Twitter and Facebook upend that natural order.

Social media are designed to look and feel as casual and interactive as possible. What platforms such as Facebook and Twitter aim to evoke is the easy-going, informal atmosphere of being home, of barbecuing in the garden with a few good friends and of backslapping with the guys or girls at the pub. They are designed to resemble the kind of intimate gathering where people let down their guard and share whatever they feel like. Where as soon as things are said, they're gone and a gaffe is washed away with a laugh, or at worst a good-humoured slap on the wrist. Where you can safely share confidences, float ideas and explore paths you wouldn't dream of letting the world at large know about just like that. The platforms have been extremely successful at creating this illusion. Many contributions have a private and personal feel: things about kids' birthdays, the dog or cat that has died, personal health trouble or the vicissitudes of caring for a sick or elderly relative. A surprisingly large proportion reads like diary entries, things that are not usually meant to be made public. Apparently people really do look upon their social-media accounts as if they are as intimate and sheltered as their private diaries, their own homes or their own local version of *Cheers*, 'where everybody knows your name'.

Next to the suggestion of casual intimacy and general goodwill, the platform designers have built in competitive elements to boost the turnover of contributions and reactions to contributions. Twitter pokes up urgency by constantly updating on-screen how many 'new' Tweets there are that you haven't read yet, and sending reminders of replies to your own tweets by email. Facebook tickles your curiosity through pop-ups warning you of any actions of your Facebook friends that might concern you, even their birthdays. The more businesslike LinkedIn actively warns its clients about their connections' new jobs and job anniversaries, and any vacancies that might interest them: come and check in with us now, don't miss out. In addition, Facebook has a real-time warning sign that tells you when someone is typing a response to one of your own posts or replies. Just like the Roman Catholic Church, they all exploit human fallibility. The Church of Rome uses the idea of everyday sinning to evoke feelings of guilt designed to drive the flock to the confessional, from which they emerge both relieved and a little more indebted to the Church that granted them its pardon once again. Likewise, the social platforms foster a constant feeling of failure. They make you feel unable to keep up, imbue you with a constant fear of lagging behind and missing out on something important.

The urgency of social media is, of course, mainly an illusion. The greater part by far of what people share there is of no interest to anyone. It's typical small talk, banal and mildly amusing at best, ill-informed, stupid and malicious at worst. Only Twitter has earned itself a real reputation as a uniquely fast conduit for spreading breaking news of calamities, real or fake. The feel of casual intimacy is illusory as well, as many have by now learned the hard way. There is nothing safe, confidential or exclusive about a social-media account. Literally anyone might pick up on what you put there and do with it as they please, whether right away or days, months or even years later. For, alone among interactive modes of communication, social media are written and read. They are permanent.

Normally, written communication consists of meticulously composed and, ideally, fully grammatical sentences. As we saw before, in

The scourge that is WhatsApp

Whether by design or not, the developers of WhatsApp have taken the exploitation of the fear of exclusion and feelings of failure to a new, hitherto unknown level. WhatsApp groups are members-only, so unlike those of Twitter and Facebook members are safe from prying eyes and unwanted commenters butting in. On the other hand, group members take it for granted that their fellow members are always immediately aware of their contributions, requests and eruptions, which puts enormous pressure on all members to keep in constant touch, day and night, seven days a week. Countless people now sleep with their smartphone active and within arm's reach. As a result WhatsApp has turned into a uniquely powerful social-control machine with flabbergasting potential for influencing and manipulating people. It affords employers, teachers, service providers and interest groups a unique measure of control over their employees, clients and members, the psychological and possibly political and moral effects of which we haven't yet begun to understand. From the point of view of the manipulator, the beauty of it is that no coercion or explicit pressure is required. People willingly subject themselves to the whip of WhatsApp.

writing errors are forbidden altogether. Among fully literate people, spotting spelling errors and grammatical or lexical mistakes in writing is one of the most popular sports of all time – it is the communicative parallel of the banana-peel joke. Such inordinate sensitivity to small imperfections shows how writing things up works like a lens, enlarging everything, making it coarser by showing the grain. Because of this, people generally prefer more formal and circumspect wording when writing. If a good friend does something stupid or misinterprets something fairly obvious in your presence, it is perfectly all right to vent an affectionate 'idiot', but answering a letter or email in which they told you about their slip-up, you would never start off with 'darling idiot' – unless perhaps you were attempting a particularly steamy love letter.

Just like errors, informality and hyperbole work very differently in black and white. So does irony. Irony is a subtle way of making known what you really think by apparently innocently stating quite the opposite. Think of yourself, fourteen years old, not making it to school on time and making up excuses for the principal about how your alarm clock has let you down and your bicycle had a flat tyre and you had to wait for ages at the railway crossing and how horrible

<table>
<tr><td>Bill Weir   ✔ @BillWeirCNN</td></tr>
<tr><td>Follow</td></tr>
<tr><td>Weather is not climate, you willfully ignorant fucksticks. MT @foxnation: Climate Doesn't Cooperate With Al Gore http://bit.ly/1qMaMKg</td></tr>
<tr><td>4:25 AM - 31 Jul 2014</td></tr>
</table>

When in July 2014 the Fox Nation website ridiculed Al Gore's Climate Reality Project for doling out ice cream on what turned out to be a cold and rainy Denver day, CNN anchor Bill Weir sent this tweet, using wording he would never use on air or on paper. He later apologized for his use of the vulgar 'fucksticks' (pricks, idiots).

it had all been, and her just faintly smiling: 'I'm sure it was.' That's irony, and without all these killing explanations, it just won't work in black and white, unless you are a particularly accomplished writer. Something similar holds for jokes. Written down and read, most jokes are just boring, boorish or misunderstood as insults. Written humour does exist, of course, but by and large it is a completely different genre with its own rules. Orally conveyed jokes usually rely on the element of surprise, the slow and artful build-up of suspense followed by a punchline that turns everything topsy-turvy. This strategy does not work if people can read at their own speed and check back at will, which is why written collections of such jokes make dull reading: the build-up of suspense is missing, and thereby the release afforded by the punchline.

To some extent, users of social media are aware of the problematic character of the combination of interactivity and the effects of permanence in black and white, hence the success of emojis. Such symbols are a crude but fairly effective means of compensating for the lack of context characteristic of writing and reading, especially the part conveyed by body language and voice quality in direct conversation. Sadly, the popularity of the handful of early and effective emojis such as :-) for happiness or agreement, ;-) for an ironic wink and :-(for disappointment, sadness or anger has led to the development of a host of new pictograms whose meanings are either too specific to be of much use, or unclear, or both, thus defeating the purpose.

@#$%!

SO HERE'S THE RUB: users of social media are duped into thinking they are taking part in a real conversation, whereas in reality they are writing the unedited minutes of that imagined conversation. Minutes are not fun to read, or even instructive; usually they are material used to check up on who said what and to quarrel over – which is exactly what happens. The pressure for fast repartee, also typical of spoken conversation, exacerbates the problem, causing people to write and reply too quickly and sloppily, producing awkwardly formulated, overstated and inconsiderate texts. These are negative effects that even email suffers from.

At the same time, what is written on social media and elsewhere on the web, which is inextricably linked to them in every sense of the word, is regarded with the same gravitas as anything in black and white, causing people – even highly educated ones – to attribute weight and trustworthiness to anything they find there. The damaging effects of this mistake go far beyond increasing the inflammatory impact of ill-considered remarks and failed attempts at humour and irony. It also helps to propagate and perpetuate misunderstandings and misinterpretations, urban myths and outright disinformation. To give an example, nowadays an unsettling number of young parents refuse to have their children vaccinated against crippling or life-threatening diseases such as measles, whooping cough and polio, not to mention COVID-19, because they think the vaccinations themselves endanger their children's health. Why do they think that? 'I read it on Facebook' and 'It says so on the Internet' are frequent answers. In short: it's in black and white, therefore it's reliable and true.

But wait! Isn't all the information that is actually reliable and well researched and as true as true can ever be also in black and white, either on the Internet or on paper? Why doesn't that enormous, constantly growing pile of true-blue tried-and-tested knowledge and information cancel out the effects of social-media mythology, misinterpretation and wilfully misleading propaganda? The answer lies in the illusion of intimacy that social-media platforms create. This illusion engenders a kind of club spirit, first and foremost among those who read little beyond social media, but even among better-educated and informed people, who are certainly not immune to it. In some sense, the information found on or through social media feels like 'our' information, put there by people who belong to the club and are therefore nice, well-intentioned and believable friends. They are certainly nicer and more empathic than the dyed-in-the-wool, aloof and arrogant professionals of the traditional media, politics and science, and therefore to be preferred and trusted above them. This is not a completely new phenomenon, nor is it limited to social media per se. For as long as they have existed, some of the traditional press media have actively and successfully created and exploited a club spirit among their subscribers, and tried to rally them behind causes of the medium's choosing. Activist papers such as *The Sun* and the *Daily Mail* in the UK, *Bild Zeitung* in Germany and *De Telegraaf* in the Netherlands are examples, as are the *New York Post* and the Fox television network in the United States. The difference is that these media make orchestrated efforts to bind and manipulate their readers and viewers in a particular direction in accordance with their own agenda, whereas the club feeling on social media derives from the general design of the platforms, but is not directed by them. On social media, the issues and directional pull are generated by the users themselves.

In turn, the club spirit among users of social media generates a measure of group solidarity, which has proven to contribute relatively little to the wider dissemination and better explanation and clarification of existing knowledge, or better understanding and appreciation of the world and its problems. Instead, it tends to unite social-media users *against* the world outside, its institutions and its wisdom, a tendency that is easily and eagerly exploited by self-appointed gurus, health freaks, paranoiacs, zealots, conspiracy theorists and political malfeasants. If populism is the frame of mind of those who feel ignored, despised and disenfranchised by the powers that be, then social media are their *samizdat*. It is their informal underground information circuit that unites them against the social, intellectual and political elites who would keep them in their place and in the dark about the true state of things. That is why many prefer to believe dubious Internet-based sources on topics ranging from nutrition, vaccination and climate change to conspiracies to take over the world by 'Bilderberg', George Soros or the European Commission, over what has become known as MSM, the mainstream media.

That's not all, for there is yet another way in which social media don't square with human intuition and expectations, and probably never will. In ordinary life, there is a huge difference between what we say about other people in their absence and what we say to them directly. Girls may tell each other that the captain of the school rugby team is a super-sexy, absolutely adorable hunk for hours, but they will never say those words to his face. Children caring for an ailing parent have lots of conversations about their charge that they wouldn't dream of sharing with him or her. At the office someone's body odour can be hotly debated among their colleagues, but it may take forever for someone to work up the courage to confront the stinker. Even then, our courageous bringer of bad tidings is likely to handle his target with kid gloves, using wording quite unlike the giggly or irritated banter that has taken place behind his colleague's back. Similarly, people greatly enjoy satirizing and imitating other people behind their backs, but doing so in their presence is generally considered painful or downright offensive. Speaking *about* someone and speaking *to* them are strictly separate domains.

The only exceptions are weddings, jubilees and the essentially awkward phenomenon of the roast. There, as part of the festivities, the protagonists are traditionally allowed to witness a carefully scripted version of what their nearest and dearest think and say about them between themselves, in the form of jocular speeches, sketches and singalongs. Even then the outcome is not always a happy one. Words about people are confrontational, and weigh on them, especially emotional and judgemental words. So much so, in fact, that the shocking scene in which someone opens and reads a letter, email, text or WhatsApp message that wasn't meant for them to read but turns out to be about them has become a staple of film, theatre and literature.

Under almost any circumstances the boundaries between communicating about someone and with someone are clear and carefully maintained. Social media, however, tear the veil between the two. The illusion of intimacy causes people to feel free to say things about other people without taking account of the fact that that *Feind hört mit*, 'the enemy is listening in', as the Nazis said. People can actually read and – still worse – re-read what others say about them or about things they value dearly. Small wonder that they tend to fly off the handle and give others a taste of their own medicine.

@#$%!

THIS IS, IN SHORT, the rather disappointing state of affairs: the incongruous combination of permanence and interactivity characteristic of social media allows endless and inordinately deep scrutiny of – thanks to the illusion of urgency – hastily jotted down, sloppily formulated, overly informal and rough remarks. In combination with the psychological emptiness of most of one's day-to-day interlocutors, and the lack of separation between the domains of talking to and talking about, it all results in a volatile, vindictive, fault-finding atmosphere and a penchant for polarization and disharmony. At the same time, compounding the issue, all those quarrelsome users are subject to the illusion of intimacy and group membership that pulls them together and creates the semblance of reliability of group members and sympathizers, and, conversely, that of malevolent deception on the part of disagreeing outsiders. Permanency is a fundamental flaw of social media, but it could be redressed at least partly by letting posts and replies automatically decay and disappear after a while, more or less as those on Snapchat do. For their records, users might be given the opportunity of storing their own contributions and those replies to them and other contributions that they consider worthwhile keeping, in a private place, but not out in the open for everyone to see, copy and comment on. This might help to make social media more like the light-hearted conversational environment they appear to be. However, no amount of redesign is going to eradicate the illusion of intimacy; that's just human nature. Nor can the problem of psychological emptiness be overcome – it is the price we pay for the possibility of contact with billions of people all over the world. Lastly, for understandable economic reasons no platform owner will be prepared to mitigate the sense of urgency that social media maintain in users, the fear of missing out. In large part, we can't do better than to educate people, both children and adults, to be aware of these conditions and learn to live with them.

@#$%!

ALTHOUGH THE DISHARMONY and misinformation with which social media are rife have turned off many people of good will, there is one type of user who could not have been better served by things as they stand. This is the user who is not at all interested in interaction, nor in listening to what others have to say. This self-centred, uniquely self-interested species is the Blowhorn, and it is often a politician.

To politicians, it is important to reach as large an audience as possible as directly as possible. This is equally true in democracies and more authoritarian societies. Direct contact with voters or subjects offers the best chances of manipulating them into accepting, believing and supporting your plans and points of view. In old-fashioned authoritarian societies, this was achieved by the state monopolizing access to the printing press and other media, the way countries such as Russia and China do today. In democracies, party rallies excepted, politicians have the forces of journalism to contend with. There, extremist politicians, regardless of their particular kind of extremism, are invariably confronted with a press the majority of which is sceptical about their ideas, limiting their chances of getting their message across to the general public undiluted. Even with sympathetic traditional media, politicians in a democracy seldom get a chance to expound their views unopposed. They will be interviewed by a trained, ideally knowledgeable and competent journalist posing critical questions, or invited to defend their position in a debate with direct competitors. In democracies, radio and, later, television have immensely increased the possibilities for politicians to reach the people directly and tap into their emotions, but there too they hardly ever get the chance to do so unchaperoned. The best they can hope for is to have an opinion or essay of their own published – but even that ultimately depends on the say-so of some editor at a newspaper or magazine. This is as it should be, of course. Politicians sell dreams, sometimes dangerous dreams, so they must be forced on every occasion to explain their ideas, the consequences of those ideas and how they propose to cope with them.

To politicians bent on disseminating their views without interference from sceptical journalists or opposing competitors, social media have proven a godsend. This is especially true of those who aim to realize their goals by sowing dissent and polarization rather than achieving consensus, people who consider the threat of angry mobs on the streets a legitimate political tool. Thanks to social media, they can tell their following and all others exactly what they want, and bypass all those annoying journalists. One controversial politician who realized the political potential of social media, notably Twitter, right from the start and was quick to exploit it was the Dutch member of parliament Geert Wilders, an invariably 'outraged' or 'livid' populist. Inexplicably, the traditional media were caught completely off-guard. They reacted not by ignoring Wilders's incendiary tweets and forcing him to be professionally interviewed to explain in detail what he thought. Instead, they repeated each of his ramblings on their pages as if God himself had spoken, accompanied by many columns of anxious, speculative exegesis. By doing so, they put themselves in the position of involuntary propagandists for his cause. Sadly, more than a decade later nothing has changed, and more and more politicians have discovered this way of not only bypassing, but actually using the press for their benefit.

The greatest example of a Blowhorn undercutting the position of professional journalism, science and scholarship by means of social media was the busily tweeting 45th president of the United States, Donald Trump. What's more, from the day of his inauguration he waged an ever-escalating war on what he calls the 'fake media' or 'fake news', meaning everyone and everything who disagrees with his views, questions his motives or does not serve his interests. Behaving like the archetypal user of social media, he even conducted diplomacy of a threatening sort from the safety of his bedroom or office, ignoring and alienating his own staff and State Department. Thanks to the illusion of intimacy and the black-and-white effect, his rants are still gospel truth to his extensive following, regardless of their

Two authoritarian political hecklers of the 21st century flex their muscles. Trump hurls threats at Iran — mark the use of capitals, the social media equivalent of yelling. His Iranian counterpart Rouhani answered, 'Americans should know that peace with Iran is the mother of all peace, and war with Iran is the mother of all wars.' This is not diplomacy. It is not even a conversation: it is an ordinary slanging match, with both participants banging their chests to impress their own following.

ill-mannered impoliteness, inconsistency or blatant falsehood. So far, most of his targets have reacted either as unpreparedly as the Dutch press did to Wilders, or just as social-media users are wont to do: with anger and counter-threats. This way, Trump, with the aid of the most advanced media ever conceived, has plunged the world back into the days when kings and schoolboys conducted diplomacy as if it were a family row, a shouting match for the benefit of their own crowd, just like that between Thaw and Coulter.

7

INFUXATION AND OTHER MIRACLES OF LANGUAGE

Νή τον κυνα!

In the public eye, swearing, cursing and other transgressions of the boundaries of verbal propriety belong largely to the frayed edges of society, the shabby and smelly slums and shanty towns that decent people shun. Although this is largely a fantasy – swearing, slights and slanging seem to be equally at home in every class and niche in society, at least in anger and behind closed doors – it is true that much of it technically belongs to the neglected fringes of grammar. Its finest flowers grow closest to the edge, where language boffins have long feared to tread. So let's do some exploring.

First of all, there is the question whether swearing occurs in all languages and cultures and has always done so. In other words, is swearing behaviour universal? The traditional answer is a tentative no, for three reasons. First, it seems that the classical Romans and Greeks swore a lot less than modern Westerners do. Not that they were squeamish; quite the contrary. But even in their raunchiest, bawdiest comedies there is very little of the cursing and swearing an author such as Shakespeare larded his plays with. If there is an oath at all, it is, so to speak, a bloody bland one. *Qõrkēto ma ton Apolō*, 'and he fucked, by Apollo!', is among the almost 3,000-year-old graffiti found on the Greek island of Thera. We hear about Socrates swearing *ny ton kuna*, 'by the dog', and Pythagoras using *ma tyn tetrakton*, 'by the tetraktys', the perfect triangle of triangles that played a central role in his philosophy. According to Diogenes Laërtius, the philosopher Zeno was in the habit of swearing 'by the caper', and the Ionian Greeks, roughly those living on the west coast of Asia Minor, were famous for their *ma tin krambin*, 'by the cabbage'. That's about it.

The second reason is that linguists and anthropologists who went charting hitherto undescribed languages in the nineteenth and twentieth centuries often failed to find much swearing among the tribes and peoples whose languages they tried to get to grips with. It has thus been stated that North American Indians don't swear. Yet many among them do so as much as the next person when they speak English or Spanish. It may of course be true that some of these indigenous cultures are indeed far less prone to the kinds of cursing and swearing Western European cultures are home to. However, there are many factors that may conspire to give a false impression.

For a start, linguists, anthropologists and missionaries – the kind of people who are most likely to go out and discover everything about exotic cultures and their languages – have their own taboos and inhibitions to contend with. Those don't make it easy for them to ask people how they verbally clobber each other or what shameful, despicable things they blurt out in anger or when hurt, frustrated or in ecstasy. Chances are, then, that most of them never broached the subject at all – even ordinary European grammarians and most lexicographers didn't. And if they did, they probably knew better than to persist at the first signs of unease, for they depended on the cooperation of the natives.

In turn, the people those missionaries and researchers visited and questioned suffered from similar qualms. One inhibiting factor is the widespread taboo on contradicting respected people or just saying no to them. Quite apart from this, it is decidedly awkward for anyone to be asked to share with strangers those aspects of their language and culture that they have been taught are improper, even in the best circumstances. It's as if when you were shopping for a pair of shoes, the shop assistant suddenly came out with: 'Please, talk dirty to me!' Even if you understood and appreciated the reasons for asking, that would not make it any easier to comply and start unloading everything you were taught not to say. The very essence of a taboo is that it must not be discussed.

While it is true that the European and American missionaries and researchers depended for their success, their livelihood and sometimes their survival on the cooperation of the natives they visited, those people (excepting only those who were averse to all contact with the world outside) had a keen interest in keeping their guests around and happy for as long as they could. Some saw them as a

Hurling abuse at people seems to have always been with us. Here, Egyptian fishermen settle their differences in the tomb of Ti at Saqqara, c. 2300 BC – the hieroglyph just right of the buttocks of the second man from the right is pretty self-explanatory, having been translated as 'Come here, you fucker!'

source of amazement and mirth, others as a fount of desirable gifts, such as cloth and clothes, colourful trinkets, mosquito nets, alcohol, high-quality tools, guns and outboard motors. Naturally, then, they would amuse and amaze their guests as best they could. This included second-guessing what the visitors hoped and expected to hear. Sometimes this led to whole 'ancient and traditional' dances, customs and rituals being invented just to please the guests. Doubtless, the same happened when people were questioned about aspects of their language, including the less savoury ones. Sometimes, also, outsiders may simply have failed to recognize what swearing and cursing there was, because the way the people they were investigating did it was just too unlike what they were used to in their own languages.

The third reason is the existence of societies like Japan. The Japanese claim never to swear, curse or rant, not even in anger or frustration. As every prisoner of war who ever suffered the attentions of the Japanese army or its dreaded military police, the Kempeitai, during the age of imperial expansion from 1894 to 1945 quickly learned, that is blatantly false, even though to this day most Japanese honestly believe it to be true. The point is that Japan is a nation so obsessed with social hierarchy, decorum and good form that among the Japanese improper behaviour itself, whether verbal or not, has become a grave taboo. This is different from Western cultures, where the verbal taboos lie with the objects or ideas swear words denote, usually belonging to the spheres of sexuality, physical or mental defects, excrement and religion. In the West, swearing is something that other, lesser people do, while restraint is a sign of social distinction. For this distinction to work, one must minimally acknowledge the existence of swearing. But in Japan, it is not only swear words that are taboo, but the phenomenon itself. This taboo is so deeply engrained in Japanese society that, when asked, even young, internationally orientated Japanese will first flatly deny the existence of swearing in their language. Only under pressure may they admit somewhat bashfully that swearing, slanging and name-calling actually do exist, and even come up with a few examples.

As with all socio-cultural taboos, the picture that arises is one of much uncertainty and confusion, tainted by wishful thinking, bashfulness, misunderstanding and hypocrisy. Nevertheless, there does not seem to be a single culture or language in which swear words and curses are truly absent, by the dog! Also, if our account of cathartic swearing in Chapter Two isn't too far off the mark, swearing and cursing are partly based in biology, as an extension of our language faculty proper. So eventually, rather than the traditional tentative 'No', the answer to the question of whether swearing is universal should be a reasonably confident 'Yes'.

@#$%!

WHAT MAKES A GOOD swear word or slur? Not every term with a negative meaning or negative connotations is necessarily a slur. To attain this lofty standing, a term must be intended and used to actually hurt, disparage or ridicule someone. Figuratively used and hyperbolic slights clearly fit the bill, as do literal slurs such as *four-eyes*, *fatso*, *carrot-head* or *schnoz* (the last for someone sporting a formidable proboscis). However, many other negatively charged terms are just that: factual descriptions of less desirable characteristics or phenomena. You wouldn't generally include *trigger-happy* among the skills section housed in your curriculum vitae, but not because it's a slur. Normally, calling someone trigger-happy is just a neutral description of an undesirable trait. One could try to use it as a slur, for instance with respect to an over-zealous, obstinate debater who always interrupts, but then one would have to add a reasonable explanation proving the relevance, the truth if you will, of the attribution. Real slurs and slights need never be explained, nor do they need to be either true or relevant.

It is surprising how few generally used slurs there are. The English language alone has more than a thousand synonyms each for *prick* and *cunt*, many with suitably rude or otherwise negative overtones. Yet hardly a handful of them are ever levelled at someone in anger or out of disdain. As a slur, *dick* is just about the only regular alternative for *prick*, and *twat* for *cunt*. For no apparent reason, it is decidedly odd to call someone a *quim*, *fig*, *slit*, *flange* or, heaven forbid, *vagina*. The same holds true for *dong*, *schlong*, *cock*, *pole*, *Pilate*, *thingy*, *third leg* and all the other more or less exotic nicknames for the male member. It would seem that other languages are no different, although choices vary.

In a language such as English, the standard repertoire can be enlarged by using one of its members as a base for something more articulate. Thus *dick* gave rise to *dickhead* and *dickwipe*, *prick* inspired *prickhead*, 'baldy'. *Cock*, itself not a usual slur, spawned *cockrash* for a supporter of the wrong soccer team and *cockwomble* for a contemptible, socially inept person. (Wombles being fictional creatures inhabiting Wimbledon Common in London; they were invented in the 1960s by the children's book author Elisabeth Beresford.) However, this is nothing compared to what the Dutch do with their staple slur, *lul*, meaning 'prick' in every sense of the English word: *lulhannes*, 'prick Hannes' (a first name associated with clumsiness), *droplul*, 'liquorice prick', *lamlul*, 'lame prick', *bloedlul*, 'blood prick', *kankerlul*, 'cancer prick', *boerenlul*, 'peasant's prick', *hondenlul*, 'dog's prick', *bokkenlul*, 'goat's prick', *paardenlul*, 'horse's prick', *ouwe lul* 'old prick', *lul met vingers*, 'prick with fingers' and the mysterious *lul de behanger*, 'prick the wallpaperer', all mean roughly the same and are all somewhat ruder and more serious than the unadorned base term. And then there is *lulletje rozenwater*, 'little prick rosewater', also known among those feigning a classical education as *penis aqua rosa*, for Johnny Too Good or someone lacking spunk or prowess.

Next to the more-or-less standard repertoire, ad hoc slurs and slights are made up on the spur of the moment, especially when tempers are bad and emotions run high – and are forgotten again. But, as the American folklorist Gershon Legman noted in regard to *motherfucker*, there is also 'a whole lesser spectrum of obviously burlesque and mocking synonyms, such as *granny-jazzer*, *mammy-jammer*, *momma-hopper* and *poppa-lopper*'. These are not euphemisms. Instead, 'they are used to raise a laugh, not to start a fight.' They are, in a sense, pastiches, satirical puns, and, as Legman goes on:

> the insulting intention in almost all these can be changed or reversed into a rough and grudging compliment by a subtle change in the tone of voice or inflection – the tune – in which they are delivered. *Lucky bastard* and *smart son-of-a-bitch*, or *bad-ass motherfucker* are nowadays terms of sincere admiration. Even *bitch* can become a compliment if said in the right way.[1]

That said, a straight slur always aims to belittle, which is reflected in the choice of term. Slurs are simplifications; they reduce someone to a single characteristic that is disapproved of. In principle, anything goes. One can berate someone for their lack of experience and call them a *greenhorn*, a *snotnose* or a *runt*, the weakest, smallest piglet in a litter. Many an adolescent with unfortunate skin blemishes has had to endure being called *zit*, *zit-face* or *blackhead*. If you look sickly, Iranians may call you a *shamshīr az kūn-i-sag dar āmadih*, 'a sword pulled out of a dog's arse'. A German might express utter contempt for a spineless prig by calling them a *Hohlkreuzpinsel*, a *Pinsel* being literally a brush but figuratively a prig, while the term *Hohlkreuz* refers to a hunched spine. However, there are certain favourite themes that occur in one language after another across the world.

One of these cultural stereotypes is, strange as it may seem, likening someone to a plant or fruit, which need not always be really negative. For instance, German, Dutch and English have *Mauerblümchen*, *muurbloempje* and *wallflower*, respectively, which carry a hint of sympathy, as does the Dutch term *oud besje*, 'little old berry', for a frail old woman. Calling someone in a deep coma a *vegetable* or *cabbage*, however, is a sign of disrespect or badly contained despair, and the American *hayseed* is as derogatory as its alternative *hick*. A bad product, of course, is a *lemon* in English, and the proverbial third wheel on the wagon is a *gooseberry* in Britain. The Germans also have *Pflaume*, 'prune', for a fool, *Pissnelke*, 'dandelion', for a boring, prudish girl and *Erdapfel* for a crude, boorish man. In Zambia, someone who won't listen to good advice is a *chumbu mushololwa*, a sweet potato that breaks when it is bent. Unintelligent Chinese are made out to be *shǎ guā*, 'stupid melon', which is reminiscent of the Dutch *achterlijke gladiool*, 'retarded gladiolus'. If Danes don't like you, they'll characterize you as a *røvbanan*, 'arse banana'. In English, *fruitcake* refers to someone who is completely insane or, like *fruit(er)* and *daisy*, to a homosexual. Italians make different choices, calling a homosexual *finocchio*, 'fennel', and using *fava*, 'bean', for someone very stupid and *carciofo*, 'artichoke', for those who are a bit less stupid but certainly too naive for their own good.

Another widespread cultural stereotype concerns the reproductive and excretory organs. *Cunt*, *prick*, *twat* and *asshole* are staples of English verbal abuse, as are the French *con*, *connard* and *conasse*, all basically meaning 'cunt' but used as 'cretin' or 'bastard'. French *casse couille*, 'ball breaker', occurs in Spanish as *hinchabolas*, 'one who swells another's balls'. Speakers of that language call a little pest *pelotudito* or, if she happens to be a girl, *pelotudita*, 'little one with balls', and will honour a sharp dresser with the moniker *culo empolvado*, 'powdered arse'. Italians yell *cazzo*, 'prick', at men and *cagna*, 'bitch', at women, but also *coglione*, 'testicle', at either: *cogliona!* Just as the Spanish do with *pelotudito/a*.

The Dutch use terms such as *lul*, 'prick', *eikel*, 'glans', and *zak* or *klootzak*, 'scrotum', for men, but against and about women they prefer *trut*, which is supposed to have originated as an onomatopoeic word for the bubbling of porridge, indicating the female organ, over the straight *kut*, 'cunt'. Exclusively applicable to women behaving stupidly, and mostly used *by* women as well, are *muts*, 'woollen cap', and *doos*, 'box'. The former probably refers to pubic hair, the latter to what's behind it.

In Swiss German, a *Fötzel*, 'little cunt', is a scoundrel, layabout or otherwise undesirable person, whereas a *Fidla* or *Fütli*, 'buttocks', is a narrow-minded woman, whose male counterpart, the narrow-minded bourgeois, is a *Fidla Bürger*, while an interfering busybody of either sex is a *Gäksnase*, 'shit-nose'. The Russians have their standard *huj* and *eldá*, 'prick', plus *pizdá*, 'cunt', as well as slights such as *huj sobačij*, 'dog's prick', and *mudák*, 'fool', from *mudó*, 'prick'. They even have a masculine cunt, *pizdún*, meaning 'weakling'. Russians also show a real fascination with their *žópa*, 'arse(hole)'; witness compounds such as *hitrožopyj*, 'smart-arse', *žópnik*, 'arser', for a sodomite, *žópoliz*, 'arse licker', as the equivalent of brown-noser, and the famous *černožopyj*, 'black-arse', for the inhabitants of the Caucasus, Chechnya in particular.

As with excretory organs, so with certain excreta and effluvia, the despicable output of the body. Shit is the most popular by far, and has been for a very long time. Some 1,500 years ago the *Lex Salica*, a body of law of the Germanic tribes, called for a fine of four gold pieces for calling someone a *cacatus*, 'shit-fellow', one more than for cutting off their finger. And remember the tenth-century phrase book containing *Vndes ars in tine naso – Canis culum in tuo naso*, 'a dog's arse up your nose'. And although the great seventeenth-century poet and playwright Ben Jonson opposed swearing, in his comedy *Bartholomew Fair* (1614) he had the character Waspe exclaim: 'Turd in your teeth!' and 'Shite o' your head!'

In present-day English one can be called a *shit*, a *shithead*, a *shit-for-brains* or, if an American hick, a *shitkicker*, while someone who spoils the fun is a *party pooper*. Russians have their *govnjuk*, 'shitter', by which they mean a bastard. In Swiss German *Fitzer* or *Pfitzer* literally means 'diarrhoea', but is also used for a sly guy or a dandy. They also call a cute child a *Gagel* or *Kakel*, meaning 'turd'. The Yoruba in and around southwestern Nigeria may disparage people as *agbégbẹ́*, 'shit carrier', referring to a member of an underclass whose job it is to clean latrines. *Stronzo*, 'shit, turd', is perhaps the most widely used slur among Italians, and an exasperated Georgian will on occasion yell *mjǧnero*, 'you shit(head)!' Dutch classroom bullies may call their victims *poepzak* and *strontzak*, 'shit-bag', or make them out to be *bangeschijters*, 'scared shitters'. Adults will call a sorry excuse for a man a *flapdrol*, 'flap-turd', the provenance of which is a total mystery. Perhaps *flap* is onomatopoeic; imagine the sound of a cow dropping a warm and squishy cowpat. A Dutchman *heeft schijt aan*, 'has shit on', anything he doesn't give a damn about, but does not use excrement just to vent his displeasure, as the Germans do with their ubiquitous *Scheisse!* Here, the Dutch prefer *kut!*, 'cunt', or some variety of good old *godverdomme*, 'Goddammit'. In this respect, the Germans are closer to the Latin world, where we find the real past masters at throwing shit around. What would French be without its *merde*, 'shit', which as an exclamation or attribute has, like *putain*, 'whore', and *putain de merde*, become as devoid of meaning as *fuck* and *fucking* in English? Could Catalan survive without its frame *mecàgum* something (*de Déu*)? Its literal meaning is 'I shit on something (by God),' but it functions like the English *fucking*. *Mecàgum la porta de Déu!* just means 'that fucking door!' Similar things exist in Spanish, worst of which is the *cago en la leche de tu madre*, 'I shit in your mother's milk,' mentioned before.

Except for the occasional *piss-willy*, meaning 'coward', urine and other effluvia such as blood, sweat, tears and semen are not used in standard slurs in modern English, although compounds and phrases with urine do exist. *Having the piss-willies* is an alternative for having the shivers, for obvious reasons, and rain may come *pissing down*. Also, you can be *pissed off* because your friend is *pissed* and wants another drink, which she can't afford since she's *piss poor*. If so, you may tell her to *piss off* before you start *taking the piss out of her*. Most of these belong to what the *Oxford English Dictionary* calls 'vulgar slang', but they are not slurs. The Dutch do have a set of pissy slurs, including *zeiker(t)*, 'pisser', *zeikvent*, 'piss-fellow', and its feminine counterpart *zeikwijf*, 'piss cow', *zeikstraal*, 'spurt of piss', *zeiksnor*, 'piss moustache', for someone who nags a lot or is a coward, and *azijnpisser*, 'vinegar-pisser', for a dour, humourless critic. All these are based on the frequently used vulgar verb *zeiken*, which literally means 'to piss', but has also come to mean 'to nag, to moan'. The Latin world believes that aggression has its seat in the testes, hence expressions such as the Spanish *estar de muy mala leche*, 'have very bad milk (that is, semen)', which means that someone is in a foul mood. The rare but extremely rude Dutch *smegmakop*, 'smegma head', seems to be in a class of its own.

Possibly the most popular cultural stereotype is reduction to an animal. An unreliable colleague, elbowing his way up, is likely to be considered a *rat*, a woman who is either too aloof or too easy a *bitch*, and someone who is physically or hierarchically unimpressive may be branded a *shrimp*. There are scores of these in almost any language one cares to look at. According to some scholars, even the modern word *dupe* developed out of an Old French animal slur, *d'huppe*, 'of the hoopoe', the poor bird being considered filthy and exceptionally foolish.

It is tempting to interpret this as the ultimate means of disparaging a person, as the renowned French cultural anthropologist Claude Lévi-Strauss did. Although we live in a world of endless shades and nuances, he argued, we view that world and think about it in terms of clear binary oppositions: good versus bad, light versus dark, straight versus crooked and, most importantly, culture versus nature and 'us' versus 'them'. According to Lévi-Strauss, characterizing undesirable people as beasts removes them from the 'us' of our species and its culture to the animal domain of nature. It is a form of both degradation and excommunication, not unlike the way the American slaveholders, ethically cornered by the French *Déclaration des droits de l'homme*, denied slaves their humanity and therefore their human rights. As we saw in Chapter Four, however, animals and their typical properties are equally frequent, if not more so, among the terms of endearment people use for their loved ones. In more than a few cases, the same animal is used both as a disparaging epithet and as an intimate token of deep affection. For Lévi-Strauss's proposal this is a problem, since making the object of one's affection think they are no longer part of the fold would be the last thing anyone would want. It follows that, whatever the explanation for the popularity of animal names in both functions, Lévi-Strauss's idea doesn't hold water. The point might rather be that animals simply are the nearest thing to us in nature, sufficiently close and familiar for us to form a reasonably clear (if possibly flawed) idea of what they are and what moves them, and sufficiently remote to make stereotyping both easy and unproblematic.

Interestingly, Lévi-Strauss's hypothesis might actually be true of ethnic and racial slurs. Unlike animal names, these do not seem to fit spheres of cuddly intimacy. No Brit will lovingly call his spouse *frog* or *Turk* or *little kraut of mine* unless she actually is French, Turkish or German, and even then it would be a strange thing to do. Perhaps *chink* might be used between a couple one-half of whom is actually Asian, but doing so would definitely be considered kinky and fit for very intimate environments only. So perhaps there is something inherently negative, a measure of 'themness', to ethnic and racial distinctions that does not apply to animals. If so, that inescapable negativity might well be the excommunicating character of ethnic and racial slurs. After all, no Russian will denigrate another Russian by calling him a Russian. You cannot very well blame someone for being part of 'us', can you? Rather they would call him something foreign: a black-arse, an Ethiopian (idiot), a Dutch prick, an Arab (thief) or a Jew (generally unsavoury) – anything except Russian. Naming someone a member of your own group, like a Russian calling someone 'a true Russian', is always a compliment, even if the group

A selection of animal names used as slurs across the world. Literal and abusive meanings are provided if not self-evident and if different from that in English.

Arabic *ḥawayaan* 'animal'; *ḥumaar* 'ass'; *ibn ilkalb* 'son of a dog'; *kalb(a)* 'dog/bitch'; **Dutch** *aap* 'monkey'; *beardmonkey* 'baardaap' someone with a (large) beard; *gorilla* 'gorilla', bulky, dangerous-looking man, security guard; (*boerenkar*) *hengst* '(farm cart) stallion', unsophisticated, inattentive ruffian; *hondsvot* 'dog's arse', despicable person; *kattenkop* 'cat's head', feisty, hot-tempered girl; *kloothommel* 'testicle bumblebee', irritating person; *koe* 'cow', big, ungainly or stupid woman; *paard* 'horse', large and ungainly or ugly woman; (*riool*) *rat* '(sewer) rat'; *rund* 'bovine', oaf; *schijtlijster* 'shit-thrush', spineless coward; *serpent* 'serpent', malicious, scheming woman; *uilskuiken* 'owl's chick', stupid bungler; *zwijn* 'swine'; **English** *adder*; *ass*; (*son-of-a-*)*bitch*; *coon* black person (American, from raccoon); *coot* elderly person; *cow*; *cur*; *dog*; *gadfly* 'horse fly', troublemaker, stirrer; (*old*) *goat*; *jackass* lecher; *leech*; *old bat* silly old woman; *pig*; *puppy*; *rat*; *serpent*; *shitehawk* 'scavenging or predatory bird', useless bungler, pauper; *shrimp* diminutive person; *swine*; **Farsi** *aghrab zir ghālih* 'scorpion under the rug', untrustworthy person; *bū ghalamūn* 'turkey', ideologically unreliable person; *fil* 'elephant', fatty; *gāv* 'cow', oaf, ill-mannered person; *khirsi* 'bear', slob; *sag* 'dog', feisty ruffian; *shutur* 'camel', big klutz; *tūlih sag* 'puppy', member of the lower class; **French** *baleine* 'whale', fat woman; *baudet* 'donkey', ignoramus; *bête* 'beast', a. uncivilized oaf, b. someone exceptionally talented at something; *chienne, chienasse* 'bitch', loose woman; *cochon(ne)* 'pig', unwashed, ill-mannered or sexually depraved person; *halouf* 'pork' (from Arabic), someone despicable; *magot* 'macaque', unpleasant, gruff man; *marsouin* 'porpoise', colonial soldier, marine; *mollusque* 'mollusc', weakling; *morue* 'cod', whore, slut; *moule à merde* 'shit mussel', idiot; *nez de boeuf* 'ox's nose', halfwit; *peau de vache* 'cow's skin', ill-natured person; *porc, porcas* 'pork', uncouth, ill-mannered man, lecher; *poulet* 'hen', a. policeman, b. Pharisee, hypocrit; *putois* 'polecat', wrongdoer; *rat* 'rat', despicable person; *tête de linotte* 'finch head', loafer, good-for-nothing; *thon* 'tuna', slut; *truie, truiasse* 'sow', unkempt woman; **German**: *Affe* 'monkey'; *Bibelhengst* 'Bible stallion', bigot, zealot; *Esel* 'ass'; *Hund* 'dog'; *Kröte* 'toad', pricktease; *Muckl* 'young bull', uncouth, bull-headed man, hick; *Neidhammel* 'jealous wether (castrated ram)', jealous oaf; *Rindvieh* 'bovine', stupid, irritating person; *Sau* 'sow', unkempt or malicious person; *Sauhund* 'pig-dog', lecher; *Ungeziefer*, 'vermin'; *Wildsau* 'wild pig', someone filthy, pervert; **Italian** *cagnaccia* 'bitch'; *cavallona* 'big horse', streetwalker; *papagallo* 'parrot', young man whistling after girls; *porcella* 'piglet', swine; *porcellino* 'piglet', mucky pup, slob; *rospo* 'toad', ugly person; *scrofa* 'pig'; *vacca* 'cow'; **Mandarin** *cí lǎo hǔ* 'old tigress', domineering shrew; *guī* 'turtle', slut; *guī gōng* 'male turtle', pimp; *sè láng* 'horny wolf', lecher or womanizer; *tū lú* 'bald donkey', dishevelled man, monk; *zhōu gǒu* 'obedient dog', collaborator; **Menominee** *anêm* 'dog'; *kko:hko:s* 'pig'; *mêhkê:nah* 'big turtle', someone talking dirty or roughly; *namê:pen* 'carp', a. sucker, b. Norwegian or Irishman; **Portuguese** *macaco* 'monkey', black person; **Spanish** *alimaña* 'vermin', scoundrel; *cabrón* 'big goat', asshole; *chancho, cochino* 'pig', poor, weak or sickly person; *gallina* 'hen', coward; *ganso* 'goose', thickhead, silly bugger; *gusamo* 'worm', despicable person; *lechuza* 'owl', gossiping old woman; *marica* 'magpie', homosexual; *moscón* 'big fly', creep, pest; *pájaro* 'bird', homosexual (Cuba); *percebe* 'barnacle', idiot; *puerco* 'pig', fat person; *rata* 'rat', miser; *urraca* 'magpie', hoarder; *víbora/viborón* 'viper', treacherous person, malicious gossip; *zorra* 'vixen', slut, whore; **Swiss German** *Chretli* 'toad', pricktease; *Huen* 'hen', stupid woman; *Mugge* (from German *Muckl*) 'young bull', slutty girl; **Turkish** *ayı* 'bear', insensitive ruffian; *domuz* 'pig'; *eşek* 'donkey'; *hayvan* 'animal'; *it-köpek* 'dog'; *katır* 'mule'; *keçi* 'goat', a. passive homosexual, b. stupid woman; *maymun* 'monkey', ugly person; *öküz* 'ox', stubborn person; **Yoruba** *ajá* 'dog', whore, slut; *ẹran* 'dull kind of animal like sheep, donkey', oaf, thickhead; *ọbọ* 'monkey', simpleton.

and its name are disparaged themselves by others. That's why certain African Americans will freely call each other 'nigger' but fly off the handle if anyone else does so.

There are, however, two exceptions. When the Swedes talk of a *norsk norrman från Norge*, a 'Norwegian Norman from Norway', they mean a stereotypical, overly serious and taciturn country Viking. Half in jest, more enlightened urban Norwegians use the same expression, which in Norwegian is *Norsk normand frå Norge*, to distance themselves somewhat from their more rustic and conservative brethren.

The other exception regards the Dutch, who are famous for their paradoxically self-deprecatory attitude. They like to think of themselves as 'just a small country', which may be true geographically, but they maintain the nineteenth-largest economy in the world, have been among the richest and happiest countries for ages, and maintain a huge cultural and intellectual heritage. In addition, they cultivate a peculiar kind of social and intellectual egalitarianism and usually keep away from nationalist and patriotic brouhaha. So when they call a compatriot *een echte Hollander*, 'a true Dutchman', it's usually not a compliment. Instead, they mean that the target shows the traditional stereotypical shortcomings of the Dutch: stinginess, stubbornness, provincialism and a lack of *savoir faire*. In fact, in such cases the speaker distances himself from the vast majority of his own people, sides with the world outside and advertises himself as above all that.

@#$%!

IT MAY SEEM ODD that the Italians and Spanish use the names of such exclusively male attributes as testicles to revile women and girls, and even give those slurs grammatically feminine forms, as in *cogliona*, 'female testicle', and *pelotudita*, 'heavily hung girl'. What it illustrates, however, is a very general process called desemanticization. Over time words that acquire a second figurative meaning, such as those that are pressed into service as slurs or swear words, tend to separate themselves from their literal and original semantic values, or lose their original meaning altogether. New generations never think twice; they just take the words and expressions they come across at face value. As a consequence, the whole idea of a testicle is immaterial to the use of either *coglione!* or *cogliona!* Their true meaning is now something like 'tosser' and 'bitch', respectively. Similarly, if you call someone a *prick*, you don't really think of the actual male member. You just mean something like 'obnoxious, stupid, despicable man'.

If you care to look, the original literal meanings are still clear to see in these cases, but often such origins have become hard or impossible to determine. Whence, to give a famous example, came 'damn' in *I don't give a damn*? Stories abound, the most attractive among them being that the phrase was coined by the Duke of Wellington, who actually had a *damm* in mind, an Indian farthing. But when push comes to shove, nobody really knows whether this or any of the alternative explanations fits the bill.

Desemanticization can become something of a problem when words and phrases leak into other languages, as the linguist Victor Friedman has shown for Macedonian.[2] In Macedonia, which has a long history of Turkish occupation, *sikter* means 'scram'. No contemporary Macedonian realizes that this is actually Turkish *siktir*, 'get fucked'. Macedonian children innocently chant *sikánani sikím* the way English children chant *eeni-meeni-mini-mo*. Neither they nor their parents have the slightest idea that it goes back to Turkish *sik* *ananı, sikeyim*, 'fuck your mother, let me fuck (her too).' Similarly, the old Slavic root **kurb* for 'chicken' lives on in Russian as *kuritsa*, 'hen'. However, for reasons unknown, it turned into *kur*, 'prick', in the Balkans. Such developments can lead to quite embarrassing situations when visiting Russians try to talk about hens in their best Czech, Bulgarian or Serbian.

In British English the opposite of this kind of desemanticization occurs: an innocuous term that becomes offensive in the language into which it leaked. *Bint* is a relatively new, highly derogatory term for a woman of Arab descent. British youths borrowed it from the Arabic they heard immigrants speak, where it simply means *girl*, picking up the misogynist connotations of the concept of women in Arab culture.

@#$%!

A MAJOR SOURCE of slights and slurs is a process with the ungainly name *pejoration*, 'worsening'. We'll call it downgrading here. Among the most important forces responsible for changes in the meanings and connotations of words over time are changes in society and technology. *Peasant*, for example, started out in Middle English as a neutral term derived from French *paysan*, 'land man', for an ordinary country-dweller. Most of these were simple farmers, not landowners, but people tilling soil that was considered the property of some nobleman, to whom they were often bound in some way. By and by a class of free farmers working their own land took shape and 'peasant' came to mean 'small, poor farmer'. At the same time the country was steadily losing cultural prestige to the evermore dominant towns, which saddled 'peasant' with unpleasant urban-born connotations of backwardness and lack of sophistication, until it had acquired its present figurative meaning of, as the OED puts it, 'ignorant, rude, or unsophisticated person'. 'Peasant' had been downgraded to a slur.

Although changes in meaning may in time affect any word, changes in appreciation, as happened with 'peasant', are possible only with terms that allow of a value judgement. By and large, this means terms relating in some way to people and their place and function in society, or to concepts that can become or cease to be taboo. *Shit*, for instance, functioned as a normal, neutral descriptive term until the eighteenth century, when it dropped out of favour for reasons unknown.

Otherwise, semantic changes generally don't trigger a change in acceptability, let alone one for the worse. Until the 1960s, *computer* denoted a person employed to do calculations with pen and paper or a mechanical adding machine. Then, quite suddenly, its reference shifted to a new and wondrous kind of machine that might appear to be any of a thousand different things at any given time. Around 1945 the inventors had bestowed the name computer on the earliest of these machines, because they were built to do exactly the same work as the old human computers, only faster and more reliably. Before long, the whole concept of human computers had vanished into thin air. This was an extraordinarily complete switch of reference that reflected a changing reality but did not touch in any way on the appreciation of the term.

Often, downgrading occurs by accident. An example is the English word 'knave'. This started out in the Germanic languages of some 1,500 years ago as *cnapa* or *cnafa*, both meaning 'boy', 'youth' or 'servant', the use youths were usually put to. In English, it slowly developed into 'knave' and acquired the negative meaning 'dishonest, unscrupulous man' in the process. Nowadays it has fallen out of favour completely, and the OED labels it archaic. In German and Dutch, however, *cnapa* went on to become *Knabe* and *knaap*, respectively, without any negative overtones at all. Today, German *Knabe* still simply means 'boy' or 'youth', while the Dutch use *knaap* mainly in a formal, technical sense as meaning 'male virgin', or for something really big. A Great Dane is a *knaap* of a dog and a humungous mistake a *knaap van een fout*.

The converse of downgrading is upgrading. A remarkable case in the European world is the knight. In fact *knight*, which also occurs in Swedish, is an outlier among Western European languages. All the other Germanic languages – and even unrelated Irish – use a variant of the German *Ritter*, while all the Romance languages have some variant of the French *chevalier*. Both terms originally just meant 'one who rides (a horse)'. In early medieval armies, horsemen counted for something more than mere footmen. Also, the armies of the day were strictly bring-your-own, so being a horseman entailed being sufficiently well-off to own a horse, which was more than most could manage.

Nevertheless, as English and Swedish usage indicates, the horseman remained an Old English *cniht*, a servant to a noble master to whom he owed allegiance. However, in the course of time courtly culture developed and the knight, *Ritter* or *chevalier* rose from a mere crofter on a horse who on occasion answered the call to arms of his liege to a kind of courtier – or, for that matter, was replaced by sons of noblemen – and became a professional, evermore elaborately armoured mounted soldier. Eventually, all over Europe the *chivalry* ended up as a prestigious, esteemed class on the fringe of nobility. The terms *knight* and *chivalry* gained prestige accordingly.

In German and Dutch, *cniht* continued for centuries on a more modest career as *knecht*, a servant, footman, farmhand or workman, until in Dutch it suddenly fell prey to the anti-authoritarian, egalitarian revolution of the 1960s. This revolution hit exceptionally hard in the Netherlands and did away with much of the country's traditional social barriers as well as the terms that marked them. *Knecht* was among the first to be downgraded into unacceptability not only because it made it very clear who was boss and who was not, but also because as a verb it meant 'to subdue' and 'to press into service'. The verb *knechten* was and still is all but equivalent to 'enslave'. Before long, in the Dutch middle-class world terms such as *ondergeschikte*, 'subordinate', and *employé*, 'employee', gave way to *medewerker*, 'co-worker', while *baas*, 'boss', and *chef*, 'chief, supervisor', were replaced by *leidinggevende*, 'manager', 'coach'. In name at least, in a few years the Netherlands became a very egalitarian society.

Around the same time that hierarchical terminology was downgrading at breakneck speed in Dutch society, sexual taboo terms underwent considerable upgrading. This was partly because of the sexual revolution, which created a much-needed openness and gave many taboo terms new cachet as being progressive and even avant-garde. Nevertheless, there was quite a stir when on 21 January 1974 the esteemed journalist Joop van Tijn enunciated, with some effort, *het zogenaamde neuken*, 'the so-called fucking', for the first time on Dutch television in what was the first fully fledged (although also decidedly funny and irreverent) sex-ed programme. It was called *Open en bloot*, a title best rendered as 'the naked truth'. The programme fitted into and helped along the razing of taboos surrounding intercourse, masturbation, sexual hygiene, contraception, sexually transmitted diseases, abortion and, ultimately, sexual orientation, and rendered the terminology necessary to discuss these subjects more acceptable.

Since then, one of the most remarkable cases of upgrading in Dutch concerns *kut*, 'cunt', as an adverb, a prefix and an exclamation of startled surprise or frustration. Until the 1970s it was absolutely not done to pronounce *kut* in public at all. Nowadays, even young girls consider their homework *kut*, hate their *kutschool*, 'cunt school', and yell *kut!* in exasperation if they miss the bus or drop their smartphone. Mind you, *kut* is still at the bad end of the scale, below neutral, but it has moved up from being completely taboo to something parents feel only occasionally obliged to tut-tut about. The same holds for *kanker*, 'cancer', which is mainly used as a prefix of disparagement, as in *kankerzooi*, 'cancer shambles', and *kankerfiets*, 'cancer bike'. Among young men it is almost as ubiquitous as *kut* nowadays, but not half a century ago the affliction was so very taboo that even in serious discussions many preferred speaking of *K* and some doctors didn't dare tell their patients what was actually wrong with them.

It will forever remain unclear whether the trail-blazing *Open en bloot* actually helped to bring down taboos, or just confirmed and highlighted moral and societal changes that were happening anyway. What is clear, however, is that there are many who try to change society and improve social justice and public morale by actively depreciating certain terms. The most obvious example is no doubt the ever-changing terminology for the African American citizenry of the United States. Having been *niggers*, then *negroes*, then *blacks*, then *Afro-Americans*, then *African Americans*, black people have now been subsumed under the somewhat broader term 'people of colour'. Each new term was coined to get rid of a predecessor that had come to accentuate the group's position as underdog in society. There are many such trajectories, from the *skivvy* of a hundred years ago, who became a *maid*, a *cleaning lady* and then a *cleaning person*, to those who went from being called *idiots* via stages such as *mentally retarded* and *mentally handicapped* to *intellectually challenged* or even *differently talented*.

Unlike the downgrading of *knave* and its replacement by *boy*, *youth* or *servant*, such changes are not spontaneous. They are actively and intentionally championed by self-proclaimed minders who often are not themselves members of the group under consideration. These efforts are characteristic of the emancipatory waves that have been rolling over Western culture since the late eighteenth century, when French *sujets*, 'subjects', renounced their subservient status and proclaimed themselves *citoyens*, 'citizens', on a par with *citoyen Capet*, their king.

Such self-proclaimed minders are convinced that declaring a term downgraded and pushing for its replacement with a new one helps to remove the stigma that affects a disadvantaged group and improves or rectifies its social standing. They have certainly proved it possible to bury displeasing terms under a taboo and replace them with more satisfactory alternatives, especially when they have gained the support of officialdom and mass media. But that's as far as it goes. The discredited terms don't usually disappear; they merely go underground to live on in informal speech and in jokes. Still worse, the typically repetitive character of such corrections suggests that the underlying problem that motivated the wish to replace such terms in the first place stays right where it was.

The reason for this lack of real success is a deep misunderstanding of the way names function. When the revolutionary French decided they would henceforth be *citoyens* instead of subjects, they had already taken leave of the *ancien régime*. The new moniker merely confirmed what had already become reality, as names always do. A new name is a consequence of some change in the real world, never its cause. *Knave*, *skivvy* and *peasant* downgraded with changes in the positions of knaves, skivvies and peasants in the greater social scheme of things. Likewise, the meaning of *computer* changed with the advent of new technology, and *knight* gained prestige only as real-life knights did. Social-justice warriors, however, as minders call themselves these days, are under the spell of the magical Great Law of Similarity. They think that if one changes the name of some thing or group for a more prestigious one, that thing or group will acquire the prestige residing in the new name. Sadly, it won't. Instead, the new term will acquire all the negative connotations the old one had.

@#$%!

SWEAR WORDS AND SLURS are rather different creatures, even though some, such as *fuck,* can be used as both. Slurs and slights damage the person they are directed at. If they are used directly against a person, they have a general unsettling effect and may harm one's self-confidence: being greeted by 'Hi, you loathsome tub of lard' or a scathing 'Look what the cat dragged in' is not going to enhance anybody's self-esteem. Slurs and slights levelled against a person in their absence eat away at the target's reputation: 'That dirty rat Harry would sell his grandmother to get his hands on a pair of Tony Lama's boots.'

Swear words and imprecations may add to the unsettling effect of directly used slurs, as in 'Bloody hell! You loathsome tub of lard,' or 'Jesus fucking Christ! Look what the cat dragged in!', but they have no impact on a target when used in his or her absence. Their main effect is to divulge the state of mind of the swearer. People's imprecations reveal their own irritation and pain, surprise and disappointment with or plain old excitement about someone or something. In short, a slur is a comment on someone *by* a speaker, whereas swearing is a comment about the emotional state *of* the speaker. The difference is to some extent reflected in the physical form of swear words.

Arguably, grammar and structured thought are the most sophisticated, most abstract products of the human mind, but the sounds by which language is expressed are not. Speech sounds are where the arcane, abstract structures of grammar and thought connect with the wet and messy world of the body and its senses. Sounds are the result of formal instructions that cause muscles to flex, membranes to tighten and relax, and air to be pushed from the lungs and out through the mouth and nasal cavity. *Mutatis mutandis*, the same is true for the gestures of sign languages. They too are first and foremost physical, sensory things.

We usually think of the five senses – vision, hearing, smell, touch and taste – as separate, unrelated entities. They just feel that way to most of us. Also, any one of them can be damaged or lost without any of the others being affected. And yet, about one in twenty people experiences strong associations between certain senses. A particular taste may be red to them, or blue, and in some, colours trigger taste sensations. The phenomenon, called synaesthesia, actually extends beyond the realm of the senses proper, into language. People report associating colours and tastes with abstract mental concepts such as numbers, letters and the names of the months. *Three* may be pale yellow, and *January* bittersweet. Such couplings exist when people see a number or read the name of a month, but also when they hear them spoken, indicating that these associations involve sounds as well as visual shapes.

If speech sounds can be connected with sensory experience, then why not with aspects of word meaning as well? Following the assertions of the Swiss linguist Ferdinand de Saussure in the late nineteenth century, linguists have assumed for more than a hundred years that there is no link between the sounds that make up a word and its meaning. In other words, there is nothing 'tably' about the word *table*, which is why its phonetic form varies randomly across languages. Danes call the thing *bord*, Turks say *masa*, Fins *pöytä* and Greeks *trapezi*. In Scottish Gaelic a table is a *klàr*, in Hausa it is a *tebur* and in Chinese a *zhuōzi*. Arbitrariness rules even among very closely related languages: witness the English *butterfly*, which is *vlinder* in Dutch, *Schmetterling* in German, *skoenlapper* in Afrikaans, *fjärel* in Swedish, *sommerfugl* in Danish and Norwegian, *fiðrildi* in Icelandic, *farfalla* in Italian, *mariposa* in Spanish, *borboleta* in Portuguese, *fluture* in Romanian and *papillon* and *papallona* in French and Catalan, respectively. But Saussure's point was merely that there need not be a relationship between sound and meaning in a word. He did not claim that there could not be one, ever.

In fact, words whose phonetic shape is linked to their meaning are not that uncommon. Best known are onomatopoeia, words that represent animal and other sounds, of which Saussure was certainly aware. *Moo, arf-arf, meow, oink-oink* and *nyam-nyam* (the last imitating the contented grunts of people stuffing themselves with good food) are examples of the most primitive kind, but we also have *bleh* for disgust and the *wham, vroom* and *vrooaaarr* familiar from comic strips. They are conventionalized imitations, meaning that they obey the limitations of the stock of distinctive sound units a particular language uses, its phonemes. This makes them into semi-words, teetering on the threshold between true imitation and actual words of a language. They can be cited in sentences, but have no grammatical status of their own. Saying that 'the infuriated chihuahua went "arf-arf"' is OK, but 'the Alsatian arf-arfed too loudly' is not. The same goes for words such as *bam, ding-dong* and *dingaling*. Instead of *arf*, English has a fully fledged verb, *bark*, for the noise dogs make, itself a linguistically more sophisticated kind of onomatopoeia, on a par with *zip, buzz, beep* and *squish*. Birds such as the *cuckoo*, the *hoopoe*, the *crow* and the *chiffchaff* are named after the sounds they produce, and therefore onomatopoeic as well. There also exists at least one onomatopoeic dismissive remark. The Japanese expression *heiten garagaragara* means something like 'I've heard enough from you, sod off.' The onomatopoeic part is *garagaragara*, mimicking the sound of shutters being pulled down.

Comic book artists often use so-called grawlix, the visual parallel of onomatopoeia.

A fairly well-kept secret is the existence in many languages of so-called ideophones, words whose sounds say something about their meaning, without actually mimicking a sound. To get an idea of what ideophones are, ask yourself which of the two shapes below fits the name *kiki* best, and which is more *bouba*-like.

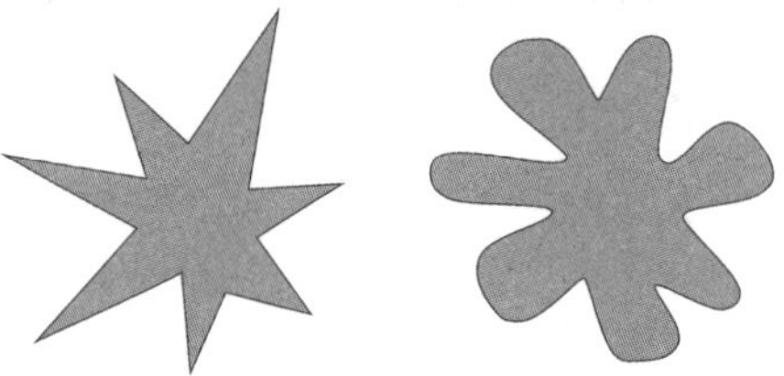

The odds are overwhelming that you have given the name *kiki* to the pointy star shape on the left and allotted *bouba* to the blob on the right. Virtually everybody does. Obviously, then, *i* and *k* sound sharper, pointier and more strident than a combination built of *b, ou* and *a*. Likewise, specific sounds and sound combinations in a word might suggest something about the way in which something is done, the way 'scamper' intuitively differs from 'run', or about the texture or hue of the thing that word denotes. If you ever indulged in assembling plastic models using Humbrol paints, you must have been struck by the evocative quality of the colour name 'olive drab', sounding exactly how it looked. Many languages, from Japanese, Basque and Turkish

Some classic ideophonic associations	
low tone high tone	large, slow, dull, dark, drab small, fast, sharp, light, nice
dark vowel (b*u*rn, g*o*ld, d*o*ll) light vowel (b*i*g, b*e*tter, n*ai*l)	heavy, thick, plump, bloated, dark light, thin, tall, fine, bright
voiced consonant (b, d, g, l, m, n, r, v, w, z) voiceless consonant (f, k, p, s, t)	heavy, soft light, hard

to African languages such as Ewe and Yoruba, are reported to possess thousands of such terms, sometimes in the form of special adverbs and adjectives that are put in only to add this kind of colouring to what's being said.

Ideophonic associations turn out to be quite strong as well as constant across languages. Recent research at the Max Planck Institute for Psycholinguistics in Nijmegen, the Netherlands, has established that people who haven't a clue about Japanese did surprisingly well at choosing the right meaning of Japanese ideophonic words. Thus, when asked whether *korokoro* was the Japanese equivalent of 'rolling' or 'floating in the air', more than three out of four of a group of some 4,000 subjects rightly chose the former. The same happened with choosing between 'dull' or 'sparkling' for *kirakira*, while virtually nobody ticked 'lanky' for *bukubuku* instead of the correct 'plump'.

Swear words and vulgar taboo terms, especially those employed in cathartic swearing, seem to be susceptible to ideophonic associations as well. A remarkable proportion of English cathartic swear words, for example, feature short, high vowels and consonants that involve interrupting the stream of air that comes from the lungs by pressing the lips together or the tongue against the palate, building up pressure. These include plosives such as *p*, *t* and *k* and hissing fricatives such as *f*, *s* and *sh*, and sounds that can be literally spat out in anger, as in *shit*, *fuck*, *damn*, *Christ* and the Cockney *cor*. The French have *con*, 'testicle', *putain*, 'whore', and *sacre dieu*, 'holy God', among their standard anger-vents, and the Germans use *Scheisse*, 'shit', and variants such as *Scheisskerl*, 'shitty guy'. The Italians blow off steam with *cazzo*, 'prick', and *vaffanculo*, 'go and do it in your arse', and the Dutch use *kut*, 'cunt', *klootzak*, 'scrotum', and *gótfurtomme*, 'goddamn', with a rasping, voiceless *g* that sounds as if you're trying to dislodge a herring bone from your throat. Clearly, in anger and in verbal abuse, aggressive terms such as *cunt* could never be replaced by more laid-back-sounding alternatives such as *vagina* or *yoni*.

Rhyming is another traditional instrument for creating slurs and slights – witness catchy Dutch slurs such as *slampamper*, 'drunk, good-for-nothing', and *urkedurker*, 'small person'. Both these nouns are so evocative that they hardly need an explanation. In fact, more often than not *urkedurker* is nowadays unthinkingly used for 'strange person, weirdo' in general, and virtually no speaker of Dutch is aware any more of the fact that *slampamper* is derived from the verb *slempen*, 'to drink excessively'. *Slampamper* has turned into a straight synonym of 'good-for-nothing'. America gave the world the *wisenheimer*, 'irritating know-it-all', and English has adjectives such as *namby-pamby*, 'weak, effete, sentimental'. This intriguing slur emerged in the eighteenth century as a ridiculing play by literary pundits such as Alexander Pope on the name of the sentimental poet Ambrose Philips, whom they despised heartily. This now standard slur was an eighteen-carat invented original, as is *fuddy-duddy*, 'old and pompous'. *Tinkiewink* and *tinkie-winkie* were borrowed from the BBC children's programme *Teletubbies* (1997–2001), and refer to an exceedingly small penis. Other rhyming slurs have been built on existing roots. *Harum-scarum*, 'reckless, impetuous', another eighteenth-century invention, is one. It's based on *hare* and *scare*, hares being notorious for their fast and unpredictable movements. *Roly-poly*, 'plump', a very weak slur these days, is another, created from *roll* in the early years of the seventeenth century.

@#$%!

A POPULAR WAY of creating slurs and slights is to use the diminutive. The purpose of diminutives is to render things smaller, less impressive, less serious and less formal. From there, it is but one step to conveying a lack of respect and a belittling attitude. Unless you are a toddler, being called *little man* or *little lady* is not a compliment. On the contrary, it's an insult. A slur.

In most European languages diminutives are formed by tacking one of a great many diminutive suffixes or 'endings' on to a word. German, for example, uses *-chen* a lot. A small *Bett*, 'bed', is *Bettchen* and a little *Mann*, 'man', *Männchen*. Italian and Spanish respectively use *-ino* and *-ito* a lot, or, for feminine words, *-ina* and *-ita*. So *signorina* is a young and unmarried *signora*, 'lady', and *chiquita* is actually not a banana but a little *chica*, 'girl'. Czech and all the other Slavic languages have lots of variants of *-ka*, as in Ivanka Trump, simply 'little Ivana', after her mother. Among today's Western European languages, Swedish and English are, to some extent, the odd ones out once more. Swedish alone prefers prefixes such as *mini-*, *lill-*, *små-* and *pytte-*, all meaning 'small'. English uses *mini-*, *little* and *small* as well, but only the first is used as a prefix, as in *minicab*. The others are straight adjectives.

Although English usually resorts to the adjectives *little* and *small* for its diminutives, it does have two diminutive suffixes as well. One is the rare *-let*, which occurs in the recent technical IT terms *servlet* and *applet*, and in *droplet*, *booklet*, *chicklet* (a small young chicken, not the chewing gum), *piglet*, *leaflet*, *platelet*, *eyelet*, *islet* and *starlet*. Only the last of these has the characteristics of a slur, patronizing at best, disparaging at worst. This may not seem like a lot, but in view of the relative scarcity of accepted slurs – I would estimate that there are fewer than five hundred among the more than 100,000 words of the English language – one in a dozen or so is an impressive score.

The other diminutive suffix in English is *-y* or *-ie*, and it looks as though it has been at least mildly denigrating for almost three centuries whenever it was applied to terms referring to people. *Darkie* has been a benevolently patronizing term for black people ever since the eighteenth century, and much later became a brand name for toothpaste. Nowadays *darkie* is taboo and *blacky* is acceptable only as a name for an animal – a literal reference to the colour of their pelt. *Preppy* also has an ominous ring, smelling of spoiled brats and snobbery. Back in the 1960s *hippies* were, in the eyes of the mainstream, people who foolishly took being *hip* and into the New Age a step too far. Quite a few of them ended up as *junkies*, the drug-addicted dregs of society. And finally, by the 1980s, a new class of Young Urban Professionals hatched and stormed London's City and New York's Wall Street as *yuppies* – half despised and half envied. And then there is the somewhat disparaging *Geordie*, a diminutive of George, which refers to the denizens of *Geordieland*, the northeast of England.

Some languages have specific suffixes that turn concepts into a negative, disparaging version of themselves. For instance, the Ojibwe, a group of North American Indian peoples based roughly around Lake Michigan, form insults by adding the suffix *-ish* to a common word. Thus *monias* means 'white man' but *moniasish* means 'damned white man'. The French discredit things by adding the suffix *-asse*. Thus a *bombasse* is a sex bomb, a *conasse* an extreme *con*, 'jerk', and *godasses* shoes you wouldn't want to be seen dead in, derived by first clipping the end of *godillot*, 'large, ungainly shoe', and then adding *-asse*. Someone *bonasse* is just too *bon*, 'good', or too naive for their own good. Even English has a pejorative suffix. It is *-o*, as in *wino*, *dumbo*, *weirdo*, *whacko* and *lingo*. Perhaps the suggestion of this suffix is why *bimbo* was borrowed from Italian, where it just means little boy, as referring to a sexy, slutty and not too bright girl. Perhaps, too, it is why *paedo*, *paedophile* clipped short, caught on with such almost perverse success.

Next to suffixes, most languages also have a stock of prefixes, elements that are attached to the beginning of words. In European languages, grammatical aspects of nouns, adjectives and verbs, such as number, grammatical gender and tense, happen to be mostly (but not exclusively) specified by means of suffixes. Thus, the English verb *tie* has the grammatical variants *tie-s*, *tie-d* and *tie-ing*, and the noun *view* has the plural form *view-s*, while *actor* and *priest* belong to the small group of English nouns that still have an explicitly feminine form: *actr-ess* and *priest-ess*. Prefixes are more likely to affect the meaning of a word. They negate or invert it, as *un-* in *untie* and *de-* in *dehydrate*; they intensify it, as *super-* in *supercharge* and *over-* in *over-state*; they tone it down as *semi-* in *semi-solid* or *under-* in *understate* and so on. Many such prefixes cannot occur as words in their own right, but need a real word to hang on to. Certain independent words, however, can also be pressed into service as prefixes, qualifying the meaning of the term on to which they are tacked. Although English and French do not, Dutch uses this strategy freely to create slurs and swear words. The adjective *rot*, 'rotten', is a case in point. It means putrid or decayed: *die rotte banaan* means 'that putrid banana', pure and simple. If *rot* is used as a prefix, however, it functions as the perfect equivalent of English *bloody* and *fucking*. *Die rotbanaan* means 'that bloody banana', and can be said of a perfectly healthy banana. Likewise, the Dutch have *klotebanaan*, 'testicles banana', *kolerebanaan*, 'cholera banana', *kutbanaan*, 'cunt banana', *pokke-banaan*, 'pox banana', *pestbanaan*, 'plague banana', *pleurisbanaan*, 'pleurisy banana', *tyfusbanaan*, 'typhoid fever banana', *teringbanaan*, 'consumption banana', and *kankerbanaan*, 'cancer banana', all meaning 'fucking banana' at different levels of emotional intensity. Cancer excepted, the illnesses used as prefixes are the same ones that are used to create frequently used curses, all meaning 'fuck you' or 'fuck him': *krijg de kolere*, 'go contract cholera', *hij kan de pokken krijgen*, '[as far as I'm concerned] he can contract pox', and so on. Telling someone *krijg de kanker*, 'go and get cancer', still seems to be out of bounds even to most Dutch people. Unlike the other illnesses, which have all virtually disappeared from modern Western life, cancer still seems to be too close to home and too real a threat to be used in a direct threat or curse.

Catalan has an intensifying prefix, *re-*, which is also put to good use in exasperated curses such as *ira de Déu, reïra de Déu!*, 'God's wrath, God's double-wrath' and *Déu, redéu i mecàgum Déu!*, 'God, double-God and I shit on God'.

Languages such as English and French keep to phrases constructed from independent words when it comes to swearing, as in French *cet banane de merde*, literally 'that banana of shit', which is the equivalent of the English 'that bloody banana'.

@#$%!

HOW SWEAR WORDS and slurs are constructed is one thing, how they function in sentences is another. First of all, there is nothing wrong with or peculiar about taboo terms and derogatory words as such. They are nouns, verbs, adjectives or adverbs like any other. From a grammatical point of view, sentences that contain them, such as 'I gave the blithering idiot a piece of my mind' or 'Those idiots even stole the bloody TV guide' are perfectly bland and utterly unremarkable. Yet there is something special about imprecations and slurs: with certain other kinds of comment they can inhabit a semi-grammatical sphere of their own.

Simply put, a sentence is a thought turned into language. It starts out with the mind picking out words and grammatical odds and ends, such as tense and number endings, from the mental lexicon and using them to construct a network of relations and dependencies that mirrors the thought as closely as possible. This network is the syntactic representation. Once it has been constructed, its parts are clustered and ordered according to the rules of a particular language, and translated into a series of phonemes, the abstract 'recipes' for the sounds that are relevant to that language, grouped into syllables. The result is a phonological representation, which is then fed to the muscles of mouth and throat, and out comes the sentence.

Of course, this is not a faithful representation of all the brain events that produce an utterance. It is only a very sketchy model of what happens. If we could see into the brain well enough to follow the actual production of language in detail, the process would probably look completely different. Messier and more chaotic, for one thing, and certainly much less linear, since we all know from experience that we do not first 'have' a complete thought and then turn it into a complete sentence, level by level, before we open our mouths. Instead, we begin speaking as soon as the first parts of what we wish to say are somehow sufficiently complete, and ready the rest 'on the fly'. Frequently, we speak faster than our thinking and our coding mechanisms can deliver the necessary goods, and we are forced to insert a pause, usually a procrastinating 'eh' or 'er'. Such pauses always occur between words, not inside them, and only in certain suitable places in a sentence.

Those same places can also accommodate slurs and imprecations. This shows that they are interjections: not fully integrated parts of the hierarchical grammatical structure of a sentence, but things that hover among its pronounceable chunks like fruit flies among plums in a fruit bowl. Here is how that semi-grammatical sphere of positions suitable for 'eh' can be filled in Edward Abbey's rendering of Hayduke's confession at the top of Chapter Two:

> 'Well, you silly bugger,' he said. 'Eh, I don't know, I guess . . . well, eh, if I can't swear I can't talk.'
>
> 'Well, God damn it,' he said. 'Eh, I don't know, I guess . . . well, eh, if I can't swear I can't talk.'
>
> 'Well, eh,' he said. 'You silly bugger, I don't know, I guess . . . well, eh, if I can't swear I can't talk.'
>
> 'Well, eh,' he said. 'God damn it, I don't know, I guess . . . well, eh, if I can't swear I can't talk.'
>
> 'Well, eh,' he said. 'Eh, I don't know, I guess . . . well, you silly bugger, if I can't swear I can't talk.'
>
> 'Well, eh,' he said. 'Eh, I don't know, I guess . . . well, God damn it, if I can't swear I can't talk.'

Interjections don't fit where there can't be an 'eh', such as between *he* and *said* in Abbey's example. You can put true adverbs there, such as *fucking* or even *bloody well*, which are just as much integral parts of the grammatical structure as *suddenly, quickly, hastily, hesitantly* and so on. But not things such as *you stupid moron* or *God damn it*, which can't be cast into adverbs.

Another indication that interjections are not really part of the grammatical structure of a sentence is that their position hardly makes a difference to the interpretation of the sentence as a whole. All the examples above mean basically the same thing; the interjection just adds 'and I think you are a silly bugger' (for asking, perhaps), or 'and I feel somewhat awkward about having to explain myself'. Compare this to the enormous difference in interpretation between 'he suddenly said he felt nauseous' and 'he said he suddenly felt nauseous'. Within the grammatical network proper, position matters a lot, even in languages with a much more dynamic word order than stodgy English. Where interjections are concerned, it generally doesn't.

Things are slightly different when slurs and imprecations occur at the very beginning or end of a sentence. As always, they can be either a comment on the situation described in the sentence they hover around or, as a slur, comment on an element inside it. Thus, in both '*You silly bugger*, did you really think you'd get that job?' and 'Did you really think you'd get that job, *you silly bugger*?', *you silly bugger* is a direct comment on the stupidity of the person indicated by 'you'. Similarly, in both '*Damn it, man*, did you really think you'd get that job?' and 'Did you really think you'd get that job? *Damn it, man*,' the interjection means that the speaker considers the whole idea of you getting the job preposterous, but it does not imply that you are to blame for not being aware of this. It might be that the speaker alone was privy to a ploy to give the position to someone else, for instance.

In these cases, however, there is a subtle difference with respect to the position of the interjection. In European languages at least, it would seem somewhat more natural for a comment on the whole situation to precede its sentence, which increases the chances for interjections at the end to be interpreted as a comment on one element of the sentence. 'Did you really think you'd get that job, *you silly bugger*?' sounds just a tad more natural than 'Did you really think you'd get that job? *Damn it, man.*' This could become a problem if the imprecation in question might be interpreted as a comment both on the sentence as a whole and on an element inside that sentence. And in January 2012 it did.

On Friday 13th of that month, the Italian sea captain Francesco Schettino wrecked his huge cruise ship *Costa Concordia* on the shores of the island of Giglio, off the Tuscan coast, and soon afterwards abandoned ship, leaving his crew of more than 1,000 and 3,206 passengers, 32 of whom would lose their lives, to fend for themselves. Learning of this, a shocked coastguard officer called Gregorio de Falco barked at Schettino over the radio: *Vada a bordo, cazzo! Cazzo* meaning *prick*, most of the press took this curt admonition to a fellow naval officer outranking him to mean 'Get back on board, you prick!' That would have been a flagrant breach of protocol. But *cazzo* also means 'damn it!', and *vada* is the formal, respectful imperative of the verb 'to go'. So what de Falco really said was 'Get back on board, sir, damn it!', where *damn it* is equivalent to 'what a shambles'. So he addressed Schettino correctly, adding some understandable cathartic swearing. However, the press and commerce preferred the more spectacular 'prick' interpretation. To this day the *Costa Concordia* disaster is avidly being exploited by the garment and fashion industries.

This obviously titillating ambiguity would never have arisen if de Falco had used any other standard Italian imprecation, such as the roughly equivalent *vaffanculo*, *porca miseria*, 'pig misery', the

Merchandizing the *Costa Concordia* tragedy.

relatively weak *dio diavolo*, 'God devil', or even the absurd *dio mot-tarello*, 'God ice cream', presumably a euphemism of *dio merda*, 'shit God', Mottarella being a mass-produced ice cream on a stick, covered in dark chocolate. Like the very rude *porco dio*, 'pig God', and *porca Madonna*, 'pig Madonna', these are never comments on a person or their qualities. This is also true of most standard imprecations in other languages, such as Spanish *joder!*, 'fuck', Dutch *kut!*, 'cunt', and (*god*) *verdomme!*, 'God damn me', or German *Scheisse!*, 'shit'. However, *cazzo* is not alone. Spanish *coño*, 'cunt', French *putain*, 'whore', and Russian *suka*, 'bitch', and *bljad*, 'whore', which in Soviet times also meant 'government operative', can give rise to similar ambiguities.

@#$%!

THIS LEAVES TWO extraordinary phenomena to be discussed. One is the Dutch *godverdomme*-phenomenon, the other the uniquely English mechanism of infuxation.

Godverdomme, pronounced with the *g*-sound of the Scottish *loch*, is pretty much the standard Dutch imprecation, comparable to English *damn (it)*, *bloody hell* or *fuck!* It is in fact a three-word phrase, *God verdo(e)me me*, 'God damn me', which has fused into a single word. In itself, this is not unusual. Over time, set phrases tend to lose both their literal meaning and their grammatical structure. They become so-called idiom chunks, immutable fossils. If, for instance, you replace *cat* with *dog* or *milkman* in the expression 'look what the cat dragged in', its special meaning is lost. All that's left is an ordinary sentence, to be taken at face value. Sometimes such phrases don't just fossilize, but actually melt into a single ready-made chunk: a word. The Italian swear word *vaffanculo* derives from the phrase *va fare in culo*, 'go and do (something) in (your) arse'. A slightly different example is what Ukrainians and Poles call the Russian curse and in Yiddish is called the Russian blessing: '*ēb tvojú mat*', which literally means 'I fucked your mother,' but serves as a general imprecation. Although the 'blessing' is always spelled as a phrase, it actually seems to have fused into a single unit that is sometimes cast as an adjective on a par with English *bloody* or *fucking*, as in '*Peredáj, ēb tvojú mat*', *sol!*', 'Pass the bloody salt.'

Godverdomme can be turned into not one, but two subtly differing adjectives: *godverdomde*, 'goddamned', and *godverdommese*, 'bloody, fucking'. Furthermore, the term is routinely clipped to either of two shortened forms, the exclamations *godver* and *verdomme*, from which two further adjectives, *godverse* and *verdomde*, are derived. The exclamation *godver* can be intensified not by a prefix like the *re-* that Catalan uses, but by repetition, assisted by an extra interposed connecting syllable, *de*. Thus you may hear a really angry or frustrated Dutchman yell – or mutter, with jaws clenched – *godverdegodverdegodverdegodver* . . . and so on, ad infinitum.

Quite apart from this, *godverdomme* is father to seven similar imprecations, also fused into single words. None of these is a euphemism. The first two have been created by just changing the *o*, the stressed, most prominent vowel in *godverdomme*, to *a* (as in 'heart') and *e* (as in 'men'), respectively. The resulting *gadverdamme* and *gedverdemme* are the only ones that are somewhat more acceptable than the original form, but that does not make them euphemisms. Rather, they have acquired a completely different meaning. Whereas *godverdomme* expresses anger or frustration, the other two express the somewhat more acceptable emotion disgust. You can say *gedverdemme* or *gadverdamme* when unwrapping a piece of greenish mouldy cheese or if you step in a dog turd, but also when confronted with a particularly low blow or a gruesome scene in a film.

The next pair of derivatives of *godverdomme* are *godvergeme*, 'God forgive me,' and *godsammesegene*, 'God shall bless me.' The latter can be clipped to *godsamme*, but neither is used as an adjective, at least not in standard Dutch. In all other respects they are perfect equivalents of *godverdomme*.

The remaining three derivatives have everything to do with French. Like *godverdomme*, the archetypal French imprecation is drawn from religion, but unlike the Dutch spell or curse, it is an invocation: *Nom de Dieu*, 'name of God'.

For centuries, Dutch and French have been neighbouring languages whose speakers did not see eye to eye most of the time. The front line in the resulting never-ending border conflict between the two languages now runs straight through the middle of Belgium, east to west and right across Brussels, the nexus of the European Union. Here the northern Flemish, speaking dialects of Dutch, and the Francophone Wallons in the south have been vying for dominance – linguistically, but also politically and economically – for hundreds of years, and still do. All the while they have – especially the Flemish – been making a point of keeping as far away from the other group's language as possible, but to no avail. The supposedly unadulteratedly Dutch alternatives the Flemish invented for terms that smacked of Latinate influence all boil down to transliterated French, and even Flemish curses are contaminated with French repertoire. As a result, both the Flemish and southerly Dutch use the Dutch *godverdomme* system and its variants, but by and large prefer *nondeju*, a bastardization of the French *nom de Dieu*. Even more curiously, the French system has leaked into the Dutch, giving rise to the popular mongrel form *godvernondeju* and, further north, the very curious *godverjume*, where the element *dom*, 'damn', in *godverdomme* has been replaced by *ju*, pronounced as a Scots person says 'you'. It is the *dieu*, 'God', part of French *nom de Dieu*.

@#$%!

THE ARCHETYPAL STANDARD IMPRECATIONS of modern English are *bloody* and *fuck(ing)*, accompanied by a host of euphemistic variants such as *ruddy*, *freaking*, *blooming* and *bleeding*. *Fuck* is unique among these on account of its unparalleled versatility. In the same way as *bloody* and all those euphemisms it can function as an intensifying attributive adjective, as in 'Pick up the *bloody*/*fucking* phone, Sarah!', and as an adverb, as in 'The XR6 is a *bloody*/*fucking* fast car.' But *fuck* alone occurs in the expression *fuck all*, meaning 'nothing', and only *fuck* can serve as a predicative adjective, as in 'This smartphone is *fucked*, ready for the bin', as a noun, as in 'Harry?! – where is that *fuck*? – Harryyyyyyyy???!!!' or 'It was cold as *fuck*,' and as a verb, in well-known expressions such as 'Stop *fucking* around,' 'Nobody *fucks* with Frank de Grave' and '*Fuck* you.'

As always, the adjectival and adverbial use of *fuck* has nothing to do with sex. Like *bloody*, it is just an expression of general stress and annoyance on the part of the speaker. The same is true of its use as a noun. Harry, the *fuck* in the example above, is simply not very popular with the speaker just now, and in 'I don't give a *fuck*,' 'fuck' is simply the equivalent of *damn*, *toss* or any other term for something worthless. However, when *fuck* functions as a verb, things are somewhat different. If you're *fucking* around, you are being ineffectual, which is in keeping with the other grammatical functions. But the expression *to fuck with someone* does have sexual overtones, in the sense that it implies exerting power over someone. It is the old sexual hierarchy rearing its ugly head once more, with the heterosexual penetrator at its top. This is also the case in *fuck you*, with its close parallel *screw you*. They are most probably clipped curses, comparable to *bless you* when somebody sneezes. Where *bless you* is short for 'may the Lord bless you,' *fuck you* might very well be understood as 'may the Lord degrade you' or 'may God bugger you.' You don't have to believe in a god to use such expressions. He doesn't matter, which is probably why no god is explicitly mentioned. The idea is just that some unidentified authority – fate, perhaps, or life itself – is invoked to let unspecified harm come to the annoying 'you' of the moment. This is how vague language can actually be without losing clarity: nobody needs an explanation to understand the meaning and connotations of such expressions, or the intentions behind them.

Together with *bloody* and the euphemistic variants such as *freaking* and *blooming*, *fucking* has one other capability, which so far seems unique among languages. These cathartic expressions can violate the integrity of a word by infuxation. Or, to be more precise and more than a little flippant: they fuck with morphemes.

Morphemes are the smallest units in a language that carry meaning. They are semantic atoms, as it were. Every word we read or hear said consists of a string of one or more morphemes. The base of each word is its root, a morpheme that can occur on its own, without anything to support it. *Go, house, green* and *before* are all roots in English, as are tens of thousands of others, from *aal*, a red cotton dye from India, to *Zyzzyva*, a South American weevil. Roots carry the core meaning of a word and can be compounded with other roots, as in *sandstorm, doorhandle* and *dogfood*. They can also be filled out and amended by prefixes and suffixes. Many of those, such as *pre-* and *anti-*, the third person singular ending *-(e)s*, as in *walks* and *goes*, or its identical twin, the indicator of plurality in nouns, as in *words* and *wishes*, are bound morphemes. They can only appear attached to a root, either directly or indirectly. How much can be 'put into' a word by sticking on prefixes and suffixes differs from one language to the next. English belongs to the poor branch of the family in this respect. Turkish, on the other hand, has no prefixes at all, but when it comes to suffixes, it can put things in a single word that the English need a whole sentence to express. The example below, based on the root *Avrupa*, 'Europe', is a contrived but fully grammatical word invented to showcase the wealth of Turkish word-formation. The second line shows the morpheme boundaries and how the whole thing is pronounced (ə sounds as *u* in *turn* and *e* in *water*). The expression is best translated as 'So you are one among those who will not be able to allow themselves to be Europeanized?'

Avrupalılaştırılamayacaklardanmısınısdır?
Avrupa-lə-lash-tər-əl-ama-yadjak-lar-dan-mə-sə-nəs-tər?

While languages can work wonders with prefixes and suffixes to flesh out a simple or compound root both semantically and grammatically, roots themselves are generally as impenetrable as atoms: it is very rare to come across what is called an infix, a morpheme that is inserted into a root, breaking it up. Within the Indo-European family, which encompasses most languages spoken between Land's End and Chittagong – the exceptions are Basque, Hungarian, Finnish, and the Semitic and Turkic languages – it occurs in only a handful of very old verb forms in Latin and in certain proper names in Central American Spanish. Standard Spanish attaches the diminutive suffix *-ito/a* to the root of a name, turning *Pabl-o* into *Pabl-ito* and *Conch-a* into *Conch-ita*. In and around Nicaragua, however, *ito* or *ita* can also be inserted into the root, just before the last vowel, losing its own. Thus little *Óscar* may become either *Óscar-ito* or *Osqu-ít-ar* and *Víctor* either *Víctor-ito* or *Vict-ít-or*.

By and large, then, we can safely say that, in Indo-European languages at least, roots are inviolable. The same is true of words as a whole. Once a word has been constructed, it is nigh impossible to break it up. Whereas we construct sentences 'on the fly', passing readied chunks on to the phonological level as soon as possible, words are fed to the phonological machine only in their entirety. As a result, there is no place inside a word for a procrastinating 'eh', for instance. A word must come out in one fell swoop, even the complex words of languages such as Turkish. And if for any reason you fail – a sneeze, or a knot in your tongue – you say the whole word again, right from the beginning.

Infuxation, not to be confused with the much broader phenomenon called tmesis, plays havoc with all this. It consists of inserting *fucking* or *bloody* or one of its euphemistic variants (or, occasionally, even some innocuous intensifier such as *very*) slap bang in the middle of a word, as in *fanfuckingtastic* or *absobloodylutely*. It is not a passing fad; the term *self-debloodyfence* dates back to 1908, when it appeared in an Australian army song called the 'Australaise'. Also, infuxation is alive and productive – witness totally ad hoc inventions such as 'you're telepathic, telekinetic, tele-fucking-everything' from Dean Koontz's horror thriller *Cold Fire* (1991).

At first glance, it would seem that anything goes and chaos rules, for infuxation can:

1. Break up idiom chunks:
Ding fucking dong, the bitch is dead; Hell's fucking bells!; damn fucking well; oh so fucking hilarious.**

2. Break up proper nouns:
Hong-*fucking*-**Kong**, *motherfucker; You're Jerry* **Ma**-*fucking-***guire***; The lowest divorce rate is in* **Massa**-*freakin'*-**chusetts***; We're not going to sing for* **Mickey**-*fucking*-**Mouse***; **Singa**-bloody-***pore***; What else can they do? Send us to* **Viet**-*fucking*-**nam***?

3. Break up combinations of prefix and root:
Well, I'm **over**-*fucking*-**whelm***ed; You're so caught up in your* **self**-*bloody*-**pity***, you can't see anyone else; Almost totally* **un**-*fucking*-**readable***.**

4. Break up roots, that is, morphemes:
Abraca-*fucking*-**dabra***!;* **abso**-*bloody*-**lutely***;* **abso**-*fucking-***lutely***; Well,* **bra**-*fucking*-**vo***, Angus!; Christ* **Al**-*fucking*-**mighty***, what was happening to him?**; **Congratu**-*ma-freaking*-**lations***!*; Congratu-very-***lat***ions, your Majesty; It's a* **cruci**-*fucking*-**fix***ion!; as of half an hour ago, the corridor is* **fan**-*fucking*-**tas***tic*; **halle**-*bloody*-**luja***;* **halle**-*fucking*-**luja****; with Captain Succorso him*-*fucking*-**self****; You don't look like your average* **horti**-*fucking*-**cultura***list; '***Im**-*bloody*-**possible***', Gerald said emphatically*; Ad* **infi**-*bloody*-**nitum***!; That makes him a* **lia**-*fucking***bili***ty;* **unbe**-*bloody*-**liev***able;* **senti**-*fuckin'*-**ment***al; That makes it* **worth**-*really-really*-**while***; Are you sure of that?* **Guaran**-*fucking*-**teed***!*

Except for those followed by an asterisk, which come from written sources, I have heard people use all these examples in actual conversations, in talk shows or in films. The roots are in bold, and it does indeed look as though no root is safe from infuxation. Nor are proper names or fossilized phrases, the idiom chunks. This shows that infuxation is blind to the grammatical structure of a sentence, whereas even interjections respect it. However, if you look a little more closely at the examples, you'll notice that infuxation is far from random. For one thing, although it breaks up morphemes, it respects syllables. As a consequence, no root that consists of only one syllable will ever be broken by infuxation. Second, in all the examples above, the insertion point is right before the syllable bearing the main stress, which is in italic.

The difference between morphemes and syllables is that morphemes are semantically loaded units that are relevant to the grammatical structure, whereas syllables are groupings of phonemes that are relevant only on the phonological level. Normal word stress, too, is a typical property of the phonological level alone. So it would seem that infuxation is subject to the following rule of the English language, which operates on the phonological level:

Rule of Infuxation (provisional)
In a word, insert an intensifying adverbial immediately before the syllable that bears the main stress.

However, examples such as ***contra**-fucking-band*, ***any**-bloody-**body***, 'Yeah, ***mazel**-fucking-tov*' and '*Per-bloody-**chlor**ide, quickly!*' prove that this cannot be the whole story. The problem is that the main stress is right on the first syllable, so that an infuxated term would end up at the left-hand edge of the word. The results, *fucking contraband* and *bloody anybody* for example, do not feel like infuxation at all, but simply ordinary constellations of a noun and its adjective. So it seems that an infuxated element must be properly inside a word, somewhere between its first and last syllables.

If the main stress is on the first syllable, the infuxated element consistently ends up right before the secondarily stressed syllable (accentuated here by ´), if there is one, as in *contrabánd*, *anybódy* and *mazel tóv*. If not, there is no infuxation, hence no **carpen-fucking-ter* or **book-fucking-shop* (a preceding asterisk is the way linguists indicate that a word or phrase is hypothetical or incorrect). But *congrátu-fucking-lations* and the impossibility of **con-fucking-grátulations* show that if both the syllable bearing the main stress and a secondarily stressed syllable are available, infuxation clings to the main stress. Let's amend the Rule of Infuxation accordingly:

Rule of Infuxation (amended)
Properly inside a word, insert an intensifying adverbial right before the most heavily stressed syllable.

One problem remains, which becomes visible in the relatively frequent *un-fucking-**belie**vable!* Here, infuxation has happened before the weak syllable 'be' instead of right before the stressed *liev*. The explanation given by the American phonologist John J. McCarthy in 1982 relies on the rhythmic, metrical structure of the phonological representation of a word, which is a bit like the metrical structure of poetry. However, whereas poetic metre groups syllables into rhythmic patterns called feet, phonological metre helps to bind phonemes and syllables into a coherent stream of instructions to the muscles of the mouth and throat. It turns the strings of isolated phonemes that the words bring with them from the lexicon into a tightly knit, smoothly rhythmic chain of motor instructions. Obviously, nothing must tamper seriously with the resulting rhythm, or the muscles won't know what to do any more. Dispensing with lots of technical detail, within *unbelievable* there is a phonological foot that spans the syllables *be* and *liev*, which infuxation would interrupt. So preferably, the infuxated term slides off the foot, as it were, and lands just left of its beginning, in front of *be*. This is a preference, however, not a cast-iron condition. In the film *Wild Child* (2008), the actress Georgia King as Harriet comes out with a hearty 'Unbebloodylievable!'

And so infuxation gets its definitive shape:

Rule of Infuxation (final)
Properly inside a word, insert an intensifying adverbial before the most heavily stressed syllable, preferably respecting the phonological meter.

> **'The Australaise' (C. J. Dennis, 1908; this version 1915), to the tune of 'Onward, Christian Soldiers'**
>
> Fellers of Australier
> Blokes an' coves an' coots
> Shift yer bloody carcases,
> Move yer bloody boots.
> Gird yer bloody loins up
> Get yer bloody gun
> Set the bloody enemy
> An' watch the blighters run.
>
> (chorus)
> Get a bloody move on,
> Have some bloody sense
> Learn the bloody art of
> Self debloodyfence.

8
EFFECTIVE INVECTIVE

I'm like a ripe turd, and the world is like an immense arse,
and so we're about to let go of each other.

With these words, on a cold February day in 1546, Martin Luther told his wife he felt death drawing near. It is but one of the many scatological jokes and rants the monk-turned-reformer was renowned and criticized for. This time, the rueful joke was on himself. But although he has been branded a German Rabelais, Luther's diatribes were often more scathing than scatological, as when he dismissed the English king Henry VIII as *ein Schwein, einen Esel, einen Misthaufen, ein Otterngezücht, einen Basilisk, einen lügenhaften, mit königlichen Kleidern angethanen Possenreißer, einen tollen Narren mit schaumenden Maul und verhuretem Gesicht* ('a swine, an ass, a dungheap, a brood of vipers, a basilisk, a fraudulent illusionist dressed up in regal attire, a crazy fool with foaming mouth and depraved looks').

Luther was a man at war with the Pope, Catholic Christianity and his bowels. He was plagued by kidney stones and constipation, and on account of the latter probably suffered from haemorrhoids and other painful anal ailments as well. Perhaps this contributed to the particularly scatological character of much of the verbal abuse he hurled at everyone who stood in his path, even in his sermons. On the other hand, much to do with bodily effluent and the way it is produced that is too smelly for modern taste wasn't all that offensive in Luther's day. In an era without any sanitation to speak of, pus, piss, shit and the stench of it were facts of everyday life. In English, for instance, the word *shit* did not fall out of favour until the eighteenth century, by the end of which it had disappeared from polite conversation and even from the dictionaries. The growth of this incipient taboo went hand in hand with the slow emergence of worries about excrement, propriety and ill health, which would not begin to materialize in the shape of serious sewerage systems and water closets until well into the nineteenth century.

Also, Luther lived in a very physical world beset with famine and plague and run by heroes: red-blooded, often coarse men with big voices who dished out their violent virility and machismo with gusto. Men like Henry VIII. Although the Church of Rome still advocated humility, modesty and turning the other cheek, neither it nor secular authorities practised any of these – which was precisely what put Luther on his dissenter's path in the first place. Hurling abuse was one way to assert one's strength, so Luther, who commanded no armies, threw shit as a weapon. It was a weapon of ridicule mainly, for the debilitating effect of associating the high and mighty with demeaning activities and vulnerable circumstances – unless you're Lyndon B. Johnson, who is said to have received people while sitting on the toilet adjoining his office, browbeating them into acquiescence from beyond the wide-open door, you can't wield power very well with your trousers round your ankles, and it's a panicky weakling who soils himself – was not lost on Luther's largely illiterate audience, the ordinary Germans whom the Church had come to despise and exploit.

In his highly successful propaganda campaign against the corrupt Mother Church, Luther had two essential allies. First, the printing press, which had only recently taken root across the German lands when on 31 October 1517 Luther, then professor of moral theology at the University of Wittenberg, first sent his 95 theses off to the Archbishop of Mainz, then posted them on the doors of All Saints' church in his home town (the customary academic noticeboard) and promptly saw them printed as well. And reprinted, and reprinted. Over the remaining three decades of his life, Luther wrote and published no fewer than 544 books, pamphlets and sermons, which on average went through five or six reprints. That's huge, by any standard. Especially in the early years, everything that came out of Luther's hands sold like hot cakes.

Luther's second highly effective ally was his lifelong friend Lucas Cranach the Elder, who illustrated much of Luther's work. In a world with an average literacy rate of about 5 per cent, rising to at most 30 per cent in the major cities, this changed a stream of texts into a true media campaign, greatly increasing both sales and the impact of every copy sold.

Two of Cranach's illustrations in Martin Luther's 1545 pamphlet *Abbildung des Papsttums* (A Portrait of the Papacy), published in reaction to Pope Paul III convoking the Council of Trent. On the left, the pope blesses his own turd as he rides a sow representing Germany, which eagerly sniffs the vile fumes. In Luther's own doggerel underneath: 'Sow, you must let yourself be ridden and be spurred on from both sides. You want a council, so I give you my shit.' The basic message is: I can sell them anything. On the right the pope, 'Doctor of theology and master of the faith', is depicted as an ass playing the bagpipes: 'The pope alone can explain Scripture and efface errors, like only the ass can play the pipes and hit all the right notes.'

But there were mighty enemies as well. First of all the papacy, which succeeded at the Council of Trent in rejecting most of the repairs and improvements Luther and other reformers had proposed, and making everyone who henceforth disagreed with official Church lore liable to excommunication. In doing so, the Church of Rome slammed the door on every critic and all criticism for centuries to come, thus forcing a definitive breach with Protestantism.

The second powerful enemy was Henry VIII, the king of England, who in 1520 wrote *Defence of the Seven Sacraments*, a fierce treatise against 'this one little monk weak in strength, but in temper more harmful than all Turks and Saracens, all Infidels anywhere', who 'has no charity, swells with vainglory, loses his reason and burns with envy'. This pleased Pope Leo x so much that he awarded Henry the title 'Defender of the Faith' – a bit hastily, as it would turn out in 1534, when Henry flew the Catholic coop and set up shop for himself. Luther countered in kind, as quoted above, which inspired Thomas More, Henry's secretary – masquerading as one Gulielmus Rosseus – to a riposte in which he too gave as good as he got, denouncing 'a certain rascal whose name was Luther, who because he had out-stripped the very devils themselves in impiety, surpassed magpies in his garrulousness, pimps in his dishonesty, prostitutes in his obscenity, and all buffoons in his buffoonery so that he might adorn his sect with worthy emblems'. 'Meanwhile,' he addresses Luther indignantly, 'for as long as your reverend paternity will be determined to tell these shameless lies, others will be permitted, on behalf of his English majesty, to throw back into your paternity's shitty mouth, truly the shit-pool of all shit, all the muck and shit which your damnable rottenness has vomited up, and to empty out all the sewers and privies on to your crown.'

Such crude ranting, whether scatological or not, is no longer considered an effective or acceptable method of public verbal warfare – although recently the 45th president of the United States did much to revive such late medieval mores – but similar barrages of abuse continued to be launched until deep in the nineteenth century. In September 1864, with the American Union at war and the election campaign for its presidency in full swing, *Harper's Magazine* complained that the Democratic candidate, former general George McClellan, had openly made the incumbent, Abraham Lincoln, out to be a 'Filthy Story-Teller, Despot, Liar, Thief, Braggart, Buffoon, Usurper, Monster, Ignoramus Abe, Old Scoundrel, Perjurer, Robber, Swindler, Tyrant, Field-Butcher' and 'Land-Pirate'. McClellan, commander in chief of the Union troops during much of the first half of the Civil War, had an axe to grind with Lincoln ever since the two fell out over McClellan's military strategy, which consisted mainly of avoiding confrontations with the Confederate enemy. Lincoln had made a mortal enemy of the overly cautious general by sending him a note saying:

My dear McClellan,
If you don't want to use the army I should like to borrow it
for a while.

Yours respectfully,
A. Lincoln

Now this was modern verbal warfare of a kind against which the dutiful but stodgy McClellan had no recourse. Lincoln's flippant sarcasm was like the new machine guns that fifty years hence, at the start of the First World War, would put paid to the time-honoured cavalry charge in a matter of hours. McClellan was deeply hurt, and after his replacement in November 1862 all he could muster was rancour. Unlike his army, he did not spare himself in campaigning against Lincoln, and promptly bit the dust. Lincoln carried 22 out of 25 states.

And yet, as old-fashionedly Lutheran as McClellan's nineteenth-century mud-slinging may seem, there is a difference. Almost all the slurs from Luther's day are attacks on someone's character. On what he *is*: a swine, an ass, a dungheap, a crazy fool. This is also true of King Henry's assessment of Luther: more garrulous than a magpie, more dishonest than a pimp, more obscene than a prostitute. They are meant to be offensive, but there is no guilt. One cannot really help being crazy, or stupid, or even dishonest or obscene like a prostitute or swine. In contrast, most of the slights McClellan levels at Lincoln are about what his opponent *does*: he tells malicious stories, lords it over others, lies, steals, brags and so on. The difference is in the presence of personal responsibility. Being called a swine relegates you to a class of creatures; being called a thief is a condemnation of your behaviour as well as an instruction to mend your wicked ways.

This difference mirrors the slow but steady growth in Western culture of the importance of the individual and his or her life. Luther's insistence that the faith was about and of the believers themselves, who were not to be herded any more like a flock of mindless, anonymous sheep, was a formative early expression of this changing view of the world and of what it means to be human. In time, it would affect everything, leading to the slow decline and ultimate marginalization of torture and corporal punishment, the abolition of slavery, the 'discovery' of the child, modern democracy and the invention of international law and human rights.

As the unrestrained mud-slinging of the Lutheran power-rant began to lose its appeal, irony and sarcasm took over. Wit started to replace shit. With that came all the dangers of misinterpretation that are inherent in irony and indirect speech. A striking early case in point is the world-famous compliment Isaac Newton paid his colleague and rival Robert Hooke in February 1676, which was neither by Newton, nor a compliment.

Hooke and Newton exemplified two contrary types of 'natural philosopher', as scientists were then called. Hooke was something of a *homo universalis*, a successful if short-tempered inventor and scholar who applied his brilliant mind to a sprawling range of subjects and problems, making many important contributions to science but never really going through with anything. Among other things, he came up with the idea of the cell in biology, was the first to describe light as a wave, was one of the first to realize that fossils were the actual remnants of extinct species, was a gifted architect and contributed much to the development of accurate watches. Newton, on the other hand, was quite the restrained, meticulous physicist and mathematician who would cause a sensation with his theories on the behaviour of matter. Together, they were the undisputed Champions League of late seventeenth-century science, forever entangled in bitter rivalry.

In those days, the centre court of British scientific life was the Royal Society, where Hooke was Curator of Experiments, which meant that he was the boss. During the autumn of 1675 there had been a discussion there about the nature of light. Such exchanges were usually conducted by scholars writing letters to the Society, which were then read out and discussed at its meetings. The Society functioned more or less as a permanent conference. At some point Hooke let on – incorrectly – that Newton's assertions about the nature of light were but a refinement of ideas of Hooke's, which he had published a decade before in *Micrographia*, his treatise on microscopy. Newton took offence at the suggestion, which, in turn, angered Hooke even more, and a serious row was brewing. But instead of having it out in the open, Hooke wrote a personal letter to Newton professing his wish to avoid unpleasant and counterproductive hostilities. Also, he purported to be 'extremely well pleased to see those notions promoted and improved which I long since began, but had not time to compleat', and acknowledged that Newton was 'every way accomplished to compleat, rectify, and reform what were the sentiments of my younger studies, which I designed to have done somewhat at myself, if my other more troublesome employments would have permitted'.

This, of course, is tantamount to saying 'You appropriated my ideas and my work.' On 5 February 1676 Newton responded, graciously agreeing that he too wished to avoid 'contention', especially in print, and therefore thought it wise to keep the conversation private. In his letter, Newton welcomed any objections and comments Hooke might have, even though the previous unpleasantness had spoiled his appetite for the subject forever. Yet, he wrote:

> you defer too much to my ability in searching into this subject. What Descartes did was a good step. You have added much several ways, and especially in considering the colours of thin plates. If I have seen farther, it is by standing on the shoulders of giants.

First of all, the compliment was something of a cliché. Its appeared originally in the works of the twelfth-century theologian John of Salisbury, who attributed it to his mentor's mentor, the French neo-Platonist philosopher Bernard of Chartres, who stated that as philosophers he and his contemporaries were but dwarves who saw further only because they could stand on the shoulders of the giants of the classical era. In addition, Newton's version of it was a painful pun on Hooke, rather than a compliment. Newton was a tall and stately man, whereas Hooke was a short and short-fused spitfire. Newton styling himself a dwarf and Hooke a giant was obviously preposterous, and his apparent magnanimity cloaked petty vindictiveness.

The bad blood between the irascible Hooke and the aloof Newton, stoked by a number of envious colleagues, persisted until Hooke died in 1703. Newton was appointed his successor at the Royal Society and went on to outshine everybody for almost a quarter of a century. By that time Hooke was all but forgotten, for in those days a loser was merely a loser. By the end of the nineteenth century, however, this was no longer true. The ongoing upgrading of the individual had spawned a new creature: the underdog.

In the late nineteenth century, when it was first recorded, the term 'underdog' just referred to the weaker party in a dog fight.

Soon, however, it came to mean something else, something that had been foreshadowed by the rags-to-riches characters of Charles Dickens, by Alexandre Dumas' *The Count of Monte Cristo* (1844–5) and especially by Edmond Rostand's play *Cyrano de Bergerac* (1897), and was soon to be epitomized by Charlie Chaplin. The underdog is a lonesome, disenfranchised loser who nonetheless commands the sympathy of the audience by refusing to succumb to overwhelming odds. Underdogs are good-hearted suckers like Chaplin, like the peasants desperately trying to preserve their world and livelihood in Robert Redford's film *The Milagro Beanfield War* (1988), or like Jeffrey Wigand, the whistleblowing chemical engineer who comes under attack when he tries to expose Big Tobacco in Michael Mann's film *The Insider* (1999). Or, of course, hopeless revolutionaries such as Fidel Castro, who had the guts to take on the whole might of the United States to rescue Cuba from its semi-colonial plight. Thanks to Washington's unrelenting animosity, Castro, victorious against all odds, could keep on playing the part of the underdog for the rest of his long life. Even his close companion Che Guevara, in truth a murderous sociopath, became a lonesome revolutionary of mythical proportions in the eyes of the world. Much helped by that single iconic portrait the photographer Alberto Korda shot at a memorial service in Havana in 1960, he grew into the archetype of the romantic and idealistic underdog, gallantly fighting an uphill battle against the forces of evil.

The rise of the underdog made putting people in their place or airing one's disapproval about them or their actions riskier than ever before. Treat someone too harshly or clearly unfairly, and chances are your audience will take pity on them and begin rooting for them. Nowadays, the public would certainly have sided with John Milton against Claude de Saumaise, a respected French Huguenot, humanist and philologist, who had fallen out with Milton over the murder of Charles I of England. In 1660, shortly after the unfortunate Milton had gone completely blind, Saumaise wrote:

> a puppy, once my pretty little man, now blear-eyed, or rather a blindling; having never had any mental vision, he has now lost his bodily sight; a silly coxcomb, fancying himself a beauty; an unclean beast, with nothing more human about him than his guttering eyelids; the fittest doom for him would be to

hang him on the highest gallows, and set his head on the
Tower of London.

The solution for modern Saumaises is to couch their criticism, disapproval, envy or plain old hatred in comedy. It is one thing to side
with the underdog, but no one wants to be the butt of a joke or even
to be associated with someone who is. Also, bringing legal action
against ridicule is best avoided, since it will most likely backfire –
even if you win.

Therefore, to be effective, modern invective must be evocative
rather than just plain rude. Mere rudeness nowadays betrays a lack
of power and control, and reflects badly on the speaker, as Twitter
is our witness. Effective invective does quite the opposite: it is maliciously comical in some way, which makes us inclined to side with the
speaker rather than their victim, and it paints a vivid (if possibly false)
picture of the latter in your mind, one of the kind you are likely never
to forget. Thus effective invective testifies to the wit of the utterer and
taints the victim forever. From then on, every time you see them or
hear about them there will be that irrepressible little voice inside you
whispering: 'Ah, that's the one who . . .'

A good example of the difference involves the British poetess and
upper-class wild child Edith Sitwell. In her book *Aspects of Modern
Poetry* (1934), she commented on the then highly influential literary
critic F. R. Leavis:

> It is sad to see Milton's great lines bobbing up and down in
> the sandy desert of Dr Leavis's mind with the grace of a fleet
> of weary camels.

This is devastating. From now on, those plodding camels will
reappear like a mirage on the horizon of your mind each time you
hear the good doctor's name mentioned, even when you have long
forgotten who originally conjured up their image. Lytton Strachey,
a renowned writer and literary critic himself, proved how difficult it
is to coin effective invective, when he in turn tried to target Sitwell:

> Then Edith Sitwell appeared, her nose longer than an ant-
> eater's, and read some of her absurd stuff.

Admittedly Sitwell sported a formidable proboscis, and perhaps its mention would have been funny or enlightening if it had been unusually swollen, or blue, or dripping profusely when she made her appearance, or if she were sticking it into somebody else's business. But simply stating what, for all its enormity, had been there for all to see for as long as Sitwell had been around, is childish playground tactics at best. All Strachey succeeds in conveying is that he despises the woman and her poetry. His remark is not about Sitwell; it's about Strachey and his personal tastes.

Another rather unpleasant character, the poet and playwright Dylan Thomas, did much better when he expressed his loathing of Sitwell by asking:

> So you've been reviewing Edith Sitwell's last piece of virgin dung, have you?

'Virgin dung' – now there is a mysteriously evocative substance, suggesting all kinds of indeterminately iffy things about the woman who supposedly produced it. It's a surreptitious play on her sexual disposition, too. Sitwell, an eccentric in every way, never married but had been rumoured to have had a year-long love affair with a gay Russian painter and costume designer called Pavel Tchelitchew.

Cantankerous Carlyle

Cantankerousness seems to be a common streak in literary big shots, and the nineteenth-century essayist and historian Thomas Carlyle was no exception. Having little regard for either William Wordsworth's poetry or the man himself, he maliciously proclaimed that: 'For prolixity, thinness, endless dilution, it excels all the other speech I had heard from mortals . . . The languid way in which he gives you a handful of numb unresponsive fingers is very significant.' Samuel Taylor Coleridge fared little better: 'Never did I see such apparatus got ready for thinking, and so little thought. He mounts scaffolding, pulleys and tackle, gathers all the tools in the neighbourhood, with noise, demonstration, precept, abuse, and sets – three bricks.'

Fed up with Carlyle's bleak commenting on all and sundry, the satirical novelist Samuel Butler sighed: 'It was very good of God to let Carlyle and Mrs Carlyle marry one another and so make only two people miserable instead of four.'

General Charles de Gaulle, 'a human giraffe, sniffing down his nostril at mortals beneath his gaze', c. 1948.

Had Thomas just used 'shit', his quip would only have attested to his *jalousie de métier*.

The renowned American political scientist Richard Wilson showed that despite Strachey's failure a mere description of a person's physique can be very effective, when he set down the French president General Charles de Gaulle as:

> An improbable creature, like a human giraffe, sniffing down his nostril at mortals beneath his gaze.

Even if you've never seen a picture of this haughty 6' 4" man, his looks and especially his demeanour become eminently clear in those sixteen words. Even pithier was the British writer and politician Clement Freud's characterization of the legendary Margaret Thatcher, the grocer's daughter from Grantham who became prime minister, privatized her country and damaged its social fabric irreparably in the process:

Attila the hen.

Both are miniature portraits in the same brilliantly evocative class as this one by the inevitable Oscar Wilde:

The English country gentleman galloping after a fox – the unspeakable in full pursuit of the uneatable.

What does it matter whether you have ever witnessed an English country gentleman in the flesh, or in pursuit? Wilde's quip conjures up a pretty good if rather farcical picture regardless. The British writer and humorist Alan Coren did the same for British bigotry when he declared that the French are

short, blue-vested people who carry their own onions when cycling abroad, and have a yard which is 3.37 inches longer than other people's.

The American businessman and architect Charles Luckman, one-time president of the Pepsodent toothpaste company, was somewhat snappier in his assessment of his own people:

The trouble with America is that there are far too many open spaces surrounded by teeth.

And it's true: Americans are wont to throw big smiles and are just about the only people who tend to make themselves heard at the other end of a train carriage or restaurant. Louis Sherwin, a Londoner who made his fortune as a scenarist during the age of silent movies, had little regard for the Hollywood crowd he found himself mixed up in:

They know one word here of more than one syllable, and that is fillum.

Outright malicious was the way Winston Churchill, ace at the icy art, cut down to size the highly principled Labour politician Sir Richard Stafford Cripps:

There, but for the grace of God, goes God.

The same goes for Thomas Carlyle's succinct review of Richard Monckton Milnes's biography *Life, Letters and Literary Remains of Keats* (1848):

fricassee of dead dog

Just like the previous examples of truly effective invective, it is a striking remark, unconventional in its imagery and somewhat paradoxical – you cannot have fricassee of live dog. There is not a single untoward word or taboo term to be seen, no anger displayed, not even the suggestion of a raised voice. Yet Carlyle's assessment is lethal. That dog will haunt anyone who tries to read Monkton Milnes's book from cover to cover. That said, it was no surprise that Carlyle disapproved of the work. Carlyle disapproved of almost anything, and certainly of Monckton Milnes, a poet and politician of an agreeably liberal disposition, whom he thought fit only for the position of 'Perpetual President of the Heaven and Hell Amalgamation Society'.

Unfortunately, what might well be considered Churchill's most evocative, funny and utterly damning ridiculing quip is probably a fake, since he expressly denied ever having said:

An empty car pulled up at number 10 Downing Street; out of it got Mr Attlee.

@#$%!

THERE AREN'T MANY PEOPLE who are capable of producing truly effective invective on the spur of the moment. It is largely a craft indulged in by professional writers, politicians and critics, who can hone their remarks to perfection behind their desks and launch them 'spontaneously' when the occasion arises. But sometimes amateurs may rise to surprising heights, especially when driven by sincere outrage at some injustice. One of these is the anonymous Liza Minnelli fan who wrote to give John Simon, drama critic of *New York* magazine, a piece of his mind:

You have obviously spent so much time with your head wedged between your buttocks that your vision has been obscured by the reflection of your own putrid entrails. If the art of literary or dramatic criticism is to remain viable, we must seek to eliminate people like you degrading the art form by taking cheap shots at performers' physical liabilities and who must darkly illuminate their critiques with pseudo-intellectual name calling. If you must persist in deriding Ms Minnelli's so-called imperfections, at least do so with the stroke of your pen rather than with the excrement of your bowels.

Another was America's 33rd president, the famously short-tempered Harry S. Truman, who in December 1950 also proved himself a devoted father when his daughter Margaret was viciously attacked in the *Washington Post* by that paper's musical editor, Paul Hume. 'Miss Truman', Hume wrote:

is a unique American phenomenon with a pleasant voice, of little size and fair quality. She is extremely attractive on stage . . . Yet Miss Truman cannot sing very well. She is flat a good deal of the time – more last night than at any time we have heard her in past years. There are few moments during her recital when one can relax and feel confident she will make her goal, which is the end of the song.

Around 6 a.m. the following morning, passers-by on Pennsylvania Avenue in Washington, DC, swore they saw the lights flicker in the White House and snow and icicles cascade from its trembling roof. Sure enough, within hours a letter from the president was delivered by official messenger to the offices of the *Washington Post*, which read as follows:

Dec. 6, 1950
Mr Hume:

I've just read your lousy review of Margaret's concert. I've come to the conclusion that you are an 'eight ulcer man on four ulcer pay'.

It seems to me that you are a frustrated old man who wishes he could have been successful. When you write such poppy-cock as was in the back section of the paper you work for it shows conclusively that you're off the beam and at least four of your ulcers are at work.

Some day I hope to meet you. When that happens you'll need a new nose, a lot of beefsteak for black eyes, and perhaps a supporter below!

Pegler, a gutter snipe, is a gentleman alongside you. I hope you'll accept that statement as a worse insult than a reflection on your ancestry.

What makes Truman's scribblings truly remarkable is that they are such a mixed bag. First, there is the incongruity of the man holding the most exalted office in the nation unabashedly levelling threats of physical violence against someone who came too close to his daughter, as any hick or street ruffian would, only not on headed paper. This is immediately followed by the oddly restrained, almost British use of 'guttersnipe' and 'worse insult than a reflection on your ancestry', avoiding all the motherfuckers, son-of-a-whores and son-of-a-bitches the hick or thug would have showered on the despicable Hume. But the really brilliant touch is the ulcers. In Truman's time, an ulcer was thought to be caused by work stress. They were, so to speak, a sign of laudable over-commitment in tough and ambitious business-men, whereas Hume, a mere art critic, only played at being a big shot – and was paid a pittance accordingly, the president assumed. The Pegler Truman referred to, by the way, was the right-wing columnist Westbrook Pegler, the Bill O'Reilly of Truman's day, who had incurred the president's special opprobrium by such pleasantries as calling him a 'thin-lipped hater'.

Real anger, rancour and disappointment may move and inspire professionals as well, sometimes with bizarre results. In 1872 Johan Rudolph Thorbecke, by far the greatest nineteenth-century politician of the Netherlands, died. Most importantly, he had revolutionized the country's constitution, essentially transforming it from an autocratic monarchy into a modern parliamentary democracy. For Multatuli, the most prominent Dutch writer and social critic of the era, it had not been enough, and he penned no fewer than 107 sarcastic epitaphs on the much-mourned statesman – and published them, although his publisher had begged him not to. For, as he wrote to a friend:

The spirit came over me, and I produced – hold on – about a hundred of them! Quality? Who'd be daft enough to suppose they'd all be as good as the next one? I know one thing: they are all 'amusing', either through the *blödsinn* characteristic of the fad of the day . . . or by their sheer number. Feels like I'm burying the bloke.

And so he kept flogging his dead horse, all of 107 times, in this manner:

Hier ligt de man die naar z'n beste weten, *Het Volk belette zich aan biefstuk ziek te eten.* *En om de gewoonte van kauwen en malen niet te verliezen,* *Gaf hij 't een papieren kieswet tussen de kiezen.*	Here lies the man who as best he could Prevented folk from eating good. And lest they'd unlearn to chew and masticate, Gave them a paper voting-law as bait.
Wandlaar die me hier begraven ziet, *Als 't sterven 'n kunst was, dan lag ik hier niet.*	You passer-by seeing my tomb, If dying were an art, I'd never have succumbed.
De man die hier begraven leit, *Stak uit in onuitstekendheid.*	The man upon whose grave you chance, Excelled in insignificance.
Ik zou me hier minder vervelen *Als ik parlementje kon spelen.*	Here I would feel less bored and spent If I could play at parliament.
Wat ook de vuige pers, conservatievelyk liegend, verkondigt, *Nooit heb ik me aan een origineel idee bezondigd.*	Whatever the vile lying conservative press may say, From original thoughts I have stayed well away.

Notice how the man accuses the 'vile lying conservative press' of keeping the people in the dark, 150 years ago. It's awfully close to today's accusations of 'fake news' hurled at the 'lying press' and 'fake media', driven by the same indignant conviction that if the press fails to report your views, it is intentionally misleading the people.

Much subtler and therefore more poignant is the epitaph the Canadian poet-politician Frank Scott composed for the man who steered Canada through the Depression and the Second World War while avoiding the bitter political infighting the country had suffered from during the First World War, William Lyon Mackenzie King:

> He skilfully avoided what was wrong
> Without saying what was right,
> And never let his on the one hand
> Know what his on the other hand was doing.

Is this really an epitaph, or a terse obituary? Epitaphs are short and sometimes aphoristic, suitable for being inscribed on a stone, whereas as a rule obituaries are longer and more biographical. Usually, they also obey the adage *de mortibus nil nisi bene*, 'about the dead, nothing but good'. But sometimes exasperation gets the better of people and makes them ignore such customs, as in the following utterly damning farewell on a grave in the cemetery of Horsley Down church in the historic county of Cumberland, England.

> Here lie the bodies of Thomas Bond, and Mary his wife.
> She was temperate, chaste, and charitable;
> BUT,
> she was proud, peevish, and passionate.
> She was an affectionate wife, and a tender mother;
> BUT,
> her husband and child, whom she loved, seldom saw her countenance without a disgusting frown, whilst she received visitors, whom she despised, with an endearing smile.
> Her behaviour was discreet towards strangers;
> BUT,
> imprudent in her family.
> Abroad, her conduct was influenced by good breeding;

BUT,

at home, by ill-temper.

She was a professed enemy to flattery, and was seldom known to praise or commend;

BUT,

the talents in which she principally excelled, were difference of opinion and discovering flaws and imperfections.

She was an admirable economist, and, without prodigality, dispensed plenty to every person in her family;

BUT,

would sacrifice their eyes to a farthing candle.

She sometimes made her husband happy, with her good qualities;

BUT,

much more frequently miserable – with her many failings; insomuch, that in thirty years cohabitation, he often lamented, that, maugre [despite] all her virtues, he had not, in the whole, enjoyed two years of matrimonial comfort.

AT LENGTH,

finding she had lost the affections of her husband, as well as the regard of the neighbours, family disputes having been divulged by servants, she died of vexation, July 20, 1768, aged 48 years. Her worn-out husband survived her four months and two days, and departed this life, Nov. 28, 1768, in the 54th year of his age.

William Bond, brother to the deceased, erected this stone, as a weekly monitor to the surviving wives of this parish, that they may avoid the infamy of having their memories handed down to posterity with a patch-work character.

@#$%!

EVEN IN THE BEST of cases there is something sad about settling scores with the dead or poking fun at them. It's hitting a man when he's down. Taking on the living is much better sport, or even ridiculing abstract things such as behaviour. Here, hyperbole and absurdism are the weapons of choice, with a sprinkling of taboo to achieve the desired shock effect. In English, you can *shit like a racehorse*, while the Dutch must *schijten als een manke hengst*, 'shit like a lame stallion'. Strangely, both phrases mean exactly the same, which goes to show that logic and rationality are out of bounds once more. That's why people of either sex have no qualms about *boring the tits off one another*, being a *vinegar tits*, 'sourpuss', when they're out of sorts or *smashed off one's tits*, 'very drunk' or, as the case may be, 'very high'. It is why it can be *cold enough to freeze the balls off a brass monkey* and why a Dutch person can claim that it's so hot *dat de reuzel je reet uitloopt*, 'that there's suet running from your arse'. And what exactly did the British comedian John Oliver mean when, in 2017, he said that Queen Elizabeth II 'has worn the shit out of a lot of hats'? In some intuitive way it makes perfect sense, but on closer inspection his words are a complete mystery.

Similar incongruity may occur in characterizations of people without anyone blinking an eye. This is what Charles Kingsley, a devout, socially engaged nineteenth-century Anglican priest and novelist, had to say about the atheist Percy Bysshe Shelley:

A lewd vegetarian.

Just think about it for a moment. It's negative, even vicious. That much is clear. Also, since Shelley had callously dumped his first wife in order to start a free-love commune with his new flame, the gifted Mary Godwin, the disparaging *lewd* is understandable. But what was Kingsley's problem with vegetarianism? Perhaps he just thought it absurd. Or maybe he thought vegetarianism incompatible with the way God had ordered the world. Anyway, even today and to people who don't know Kingsley from Adam, the combination 'lewd vegetarian' sounds ominous. Smut is contagious.

Many a good quip relies on precisely this kind of cloaked lack of coherence. Take Mark Twain's assessment of Richard Wagner, the influential Viennese music critic Eduard Hanslick's of Pyotr Ilyich Tchaikovsky's work and Benjamin Disraeli's opinion of his eternal political rival William Gladstone:

Wagner's music is better than it sounds.

Music that stinks to the ear.

He has not a single redeeming defect.

Or Rudyard Kipling's absurdly misogynist observation:

A woman is only a woman, but a good cigar is a smoke.

The equally misogynist Samuel Johnson, on the other hand, was a wonder of transparency, yet fun, when he remarked on the remarriage of a widower:

Alas! Another instance of the triumph of hope over experience.

However, as a sociological observer and linguistic prankster, he was beaten fair and square by G. K. Chesterton, when the latter commented on the success of the Suffragette movement in bringing women out of the house and into the workplace:

Twenty million young women rose to their feet with the cry 'We will not be dictated to,' and promptly became stenographers.

All these were – or at least may have been – carefully prepared at the writing table before they were published or 'spontaneously' dropped. Few people are capable of quick and inspired repartee, and the quips of those who are, are seldom recorded. One exception is the former tennis ace and inveterate bad boy John McEnroe, who in 1980 publicly boxed the ears of an unobliging line judge at the u.s. Open:

You can't see as well as these fuckin' flowers, and they're fuckin' plastic!

Equally vicious, but far more stylish than the short-fused American, was Edward Heath, who was vehemently disliked by Margaret Thatcher. When asked why he thought this was so, he simply answered:

I am not a doctor.

That said it all. Another exceptionally quick wit was Alexandre Dumas, who was heard to respond as follows to someone asking what his father was:

My father was a Creole, his father was a negro, and his father
a monkey. My family, it seems, begins where yours left off.

The first part of Dumas' remark was actually true: his grandmother
had been a Haitian slave. But her husband was old Norman nobility,
which, under nineteenth-century conditions, provided Dumas with
the guts and arrogance to clobber his interlocutor in this way.

Another past master at ridiculing people on the spur of the
moment was Winston Churchill. When the MP Bessie Braddock
admonished him, 'Winston, you're drunk,' the woozy politician
murmured over his cigar:

Bessie, you're ugly. And tomorrow morning I shall be sober.

He survived, which proves that Bessie wasn't a bad sort, unlike
Lady Astor, who once told Churchill, 'If you were my husband, I
should flavour your coffee with poison,' to which he replied,

Madam, if I were your husband, I should drink it.

@#$%!

'I HAVE NO PATIENCE with the sort of trash you send me out by way
of books,' Lord Byron wrote to his close friend and publisher John
Murray on 12 September 1821:

Campbell is lecturing – Moore idling – Southey twaddling –
Wordsworth drivelling – Coleridge muddling – Joanna Baillie
piddling – Bowles quibbling, squabbling, and snivelling.

This is the true wordsmith at work, who cannot help putting his dissatisfaction in stylized, almost poetic terms. But it is not just poets
who give their invective a literary dusting; witness James Abbott
McNeill Whistler, a subtle painter of a quarrelsome disposition with
a strong conviction that art had no responsibility but to itself and was
there to improve upon Nature, which he thought was 'very rarely
right'. In 1859, at the age of 25, the American-born artist landed in
London, where he became close friends with Oscar Wilde. All went
awry when in 1885 Wilde, always flippant, reviewed Whistler's first
book, *Ten O'Clock Lecture* (1885), and praised its author as follows:

For that he is indeed one of the very greatest masters of painting is my opinion. And I may add that in this opinion Mr Whistler himself entirely concurs.

Whistler felt slighted and ridiculed by that last remark; Wilde had, perhaps inadvertently, hit too tender a nerve. As a result the two became forever embroiled, and eventually Whistler fired the following devastating broadside against his nemesis in a letter to *The World*:

What has Oscar in common with Art? Except that he dines at our tables and picks from our platters the plums for the pudding he peddles in the provinces. Oscar – the amiable, irresponsible, esurient Oscar – with no more sense of a picture than the fit of a coat, has the courage of the opinions . . . of others!

It is easy to imagine Whistler scribbling away diligently, trying to get all those pithy p's in line on their way down to the pits: the petty-bourgeois, puny and profoundly pitiful *provinces*. Even wily Wilde had no repartee beyond calling Whistler venomous, vulgar and, again, rather too full of himself.

Much later, in April 1912, a manuscript submitted by the inscrutable Gertrude Stein drove the London publisher Arthur Field to such exasperation that he gave her some of her own medicine:

Dear Madam,
I am only one, only one, only one. Only one being, one at the same time. Not two, not three, only one. Only one life to live, only sixty minutes in one hour. Only one pair of eyes. Only one brain. Only one being. Being only one, having only one pair of eyes, having only one time, having only one life, I cannot read your MS three or four times. Not even one time. Only one look, only one look is enough. Hardly one copy would sell here. Hardly one. Hardly one. Many thanks. I am returning the MS by registered post. Only one MS by one post.

So far people were only dabbling in literary and poetic language, but on many occasions, literary people have sat down to write actual poems, or doggerel, as the case may be, to give someone a piece of their mind. In *The Little Review* of May 1929 Ernest Hemingway, for one, took heartfelt if poetically meagre revenge on the literary critic Lee Wilson Dodd for giving Hemingway's *Men Without Women* a poor review in the *Saturday Review of Literature*:

> Valentine – for a Mr Lee Wilson Dodd and Any of his Friends
>   Who Want It
> Sing a song of critics
> pockets full of lye
> four and twenty critics
> hope that you will die
> hope that you will peter out
> hope that you will fail
> so they can be the first one
> be the first to hail
> any happy weakening or sign of quick decay
> (All very much alike, weariness too great,
> sordid small catastrophes, stack the cards on fate,
> very vulgar people, annals of the callous,
> dope fiends, soldiers, prostitutes,
> men without a gallus)
> If you do not like them lads
> one thing you can do
> stick them up your asses lads
> My Valentine to you.

In 1928 D. H. Lawrence had acquired notoriety with his sexually explicit shock-novel *Lady Chatterley's Lover*, published in Florence to avoid problems with the British censors. Next to writing, Lawrence also painted, and when the poet and art critic T. W. Earp took a dim view of his equally shocking exhibition at the Warren Gallery in London the following year – which was duly raided by the police, who confiscated thirteen paintings – he made mincemeat of the man in far fewer words:

> I heard a little chicken chirp:
> My name is Thomas, Thomas Earp,
> and I can neither paint nor write,
> I can only put other people right.

That sums up pretty neatly what an art critic really is. Seventeen years earlier, however, Lawrence had fled England for Germany with his lover Frieda Weekley, a married mother of three torn between him and her husband, who desperately wanted her back. Already at a low point, Lawrence was told by the publisher William Heinemann that he would not consider the draft of what became Lawrence's widely acclaimed *Sons and Lovers* for publication. Then, in a letter to a friend dated 3 July 1912, Lawrence went off on a rant against English people in general, a rant so insane that it became comical in spite of its acrimonious self-pitying fury:

> Curse the blasted, jelly-boned swines, the slimy, the belly-wriggling invertebrates, the miserable sodding rotters, the flaming sods, the snivelling, dribbling, dithering, palsied, pulseless lot that make up England today. They've got white of egg in their veins, and their spunk is that watery it's a marvel they can breed. They can nothing but frog-spawn – the gib-berers! God, how I hate them! God curse them, funkers. God blast them, wish-wash. Exterminate them, slime.
>
> . . .
>
> Why, why, why was I born an Englishman! – my cursed, rotten-boned, pappy-hearted countrymen, why was I sent to them. Christ on the cross must have hated his countrymen. 'Crucify me, you swine.' – 'Put in your nails and spear, you bloody nasal sour-blooded swine, I laugh last.' God, how I hate them – I nauseate – they stink in sourness.
>
> They deserve it that every great man should drown himself. But not I (I am a bit great).

Sometimes the critic's critic hides among the public and is truly indignant about someone's conduct. On 20 December 1980, twelve days after a seriously deranged ex-fan, Mark Chapman, shot John Lennon in front of his home in Manhattan, the journalist Pete Hamill published a long, self-gratifying sob story about him and his hero Lennon in *New York* magazine. Soon afterwards a vitriolic diatribe by a never identified author hiding behind the pseudonym Donald Charles began to circulate through the city, hopping, in those pre-digital days, from one photocopying machine to the next:

Peter Hamill meretricious
Vainglorious and ambitious
Dirty, evil, credit-seeking
Whose work is mewling machoid squeaking
Pete back-of-taxi-cab disrober
Pete hateful drunk, more hateful sober
Windbag Hamill, sulphurous dog fart
Failed scripter of Amelia Earhart
Hamill balding, warty, meaty
Brother out-law of Warren Beatty
Hamill of the yellow eye
Hamill who deserves to die
Hamill tedious, Hamill grating
Hamill half-blind from masturbating
Hamill rapturous at pennin'
Eulogies for poor John Lennon

Hamill sneaking and obsequious
Hamill sly and proud and devious
Hamill wrongheaded, Hamill boring
Hamill crass who makes for snoring
Pete fired by the *Daily News*
Pete ardent swain of jet/set cooze
Hamill pushy, Hamill rude
Hamill disgusting clothed or nude
Hamill far above his station
An unsuitable presence at any occasion
Title defender on his knees
Bootlicker to celebrities
Hamill facile, Hamill banal
Hamill flotsam *du canal*
Hamill gate-crashing at Elaines
Name-dropping on Long Island trains
Hamill presumptuous, Hamill spiteful
Pseudo-tactful, pseudo-insightful
Phony kind and ersatz tough
Heart full of green and runny stuff
Hamill noisy, vulgar, coarse
Hamill's breath would stun a horse

Hamill inflated, Hamill droopy
Hamill, the press-card-flashing groupie
Pete supercilious, arch, superior
Hamill palpably inferior
Hamill pretentious pompous ass
Aspiring to the working class
Pete made-for-television man
Pete cocaine dealer to Duran
Pete ugly, greedy, graspy, grabby
Stage-Irish Hamill, Hamill flabby
Pete impotent, Pete kiss and tell
Pete of the damp and cheesy smell . . .

Enough! Why beat my broadsword blunt
Belaboring this stupid cunt?
But bear in mind I'll start again
If Hamill ever lifts his pen
To violate the taste of men in
More drool about poor dead John Lennon.

However forced and stunted in places, it is honest in its outrage and among the best proofs of the force of repetition ever. But poetic invective need not be bitter and strident, even when it's personal. In Julius Caesar's days, the great Roman poet Catullus told off the pickpocket Vibennius, who worked the local bathhouse with his son, who offered special services – a great decoy. Catullus' disdain for the villainous pair is obvious, but there is also an almost paternal lightness of tone:

O furum optime balneariorum	Of all the bathhouse thieves most bad,
Vibenni pater et cinaede fili	old Vibennius and you, queer lad
(nam dextra pater inquinatiore,	(while father does his dirty tricks,
culo filius est uoraciore),	his son's arsehole gobbles pricks),
cur non exilium malasque in oras	please leave for exile, pa and son,
itis? Quandoquidem patris rapinae	since all know by whom they've been done
notae sunt populo, et natis pilosas,	and son, there surely is no critter
fili, non potes asse uenditare.	who'll pay to use your shaggy shitter.

Roughly a century later the accomplished satirist Martial, an exceptionally keen observer, wrote highly popular epigrams including this one:

De cathedra quotiens surgis – iam saepe notavi – *pedicant miserae, Lesbia, te tunicae.* *Quas cum conata es dextra, conata sinistra* *vellere, cum lacrimis eximis et gemitu:* *sic constringuntur magni Symplegade culi* *et nimias intrant Cyaneasque natis.* *Emendare cupis vitum deforme? docebo:* *Lesbia, nec surgas censeo nec sedea.*	When you stand up I have – too often – seen your tunic, Lesbia, wedged between, and laboriously, with left, then right you groaningly correct the sight. How tightly press those clashing rocks your great Cyanean buttocks! How to avoid these ugly scenes? Don't rise, nor sit down, by all means.

It's comical, lively and embarrassing, and borders on the bawdy. No wonder Martial's work was popular among legionnaires in faraway quarters.

Both Catullus and Martial show us the first law of comical invective: sex. As today, sex sold in antiquity and ever after, everywhere. Take, for instance, the Persian Arabic tradition of *hijâ*, obscene epigrams used to insult people, which blossomed from the eighth to the eleventh century:

Wajkuha yâ Ja'far fî qubḥih *'ûlâ min al-awrat bi al-sitr.*	Your face, O Ja'far, in its ugliness, is more in need of covering than your pudenda.

Liḥyatuh fî wajhih baẓr *unfuh fî wajhih kabr.*	The beard on his face is an uncircumcised clitoris, the nose in that face buried in it.

| *An surkh ímâmah bar sar-i û* | That red turban on his head |
| *chûn âzhakh-i zisht bar sar-i kîr.* | [is] like the ugly pimple on a cock. |

| *Az bakhîlî kih hast kîrashrâ* | He is such a tightwad that he doesn't |
| *bi kus-i zan darûn hamah nakunad.* | even put his prick all the way into his wife's cunt. |

This is sexual imagery used to shock, scoff and ridicule, pure and simple. Equally irreverent, but good-natured instead of malicious, is this limerick on Albert Einstein's Law of Conservation of Energy, followed by two that try to laugh away some of people's deepest and most painful uncertainties. It's bawdy humour at its best: a silver cloud with a thin dark lining.

> A four-footer, a really thin runt
> Had a cock that was short, thick and blunt,
> With a very flat head:
> Tetrahedral. He said,
> 'Ecstasy equals square mini-cunt!'

> There was a young damsel named Baker,
> Who was poked in a pew by a Quaker.
> He yelled, 'My God! What
> Dost thou call this . . . a twat?
> Why, the entrance is more than an acre!'

> There was a young fellow named Paul,
> Who confessed, 'I have only one ball
> But the size of my prick
> Is God's dirtiest trick,
> For the girls always ask: "Is that all?"'

Rather more enigmatic is the unabashedly sexual content of the following Hebrew nursery rhyme, to the tune of 'Baa Baa Black Sheep', strangely clashing with the asexual world of babies and nappies:

Kus imxem beyn ba'ecim	Your mother's cunt between the trees,
Bi tatil šaloš beycim.	She will lay three eggs.
Aḥat li, aḥat lexa,	One for me, one for you,
Ve'od abat bekus imxa.	And another one in your mother's cunt.

Whenever there is sex in the air, power is not far away, nor is malicious glee. Nothing inspires people more than another person's misfortune. So when in 1963, in the midst of the Cold War, the British defence minister John Profumo's life and career came crashing down around him because of a short-lived affair with Christine Keeler, a call girl who was rumoured to have carried on with the Soviet naval attaché Yevgeni Ivanov at the same time, it did not take long for jocular limericks such as this to become popular:

> 'What have you done,' cried Christine,
> 'You've wrecked the whole party machine!
> To lie in the nude
> May be rude,
> But to lie in the House is obscene!'

The point was that Profumo had first categorically denied the affair and threatened to take legal action against the press, and then, faced with the inevitable, admitted to it. His political and public lives were over, but he atoned for his fateful transgression by many years of volunteer work at Toynbee Hall, a London charity.

In a different, far more sinister way, sexuality and power mix in this Turkish rhyme, celebrating the Balkan tradition of Muslim men raping 'infidel' women during the centuries of Ottoman occupation:

Am karakaşlı	Black-browed cunt
Sik soğan başlı.	Onion-headed prick.
Am dedi 'kaçarım'.	Cunt said, 'I flee.'
Sik dedi 'koçarım:	Prick said, 'I pursue thee:
Nerede tutarım,	Where I catch,
Orada sikerim'.	There I fuck.'

Here 'black-browed' identifies the owner as an 'infidel', since Muslim women must shave their privates. The 'onion-headed prick' is a circumcised one, hence belonging to a Muslim, in this case a Turk. Imagine the threat emanating from a band of soldiers or tax collectors chanting something like this.

Although it often does, political and socio-cultural poetic invective need not involve any bawdiness at all. This nasty little gem from 1940 succeeds in packing both racial and antisemitic hatred with deep resentment against Franklin Roosevelt, who ran for a third term as president that year – and won – into its four little lines:

> Roses are red, violets are blue
> You court the niggers, I'll court the Jews
> And we'll stay in the White House
> As long as we choose.

By the late 1960s some black and subversive young American poets had decided that enough was enough. The civil rights movement had not sufficiently delivered on its promises, and it was time for more radical measures. These were the years of the Black Panthers, Stokely Carmichael's Black Power and black nationalism, and the poets were black people writing for a black audience. They went for polarization and confrontation as a means to bolster black identity instead of trying to break down the apparently unassailable social barriers between the black and white communities. To do so they deliberately focused on filth and excrement, in order to maximize the contrast and paint the dominant 'other side' and black people sucking up to it in the most garish colours imaginable. Among them was Herbert Lee Pitts, who wrote verse foaming with rage such as this:

> Black revolutionary
> Got his pad
> In Greenwich Village
> Next to a white
> Girl named Sue
> If you want him
> You gotta' go up
> Sue's ass too
> His face so far in shit even he can't find it.

These poets were dead serious social-justice warriors. They had no doubts, no illusions, no time for playful irreverence. With Pitts, we are right back in the unforgiving days of Martin Luther.

Thankfully, others kept a less cheerless outlook on life, maintaining a dialogue of sorts, as in this anonymous poem called 'Honkey Chutzpah', the white guy's gall:

> Me
> When I was born, I was black.
> When I grew up, I was black.
> When I am sick, I am black.
> When I go in the sun, I am black.
> When I die, I am black.
>
> BUT YOU WHITE FOLKS!
> When you are born, you are pink.
> When you grow up, you are white.
> When you are sick, you are green.
> When you go in the sun, you are red.
> When you go in the cold, you are blue.
> When you die, you are purple
>
> And you have the fucking nerve
> to call me coloured?

Poetic invective can be purely political as well. In 1964, for instance, the Canadian poet and communist activist Joe Wallace assessed the geopolitical position of his country succinctly in a four-line poem:

> Ours is a sovereign nation
> Bows to no foreign will
> But whenever they cough in Washington
> They spit on Parliament Hill.

It is a good-humoured, matter-of-fact observation on international relations, put well enough to stick in the mind. However, all too often international politics are conducted through the mayhem of war, invasion and oppression. Such bitter experiences call for bitter

膿膿膿膿膿膿膿膿膿膿膿膿膿膿膿膿
膿膿膿膿膿膿膿膿膿膿膿膿膿膿膿膿
膿膿膿膿膿膿膿膿膿膿膿膿膿膿膿膿
膿膿膿膿膿膿膿膿膿膿膿膿膿膿膿膿
膿膿膿膿膿膿膿膿膿膿膿膿膿膿膿膿
膿膿膿膿膿膿膿膿膿膿膿膿膿膿膿膿
膿膿膿膿膿膿膿膿膿膿膿膿膿膿膿膿
膿膿膿膿膿膿膿　海　膿膿膿膿膿膿
膿膿膿膿膿膿膿　　　膿膿膿膿膿膿
膿膿膿膿膿膿膿膿膿膿膿膿膿膿膿膿
膿膿膿膿膿膿膿膿膿膿膿膿膿膿膿膿
膿膿膿膿膿膿膿膿膿膿膿膿膿膿膿膿
膿膿膿膿膿膿膿膿膿膿膿膿膿膿膿膿
膿膿膿膿膿膿膿膿膿膿膿膿膿膿膿膿
膿膿膿膿膿膿膿膿膿膿膿膿膿膿膿膿
膿膿膿膿膿膿膿膿膿膿膿膿膿膿膿膿

Umi-umi ('Pus-sea'). Out of just two Chinese characters, hǎi, 海, 'sea', and nō, 膿, 'pus, discharge', both pronounced as 'umi' in Japanese, an anonymous Japanese artist created this uniquely stylized, almost abstract invective: a scathing commentary on the state of the environment and what we do about it. Just look and let it sink in.

poems, such as 'A Certain Statesman' by Osbert Sitwell, brother to Edith and blessed with an equally intimidating nose. Sitwell published it in 1919 in the *Daily Herald*, the only British newspaper that had reported critically on the way the Allied authorities conducted the Great War. In its aftermath the paper had become a refuge for intellectuals, many of whom opposed Britain's involvement in the Allied intervention in the Russian civil war in the Baltics in 1918–19. The government, worried about morale, had considered trying to silence the unruly lot by prosecuting the paper, but in the end left it at an order to all commanding officers to have it quietly burned whenever they found it in their barracks and camps, in order to keep its subversive contents from the troops. The poem is a sardonic satire on this unsavoury demarche and on the rather too gung-ho

Winston Churchill, who as First Lord of the Admiralty had largely been responsible for the botched invasion of the Turkish Gallipoli peninsula in the spring of 1915 as well.

> The DAILY HERALD
> Is unkind,
> It has been horrid
> About my nice new war.
> I shall burn the DAILY HERALD.
>
> I think, myself,
> That my new war
> Is one of the nicest we've had;
> It is not war really,
> It is only a training for the next one,
> And saves the expense
> Of Army Manoeuvres.
> Besides, we have not declared war;
> We are merely restoring order –
> As the Germans did in Belgium,
> And as I hope to do later
> In Ireland.
> I never really liked
> The late Tsar;
> He was very weak and reactionary . . .
>
> As I said in a great speech
> After the last great war,
> I begin to fear
> That the nation's heroic mood
> Is over.
> Only three years ago
> I was allowed to waste
> A million lives in Gallipoli,
> But now
> They object
> To my gambling
> With a few thousand men
> In Russia!

It does seem a shame.
I shall burn the DAILY HERALD.

By far the most widely known example of modern war poetry is 'In Flanders Fields', written by the Canadian army surgeon John McCrae, which struck a quite different note. It is often mistaken for a sad, resigned lament for the dead, and indeed, that is how it begins. But halfway through it turns into an urgent call by those who fell on the living to keep fighting the enemy in order to avenge their death and give meaning to it:

> Take up our quarrel with the foe:
> To you from failing hands we throw
> The torch; be yours to hold it high.
> If ye break faith with us who die
> We shall not sleep, though poppies grow
> In Flanders fields.

No pacifism for Dr McCrae, who, by the way, joined the ranks of the 'us who die' in January 1918. He succumbed to meningitis and pneumonia at the Canadian General Hospital in Boulogne, which he commanded. Yet the acrimonious undertone of 'In Flanders Fields' is a far cry from the poetic piece of unrestrained and undiscriminating hate-mongering Saudi television broadcast time and time again during the Gulf War of 1990–91 against Saddam Hussein:

> Sadaam, oh Sadaam
> Thou flesh-knotter you
> Claim not to be Muslim
> For you are truly a Jew
> Your deeds have proved ugly
> Your face is darkest black
> And we will set fire
> To your bottom and your back.

Occasionally, war poetry can be comical and light-hearted too. On 19 April 1775, at the very beginning of the American War of Independence, rebellious Americans could hardly believe they had actually forced a column of seven hundred professional British troops to abort their raid on Lexington and Concord and hastily retreat to Boston. The British lost 273 men, the Americans 95. Triumphantly, one 'Paddy' wrote in the *South Carolina Gazette*:

> How brave you went out with muskets all bright,
> and thought to befrighten the folks with the sight;
> but when you got there how they powder'd your pums,
> and all the way home how they pepper'd your bums,
> and is it not, honies, a comical farce,
> to be proud in the face, and be shot in the arse.

Usually, however, fear and loathing prevail, as in this anxious English lullaby, which became popular around 1798, when Napoleon was planning the invasion of Britain:

> Baby, baby, naughty baby
> Hush, you squalling thing I say;
> Hush your squalling or it may be
> Bonaparte may pass this way.

The dreaded invasion never materialized, but the fright was obviously real enough to reach even the baby cot. Real enough, too, for patriotic poems to be composed in order to drum up sufficient volunteers to withstand the approaching French onslaught. These people knew their Bible, what with the reversal of the prediction of Isaiah 2:4 about swords that will be beaten into ploughshares:

> Let France in savage accents sing
> Her bloody revolution;
> We prize our Country, love our King,
> Adore our Constitution;
> For these we'll every danger face,
> And quit our rustic labours;
> Our ploughs to firelocks shall give place,
> Our scythes be changed to sabres.
> And clad in arms our song shall be,
> 'O give us Death – or Victory!'

In times of war, fear and aggression are normal fare, but hate changes the game completely. Most wars are about gaining something: territory, spoils, forcing your preferred religious agenda on others or strengthening one's position with respect to rivals. So there is a more or less clear objective, and as soon as that goal has been achieved, the fighting ends, or a new, different objective is put in its place. Sometimes, a war won't stop; it festers on although its purpose is no longer clear. If so, to keep it going *is* the objective. An example is the war in East Ukraine that began in 2014, which served only to keep Ukraine busy and unstable, and so keep it from prospering. Still, had Moscow decided that the need for that war had passed, hostilities would have ceased. To this extent war is, as Carl von Clausewitz thought, a more or less rational instrument of politics.

Hate changes all that. It turns warfare into an unmanageable killing spree, as blind and ruthless as a deadly epidemic. Hate is the Holocaust. Hate is the genocide in Rwanda, the bloodbaths in Liberia and Darfur, Kashmir and countless other places. Hate knows no objective other than to harm, maim and kill for no real reason, not even greed or personal gain. Hate never stops of its own accord.

Little wonder, then, that when in 1914 the German nationalist poet Ernst Lissauer published his 'Haßgesang gegen England' (Hate Song Against England), many were appalled even in his own country. Here is the first part of it, after which it just goes on and on:

Haßgesang gegen England	Hate Song Against England
Was schiert uns Russe und Franzos,	Who cares 'bout Russian or Frog,
Schuß wieder Schuß und Stoß um Stoß,	shot for shot and blow for blow,
Wir lieben sie nicht,	We love them not,
Wir Haßen sie nicht,	We hate them not,
Wir schützen Weichsel und Wasgaupaß,	We shield Weichsel and Wasgaupass,
Wir haben nur ein einzigen Haß	We all have but one single hate
Wir haben alle nur einen Feind:	We all have but one enemy:
Den Ihr alle wisst, den Ihr alle wißt,	Who you all know, who you all know,
Er sitzt geduckt hinter der grauen Flut,	Throngs behind the grey grey sea,
Voll Neid, voll Wut, voll Schläue,	Filled with anger and spite, wily
voll List,	and sly,

Durch wasser getrennt, die sind dicker als Blut.	Set apart by water, they are thicker than blood.
Wir wollen treten in ein Gericht,	We wish to stand up in a court,
Einen Schwur zu schwören, Gesicht in Gesicht,	to swear a dear oath, face to face,
Einen Schwur von Erz, den verbläst kein Wind,	An iron oath no wind can blow away,
Einen Schwur für Kind und Kindeskind.	An oath for child and grandchild,
Vernehmt das Wort, sagt nach das Wort,	Now hear the word, repeat the word,
Es wälze sich durch ganz Deutschland fort:	let it roll through all the Nation:
Wir wollen nicht lassen von unserm Haß,	We won't renege on our hate,
Wir haben alle nur einen Haß,	We all share but a single hate,
Wir lieben vereint, wir Hassen vereint,	We love as one, we hate as one,
Wir haben alle nur einen Feind:	We all have but one enemy:
England!	England!

The German Imperial government, however, was so pleased with it that it had millions of copies printed and distributed to every soldier in the German army. They even wanted to put it in schoolbooks, but by that time Lissauer, unnerved by the many negative reactions and perhaps having become aware of the dangerous monstrosity of his creation, shrank back from allowing them to do so. After the Great War was over, he claimed he had never intended the poem to be taken seriously. For all his loyalty to the German cause, Lissauer died in Vienna in 1937, a lonely, disillusioned man.

It goes to show that practising invective is not without risk, as Whistler too found towards the end of his life:

I'm lonesome. They are all dying. I have hardly a warm personal enemy left.

9

SONG AND DANCE AND GAMES PEOPLE PLAY

In the early summer of 2014 all eyes in Mexico were fixed upon the national football team, which seemed – fingers crossed – well on its way to winning the Copa Mundial. Then, on the fateful evening of 29 June, in the very last minute of the game, the Mexican dream shattered. By a penalty. An unjust penalty, Mexican sentiment dictated. Soon afterwards a furious fifteen-year-old Mexican girl appeared on YouTube brandishing a ukulele and gave voice to the frustration of her people in a song that ran like this:

Era dos mil catorce, Junio veintinueve	It was 2014, 29 June
El gran Sol brasileño está como nieve	The great Brazilian Sun is like snow
Bendita selección, no podría ser real,	Blessed selection, it was unreal,
El Piojo nos llevaba . . . directo	The Louse took us . . . straight
a la final,	to the finals,
A ganar el mundial.	To win the world cup.
Gio metió un golazo, Ochoa fue	Gio scored a goal, Ochoa was
un Dios,	a God,
El público se unía en esta ovación:	The audience joined in this ovation:
Ehh . . . ¡Puto!	Oooooh . . . bloody hell!
Pinches holandeses, nos sacaron del	The fucking Dutch kicked us out
mundial	
Con sus penaltis fingidos y malicia	With their feigned penalties and
natural	mean disposition

Robben gran actor, árbitro cegatón	Robben the fraud and a blind referee,
Nuestra gran de Satanás,	Our bane,
Nos mandaron un cabrón, punto de lanza	Stabbed us in the back.
Tenía que haber un truco, el árbitro era un Puto	It had to be a double-cross, the referee was a Shit
Y al final no vio el truco.	And in the end failed to see the ploy.
. . .	. . .
Pinchi Robben-simio	That fucking ape Robben
Ehh . . . ¡Puto!	Oooooh . . . bloody hell!
. . .	. . .
Costa Rica que se chingue a Holanda	May Costa Rica screw Holland
¡Y que pierda toda Europa!	And may all of Europe lose.

The performance was an immediate hit, but before long the girl, who called herself Dizzymissdc, was beset by indignant tut-tutters for her rude language and her 'discriminatory' and 'homophobic' attitudes. It got so bad that she felt compelled to explain – but not apologize – in an open letter that the whole thing was not an outpouring of hate but a satirical joke: a mirror held up to the Mexicans, showing them exactly what they were actually saying to each other and how bizarrely they were behaving where football was concerned.

The episode shows us two things. First, taking the girl's word for her intentions, it illustrates how dangerously difficult it is to practise irony, sarcasm and satire. Before you know it, people fail to see what you're up to and will judge you for saying the exact opposite of what you meant. Second, it proves that battle songs and hate songs are not a thing of the past, but a genre that is both alive and taken seriously.

Perhaps the most bloodthirsty battle song still to be sung regularly is the French National Anthem. It was written during the night of 25–26 April 1792 by a captain of the French Rhine army at Strasbourg, Claude Joseph Rouget de Lisle. Because the mighty armies of the Austrian empire were rapidly closing in on the city, its mayor had ordered Rouget de Lisle to create a song to bolster the morale of the inexperienced and badly appointed *sans-culottes* who must defend it. The captain presently and successfully obliged, and his song caught on immediately with the troops and elsewhere. Soon, it was also adopted by the volunteers from around Marseilles who made up the bulk of the French Alsace army, which carried a both unexpected and decisive victory over the dreaded Prussians at Valmy on 20 September that year. In memory of the gallantry of the Marseillais on that day, the song has been known as *La Marseillaise* ever since.

Its fourth stanza, followed by the refrain and the last, 'children's', stanza, give a good impression of its arousing quality and heated, violent patriotism:

Tremblez tyrans, et vous perfides	Now tremble, you traitors and tyrants,
L'opprobe de tous les partis.	You every party's disgrace!
Tremblez, vos projets parricides	Tremble now, your parricidal plans
Vont enfin recevoir leur prix!	Will be finally foiled these days!
Vont enfin recevoir leur prix!	Will be finally foiled these days!
Tout est soldat pour vous combattre.	Every man soldiers up to fight you
S'ils tombent nos jeunes héros,	And should our young heroes fall
La terre en produit de nouveaux	The earth will soon replace them all
Contre vous, tous prêts à se battre!	Trained to fight, and ready to attack you!
Aux armes, citoyens,	To arms, you citizens,
Formez vos bataillons.	Form up, musket and lance.
Marchons! Marchons!	Advance! Advance!
Qu'un sang impur	Let impure blood
Abreuve nos sillons.	Suffuse the soil of France.
Nous entrerons dans la carrière	We shall march on to the battleground
Quand nos aînés n'y seront plus,	When our parents will have gone.
Nous y trouverons leur poussière	We shall sense their ashes in the ground
Et la trace de leur vertus!	And the traces of their virtue!
Et la trace de leur vertus!	And the traces of their virtue!
Bien moins jaloux de leur survivre	We would rather than to survive them

Que de partager leur cercueil.	Share their wooden places of rest.
Nous aurons le sublime orgueil	We pledge we shall do our very best
De les venger ou de les suivre.	To avenge them, or to follow them.

Songs – not just battle songs – have always been an effective means for propping up morale and strengthening group cohesion in difficult or demanding circumstances. Sea shanties, for example, first and foremost serve to coordinate heavy and monotonous work such as pumping, rowing and pulling ropes. In the days before everything became mechanized, songs also helped pile-driving crews, peasants mowing and harvesting, slaves on plantations and soldiers marching to combine forces efficiently – and let's not forget the songs children make up and pass on to each other, to structure games such as skipping or bouncing balls. With some games the singing is actually essential to the game, such as 'Poor Mary', the Japanese *Kagomi, kagomi*, 'Look into my basket', and the French *jeu du mouchoir*, 'handkerchief game', known as *zakdoekje leggen*, 'drop the hanky', in Dutch and *Plumpsack*, 'knapsack', in German.

When authorities are listening in, the wording of work songs tends to be either patriotic or bland. The seasoned infantrymen of Nazi Germany, for instance, marched into the Second World War singing about *Erika*, a little flower blooming on the heath, which made them think of the dutiful loved one waiting patiently for the soldier to come home. Similarly, the chants of slaves on American plantations generally had a devoutly religious aspect. However, when the boss wasn't looking, lyrics were often replaced by far more salacious wording. Erika and all her sisters promptly turned into wanton sluts, about whom the severely disciplined and indoctrinated Nazi forces blared equally lustfully as 2,000 years ago Caesar's legionnaires sang, 'Beware civilians, lock up your wives and daughters, for here come the bald guy's randy ruffians!'

Through the ages, singing songs brimming with sexual innuendo and outright pornographic ditties seems to have been an irrepressible urge everywhere, in virtually all circles. Most of this was passed on orally and never recorded; the rest was often repressed. The richest fount of extant seventeenth- and eighteenth-century printed smut is the Netherlands, then by far the largest producer and distributor of political, philosophical, subversive and otherwise iffy printed material in the world. Because of its relatively tolerant political and religious climate, many thinkers from more repressive countries such as England and France had their works printed there, even when Dutch printers were notorious for pirating authors' works. This got so bad that Voltaire is said to have complained that the Dutch were publishing books by him that he hadn't even written yet. The same keen eye for profit made the printers produce hundreds, if not thousands of bawdy songbooks, which found their way on to the markets in considerable numbers. Just like modern pornography, it was excellent business, mainly conducted below the counter but otherwise unhampered. Many of these booklets were published anonymously, but not all. Some were even written or compiled by women.

A good example of this popular kind of bawdy stuff is the fragment below from a song published in an anthology in 1714, about an amorous interlude between a lustful young man called Krelis and a slightly unwilling damsel named Bregje. Once his hands have surreptitiously found their way under her skirts, she protests, and he starts pleading:

Krelis: *Ach zoete meisje, word niet kwaad,* *Ik voel maar hoe gij ermee staat.* *Laat ik een reisje, wel zoete meisje,* *Jouw poezel, zoet en blanke vleisje.* *Ai, met permissie, doch niet te grof,* *Eventjes maar, 't is met verlof.* Bregje: *Wel nou, jou gekje, doe het maar,* *Ik zal 't mooi zeggen tegen vaër* *En tegen moertje,* *Dat gij, jou loertje,* *Van mij, o jeetje, maakt een hoertje* *En hier in deez'wei verkracht,* *Had gij dat, schobberdje, wel gedacht?*	Krelis: O sweetie-pie, don't get me wrong, I'm only feeling whether you're turned on. Come on, just let me stroke, my sweet, Your juicy, gentle, soft white meat. With your permission, just a while, And none too rough, in proper style. Bregje: Well, all right silly, go ahead, But I shall surely tell my dad And mama as well, That you, rakehell, Turn me into a hussy, o hell, And rape me here in the green grass, Did you think *that* would come to pass?

With the advent of photography in the nineteenth century and improving printing technology, pornography moved from lyrics to images. In doing so, it also changed character. People seldom sing alone; they sing together or to an audience. Singing is sharing. Looking at pictures, however, is not normally a social event, except for the neighbours' dreaded slide show of their wedding, newborn child or holidays in an all-inclusive resort in Turkey. And so enjoying pornography became a much more individual and private, furtive experience.

What remained were the coordinating, bonding and entertaining functions of singing. Most workers' shanties have disappeared as a consequence of mechanization, but not soldiers' and students' songs. Curiously, unofficial army chants are as smutty and improper today as they have ever been, as are the songs that help the members of student societies define and maintain their identity as a group, and set them apart from outsiders. This one, for instance, is sung by the Areopagos chapter of the Amsterdam Christian Student Society LANX:

Een pittige penis	A savoury penis
Al in je lijf.	Up your bod.
Oeh-ah!	Ooh-ah!
Een vlezig deel	A succulent member,
Als tijdverdrijf	A pastime rod.
Oeh-ah!	Ooh-ah!

Dat is het mooiste dat je je kan
   de-henken
	It is the loveliest thing you can
	   dre-heam up,

Hier is de spuit	Here is my spout,
Oeh-ah!	Ooh-ah!
Bij mij kun je tanken!	I'm ready to fill y'up!

Typically, this song is sung with equal gusto by both sexes, although female students sometimes look a bit puzzled at first by the uniquely masculine turn the song takes in its last three lines. As before, it is neither reality nor logic that matters, but the guiltily conspiratorial effect of singing such deliciously squalid improprieties out loud. It's all about the thrill and the sheer fun of it. But why is it funny? What's so good about the thrill? To see this, we must make a short excursion into the inner workings of humour.

@#$%!

ON 11 DECEMBER 2017, as the #MeToo storm was gathering force, the American biological anthropologist Amy Parish tweeted:

> ♪♫'A secretary is not a toy,
> No, my boy, not a toy.
> A secretary is not a pet
> Nor an e-rector set.
> It happened to Charlie McCoy, boy:
> They fired him like a shot
> The day the fellow forgot
> A secretary is not a toy.'♪♫
> #WordsToLiveBy #ModernTimes #SexualHarassment

Judging by its form, it seems intended as spirited, inspirational and funny with a twist, a humorous reminder. But for all its rhythm, rhyme and musical frills it is none of those things. It isn't funny, it isn't humorous and lacks a twist. It is, in fact, a dispiritingly unidimensional, patronizing admonishment to behave according to Parish's norms or else, as dull and stifling as pre-Second World War canonized children's verse, when T. S. Eliot's 'Macavity: The Mystery Cat' counted as the apogee of flippancy.

The reason for all this is that Parish failed to heed both the laws that underlie all humour. One is the Banana Peel Law:

The Banana Peel Law
Things can be funny only if a rule or taboo is broken.

At its crudest, humour is amusement at the misfortune of others, as is the case with the archetypal man who slips on a banana skin – it breaks both the rules of normalcy and the taboo on losing personal decorum. *Schadenfreude*, 'damage joy', as the Germans aptly named it, is the bedrock on which Punch and Judy, practical jokes and slapstick rest. The immensely successful films of Stan Laurel and Oliver Hardy, Charlie Chaplin, Buster Keaton, the Keystone Cops and all the other Hollywood comedies of the silent-movie era usually consist of little more than a procession of evermore bizarre ways of endangering, hurting and maiming people. The same is true of highly popular cartoons such as those featuring Donald Duck, Popeye, Tom and Jerry and so on and so forth – and these were (and are) made for children.

As do most implications, the Banana Peel Law works one way only. Although it is true that some rule or expectation must be broken for a situation to become funny, it does not follow that breaking a rule or a bone automatically raises a laugh. From a rational point of view, there is never anything amusing about someone breaking a leg or worse, and emotionally many mishaps are just too tragic or abhorrent to appeal to our sense of humour. That said, the fact remains that there exists an uneasy link between laughing on the one hand and fright, fear or tension on the other. We have all experienced the way a banana-skin situation can instantly invoke contrary emotions of fright and amusement in us, sometimes resulting in a nervous giggle, the outward expression of this internal emotional conflict. It's very different from the nervous smile, which is essentially a subservient smile, part of the repertoire of the ancient animal communication system in us. The nervous smile signals no internal conflict, it just acknowledges some stronger party's authority.

The link between laughter and the positive feelings that come with it, on the one hand, and emotions such as fright, shock and fear on the other shows that fun is itself a form of stress. We usually think of stress as negative, something we do well to avoid. But that is not entirely true. In fact, up to a point our minds crave stress. Our brains must constantly be kept on their toes by being fed new sensations, or they'll stop functioning properly. Sensory deprivation is one of the surest ways to rob healthy people of their sanity: just put someone in an empty, featureless and soundproof cell, and let him rot there.

To see why this is so, consider how we find our way around the world we live in. We do so by means of a model of the world that we keep in our brain. Part of this model is biologically given – the things we call instinctive knowledge. But we construct the greater part of it during childhood from experience, through inference and by being taught, and we keep extending, adjusting and fine-tuning it all our lives, every waking hour of every day. It is this model that makes sense of the myriad chaotic sensory impressions the world bombards us with. It specifies the characteristics of some stone-and-glass structure as matching the concept 'office', as well as your relationship to it, and lists certain people as 'colleagues'. It specifies that those long, narrow stretches of stone and asphalt traversing the surface of the Earth are called 'roads', as well as what they are there for. And so on.

Without the mental model we could not function, for although the roads you travel along are physical things in the physical world, their meaning and use are not. Information about what a road is for and how to use it can be found only in the model, just like the route from your house to the office. Likewise, the world out there is full of patches of orderly planted soil, but 'our garden' exists only in the mind, as part of the model. Thanks to this model we know what coffee is, how to behave in a sauna, how to handle money, what to expect from a bulldog, a bartender and a bailiff, and so on. So, in fact, we do not really interact directly with things in the physical world at all. Rather, we interact with the representation of the world in our brain, which then instructs our muscles accordingly.

This works only, of course, as long as our model maps on to the real world to a sufficient degree. It need not be 100 per cent accurate; it may even contain gaping holes and gross misconceptions, as long as these do not render our actions erratic and inappropriate to a situation. Thus the quality of a farmer's model will not suffer from the idea that the Earth is flat, but a surveyor's will. Rather than fully accurate, the model must be flexible and adjustable, because the physical world is constantly changing, sometimes in unpredictable ways.

Flexibility, however, comes at a cost. It makes the model unstable. As a consequence, it must continuously be checked against the physical world to keep the two in sync. This is done by means of the small sensory events that happen to us all the time. These events are in fact small reality checks. Dreams show us just how important this constant vigilance is. As soon as our senses shut down and the calibration process stops when we go to sleep, parts of the model start derailing, leading to the absurd and incongruous brain activity we call dreaming.

In order to make sure that we get sufficient input at all times, nature has installed a reward mechanism in us. The everyday flow of small stress events not only keeps us on track but actually makes us happy. The little jolt such events give the mind brings about a form of well-being we call fun. People doing dull, repetitive work easily lose focus and get depressed or restive, unless their rut is regularly broken by some diversion causing a sufficient amount of fun: getting a cup of coffee, some gossip, a jocular remark, a small prank or even simply listening to the radio while working.

The lengths to which people will go to keep the flow of incoming sensations going can be seen on the beach or beside a swimming pool, where people lounge to relax and work on their tan, which literally means doing nothing. Such *dolce far niente* is actually quite an achievement. Without the help of drugs, very few people are capable of lying around fully awake for longer than a few minutes literally without doing anything at all. So sunbathers take precautions. To quench their constant thirst for input, they put in earphones to let music entertain their brains. Or they bring a magazine, a pulp novel or a crossword to busy themselves with. Meanwhile, of course, they also surreptitiously spy on their fellow sunbathers from behind their sunglasses.

The five senses are important sources – in animals probably the only sources – of the kinds of impulse that keep the brain sufficiently entertained. Experiences such as getting hot under the collar from spying an enticing man or woman, getting goosebumps from merely brushing inadvertently against a desirable person's skin, enjoying music or basking in the smell of roses are straightforward instances of external sensory stimuli triggering a delightful response from some part of the brain dedicated to that particular kind of input. But getting a whiff of some bad smell, an unsettling sight such as someone with an ugly physical defect or an unfriendly looking dog, or unexpectedly touching something sticky cause a kind of fun as well – if such experiences are bad enough, they may trigger nervous laughter. This indicates that it is the thrill that we crave. It's all about the jolt, not just a positive experience. That is why such doubtful experiences figure in pranks so often.

The five senses are all we need for *Schadenfreude* to occur. But *Schadenfreude* is only one type of entertainment for the brain. The joy of reading a funny story or poem is different; it is not in perceiving the printed letters. Likewise, the fun of a joke is not in hearing its sounds being uttered. Appreciating jokes and wordplay, or funny stories, anecdotes, poems, lyrics, imitations and cartoons – which we'll call true humour – involves an actual sixth sense, one that interprets and transforms certain aural or visual impressions, then feeds the result back to the brain as a sensation. This sixth sense is the brain itself, which turns humorous input into fun. The involvement

The humorous effect of breaking expectations.

of this sixth sense also changes the character of our experience. Whereas *Schadenfreude* is laughing *at* someone, true humour is a matter of laughing *with* someone about something. And to be able to do so, we have to recognize humour as such. This is the Banana Peel Awareness Law, the second law underlying all humour except simple, unadulterated *Schadenfreude*:

The Banana Peel Awareness Law
Schadenfreude excepted,
1. anything humorous must be marked as such;
2. the target must be willing and able to suspend their mistrust.

For true humour to work, then, two additional demands must be met. In natural circumstances, meaning direct conversation, any attempt at humour will be marked by tiny clues, such as a raised eyebrow, a special tone of voice, hands making the quotation marks gesture or any of a thousand other little things. In telling jokes, standard formats also work as indicators. If someone says 'A man goes to the doctor and says . . .' or 'A priest, a rabbi and a Buddhist monk are travelling on a train . . .', you immediately know that they are telling a joke. Equally easy to spot is the typical opening question of a

Q-and-A-joke: 'How does an Irishman . . .?' Each of these hackneyed formulas signals: attention, what follows is supposed to be funny! And, of course, if you sit down to watch a comedy or funny talk show on television or go to a see a comedian in a theatre, the whole setting prepares you for a barrage of humoristic stuff.

Second, for humour to work, the target must cooperate. Impulses coming from the environment are always signals that something has changed. They are disruptions of homeostasis and as such cause for concern. It might be nothing, but by the same token, the impulse signals danger. Therefore, the brain will first look upon any sensory impulse with distrust. Thankfully, there are factors that may help people to suspend this distrust, so that they can detect and appreciate the humorous element in what they see or hear, or in the situation as a whole.

One factor is a safe and trusted environment. Humour is easily appreciated in the company of familiar colleagues, friends and well-liked family members. In these environments, most everyday humour is couched in perfectly normal behaviour and conversation. It adds zest to ordinary life as a dash of Tabasco does to an otherwise bland cocktail, and does its work virtually unnoticed. Even more conducive to humour are environments specifically marked for merriment, such as campfires, pubs and parties. There, eruptions of laughter occur much more frequently than at home or in the office. Most explicitly geared to humour is the cabaret. People queue up and pay good money to get in there and let some comedian entertain but also lambast and ridicule them. These people are not masochists, they are fun seekers. Many among us consider being chided and embarrassed in the collective safety of a theatre audience a thrill and great fun.

On the other hand, there is hardly any room for humour in environments where people do not trust one another or when there is a considerable unbalance of power. If, in such a situation, the weaker party makes an attempt at humour, he merely shows a lack of appreciation of the situation. Attempts at humour by the stronger party are not funny either; they merely betray a lack of respect for their interlocutor, or constitute a threat. Nobody laughed unconcernedly with Joseph Stalin. In a board meeting, nobody laughs unconcernedly at an unpredictable CEO trying to be funny.

Another factor is the target's character and personality. Some people are just more likely than others to take things literally. A lot of the run-of-the-mill little quips and jokes in ordinary conversation will be lost on them. Explaining to them that something was said in jest usually defeats the purpose, since humour depends in part on surprise. Suspicious, insecure or depressed people have little time for flippancy and absurdity either, as do people with an inflated self-image.

The set of convictions, values and principles a person adheres to plays a prominent role as well. Ethical, religious and political beliefs, especially if they are not mainstream, easily take on puritanical, absolutist proportions. If so, they proscribe making light of anything even remotely bearing on them. The one thing uniting all true fanatics is their dour conformism and lack of a sense of humour. The attitude of people such as the Spanish king Philip II or Ayatollah Khomeini is the attitude the cultural critic H. L. Mencken had in mind when he characterized puritanism as 'the haunting fear that someone, somewhere, may be happy'. People like that may grin, but they won't laugh. To them, humour is merely offensive.

This is not an accident. Humour, relying on absurdity, on breaking taboos and flaunting rules, naturally flies in the face of the conformism of zealots and fanatics and their typical obsession with what they consider to be propriety and decency. They share man's biological craving for sensory impulses, of course, but they'll do all they can to ignore and deny the fun aspect of them. They may, however, allow themselves a modicum of *Schadenfreude* of the 'serves them right' kind.

The Banana Peel Law explains why a decent joke or humorous anecdote will be off-colour rather than true-blue. A call for proper behaviour and respecting rules and boundaries will never elicit a hearty laugh, although it may cause a mirthless, scornful one. It will turn funny only if it is sufficiently overstated to become ridiculous.

The Law also explains why successful jokes and other humour so often hinge on stereotypes and prejudice, much to the chagrin of adherents of political correctness. Real insider jokes target something familiar to the members of a small, exclusive group alone: a colleague, friend or relative, a particular way of doing things or a department of their own organization. Such jokes fall flat in the world outside, where they are not understood. Jokes may spread far enough and be retold often enough to be considered successful only if everybody 'gets' them, so they must be about people and subjects that everybody is familiar with as a matter of course, whether they like them or not: celebrities, stereotypes and widely shared prejudice. Also, for a joke to work, it must be clear to all listeners which rule, taboo or expectation is being infringed upon. As a consequence people build jokes around the most widely known and most commonly entertained rules, taboos and expectations. The overwhelming majority of new jokes will therefore be sexist, racist, cruel or simply absurd, or they will be dull and disappear.

Here are two examples of sex-driven jokes in one of the great joking genres, the riddle:

Q: Why do women fake orgasm?
A: Because men fake foreplay.

Q: Where did O. J. Simpson move to after the trial?
A: Arkansas, because there everybody has the same DNA.

Both are funny because they break not only a taboo, but an expectation: after a second or so you realize that they are about something different from what is apparent at first. The orgasm joke is not about the wily ways of women, but about the sexual shortcomings of men. The other is not about O. J. Simpson, the former football and film celebrity who, in 1995, was spectacularly acquitted of murdering his ex-wife and her lover in spite of reasonably solid DNA evidence. In fact, it derides the poor Arkansans for their purported incestuous leanings. It is, to all intents and purposes, an ethnic joke and a social slur.

Owing to the Banana Peel Awareness Law, jokes are both culturally bound and perishable. With its insiders' reference to Arkansan culture and habits, the Simpson joke will be appreciated best by Americans, who share or at least know about this particular prejudice. As the details of the case are fading from America's collective memory, it is also nearing its sell-by date. Here is a definitely outdated ethnic joke of the same type about American whites but really on American blacks. It's from way before the era of hoodies and gangsta-culture, of a time when golfers wore two-tones, plus-fours and colourful sweaters, and fashionable black youngsters did the same:

Q: Why do whities play golf?
A: So that they can dress up as negroes.

Although many take exception to ethnic jokes, they seem to be a universal part of human culture, and usually just silly. One example is this play on some deeply ingrained Western stereotypes:

> *Q: What is hell?*
> *A: A place where the French are the mechanics, the English the cooks and the Americans the lovers.*

Even more typically American than the Simpson joke are these:

> *Q: How do you know a West Virginian is rich?*
> *A: If he has two junked-up cars in his front yard.*

> *Q: How can you tell whether someone from Tennessee is level-headed?*
> *A: When there's tobacco juice running down both sides of his chin.*

The three jokes above show that the notion 'ethnic' is to be taken very loosely. Ethnic jokes may just as easily target nationalities or any other social grouping. The first riddle below is on the Swiss; the second is a Swiss joke on the Austrians, who live next door to them.

> *Q: What's brown and full of holes?*
> *A: Swiss shit.*

> *Q: Why is the Austrian flag red-white-red?*
> *A: So that they can't hang it upside down.*

The second one was coined by the Swiss in 1981 and angered Austria to the point of lodging an official diplomatic complaint with the Swiss embassy. That was rather too much of an honour, one would say, for a rather lame joke that wasn't even original, but recycled from older, similar jokes.

This is another characteristic of ethnic jokes. They are quite often recycled, meaning that their target is easily replaced, depending on the part of the world and the environment in which they are told. Here is a somewhat crude illustration from the Netherlands:

> *Q: How do you know it was a Turk who broke into your home?*
> *A: When your dustbin's been cleared out and your dog's been*
> *raped.*

Israelis tell the same joke about 'Polacks', but in the right circumstances the Turk might equally well be replaced by an Arab,
a refugee, an Irishman, an Islamic terrorist, a Chechen, a Dalit, a
junkie, a Scouser, a Chelsea fan, a poor maths student or any other
purportedly unsavoury, sexually frustrated type. Another example
is this American joke, also easily transferable to any number of
disreputable minorities:

> *Q: What's a hillbilly virgin?*
> *A: An eight-year-old who can run faster than her brothers.*

Like the Turkish immigrant workers and their offspring in the
Netherlands and Germany, the Kurdish and Georgian minorities
are pet targets in Israel, as are the Germans in Austria and non-
indigenous group are anywhere. Here are a few more recycled jokes,
recorded in Israel:

> *Q: Why do they smear shit on the ceiling at a Georgian wedding?*
> *A: So the flies will leave the bride.*

> *Q: How does a Georgian commit suicide?*
> *A: By smelling his armpit.*

> *Q: How does a Kurd commit suicide?*
> *A: By telling this last joke to a Georgian.*

This last joke is a bit different. It is not just in bad taste and outrageously silly like the others. Instead, it is a thinly veiled warning
about the supposed volatility of Georgians. Not so funny in quite a
different way is this one from, of all places, Germany:

> *Q: How many Turks fit into a Volkswagen?*
> *A: 20,000: two in front, two in the back, and the rest in the*
> *ashtray.*

It seems a meaningless non-starter until you realize the revolting truth: it is a stupidly recycled Holocaust joke, with Turks blithely substituted for Jews.

With that, we enter the realm of the racist joke. Although the edges are blurred, truly racist jokes differ from ethnic jokes in at least three ways. First, racist jokes tend to lose a lot of their edge when the target is replaced by a non-racial one, and it is more difficult to find worthy alternatives than it is with merely ethnic jokes. Second, they are primarily about reinforcing the pecking order, not about funny habits and unsavoury peculiarities of the target. Third, racist jokes tend to be more vicious, meant to belittle and disparage people, rather than make fun of them. Consider the following three, two riddles and one example of the other great jocular genre, the anecdote:

Q: Why do they draft Puerto Ricans into the army?
A: So that the niggers have someone to look down on.

Q: What's the difference between a Negro and a Polack pissing in the sink?
A: The Negro first takes out the dishes.

A black fellow walks into a bar and says to a white man: 'I's Biggs and I's black and I loves to fuck white women.' The white man doesn't know what to say and slinks away. Then Biggs sees a Mexican and tells him: 'I's Biggs and I's black and I loves to fuck white women.' The Mexican is scared out of his wits and runs off. Now Biggs turns to the only customer left, a Polack: 'I's Biggs and I's black and I loves to fuck white women.' The Polack gives him a broad smile and says: 'Hey, I don't blame you. I wouldn't fuck a nigger either.'

The anecdote is, in fact, exceptionally well composed. It is a racist joke on black people and an ethnic joke on the racist tendencies of American Poles cleverly rolled into one, raising the question who is the real dupe here. Is it the obviously none-too-clever black man, or the callously racist Pole? Or even the spineless white man or the panicky Mexican? Nobody seems to come away from this bar unblemished.

Clearly, not all is what it seems where racism in jokes is concerned. The riddle below is more like a bitter comment on reality than a racist joke. The Dutch anecdote following it is a particularly vile mixture of pornography, racism and misogyny:

Q: When does a 'black gentleman' become a nigger?
A: As soon as he leaves the room.

An Arab immigrant woman went shopping but tripped and fell into a muddy ditch along the way. She's in up to her bosom, can't climb out and can't swim. The only thing preventing her from sinking deeper and drowning are the few reeds she's clutching. She cries out for help, and a man comes to the rescue. 'I'll help you out,' he says, 'but on condition that you wank my willy.' 'No, no,' the woman cries, 'no possible! Very bad!' 'Whatever,' the man shrugs and walks away. After a few minutes – she is now in to her armpits – a man walking his dog hears her bawling and offers to pull her out on condition that she suck his dog's prick. 'Oh, no!' she wails. 'Isse bad, isse no good.' 'Suit yourself,' the man says and continues on his way. Then – she is now in to her chin and seriously panicking – a third man comes along and she cries out to him: 'Please help me! Me wank willy, me suck doggie, me do anything!' 'What? You filthy whore!' the man barks and pushes her under.

No group has been more generally reviled and abused in quips and jokes as well as in real life than women. As the twentieth-century humorist, cartoonist and author James Thurber stated almost a lifetime ago: 'a woman's place is in the wrong,' and boy, have the men of the world helped to keep her there! Long before Thurber, in 1844, Friedrich Nietzsche said that *Wenn ein Weib gelehrte Neigungen hat, so ist gewöhnlich etwas an ihrer Geschlechtlichkeit nicht in Ordnung,* 'When a woman is inclined to learning, there is usually something wrong with her sex apparatus,' which is funny only on account of its preposterous pomposity, coming from a man who was too troubled to manage his own life, let alone comment on anybody else's. Almost nineteen centuries before that, Ovid noted in his *Amores* (1:8) that 'she is chaste, whom nobody has asked.' Misogyny also occurs in the shape of riddle-jokes:

> *Q: What are a woman's favourite animals?*
> *A: A mink for her back, a Jaguar for her garage, a tiger for her bed and a jackass to pay for it all.*

There are endless jokes like this, all confirming the stereotypes of womanhood as hormone-ruled gold-diggers or cute-but-inane brainless toys:

> *A blonde goes to have her hair done. As she sits down in the chair, the hairdresser asks her to take off her headphones. 'Oh, no,' the girl coos, 'I just can't do without them.' When the hairdresser asks why not, the blonde lifts one earpiece slightly and motions her to come closer. The hairdresser bends over to listen in and hears a soothing voice intone: 'Now breathe in . . . and breathe out . . . Breathe in . . . and breathe out.'*

Whereas blondes are portrayed as stupid but somehow endearing in jokes, certain other types of woman are treated far more harshly. Americans seem to have it in especially for the overly fussy, imposing kind they call Jewish mothers and their spoiled, self-obsessed daughters, the Jewish American Princesses:

> *Q: What's the difference between poverty and a Jewish wife?*
> *A: Poverty sucks.*

> *Q: Why does the Jewish American Princess prefer intercourse doggy-style?*
> *A: Because she hates to see anyone else have a good time.*

> *Q: What does a Jewish American Princess do with her asshole every morning?*
> *A: She sends him off to work.*

Strangely, men who figure in misogynous jokes tend to be tarred with the same brush, from the 'asshole' married to the Jewish American Princess to the 'jackass to pay for it all' before. Strangely, too, the overwhelming majority of sexist jokes seem to be misogynous. If nothing else, joking can be a form of resistance, of protest. Jokes are first supposed to make you sit up and laugh, and will then, sometimes, make you consider that it is actually about a disgrace. In that sense, jokes can be wake-up calls, but women do not seem to make much use of them. And if they do, the results often seem equivocal at best. Parish's unfunny verse is one example; another is this deeply embittered attempt at a quip from 1967 by the radical feminist Valerie Solanas in her scum *Manifesto*, a year before she went out and shot Andy Warhol:

> *To call a man an animal is to flatter him; he's a machine, a walking dildo.*

Although women clearly appreciate and eagerly engage in humour in many ways, quipping and telling jokes are perhaps simply more of a male thing.

Strangest of all, when women do lash out, quite a few of their quips and jokes are misogynous too. Consider this one, by the unparalleled Dorothy Parker about a guest at one of her parties who was basking in more male attention than her hostess could stomach:

> *That woman can speak eighteen languages and she can't say 'no' in any of them.*

This comes close to the cinematographic legend Otto Preminger's assessment of Marilyn Monroe as 'a vacuum with nipples'. It's only seldom that the tables are really turned: for once the guy is at the butt end.

> *Q: What did the woman say to the guy who told her he'd love to get into her pants?*
> *A: Sorry, you can't, there's already an asshole in there.*

It effectively thrashes the kind of man the legendary actress, scenarist, minx and mischief-maker Mae West may have had in mind when, some time in the 1930s, she remarked that 'his mother should have thrown him away and kept the stork'. Or the 1950s sex bomb Jayne Mansfield when she defined the male of the species as 'a creature with two legs and eight hands'.

That said, women surely can be just as brutally and irreverently jocular as any man. The long, dry summer of 2018 had just confronted the devoutly Christian Dutch Minister of Agriculture, Carola Schouten, with dramatically bad fruit harvests, threatening the livelihoods of many farmers, when parliament began harassing her about health problems in hairless Sphynx cats. She got up, grinned mischievously at the members gathered before her and said: 'Undersized prunes and bald pussies, that sort of sums up my policy domain,' *pruim*, 'prune', being a very vulgar synonym for cunt in Dutch.

Schouten's remark illustrates another great pillar of humour, the pun. A pun is a quip or joke that exploits ambiguity and multiple meanings of words, and the formal properties of words and how they sound. Here are examples of 'sounds-like', 'also means' and 'is also associated with', respectively:

Q: *What's a necrophiliac?*
A: *One who believes love is just around the coroner.*

Q: *What do you call someone with herpes and* AIDS?
A: *An incurable romantic.*

Q: *What did the husband do when he heard that his wife was having an affair with his best friend?*
A: *He ran home and shot the dog.*

Puns are invariably about mishearing and misunderstanding, rendering them virtually untranslatable, sometimes even between varieties of the same language. This one, for instance, will not go down very well with British people unfamiliar with the American slang term 'upchuck' for vomiting:

Q: *Why did Prince Charles and Lady Di want to name their baby 'Up'?*
A: *So they could sign their Christmas cards 'Up, Chuck and Di.'*

Another unmistakeably American pun is this one:

Two black whores – or 'hos', as they call themselves – got tired of the winters in Detroit and Chicago and moved to Arizona. There they ran into a couple of Native American women. 'Hey, you be Indians?' asked one.

> *'Why yes, I'm a Navajo and my friend here, Gray Dove, is an Arapaho.'*
>
> *'Well, sheee-it! If dat don't beat all. I be a Detroit ho, and Maizie Lou here be a Chicago ho!'*

Yet, despite all the smut and innuendo characteristic of much humour, it can exist without any form of impropriety, stereotyping or breaking of taboos. Such jokes play havoc with expectations and normalcy. One example is such purely absurdist jokes as the following one, which I can personally attest is capable of having large numbers of people, especially young people, in titters:

> *Q: What's red and lonely and lies on the roof in the gutter?*
> *A: A dead toy fire truck.*

And, of course, there's T. S. Eliot's mystery cat Macavity, that masterpiece of double entendre that in Ulysses' footsteps explores identity and the fine line between the possible and the absurd, subjects of great intrigue to children:

> Macavity, Macavity, there's no one like Macavity,
> . . .
> There never was a Cat of such deceitfulness and suavity.
> He always has an alibi, and one or two to spare:
> At whatever time the deed took place – MACAVITY WASN'T
>   THERE!

@#$%!

JOKES, SONGS AND VERSES also serve to comment on social and political conditions, and to allay fears and unhappiness caused by events that are beyond people's control. During the 1980s there were two unprecedented, seemingly uncontrollable new threats to the world: AIDS and, in 1986, the nuclear disaster at Chernobyl in Ukraine, then still very much part of the Soviet Union. Both engendered a lot of fear among the population at large, the way reports of the Black Death raging through neighbouring lands must have scared people in the fourteenth century. Both, too, quickly gave rise to lots of callous, cruel jokes including the three riddles and the anecdote below:

Q: What's meaner than a pitbull with AIDS?
A: The guy who gave it to him.

Q: Who has AIDS?
A: Those who have stopped laughing about it.

Q: How many people really died as a result of Chernobyl?
A: Just two! The one who was on duty at the reactor the night of the accident, and the one who brought the news to Moscow.

In the year 2086 an old man and a young boy are wandering through the Ukrainian desert. In the distance they see several huge mounds. 'What is that, Grandpa?' asks the boy.

'That was once the great city of Kiev, but, alas, nobody lives there any more,' says the old man and pats the boy on his head.

They continue to wander and soon they see a huge cement pyramid off in the distance. The boy asks 'What is that, grandpa?'

'That was once a nuclear power plant, but a hundred years ago they had a small accident there. It was nothing serious – the negative effects of the problem were quickly brought under control and everything returned to normal,' says the old man, patting the boy on his other head.

It was as if people, after the first panic, were trying to regain control of their shaking limbs and shocked minds by ridiculing events, thus making them acceptable. An extraordinarily striking example is this improbable children's song, which appeared out of nowhere and could be heard in playgrounds all over Poland (one of the first countries to be hit by Chernobyl's radioactive fallout cloud) within a week of the disaster:

Dylu, dylu	Dilly, dilly
W Czernobylu	In Chernobylly.
Raz, dwa, trzy; raz, dwa, trzy.	One, two, three; one, two, three
Na białaczkę umrzesz ty.	Leukaemia will kill thee.

Interestingly, the equally shocking advent of large-scale Islamic terrorism with the attack on the Twin Towers on 11 September 2001 did not cause anything of the sort, nor did any later attacks or, for that matter, Anders Breivik's anti-Islamic onslaught on social-democratic youths in Norway. Also, AIDS and Chernobyl jokes were part of the public domain, circulating among ordinary people in the street, in bars, offices and schools. What jokes there are about Islamic terrorism seem to be largely confined to the Internet, and are exceedingly lame at that. One reason for this might be that in a way, Chernobyl and AIDS hit much closer to home. In both these cases, literally everybody appeared to be personally and immediately at risk. As far as people knew in the early 1980s, AIDS was 100 per cent lethal and could be contracted from a toilet seat, mucus, a doorknob or simply shaking hands with someone. As regards the melting power plant, there was simply no escaping the fallout clouds that swept across much of the world. Things came with the wind. Terrorism is different. It is beyond your control and it's shocking and gruesome, but it is primarily something perpetrated by other people in the name of some group of people. With terrorism, there is not only a beleaguered 'us', but a 'them' to be blamed. And when you first hear about a terrorist attack, it's usually over and done with and it hasn't hit you. The threat has passed.

Songs are an important way for us to deal with other things beyond our control, as well. One might well suppose that one-third of the world's lyrics are about unattainable and unrequited love and that another third lament love lost. Much of the rest deals with human relations in general and the various disappointments life tends to have in store for each of us. 'Trouble is a man,' sang Sarah Vaughan, and half of womanhood nodded their approval. In response, songwriter Eddie Boyd complained about the years of work he invested in a woman, only to be kicked out in the end. With 'Young Girl, Get Out of My Life', Gary Puckett bewailed his incapacity to control his lust for an anonymous Lolita.

Way back in 1975 Tom Waits summed up *la condition humaine* – or, rather, *la condition de l'homme* – in just four words: warm beer, cold women. It was not only succinct, it also had that typical whiff of self-pity that permeates one of the greatest musical genres dealing with the vicissitudes of life: the blues. An astounding number of blues lyrics are about men who can't hack it and blame everybody but themselves for their misfortune. Their wives and girlfriends desert them and leave them at a complete loss, asking, 'Won't somebody send her home to me?' Some have become so destitute that they can't even make that desperate all-important phone call: 'Somebody loan me a dime.' They are so insecure that they immediately buy a gun and, like Jimi Hendrix's Joe, shoot their woman down on rumours about her messin' around town, or, as in Ray Charles's 'Rainy Night in Georgia' (1960), disintegrate into hopeless and homeless drunks searching for a warm, dry spot to spend the night with their suitcase. They care for nothing but drug-induced stupor, as in the much-recorded 'Gin House Blues'. In the best of cases they come back after months of unclarified absence to find their baby has changed the locks, and decide to saunter on to the house on the other side of the hill, for if the hag won't have him, he's sure her sister will. Hendrix's 'Red House' (1966), where this scenario plays out, is flippantly funny and definitely rakish, but that doesn't change the fact that, as do a thousand other blues classics, it portrays men as feckless, unreliable losers and scroungers.

Blues is by far the best known of such traditions, but by no means the only one. In the heyday of Greek shipping, the Athenian underworld created its own musical tradition called *rebetika*, full of men loudly posturing while spectacularly failing to hold their own against rivals, drugs and women, as in this example by Kostis from 1910:

Ap' tón kairó poú árkhisa tín préza ná phothmáro	Ever since I started smoking heroin
O kósmos m' aparníthike, dén xéro tí ná káno	the world has turned its back on me, I don't know what to do.
Ap' tís mitiés poú trávaga árkhisa kai velóni	I started snorting it, then turned to the needle,
Kaí tó kormí mou árkhise sigá-sigá ná lióoi.	and my body began slowly to waste away.
Típota dén m' apómine stón kósmo yiá ná káno,	There's nothing left for me to do in this world,
aphoú i préza m' ékane stoús drómous ná petháno.	since heroin has caused me to die in the streets.

It can't get much worse than this, one would think, but just like the blues, *rebetika* sets down women as the greatest danger of all, ruining a man's life in the blink of an] eye. This one, entitled 'Paixte Bouzoúkia', play the bouzouki, is by Vassilis Tsitsanis:

<table>
<tr><td>

Póso vasanístika kontá sou,

póso plírosa tín aponiá sou.

Kakoúrga sí mou tó 'klises tó spíti,

kaí tóra khairessi poú m' ékanes alíti.

Refrain:
Paixte bouzoúkia, paixte paidiá,
miá ponneméni psikhí tó zitá,

paikhte apópse ná spási, paidiá,
toú alíti i kardiá.

Tí zoí mou épaixa mé séna,
tí zimiá sou plírosa mé aíma.

O, ti k' án íkha se miá níkhta tó 'kho khási.
yiatí stí mávri sou psikhí édosa vási.

[Refrain]

Dío kardiés aphínis més' stó kláma.
pónese ki i dólia mou i mána,
poú mé megálose mé píkres, mé nikhtéria,

yiá ná mé pníxoune tá dió sou mávra khéria

</td><td>

How I've suffered since I've been with you,
how hard I've paid for your lack of caring.
Evil woman, you shut me out of the house
and now you're rejoicing that you have turned me into a bum.

Refrain:
Play the bouzoukis, play, lads,
because a suffering soul is asking you.
Play tonight, boys, so that
a poor bum's heart can break.

I gambled my life with you,
I paid for the damage you did with blood.
Anything I ever had I lost in one night
because I placed my trust in your black soul.

[Refrain]

You've left two hearts in mourning.
My poor mother is suffering too,
she who brought me up with so much
night-time suffering,
so that your two black hands could strangle me.

</td></tr>
</table>

Sometimes, however, singers don't take it lying down, but actively lash out at those who make their lives miserable – as Carly Simon did in her most famous song, 'You're So Vain' (1972). In it, she expressed her bitter disappointment about an ex-lover so self-centred that she suspected him of wallowing in her accusatory lament, just loving the attention. Although angry and full of disdain, it was a clever and subtle act of revenge.

A year or two before, in 1970, Neil Young had dealt a far less subtle blow by coming up with 'Southern Man', in which he expressed in no uncertain terms his frustration at and anger about the bigotry and racism still rampant in the southern United States. The record was a hit, but otherwise nothing happened, so two years later Young – a Canadian and therefore considered an undesirable foreign meddler in American affairs anyway – added insult to injury with the provocatively condescending 'Alabama'. The song was a scathing portrayal of Cotton State folk as ignorant and bigoted rednecks, stubborn stuck-in-the-mud hicks.

This time the hicks rose to the bait. Or, at least, after another two years the rock band Lynyrd Skynyrd did, in a biting song called 'Sweet Home Alabama'. It starts out extolling the sunny skies of their home turf and asserting that they did not need interlopers like Neil Young down there, thank you very much. But then the song becomes exceptionally vicious, turning into a political statement in classic secessionist style. The 'Gov'nor' Lynyrd Skynyrd says every Alabaman loves is none other than the highly controversial George Wallace, the man who in June 1963 had personally stood blocking the doorway of the Foster Auditorium at the University of Alabama to prevent the first black students from enrolling, and ten years later, when the song was written, was still a staunch segregationist. Meanwhile Watergate, right then the biggest political scandal in the history of the United States, and the only one ever to cause an incumbent president to flee office, is dismissed as Yankee hobbyism.

'Sweet Home Alabama' is proof not just that the American Civil War has never really ended, but also that even today, songs and rhymes are serious weapons of verbal warfare. Lynyrd Skynyrd just latched on to a worldwide, centuries-old tradition of ritualized slanging matches.

@#$%!

ONE OF THE LANGUAGES spoken in Ghana is Fante, a tone language with a high and a low tone (indicated by ´ and `, respectively). A popular children's game among its speakers is *aborome*, a kind of foul-mouthing competition. The game starts off with one child (A) challenging another (B) and the other accepting it, in this way:

A: *Mègyè wò mègyé wó mégyè wò.*	I claim from you [three times].
B: *Mèdzè bìntúw mékyè wò.*	I give you shit as a gift.

Now the idea is for the challenger to set challenges, to which the other must reply with some abusive or vulgar expression. The retort may be personal and meaningful, but need not be either. It must, however, rhyme the Fante way, which means tonal rhyme: the retort must end in the same tonal pattern as the challenge. Here are a few examples to illustrate the idea, with rhymes underlined:

A: *Nyànkómásé ábò<u>ròbè bún</u>*	unripe pineapple in the town of Nyankomase
B: *wɔdzè wó bɛyè é<u>yì kèsé</u>*	you will be used during a great funeral
A: *ǹkàmpòf <u>àsé sùnkàmm</u>*	darkness beneath the bamboo tree
B: *wósè àsé bìndàmm*	filth beneath your teeth
A: *sógyànyí à ɔróbɔ ǹsìrà*	a soldier marching
B: *wó nà né twɛ à órútù mìrìká*	your mother's cunt running
A: *sɛ́ yé{rékɔ o <u>sɛ́ yérébà</u>?*	are we going, are we coming
B: *kónkóntsímá <u>bédzí wó nà</u>*	a tadpole will fuck your mother

The game often has competitors and bystanders in titters and nobody takes offence. For the children, it's a great way to display and hone their verbal prowess. *Aborome* is somewhat reminiscent of the Western echoing game:

A: *Pass the salt, please?*
B: *Hair on your knees!*

> A: *Look at those beautiful stars!*
> B: *Hair on your arse!*

A similar game is played among Turkish boys ranging from eight years old to when they properly enter puberty. The subject-matter is always sexually abusive and would seem a bit beyond the knowledge and understanding of the ordinary eight- or nine-year-old. Once more, literal meaning takes a back seat to metaphor and loose associations. The idea is for one boy to best another at insulting his mother or sister, to force the other into a passive homosexual role, or to display a superior command of the large stock of traditional set retorts. Rhyme is imperative once more, and the retort must end-rhyme with the challenge. As an exception, the rhyme may be inside the retort, as in the last of the examples below:

A: *Ayı!*	[lit. bear!] You clumsy sow!
B: *Sana girsin keman yayi!*	Get fucked by a violin bow!
A: *İbne!*	You pansy!
B: *Sen ibneysen bana ne?*	What do I care if you're a nancy?
A: *Halep yikildi.*	Aleppo was flattened.
B: *İçine tikildi.*	It was crammed inside (you).
A: *It oğlu it!*	You dog, son of a bitch!
B: *İti allah yaratmış,*	Allah created every dog breed,
Ananın amını kim kanatmış?	but who made your mother's cunt bleed?

In the female communities of the polygamous Yoruba people, who live in and around western Nigeria, women are explicitly instructed in creating and using ritual insults called *èébú*. These are used by adults in ritual battles less innocuous than the children's games above. It is not always easy to control tempers in the face of such taunts, and it may come to blows. That said, one cannot deny the artistic flair the Yoruba put into these ritualized insults:

onígbèsè tíí f'adìẹ sìnkú	Squanderer who feasts funeral guests on chicken [beef is far cheaper]
akíyẹ̀yẹ́ tíí relé àna rèé kú sí	Shameless nincompoop who goes to his in-laws' house to die [then, they must wash him, but they are not supposed to see him naked]
a-tóó-kú-má-kŭ	Should have died long ago but refused to oblige
okó ṣíkírí bi okó lúbẹ́	[With a] prick as tiny as a *lúbẹ́*'s [a tiny dog]

The same was true of the medieval Germanic practice called *flyting*, a traditional poetic form of boasting about oneself and insulting others, mostly indulged in by hot-headed poets and leaders full of drink. Lately, *flyting* seems to have revived to some extent in the much watered-down and polished-up form of the roast. Perhaps the best example of *flyting* that has been preserved is the Scotsman William Dunbar's *The Flyting of Dunbar and Kennedie*, which dates back to some time around the year 1500. Although the meanings of some of the words are forever shrouded in the mists of time, a few lines suffice to show its malicious and infuriating intent:

Mauch muttoun, byt buttoun, *peilit gluttoun, air to Hilhous;*	Maggoty mutton, bitten button, Shaven [that is, cheap] glutton, heir to Hilhous;
Rank beggar, ostir dregar, *foule fleggar in the flet;* *Chittirlilling, ruch lilling, lik* *schilling in the milhous;* *Baird rehator, theif of natur,* *fals tratour, feyindis gett.*	Despicable beggar, oyster dredger, Foul ogre behind the hearth; Chittirllilling, shoddy sod, meaningless Speck of chaff in the mill; Bearded bootlicker, thief by nature, False traitor, fiendish get.

Similar traditions have been reported from all cultures and climates. The Inuit of Greenland stage insulting song duels, and in Trinidad even the calypso originated as a musical means of bearding and insulting politicians. More than a hundred years ago a tradition emerged among young black people living in the ghettos of the United States called *sounding, signifying* or *the dozens*. Like *èébú*, *flyting* and the rest, it is essentially a verbal battle between dominant young men to enhance their prestige among their peers and damage the status of their opponent by insult and ridicule. Like the other traditions, it is not without risk: too sharp a tongue may well be met by even sharper steel or worse.

Playing the dozens involves an exchange of mostly sexually insulting taunts called 'raps' and rhyming retorts called 'caps'. In time, it has given rise to a whole new and highly successful musical tradition: rap. In it, the tit-for-tat character of the original tradition is largely lost, but the emphasis on insult, sexual abuse and depravity has, if anything, been strengthened. It has also been mixed with typical elements of prison and street culture. In doing so, disadvantaged youths turned the demeaning aspects of their marginal social position, including those of delinquency and prison life, into a show of desperate heroism. They appropriated the prisoner's fate of not being allowed to wear a belt or shoelaces as fashion statements the way others in history appropriated some particular slur or derogatory nickname as a *nom de guerre*. And they adopted the violent authoritarianism and rank misogyny that are defining characteristics of criminal life everywhere as mainstays of their musical culture.

@#$%!

IF IT HASN'T BEEN painted over by now, it should still be there on the wall of one of the toilets at the Faskally Caravan Park, just north of Pitlochry in Scotland:

Stamp your feet, jump with joy, I got here before Kilroy!

It is a perfect example of the most artsy kind of verbal warfare there is: graffiti. Graffiti in the modern sense of the word is a pure act of both self-assertion and self-expression, the quintessence of modern art. That said, there is but little progress in graffiti. Probably the oldest graffiti ever discovered in Europe dates back to 800 BCE. It was found on rock surfaces on a tiny island called Thera, also known as Santorini, in the Aegean Sea north of Crete. Here are four examples:

Pheidipidas ōiphe	Phidippidas screwed
Timagoras kai Enpherēs kai egŏ iph[omes]	Timagoras and Enpheres and I fucked
Enphülos tade – pornos	Enphulos, these things – the whore!
qŏrkēto ma ton Apolō	And he fucked, by Apollo!

Similar bouts of male (and in these cases apparently homosexual) boasting still abound in public toilets and on school desks around the world. Furtively scrawled graffiti was and still is a means of safely expressing things that are too intimate, too taboo even to mention to friends. Writing graffiti is shouting into a bucket, but it's also putting out a territorial scent mark, hence perhaps the positively mystical attraction of the most archetypal modern graffito of all:

Kilroy was here

'Kilroy' was immensely popular all over the Western world during the Second World War and the decades that followed, but, as with most good jokes, nobody knows where or how it originated. All we know for certain is that it pre-dates 13 May 1937. At that time, the vaults of Fort Knox in Kentucky were being stacked wall to wall with bars of gold and sealed. The bars weren't touched until an audit was ordered in the 1970s. Then, workers removing the precious metal could not believe their eyes when, baring one wall the gold was stacked against, they discovered 'Kilroy was here, 5/13/37' written upon it in white chalk.

Although at first glance the world of graffiti seems a chaotic free-for-all, it actually shows a fairly clear set of characteristics. The first of these was once noted on a wall by an anonymous scribbler:

Graffiti should be obscene and not heard

This not only nicely points out the furtiveness of graffiti and its preferred subject matter, but shows that good graffiti is usually a succinct pun. In this graffiti resembles its upmarket cousin the epigram. And not in this alone; even the names of the two genres emphasize their relatedness. The modern term 'graffiti' derives from Italian *graffiare*, to scratch. 'Epigram' derives from the Greek *epi grafein*, to inscribe. Just how close graffiti is to epigrams was shown by the great Roman poet Martial when one Ligurra expressed his anxiety about becoming the target of Martial's sharp and witty pen:

Versus et breve vividumque carmen	Poor Ligurra! You are sore afraid
In te ne faciam, times, Ligurra,	I'll write some pungent epigram to whack you –
	A vivid little squib, or verses made
Et dignus cupis hoc metu videri.	To flame your envy-driven ass. In fact you
Sed frustra metuis cupisque frustra.	Dream about being worthy to shed blood
In tauros Libyci ruunt leones,	As the chosen target of my lance.
Non sunt papilionibus molesti.	Forget it, pal – you're just a piece of crud.
Quaeras, censeo, si legi laboras,	Lions hunt bulls, not butterflies and ants.
Nigri fornicis ebrium poetam,	If you want fame, go find somebody fitter:
Qui carbone rudi putrique creta	A sot-brained rapper from the ghetto slums
Scribit carmina, quae legunt cacantes.	Who'll chalk you up in toilets, where a shitter
	Can read about you with the other bums.
Frons haec stigmate non mea notanda est.	Me go after you? Please understand:
	Your brow's too low to take my high-class brand.
(Epigram XII.61)	(translation by Joseph S. Salemi)

It is immediately clear from Martial's epigram that graffiti has always been associated with places like public loos. In fact, 2,000 years ago it got so bad that Roman authorities put religious effigies on latrine walls to dissuade people from scrawling all over them. From the ruins of Pompeii, no fewer than 15,000 graffiti in charcoal or chalk, or scratched into walls, have been recovered – an amazing number, considering how few people could read and write in those days. The situation moved one Pompeiian to lament:

Admiror, paries, te non cecidisse ruinis *qui tot scriptorum taedia sustineas*	Wall, I'm amazed you haven't fallen in ruins since you bear so many writers' follies

The millennia-old ties between graffiti and lavatories have given rise to a whole subgenre, scatological graffiti. Here are a few classic examples:

While I read the writing on the walls,
I shit and stink and scratch my balls

Sam, Sam, the janitor man
Chief Superintendant of the crapping can.
He washes out bowls and picks up towels
And listens to the roar of other men's bowels

Here I sit, broken hearted:
Tried to shit but only farted

Ici tombent en ruine *Les merveilles de la cuisine*	In this place go to ruin the miracles of French cuisine

All shithouse poets, when they die,
Will find erected to the sky
A lasting tribute to their wit:
A monument of solid shit

La mierda no es pintura *El dedo no es papel* *Cuando cagas, hijo de puta,* *Limpiate con el papel.*	Shit is not paint, Your finger not paper, When you shit, you son of a bitch Wipe your arse with paper.

Malerei ist fein und zierlich	Painting is fine and gracious
Aber nicht an diesem Ort	But not in this particular spot
Wo der Finger dient als Pinsel	Where the finger serves as paint
Und der Arsch als Farbdepot	brush
	And the arse as pigment pot

In 1731 a man calling himself Hurlo Thrumbo, possibly a pseudo-nym of the lexicographer and writer Samuel Johnson, served up an impressive collection of contemporary graffiti in *The Merry Thought; or, the Glass-Window and Bog-House Miscellany*. In a 'bog-house' at Epsom Wells he found this comment on the lack of originality that is indeed typical of most graffiti:

> *Privies are now receptacles of wit*
> *And every fool that hither comes to shit*
> *Affects to write what other fools have writ.*

This too was nothing new. A good many of the graffiti found in Pompeii were mere quotations – often warped ones, as if the writers had never seen the originals but relied on their memory of hearing them recited – from works by poets such as Virgil, Ovid and Martial.

Scatology apart, sex in the broadest sense of the word is the central theme of graffiti. It is almost always there, even in graffiti that deals with other subjects. Puns with sexual content, brimming with innuendo, abound:

> *Rugby is a game played by gentlemen with odd-shaped balls*

> *Be security-conscious: 80% of people are caused by accidents*

> *Buggery is boring; incest is relatively boring; necrophilia is dead boring*

> *Is a lady barrister without her briefs a solicitor?*

Political graffiti is relatively rare and mainly consists of straightforward war cries such as 'Kill all Taigs' or 'Yankee go home.' The same goes for personal attacks, such as this one from Pompeii:

Cosmus Equitiaes magnus cinaedus et fellator est suris apertis	Cosmus, slave of Equitias, is a big queer and cocksucker with his legs wide open

Religious graffiti is rarer still, as are references to literature, but they do occasionally occur:

Where will you be on the Day of Judgement?
[in a different hand] *Still here waiting for that number 95 bus*

Come home Oedipus, all is forgiven – Mum

Back in a minute – Godot

As the Day of Judgement example above illustrates, graffiti is also often competitive. That is, people often try to best a writer by answering graffiti in an absurd way, like giants settling on the shoulders of dwarves:

A: *I hate graffiti*
B: *I hate all Italian dishes*

A: *I buy petrol, therefore I exist*
B: *I just wankalong*
C: *I slit wrists*

A: *John Wayne is a closet queen*
B: *Ellery Queene is a closet john*
C: *Queen Elizabeth is a water closet*
D: *Victoria was a queen of the closet*
E: *The queen of spades is a man*
F: *The johns in the Queen Elizabeth don't work*

A: *A watched proverb butters no parsnips*
    [a mix-up of the proverbs 'Words butter no parsnips'
    and 'A watched pot never boils']
B: *A buttered parsnip watches no proverbs either*
C: *A buttered watch parsnips no proverbs*

D: *Melted butter never watches parsnips*
E: *A parsnip buttered proverbs no grunch but the eggplant*
   over there
F: *A panned pars nips no butter*

So far, it is not clear whether the advent of social media will have a noticeable effect on the nigh-immutable traditions of graffiti. It could, because – at least for the time being – social media such as Twitter offer a completely new low-threshold way of just making fun, making a point, venting one's frustration or attacking people without revealing one's identity. After all, the wisdom of the walls has it that:

To err is human, but it takes a computer to completely fuck things up.

10
THE POLITICS OF SWEARING

Swearing, cursing, insults and taboo words never worried worldly authorities much, except when an infraction of order resulted – in other words, when foul-mouthing became political. But once they do take up arms against a sea of offensive language, they often threaten all offenders with grave punishment and are likely to follow up on those threats. There are many motivations for taking action of that kind, which ultimately all boil down to the need to preserve the fabric of political power, a fabric that is only too vulnerable to the effects of well-chosen words – or ill-chosen ones, depending on one's point of view.

When push comes to shove, political power is invariably about the emperor's new clothes. In this respect, there is essentially no difference between the prime minister of a modern democracy, the archetypal despot or the sly ruffian leading a chapter of Hells Angels. Their power depends only to a very limited degree on their ability to do right by their people and protect them. Many leaders cannot or will not do so, are even *seen* to be unable or unwilling to do so, but remain in power regardless. What really matters is that people keep *thinking* their leader is able to enforce his authority and control them. The moment this belief starts wavering, the whole power structure begins to crumble. That is when ambitious princes, competing tribal leaders, runners-up on the party ladder, disgruntled courtiers or scheming generals seize the opportunity to put themselves in the driving seat. Or, on occasion, it is when the people themselves rise against their rulers and take matters into their own hands. In short, political power is all about reputation, which is how people view political pundits, and about face, which is how these pundits understand their own reputation.

An illustration both apt and terrible is the way a century ago the Central Powers Germany and Austria ultimately lost the First World War. By early 1918 the Central and Allied armies on the Western front had been bogged down in the mud of Belgium and France for more than three years, without either side having succeeded in making any serious headway. Millions of soldiers had been torn to pieces by shellfire, machine-gunned to bits, disembowelled by bayonets and bullets, and scorched and flayed alive by gas and fire, and still there was no prospect of an end to the carnage. This was an industrial war, a mindless process churning out thousands of cripples and corpses a day. It was fought in a surrealistic world of its own creation, where nothing natural had survived the years of relentless shelling. Not a house, not a tree, not even the soil itself remained untouched.

When they were not being bombed or attacked, and were not sent into the barbed-wire wilderness called no-man's-land to attack, life was hardly better for the troops. The filth and the stench were sickening, the men were besieged by rats, lice and dysentery, rations were low and of poor quality, and discipline was harsh. Especially on the German side, life in the trenches had become virtually unbearable. The German Reich and Austria, boxed in between enemies on all sides and cut off from the world markets by an effective British sea blockade, were by now desperately short of almost everything. Famine threatened the families of the enlisted men fighting the war. There was no tobacco any more, no cheese, no milk, no meat, no decent bread, no soap. And yet, despite all the hardship, despite the countless broken promises that the next offensive would be the last and decide the war, and despite all the dead and dying, the German soldiers held out and stolidly went on with the business of fighting for their kaiser.

Then, in the early spring of 1918, things seemed to look up for the Germans. The Russians, busy with their own Revolution, suddenly bowed out of the war at Brest, not only yielding most of what is now the Baltics, Poland, Belarus and the Ukraine to the kaiser, but freeing up most of the German troops manning the Eastern front. They were rapidly redeployed in the west, where the German High Command was planning a desperate gamble to force the outcome of the war by going 'all in'. This time, it seemed to work. Once the offensive called *Kaiserschlacht*, 'Emperor's battle', was launched, the Germans cut through the Allied defences and advanced many miles in a matter of days. But after about a month of fierce fighting, the military results proved so-so at best. Yes, a considerable amount of territory had been gained, but almost 350,000 men had died, gone missing or been taken prisoner. And once again nothing essential had changed.

Or so it seemed, for this modest and costly success actually heralded Germany's undoing. In the Allied trenches they overran, the conquering German troops for the first time saw how the other half lived, and it was not at all what they had expected. They had been told by the German leadership that the Allied forces suffered far more than they did, with worse rations and worse amenities. Instead, the British, the French and the newly arrived Americans turned out to be enjoying real cigarettes, real cream and far more comfortable quarters than their own. At that point, the German troops began to realize that they had been lied to and cheated on a grand scale. Suddenly, the kaiser had no clothes on. He, his ministers and the High Command had obviously been making a shambles of the Reich, while pretending to do better than anybody else. The spell was broken, the imperial magic gone, and this realization accomplished what no quantity of shells, grenades or gas had been able to achieve: in the summer of 1918, the German army began to crumble. More and more soldiers failed to see the point in continuing a fight that they considered theirs no longer. A few months later Germany fell prey to chaos and revolution, leaving the once godlike kaiser no choice but to throw himself on the mercy of the Dutch, who grudgingly granted him shelter at Doorn in the Netherlands. There he spent the rest of his life on a country estate, bossing around servants and felling trees as a hobby.

The demise of the second German Reich towards the end of 1918 is by no means the only dramatic example of what loss of reputation can do to a ruler. Another is the fall of Richard Nixon, so far the only American president ever forced to give up his office untimely. Nixon had succeeded Lyndon B. Johnson in 1969 and had curried much favour with the whole world by opening up diplomatic relations with and even paying a visit to Mao Zedong's China, at that time a hermetically closed, enigmatic realm. So much, in fact, that he carried no fewer than 49 states in the presidential elections of 1972. But Nixon's second term started badly with allegations of tax evasion and bribery against Vice-President Spiro Agnew, who would step down in October 1973, and the outbreak of the Watergate scandal. Officially, it was 'Watergate', essentially a botched ploy to spy on and destabilize the competition – the Democratic Party – that eventually put paid to Nixon's presidency. But a sufficiently large part of his constituency and, equally importantly, the senators and congressmen whose livelihood depended on that constituency were quite prepared to forgive their crook of a president his dodgy deeds and silly schemes. Any political constituency is so disposed. Consciously or subconsciously, most people understand that someone completely honest, someone who always does the right thing, does not stand a snowball's chance in hell in that rat race called politics. Long before the presidencies and party leaderships – the highest peaks in the political landscape – first appear on the horizon, they will have been devoured by less scrupulous, more ruthlessly ambitious contenders. Tripping up competitors, colleagues and even friends, and selling them out, is par for the course.

What Nixon's voters could not stomach was a cascade of quite different revelations. First, there was the discovery that he had surreptitiously been taping every word that was said in the White House for years. Few people knew or realized at the time that this was hardly new. All presidents from Franklin Roosevelt onwards had been taping conversations in the Oval Office and perhaps elsewhere on the sly. The only difference was that Nixon was the first to record literally everything. During his administration, there was no start and stop button to press, no choosing which conversations were worth recording. In this day and age, in our world of nationwide cctv, spying drones, the National Security Agency's Prism programme, Echelon, all-encompassing social surveillance in China and whatnot, this may not seem like much, but back then it came as a real shock to the American public.

Nixon's apparent paranoia made the first serious dent in the confidence of his voters. Things got worse when the president first tried to wriggle out of disclosing his tapes like a child not wanting to let go of a toy, and really went wrong when he tried to have the dogs called off by handing over 1,200 pages of redacted typewritten transcripts of part of the material. When these were published in April 1974, it was not what was there that bowled every upstanding American citizen over, but what was missing. The pages were riddled with the phrase 'expletive deleted'. The president of Middle America, who took pains never to utter an offensive word in public, the man who claimed to be the voice of the 'silent majority', this self-professed champion of decency, propriety and family values turned out to swear and curse and demean people in the relative privacy of his office with extreme gusto. On the one hand, the transcripts and their unedited versions, which in time became public knowledge as well, caused great 'I told you so' fun among Nixon's enemies, to the extent that on the strength of Nixon's angry quip, 'That asshole [Pierre] Trudeau is something else,' on 21 October 1974, 'that asshole' became a popular nickname for the poor prime minister among Canadians. On the other hand, Nixon's carefully groomed image as an astute statesman and steadfast defender of the decent people had irreparably shattered.

Then, and only then, political support for the president began melting away. The famous 'smoking gun' tape, on which he was heard to agree with his cronies on an attempt to try to stop the FBI from investigating the Watergate break-in – thereby unmistakeably obstructing the course of justice – just gave Congress and Senate a solid reason for abandoning their president. That was the end of the career of Tricky Dick, as Nixon had been known since his ruthlessly slick senatorial campaign in 1950.

More recently, if less spectacularly, the reputation of Nicolas Sarkozy, president of France from 2007 to 2012, was seriously damaged by a stupid incident at an agricultural fair in February 2008. As Sarkozy, a flashy right-winger not all that popular among the struggling farmers of France, made his way through the crowd into the venue, shaking hands here and there, an elderly man refused him: *Ah non, touche-moi pas! Tu me salis!*, 'Oi! Keep your filthy hands off me!' *Casse-toi alors, pauv' con!*', 'Fuck off then, loser', the bling-bling president retorted without missing a beat. It was bad form all round, but from some poor bugger uncivil behaviour might be expected – in fact, nobody even bothered to check who the man was, and his identity remains a mystery even today. Coming from the president of France, however, such language was unworthy and disgraceful, showing him off as a petty person who lacked both the class and the self-control his lofty office required. Sarkozy proved himself another emperor in birthday suit, and it took all his skill to weather the ensuing storm of indignation.

Something similar happened to Sarkozy's successor, the socialist François Hollande, when in the summer of 2014 his ex-partner Valérie Trierweiler published a book about their none-too-happy love affair. In it she revealed how after two years it had ended with a bang when she found out that the actress Julie Gayet had surreptitiously succeeded her in her role as amorous interloper at the Élysée Palace. Trierweiler, every inch the archetypal vindictive ex, was even more unpopular than Hollande himself, so the French no more than shrugged at most of her indiscretions. But not at her imputation that in the privacy of the presidential chambers, the socialist president was wont to refer to the French poor – the group whose interests he was supposed to have closest at heart – as *les sens-dents*, 'the toothless'. That did strike a nerve, damaging Hollande's already weak position even further.

It would seem that French presidents never learn. In the summer of 2018 disgruntled lower-middle-class French began protesting in large numbers against the politics of Hollande's successor, Emmanuel Macron, who had won the presidency on the promise that he would do things completely differently: away with the old party aristocracy, away with the disparaging arrogance of the political elite towards the people whose interests they were supposed to protect. But in the first year he had abolished taxes for the super-rich and cut pensions and other benefits for the less well-to-do. In the midst of austerity programmes, he had begun to restore the lavish splendour of the Élysée Palace, spending a taxpayer's fortune on an extravagant dinner service of costly Sèvres porcelain for it. And he had told his voters that they were 'nothing in life' and unruly *Gaulois*, 'Gauls', unwilling to change. Also, he snapped at some hapless unemployed to 'Cross the street, you'll surely find jobs there.' This was *exactly* the opposite of what he had promised, and it was enough for large numbers of people to don the now famous yellow vest every Frenchman is obliged to keep in his car, and take to the streets.

That is not to say that rulers should always avoid uncouth behaviour and improper language in order to safeguard their image and reputation. A president of the Hells Angels is not expected to pussyfoot around, and certain politicians can get away with extremely uncivil behaviour and even with complete poppycock and blatant lies. But two conditions must always be met: be consistent and don't bite the hand that feeds you.

Kaiser Wilhelm II, Richard Nixon, Nicolas Sarkozy and François Hollande failed to obey these conditions by feigning propriety while blatantly lying to and disparaging the people they had vowed to lead, represent and protect, and by not living up to the standards set by themselves and their position. Three other luminaries of our times prove that rulers can indeed get away unpunished with quite surprising, even scandalous behaviour if they do obey those two principles. They are Silvio Berlusconi, Vladimir Putin and Donald Trump.

Berlusconi entered the political arena in 1993 as a maverick and has always meticulously cultivated that image, with amazing success. Already a renowned media tycoon and popular with a large part of the population as the owner of the prominent soccer team AC Milan, he presented himself to the Italian public as an unconventional businessman. Here was an energetic man with a talent for success, a powerhouse come to clear up the total mess the political establishment had landed the country in. The unlikely name he gave to the party he created, *Forza Italia!*, 'Go, Italy!', said it all, and it was exactly what the Italians wanted to hear. Within a year Berlusconi went from being a successful businessman to being prime minister of Italy.

However, it soon transpired that Berlusconi never put the national interest before his own. Not only did he run the country – or pretend to, at any rate – as a business, an idea that was very much *en vogue* in the 1990s, but he ran it as if it were *his own* business, or a subsidiary thereof. Right from the start, much of his energy went into putting legislation in place that was favourable to his companies and himself, and shielded him from the missteps he had perpetrated while becoming and staying rich – mainly corruption and tax fraud. Meanwhile, he began tightening his grip on the Italian mass media, simply by buying them up. That way, some voices warned, the general public could be kept largely ignorant of what Berlusconi did not want them to know, and critical voices could be muffled.

This did not go unnoticed by the Italian judiciary or in the political world at home and abroad, and nor did a series of evermore bizarre incidents and scandals. In the summer of 2003, during the first meeting of the European Union council that Berlusconi chaired, he told Martin Schulz, a German member of the European Parliament, that he would be the perfect candidate to play the part of KAPO, a collaborating inmate of a Nazi concentration camp guarding other inmates, in a film then being made. The huge consternation that ensued abated only after Berlusconi apologized to the German chancellor, Gerhardt Schröder – or seemed to do so, for later Berlusconi denied ever having offered an apology. Not two months later Berlusconi declared publicly that the former fascist dictator Benito Mussolini,

Adolf Hitler's closest ally, had had no blood on his hands: 'He never killed anyone, he just forced people to go on vacation.' There was a certain amount of international outcry, but the Italian people did not care much. As mentioned earlier, there were still quite a few Italians around who could privately be heard sighing *se fosse ancora Lui*, 'if only He were still here,' meaning Mussolini, whenever trains ran late or a strike struck.

Four years later Berlusconi called left-wing voters 'mentally deranged', adding that they ought to be institutionalized. Shortly after Barack Obama became the first black president of the United States in 2008, he told the Russian president Dmitry Medvedev about this new guy in the White House, who is 'handsome, young and well-bronzed'. He parried accusations of racism by saying he meant it as a compliment. When in April of the following year an earthquake destroyed the city of L'Aquila in central Italy, forcing thousands to live in tents, he quipped that these homeless should look upon their plight as a 'weekend on a campsite' (there is something about Berlusconi and involuntary holidays). Meanwhile he ridiculed the entire leadership of NATO by unconcernedly pottering about telephoning the Turkish president Recep Tayyip Erdoğan while the German chancellor, Angela Merkel, stood waiting to officially welcome him. What Berlusconi thinks of Merkel became eminently clear when a phone tap by the justice department revealed him calling her a *culona inchiavabile*, a 'great unfuckable arse'.

Regardless, Berlusconi essentially got off scot-free every time. He even survived the sexual scandal surrounding his so-called bunga-bunga parties, involving underage prostitutes. And although Berlusconi did not really put the Italian economy in order, even by 2014 had not made good on his promise to provide adequate new housing for the victims of the earthquake in L'Aquila, and broke almost every other vow he had made. Well . . . hey, this was Silvio, this was the man who told the rest of the world what's what, the flashy, vulgar self-made guy who knew the street and got rich and now unconcernedly walked among world leaders, and so partly restored the badly damaged face of his frustrated, often ridiculed country. His ridiculing of the high and mighty was a wink to ordinary middle-of-the-road Italians, and they loved him for it. He was always in character, always consistent, and a great many Italians considered the *cavaliere* their knight in shining armour.

Berlusconi finally lost his seat in parliament in 2014, after having irrevocably been found guilty in one of the few tax-fraud cases that he had not been able to defuse. The judiciary may have had him by the balls, but the old fox maintained a considerable following and even threatened to make a comeback in politics. Chances are that in a few years' time, Italians grumpily sighing *se fosse ancora Lui* will be thinking not of Mussolini any more, but of their own hero, Silvio Berlusconi.

If the extravagant Berlusconi spoke out of line and behaved churlishly, it was because that was in his character: he wanted to reaffirm his bond with his voters and – lest we forget – consumers, and more often than not he did it with a flourish and a dash of humour. Berlusconi obviously enjoyed his pranks and the uproar they caused; he was his own biggest fan. Not so the Russian president, Vladimir Putin. There is no trace of humour in this dour man, no sign of mirth. His preferred role is that of the stern, fearless strongman, the antithesis of the glib diplomats of the modern Western world. He used to make a point of slumping in his chair looking bored, legs wide apart, when visiting distinguished and powerful leaders abroad, like a latter-day Al Bundy longing for his TV guide. He loved to flaunt his naked torso on horseback, fishing or hunting, preferably in more or less martial attire, and he openly flirts with the world of criminal motorcycle gangs, bolstering his image as a thug of thugs. In fact, his single original contribution to world culture has been his improvement on the old adage 'If you can't beat them, join them,' when he said, in relation to his warm ties with such unsavoury elements as the Night Wolves Gang: 'If you can't beat them, lead them.'

Unlike Berlusconi's, Putin's rudeness is not meant as a bonding agent with the average Ivan, but merely to impress them. Unlike Berlusconi, Putin is not a salesman and has no time for grand gestures. He prefers the blunt statement, the flat denial, the blatant lie, the direct threat and an attitude of impertinent indifference. He cultivates this disrespectful image with great care, because it serves him very well both in Russia and abroad.

Putin's agenda is about putting Russia back on the world map as a superpower, with himself in charge. To this end, he exploits the old and widespread belief among Russians that they are a special people with a unique, superior culture and a historic destiny, not entirely unlike the way Americans feel about themselves and their country.

Vladimir Putin among bikers near Sebastopol, July 2010.

However, it is hard to ignore the state of disrepair Russia is in, both socially and economically. On top of that, parts of the Russian population, in particular those who made up the old Soviet establishment, feel disparaged and looked down upon by the West. This double insecurity, this jealous rancour, is what Putin taps into, by making a great show of giving all those fanciful arrogant Westerners the finger. And most Russians love it. Putin is their hero, the big brother who has finally come home to teach those bullies out there in the West a lesson. At the same time, he is well aware that his style irks and bewilders Western politicians. That too is a good thing, for he is not out to make friends with anyone. Superior countries don't have friends; they have vassals. He wishes to command if not respect, then at least awe. It may not be a pleasant sight, but Putin's behaviour is totally consistent and gives the Russians the impression that he is serving their interests. That is why, just like Berlusconi, he can misbehave and even lie openly without losing prestige.

Put Silvio Berlusconi and Vladimir Putin into a duck press, squeeze out Berlusconi's sense of humour and Putin's show of physical prowess, square the dregs and you end up with Donald Trump.

He is an utterly improbable character, who became president of the United States against all expectations, even his own. The kind of man nobody wants to live next door to, but whom the American disgruntled loved being in the White House telling the rest of the country and the world beyond who's boss. In 2016 Trump was heralded as an unprecedented and unique force of nature, but his programmes and ideas were a mix of those of the other two gentlemen. He was not their epigone. He was just the same kind of man, successful for the same kinds of reasons. Like the other two, he was free to be as rude and offensive as he liked, to act as impulsively, unreasonably and irresponsibly as he wanted, to claim other people's successes as his own and to lie through his teeth. He could even break certain promises, but he had to keep those on account of which he got elected, even if they were counterproductive and irresponsible. In fact, he *must* do all these things, it was expected of him.

@#$%!

MAKING MISTAKES is not the only way in which an authority figure may lose face. Another is failing to fend off attacks by others. Such attacks can be directed against their person, their legitimacy or their ability to hold sway, but may also threaten the socio-political fabric, which it is the first task of any political leader to protect and preserve.

People all over the world have always had the same basic interests. What they want for themselves and their families is a reasonably safe and comfortable life. This means more than just having enough to eat and a warm and dry place to sleep; Bertolt Brecht's adage *Erst kommt das Fressen, dann kommt die Moral,* 'food comes first, morality later,' is fundamentally wrong. Surely, nobody chewing the bark off the trees for want of proper food is happy. But without a certain level of social order and public organization, absence of hunger means very little. Without some kind of morale, what ensues is Thomas Hobbes's spectre: a war of everyone against all others, and an endless unequal battle of each individual against predators, disease and the forces of nature. For who can be trusted, whose behaviour is even slightly predictable, if people do not share at least some values and some rules of conduct? And what does that spell for the continued availability of Brecht's *Fressen*? So if there is to be any prosperity and any safety at all, some form of social order must be created and maintained.

– In the spring of 2014, in a restaurant in the American town of Wolfeboro, New Hampshire, a woman overheard 82-year-old local police commissioner Robert Copeland calling President Barack Obama a 'fucking nigger'. She protested, but Copeland would not budge then or later. His stubborn refusal to take back his words and apologize caused such uproar among the nearly 7,000 inhabitants of the town that after long and bitter resistance, Copeland was forced to throw in his baton and resign from office.

– At about the same time Maya Peterson, the first female president of the student body of Lawrenceville School and black to boot, was forced by the authorities of that illustrious institution – the most expensive boarding school in the United States – to resign her position 'or else', because of a rather unremarkable photo she'd put up on Instagram. In it, she posed in a Yale sweater, holding an ice-hockey stick and looking very cockily into the camera. She had added hashtags such as #confederate and #peakedinhighschool to make it clear that she was mocking the typical Lawrentian: a conceited, bigoted, humourless right-wing white male. Her reason for doing so were protests by some of these students against her yearbook photo, in which she and some friends made the Black Power salute. She was right about the bigotry and the lack of humour; the school did not take kindly to being bearded by a black girl and forced her out after she had explained that she was indeed 'making a mockery of the right-wing, confederate-flag-hanging, openly misogynistic Lawrentians'.

– On 17 October 2013 the French politician Anne-Sophie Leclère posted a picture on Facebook that would land her in prison. On the left was a monkey over the legend 'at 18 months', on the right the French Guiana-born Minister of Justice, Christiane Taubira, with the text 'today'. 'She is a savage,' Leclère explained to the media. 'When she talks about things on the telly . . . she throws you a devilish smile. The bottom line is, I'd rather see her squatting in a tree among the branches than in the cabinet.' Although Leclère maintained that all this was just a joke and that racism had 'nothing to do with it. A monkey is still an animal, a black is a human being,' she was sentenced to nine months in prison, loss of the right to stand for office for five years, and a €50,000 fine.

– In March 2011 the British fashion designer John Galliano lost his position as chief designer at Christian Dior after an incident in the Marais, a stylish central Paris neighbourhood – formerly predominantly Jewish – that in recent years has become quite the place to live among the well-to-do gay community. For reasons that are unclear Galliano, sitting pissed up to the eyeballs on the terrace of the trendy Café La Perle, fell out with a couple and was subsequently filmed by a bystander slurring his way through 'I love Hitler. People like you would be dead today. Your mothers, your forefathers would be fucking gassed and fucking dead.' It took him three and a half years of grovelling and making amends to return to the fashion scene, this time as creative director with Maison Martin Margiela.

– In the afternoon of 11 September 2001 Jo Moore, Special Adviser to Stephen Byers, the British Secretary of State for Transport, witnessed the devastating attack by Mohammed Atta and his men on the Twin Towers in New York. Watching the horror, a thought struck her. She turned to her keyboard and tapped out an email to the press office of the department: 'It's now a very good day to get out anything we want to bury. Councillors' expenses?' At first, nothing happened, but after a few weeks someone leaked Moore's message to the press and she duly apologized. Again, all seemed well, but on 13 February 2002 a subsequent leak suggested that she had tried to 'bury' unwelcome stuff once more, this time under the interment of Princess Margaret. Although it remains unclear whether she really had done so or had been framed, Moore resigned two days later, turned her back on Whitehall and became a teacher.

– On 6 March 1987 the *Herald of Free Enterprise*, a Channel ferry bound for Dover, sailed from the Belgian port of Zeebrugge without closing her front loading doors and soon capsized, killing 193 passengers. To the embarrassment of many, this tragedy inspired the British Transport Minister Nicholas Ridley to declare shortly afterwards that he would not pursue some policy 'with bow doors open'. That time, Prime Minister Margaret Thatcher saved him, but she did not do so three years later, when in an interview in *The Spectator* he characterized the plans for the European Economic and Monetary Union as 'a German racket designed to take over the whole of Europe', no better than giving up sovereignty to Hitler. On 14 July 1990 he handed in his resignation.

– Considering her appalling lack of tact, it took the British Junior Health Minister Edwina Currie surprisingly long to be axed. In 1986, just months after being appointed, she was heard saying that 'good Christian people' don't get AIDS. Some time later she urged old people too poor to pay the heating bill to wrap up warmly in winter, and declared that Geordies – people living in the northeast of England – usually died of 'ignorance and chips'. Ironically, what did cost her her cabinet post was not another of her lurid opinions, but a statement of fact that was essentially correct. On 3 December 1988 she issued an official warning that 'most of the egg production in this country, sadly, is now affected with salmonella.' Within days, egg sales in Great Britain more than halved, for which Currie was blamed. Only she had been misunderstood. By 'egg production' she had not meant the product – the actual eggs – but the hens that produced them. But the damage was done. Nobody wanted to hear any more, and Currie went back to being a lowly MP.

– The American Secretary of the Interior James G. Watt was a loose cannon if ever there was one. Watt fervently opposed affirmative action, the controversial government policy promoting the emancipation of black people, women and other 'minorities'. Moreover, he had no time for environmentalist nonsense, being very much in favour of the commercial exploitation of federal forests and open land. It made him enemies. He was even rumoured to have said, 'After the last tree is felled, Christ will come back.' Whether or not he actually did is immaterial, for in October 1983 he single-handedly ended his political career. In an effort to deride the excesses of affirmative action, he characterized a committee he was chairing as 'every kind of mix you can have. I have a black, I have a woman, two Jews and a cripple.' It was the word 'cripple' that tripped him up. He resigned within weeks.

– In 1974 the United States Secretary for Agriculture Earl Butz put his country in a tight spot at the World Food Conference by deriding the pope's opposition to birth control. His jocular and essentially correct 'He no playa the game, he no maka the rules,' spoken in a mock Italian accent, did not go down well with so many important people that he was forced to make a formal apology. All went well until he slipped up again in 1976 in a raunchy aeroplane conversation with singers Sonny Bono and Pat Boone and former adviser to President Nixon John Dean. Asked by Boone why the Republican party could not attract more black voters, Butz professed: 'I'll tell you what the coloureds want. It's three things: first, a tight pussy; second, loose shoes; and third, a warm place to shit.' They all laughed, but Dean ratted Butz out to *Rolling Stone* magazine a while later. That was the end of Butz's political career.

Any social order rests on two cornerstones and some form of authority to guarantee their integrity and deal with infractions, calamities and unexpected situations. The first of these cornerstones is the integrity of the family and its fortune. The family affords protection for its children, mutual assistance for the adults and care for the elderly and infirm. It is the seat of the family fortune – money, land, a flock of animals, a workshop and so on – which is the source of prosperity and stability for all members.

The other cornerstone of social order is the trust necessary for transactions between people to work. The transfer of goods and services between parties often involves promises, but it is not humanly possible to keep tabs on everything and everyone all the time. So trust is essential. You would not put your money in a bank if you did not trust it to keep the cash safe and return it to you when you asked for it. Nor would you pay for a subscription to a magazine if you weren't sure that they would actually send it, or put anything in the post if it was likely to be stolen underway. This is why a person's word is so important in all cultures.

Looking at the world from a modern European perspective, from countries with effective administrations and brimming with laws, protocols, organizations and institutions that ensure our welfare, it is all too easy to underestimate the importance of both the family and a person's word in times less abundantly appointed. We may not be all that happy with the sometimes stifling red tape that rules our lives, but think for a minute about how even our own immensely rich neck of the global woods looked only a few generations ago. It was a world without anything like a state pension, child support, unemployment benefits or health insurance. A relatively simple world, but insecure and hard to live in, even for the few who were fortunate enough to be able to afford good housing and plenty of food and drink. Between themselves, Charles Dickens and Jane Austen painted a pretty good picture of Europe before the turn of the twentieth century. Middle-class people lived on the muddy, slippery shores of an ocean of poverty. Destitution lurked around the corner, just one stroke of bad luck, one bad investment, illness or fire away. Their first priority was to keep what family fortune there was intact for the present generation and the next.

Apart from the usual precautions against theft and robbery, sexual integrity was paramount. The last thing anyone would want was a cuckoo in the nest, nibbling away at the family reserves. It is not an accident that much swearing and name-calling is directed against sexual impropriety. *Bastard*, the venerable English slur *whoreson*, the Black American *motherfucker*, *bint iššaṛmuuṭa* and *ibn il'aḥba*, 'daughter/son of a whore', from the Arabic world, Polish *kurwa (jego) mać*, 'whore your mother', Yoruba *ọmáàlè*, 'child of concubine: bastard' and Spanish *hijo de puta* all testify to the deep fear of interlopers. Nor is it surprising that all societies have laws and principles regulating who can play what carnal games, and with whom. The sole apparent exception – the relaxed, sexually libertarian society of Samoa that the anthropologist Margaret Mead made famous in 1928 – eventually turned out not to exist. In societies with strict divorce laws, adultery would typically be one of the few accepted grounds for terminating a marriage. In the Netherlands it was the only accepted reason for getting a divorce until 1971, a circumstance that gave rise to the so-called great lie, spouses falsely admitting to adultery in order to be able to break out of a soured marriage. In Great Britain adultery, understood as extramarital intercourse with a member of the opposite sex (probably because homosexual transgressions cannot result in offspring), is still the most prominent of the five grounds for divorce.

Laws against adultery and incest are also among the oldest in the world. The most obvious example is the biblical commandment 'Thou shalt not commit adultery' of Exodus 20:14. It is by no means the first, however. Hammurabi's Code of Laws, dating back to 1780 BCE and representing the apogee rather than the beginning of a still older tradition of legislation, contains detailed rules concerning marriage, divorce, adoption, inheritance and the sexual transgressions adultery and incest. Hammurabi's punishment for an adulterous wife is to be drowned (law 143). The father who commits incest with his daughter incurs banishment (law 154), and mothers and sons who engage in the kind of incest Oedipus committed both risk being burned to death (law 157). In today's Western world such punishments are generally considered barbaric, but not necessarily elsewhere. In many parts of the Muslim world stoning is still an accepted sanction against adulterous women, and corporal punishment such as caning or whipping for lesser crimes like kissing or holding hands while not married are not only accepted but on the rise. In Europe and in slightly more than half of the states of the United States of America, adultery is no longer a criminal offence. However, in recent years it has been replaced by a growing obsession with sex offenders and especially paedophiles that sometimes borders on an all-out witch-hunt.

Remarkably, Hammurabi's Code does not mention homosexuality. The Bible does, however. Leviticus demands that not only all adulterers be put to death, but the man who lies 'with mankind, as he lieth with a woman' (Leviticus 20:13). This is still the case in many parts of the world. Tolerance towards homosexuals is a fairly recent phenomenon, mostly restricted to northwestern Europe and parts of North America.

To some extent, the traditionally negative attitude towards homosexuality is understandable. By their very existence, homosexuals seem to thumb their noses at all the preciously upheld traditional codes of sexual conduct. In that sense, they inspire uncertainty, which is for most people a very unwelcome emotion. As a consequence a fair number of societies – Iran and Turkey are examples, but also parts of Africa and Eastern Asia – stringently claim that homosexuality simply does not exist in their country. Yet they all have punishments to guarantee that homosexuals know better than to flaunt their orientation. Russia is one country where the government has begun to blame homosexuals for almost anything in much the same way that the Jews were blamed for everything during the interwar period, including suggestions of a malevolent worldwide conspiracy. To give an example: in 2013 all sorts of Russian businesses – pharmacies, supermarkets, purveyors of stationery – were 'exposed' as fronts for the international homosexual conspiracy to defile and demoralize Russia, simply because their company logo sported a rainbow.

The existence of so many laws and threats regarding sexual conduct alone bears witness to the fact that boys will be just that, and girls will be girls, regardless. Another interesting consequence of the chasm between laws, principles and good intentions on the one hand and the messiness of real life on the other is that sexual transgressions per se need not be detrimental to a leader's prestige. As with words, powerful people may transgress the boundaries of propriety without sanction, provided certain conditions are met.

In Fascist Italy, it was not much of a secret that Benito Mussolini received delectable young ladies daily in his office, the colossal *Sala del Mappamondo*, the World Map Room, in the Palazzo Venezia in Rome, enjoying them between *pasta* and *postre*. It was only natural that the duce, endowed with a libido befitting his station, should have to let off steam every now and then. In February 1899, some twenty years before Mussolini came to power, the French had just smiled when their president Felix Fauré suddenly died at the Élysée Palace in the arms of his mistress, a demi-mondaine called Marguerite Steinheil, if not actually in the act. One-time vice-president of the United States Nelson Rockefeller met with *mort douce*, sweet death, at night in the sole company of a female not his spouse, as well, and it did not hurt his reputation in any way. One of the most amazing things about the presidency of John F. Kennedy is the silence surrounding his voracious sexual appetite. Not a skirt was safe when he was around. As soon as First Lady Jackie Kennedy was away from the White House – which was every weekend at least – so many unfamiliar women sped through the corridors to help relieve the president that the Secret Service, responsible for the safety of the First Family, eventually gave up checking and just ignored them. Not one woman, not one cuckolded husband complained, then or afterwards.

Even Bill Clinton, who was effectively caught with his pants down – although the 42nd president of the United States would certainly object that it was a matter of opinion what 'pants' and 'down' really meant – came away from the Monica Lewinsky scandal unscathed. Neither the widely advertised embarrassing find of his semen on the intern's dress nor his hedging and sometimes blatant lying could hurt him. He simply went on to become one of the most respected and highly paid public speakers in the world. Meanwhile Jacques Chirac, president of France from 1997 to 2007, was known in high circles as *monsieur vingt minutes, avec douche*, 'Mr Twenty Minutes, shower included'. And then there was Chirac's infamous compatriot Dominique Strauss-Kahn. He was a man with a brilliant career at the International Monetary Fund who had been Secretary of State three times and seemed destined to become president of France in 2012. At the same time DSK, as he was fondly known, was a pathological womanizer, which earned him a second nickname: *monsieur trente centimètres*, 'Mr Twelve Inches'. His extravagant sexual tastes had never been a problem, until in April 2011 a New York chambermaid accused him of forcing her to perform sex on the way from shaving mirror to trouser stand. DSK was duly arrested and at that moment fell from the ranks of those who were not hurt by their promiscuous behaviour, to suffer the sorry fate of men like John Profumo.

What had changed? Why did this chambermaid matter, whereas the countless women with whom DSK had had his way before had not? The difference was that DSK's earlier adventures had somehow been perceived as natural for a man in his position. Far from commendable, to be sure, distasteful and perhaps reprehensible, but not incongruous. He was a libidinous and powerful man. Regardless of laws and morality, such men are expected to show some alpha-male behaviour, up to and including swinging their dicks a lot, like animals staking out their territory. It had been the same with Fauré,

Mussolini, Rockefeller, Kennedy (a sexy charmer if ever there was one) and Clinton, who also had that rakish twinkle in the eye that made many forgive him almost anything. What was not acceptable, however, was sexually manhandling a powerless underling, a purely accidental bystander. That amounted to biting the hand of the public that fed him. It was unbecoming conduct, turning DSK from an intimidating but respected powerhouse into a creepy rapist, an unsavoury bully of the kind people fear but do not respect.

A good illustration of how quickly attitudes may change towards what is and is not acceptable bad behaviour is the case of Jack de Vries, a former spin doctor for the Dutch Christian Democrats, as always the gallant champions of family values. Three years after he had been appointed Undersecretary for Defence in 2007, his wife found out that in the course of several trips to the Dutch troops in Afghanistan her husband's relationship with his personal secretary had developed into a full-blown love affair, and summarily kicked him out of their house. For security reasons, the suddenly homeless undersecretary was put up in an army barracks for a while, which did not go unnoticed. Within days his marital problems and his affair were public knowledge. De Vries was sufficiently popular not to be hurt too much by remarks about yet another Christian Democrat saint in public who sinned in secret. What was unacceptable and forced him to resign was something people would hardly have cared about in Profumo's day: the inequality between him and his lover, the simple fact that he was her boss.

Sexual transgressions by powerful people are subject to the same rules as verbal ones. As long as transgressions are perceived as somehow in character with both the person and their position, prestige remains intact. It is lost only when behaviour is incongruous or when there are complicating factors of an embarrassing kind. Or if someone just goes way too far and bites the hand that feeds them, as DSK did.

Unhampered and reliable political and commercial relations are no less important than sexual integrity. Especially during times when the political power structure rested on personal loyalty between a king and his peers, and commercial relations depended on the self-professed honesty of the partners involved, the solemnity and sincerity of oaths and a person's word were not to be taken lightly. In a way, people who swore and cursed for no good reason had the same upsetting effect with respect to the integrity of the indispensable loyalty network as homosexuality had on the house of cards of sexual integrity: they thumbed their noses at it and by doing so trivialized it. It is no surprise, then, that rulers have tried time and time again to curb people's mouths. In France, King Louis XI, better known as St Louis, decreed during the thirteenth century that swearers should have their faces marked with a branding iron. Even earlier, Henry I of England, son of William the Conqueror, had drawn up a list of fines for swearing at the royal palace, ranging from 40 shillings for a foul-mouthed duke to half a mark for a yeoman. Pages, who were supposed to have no money at all, would simply be whipped.

None of these or many other measures had more than a fleeting effect on people's behaviour. Not even threatening to rip out a swearer's tongue, and following up on it. In 1543 Thomas Becon lamented that:

> this damnable use of swearing hath so greatly prevailed among them that profess Christ that it is also crept into the breasts of young children. It is not a rare thing now-a-days to hear boys and mothers tear the most blessed body of Christ with their blasphemous oaths, even from the top to the toe. What marvel is it then though they be abominable swearers when they come to age? But whence learn they this? Verily from their parents and such as bring them up.[1]

Apparently, not much has changed on this score.

As would be expected, the English Puritans did everything they could to stamp out all 'impious expressions' by means of harsh repression. In 1635 they even established a public department for the enforcement of the laws against swearing, only to be outdone by the Scottish Parliament in 1649, when it declared cursing a parent to be a capital offence. These were truly Talibanesque times, both in Britain and elsewhere in Europe, but they were soon to end. In the summer of 1648 the Peace of Westphalia ended the religious wars that had been ravaging the continent, and by 1661 the English Puritans lost their power when England, Scotland and Ireland were united under King Charles II, a most unpuritanical figure, who liked to teach his mistresses how to curse most vilely.

The moment the heavy lid of Puritan oppression was taken off society marked the start of a period of playful libertinism not unlike that which began in the 1960s and lasted until roughly 2001. Anything went, for a while. But soon the first Societies for the Reformation of Manners raised their worrisome heads, and by 1700 actors and playwrights had largely succumbed to their pressure. Censorship was back, and it was here to stay.

@#$%!

CENSORSHIP COMES IN MANY GUISES, but its objective is always the same: to keep people from entertaining ideas and adopting habits and policies the powers that be prefer them not to indulge in. One important part of this is keeping people in the dark about much of what those powers themselves think and do. The other is to prevent potentially disruptive ideas from forming, spreading and taking root among the population. All these efforts, whether made by governments to control the population or by companies, parties and associations to control their staff or membership, are clearly political in nature. They serve to maintain the existing balance of power and the social status quo.

Cultural censorship, as exemplified by de-platforming, bowdlerizing, historical cleansing and tabooing terms and expressions, would appear to be different. First of all, it originates not in the state but in the personal views of private people. And whereas secular censorship – that is, censorship by the state or some other hierarchical institution – is mainly about secrecy, guarding the reputation of the powerful and maintaining social order, cultural and moral censorship centre on obscenity. Cultural censorship is the weapon of reactionaries and idealists alike. The former wish to preserve a society's cultural and moral status quo, the latter to mould the minds of people according to a preferred world-view by tabooing and demonizing any ideas that don't agree with it. So when push comes to shove, cultural censorship is about power and control as well, which entails that all censorship is essentially political.

Sometimes, these two kinds of censorship blend into one, as happened in 2014 when the Russian Parliament with Putin's blessing adopted a law banning 'indiscriminate profanity'. The people behind the law claimed that they wished to protect 'Received Russian' from the onslaught of the thousands of extremely juicy profane expressions and expletives that the Russians have always been masters at coining. Critics of the regime, however, considered it a revival of Soviet conservatism. On the other hand, since the law does not specify what exactly constitutes indiscriminate profanity, and Russians do seem to swear rather a lot, it may just serve as a vague arbitrary threat, yet another means to intimidate the population into docility.

The Roman Catholic Church offers what may well be the greatest example in history of the efficacy of a very simple form of censorship. For approximately fifteen centuries, its innumerable members were kept in the dark about what actually was in the Bible, the Holy Writ on which the Church based its authority. This was done by keeping it as well as the liturgy in Latin, a language that, after the demise of the Roman Empire, was understood only by the better-educated few. Effectively, this turned the whole thing into one great mystery – quite a plus for a religion – even to parts of the clergy, many of whom weren't too well versed in Latin either.

This passive form of censoring served the Church well for a thousand years, until reformers such as Martin Luther appeared on the scene, claiming, among other things, that religion belonged not to a privileged caste of priests, to exploit economically and politically as they saw fit, but to the faithful. Rome and its clergy stuck to their guns, and eventually Western Christianity was torn limb from limb by the Reformation. It wasn't until 1965 that Rome grudgingly gave up on its exclusively Latin liturgy. What followed looked a lot like the developments in England after the demise of Puritan oppression: a frenzy of religious libertinism and experimentation, followed by a clampdown by conservative clergy. Meanwhile, the Church had easily lost more than half of its flock in northwestern Europe, and much of its socio-political influence.

There is a lesson in this to all incumbent and aspiring authoritarian rulers, including the civil servants of the modern democracies: if you empower the people, there is no limit to what might happen. The Church of Rome paid dearly for its modernization, although it really had no alternative. Similarly, as educational standards rose and their mystical gloss dulled, physicians saw their patients become steadily less deferential and more demanding, even though the profession actually had much more to offer. Then the Internet came along to pour yet more oil on the fire. From a place where doctors held sway with quiet, unquestioned authority, the surgery has gone some way towards becoming a medieval stronghold beleaguered by people clamouring for diagnoses, treatments, pills and whatever else they feel entitled to.

So far, Islam has not suffered a similar fate, although throughout its existence it has practised a similar form of passive censorship. The Quran, supposedly dictated by God to the Prophet Muhammad, is in classical Arabic or Fuṣḥā, a dialect that nobody uses in everyday life and that isn't taught in schools. To read the Book, one must put in considerable extra effort. There is no prohibition on translations, but warnings apply that no translation can ever do justice to the real thing. Thus, the imams, muftis and mullahs, who do put in the effort of learning Fuṣḥā, always have a comfortable head start when it comes to interpreting their Holy Writ.

Neither Roman Catholicism nor Islam has left it at that. Both employed and continue to employ more active forms of censorship as well. Islam in principle prohibits all images of humans as a form of idolatry. Furthermore, unwelcome books can be outlawed by fatwa, as Salman Rushdie learned the hard way in 1989, when his *Satanic Verses* angered Ayatollah Khomeini, the leader of the Iranian religious junta.

Although the term 'censorship' and the practice of monitoring public morale date back to Roman antiquity and, especially following the invention of moveable type around 1450, many attempts to suppress unwelcome information had been made by worldly and religious authorities alike, it was the Church of Rome that first instituted a regulated all-encompassing system of 'modern' censoring in 1559. The *Index librorum prohibitorum*, or 'list of forbidden books', as the system was called, was based on ten rules formulated at the Council of Trent, and kept up to date by the Sacred Congregation of the Index, a Papal department created especially to this end in 1571. The Index, as it was referred to for short, persisted until 1966. At that time it contained roughly 4,000 titles, including works by such diverse writers as John Calvin, René Descartes, Laurence Sterne, Stendhal, Heinrich Heine, Gabriele D'Annunzio, Alberto Moravia and Simone de Beauvoir. Of course, placing them on the Index did not make disagreeable works go away completely, much less the unwelcome ideas they embodied. It did, however, hamper their distribution and came in handy when grounds were sought for curbing unruly intellectuals and freethinkers. Most important of all, it sent a powerful message to society at large about what the authorities deemed acceptable and what was considered dangerous thought that people would do well not to engage in.

In true Roman Catholic style, in 1589 the Church forbade believers even to own a copy of the Index itself, meaning the mere *list*, as well. This rendered the Index almost as mysterious as the Latin liturgy, and gave clergy the opportunity of bullying their parishioners through finding fault with their reading. Thus it became one more instrument for intimidating the flock and inspiring feelings of guilt and inadequacy among it, the lifeblood of all the great religions.

While for a long time the Index was reasonably effective in suppressing the spread of works that were deemed immoral, heretical or seditious, it did little to prevent their inception and had no immediate effect on the fast-growing flood of occasional pamphlets, flyers and – from 1609, when the first fledgling regular newsletter, the *Relation aller Fürnemmen und gedenckwürdigen Historien* (Account of All the Important and Memorable News), took wing in Strasbourg – newspapers. But there were plenty of other ways for authorities to do this: importation bans, for instance, and taxes on the printed materials themselves, on paper and other necessary materials, or on their distribution. Before the age of broadcast media, an even more effective and simple method of controlling what might meet the public eye proved to be controlling the number of printers and their behaviour by means of licensing. In England this was done through the Stationers' Company, nowadays a trade association but originally a medieval guild founded in 1403. This institution was granted a monopoly on the printing trade in 1557. From then on, only the 21 licensed printers in London and two universities could legally own and operate printing presses. Of course, these chosen few toed the line for fear of being reprimanded or even losing their licence.

As the demand for books, treatises and newspapers kept growing, English regulation was intensified by the Licensing Act 1662, entitled 'An Act for preventing the frequent Abuses in printing seditious treasonable and unlicensed Books and Pamphlets and for regulating of Printing and Printing Presses'. With it came an official licenser, a kind of one-man inquisition in the person of Roger L'Estrange, with powers not unlike those of the Nazi Gestapo during the Second World War. He could search anyone's premises on the least suspicion of the presence of illegal printing equipment, seize what he found and have the owners arrested and brought to justice.

L'Estrange performed these duties with great as well as partisan zeal, and succeeded in reducing both the stream of publications and the public debate on political matters to a mere trickle. He managed, for instance, to close down virtually all newspapers except his own favourite, the *London Gazette*.

Until this time censorship had been mainly indirect. It regulated the general flow of print as a tap regulates the flow of water. Catholic authors were encouraged to present their manuscripts to the Sacred Congregation before publication to avoid a ban, but there was little systematic interference with what exactly was being published. In England this now changed; the licenser was there for prevention. All risky materials could and should be presented to him for permission to print before publication. In time, the Licensing Act itself developed into copyright law and gave way to more specific libel, obscenity and secrecy laws. But while at some point during the eighteenth century the official licenser disappeared as well, the practice of censoring theatrical plays – first from the late sixteenth century by the Master of the Revels, and later by the Lord Chamberlain's Office – continued until it was finally abolished in 1968. Upon learning that more than sixty cuts had been made in the manuscript of one of his plays, Sir Lawrence Evelyn Jones made an appointment with the censor, and 'apart from some perfectly loyal references to Queen Victoria, who, with God, is unmentionable on the stage, and a third "bloody" (the allowance is two), all the cuts were restored.'[2] This was in 1939, 25 years after the outcry over *Pygmalion*, when Queen Victoria had been good and dead for nigh on four decades!

The details are different every time, but in the course of history similar developments took place in every more or less literate society on Earth. In many, blatantly political censorship is still very much alive, aiming to stamp out any criticism of the government or its ideology. A poignant recent example is what happened when the Chinese democracy advocate Liu Xiaobo was awarded the Nobel Peace Prize in 2010. Liu had been imprisoned the year before on account of his sustained criticism of China's undemocratic one-party regime and grubby human-rights situation. Immediately the state-controlled Chinese media were instructed not to let on about what happened, and duly obliged. CNN, which is available in some hotels and expats' compounds, was blacked out, as were all text messages containing his name. The Great Firewall, China's Internet-censoring effort, did its job and Liu's wife was put under house arrest and told not to contact anyone. Unbeknown to the Chinese people, their Nobel laureate festered in prison until 2017, when he was diagnosed with liver cancer and allowed to go to hospital. He died within three weeks.

Such ruthless censorship works quite well. Most Chinese have no idea that Liu ever existed, and where information did leak through the cracks it sent a very clear message: Don't you dare question authorities or raise your voice in any way, or we'll come down on you like a ton of bricks.

Meanwhile, something peculiar happened in those countries that some three hundred years ago began to show the first signs of developing towards what we now call modern democracies. As little by little the influence on policy of ever larger circles of the citizenry grew, more and more people outside the traditional tiny coteries of the courts had to be sufficiently well informed to propose and support sensible arguments and decisions. This development rationalized politics, away from the old authoritarian styles of government driven by faith, family ties and a ruler's fancy. To some extent, declarations of undying loyalty or enmity were replaced by information, debate, discussion and, ultimately, compromise. As far as we know, something like this first happened in classical Athens and in the Roman Republic, where it ultimately failed. However, as the Enlightenment got underway, it became apparent that such a process had started anew, for instance in the English Bill of Rights of 1689, which granted the right to speak freely in parliament. The American and French revolutions took the idea further, expanding it into what we now know as the freedoms of speech and press, of assembly and of receiving information, applying to everyone.

These freedoms are essential for the citizenry to be able to partake in managing society. They are also fundamentally incompatible with across-the-board censorship of the kind L'Estrange practised. Nevertheless, even democratic governments and their political elites have a vested interest in controlling and limiting the flow of information. Rightly or wrongly, they have secrets to protect, and they are responsible for keeping public order – there is a limit to the amount of infighting and upheaval a society can sustain without falling apart. Also, they have an obligation to protect the rights and freedoms of *all* their citizens, both from external dangers and from each other.

One result of this paradoxical political challenge has been that by and by general repression of non-mainstream opinions has given way to more specific laws imposing specific limitations on the freedom of speech. In terms of suppression, some of these are little better than the old ways, such as the British Official Secrets Act and the Patriot Act the Americans set up after the shocking attacks of 11 September 2001. Others, obscenity laws for example, often proved hardly tenable in the face of changing public morale, and became sources of controversy that focused attention on just the kind of smut they had been designed to eradicate or, failing that, keep under wraps.

The other result was that a great deal of censorship became privatized. An early example of this was Thomas Bowdler's initiative to expurgate Shakespeare's works. The preface to *The Family Shakespeare*, which was published in 1818, stated that the good doctor had intended:

> to present to the public an edition of his Plays, which the parent, the guardian, and the instructor of youth, may place without fear in the hands of the pupil; and from which the pupil may derive instruction as well as pleasure; may improve his moral principles, while he refines his taste; and without incurring the danger of being hurt with any indelicacy of expression.

Although *The Family Shakespeare* was a success that inspired quite a few similar undertakings, and although Bowdler's name became an eponym, many of his contemporaries had reservations. Right from the start, 'bowdlerization' had a negative ring, closer to eviscerating literature than to giving it a much-needed polish.

Nevertheless, censorship in the burgeoning democracies of the Western world flourished, especially where morality and royals were concerned. Lese-majesty, insulting the monarch, was an actively and eagerly prosecuted crime, and until the 1960s both public authorities and private institutions more or less effectively curtailed the possibilities for authors, artists, cineastes and pornographers to confront the public with ideas and images considered undesirable or improper. Ever since the British Board of Film Censors, now the British Board of Film Classification, was instituted by the industry in 1912, no film, video or television producer in their right mind would invest

BBC radio and related television programmes such as *Top of the Pops* have quite a reputation for suppressing music that does not meet their standards of taste and decency. Poppy use of classical themes was long frowned upon, just like making light of religion. But worst of all were references to death, sex and drugs, the very staples of rock 'n' roll. For these reasons, songs such as T. Texas Tyler's 'Deck of Cards' (1948), Ella Fitzgerald's 'Love for Sale' (1956) and 'Bewitched, Bothered and Bewildered' (1958), plus 'I Am the Walrus', 'Lucy in the Sky with Diamonds' and 'A Day in the Life' (all 1967) and 'Come Together' by the Beatles (1969) were banned from Britain's airwaves. The same fate befell Billie Holiday's 'Gloomy Sunday' (1941), 'Leader of the Pack' by the Shangri-Las (1964), the Troggs' hit single 'I Can't Control Myself' (1966) and of course the apogee of the art of heavy breathing, 'Je t'aime . . . moi non plus', moaned by Jane Birkin and Serge Gainsbourg in 1969. In 1977 Ian Dury virtually asked for a ban with 'Sex & Drugs & Rock & Roll' – and got his wish. Although the BBC claims to have given up on banning around 2010, it banned Frenzo Harami's 'Chaabian Boys' in 2019, even after it had been purged of swearing, for references to organized prostitution. And in 2020 BBC Radio 1 would allow 'Fairytale of New York', a Christmas classic by Kirsty MacColl and the Pogues, in a bowdlerized version only, because its 'young listeners were particularly sensitive to derogatory terms for gender and sexuality'.

Way back in 1965, the Who found no favour with their rebellious 'My Generation', and the Sex Pistols were duly rapped on the knuckles for their shocking 1977 hit 'God Save the Queen ("the fascist regime")'; at the BBC, the monarchy remains inviolable. Speaking of queens, the Tom Robinson Band saw Auntie close the door on 'Glad to Be Gay' the following year. The same thing happened to George Michael with 'I Want Your Sex' in 1987, and, decades before, Louis Prima with 'Please No Squeeza da Banana' (1945). Unsurprisingly, 'Too Drunk to Fuck' by the Dead Kennedys (1981) and 'Fucking in Heaven' by Fat Boy Slim (1998) got the hatchet as well. Even 'My Little Ukulele' by Joe Brown and the Bruvvers did not pass muster in 1963, let alone George Formby's original, 'With My Little Ukulele in My Hand', thirty years before that. Sometimes, a ban was limited to a phrase or word. Thus in 1967 the Rolling Stones were ordered to change 'Let's Spend the Night Together' into 'Let's Spend Some Time Together', while the Kinks had to replace the brand name 'Coca Cola' in 'Lola' with 'cherry cola'.

In a number of cases songs were banned for political reasons. This happened, among others, to Noël Coward's 'Don't Let's Be Beastly to the Germans'

(1943), 'Eve of Destruction' by Barry McGuire (1965), 'Give Ireland Back to the Irish' by Wings (1972), 'Killing an Arab' by the Cure (1979) during the Gulf War of 1990–91 and 'Ding-Dong! The Witch Is Dead', from the 1939 musical *The Wizard of Oz*, when it spontaneously rose to number two in the charts after the death of Margaret Thatcher in 2013. In 1982 it was the Australian band Split Enz's misfortune to run into the Falklands War with their 'Six Months in a Leaky Boat'.

There is a strange irony in that among the earliest pieces of music ever banned by the BBC were 'Radio Times' by the BBC's own Dance Orchestra (1935) and, in 1932, 'We Can't Let You Broadcast That' by Norman Long. Other than that, only one thing is for sure: at the BBC, a dirty mind is a joy forever. (Source: Wikipedia's List of Songs Banned by the BBC)

in anything that might not get a rating from it. Without a rating, distributing your product would be nigh impossible. Other countries developed their own comparable systems of private censorship and self-regulation, journalistic codes and standards. Such codes and standards always purport to enhance quality and protect integrity, but often border on censorship and promote self-censorship.

In some cases, private initiative takes the place of state censorship. This happened, for instance, in December 2010, shortly after WikiLeaks had published thousands of diplomatic cables showing – what a surprise – that American embassies facilitated espionage. Soon PayPal and all American credit-card companies were refusing to process transactions involving WikiLeaks, in an attempt to starve the platform out of existence. A few years before this, something similar had happened in the Netherlands. An association of anti-monarchists and one advocating paedophilia, both perfectly legal at the time, found it impossible to open a bank account anywhere. In the twenty-first century such denial of service is tantamount to putting an organization out of business. These were in fact early examples of what later became known as cancel culture.

From about 2010 the advent of social media sparked a whole new and rather frightening form of private censorship. Initially, following the lead of Internet service providers, social-media platforms such as Facebook, YouTube and Twitter saw themselves as equivalent to traditional telephone companies and postal services. They were mere facilitators, providing the means for people to reach out to each other and interact, but not involved in or responsible for the uses to which their clients put their services. Strangely, the prudish and turnover-conscious Facebook did not abide by its own self-image right from the beginning. It was quick to ban any image even remotely interpretable as referring to sexuality – an ironic policy for a platform that had started out as a student site for rating dateable girls. Soon the others too began monitoring and censoring the content that was uploaded. These activities were partly inspired by the growing waves of truly nasty smut and violent verbal abuse that flooded the 'socials'. More and more, too, they were caused by pressure from governments and private parties who worried about these vast and unregulated playpens for the great unwashed. Inexorably, they forced first the access and service providers, and then the social-media platforms, into the position of publishers, who could be held responsible for what materials they made available through their channels. By 2018 each platform had strict policies in place, with hundreds, maybe thousands of censors busily scouring servers and blocking the accounts of any user they deemed guilty of overstepping the bounds.

Although efforts to spare users of social media unsought confrontation with revolting images and footage of torture, executions, sadistic child abuse and the like are understandable and perhaps even commendable, the ways the platforms operate are, mildly put, problematic. First, private companies are concerned with their own continuity and profitability rather than with principles of legal and moral propriety and civil rights. Faced with pressure from governments and activist fanatics they will invariably play it safe. Therefore, no matter how meticulously they formulate their criteria and how scrupulously they apply them, they will inevitably cast their nets wide and in doing so maximize the number of unacceptable utterances, for fear of letting anything slip through that they might be held accountable for. Nor does any company wish to jeopardize its access to, say, the Chinese market, making them vulnerable to blackmail. This approach flies squarely in the face of freedom of expression, which is expressly designed to do the opposite. Freedom of expression, however formulated, first grants people the right to vent their ideas, opinions and whatever else they want to share. Only then, if there is reason to do so, can utterances and their producers be subjected to judicial scrutiny and, eventually, prosecution, on clear and specific legal grounds. To authoritarian regimes all this doesn't make a difference, but a free flow of ideas and information is the lifeblood of any democracy worth its salt. To them, any obstruction of it is a serious problem and a danger.

Second, what with the speed and size of the Internet, much of the censoring is done by sloppily trained people who must hastily judge huge amounts of material in languages they don't necessarily speak, stemming from cultures they don't understand. More and more frequently, this leads to errors and unwarranted interruption of service to innocent, well-intentioned clients. To give one example: in early June 2019 YouTube closed down the channel of the Regional Archives of the Dutch city of Alkmaar, a respected historical institution, on grounds of purported hate-mongering. All the archives had done was publish some educational videos in connection with the 75th anniversary of the Allied invasion in Normandy, which included Second World War footage showing a swastika and a propaganda film featuring marching members of the Dutch National Socialist Movement. It goes to show the mindless shallowness of Internet censorship, its arbitrariness and above all its detrimental irrelevance.

At the same time, partly owing to the sheer amount of horrendous filth floating around on the Internet, these human censors are waging an impossible war that wreaks havoc with their mental health. This is one of many reasons for so much energy being directed towards developing artificial intelligence to do the job for them. Computers don't care, is the idea. They don't get upset or tired, they just get on with the job at hand as relentlessly as they are impartial. Unfortunately, this not only sounds too good to be true, it *is* too good to be true. Yes, computers do not get upset or tired, and they are certainly relentless, but they are just as biased and fallible as the people who programmed them, or worse.

Computers are much faster and far more reliable than people at carrying out well-defined, highly standardized tasks: things like welding together parts of a car arriving on a meticulously organized conveyor belt, making minute high-precision cuts in human flesh when instructed to do so by a human surgeon behind a microscope, or doing complex mathematical, statistical and financial calculations. But they cannot deal very well with the surprises, the variability and the ambiguity that the messy world of human life is rife with. Here is why.

Basically, computer programs consist of two kinds of operation: loops and algorithms. Loops are good for monitoring situations. They are like the thermostat that checks the temperature in your living room and checks it again, and again, and again, and again, until kingdom come or some external force – you, for instance – turns it off. An algorithm, on the other hand, is a decision procedure. It consists of an ordered set of explicit instructions that will always answer a specific question put to it within a limited amount of time and then stop. It is the part of your heating system that turns the boiler on or off with each temperature check by the thermostat: is the temperature below 20°C? Then if the boiler is off, turn it on. And conversely.

It is easy enough to program a way of making the right decisions within small-scale and closed universes as simple as central heating. However, as systems get more complex, so does the task of the programmer. There are not just more decision-making processes to identify, break down to the last detail and put back together in the form of an algorithm, but also these processes must interact with one another in many ways. Soon human programmers lose oversight and have to take recourse in mathematical techniques to ensure that their programs are sound and actually do what they designed them to do. In this way, remarkable successes have been achieved, such as uncannily real flight simulators, automatic pilots and, perhaps most spectacular of all, facial recognition. Still, the last skill is basically a matter of matching a few score points and relative distances in one isolated environment, the general layout of the human face. From 'This is a face, tell me which picture in our carefully designed photo database it matches best' to 'Here's a picture, tell me what's in it and what it means' is a giant leap.

Interpreting random pictures, which is what the social-media platforms want, involves so many environments, circumstances, shapes, movements, hues and connotations that no number of programmers, however clever, could ever hope to finish the job of building and integrating all the necessary loops and algorithms, assuming that they even knew how to go about it. But since they are indeed clever, computer scientists realized this very early on and started to work on a completely different technique: so-called neural networks.

Unlike traditional computer programs, human brains are excellent at performing poorly defined complex tasks such as interpreting pictures. Brains basically consist of a huge mass of interconnected neurons. As far as we know, they develop and perfect many of their skills by fine-tuning the strength of these connections on the basis of exposure and experience. Neural networks are an attempt at mimicking such brains. They are electronic networks of interconnected nodules that can change and reconfigure their own connections. By feeding it pictures and telling it whether it reacts well or poorly, we can train the network to react the way we want it to, much as we train a dog to perform tricks. For instance, we can train a neural network to raise the alarm whenever it 'sees' something resembling a swastika or fascist boots marching. Or a bare nipple.

To some extent, neural networks have been successful, but these successes come at high cost. The price is loss of certainty and control. Traditional programs may be cumbersome and limited in scope, but if they are constructed with sufficiently meticulous care you can be absolutely certain of what they do, step by step, instruction by instruction. Such programs are completely predictable. Neural networks, on the other hand, are black boxes. All we can see is what final answer they produce to questions we put in, as when we show a network a picture and it answers 'porn!' The thing is that we have no idea what happens in between. How and why the network arrives at some conclusion remains a mystery, even if we opened up the box and inspected its contents. As a consequence, we can never be sure it will give the same answer to what we think is the same question every time. It might even acquire highly undesirable operational characteristics without us noticing or being able to correct it.

A famous example of the practical dangers that lurk here comes to us from the Cold War. Around 1980 NATO felt the need for a system that could automatically detect the presence of Soviet tank formations hidden in the woods of Central Europe from aerial photographs. Researchers set to work, training a neural network by means of an extensive set of photographs already taken by NATO's most hush-hush satellites and spy planes, and analysed by hand. After a while the network caught on, and before long it was time for a demonstration to NATO's top brass. On this occasion, a new set of photographs was used, and Murphy's Law struck: the system got almost nothing right. Nobody understood why until, one day, a researcher took another good look at the original set of photographs. Suddenly it hit him: by chance, the vast majority of photos without tank formations had been made on overcast days, whereas those that did contain tank formations had mostly been taken in bright sunshine. The neural network had never 'understood' anything at all about tank formations. All it had learned to do was differentiate between high-contrast photographs and low-contrast ones.

Four decades on, in 2017, a group of dermatologists claimed in the journal *Nature* that they had developed a neural network that was better at detecting moles that were likely to develop into skin cancer than experienced live dermatologists, albeit by a margin of only 0.5–1.5 per cent.[3] Soon, however, they realized – and made public – that there was something fishy about their results. It turned out that among the photos the system had been trained on, most that showed suspicious moles also included a ruler, since dermatologists tend to include a ruler in photos they take of iffy moles, to give their colleagues an idea of size. So the system registered rulers rather than cancer. To make matters worse, both the system and dermatologists generally scored slightly below 50 per cent, meaning that similar results might have been achieved by throwing dice. Nevertheless, the original paper has been cited more than a thousand times in professional papers, books and the media to sing the praises of artificial intelligence.

The existence of such inherent pitfalls is something to keep in mind for anyone tempted to entrust neural networks with real decisions about real people. And it gets worse. When digital storage became cheap and abundant, another magic approach to dealing with complex, swampy problems marched on to the scene: Big Data. Broadly speaking, the idea is to amass as many data as you can on some subject, and mine them for correlations. As the multitude of data increases, the patterns of correlations detected are supposed to give an evermore reliable description of the subject, a description on which decisions can be based. A simple example is the correlation between people's abode and their economic position, which banks use to determine eligibility for loans and insurers to assess risks and premiums. Such assessment strategies are fraught with problems.

First of all, they are statistical in nature. This means that the implications found are applicable only to large groups of subjects. They are relevant for the average individual, but not necessarily to any particular person. If a random 2.5 per cent of the population of a country will develop a particular kind of cancer, it makes no sense to spread facilities evenly across the country, because no patient wants 2.5 per cent care. Any individual patient either falls 100 per cent prey to the disease or not at all, and if she does, she needs access to all the relevant facilities, in the same place. Also, increases in the average income of the relatively rich will lead to increased sales of swimming pools. Not so, again, on the level of the well-to-do individual. Those without a pool may decide to call a supplier, but no matter how lavish the pay rise, virtually nobody will purchase a second swimming pool.

Next, there is a problem with correlations per se. If two phenomena correlate, it means that they typically tend to occur together, nothing more. However, people have an irrepressible inclination to interpret correlations as causal relationships: if two phenomena more or less consistently co-occur, we tend to think that one causes the other. But no: women over fifty strongly tend to be grandmothers, but reaching fifty does not cause anyone to become a grandmother, nor does the birth of a grandchild turn anyone into a quinquagenarian. The correlation is driven by a third independent factor: the fact that younger women, daughters, tend to become mothers themselves around the time their mothers reach fifty. Likewise, in Christian countries you will find that in general the geographical distributions of cancer casualties and churches are positively correlated. This does not mean, however, that people take refuge in religion once they have been diagnosed with the dreaded disease, nor that Christianity is carcinogenic. It is just a reflection of the size of towns: the bigger a town, the higher the number of both churches and cancer patients. The bottom line is that, counter to common wisdom, things that walk like ducks and talk like ducks need not always be ducks at all. However, Big Data, manipulated by people, is likely to treat them as if they are.

Then there is the matter of reliability. Using Big Data or, for that matter, any other modelling and decision-making strategy, it is often fairly easy to achieve a level of reliability in the order of 70–80 per cent. This sounds impressive, but it means that between two and three out of every ten results are wrong. That's two or three people out of every ten who are either refused a mortgage for no reason, or granted one they cannot afford. It's two or three people out of every ten being diagnosed with an illness they don't have, or falsely declared healthy. It also means two or three out of every ten reported social-media accounts are shut down for no good reason, and two or three out of every ten banned pictures or texts should not have been banned at all.

Two to three wrong outcomes in every ten are just about the odds that you won't make it to the other side of a not too busy motorway on foot. Nobody in their right mind would accept such odds in matters of any importance. A fair practical example of what something like 70–80 per cent reliability means is Google Translate. It is absolutely impressive and does open doors to otherwise totally inaccessible worlds, but it lets you down far too often and its results often don't even begin to look like a competent translation. The bad news is that each 1 per cent increase in reliability seems to require double the effort that was needed to achieve the last one. There are, and have been for years, scores of highly promising systems, but most of them never improve significantly beyond being just that.

The last and probably most pernicious problem with automatic systems of any kind are people. Although we recognize and value the disinterested neutrality of computers, the programs that make these machines come to life are written, interpreted, trained and tuned by people, people who bring their biases, predilections and prejudice willy-nilly to the task. In all systems that have a social dimension, subjective and ideological elements are implicitly present. Sometimes these have been put in on purpose, sometimes inadvertently, but in either case they affect the decisions the government, social services, insurers, banks, Internet censors and a host of other institutions make regarding us, their clients and interlocutors.

People are also notoriously fallible. They will make mistakes when designing a program, when working with programs and when entering new data or updating existing information. Sometimes, errors will percolate through systems, doing even more damage. In time, any database will degrade by amassing more and more data that are no longer relevant or correct, and erroneous input. In this world, the only unshakeable truth is the old programmers' adage 'Garbage in, garbage out.'

@#$%!

IN THE UNITED STATES, the First Amendment to the Constitution had made it impossible for state and federal governments to openly institute preventive censorship from the beginning. In a country with a government of the people, this was not a serious problem for the authorities as long as they were able to keep their own secrets. Until modern mass media came upon the scene, keeping state secrets was not too difficult, while moral censorship could be left to the churches and private societies. For a long time America showed the world that vigorous and unfettered public debate need not endanger the stability of a nation, as was widely believed. For example, at the start of both the world wars of the twentieth century the country was deeply divided on the matter of whether or not to join the fight, but once by hook or by crook the die was cast, the nation fell in line and went to war as one.

That is not to say that there were no attempts to deny people the right to speak out, but these came under a different flag. In the eyes of most people in the West, the end of the Second World War had brought not peace but the opening manoeuvres of a new, even more terrifying war, this time with the impressive and expansive Soviet Union. The Soviets had not only borne much of the brunt of the German attack on the world and come out on top, but also underwrote a revolutionary policy aimed at spreading their communist ideology and system across the entire world. In this sense their intentions seemed a lot like those of today's Islamic extremists. The difference was that by the late 1940s the Soviet Union looked strong enough to actually pull it off. Whether this was true or not is immaterial. What counted was the fear, stoked to incredible heights by first the new threat of atomic warfare, and then the war that broke out in Korea, with the old Western Allies and eventually the Chinese Communists joining in. Korea was in fact a small-scale Third World War, and the West looked under siege instead of victorious. This atmosphere became a hotbed for fear-mongers such as the United States senator Joseph McCarthy and his House Un-American Activities Committee. Before he was shown up as an overly ambitious fraud, McCarthy went a long way in trying to root out and lock up supposed communists and fellow travellers and bullying most even remotely liberal-minded Americans into silence, ruining thousands of careers and lives in the process.

On a more cultural note, there was the film industry's Motion Picture Production Code or Hays Code, a self-imposed set of moral guidelines that was enforced from 1934 onwards, mainly to prevent even more stifling interference by the government. This was a real danger. Many considered Hollywood a cesspool of scandal and depravity best closed down. Others objected to its putting social problems such as poverty, corruption, crime, injustice, sex and segregation on the agenda, and yet others loathed the extreme violence it portrayed. Government censorship had indeed loomed large since 1915, when in *Mutual v. Ohio* the Supreme Court had excepted film from Constitutional protection, expounding that motion pictures were:

> not to be regarded, nor intended to be regarded as part of the press of the country or as organs of public opinion. They are mere representations of events, of ideas and sentiments published or known; vivid, useful and entertaining, no doubt, but … capable of evil, having power for it, the greater because of their attractiveness and manner of exhibition.

As a consequence, film became the first of only two forms of expression that could be legally and preventively censored in the United States – the other one is television, where, with the exception of Elvis's scandalous hips in 1957, censorship didn't begin until 1978. Although the Supreme Court's decision was revoked in 1952, the Hays Code, further tightened up in 1951, formally remained in effect until 1968, when it succumbed to the times that were a'changing and was replaced by a ratings system.

At that point the United States and, in its wake, the rest of the Western world were stunned by a completely new, shattering phenomenon: the uncensored war. Until then, the many small wars after 1945 – those in the Dutch East Indies, Korea and French Indo-China; and the African decolonization brawls, which, in the words of Matthew Broderick's character in the opening sequence of Mike Nichols's film *Biloxi Blues* (1988), had come to seem 'a lot bigger now than the Big One was' – had all been endorsed by the Western peoples involved in them. But not this time. The initially small scale anti-communist containment war America had let itself be drawn into in Vietnam not only got dramatically out of hand, but also almost tore the nation to pieces and gave it a trauma that lasted for at least fifteen years. What had changed?

The answer is threefold. First, as Steven Pinker first pointed out, there has been a slow but inexorable increase in appreciation for human life among Western cultures over the past few centuries.

Until the days of Napoleon, whoever found themselves in the way of warring armies had better run fast just to save their skin, while hardly anybody complained about more than 10,000 dead and seriously wounded falling on battlefields such as Marengo in a matter of hours. A century later, when the First World War was raging, such carnage was widely considered an outrage (although that did nothing to stop it). Nowadays each individual casualty causes acute distress, and serious pains are taken to avoid civilian deaths. The bottom line is that regardless of all the atrocities that were perpetrated, over generations Western societies have been growing less violent and less tolerant of violence.

Second, the reconstitution of Western Europe and Japan after the Second World War had sparked an unprecedented technological, medical and economic upsurge. As a result, people in the West in general were fast becoming far richer, better educated, healthier and better cared for than ever before. In spite of the threats posed by the Cold War, this engendered a deep-rooted optimism everywhere and high expectations among the young, who naturally took their historically unique health and economic freedom for granted and wanted cultural and sexual liberties to match. They increasingly felt that the morale and world-view of their parents, understandably steeped in war and authoritarianism, stood in their way: peace, man! Precisely then, halfway through the 1960s, the American young began to be drafted for duty in some hideous Southeast Asian hellhole instead.

The most important factor, however, was television. News of what went on in the world had always been slow, distorted and somewhat remote. People mainly knew about the vicissitudes of war through the biased and embellished stories of veterans and second- or third-hand renderings of written reports, often no more than hearsay, in newspapers. Radio and film had begun to improve things somewhat, but film was cumbersome and expensive. Either directly or indirectly, film remained firmly in the hands of officialdom and propaganda services and was easily censored before reaching the theatres. Radio, by its nature, remained somewhat abstract. Now, however, Americans had television, and for the first time the home front was directly confronted with what actually went on in the business known as war. It was not a pretty sight.

Thanks to both the First Amendment and the inexperience of the army and politicians, Vietnam burst into the living room full blast.

Reporters travelled Vietnam unhindered, hitching rides with the military to go wherever the action was, sometimes even on helicopters, filming and photographing all there was to see, including the horrors. As a result, the prestige of the army and support for the war steadily eroded as the conflict turned into a hopeless quagmire that it took America 58,000 dead boys to extricate itself from.

After the pull-out of 1975, the American authorities sat licking their wounds and vowed 'Never again,' Constitutional Amendments or not. Their first reaction was simply to close the doors on the media when the next real war came, the liberation of Saddam Hussein-occupied Kuwait and the incursion into Iraq known as Operation Desert Storm in early 1991. Reporters were kept away from the real theatre and fed only army-controlled and -produced scraps and statements. The world got to see little more than propagandistic army-made videos of spectacular precision bombardments, presented by General Norman Schwarzkopf, commander of the Coalition Forces. The only independent reporting available was done by the fledgling cnn, the bbc and a few others from Baghdad, the enemy capital.

The American authorities took a lot of flak for their extreme lack of openness, and by the time the second Gulf War came around in March 2003, the military had come up with a way to keep the media both under control and on their side. It was called 'embedded journalism'. Purportedly for reasons of safety, the army offered journalists of its choosing an all-inclusive war trip and access to all sorts of juicy information, to the exclusion of all others. The few diehards who tried to cover operations independently were refused protection and all cooperation. In this way, the army almost completely controlled and manipulated the flow of information. On the one hand, it alone determined what the embedded reporters got to hear, and when. The lucky guests, on the other, knew better than to cross their host, and duly censored themselves.

In 1978, ten years after the demise of the Hays Code, broadcast radio and, in its wake, television became the second medium to be denied the full protection of the First Amendment, this time primarily on grounds of privacy. In *Federal Communications Commission (FCC) v. Pacifica*, a divided Supreme Court ruled about radio that:

> patently offensive, indecent material presented over the air-
> waves confronts the citizen, not only in public, but also in

the privacy of the home, where the individual's right to be left alone plainly outweighs the First Amendment rights of an intruder. Because the broadcast audience is constantly tuning in and out, prior warnings cannot completely protect the listener or viewer from unexpected program content. To say that one may avoid further offense by turning off the radio when he hears indecent language is like saying that the remedy for an assault is to run away after the first blow.

This line of reasoning is patently wrong. The notion of privacy as 'the right to be left alone', which goes back to the prominent Supreme Court judge Louis Brandeis, refers to active intrusions by peeping Toms, aggressive Bible thumpers and stalkers, or rather too nosy or obtrusive authorities and private parties. But broadcasters aren't intruders. They do not spy on their audience, nor do they ring anyone's doorbell uninvited and put their foot in the door. It is the viewer who is actively 'tuning in and out', eagerly searching for something she likes – and runs into things she does not like in the process. That's life. It is much like going to the farmers' market looking for cauliflower and happening on boxes of uncannily shaped figs and penis-like asparagus on the way. Complete protection from the unexpected and unwanted is an impossibility. It is also extremely undesirable in a society where the people are supposed to be knowledgeable and responsible enough to govern themselves.

Nevertheless, the ruling stands to this day. By 2003, when U2's Bono accepted his Golden Globe saying it was 'really fucking brilliant', the atmosphere had become sufficiently stifling to let the FCC, relentlessly egged on by the Parents' Television Council, a conservative pressure group not unlike Mary Whitehouse's, threaten the networks that had aired the 'obscene and indecent' ceremony that 'broadcasters are on clear notice that, in the future, they will be subject to potential enforcement action for any broadcast of the "F-Word" or a variation thereof.' A year later the Commission made good on its threat by fining CBS to the tune of $550,000 for airing Janet Jackson's so-called wardrobe malfunction at the Super Bowl Halftime Show, grandiosely referred to as 'Nipple-gate', but amounted to no more than a hardly noticeable glimpse of an intentionally, half-heartedly exposed right breast. The fine was struck down after seven years, but by then a lot of damage had been done.

Networks had become as squeamish about what they broadcast, beeped or cut out as a retirement home full of Victorian virgins.

The reason for the tenacity of a Supreme Court ruling that almost half of the court considered wrong, and the vigour with which it was acted on by the FCC, lies in a second argument adduced in it: fleeting, even inadvertent exposure to inappropriate language on the radio 'could have enlarged a child's vocabulary in an instant'. As the FCC later put it in its warning to over-enthusiastic Golden Globe winners: 'We believe that even isolated broadcasts of the "F-Word" in situations such as that here could do so as well, in a manner that many, if not most, parents would find highly detrimental and objectionable.' This, of course, could not be allowed to happen in view of 'parents' claims to authority in their own household'.

While it is hard to see what harm a child could come to by merely acquiring the word 'fucking' in the sense of 'very' or 'truly' among the tens of thousands of words the average youngster picks up before reaching puberty, the idea was seized on by conservative citizens, insecure parents and other groups with an interest in blinkering society alike, to surface during the 1990s as the catch-all argument for censuring anything from broadcasts to schoolbooks and literature: 'not suitable for minors'. Under this aegis, everything that wasn't undilutedly mainstream could be curtailed, emasculated or simply suppressed, since restricting accessibility to minors automatically also hampered adults. School boards, private moralistic societies and – later – social-justice warriors have enthusiastically grabbed their chance to cleanse books and other media, purging them of anything unwelcome, un-Christian and un-American. Together with the politically correct obsession with f-, n- and God knows what other unspeakable words and the modern trend in American academia of 'de-platforming' people with undesirable opinions, it has created a remarkably tense and taboo-ridden atmosphere in a country that prides itself on being the ultimate champion of free speech.

@#$%!

FREE SPEECH OR, BETTER, freedom of expression is the principal cornerstone of any democracy, but it is also an uneasy and therefore precarious blessing. The French *Déclaration des droits de l'homme* put it like this in 1789:

Most of the institutions people have built serve a clear, specific goal. Companies produce commodities and services, courts exist to dispense justice and museums provide aesthetic pleasure and a sense of our place in history. Not so, however, in the case of public discourse, says the Yale law professor Robert Post. While the others strive to realize their respective purposes, 'the objective of public discourse is to determine what our purposes are.'[4] This renders public discourse vital to any democracy, since all our policies and laws are based on its outcomes. As a consequence, unfettered freedom of expression is equally vital, for 'we', as a society, can establish sufficiently widely supported purposes only by computing and negotiating sets of carefully weighted averages of myriad individual wants and wishes. This can be done only if everyone is able to voice their preferences and ideas on any subject, even when ideas and preferences are voiced that you or even 'everyone' find reprehensible or stupid. Then, too, it is simply not for you to say that what someone else thinks does not matter or must be repressed, and conversely. Yet this is precisely what hate speech sets out to do.

Hate speech refers to the public act of demonizing and thus marginalizing people on grounds of some group characteristic, in the worst cases calling for violence against them. The pattern is always the same: communists, fascists, liberals, blacks, whites, Hindus, atheists, Jains, heretics, black-arses, Tutsis, Boers, migrants, homosexuals or sexists are undesirable vermin; Mary and her friends are sexists, so they should be silenced, locked up or worse.

On account of its historically proven lethal potential, quite a few democracies have developed laws to curb hate speech. This may have some educational effect, although how much and on whom remains unclear. Paradoxically, however, criminalizing hate speech may do more harm than good. First of all, prosecution cannot make it go away; it just drives hate speech underground to fester in the dark and putrefy minds there. At the same time it undercuts the legitimacy of democracy itself by infringing directly upon the pivotal principle of equal rights, sending a message that democracy is there only for 'us, who are in the right', not for the rest. Finally, it tends to spawn lengthy, sensational and highly divisive judicial bickering, usually with unsatisfactory outcomes for all concerned and for society as a whole. It would perhaps be wiser for legislators to keep from criminalizing and trying hard to define crimes of expression such as insults, abuse, humiliation and offence, or even, as in Germany, speech that 'violates the dignity of an individual'. In the verbal arena, they might do well to restrict themselves to direct calls for violence, concrete threats and intimidation – far clearer and unequivocally provable offences that are punishable in any case – and leave the rest to public discourse.

> Article 11. The free interchange of thoughts and opinions is one of the dearest human rights. Therefore, any citizen may speak, write and print freely, under the sole condition that he answer to charges of abusing this freedom as specified by law.[5]

In one version or another, this idea has found its way into the laws and constitutions of all modern democracies. Together with universal suffrage, the right to freely inform and be informed by others is the backbone of democracy, but this does not mean that people find it easy to live up to. The trouble is that nobody has a problem with others expressing what they themselves agree with. So freedom of speech, as it is often called for short, becomes meaningful only when people say, write or print things that you deeply disagree with or that strike you as reprehensible. Rather than a privilege to claim for ourselves, it is the right we grant to *others* not to be bowdlerized, culturally cleansed, de-platformed or preventively censored, however much we would like to do just that. It charges us all with the painful obligation to tolerate the expression of what we consider stupid, banal, immoral, offensive or otherwise despicable, all the things we'd much rather not hear or expose our children to. Only after the fact, if there is reason to believe that a specific law has been violated, can a person be held to account for what he said or showed.

While freedom of expression gives you the right to say basically what you want and obliges the state to protect your freedom to do so, nobody is obliged to agree with or like what you say. Therefore, it is important to keep in mind that there may be serious consequences. While you have little to fear from the state as long as you don't break a specific law, other parties may be less forgiving, and have every right to be – although not necessarily to act on their indignation. If you vent a dissenting opinion, people may be offended or even try to intimidate you into shutting up. For instance, in France, the Netherlands and Belgium, strongly right-wing political parties have been isolated and ignored in parliament by all the rest for many years – it is hard to do politics when nobody wants to enter into a debate with you. If you scold someone or spread malicious gossip about them, chances are they will become angry and retaliate. Furthermore, there are numerous situations where people are required to sign non-disclosure agreements, which they do well to honour. Many employees who thought they could freely discuss their boss with friends on Facebook, or even on their company's intranet, landed in a real pickle, up to losing their jobs when their superiors found out about it. In July 2019 even Sir Kim Darroch, British Ambassador to the United States, lost his job over leaked diplomatic emails in which he assessed then President Trump as a chaotic and incompetent simpleton.

Before the invention of freedom of expression, people had always found ways to make critical points in veiled, roundabout ways. They took refuge in allegory and fables and often published anonymously or used a pseudonym. These were risky stratagems, for if they were found out, it was clear from their subterfuge alone that they had intentionally been criticizing, if not actually undermining, the state and its representatives. Nowadays, in countries where freedom of expression is seriously limited, such as Russia, or non-existent, as in China, people once more play risky games of hide-and-seek with the government. In Russia in 2017, the Ukrainian film director Oleg Sentsov was sentenced to twenty years' imprisonment, ostensibly for terrorist activities but in reality for protesting against the Russian annexation of the Crimea. In China, people cannot mention Winnie the Pooh on the government-controlled social-media service Weibo, presumably because that term has been used to refer unobtrusively to China's chubby strongman Xi Jinping.

Given enough money, effective censorship does not have to resort to such rough measures. The old strategy of controlling the presses still functions as well as ever. In Italy, Silvio Berlusconi's company Mediaset successively gobbled up virtually all of the media, which were then placed under orders not to publish anything that might be awkward for the *cavaliere*. Most of the British printed press has been suffering from a serious right-wing bias for decades now, which has everything to do with its ownership. And following the Umbrella Revolution of 2014 in Hong Kong, when China wanted to stem the flow of critical and anti-Chinese publications from the city, it simply bought Sino United, the conglomerate of publishers and bookshops that controls 80 per cent of the city's written output. Sino United was immediately ordered to give anything referring to the Umbrella Revolution a wide berth.

George Orwell got the inspiration for the Ministry of Truth that dominates his *Nineteen Eighty-Four* (1949) as a BBC employee during the Second World War, when a British Ministry of Information put out the government's preferred version of the truth from Senate House in London. It was thankfully dismantled once conditions of war no longer applied, for a free press is usually best served by governments not interfering. A quick look at the 2019 World Press Freedom Index compiled by Reporters Without Borders is enough to show that countries that care so much for their press that they sport either a Ministry of Information or one of Communication (as distinct from Ministries of Information and Communication Technology) are likely to censor and hinder independent critical journalism. No fewer than 43 countries out of the 50 that do feature in the lower half of the index, where freedom of the press and civil liberties are seriously compromised. The average score of a country with such a ministry was 129, worse by 1.5 points than two years before and squarely within the worst third of the index. This makes the presence of a Ministry of Information a reliable indication of undesirable conditions.

Country	Ministry Title	Position
Ghana	Ministry of Information	27
Tonga	Ministry of Information & Communications	45
Malawi	Ministry of Information, Communication Technology and Civic Education	68
Togo	Ministry of Communication, Culture & Civic Education	76
Bhutan	Ministry of Information and Communications	80
Israel	Ministry of Information	88
Serbia	Ministry of Culture and Information	90
Liberia	Ministry of Information	93
Kenya	Ministry of Information, Communications and Technology	100
Lebanon	Ministry of Information	101
Ukraine	Ministry of Information Policy	102
Nepal	Ministry of Information and Communications	106
Kuwait	Ministry of Information	108
Bolivia	Ministerio de Comunicación	113
Congo	Ministry of Communication	117

11

THE NAMES OF THE LORD, THE STATE AND THE INSECURE

If God would allow himself to be caught in the Living Dust once again, He will return as an ass, capable of formulating a few syllables at best, ignored and maligned and flogged, but I shall understand Him and immediately go to bed with Him but I'll swathe His little hooves, lest I would be scratched too badly when He thrashes about in coming.[1]

In early 1966, as the sexual, secularizing and cultural revolutions that swept the Western world during the 1960s were gathering steam, this one sentence from a 'Letter to My Bank', published in the first issue of the literary journal *Dialogue: Magazine for Homosexuality and Society*, sparked the most spectacular blasphemy trial in Dutch history. The oddly irreverent allusions to homosexuality and bestiality were too much for people and institutions that already felt their traditional hold on society slipping, from ultra-orthodox protestants such as the Member of Parliament Cor van Dis to the Socialist Justice Minister Ivo Samkalden. However, before the judiciary could decide whether or not to actually prosecute, the author – the novelist and public figure Gerard Reve – forced their hand by publicly demanding to stand trial in order to exonerate himself from any charges of blasphemy.

There was always a whiff of scandal about Reve. Six years before, after his marriage of eleven years had collapsed, he had come out as one of the first openly declared homosexuals in the country. And right now, when Roman Catholics were beginning to flee the Mother Church in droves, this alleged blasphemer, born to a staunchly communist family, was clamorously converting to Catholicism, adding insult to injury by publishing a book called *Nearer to Thee*, which contained the following gem:

And God himself would come by in the guise of a one-year-old, mouse grey ass and stand at the door and ring and say:

'Gerard, that book of yours – do you know I cried at some passages?' 'My Lord and my God! Hallowed be Thy name in all Eternity! I love You so terribly much', I would try to say, but I'd start blubbering before I was half way through, and begin to kiss Him and pull Him inside, and after an impressive clambering effort in order to make our way up the stairs to the little bedroom, I'd possess Him three times in a row in His Secret Orifice, and then give Him a complimentary copy, not sewn but bound – no time for narrow-minded stinginess – and inscribed: 'For the Eternal. Without Words.'[2]

The case went before the court and in due course Reve was acquitted, even though the court did consider his writings blasphemous. The thing was that Dutch blasphemy law, adopted only in 1932, stipulated that blasphemy was punishable only if it was malicious, positively intended to deride and hurt. In the intractable amalgam of pompous hyperbole, bawdy comedy, good-humoured irony and piteous complaints mixed with deadpan seriousness that made up Reve's writing – and, indeed, his demeanour and idiom in real life, for Reve and his work were truly one – the court could not discern any malevolence towards anyone. Nor could society at large, it would seem: a year after his acquittal Reve was awarded the most prestigious literary prize in the Netherlands by the state itself. When it was presented to him on national television by Marga Klompé, the very first female cabinet minister in Dutch history, he promptly kissed her on camera, causing considerable though mainly good-natured upheaval once again.

The Reve trial was atypical in two ways. First, for the two years it took to reach a definitive verdict, it caused far more hilarity than indignation among even those who seriously frowned on depravities such as homosexuality, bestiality and making fun of the Lord. In this respect, it both exemplified and reinforced the final loosening of the religious fetters that had kept society hemmed in for so long. Second, it was one of the very few blasphemy trials in history that genuinely seemed to lack a political dimension – which is probably why it basically ended in a laugh instead of a tragedy.

As a rule, however, blasphemy trials are no laughing matter. Most have very little to do with honest religious convictions and everything with exerting political power. On 7 October 2019, for

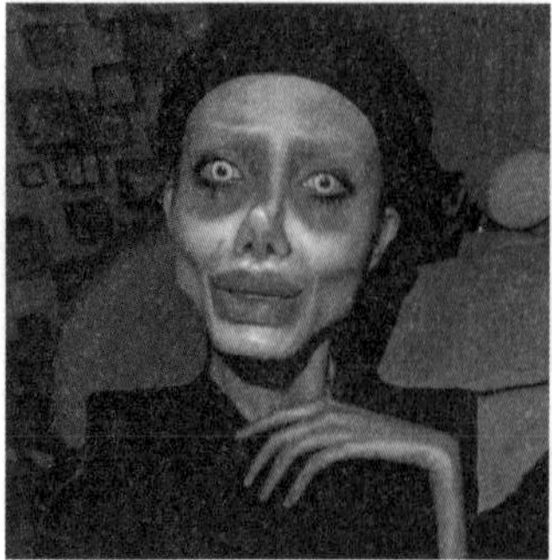

Iranian Instagram celebrity Sahar Tabar as Angelina Jolie and, in the middle, as herself.

instance, 22-year-old Sahar Tabar was arrested in Iran on charges of blasphemy, incitement and corrupting the young. Her crime lay in the eerie zombie-like imitations of the film star Angelina Jolie's face wrecked by cosmetic surgery that she had been publishing on Instagram since 2017. In her case, blasphemy meant that she had been flouting the cultural doctrine of the theocratic regime. In the eyes of the ayatollahs, Islamic precepts restricting the freedom of women, such as dressing demurely and covering both head and body in public, including on social media platforms such as Instagram, are essential to the nation's survival. For, as one prominent officer in the Revolutionary Guard put it: 'the enemy is trying to make our national culture adopt a Western life style' – which would be the end of the Iranian powers that be. The ayatollahs' problem is that Iranian women – probably with the tacit support of at least some of the men – are doing just that no matter what. And they are doing it with a vengeance: in their plight, they have begun idolizing the Western decadence of cosmetic surgery as a way of asserting and expressing themselves; no country tops Iran when it comes to nose-jobs per capita. In this light, it is no wonder that Tabar's silly mischief hit a sore nerve with the authorities.

Iran has quite a reputation when it comes to fanatical religious oppression, largely owing to the fatwa that Ayatollah Ruhollah Khomeini issued on Valentine's Day in 1989 against the British author Salman Rushdie. In it, he called upon every upstanding Muslim to kill the writer and his associates, who – according to Khomeini – had blasphemously offended Allah and his prophet by helping Rushdie to write and publish his book *The Satanic Verses* (1988). It gave rise to bloodthirsty demonstrations and book-burnings throughout the

Muslim world and the Islamic diaspora, including Great Britain, and ruined Rushdie's life. He spent years in hiding under heavy guard, and eventually fled Britain for New York. Of course, the Ayatollah had no jurisdiction beyond the Iranian borders, and no right whatsoever to incite citizens of other countries to commit murder, whatever their religion. Khomeini's murder contract flew in the face of every reasonable conception of international law and order. By issuing it he proved himself the twentieth-century incarnation of the barbarian banging on the gates of civilization.

Astonishingly, quite a few political and cultural pundits in the West responded by actually opening those gates, in anticipation of the great wave of politically correct kowtowing to all who present themselves as disenfranchised minorities that would soon follow. One of those was the British Labour MP Bernie Grant, who, a day after the fatwa was issued, asserted in parliament that 'Burning books is not a big issue for blacks,' and that objecting to it proved that 'the whites wanted to impose their values on the world.'[3] It was an early example of the neo-racist rhetoric that has been growing stronger and more disruptive in the West ever since.

Of course, nobody among the vociferous mobs of Muslim book-burners and would-be killers had read Rushdie's work or even heard of him until then. They were useful idiots, expendable pawns in the sinister political game Khomeini was playing – a game with two objectives. One was for Khomeini to make good as best he could on his old vow to export his Islamic Revolution, an ambition that had been shelved during the eight long years of the war Iran had been waging with Iraq since 1980. And the other? Half a year after the atrocities that had cost close to a million lives had come to an end, Iran was demoralized and economically in a bad way. While Iraq had not actually won the war, Iran felt it had largely lost it and had meanwhile been subjected to crippling sanctions that would persist until 2016. In the face of all that hardship, what could be a better way of rallying the people behind the Ayatollah's disastrous regime once again than to create a new, far less lethal foreign enemy to fight, in the shape of the very antithesis of Khomeini and his cronies: the intellectually bespectacled, urbane person of the Indian-born apostate Muslim writer Rushdie?

Pakistan is another society where blasphemy is a political weapon, to which end the country has adopted the harshest blasphemy laws in the modern world. Under these laws, a young woman called Asia

> **Khomeini's fatwa against Salman Rushdie, issued 14 February 1989**
>
> I inform all zealous Muslims of the world that the author of the book entitled *The Satanic Verses* – which has been compiled, printed and published in opposition to Islam, the Prophet and the Quran – and all those involved in the publication who were aware of its contents are sentenced to death.
>
> I call upon all zealous Muslims to execute them quickly, wherever they may be found, so that no one else will dare to insult the Muslim sanctities. God willing, whoever is killed on this path is a martyr.
>
> In addition, anyone who has access to the author of this book but does not possess the power to execute him should report him to the people so that he may be punished for his actions.[4]

Bibi was condemned to death in 2010. In 2009 a couple of women from her village of Ittanwali in Punjab had denounced Bibi, an illiterate member of the tiny Christian minority in the country, for having insulted Muhammad when they had been picking fruit together. Bibi had offered her later accusers some water, which they, pious Muslims, had of course refused: it had been rendered unclean by having been passed to them by a Christian. Then, they said, Bibi had asserted her belief in Jesus Christ, who had died on the Cross for the sins of the people, allegedly adding: 'And what did Muhammad ever do to save mankind?' That was all, but in the best Muslim tradition Maulana Yousef Qureshi, a prominent imam in Peshawar, publicly pledged to award some £4,000 to whoever took Bibi's life, and on 11 November 2010 she was officially convicted as well. Pending appeals she disappeared into solitary confinement for eight years, where she was badly treated even by Pakistani standards. Both the governor of Punjab and the Catholic Minister of Religious Minorities, who were in favour of reforming the blasphemy laws, were murdered along the way. The former was shot by his own bodyguard, Mumtaz Quadri. Quadri was hanged for his crime in 2016, and the Taliban celebrated the occasion by a suicide bombing on a court of law, taking seventeen lives. After this, nobody in Pakistan dared to mention reform any more. In total, 65 people have been murdered there in connection with blasphemy between 1990 and 2016, and seventeen were on death row awaiting execution in that year.

In 2018 Bibi, who had always denied the accusations, was finally acquitted for lack of proof, but she could not safely be released on to the streets, where hordes of extremist Muslims were clamouring for her death. It was seven months before she could finally be spirited away to Canada.

Although Iran and Pakistan are both Islamic republics, the cases of Rushdie and Bibi differ significantly. In Rushdie's case it was the state itself that went for the writer's jugular in order to further its own interests. Secular and religious authority are one and the same in Iran. In Pakistan, however, religious and secular authorities are not identical. What is more, they differ in their opinions on religious matters, including blasphemy. Bibi got caught up in the ongoing internal power struggle between political factions, with the Sunni community, to which the majority of the population belongs, defending its privileged position of power against all perceived competitors, Islamic or not, by means of intimidation and, if necessary, violence, even murder, sanctioned by Muhammad. As is the case everywhere in Islam, their strong arm is the illiterate, ignorant rabble that is sent out into the streets to put the fear of God into everyone.

A very old variety of blasphemy is exploited by modern Thailand. Most Westerners regard the country as a nation of extremely friendly and accommodating people, born to serve the modern tourist's every need. In fact the Thai have a long and turbulent history full of war and strife, punctuated by countless military coups and juntas. In the course of eight bumpy centuries, the Thai developed a unique concept of absolute kingship, based on Hindu and Buddhist ideas. On the one hand, the monarch and his people are thought to share a deep and mystical unifying bond. On the other, as an incarnation of any of a number of Hindu gods, the ruler enjoys semi-divine status. This puts him in a fundamentally different class from mere mortals. As a consequence, Thai rulers are not only legitimized by the highest supernatural authority, but actually embody it. If they do well they are likely to achieve truly divine status with the populace, always the cornerstone of monarchical power. This was certainly the case with Bhumibol or Rama ix, the longest reigning king of the ruling Chakri dynasty, who died in 2016.

This semi-divine royal prestige is exploited relentlessly by whoever happens to be in power, by means of a set of laws forbidding almost any criticism of religious customs, notions and entities or the monarchy. In 2017 a man was sentenced to 35 years in prison for sharing photos of royals with comments on Facebook. What he had written remains a mystery; the posts are gone and the trial was conducted in camera. That same year another Thai, a 28-year-old who had been arrested at a peaceful protest some nine months before, was sentenced to eleven years and four months in prison, also for having offended the king in a Facebook post. At the behest of the Thai authorities Facebook took down more than three hundred pages containing 'improper' content around the same time. Critics who try to escape the wrath of king and government by going into exile tend to disappear or turn up dead, in one case with their stomach pumped full of mortar. In Thailand, lese-majesty is a very, very dangerous game, and functions as an effective means of subduing unruly subjects.

It was logical for blasphemy to be a serious offence in medieval and earlier cultures, when a person's oath was the only guarantee and gods were the supreme guarantors. It is also logical for blasphemy and lese-majesty to be closely connected political offences in authoritarian nations with a close bond between secular and divine power. In theocracies such as Iran they are one and the same, and the rulers are priests who merely represent the interests of a supreme being that, although omnipotent, invariably has trouble making itself understood. Something slightly different applies in systems where rulers are legitimized by claiming to be divine themselves. Starting with Augustus, Roman emperors let themselves be deified in life, thus adding to their already exalted status and shielding themselves from criticism. Many Asian rulers and most of the pre-Columbian kings of the Americas did the same. Thailand and Japan are present-day examples.

Other kings legitimized their grip on society 'by the grace of God', a move that grants considerable power to that god's representatives on Earth, usually some priest caste or church. Medieval European history is rife with conflicts between secular rulers and the Papacy that arose from this idea.

From the beginning of the modern age in Europe, however, monarchs and emperors there gained new confidence. They generally began to take leave of divine legitimization, substituting the new concept of the nation for it. *L'état, c'est moi* ('I am the state'), the French king Louis XIV is said to have snarled at his parliament in 1655. God had to some extent become expendable, and Louis and all rulers like him styled themselves as absolute monarchs, accountable to nobody, not even God. Yet they were still divine, in the sense that they embodied the supreme being, now identified as the nation, which existed only through them.

However, once the nation had become the fundamental legitimizing concept, it did not take long for the people to realize that it was they who incarnated it rather than the king, and to start making claims of their own. In 1776 the British colonies in North America were the first to do away completely with rulers sanctioned from on high or personifying the nation. 'We, George III, by the grace of God' was summarily replaced by 'We, the people'. Within sixteen years the French had followed suit, identifying the *citoyen* as the root of legitimate power, instead of God or a king. These were radical experiments with non-authoritarian self-government. They were early and somewhat crude attempts at what we now know as modern democracy.

In the course of this long-term trend, blasphemy as an offence lost much of its sting, being replaced first by lese-majesty and much later still, as all sorts of minorities among 'the people' began emancipating, by the offences of defamation and hate speech. That is not to say, however, that in the budding democratic world blasphemy as an offence just faded away. Nor, for that matter, did lese-majesty. There were two reasons for this.

First, although the absolute rulers and, later, the majority of modern politicians did not feel they needed divine justification for their power and position, the churches and their obedient flocks remained highly influential and therefore essential allies, which, if neglected or thwarted, could easily turn into formidable enemies. Best then to keep on their good side, honour them and use them to your advantage. This is precisely what Vladimir Putin, formally leading the irreligious Russian democracy but in reality a latter-day absolutist, has been doing ever since he came to power. This is why the Russian state punished Nadezjda Tolokonnikova and Maria Aljochina of the girl band Pussy Riot so harshly for committing blasphemy. Not on account of the ungodly racket they made, but for doing so in a Russian Orthodox cathedral – for all of one and a half minutes, after which churchwardens burst in and seized them. Both women served two years in a prison camp.

Another pillar of society to cultivate, especially in today's Russia, are patriotic conservatives. Hence the stiff fine plus suspended sentence of fifteen days in jail a 22-year-old Russian woman received for lese-majesty in the guise of 'disrespect for the state' in 2019. Her offence had been an Instagram post in which she did a reggaethon dance routine in front of a Soviet war memorial.

A similar development can be seen in the still fragile democracies of the former Warsaw Pact nations. There are clear reactionary tendencies in countries such as Hungary and Poland, where large groups prefer the authoritarian predictability of yore to the apparent fickleness, profligacy and scandals of democratic politics. To their leaders the Church, which loathed the communists but is equally averse to the individual freedom that democracy requires, is an essential ally. Hence the prosecution of someone like Elżbieta Podleśna in Poland in 2019 for 'insulting religious feelings' – all she had done was distribute posters of the Madonna with a rainbow aureole, as an appeal for sexual tolerance.

This brings us to the second reason. Even stronger than recent events in Eastern Europe, the fate of the early democratic experiments shows that there is a deep authoritarian streak in people. Much as they like freedom and self-determination, they also have a yen for someone or something bigger than themselves, something to obey and follow and afford them a sense of belonging. Twelve years after the citizens of France had vigorously shaken off the shackles of absolutist monarchy in the name of freedom, equality and brotherhood, they cheered their heads off when Napoleon Bonaparte crowned himself emperor of France at Reims. Ten years and rivers of blood after that, the Vienna peace conference reinstated old-fashioned monarchical rule everywhere in Europe. In time the presidency of the United States of America, decked out with near-regal executive powers already, took on all the trappings of an absolutist royal court, albeit limited in duration. It was not a coincidence that John and Jackie Kennedy, inspired by the musical of the same name (1960), at once fondly and ambitiously referred to their presidency as well as their household as Camelot, the court of the legendary King Arthur.

In the course of the nineteenth century, democracy nonetheless gained ground across Europe, resulting in today's patchwork of republics sprinkled with a handful of constitutional monarchies: the United Kingdom, the Netherlands, Belgium, Spain, Norway, Sweden and Denmark. With the exception of Spain these are, together with the United States and Switzerland, the oldest and most stable modern democracies in the world. In view of the remarkably large popular support for the royal families involved, it would seem that the typical combination of an open, democratic society with the kind of largely ceremonial kingship that has evolved over the past two hundred years offers a psychologically ideal mix of emancipated citizenship and something awe-inspiring and innocently authoritarian to belong to and identify with.

The rise of democracy in Europe was neither smooth nor steady. Along the way a wholly new, brutal kind of regime sprang from it, one that would dominate and shape much of the twentieth century. From the late nineteenth century onwards, new inventions such as the telephone, motorized transport, photography, film, fingerprinting, radio, recording and bugging devices and evermore efficient handheld weaponry afforded authorities unprecedented and hitherto unimaginable means of controlling, manipulating and subduing populations. They enabled authoritarian cliques and strongmen, with the help of the oppressed and the disgruntled, to establish the first totalitarian states in history: first in Russia in 1918, then, during the 1920s, in Italy and finally, from 1930 onwards, in Germany.

Totalitarian states are miracles of cynical sophistication compared to old-fashioned absolute monarchies and crude dictatorships. Without exception they are set up and ruled by a tiny class of self-appointed revolutionaries who claim to be exclusively privy to a mystical 'will of the people', as the king-priests of yore claimed a unique familiarity with the will of the gods. Their knowledge not only entitles but obliges them to impose this popular will, regardless of how the people themselves feel about it all. The new technology gave them the means to do so and to build societies suffused with ideology and political control, everywhere, every day, for everyone. They turned out to be societies driven by paranoia, where security always trumps safety.

Still, each of the great totalitarian regimes of the twentieth century differed from the others. The Soviet party elite turned their nation into an immense prison stretching across eleven time zones, which – except during the worst part of Stalin's rule – they ran as a collective. Mussolini's regime was more of a cult, with Il Duce personifying his nation. But only Adolf Hitler, with the aid of his propaganda minister Joseph Goebbels, truly *was* his Reich, much more than Louis XIV ever even pretended to be. One cannot take the

Nazi slogan *Ein Volk, ein Reich, ein Führer* (One people, one nation, one leader) too literally. The fundamental, mystical notion of the *Volk* was embodied in the territorial *Reich*, itself in turn incarnated in the *Führer*, with whom everything began and ended. By the process of *Gleichschaltung*, 'coordination', every aspect of daily life became steeped in Nazism, and joining ranks with the Nazis through membership of either the NSDAP or the SS became unavoidable for anyone who aspired to a career beyond a menial job. The unprecedented mass complicity this generated might in part explain why there was so little opposition and why the Germans went on waging the war for so long after it had become clear that they must lose it.

During the first half of the twentieth century authoritarian regimes flared up in other European countries as well. Spain and Portugal were autocracies from the 1930s until the 1970s, and the countries of the Warsaw Pact were under communist totalitarian rule from the late 1940s until November 1989. Lastly, there was the military junta that held Greece to ransom from 1967 until 1974. Surprisingly, for all their apparent strength, suppressive force and evermore sophisticated censoring and indoctrination, none of the authoritarian regimes in Europe survived. In the end they all reverted to democracy, or completed their interrupted development towards becoming modern democracies, rife with indecision, squabbling and contradiction, scandal and ridicule of the powerful.

As Winston Churchill put it in the British House of Commons in November 1947: 'Many forms of Government have been tried, and will be tried in this world of sin and woe. No one pretends that democracy is perfect or all-wise. Indeed it has been said that democracy is the worst form of Government except for all those other forms that have been tried from time to time.' So what is it that gives this worst of all systems bar the rest its unique resilience and allure? Certainly not that it is free of indoctrination. Children in democracies are ideologically indoctrinated just as thoroughly and as biased as in any authoritarian society. The difference is that whatever else children are taught, from the 'grandeur' of the Nation in France to allegiance to the flag in the United States, their indoctrination is rooted in the connected values of individual freedom and equal rights. From these flow both freedom of speech and association, and awareness of the fact that different views and opinions can and do coexist and can be tried and tested by openly discussing them.

The false lure of cultural relativism

The old adage 'When in Rome, do as the Romans do' is often taken to express the essence of cultural relativism. In truth, however, it does nothing of the kind. 'When in Rome' reflects an immensely old and important strategy of rational compromise. As long as you're on someone else's turf, you show respect for and abide by the rules of the house, even if they clash with your own, up to a point. The host, on the other hand, will allow guests a certain leeway in the observance of rules and mores that they may not be conversant with. Together these constitute the core of the age-old ethics called hospitality, without which strangers would not be able to contact and communicate with each other at all. It is essentially tit-for-tat on a footing of pretended equality. Without it, there could never have been long-distance trade, cultural and scientific exchange or diplomacy. Most essentially, it is dynamic in that it promotes thinking about one's own and one another's cultures and hence sparks new syntheses. It brings people together and creates intercultural ties and progress.

Cultural relativism, on the other hand, is an ideology that denies the existence of any universally held moral values. Hence, all cultures are equivalent and, since in the absence of universal values there need not be any common ground, incomprehensible to outsiders. Therefore, any culture can only be evaluated and judged by its own members in terms of its own beliefs, morals and values. Although at first glance this seems a very tolerant, even magnanimous stance, it is in fact quite the opposite.

To begin with, there is no element of compromise and no need or willingness to find points of agreement, for to the cultural relativist, there may not be any. As a consequence no effort is made to try and understand the other, and perhaps achieve a new synthesis that might benefit both parties. There is no prospect of any rapprochement at all, only cultural isolationism and moral inertia. At best, cultural relativism embodies the barren indifference of 'You go your way, and I'll go mine.'

Cultural relativism also lacks the reciprocity that is essential to establishing meaningful intercultural contact. Whereas hospitality is a carefully balanced game of give-and-take between guest and host, leading to better mutual understanding, cultural relativism is necessarily a one-way street. Let us not forget that cultural relativism is a typically modern Western hobby. All other cultures consider themselves superior to all others as a matter of course, or they would have changed. So, with respect to the non-Western world, cultural relativists give 'respect' without getting anything in return except, perhaps, scorn and ridicule. At best they are considered useful idiots.

> Last but not least, there is not even equality in cultural relativism, real or pretended. The so-called respect cultural relativists grant to 'others' is just old-fashioned colonial paternalism. When push comes to shove, it's Western rich kids allowing non-Westerners their quaintly backward cultural aberrations, including misogyny, repressive – and by Western standards sometimes criminal – customs and antisocial tendencies. Cultural relativism is the lazily cynical modern variant of 'They don't know any better.'

In other words, through verbal warfare. In a democratic society, there simply is no gospel truth. This does not imply any kind of cultural relativism, the idea that any cultural custom is fundamentally as good as the next one. On the contrary, it entails that no authority, idea, custom or practice is beyond criticism.

In authoritarian societies, on the other hand, the goal of indoctrination is to imprint upon all minds one unquestionable view of society and the individual's place in it, to the exclusion of all others. In such cultures, the author Ben Macintyre wrote in 2018, 'the individual is encouraged to consider the interests of society before personal welfare: from Nazi Germany to communist Russia to Cambodia under the Khmer Rouge and North Korea today, a willingness to betray those nearest to you for the greater good was the ultimate mark of committed citizenship and ideological purity.' These same characteristics also apply to the societies of the Islamic world, steeped in aggressive disdain for all dissenters and suffocating under the pressure of clan-thinking centred on the family and its honour.

The consequences of this juxtaposition between democracy on the one hand and all forms of authoritarianism on the other are dramatic. Without exception, the standard of living in the present Western democracies has improved spectacularly over the past two or three centuries, across all segments of society. As a result, life there has become immensely more comfortable, healthy and safe. At some point during early modernity, a snowball started rolling in the Western world that, in time, developed into an ever-growing avalanche of new scientific insights, technological innovation and artistic variety. Nothing of the kind happened anywhere else.

Until around the year 1500 there had been little to choose between the European, African, Asian and American worlds in terms of knowledge, art, wealth, health and respect for human life. Life had been roughly equally poor, nasty, brutish and short everywhere, even for the happy few. Technologically cultures did not differ much, except for the Americas suffering from a lack of strategic raw materials such as iron and large domesticable animals for transport, labour and warfare. China alone was some significant paces ahead of the rest of the world. It had an advanced bureaucracy and had invented, among other things, gunpowder, rocketry, paper and a kind of typesetting way before anyone else. Under Admiral Zheng He it had explored the oceans in ships larger than the world had ever seen, reaching East Africa when the Portuguese first ventured beyond Ceuta on the northwest African coast. But virtually nobody outside the realm knew or cared. Nor did the Chinese themselves, apparently, for they went on to squander most of their achievements, to end up a shambles by the end of the nineteenth century, helpless carrion gnawed at by hungry vultures from the West. By that time, too, Africa and large parts of Southern Asia had been divided between the European powers, and the once so powerful Ottoman Empire lingered as a mismanaged, poverty-stricken relic of the Middle Ages.

Usually, the reason given for this abysmal rift evolving between the West and the rest is the Enlightenment, which transformed Western culture in the eighteenth century. But the Enlightenment was itself a result rather than a reason. It was important, but also just another phase in a process that had begun many centuries before. A process whose real prime mover was, surprisingly, the medieval Roman Catholic Church.

From the days of the first kingdoms, religion and secular power had been inextricably intertwined as a matter of course. Kings could be gods, demi-gods or incarnations of gods, or they were high priests or at the very least ordained and supported by a religious caste. Of course, the three great monotheistic religions denied their kings divine status. This was not a problem for the Jews, who, lacking a territorial history since the days of the Roman Empire, had neither kings nor secular power to manage. In Islam secular and religious structures remained hardly distinguishable. Islam assumed and retained a fairly flat, decentralized structure, remaining close to the people and creeping into society's every capillary. The Christian Mother Church, however, took a radically different tack. It modelled itself on secular, hierarchical and centralist power structures, putting a pope at the very top as the sole representative of Jesus Christ on Earth. In doing so, it positioned itself with respect to secular rulers not as a spiritual guide to trust in, the way older cultures had looked to priests, oracles and soothsayers for guidance, but as a competitor. From the eighth century onwards it even maintained its own papal state. But by joining the rulers and their game, the Church automatically distanced itself from its flock. It was no longer naturally omnipresent like the air people breathe, but one of a set of identifiable institutions vying for worldly power and control, usually at the cost of ordinary people.

Together with the strict pecking order, which was expressed in terms of privilege, prestige and power, this alienation from ordinary folk further fostered elitist, snobbish tendencies that were latent among the ambitious clergy anyway. For weren't they the saintly guardians of holy knowledge and literacy in an otherwise barbarous, tumultuously violent world? As a result, as Barbara Ehrenreich argues, the clergy quite literally began to push believers out of their churches, putting an end to much of their traditional communal use as a venue for anything from town-hall meetings to feasts. Unwittingly, the Church itself set in motion the process that would ultimately result in the separation of Church and State as we know it.

The very same snobbism engendered irrepressible greed and corruption among religious dignitaries. This was regularly protested against by religious reformers and purists, usually by founding a new, still more virtuous and ascetic religious order, or by renouncing the Church altogether for a life of persecution for heresy. In the end, more precisely in 1517, the disgruntled German monk Martin Luther sparked the Reformation in Europe. His idea was to give the Church – which he said had been usurped by a gluttonous, hubristic and corrupt clergy – back to the believers. According to him, this could best be achieved by affording the people a Bible and liturgy in the vernacular. His insistence on religion being a matter of a personal relationship between a believer and God gave unprecedented prominence to the individual and also stressed the importance of literacy. Thus Luther and the Mother Church together planted the seeds from which would eventually grow the Enlightenment and all that it entailed.

Next to individual freedom and unsurpassed and uniquely widespread physical, economic and cultural prosperity, modern democracies turn out to have yet another attractive characteristic. Mature democracies seem less likely to go in for unprovoked adventures of conquest than other kinds of culture. The wars modern democracies have fought since the beginning of the twentieth century were overwhelmingly either started by an undemocratic regime or part of some process of decolonization. Across Western Europe, international peace has reigned for three quarters of a century, since 1945 – an unprecedented miracle. Even the bloody conflicts in the Balkans during the 1990s were the result of strongmen such as Slobodan Milošević, Franjo Tuđman and Radovan Karadžić grabbing their chance in the chaos following the fall of the Warsaw Pact and the disintegration of Yugoslavia after the demise of its dictator, Marshal Tito.

There are exceptions, though, such as several conflicts between India and Pakistan and the *konfrontasie*, 'confrontation', the undeclared war between aggressor Indonesia and fledgling Malaysia from 1962 to 1966, all involving young and unstable but formally democratic nations. And, of course, there is the behaviour of the United States, which not only ignominiously carried the can for defeated colonialist France in Indo-China, but waged several wars of aggression against small American nations such as Panama, Nicaragua and tiny Grenada, as well as helping to stage right-wing coups in a gamut of countries from Iran to El Salvador. On balance, however, it seems correct to state that mature democracies tend to keep verbal warfare verbal in dealing with each other, whereas authoritarian regimes stifle it and prefer to put stick about.

@#$%!

IN THE WEST, the Enlightenment changed the way people related to nature, God and society. As a consequence, it also affected the way people personally appreciated blasphemy. Instead of a public crime against social order, it came to be understood as a symptom of some form of mental indisposition, something much more private. In due course this came to be reflected in the laws of most Western nations. The old harsh laws requiring corporal punishment and mutilation or worse with an eye to maintaining public order gave way to more lenient measures. Here and there blasphemy laws disappeared altogether, at least for a while. 'God can preserve His own rights by Himself, no human laws are needed for this purpose,' the Dutch Minister of Justice Anthony Modderman told his parliament as early as 1880. But of course this did not stop people from taking offence.

On the whole, among the democracies of the West the twentieth century was a period of more or less steady relaxation of social standards and protocols. As prosperity and the average level of education increased, class barriers weakened and taboos shattered. In Europe, although not in America, the churches lost much of their hold over people's lives and thinking. Those who saw this as growing evidence of dangerously loose morals, people such as Mary Whitehouse in Britain, had a hard time of it. Large parts of society – ordinary folk, women and the young – were aching for emancipation and liberation. And, especially after the Second World War, they began taking what they thought of as naturally theirs. Ostensibly, this culminated in the hippie movement of the late 1960s with its not all that constructive, naively self-indulgent motto: tune in, turn on, drop out.

But behind the hippie histrionics hid an unsung, highly important achievement of the older half of the so-called Silent Generation, those who had had their adolescence stolen from them by the Second World War. They had come of age in a highly militarized and therefore necessarily conservative and authoritarian setting. Nevertheless, in their late thirties or early forties many of them actually did what their hippie children professed to be doing, up to a point. Once the 1960s broke, they hesitantly did tune in and did turn on. And, unlike their children, to whom the new freedoms came as a matter of course, they actually changed their mentality, their understanding of events and what they meant. But they did not drop out, and by doing so they kept society afloat, and the processes of liberation and emancipation with it.

At the same time, however, the seeds of backlash were already being sown, primarily in academic circles in the United States. The term 'politically correct' or 'PC' began popping up there from the late 1960s. At first it seems to have been used as a slur on bigoted Maoists and similar far-left hardliners, but soon the term was adopted by people with a somewhat different mindset: people who considered themselves progressive and endorsed Women's Lib and the emancipation of black and indigenous America, for instance. Other than the familiar Maoists, Leninists, Trotskyists and whatnot, they aimed not to bring about a proletarian revolution, but to end all inequity between what they considered the sexually, racially or culturally oppressed on the one hand and privileged groups in society on the other – from the male chauvinist pig of the late 1960s to today's angry white man. What remained, albeit with the best intentions, was the bigotry, the obstinate attachment to one's own beliefs and intolerance of other people's beliefs and practices. From its beginning, political correctness was all about guilt and retribution. While the 1960s were bent on promoting equality by empowering people through enlarging their freedom and their potential for self-expression, political correctness sought to root out the inequality in society by denying people what it saw as privilege and cultural appropriation. While the essence of the decade lay in breaking taboos and the unabashed exploration of new territory, politically correct thinking was all about creating taboos, inducing shame and putting up new, 'correct', fences. Whereas the 1960s were a celebration of the joys of unprecedented freedom of thought and expression – in theory, anyway – the politically correct movement was out to impose its own ideology on everybody. And it did so, primarily, by lashing out at people's speech, by attacking and tabooing terminology that was deemed racist, sexist or in some other way undesirable.

The result has been a never-ending cascade of terms being deprecated and replaced by more circumspect new euphemisms, in the bowdlerization and banning of children's books, in emasculating the names of sports teams and even in changing colour names that were considered racist or appropriated from indigenous people. It has also resulted in evermore complex ways of indicating people's ethnic background. Ironically, while the main idea behind this was to reduce and ultimately put an end to the racist fixation on ethnicity that has pervaded American society from its inception, it drew even more attention to the matter, keeping everyone permanently on edge. Of course, except for the public debate souring, nothing substantial changed. When all is said and done, political correctness is just smoke and mirrors. It is all about appearances, with one exception. To Americans the word 'negro' (and, of course, 'nigger') had long been used to refer to people who were not only black but second-rate citizens, subject to systematic and intentional, officially sanctioned and enforced segregation and discrimination – in short: actual racism. On paper, at least, such people did not exist once the Civil Rights Act of 1964 had been passed, so in America 'negro', which was inextricably bound to these obsolete ideas and practices, had to go. The understandable anger and resentment among the long-repressed black people were too great even to let it live on as a neutral term referring to black people 'back in the day'.

The rise of political correctness and its subsequent spread to Europe during the 1970s is yet another instance of the old spectre of authoritarianism that lurks in the cellars of all modern democracies rearing its ugly head, in a new, different guise. This time there was no ideologically extremist cabal that raised a violent militia and used it or the army to force its will on a nation. This time the driving force was a loosely knit conglomerate of academic social-justice warriors *avant la lettre*, using the rapidly growing, impressionable student body to push their agenda all over the Western democratic world. Inspired, in part, by philosophers such as Jacques Derrida and Michel Foucault, they considered that knowledge and truth were social constructs, more like shared opinions based on the ideas and convictions of individuals at some point in time than immutable facts or logical conclusions. From their emancipatory, politicized agenda it follows that these opinions are highly moralistic. So, to the politically correct mind, objectivity and disinterested truth are just naive illusions or worse: ploys of the privileged to protect their dominant positions.

In the same vein, politically correct thinking embraced the notion of cultural relativism, the idea that a culture can be judged only on its own terms, which amounts to not at all. Thus, PC-adepts can easily turn a blind eye to aspects of minority cultures in the West that are undesirable or reprehensible to those outside them, such as genital mutilation, the violent repression of homosexuality, forced marriages and honour killings. It explains, for instance, how modern feminism can stand up for the right of Muslim women in the West to wear the burka their male oppressors impose on them, while ignoring the struggle for freedom of their sisters in Iran and elsewhere in the Islamic world. Such muddled inconsistency, such cognitive dissonance is only to be expected once you throw away the yardsticks of fact, objectivity and logic.

This lack of an external, independent yardstick entails that all tenets of political correctness are baseless. They float anchorless in seas of opinionated and unabashedly prejudiced relativity. In such dire straits there are four straws to clutch at: the consensus of the PC peer group, the authority of captains of that peer group, denial and disparagement. These are precisely what the politically correct cling to. Propositions and judgements are considered valid and acceptable because 'everybody' tells one another that they are, or because some race-gender-culture scholar says they are. Denial comes in the form of a refusal to enter into open debate with critics and opponents, preferring to try to 'de-platform' the opposition. A favourite tactic is intimidation and disparagement by name-calling, to which end the concept of phobia has been usurped and warped. According to circumstance, critics are vociferously decried as for instance homophobes, Islamophobes, transphobes or whatever else comes in handy. However, these are nonsensical slurs. A phobia is an irrational but irrepressible fear of something, a phenomenon primarily rooted in biology. By contrast, what the politically correct accuse one of by such terms is a voluntary and therefore reprehensible hatred of something, which is a cultural phenomenon. Nevertheless, the tactic has proven highly effective, especially among the vacillating majority, always afraid of ending up on the wrong side of the stick. It frames all those who disagree as despicable Neanderthals nobody would want to associate with, and thus splits society into virtually irreconcilable camps. By doing so, and by its fluid, self-serving concept of what is right or wrong, it even paved the way for what we now call alternative facts and fake news. In this poisoned atmosphere, using politically incorrect terms has become the new sacrilege, blasphemy against the new gods of cultural relativity and 'inclusiveness', who in fact exclude all dissenters.

By now, it will be clear that political correctness and the identity politics it spawned are not just anti-intellectual, anti-rational and totalitarian, but also have all the trimmings of a religious sect. It even has its own revelation, in the form of the mystical notion of being 'woke'. Those who are 'woke' are privy to a higher understanding of the way things are. They have entered into a superior class (precisely the thing political correctness was invented to eliminate) that has knowledge of some ultimate, absolute truth, the very thing political correctness denies exists. Moreover, since truth and validity are a matter of consensus and authority, the interests of the collective come before those of the individual. In the PC world, a good person is one who unquestioningly subjects herself to the entire philosophy. Like any other sect, the politically correct sphere is a Hotel California, where you can check in any time you like, but you can never leave.[5]

> ## Cancel culture and de-platforming in academia
>
> Whereas hate speech typically targets groups and individuals as representatives of a group, de-platforming and cancel culture are acts of collective aggression against an individual as a person. De-platforming occurs mostly in and around universities. It aims to deny people access to the public and academic discourse by intimidating them, demanding their dismissal and sabotaging venues where they speak, in the hope of turning academia – and ultimately the world – into a 'safe space'. But universities worth their salt are anything but safe spaces. They are places of adventure, of intellectual daring and discovery, of discord, occasional brinkmanship and frequent failure; places where commitment and good work are respected but nothing is holy or beyond scrutiny. Guided by the facts as best we know them, science and scholarship are fundamentally undemocratic. All they share with democracy is the absolute need for unfettered discourse. De-platforming is, apart from being very threatening to its victims, a dangerously detrimental form of obscurantism and bigotry every student, scholar and scientist should do their utmost to fight.
>
> Even more malignant is cancel culture. Just take a moment to contemplate the very concept of cancelling people. It means to wipe them out, erase them from society. It is what happened to Kevin Spacey, Woody Allen and a fast-growing list of others – all the way down in time to Christopher Columbus, and who knows, beyond. Despite not being tried or convicted in a court of law, they are quite literally struck from the record, even to the point that their creative contributions cannot be shown or viewed in peace any more. They have been morally murdered, and the corporate world and creative industry, demonstrating a spine made exclusively out of loose change, have proven quick to oblige. Cancelling is criminal vigilante justice and medieval witch-hunt rolled into one, and a grave danger to everything most people in modern democracies hold dear.

It is probably this religious character that explains the astonishing success of politically correct thinking, both inside and outside academia. American culture has always been highly susceptible to sectarian religiosity, and in Europe it filled the vacuum left by the retreating traditional churches. To many, the politically correct ideology offers a semblance of security and belonging in an insecure, lonely world.

@#$%!

THE BIG QUESTION IS, of course, why modern democracy, with all that it has going for it, is beleaguered time and time again by authoritarian forces, with no guarantee that these forces might not one day win. They do, as a matter of fact. It happened in Italy, in Spain and ultimately in Germany. It also happened in Iran and possibly in the Philippines when Rodrigo Duterte was elected, and it keeps happening in fledgling democracies all over Central and Southern America. Even the 45th president of the United States openly flirted with such ideas as presidency for life and physically violent defence of his rule. The answer probably lies in feelings of insecurity.

By definition, democracy does not issue its citizens with clear marching orders, making it easy on them to do the right thing. Instead, it saddles people with a grave responsibility: go and fend for yourselves, for those who are dear to you, and even for people whom you don't much like, care about or agree with on anything. It tells you to keep society in order, but it does not say how. That's political freedom for you: essentially, it leaves the citizen at a loss. Most people cope with this by either joining the bandwagon of some established political party or not partaking in the democratic process at all, abiding by the law and offering silent support but leaving it to others to do the maintenance and development. Some, however, fall for the lure of an easier solution, of putting all your eggs in the basket of some leader, religious movement or extremist political or cultural ideology. It would seem that this latter group comprises up to 30 per cent of the adult population in all Western democracies. Not sufficient for democracy to collapse, but large enough to pose a real threat in the hands of a determined well-organized group of agitators.

Without exception such leaders, movements and ideologies, if they win, run into the eternal deficiencies of authoritarian rule: rampant corruption, intellectual, scientific and technological stagnation, and an uncooperative workforce. Those who bear guns have few real friends. Unfortunately, this is not a guarantee that all will be well in the end.

@#$%!

AT THE HEIGHT of the French student rebellion of May 1968, Daniel Cohn-Bendit, their best-known frontman, was rumoured to be en route to the Netherlands to spread the revolution. Scared out of his wits, a Dutch MP interpellated the Minister of Justice whether this 'foreigner of anarchist and revolutionary views' could be stopped at the border. Minister Carel Polak suavely replied: 'Democracy is not for the fainthearted.'[6]

Instead of succumbing to fear, Polak hung on to the combined principles of democracy and freedom of speech, and rightly so. For any kind of democracy to work takes a certain confidence in themselves and in their fellow citizens on the part of the people. Not much, but just enough to trust that the country will not plunge into chaos at the first villain 'of anarchist and revolutionary views' crossing its borders. This shared trust, a relatively small matter, might well be the primary reason for the vitality and resilience modern democracy has shown over the past century, for it offers a huge return on investment, in two ways.

> ## How can democracy be based on both trust and 'organized distrust'?
>
> Trust is the linchpin of any functional democracy, yet the system is often paradoxically called 'organized distrust', its very opposite. This is a paradox but not a contradiction. On the one hand, for a democracy to work there must be sufficient trust between citizens, as well as between citizens and officials. Citizens must be prepared to relegate permanently to the state most of their powers to protect their personal interests, hoping that in the long run they will, on balance, be better off.
>
> On the other hand, however, there is the question of who can be entrusted with the powers that those citizens so daringly relinquish. Plato thought experts were the answer: wise philosophers whose good intentions could be relied on. Indeed, many indigenous peoples have taken this road, relegating power to elders and shamans, men (and sometimes women) of experience who are supposed to know best. To some extent this works, but only in societies small enough for everybody to know each other personally. Anonymity is the enemy of entrusted power. As societies grow larger, these intimately known, authoritative elders degrade into distant, indifferent tyrants. So the democrat's answer to the question of whom to trust with all that power is: nobody.
>
> The consequence is that everybody is equally responsible and hence must have an equal share of power. This is why democracy is called organized distrust. For all sorts of practical reasons, citizens of larger democracies have found ways to delegate their share of public responsibility, which has resulted in the wide array of representative democracies that exists today.

First, a small measure of mutual trust helps to keep Hobbes's all-devouring monsters from our doorstep. Trust by itself generates social and political stability, which in turn help to bolster confidence and trust, and so on. This may be why in any well-rooted democracy a lot of people loudly complain, but very few of those seriously go in for solutions outside the system. Even most of those who call their prime minister a tyrant, their president a traitor and a dictator and their representatives untrustworthy lying scum don't really wish for regime change. They want things as they are, only better.

But the greatest dividend of democracy comes in the form of a solution to the most dangerous power problem facing any society: the matter of succession. Since we are all mortals, any king, caudillo or comrade-number-one will at some point begin to lose strength and face, which is when ambitious would-be usurpers move in. More often than not, it all ends in a country in turmoil with much thieving, robbing and bloodshed. Authoritarian rulers have always known this, of course, and many make an effort to ensure a smooth transfer of power. But except for the occasional monarchy that is strong enough and sufficiently well organized and well connected to remain in power for a number of generations, they are typically bad at it. In most cases, insecurity about their own position makes them do away with most competent candidates for succession, who come to be seen as dangerous competitors, right from the kings of Sumer and the emperors of Rome down to present-day Kim Jong-un. And each time, ordinary people must foot the bill and are rewarded with bad, unjust governance.

Here, for instance, is how, according to the seventeenth-century Spanish missionary Antonio de Teruel, King Garcia II Nkanga a Lukeni of Kongo viewed his own position. In 1645 Garcia had availed himself of the elective throne of Kongo 'with violence and against the will of his vassals', writes the missionary. 'He knew that they had no love for him, and so he was wary of them, never eating with his nobles as was the tradition of the Kings.' Still worse, 'he feared everyone, and if he suspected anyone of treachery he would find an excuse to send them to another Province, and order them to be executed when they least suspected it.'[7]

Of course, politicians in a democracy are no better. They fear the talented upstarts in their parties just as much as the junta general fears the up-and-coming charismatic young colonel, and are just as eager to trip them up. They too fear for their own position and wish to stay in power past their sell-by date. Sometimes whole parties are torn asunder by internal strife for this reason. The big difference is that in a mature democracy, all this happens at the level of individual parties, and hardly affects the functioning of the state and the security of the population. Democratic leaders have much less potentially disruptive power than their authoritarian colleagues, but they are also more expendable. The system of free and fair elections at set intervals offers a stable, well-understood and widely supported procedure for the transfer of power, which – and this is essential – is independent of those vying for it. The process of forming a new government may be messy, lengthy and frustrating, but in the end there always will be one, while everything keeps running smoothly. This, then, is the greatest advantage of democracy over all other political systems: basic universal security, rooted in universal suffrage, the rule of law and reliable procedures for the transfer of power.

@#$%!

THIS CONFIDENCE GAP between authoritarian and democratic rule is also reflected in how governments, religions and people cope with satire. Next to their succession, the greatest problem of both secular and religious authoritarian rulers has always been how they could be sure that the information they received was accurate and their reasoning sound. Any despot ultimately surrounds himself with sycophants, yes-men who may or may not be loyal to him, but can never be trusted to speak their minds. For to do so may easily cut short a promising career – or even a life – if what comes out is unwanted. Even the most suspicious and short-fused of dictators need a modicum of rational and realistic criticism to be able to defend their position, but allowing people of importance to disagree with the chief might signal weakness and dependency. Therefore, providing criticism and putting things into perspective became the task of the court jester, whose comments were tolerated because they clearly seemed not serious and whose jocular advice could be ignored without loss of face. Irreverent carnivalesque distortion was vital for a jester's criticism to be acceptable, and if it was not there was always the chop.

Away from the courts, among the ordinary people, humour acquired a similar function. Straight, serious criticism of those in power might easily be branded seditious and trigger violent

Comedian politicians

Over the past few decades, Western democracies have seen the rise of a new phenomenon: the satirical populist politician, whose criticism is acceptable to people who usually don't want to hear about politics at all. The first of these was Coluche, a French comedian of the Mitterrand era, who made a bid for the presidency of France in 1980. At one point he had the support of no less than 16 per cent of the French electorate. But before he could be put to the test, he dropped out of the race on account of death threats he had been receiving. More successful was Beppe Grillo, the Italian comedian who started the Movimento Cinque Stelle (Five Stars Movement) in 2009 and in 2013 made it the biggest party in the Italian parliament. Grillo kept up his biting political satire in support of his movement, but never went into parliament himself. In May 2019 Volodymyr Zelensky, a man with no background in politics, became the first comedian to go all the way by winning the general elections and becoming president of Ukraine. It would seem that the greatest asset of such candidates is the fact that they are so refreshingly not part of the political establishment, as well as free of any stains of favouritism and corruption. Once in office, Zelensky at least has proved himself a sincere and true people's president, wielding his thespian talents as an impressive weapon.

suppression. Couching criticism in the age-old literary form of allegory was one way of trying to avoid this. Making these allegories funny was another. Yes, it was still criticism, but it was 'just' a joke. Also, in order to take punitive measures, a ruler had to acknowledge that the veiled criticism was directed at him, and in doing so concede that it held water. It also entailed acknowledging that one was the butt of a joke, which meant loss of face. Together, this has always made satire a powerful form of criticism, infuriatingly difficult to contend with.

But what *is* this thing called satire? One thing we can say with confidence is that its function is to expose aspects of politics, cultures and religions that are considered hollow, unjust and immoral by ridiculing, simplifying and distorting them. Distortion is at its core, and its weapons of choice are hyperbole, parody and caricature – not mere exaggeration, imitation and portrayal, which belong to the armoury of the straight bully. Like bullying, satire aims to unsettle people, sometimes even to intimidate them, and to show them up as ridiculous, banal and trivial. The principled difference between the two regards the choice of target. Bullying is always deeply and exclusively personal; it is impossible to bully an institution, or someone's social status or profession. When it is funny, bullying is a form of *Schadenfreude*, laughter at the expense of someone who is weak or at a disadvantage. Bullying exploits personal weakness by exerting crass authority. Satire, on the other hand, is essentially anti-authoritarian. Even if a satirical attack seems personal, the real target is an institution or situation that person represents. One can satirize a functionary, a member of some group, a promotor of some idea or a fighter against it, but not a mere private person. Satire is poking fun at power and dominance and the pretence of superiority as exemplified by sects, religions and ideologies. Rightly or wrongly it questions and exposes what it considers to be the hollow hypocrisy of the powerful and the dominant, both authoritarian entities. This is why one of satire's favourite targets is that most dominant group of all: mainstream citizenry with its stuffy moral values, which it so often fails to uphold.

The comfortably powerful often derive considerable pleasure from the ways in which they are satirized. The largely symbolic, firmly entrenched monarchies of present-day Europe, for example, hardly ever comment on satire. And if they do, they try to get in on the fun. The originally American phenomenon of the roast (which is, as the *Oxford English Dictionary* puts it, 'a banquet at which the guest of honour is subjected to good-natured ridicule') is another illustration of confidently powerful people effectively joining forces with those who satirize them, all the way up to most of America's more recent presidents at the annual White House Correspondents' Dinner. This is something that it takes real self-confidence to do, including the firm conviction that those who ridicule you are critical of you, but not malevolent. If they pull it off, they actually turn ridicule to their advantage, strengthening their prestige by confirming and advertising both easy self-assuredness and gracious magnanimity.

This highly effective way of neutering ridicule is out of reach to those who are insufficiently secure or feel threatened by satire. It is not a coincidence that, as president of the United States, Donald Trump, who fears and loathes the press more than anything in the world, preferred to forgo the Correspondents' Dinner and in time even forbade his staff to attend.

Coping with satire by ignoring it, enjoying it or feigning to do so is yet another hallmark of modern democracy. With the July Revolution of 1830, France stumbled one step ahead on the way to becoming such a democracy by ousting the oppressive King Charles x and replacing him with his cousin, the much more liberal-minded *roi-bourgeois*, 'citizen-king', Louis-Philippe and a more modern constitution. The new king's mission was, in his own words, to find 'the right middle, equally removed from the excesses of popular power and the abuses of royal power'.[8] This involved much more lenient censorship laws, inspiring a small group including the printer and editor Charles Philipon and the young cartoonist Honoré Daumier to start a satirical weekly called *La Caricature*. In it, the king was roundly ridiculed, squarely attacked and given a second life as *le poire*, 'the pear'. If we can trust the testimony of the German poet Heinrich Heine, Louis-Philippe loved this satirical attention, but that didn't stop him, and it certainly did not stop his government, from clamping down on the band of political satirical gadflies so hard that by 1840 the British cultural satirist William Makepeace Thackeray wondered: 'Half-a-dozen poor artists on the one side, and his Majesty Louis-Philippe, his august family, and the numberless placemen and supporters of his monarchy, on the other.' Three troubled years later *La Caricature* finally gave in.

Obviously, the French leadership did not feel sufficiently secure to condone cartoons that were, as Thackeray wrote, 'so ludicrously mean, and so often appropriate'. And they were right in a sense. In February 1848, not quite eighteen years after one revolution had landed Louis-Philippe on the French throne, another pulled it out from under him. This time the French decided to say goodbye to monarchy for good, and went for a republic.

The enormous force of suppressive power that regimes deploy time and time again to smother Thackeray's 'half-a-dozen poor artists' makes one wonder why authorities in general so fear and loathe the occasional unarmed satirist who is not out for their job. For, let's face it, no leader, regime or even democratic government has ever been toppled by a cartoon or a sketch. By themselves satirists don't cause anything more than occasional upheaval. They don't set any agenda. Instead they comment on and hopefully induce people to reflect on things that are already happening, and there's an end of it.

The explanation may well be that, although satire attacks abstract entities such as institutions, ideas and taboos, ordinary people always bear the brunt of it. Consider how the scathingly satirical French

LES POIRES,

Faites à la cour d'assises de Paris par le directeur de la CARICATURE.

Vendues pour payer les 6,000 fr. d'amende du journal le *Charivari*.

(CHEZ AUBERT, GALERIE VÉRO-DODAT.)

Si, pour reconnaître le monarque dans une caricature, vous n'attendez pas qu'il soit désigné autrement que par la ressemblance, vous tomberez dans l'absurde. Voyez ces croquis informes, auxquels j'aurais peut-être dû borner ma défense :

Ce croquis ressemble à Louis-Philippe, vous condamnerez donc ?

Alors il faudra condamner celui-ci, qui ressemble au premier.

Puis condamner cet autre, qui ressemble au second.

Et enfin, si vous êtes conséquens, vous ne sauriez absoudre cette poire, qui ressemble aux croquis précédens.

Ainsi, pour une poire, pour une brioche, et pour toutes les têtes grotesques dans lesquelles le hasard ou la malice aura placé cette triste ressemblance, vous pourrez infliger à l'auteur cinq ans de prison et cinq mille francs d'amende !!
Avouez, Messieurs, que c'est là une singulière liberté de la presse !!

Louis-Philippe turning into a pear step by step. It is really a defence against censorship: if you ban caricatures of the king for their likeness, like the one top left, you must ban the sketch to the right of it as well, on account of its likeness to the first, and so on. So the censor inevitably ends up banning everything down to an innocent pear, which is absurd. Therefore, the press must be free. From *Le Charivari*, III/17 (17 January 1834).

weekly *Charlie Hebdo* reacted after the barbaric massacre of eight of its writers and cartoonists, a visitor, a bystander and two policemen by two al-Qaeda extremists on 7 January 2015. What was left of the editorial staff showed its temerity and resilience by putting out a new issue on the fourteenth, not missing a beat. Its Islam-green cover featured a tearfully regretful prophet Muhammad holding a sign saying 'I am Charlie,' the meme expressing solidarity with the cartoonists that had swept the world in the days after the atrocity. Over his head were the words 'All is forgiven.' It was a brave and magnanimous offer of mutual reconciliation, while reserving the right to satirize anybody and anything, including the Prophet.

This was, at least, how it looked to enlightened Westerners. Not, obviously, to millions of incendiary Muslims. The issue kindled new flames of hatred and violence among them, resulting, for instance, in ten murders and some 45 torched Christian churches in Niger. The Turkish national daily *Cumhuriyet*, which had published four pages from the issue of *Charlie Hebdo* but not its cover, ran into trouble anyway because two of its columnists, Hikmet Çetinkaya and Ceyda Karan, included a thumbnail of it by way of illustration. An astonishing 1,280 people – among them close family members of the Turkish president Recep Tayyip Erdoğan – brought complaints, and both columnists were arrested. In April 2016 they were found guilty of 'inciting public hatred', whatever that means, and sentenced to two years behind bars. Curiously, they were never prosecuted for blasphemy and were acquitted of the charge of 'insulting religious values'. So why the hubbub; what sparked all that anger among Muslims?

The answer is that many Muslims registered something quite different from an illegal depiction of their prophet. What they saw on the cover of *Charlie Hebdo* was just a stupid-looking, ugly, somewhat dishevelled sorry little sod, and he was *them*. They felt personally belittled, derided and insulted. Not all Muslims, of course, but at least the underprivileged and the insecure and their spokespeople. Little people eking out a meagre existence in some corrupt and badly administrated Middle Eastern or African hellhole, or surviving as second-rate citizens in the projects and *banlieues* of the West, clinging to tradition and religious identity to keep mentally afloat. To them, the cover just added insult to injury.

So it goes. What is intended and published as satire, as an attempt to expose the hollowness of some institution, religious or otherwise, is often read and understood as plain bullying by those who adhere to that institution. Disparagement of an institution is easily interpreted as disparagement of their very person by people who are not snugly secure or truly and deeply arrogant. What we see here is a mix-up of spheres, which, as we saw in Chapter Four, determine what is appropriate and what is not. Satirists, with their focus on institutions, ideologies and religions, operate in the public sphere of newspapers, magazines, blogs and television shows. Those without an interest in the matter at hand usually sort of understand this; they just laugh or tut-tut at irreverent texts, sketches or cartoons and the upheaval they cause. Those who incarnate or adhere to the object of ridicule, however, often react from their private sphere: they take it personally.

This partly explains why satire is much more accepted in democratic societies than in authoritarian ones. If in a democratic society bigwigs fall from power, all they stand to lose is a job, so they can afford a few jesters and pranksters nibbling at their thrones. In fact, doing so may even be interpreted as strength and curry extra favour with the electorate on which they depend. The position of authoritarian leaders and their associates is generally much more precarious. They have gone all in; falling from power may cost them their fortune, their freedom and even their lives, so preservation of face and the pretence of being in complete control are paramount. Although some don't start out this way, ultimately they all embrace some version of Caligula's motto *oderint dum metuant*, 'I don't care if they hate me, as long as they fear me.' From their point of view, everything is personal and any criticism of their functioning is a threat to their personal security.

The other half of the explanation is that to such people and their entourage, satire is even worse than straight, serious criticism. Authoritarian leaders live by enforcing strict obeisance to their rules and suppressing any doubt regarding their ability to do so. This is completely incompatible with any kind of humour. In Chapter Nine we saw how by the Banana Peel Law humour – any kind of humour – involves breaking some expectation, rule or taboo, and how smiles and laughter may signal internal conflict, unease and subservience.

Remarkably, the tolerance of satire is limited to the public domain even in democratic societies. Outside it, within companies, institutions, schools and the civil service for instance, unsolicited criticism and satire are often just as unwelcome and dangerous as in

We know from films and snapshots made at his retreat in Berchtesgaden that Adolf Hitler could look happy, smile merrily and enter into friendly conversation with both adults and children. But one wouldn't say so from looking at his official portraits (seen here in a photograph, from c. 1933, centre bottom left) or the footage of his public performances. The same holds for Stalin, who must have been a fearsome party animal and apparently liked a good joke, if only anyone dared tell one. He too looks stern and decisive in his official portraits. As for Ayatollah Khomeini, there actually exist one or two snapshots of him laughing, but his official portraits (seen here in a photograph from late 1970s, centre top left) show a man who deeply abhorred and despised laughter and merriment; a true puritan, driven by the haunting fear that someone, somewhere may be happy, as H. L. Mencken once put it. Going further back in history, the pattern among authorities like kings, nobles and dignitaries continues, not only in paintings, but in their portraits on coins and in statues. There is hardly a smile to be found. They generally look aloof like the emperor Octavian Augustus (seen here in a detail of a marble statue, 1st century AD, centre bottom right) or Louis XIV (seen here in a detail of the portrait by Hyacinthe Rigaud from 1701, far right), intimidating like Henry VIII (seen here in a portrait by workshop of Hans Holbein the Younger, 1537–47, far left) or fierce like the third Duke of Alba, Fernando Álvarez de Toledo (seen here in a portrait by Antonis Mor, 1549). Even Jesus, despite all his other cheeks and meekness, is never portrayed openly smiling, except in post-modern hippie art. The Madonna does smile, but with eyes cast down. Hers is the modest smile of female subservience. Among the gods, only Buddha smiles, because he does not care about power and authority and does not need anyone's obedience.

any authoritarian society. Generally, then, satire can flourish within non-hierarchical, democratic settings only. And even there, even under the best of economic and social circumstances, escaping the clutches of victimhood by not taking everything personally is a feat of emancipation many fail to pull off.

@#$%!

SOME PEOPLE BRUISE easily, some don't. Those who do are usually advised to avoid bumpy rides and other risky situations. Some fruit and most fish bruise easily as well, which is why we are advised to handle them with care. Things are simple in the physical world, and relations between causes and effects are often straightforward and predictable. When it comes to psychological wounding, however, things are rather more complex and far less manageable. Not rarely its effects are surprising, and in some cases its consequences are as far-reaching as they are undesirable.

Giving and taking offence is a case in point. Offence is by no means limited to verbal communication. On the contrary, one can hardly imagine a mode of expression that is not likely to cause psychological bruising in the right – or should we say wrong – circumstances. Wearing the wrong clothes, making an inappropriate or misunderstood gesture, arriving too early or too late, giving the wrong token of appreciation, reacting too quickly and vociferously, or too slowly and perfunctorily, these have all been the cause of bitter enmity between individuals, families and whole nations. Remarkably, offence is as easily given by failing to do something as by doing the wrong thing, as I once learned the hard way at the bar of the Blarney Stone, an Irish pub in Dorchester, on the outskirts of Boston, Massachusetts. To my uneasy surprise, I and my order for a pint of beer were both stubbornly ignored. It was clear that something was wrong, but for the life of me I could not see what. The awkward stalemate lasted until a new arrival joined me at the bar and I told him I was from the Netherlands – before I had finished my sentence my pint materialized in front of me, accompanied by a profusion of apologies from the bartender. This was in 1982, at the height of the Troubles in Northern Ireland, and my accent, my age and my crewcut had caused me to be mistaken for a British squaddie.

Offence is all in the mind of the offended, but this is something people seldom realize, partly because of the misleading terminology we use. Malice aside, someone who gives offence actually does not 'give' anything at all. They need not even be aware that their presence or behaviour has a negative effect on anyone, as when someone insufficiently acquainted with the mores enters a sauna in swimwear, or a friendly Western tourist goes about Southeast Asia patting children on the head, to the horror of the locals. Even if people become aware that something is wrong, they need not know why. Someone may even stumble unintentionally into a situation and cause offence in spite of any apologies, as can happen when a man enters the ladies' lavatory by mistake. Conversely, taking offence does not mean that anything is taken from the offending party. Being offended is a self-induced state of indignation and painful insecurity, caused by a perceived infringement of one's dignity, face or peace of mind. People can be and do remain very offended even after it has become entirely clear that no such infringement was intended, such as when some poor innocent fails to turn up at a date or appointment for reasons beyond their control.

That said, it is of course entirely possible for someone actively to offend others. One way of doing so is to behave impolitely or rudely. By this, we mean that one could know or should know about certain sensitivities in others, but refuses to acknowledge them. Often such behaviour arises from a mere lack of consideration or respect, or as a means of pulling rank, but it might also be that showing consideration flies in the face of one's own values and sensitivities. Cultures can clash painfully, creating awkward situations for all involved, even on a small scale. Think of that time, for instance, when as a child you were invited to eat at a friend's house, only to find that your friend's family were seriously into some other religion than yours, and started saying grace their way. What to do in such a situation? Is it best hypocritically to join in as best you can, or to be true to yourself, keep perfectly still and pretend you're not there for the duration? Either way, your hosts may choose to be offended by your behaviour.

Such situations are problems of the 'when in Rome' kind. In dealing with parties whose culture, ideology and morals clash with yours, how indulgent must one be and where should a line be drawn? These are problems that have become very real and urgent owing to the mass-migration that began with the dismantling of the colonial empires after the Second World War. From then on, from the point of view of modern democracy, 'Rome' meant Europe, Australia and the United States. For various reasons, the Western world has accommodated huge numbers of immigrants, many of whom, especially in Europe, arrived convinced that they would one day, when circumstances were better, return to the old country. In their eyes, this decreased the need to 'do as the Romans do'. They considered themselves guests who went through the Western motions but whose first duty was to preserve their own culture, so that they would blend back in on their return home. In time, this has turned out to be a pipe dream for virtually all of them. Checking back, they found that back home the culture they had worked hard to preserve had changed too much itself for them to feel at home there any more. Meanwhile their children had become caught in the anomic middle between one culture that no longer fit their parents' teachings and another that those same parents had failed to make them fully conversant with. The result is that, although many have found their way and blended into society, many others do not feel accepted by the indigenous population and give up on Rome, withdrawing into a cultural and religious parallel world, segregated from mainstream society, but bent on furthering their interests and promoting their own, usually somewhat puritanical version of their old culture. What nobody could foresee at the outset was how new technology such as satellite television, the Internet and modern international banking would make living in the West in a non-Western bubble easier than ever. Worse, it gave the countries from which the immigrants came an iron grip on their diasporas.

Rome, or mainstream Western culture, on the other hand, for a long time neglected the plight of many of its new inhabitants, not quite knowing what to do about them, or caring much. As guests, they were given considerable leeway and were in most countries even supported in preserving their old culture and its institutions, at the cost of their acculturation in their new homelands. When they were no longer guests, the West found that large groups of mostly Islamic immigrants and their children had become alienated and advocated cultural and religious ideas that conflicted with deeply held Western values and morals, and in some cases were incompatible with modern democracy. Thus the indigenous majority of the West finds itself in a dilemma. On the one hand, its core values of equality and individual freedom of speech, thought and expression urge it to respect the ideas and wishes of all citizens. On the other, it cannot afford to let authoritarian minorities endanger its goose with the golden eggs – modern democratic culture – by refusing to at least respect those same core values. For now, the sad status quo is that both groups are likely to take offence at each other's practices at every occasion.

The one kind of offence in which the one giving offence is truly instrumental is the insult. An insult is an intentional attempt to wound someone's ego. It relates to other kinds of giving offence more or less like premeditated murder to involuntary manslaughter. Still, even with insults, it is the target who calls the shots. Try as you may, if someone refuses to rise to the bait – or, at least, pretends sufficiently well not to do so – the taunter is left with nothing. As with satire, ignoring insults and offensive behaviour is often the most effective way of dealing with them.

In modern secular societies, defamation laws against offence and insult have largely filled up the vacuum left by good old blasphemy. This is in many ways a lamentable mishap. First of all, the fashionable idea that a right should exist not to be offended, usually promoted by people who wish to curb the freedom of speech, holds no water. We have seen that offence becomes meaningful only when it is taken: whether to feel offended or not is an arbitrary choice by the offended party. But no right can exist that protects arbitrary choices, because it would subject everybody to the whims of everybody else. That is not a right, it is chaos. Rights put fences between the spheres of freedom of people and institutions. My right to corporeal integrity is your obligation not to physically harm me. Your right to free speech is my obligation not to prevent you from speaking out, and my right to privacy is your obligation not to come snooping around my door. In order for such fundamental rights to work, it must be eminently clear where the fence posts are. In other words, they must be very specific and predictable, and simple enough to be understood and complied with by everyone. An obligation not to infringe a person's arbitrary whim is none of these things. It's meaningless.

Apart from this, the main problem with laws criminalizing defamation is that they grant a specific role to the irrational and the supernatural in legal systems that neither can nor should accommodate them. The legal systems of modern democracies are designed to function fairly and reliably, and do so on the basis of three cornerstones: objectively verifiable fact, sound rational reasoning and disinterested impartiality on the part of judges. Such legal systems are strictly of this world. Subjective and irrational notions such as drives and intentions must play a role only if they cannot be avoided, such as when it has to be decided whether a murder was premeditated or not. Even then judges rely heavily on objectively observable facts and clues and sworn eyewitness testimonies. Of course there are judgments to be made that defy objective observability to a degree, such as whether a particular perpetrator can be held accountable for what they did, or only partly, or not at all. The subjective aspect is precisely why such cases are hellishly difficult to decide and likely to cause unfortunate amounts of upheaval. But, even then, judges will clutch at any objectively observable straw they can find, such as professional psychiatric evaluations. Moreover, in criminal law, these subjective and not entirely rational aspects always regard the circumstances surrounding a crime, never the actual crime itself.

Objective observability, the first cornerstone, means two things. First, different people must be able to 'see' the fact in question independently of each other. Second, when they observe such a fact, they must see the same thing. For example, a broken pot is a broken pot whoever looks at it, and everybody will say so. However, if one person spies a beautiful Baroque vase, the same thing may strike the next as an ugly piece of frilly earthenware junk. Both see the same thing, but differently. This makes 'broken' an objectively verifiable property, but not 'beautiful', which is a personal emotional choice instead.

The second cornerstone, sound rational reasoning, is a guarantee against arbitrariness and unpredictability. It ensures that the court will take the provisions of the law as both its point of departure and its yardstick, that it will respect the principles of common logic and refrain from introducing unfathomable arguments from magic, religion or superstition. A criminal lawyer arguing that his client's infelicitous exploits should be blamed on it being Friday the 13th won't curry any favour.

Third, disinterested impartiality must guarantee that any judgment reached is based on the character and circumstances of the crime committed, not on the colour of the hair or the name of the person in the dock, or the amount the defence offered the court to fix the match.

All three of these cornerstones are violated in defamation cases, whether or not they involve a god. The main problem is the lack of anything objectively verifiable. It is impossible to ascertain whether someone has been offended or insulted other than by their say-so. There is no corpus delicti and no objectively ascertainable damage, elements without which no other case would ever go to trial. Insulted people are plaintiff, victim and sole witness at once. But they are also the investigating officer, since the only 'evidence' is locked up inside their minds.

Since there is nothing factual to begin with, any rational discussion is impossible. Essentially, the plaintiff should always win, since what judge or jury can disagree with a person's assessment of their own feelings? Likewise, impartiality becomes difficult, for in the absence of anything tangible or verifiable, what is there for a judge to base his verdict on except his opinion of the plaintiff, his own idea about how offended he himself would be by the insult in question, and his personal appraisal of accuser and accused?

Things get even worse when a god is involved. Of course, someone can claim that their religious feelings have been hurt, for which many countries have extra legal provisions. But religious claimants also tend to go to court on the grounds that not they but their god has been offended, or one of his associates. Here people bring complaints on behalf of somebody else who refuses to appear in person or even to endorse his representative. Someone who, in all cases, the majority of the world population will swear doesn't even exist. Under proper rule of law, this is as unique as it is absurd.

Religious and activist parties will also bring cases by proxy, saying their group has been offended, or their creed. In some countries, the law even specifies that offending an individual is not a criminal offence, but offending a group is. In such cases, neither the group nor a representative sample of it is ever examined or called up to testify in court to the degree and sincerity of their offendedness. Again, the say-so of the plaintiff is all that matters, turning justice into a travesty of itself.

All this would perhaps be excusable if it yielded positive results, but it does not. It is simply bad justice, spawning expensive and protracted procedures that at best end in unsatisfactory compromise and chaos, exactly like many old-fashioned blasphemy trials. Or, rarely, in a laugh, as happened with Reve. The best thing by far would be to scrap the defamation laws and relegate rows about insult and offence to the private sphere, where they belong. They are better suited to the unsavoury logic of Raqqa, Syria, under ISIS, where, when an old man was mercilessly flogged, the reporter Azadeh Moaveni recorded this comment:

> 'He cried the whole time,' Aws said. 'It was lucky for him that he had cursed Allah, because Allah shows mercy. If he'd cursed the Prophet, they would have killed him.'[9]

12

THE FIFTEEN LAWS OF PROPAGANDA

Please remain. You furnish the pictures and I'll furnish the war.

This was the telegram that the American newspaper mogul William Randolph Hearst reportedly sent to Frederic Remington, the renowned artist he had dispatched to Cuba in January 1898 to illustrate the revolution that was expected to flare up there, ending the bloody deadlock that had existed between the Spanish colonial army and local insurgents for years. The problem was, as Remington soon complained, that 'Everything is quiet. There is no trouble. There will be no war. I wish to return.'

Hearst didn't need long to make good on his promise. In the evening hours of 15 February the armoured cruiser USS *Maine* blew up to smithereens at the dockside in Havana, where it had been stationed to protect American interests in unstable Cuba, killing 260 officers and crew. Captain Charles Sigsbee of the unfortunate vessel remained convinced that it had been an accident, but Hearst's newspapers strenuously made out that the sinister Spaniards had attacked the unsuspecting Americans with a secret mine or torpedo. These sustained allegations brought to boiling point the enmity that was already brewing among the Americans towards the cruel colonialist Spanish, and by 20 April Hearst's Spanish–American War was a fact.

Or so they say.

There is no doubt that the American press did all it could to turn public opinion against Spain and did not shy from spreading hoaxes and lies to achieve its belligerent goals. But its propaganda did not succeed in turning the *Maine* disaster into a direct *casus belli*. Nor is it likely that Hearst was personally involved. In the unabashedly imperialistic world in which he lived, it was only natural for the United States to carve out its own empire. Doing so was its so-called

$50,000 REWARD.—WHO DESTROYED THE MAINE?—$50,000 REWARD.

EDITION FOR GREATER NEW YORK.

NEW YORK JOURNAL

AND ADVERTISER.

NO. 5,572.   Copyright, 1898, by W. R. Hearst.—NEW YORK, THURSDAY, FEBRUARY 17, 1898.—16 PAGES.   PRICE ONE CENT In Greater New York Elsewhere and Jersey City. TWO CENTS.

DESTRUCTION OF THE WAR SHIP MAINE WAS THE WORK OF AN ENEMY.

$50,000!

$50,000 REWARD!
For the Detection of the Perpetrator of the Maine Outrage!

The New York Journal hereby offers a reward of **$50,000 CASH** for information, **FURNISHED TO IT EXCLUSIVELY,** which shall lead to the detection and conviction of the person, persons or government criminally responsible for the explosion which resulted in the destruction, at Havana, of the United States war ship Maine and the loss of 258 lives of American sailors.

The **$50,000 CASH** offered for the above information is on deposit with Wells, Fargo & Co.

No one is barred, be he the humble but misguided seaman eking out a few miserable dollars by acting as a spy, or the attache of a government secret service, plotting, by any devilish means, to revenge fancied insults or cripple menacing countries.

This offer has been cabled to Europe and will be made public in every capital of the Continent and in London this morning.

The Journal believes that any man who can be bought to commit murder can also be bought to betray his comrades. **FOR THE PERPETRATOR OF THIS OUTRAGE HAD ACCOMPLICES.**

W. R. HEARST.

Assistant Secretary Roosevelt Convinced the Explosion of the War Ship Was Not an Accident.

The Journal Offers $50,000 Reward for the Conviction of the Criminals Who Sent 258 American Sailors to Their Death. Naval Officers Unanimous That the Ship Was Destroyed on Purpose.

$50,000!

$50,000 REWARD!
For the Detection of the Perpetrator of the Maine Outrage!

The New York Journal hereby offers a reward of **$50,000 CASH** for information, **FURNISHED TO IT EXCLUSIVELY,** which shall lead to the detection and conviction of the person, persons or government criminally responsible for the explosion which resulted in the destruction, at Havana, of the United States war ship Maine and the loss of 258 lives of American sailors.

The **$50,000 CASH** offered for the above information is on deposit with Wells, Fargo & Co.

No one is barred, be he the humble, but misguided, seaman eking out a few miserable dollars by acting as a spy, or the attache of a government secret service, plotting, by any devilish means, to revenge fancied insults or cripple menacing countries.

This offer has been cabled to Europe and will be made public in every capital of the Continent and in London this morning.

The Journal believes that any man who can be bought to commit murder can also be bought to betray his comrades. **FOR THE PERPETRATOR OF THIS OUTRAGE HAD ACCOMPLICES.**

W. R. HEARST.

NAVAL OFFICERS THINK THE MAINE WAS DESTROYED BY A SPANISH MINE.

George Eugene Bryson, the Journal's special correspondent at Havana, cables that it is the secret opinion of many Spaniards in the Cuban capital that the Maine was destroyed and 258 of her men killed by means of a submarine mine, or fixed torpedo. This is the opinion of several American naval authorities. The Spaniards, it is believed, arranged to have the Maine anchored over one of the harbor mines. Wires connected the mine with a powder magazine, and it is thought the explosion was caused by sending an electric current through the wire. If this can be proven, the brutal nature of the Spaniards will be shown by the fact that they waited to spring the mine until after all the men had retired for the night. The Maltese cross in the picture shows where the mine may have been fired.

Hidden Mine or a Sunken Torpedo Believed to Have Been the Weapon Used Against the American Man-of-War---Officers and Men Tell Thrilling Stories of Being Blown Into the Air Amid a Mass of Shattered Steel and Exploding Shells---Survivors Brought to Key West Scout the Idea of Accident---Spanish Officials Protest Too Much---Our Cabinet Orders a Searching Inquiry---Journal Sends Divers to Havana to Report Upon the Condition of the Wreck. Was the Vessel Anchored Over a Mine?

BY CAPTAIN E. L. ZALINSKI, U. S. A.

(Captain Zalinski is the inventor of the famous dynamite gun, which would be the principal factor in our coast defence in case of war.)

Assistant Secretary of the Navy Theodore Roosevelt says he is convinced that the destruction of the Maine in Havana Harbor was not an accident. The Journal offers a reward of $50,000 for exclusive evidence that will convict the person, persons or Government criminally responsible for the destruction of the American battle ship and the death of 258 of its crew.

The suspicion that the Maine was deliberately blown up grows stronger every hour. Not a single fact to the contrary has been produced.

Captain Sigsbee, of the Maine, and Consul-General Lee both urge that public opinion be suspended until they have completed their investigation. They are taking the course of tactful men who are convinced that there has been treachery.

Washington reports very late that Captain Sigsbee had feared some such event as a hidden mine. The English cipher code was used all day yesterday by the naval officers in cabling instead of the usual American code.

One of Randolph Hearst's newspapers, the *New York Journal and Advertiser*, on the uss *Maine* disaster, 17 February 1898. The daily offers a $50,000 reward for 'detection of the perpetrator', a stunning $1.5 million today.

Manifest Destiny. And if the formally anti-colonialist nation could achieve this at the expense of its closest rival, colonialist Spain, so much the better. The sinking of the *Maine* came in handy, but without it – and without Hearst's promise to Remington – war would have ensued anyway.

Then there is that pesky 'reportedly' in the first sentence of this chapter. The thing is, nobody has ever found one shred of evidence that Hearst's cable was sent. All we have to go on is the say-so of a contemporary reporter called James Creeley, who wasn't anywhere near at the time and was known to invent stories more readily than Boris Johnson did when he was Brussels correspondent of the *Daily Telegraph*. So it would seem that, intentionally or not, Creeley single-handedly performed one of the greater propaganda achievements in history. More than a century has passed and the Spanish–American War has been all but forgotten, but the Hearst–Remington story keeps popping up, forever boosting the myth of the all-powerful newsman who can make war or peace with a snap of his fingers.

In reality, media tycoons such as Hearst, Joseph Pulitzer, Lord Northcliffe, Rupert Murdoch and Robert Maxwell were capable of inflicting enormous damage on anyone or anything they disapproved of, but that was more or less it. These people ruined lives, not countries. They were able to put murderous mobs on to the streets, clamouring for someone's hide. They blackmailed politicians, broke the careers of quite a few and intimidated many. But they could not sway politics. That said, the power of propaganda to influence people's minds and views is felt to be as huge as it is menacing, which gives us good reason to ask what propaganda really is and how it works.

Even though satire can be and often is part of propaganda efforts, propaganda is in many ways the antithesis of that noble art. As we saw in Chapter Eleven, satire is essentially a critique of the powerful and the dominant, aimed at making them think again about their plans, ways and convictions. Its products are doubt, reflection and arousal through irritation, engendered primarily by way of distortion and ridicule. In a nutshell, satire is a way of calling people out to think for themselves. Propaganda, on the other hand, is first and foremost an instrument of the powerful and the dominant, aiming to implant and maintain certain beliefs and convictions in people. This is done by overt and covert persuasion and temptation, nudging and a fair bit of threatening, fear-mongering and deception. Its ultimate products are unquestioning loyalty, orthodoxy and the comfort of fitting in with the winners who are correct. Propaganda, in other words, is a way of instilling in people the thoughts you want them to think. It is, in the most literal sense of the word, make-believe.

Both satire and propaganda serve the interests of their practitioners. The satirist tries to rouse you from the comfortable bed of conventional wisdom to go and develop new, hopefully 'better' ideas, whereas the propagandist wishes to hoist you on to the bandwagon of her own particular views. Halfway between these extremes lives a third, equally important social force, the educator. Educators are disinterested dispensers of such wisdom as twice two makes four, hot

Sometimes, political propaganda is cloaked as satire, as in this Ben Garrison cartoon called *Democrat Slavery, then and now*. It looks like irreverent banter, but actually tells you exactly what to think and accept as the truth. An excellent example of the opposite, satire disguised as propaganda, was the cover of *Charlie Hebdo* of 10 August 2016, which was republished in *Paris Match* but I cannot show here for reasons explained in Chapter Eleven, on pp. 361–4.¹ Its general design is exactly that of classical propaganda posters, with a ridiculously exhilarated naked Muslim couple storming down a sunny beach, over the Zappaesque slogan *Musulmans . . . décoincez vous!*, 'Muslims . . . free yourselves!' So it is propaganda for Muslims living in the Western world to join the world they partake of, break the fetters of stifling convention and social control, and start thinking for themselves. Precisely this, breaking taboos and questioning convention and stereotypes by ridiculing them, is the essence of satire.

stoves and wall sockets are dangerous, the English gerund is formed in -ing, Bamako is the capital of Mali, or the Dutch navy torched the English fleet at Chatham in 1667 and absconded with its flagship, the *Royal Charles*. By themselves, such titbits of information are divorced from what people think, want and consider right. We call them facts, and their main dispensers are sensible parents and ditto teachers, newspapers and other media, who try to show their children, pupils, readers, listeners and viewers what the world looks like and how it is structured. Unlike satirists and propagandists, educators wish not to make you think differently about things, but to bestow on you the knowledge and skill to be able to think and understand at all. Together with satirists and propagandists, these educators shape how we see the world and function within it.

The satirist, the propagandist and the educator are not different kinds of people, but social roles that we all play at times, often simultaneously. While responsible parents teach their toddlers the facts of the domestic world, such as how to operate things and what to avoid, they also indoctrinate them with moral standards and received prejudice – they engage in socio-cultural propaganda. And, as the history teacher is throwing light on what happened in the past that made your country into what it is today, he inevitably also paints an idealized, eclectic and, depending on his views and on social pressure, more or less patriotic picture of these events – that's socio-political propaganda. Even maths teachers, who deal in implacably hard facts and indisputable truths like no others, will sometimes extol the beauty of certain numbers or the elegance of some formula or method, in a mixture of heartfelt enthusiasm and professional propagandism. Most of the time people aren't even aware which role they are playing and whether they are communicating facts or opinions – or whether what they say is even true.

@#$%!

ONE OF THE GREAT PROBLEMS of our existence is that there is a huge difference between the world as it presents itself to us and the world as people would prefer it to be; reality seldom conforms completely to people's desires and their ideas about things. If we want to understand the world as it is, instead of just accepting the picture of it that someone wants us to believe, it is of the utmost importance to be able to separate facts from value judgements, wishes, ideals and other opinions. Also, it is essential to realize that discussions about facts, opinions and the idea of truth are never about things in the world themselves, such as 'dustbin', 'children' or 'Prince Harry', but exclusively about propositions. That is: they are about the things we *say* about things in the world, such as 'This is a dustbin,' 'The dustbin smells bad,' 'Children are not allowed to vote' or 'Prince Harry is a nice guy.'

That said, how do we recognize a proposition as a fact, as distinct from an opinion? Here's a practical set of three criteria:

1 Intersubjectivity. Facts do not depend on a particular observer, whereas opinions do. If two or more random people run into the same fact – by direct experience or by being told about it – they experience the same thing and will report the same way about it. By this test 'Prince Harry is a redhead' is a fact, for the time being, as are 'two plus two equals four' and 'Bamako is the capital of Mali.' 'Prince Harry is a nice guy,' however, is not. This remark may strike different people quite differently, depending on their knowledge of and personal appreciation of the man.

2 You cannot joke about, ridicule or deride a fact. It is plainly pointless to snigger 'Yeah, Prince Harry is a redhead, ha-ha!', whereas 'Yeah, Prince Harry is a nice guy, ha-ha!' is something at least some people would find both funny and to the point, while others would consider it in bad taste.

3 You cannot deny or disagree with a fact. 'I don't think Prince Harry is a redhead' is just stupid, whereas 'I don't think Prince Harry is a nice guy' is a valid opinion.

If something you're told passes all three of these tests, and only then, you can be pretty sure it's a fact.

A large part of the body of facts is comprised of what we might call natural facts: aspects of the natural world that exist regardless of our own existence. This includes natural laws such as those of arithmetic and logic, and propositions strictly derived from them. It also comprises a plethora of phenomena such as temperature, seasons and tides, geological conditions and observations about them such as 'It's spring' or 'It's ebb' or 'Mount Everest is the highest mountain on Earth.' Moreover, it includes observations about people and the endless variety of artefacts they have created taken purely as objects of the world around us, as in 'Prince Harry is a redhead,' 'Mary has a mole on her upper lip' or, far more complex, 'An electric car travels less far in cold weather.'

There is, next to these natural facts, also a huge category of abstract man-made facts. These are, broadly speaking, of two kinds. First there are the facts concerning concepts and institutions that exist only because we thought of them, and will vanish with us. These are hugely important ideas that shape much of our lives, such as economy, money, monarchy, music, law, justice, freedom, India and the alphabet. Although they are mere figments of our imagination, observations such as 'The Russian rouble sells at about seventy to a euro,' 'Boz Scaggs's "Loan Me a Dime" is a twelve-bar blues' and 'Shoplifting is punishable by imprisonment for a period of no more than six weeks' are all facts that pass the three tests above. Like natural facts, everyone can verify them by checking with their bank, looking at the relevant musical score or consulting the penal code.

The other kind are historical facts. Historical facts are much like abstract facts, except that it is not always possible to verify them by personal observation. In the case of the Dutch taking the *Royal Charles*, we can – the carving of the Royal arms on the ship's transom is still on display as a trophy at the Rijksmuseum in Amsterdam. Solid proof. Usually, however, historical facts exist only because we carry them in our memories, noted them down in newspapers, books and archives, and tell each other about them. That Caesar vanquished Vercingetorix at Alesia more than 2,000 years ago counts as a fact only because we accept Caesar's own word for it, and that of his contemporaries; no undisputed trace of the battle, or even of Alesia itself, has ever been found. As a result, historical facts are almost always squishy and sketchy, stories full of holes and conjecture, based on a rickety consensus. Facts, therefore, are not always clear.

As the uncertain status of historical facts suggests, but contrary to what many people think, facts are not absolute either. To begin with, only natural facts are universal, meaning that they hold the same way for anyone across the world. Many man-made facts do not. To give an example, it is a fact that Bamako is the capital of Mali. But any one of the insurgent parties there might declare themselves the

> ## So how about denying the Holocaust?
>
> According to our three criteria, facts cannot be denied, or at least it must be senseless to do so, such as stating that Prince Harry is not a redhead or flu is not a disease. So why are there countries that consider denying the Holocaust a criminal offence? Within reason, denying the Holocaust is nonsensical and meaningless. There is just far too much documentary, pictorial and physical evidence on a thousand different aspects of it, coming from countless different sources. And countless eyewitnesses – victims, liberators and the occasional perpetrator – have spoken out. They cannot all be wrong or deluded. So why bother?
>
> The point is that *beyond reason* anything goes. Without reason, there is no sound reasoning, nor are there defining criteria. Without reason, only obstinate prejudice remains. Most of those who seriously deny the Holocaust, or certain aspects of it, don't offer much in the way of proof other than unattested conspiracy theories. Yet it is widely feared that vociferously repeating such unmotivated denials may diminish the awe with which people regard this so far uniquely industrial genocide and thus increase the risk of similar atrocities happening in the future.
>
> Criminalizing the mere expression of particular opinions is problematic in countries that subscribe to the principle of freedom of expression, itself an important safeguard against the rise of the kind of totalitarian regime that might precipitate another Holocaust. But fear proves once again to be a strong motivator. By 2017, denying genocides had become a criminal offence in almost twenty European countries and a few elsewhere. About half of them limit their legislation exclusively to the Holocaust of the Second World War; in most of the others it applies to all genocides. In a few, it covers other crimes against humanity and war crimes as well. Meanwhile Turkey goes the other way with one of its own national traumas. In 2017 its parliament issued a ban on the use of the term 'Armenian genocide' on its premises. After a hundred years, that remains the unmentionable genocide.

rightful government and Timbuktu their capital. Then that would be a fact too – for some, at least. Or, conversely, one might say that the notion 'capital of Mali' would have lost its factual status and become a matter of opinion.

This immediately suggests that facts also need not be set in stone for all eternity. The only things actually written in stone are fossils, and even they are the source of much controversy. Historical events and figures are likely to be forgotten or reappraised and the laws on shoplifting may change. Even many natural facts are perishable goods. Prince Harry's hair will turn grey, Mount Everest will eventually erode badly enough to lose its exalted status and the Earth's magnetic field may reverse. Facts aren't absolute in yet another way as well, especially those that aren't self-evident but have to be painstakingly discovered and deduced. To do so is the job of science. Scientists have been digging for the facts of life, our world and the universe for centuries now, and while they have come up with a wealth of insights, many of which have radically changed and improved our lives, most of them feel that they have only just begun. The theories they construct of how aspects of the world work – the facts of science, in other words – are always work in progress. Invariably they come with the implicit caveat 'as best we know now'. With time, many of these theories will be amended or abandoned for new, better ones. This is a point that is rarely acknowledged by the media, who like their facts to be spectacular, fresh and final. The same holds for the population at large, who prefer unequivocal certainties over the inscrutable risks and maybes that science tends to serve up.

Lastly, facts need not even be true or provable. Sunrise is a case in point. The rising of the sun each morning is one of the most deepseated, familiar and universally shared certainties of life. Yet, as a matter of fact sunrise does not exist. What we experience is not the sun rising to begin a westward trajectory shining down on to the world, but the effect of the Earth rolling us into the path of the sun's radiation. People have been aware of this fact at least since the days of Nicolaus Copernicus, almost half a millennium ago. Still, even today's nerdiest, most unromantic physicists experience sunrise as a reality, a fact of life, as well. Part of the reason for this incongruous behaviour lies in how we relate to the world around us. Our brains construct their own conceptual world from the way the world presents itself to us through the senses, which includes all that we are told. These perceptual concepts are what is involved in our thinking about and acting in the world, not the actual physical entities they are said to refer to. If these concepts get reinforced regularly enough, they don't go away when we are presented with a second, often more abstract explanation of the same events. In our minds, both ideas will coexist in peaceful contradiction.

This explains first and foremost why we are just as comfortable with abstract, man-made notions such as economy and law, which cannot be attested independently, as with the plain old facts of our physical environment. It also throws light on the ease with which we absorb things we are told about but never perceive directly, such as atoms or the customs of extinct Amazonian tribes. Moreover, it is why we accept Winnie the Pooh, Donald Duck and Batman so readily and without getting confused, even though we know full well that animals can't speak, people can't fly around in a bat cape and Gotham City does not exist. It also explains why we accept historical facts as intersubjective, undisputable facts on the basis of some vague kind of consensus alone – the Hearst telegram is an example of this, but also the French queen Marie Antoinette's well-known, shockingly callous but equally shockingly unverifiable comment *Qu'ils mangent de la brioche*, 'Let them eat cake,' on the hungry populace of Paris clamouring about the dearth of bread in the city. And, last but not least, it explains why we are wont to take gossip for fact.[2]

Although our three criteria identify a huge mixed bag of notions as facts, the array of notions they exclude is even larger. It consists of opinions and bodily sensations. By bodily sensations we mean emotions such as joy, arousal, desire, nervousness, sadness, guilt, shame, remorse, mistrust, fear, anger and pique as well as internal bodily signals such as pain, itch and feeling hungry, hot, cold or tired, and more permanent feelings having to do with belonging, attachment, love and loyalty, identity, sexual orientation and so on. Although all these feelings and conditions are extremely real and true to whoever experiences them, none of them can be observed and ascertained directly, or 'co-felt', by others. For instance, notwithstanding today's technological wealth and medical prowess, all a doctor can do to assess whether you are in pain and how badly, is to ask you. Or prod and ask 'Does this hurt?' With the exception of general stress, which is presumably reflected by the level of the hormone cortisol in the bloodstream, the rest are no different, they all fail the intersubjectivity test and the other two; your claim to be in pain, for instance, can be met with ridicule ('Yeah, you're in pain, ha-ha!') and denied or disagreed with ('Pain? Don't be such a sissy, or I'll show you pain!'). The consequence is that such sensations are not facts. Normally, people will trust each other enough to accept someone's claims about their internal state and the outward signs they show as a matter of fact, but that's just a privilege liable to be revoked at any time, for instance if someone turns out to feign illness, remorse or fatigue.

As non-facts, propositions about bodily sensations are always fraught with judgements, either positive or negative. All bodily sensations mean something to their owner, so to speak. 'I'm hungry' is not a neutral statement; it necessarily implies a desire to eat, a form of dissatisfaction. Perhaps certain extreme ascetics or fanatical anorexics derive some sort of gratification from going hungry, but nobody can be truly indifferent to it. If you are, you're simply not hungry. The same holds for things like 'I'm sad' and 'I'm happy', while feeling mistrustful always means that, in your opinion, something's rotten in the state of Denmark. And who could ever state 'I'm in love' and feel nothing about it, even in jest?

All other propositions – meaning everything we claim, assert, deny, question or conclude about anyone or anything – are opinions. In the same way as propositions about bodily sensations, they are statements not about the world as it is, but about how we feel about things. As does our example 'Prince Harry is a nice guy,' they all imply a judgement on a scale running from good to bad on some dimension. They are about desirability, justifiability and approval.

In a world populated with facts, bodily sensations and opinions, where is truth? This may come as a shock, but when push comes to shove, truth is a rather useless notion. Most of the great philosophers, from Plato through Kierkegaard, Kant and Nietzsche to Foucault and Derrida have tried to come to grips with it – and failed.

The main problem is the question of absolute and objective truth. Is there a universal truth that holds for all people, a yardstick by which everything else can be measured and rated? If there is not, as postmodernists hold, then everything is a matter of opinion. Bluntly put, in such a postmodern world truth is simply what anyone holds true, so nobody can claim knowledge or ownership of better 'truths' than anybody else. Such relativism foils any intercultural criticism, and in fact any ethical criticism, or even any ethics at all, since any norm and any value is as valid as the next one. If universal truths do exist, on the other hand, a different can of worms opens.

Absolute truths imply the existence of absolute values, superior to all others. This is a popular idea, but it has at least two problems. Most attention has been devoted to one of these, the internal conflicts that ensue. Suppose that one universal value is that lying is absolutely wrong, and another that wilfully killing people or putting them in harm's way is absolutely wrong as well. Then what should a virtuous person do if a band of killers came to his door and demanded the address of one of his friends? Should he lie in an attempt to save the friend, or piously rat him out to his prospective murderers? This extremely realistic conundrum – the killers could be an ss Sonderkommando, a band of drugged-up Charles Taylor mercenaries, a Janjaweed detail, members of a Mexican drugs cartel or any of a thousand other nasty militias around the world – is known as the 'dirty hands' problem, and no philosopher has ever come up with a satisfactory answer, other than conceding what the Germans seem to have always known: *jede Konsequenz führt zum Teufel,* 'consistency always ends up on the Devil's doorstep.'

The second, even more pressing problem with absolute truth is where to find and how to recognize it. There are many who claim to have the answers, but no two groups ever agree. Even the great philosophers simply took it for granted that their own values and those of their own society were the superior ones. In the aftermath of the Second World War the Western Allies imposed Universal Human Rights on the world as absolute truths through the United Nations, but it is clear that many parties outside and even within the Western world view those rights strictly opportunistically. Regimes in Africa and the Middle East will at best pay lip-service to human rights as long as doing so suits their purposes, as will those of countries such as China, Russia and even Brazil.

Now it becomes clear what the real problem with the notion of truth is: essentially, truth is a matter of consensus, nothing more. 'The rouble sells at about seventy to a euro' is true as long as 'we', as represented by the financial markets, keep agreeing that this is so, and not a second longer. And the universality of human rights is merely the 'stuff as dreams are made on' unless everybody agrees to acknowledge and uphold them, for whatever reasons.

Take criminal justice. Suppose some pedestrian has been hit and killed in what looks like a car accident, but might be something more sinister. When the driver is brought to trial, the judge will first try to establish the facts of the matter from the police dossier – damage to the car and victim, the presence of skid marks, results of a breathalyser test administered at the scene, eyewitness statements and so on. If at that point it transpires that the whole thing was indeed a stupid accident, a mishap that could not be helped, then the truth equals the facts, pure and simple. But if doubts remain, if the facts are incomplete or don't add up, things get hairier. Then, the judge must try to find out about the internal condition of the driver on trial, assess whether he had been tired, sleepy, agitated, under pressure, angry, depressed or otherwise psychologically or physically impaired at the time, none of which can be ascertained directly or objectively. Perhaps even murkier issues such as the intentions and mental capacities of the defendant must be probed, and psychiatric experts consulted. In the end whatever experts, judge and, if applicable, jury agree on, counts as 'the truth'. The stubborn regularity with which serious judicial errors occur shows how often truth later turns out not to be true at all.

In short: truth is consensus and consensus tends to be closer to shared prejudice and received ideas than to reality. And so we are trapped in a world where facts need not be absolute, perennial or even real, where we just have to take someone's word for most of the core aspects of human life – our bodily sensations – and where all the rest is a matter of opinion. Is it at all possible for us to understand such a world as it really is? Is it possible to separate the wheat from the chaff, the facts from honest opinions and those from mere cock-and-bull stories and, further down the slope, malicious lies? Or are we doomed to sink into a bottomless quagmire of relativism trying?

Thankfully, we are not. First of all, we have a means of identifying facts, such as they are. It need not bother us too much that facts are not all as immutable as they are usually made out to be, and sometimes inconsistent, for we can understand the world only as it presents itself to us. So if it presents itself to us differently over time or even in incongruous ways, as in the case of sunrise versus cosmological fact, then the facts should reflect this. Furthermore, the facts of logic provide us with a reliable means of interrelating facts and making valid deductions and judicious inferences, allowing us to develop more complex, more insightful and more reliable ideas.

Next, although universal agreement is a *rara avis* indeed, there are a few values that can safely be presumed universal. For instance, people all over the world generally value a safe life free from hunger, want and oppression above a poor and perilous existence filled with abuse. Although there will always be adventurers and thrill-seekers, the overwhelming majority values stability and predictability over chaos, at least for themselves, their children, other close relatives and friends. So much so, in fact, that they are willing to work hard for it. This shows up in people's behaviour, which creates its own facts. Facts such as the emergence of forms of social organization, of religious rule systems and traditions, each of which has been more or less successful at providing safety and sustenance, sparking creativity and innovation, and providing people with happiness, contentment and sufficient freedom to realize their potential – all of which can be deemed universal values. In today's mobile world, migration patterns are not random. They reflect how people in general appreciate the ways different societies are organized, even if they are not fully aware of this themselves. Results are what counts here. Results are what make people flee one region and flock to another. And those results are raw, tangible facts, not fancies.

Together, facts, the smattering of universal values and the behavioural facts those generate should suffice to enable us to get to grips with the world. As for cultural relativism, it is as the great scientist Richard Feynman once said: Show me one man in an airplane at 10,000 feet willing to trade the laws of physics for a magic carpet, and I'll show you a true believer.

The existence of at least some universal values entails an equally universal desire for a measure of frankness and sincerity in communicating our ideas and intentions. For in the absence of cultural relativity and the presence of relentless natural facts, what we communicate to one another does matter. That is why propaganda, the art of making people see things your way, matters as well.

@#$%!

BY AND LARGE, the concept of propaganda has a strong whiff of indirection and bad faith about it. The reason for this is not just that a fair proportion of propagandistic efforts have indeed been deceptive and ill-intentioned. Equally influential is the common tendency of philosophers and other investigators of the phenomenon to approach it from an ethical point of view. In doing so, they plunge straight into moral quicksand. Their own values become an integral part of the discussion from the start, rendering an open, impartial assessment of the phenomenon nigh impossible. Worse, it also precludes the possibility of reaching out to and connecting with those who do not share these values and biases in the first place, so that much discussion is reduced to preaching to the choir. So let's try and find out what propaganda is and how it works, rather than what we feel about it and about those using it, by looking at the phenomenon from a factual perspective, keeping away from moral notions such as good and bad as best we can.

A number of common misunderstandings cloud our understanding of the art of making people see things our way. The first of these is that propaganda falls within the exclusive remit of governments and corporations. While it is true that the oldest recognizable examples of propaganda, such as the use of inscriptions on buildings or the portraits of rulers on coins, were state affairs, the propaganda war Martin Luther waged on the pope and his perverted paladins was not. Here was an angry monk who, initially at least, took on the mighty Mother Church almost single-handedly, and did so by means of a stubborn and highly successful propaganda campaign of his own invention, making full use of the newly invented mass medium of his time: the printing press. By means of a never-ending barrage of books, treatises, letters and often bawdy and satirical pamphlets, he succeeded in turning the minds of great numbers of Christians and giving his reform initiative clout on an unprecedented scale, to earth-shattering effect.

A modern example of an individual launching a successful propaganda campaign is Greta Thunberg, the then fifteen-year-old from Stockholm who on 20 August 2018, instead of returning to school as she was supposed to, made camp outside the Riksdag, the home of the Swedish parliament, with a sign saying *Skolstrejk för klimatet*, 'School strike for the climate'. Those three words were her version of Luther's 95 theses. They were picked up relatively quickly by the media, and Thunberg turned out to hit a nerve among activists and adolescents across the world.

Luther's and Thunberg's campaigns conform to the standard idea of propaganda as requiring three elements to be successful: a highly motivated prime mover, a mass medium and a large target group to be converted and carry the torch further. However, none of these is indispensable. Take a classroom with one pupil starting a gossip and smear campaign to ostracize a classmate. This is a highly frequent, classic form of propaganda against a person, malignant and often painfully effective. Yet there is no mass medium involved – although in this age of social media there can be – and the target group is tiny. This kind of smear campaign occurs not only in schools, but typically in the workplace, always with the same two-pronged goal. The idea is not just to make someone's life miserable or chase them away; it is first and foremost to enhance the status of the mover with his followers and increase his hold over them.

Successful propaganda campaigns can even come alive without a prime mover. James Creeley's bit of gossip about William Randolph Hearst promising to provide a war was probably just intended as a juicy titbit of the kind Creeley liked to invent. He had no reason to embark on a long-lasting propaganda effort to enhance the awe in which press tycoons were held, but that is precisely what it became. Even in 2019, the best-selling author Tom Rob Smith created *MotherFatherSon* for the BBC, a chilling miniseries starring Richard Gere as precisely the kind of media tycoon Creeley had sketched 120 years earlier, the kind that could and would topple governments and make whole nations do their bidding at the drop of a hat.

Creeley was what one might call an unintentional mover. Much more bizarre were the events that led to the downfall of the Oisterwijk furniture factory. This factory was a well-established, prospering Dutch business, proudly advertising its traditional, heavy, solid oak furniture on radio and television. But then, at some point during the late 1970s, a story popped up out of nowhere about a man who had tried to shorten the legs of his Oisterwijk table, only to find that they weren't solid oak at all, but a thin oak casing filled with concrete. It was an archetypal urban legend: everybody said they knew someone who swore he had heard it from the guy himself, but nobody had first-hand knowledge and no proof was ever offered. Sadly, the story just wouldn't go away. Fewer and fewer people would risk being ridiculed by their friends and neighbours for putting 'that stuff' in their house, and in 1989 the factory went belly-up.

This was propaganda with great, even lethal impact, driven by nobody and without any involvement of the media. The story wasn't advertised in the papers and never became the subject of any talk shows or radio programmes. It just went round and round like the common cold. It wasn't a unique incident, either. Procter & Gamble, one of the world's largest manufacturers of household products, suffered for decades from a rumour that its trademark of a man in the moon and a sprinkling of stars was really a satanic symbol. The rumour had initially been floated by certain Christian fundamentalist groups, but quickly acquired a life of its own. Although P&G is still going strong, it eventually felt compelled to redesign its trademark, getting rid completely of both man and stars. For centuries, also, stories have been doing the rounds about Jews, Freemasons, heretics, witches and other reclusive or eccentric social groups associating with the Devil at secret gatherings, sacrificing and eating stolen babies and drinking their blood. From time to time religious firebrands and authorities in need of a scapegoat have availed themselves of such horror stories to use them as propaganda, inciting pogroms against such groups for any number of reasons, but they did not invent them. The potentially violent undercurrents were already there, festering, without there ever having been any identifiable movers.

What it shows is that in the absence of movers and media, propaganda can be sustained and reinforced by just a willing 'target' group. It also shows that to carry propaganda further, making new converts, the target audience need not even actually believe what is being propagated. Many will spread the message simply because it is fun to be in on a kind of secret, because 'everybody' does it or because of a deep-seated fear and distrust of people who somehow aren't 'us': 'I know it sounds crazy, but where there's smoke . . .' In successful propaganda, groups of converts can fuel and extend themselves, somewhat like Baron Münchhausen pulled himself out of the swamp by his own hair. And if there is an active, clearly identifiable mover, their vociferous presence will enhance his or her status among yet other target groups, as happened to Thunberg.

It is not always easy to distinguish unintentional propaganda from covert propaganda, the kind where some prime mover carefully orchestrates a campaign but hides from view. Many, but certainly not all, conspiracy theories are of this ignominious ilk, as are most atrocity stories. In April 1917, for instance, right in the middle of the First World War, the British Ministry of Information surreptitiously spread a shocking story to the media about a factory in Germany where the corpses of war casualties were processed and recycled into all sorts of materials the Central Powers were short of, such as grease, soap and glycerine. This apparent testimony to the appalling barbarity of the Hun was widely believed, not least because the reports in the British press named both a German and a Belgian source, thus enhancing credibility, while hiding the fact that the Belgian version contained a crucial mistranslation. The German original had been about a processing plant for dead *animals*, mainly horses, but

How propaganda came to be called just that

While propaganda as an activity may well be as old as language itself, its name was coined only some four hundred years ago in Rome. From 1572 to 1582 Pope Gregory XIII regularly convened with a few of his cardinals to discuss ways of combating the Reformation. These meetings came to be referred to as *Congregatio de Propaganda Fide*, meetings on how to propagate the faith. Forty years on, in 1622, his successor, Gregory XV, instituted a permanent committee to oversee the Church's missionary activities and gave it the same name. The institution, nowadays known as the Congregation for the Evangelization of Peoples, held sway over all territories where no fully fledged episcopal hierarchy existed, and became quite powerful. In time the phrase, reduced to its core, *propaganda*, came to refer to the activities of the committee and hence to efforts to spread religious or political doctrines in general.

the German *Kadaver*, 'carcass', had been mistranslated as *corpse*, human remains – which the British authorities seized on as a propagandistic godsend. It was more than seven years before the British Foreign Secretary Austen Chamberlain admitted to parliament that the British people had intentionally been fed fake news by their own government.

With the advent of social media, a whole new world of covert propaganda has emerged. Its main purpose does not seem to be to instil certain beliefs in people. Rather, it aims to confuse them into regarding everything they're told with suspicion. Whether overt or covert, intentional propaganda always serves the interest of its mover. This can be one or a combination of three things: bringing about, maintaining and defending some morally charged ideal, garnering wealth or maintaining and increasing one's power.

Political and religious propaganda are prime examples of moral propaganda. In political propaganda, the ultimate goal is to bring about, maintain and defend some kind of utopia where everybody is equal or, conversely, knows their place. The purpose of religious propaganda is invariably to establish the rule of the 'correct' faith in honour of its supreme being, to which purpose as many souls as possible must be recruited.

Essentially, these kinds of propaganda are the same song sung to different tunes. Both are grounded in a few core emotions. Most prominent among these is insecurity. Political propaganda exploits feelings of insecurity by promising better justice and safety and less corruption and crime. A clean sweep! Religious propaganda taps into insecurity about the mysteries of fate and death. Some religions promise protection from the cruel quirks of fate through obeying a moral code and performing certain offices, others offer ways of achieving a mental state that is supposed to render the twists of fate meaningless. They also lure new recruits with promises of an afterlife or a return to this world.

Apart from insecurity, political propaganda runs on resentment: feelings of being short-changed. At one end of the political spectrum we find the grudges of the poor and the disenfranchised, whose fair share of freedom and the fruits of their labour are unjustly denied them by the rich and by unfairly competing other groups. At the other extreme, there are the gripes of the well-to-do who fear that their well-deserved traditional privileges and hard-earned or rightfully inherited fortunes might be squandered on or even confiscated by the great unwashed.

Religious propaganda does not draw on grudges against others. Instead, it exploits feelings of personal guilt and inadequacy. That is why so many religions impose arbitrary demands and prohibitions on their flocks, the sole common characteristic of which is that they are nigh impossible to comply with fully. Complex and irrational dietary laws, prayer duties that disrupt the working day, periodical fasting, sexual abstinence, celibacy, all are designed to trip up the believer, whose indebtedness to and dependence on the magnanimity and forgiveness of their Lord and Church increases with each lapse.

Apart from straight religious and political causes, moral propaganda has served virtually every morally charged issue imaginable and continues to do so, often with political, religious or semi-religious overtones mixed in. A clear example is Amnesty International's unique long-standing campaign to kindle and maintain awareness of the plight of political prisoners, which over the past few years has regretfully been watered down into a general concern for human rights. Inevitably, the organization's activities are political in that they touch on some of the nastier practices regimes get up to, but it has always taken pains not to take a political stand. On a different note, it is no accident that most pro-life campaigners who try to dissuade women from aborting their unwelcome foetuses are motivated by religion, but recruitment into their congregation is not their first concern.

Some of the broad array of groups that clamour for better care of the environment and the climate show signs of para-religious inspiration. Something similar applies to the anti-vaccination fad sweeping through the Western world. An example of propaganda without any obvious political or religious ties is offered by the now banned Pro-Ana websites promoting anorexia nervosa among the young – an ideal inspired by a hard-to-fathom kind of self-deprecation.

Gaining power, not ideals, is what primarily drives the movers of what, for want of a better term, we'll call personal propaganda. The idea is to bind members of a target group to the mover and increase their hold over them by ganging up on a third party. Such propaganda exploits deep-seated group-preservation and hunting instincts. The clearest example is the classroom campaign, led by the classroom bully or the most popular girl. By continually picking on a lesser being – usually someone who suffers from some slight social handicap – they force other group members to declare their allegiance: either they are with the bully or they stand with the unattractive underdog. Once someone sides with the top dogs, he or she has become complicit to their mauling of the victim and forever bound to support and obey them, or they'll become the new dupe. Those who don't comply, even passively, have to face the wrath of an ever stronger and more determined adversary. This may sound like a typical Hollywood coming-of-age nightmare, but it is only too real. It is also precisely what malicious gossip and the tabloids centre around; it is an important part of how the genocide of 1994 in Rwanda came about and also of how Nazi Germany worked.

Whereas the morality of moral propaganda, including political and religious propaganda, depends on the cause advocated and the manner in which the campaign is conducted, personal propaganda per se is clearly immoral by most people's standards, on account of its callously sacrificing more or less randomly chosen scapegoats. The third kind of propaganda is in principle amoral. It is commercial propaganda, better known as advertising and public relations. Commercial propaganda is not about seeking power, nor do commercial movers try to make their targets 'think their way' by imprinting ideas and ideals that matter to them on their target group. In fact, the content of their messages means nothing to them. Its only quality is its potential to persuade targets to spend their money on the products the mover is offering.

The archetypal instrument of commercial propaganda is advertising, which has evolved a long way from its most primitive 'Buy Dr Doxey's Elixir, the best cure for any ailment' form. Although advertisements these days may still point to the unique advantages of a product, as in 'today's e-car of the future' or 'the professional's favourite', they often merely show the product or the product name. Instead of praise, modern ads are loaded with all sorts of subtext offering the target something desirable to identify with *as a person*. A bottom of the market product such as margarine is likely to be advertised by showing young and obviously happy, upwardly mobile people enjoying the stuff at a carefree summer picnic. What beleaguered Average Jane would not secretly, on a visceral level, wish to live like that? Washing powder is presented by a housewife (or increasingly, now, a house-husband) who obviously, between managing both a job and a sweet but useless family, remains in effortless control and finds time to keep smiling. She's exactly the kind of woman real stay-at-home mums would love and their husbands would adore them to be. The product is not just a commodity but both a passport to and proof of a better, more rewarding life. If there is irony, it is laid on so thick that the message 'we know better, don't we' is inescapable even for the dullest, least ambitious of targets. Such campaigns aim to bring about a bond between a brand and the target audience, positioning the product as a reliable and loyal but undemanding friend.

In fact, of course, the loyalty must go the other way. Advertising a new product successfully is one thing, but the real challenge comes when the novelty wears off. Then one has to keep people buying the products advertised in the face of all existing and newly arriving competition, by building brand loyalty. In this respect, commercial propaganda is a lot like the personal propaganda of the classroom bully. The bully establishes a guilty bond with his followers by making them complicit in the ostracism of a more or less random victim. Manufacturers and retailers bind their customers by plying them with freebies, coupons, 'exclusive' offers, air miles, frequent-flyer points and other loyalty programmes. In both cases, the driving emotions are indebtedness, complicity and a sense of belonging. It is hardly a coincidence that both classroom bullies and loyalty programmes use the concept of a club so often.

As with the social roles of satirists, propagandists and educators, the boundaries between moral, personal and commercial propaganda are fuzzy. They differ in their ends but use each other's techniques as expediency demands. That said, all propaganda obeys these fifteen laws.

1. The law of conservation and confirmation

As Mark Twain once put it, it is easier to fool people than to convince them they have been fooled. What he had actually stumbled upon was the principle of loss aversion, our deep-seated tendency to feel the sting of losing something more keenly than the joy of acquisition. Loss aversion is behind the mixed feelings that go with buying something expensive that you really want to have. You do fork out the money, but chances are you'll say or at least think something half regretful like 'well, it's an arm and a leg, let's hope it's worth it.' This is actually a good thing, otherwise we would buy things that took our fancy at any price. In other words we would be prone to taking unlimited risks, which would not bode well for our evolutionary chances.

Emotionally, ideas and convictions are just like money and commodities, which is why on the whole people tend to be somewhat conservative. This means that it is relatively hard to turn people once they have made up their minds, but fairly easy to keep them on your side once they have been recruited. It just takes two things. First of all, give them something to lose. Second, don't make them lose the illusions and expectations you have given them.

There are myriad ways of giving people something to lose, especially in commercial propaganda. But apart from all the loyalty programmes, the idea of belonging, which comes with simply climbing on to somebody's bandwagon, is precious in itself. Soccer fans who staunchly keep supporting their consistently underperforming team are an example, as are the many people who remain sworn to their brand of car for decades, although the models and specifications change every year.

As a person, all you have to do to leave your followers' illusions and expectations intact is to remain true to yourself. This is the lesson the careers of the American presidents Nixon, Clinton and Trump teach us, all three of whom had to face the threat of impeachment. Nixon's voter base and his support among the party elite remained intact throughout the Watergate scandal and all that came with it. Some of it was clearly criminal, but to his fans it was simply typical of Tricky Dick to fight dirty, and therefore not a problem. Support for Nixon crumbled only when the transcripts of his conversations at the White House showed him up not to be the staunch champion of American family values that he had always pretended to be, as we saw in Chapter Ten. Nixon proved himself a fake. Behind closed doors he turned out to swear and rant like a lumberjack who had hacked his own leg off. People felt betrayed, and all Nixon could do to save his skin was resign and run for the hills of Yorba Linda, California. Two decades after that, Bill Clinton survived the highly unsavoury Monica Lewinsky scandal and became one of the most popular and expensive public speakers of his time, simply because he obviously was that kind of man, a charmer with a roving eye. After another twenty years, Donald Trump entered the White House to give a whole new meaning to the concept of the presidency. He was voted in by those who wanted to teach those glib, elitist politicians in their DC bubble a lesson. They really wanted an uncouth, loudmouthed brawler there, to kick ass and make an even greater mess of what they saw as a pigsty of iniquity anyway. They meant Trump's presidency to be a bar fight and Trump obliged, in return for which his voters were quite prepared even to condone his bragging about grabbing women by the pussy. Like Clinton's, Trump's misbehaviour was in character, which is all that matters.

A slightly different but related lesson lies in the appreciation of a fourth president, John F. Kennedy. Behind the scenes of the fairy-tale Camelot household of King Jack and Queen Jacky, the president was a philanderer if ever there was one, bad back notwithstanding. But strangely, in the still fairly puritanical America of the early 1960s nobody wanted to know, not before and certainly not after his tragic assassination. He was and had to remain a hero, the fairy tale intact, his philandering simply ignored or rationalized as proof of welcome energetic virility.

The treatment bestowed upon the Kennedys was a good example of confirmation bias, a tendency in us all to ignore information that does not fit what we know and think already, and to overrate news that confirms our existing beliefs. Confirmation bias might go back to the hunter-gatherer past of our distant forebears. It would be most efficient if they could keep their attention focused on spotting the tubers or plants of choice, ignoring all others. Aeons later, it is how prejudices get confirmed and strengthened with every incident. For instance, if we feel that nowadays children are noisy, obnoxious brats, every bold little loudmouth we encounter will confirm and bolster our conviction, but we'll overlook all the little ones who go about their business unobtrusively.

In extreme cases, confirmation bias turns into what is called cognitive dissonance: ignoring and denying the facts even though they are staring you in the face. During a visit to the city of Bukavu in Congo in 2006, a Mai Mai colonel explained to the writer John le Carré the *dawa*, the magic powers this most dangerous militia possessed. According to the colonel these powers make bullets fired at the Mai Mai swerve, or turn them into harmless *mai*, water. 'When you are face to face with an AK47 that is firing straight at you and nothing happens, you know your *dawa* is authentic,' he asserted confidently. But if that is the case, Le Carré ventured cautiously, how do the Mai Mai explain their dead and wounded? Unfazed, the colonel replied: 'If one of our warriors is struck down, it is because he is a thief or rapist or has disobeyed our rituals or was harbouring bad thoughts about a comrade when he went into battle. Our dead are our sinners.' *Dawa* works flawlessly, and if it does not, it's not *dawa* but the victim who is to blame, for *dawa* works flawlessly. This is truly the apogee of the art of propaganda, getting people to actually believe and propagate blatant nonsense by handing them such hermetic, circular reasoning. Of course cognitive dissonance is absurd. But it is also real and an attractive propaganda ploy. It is, for example, the bedrock of Christianity.[3]

As we have all been taught, the Christian God is a benevolent, merciful God, with humankind's best interests at heart. But we've also been taught that He is almighty and rules the world alone, an omnipotent monopolist. This implies that literally everything that happens on Earth is ultimately caused by Him. So, a Le Carré interviewing God might ask how He justifies the fact that Earth is such a gruesome place, where criminals and psychopaths get away with wholesale slaughter and upstanding, pious Christians are regularly subjected to gross injustice and visited by unspeakable horrors. God would answer that it is all for the best. We are all sinners by definition, and He works in mysterious ways that people are just too dense to understand. As a result, true-blue Christians let God rob them of their worldly goods and loved ones and then turn to Him for solace and forgiveness. Our dead and bereaved are our sinners.

2. If you can't convince, confuse

It is not easy to shake the convictions of people living in stable, relatively rich and well-organized environments like most Western democracies. Citizens of countries from Ireland to Greece will complain loudly and bitterly about the flaws of their politicians, bureaucrats and institutions, but when push comes to shove, they simply have too much to lose. Hence it is highly unlikely for the overwhelming majority of them to fall for some foreign regime's boasting, wild promises or scathing commentaries on their depraved way of life. Nor will obvious one-off stunts, such as the aid convoy Russia sent to COVID-19-struck Italy in the spring of 2020, or the less publicized ones it sent to Central and Eastern European states that were once part of the Warsaw Pact but are now part of the European Union, do much to turn minds.

Worse, obvious political propaganda efforts may well backfire in such circumstances, showing the propagandist up as a weak and insincere bragger. During the interwar period, for instance, when the self-confidence of the West had been badly shaken by the First World War and then again by the Depression, straightforward Soviet propaganda did succeed in winning the hearts and minds of a considerable number of Western Europeans and Americans, simple folk and high-minded intellectuals alike. These people did not necessarily become card-carrying communists (although quite a few did), but they were duly impressed with what they were told and shown by those darned young Soviets, and felt genuine sympathy for them and their achievements. In 1932, for instance, George Bernard Shaw, on returning from a sponsored trip to Russia, enthused in the *Manchester Guardian*:

> Increasing unemployment and the failure of private capital to cope with it throughout the rest of the world is causing persons of all classes and parties to watch with increasing interest the progress of the Soviet Union . . . Everywhere we saw hopeful and enthusiastic working-class, self-respecting, free up to the limits imposed on them by nature . . . setting an example of industry and conduct which would greatly enrich us if our systems supplied our workers with any incentive to follow it.[4]

Even at that time, not everyone shared the enthousiasm of, as Winston Churchill commented, 'the World's most famous intellectual Clown and Pantaloon in one'.[5] From the aftermath of the Second World War onwards, as more became known about the sacrifice behind those achievements, and about actual living conditions, shortages and oppression in the Soviet world, such testimonials and chest-beating success stories found a receptive ear only among the already converted. Far from garnering sympathy in the West and generating doubts about the merits of capitalism, they stiffened Westerners in their existing political beliefs. The Soviet Union had simply lost credibility.

The first thing to do, then, if you wish to make a comfortable, confident and well-organized target group with entrenched views and opinions even begin to think your way, would be to unsettle their unquestioned certainties. The Soviet Union never found an effective way to achieve this, but thanks to the advent of social media its successor, Putin's Russia, has.

The idea is not to make people think anything in particular, but to confuse them into not knowing what to think and whom to trust. In order to do so, you must establish a number of seemingly credible sources of news on the Internet, and have them spew out a never-ending hotchpotch of true, skewed and patently untrue messages. Some will be formulated matter-of-factly, others will hit a conspiratorial note, and yet others will be set in shrilly sensational colours. Next, you create an army of trolls. These are social-media accounts set up especially for your purposes, managed either by real people or simply by a bot, a computer program. These trolls then seed social media with your messages, where they will be picked up and relayed further by unsuspecting people, conspiracy theorists, paranoiacs and other useful idiots.

A fair proportion of the output deals with potentially divisive subjects such as immigration, religious and ethnic strife, and social privilege. Another important ingredient will be items that call into question the capabilities and intentions of governments and political functionaries and their supposed ties with real and imagined interest groups. The idea is to present all sorts of alternative versions and 'explanations' of whatever is published by the established newspapers and other media, in order to undermine public trust in what they call mainstream media (MSM), and make people lose track of what is reliable information and what is not. Or even to confuse them into thinking that there is no such thing as a trustworthy explanation or fair representation of the facts. Or, still worse, to make them doubt that facts one can rely on do exist at all. Mark, by the way, that information need not be 100 per cent correct and complete to be reliable. What counts is that reporters are sufficiently skilled and earnestly try to report the facts and people's opinions as best they can, refraining from pushing hidden agendas and being clear about their biases.

Just as the British gave both a German and a Belgian source for their corpse factory story during the First World War, these news sites are preferably based in different countries, thus adding to their appearance of respectability. It's a volatile world where sites come and go, but a few apparently stable examples are Sputnik, the official Russian press agency (formerly Novosty and Voice of Russia), Russia Today (RT), Voice of Europe, Infowars, JD Report, the Chinese Global Times, SCEPTR.net, which hails from Belgium, and the Dutch ninefornews.nl and fenixx.org. Some American examples are the left-leaning Palmer Report, right-wing Breitbart and, to some extent, Fox. These last aren't mere stooges of Russia: they too push an agenda of confusing people with 'alternative facts' rather than informing and empowering them. During the Trump years developments within the United States made it crystal-clear just how politically divisive and socially disruptive these tactics really are.

This strategy is not only used in political propaganda. Aggressive private interest groups such as anti-vaxxers and pro-lifers do the same. They set up websites touting a mishmash of fact, fantasy, intentional misinformation and atrocity stories, the contents of which are willingly spread by the same useful idiots. Just like political confusers, they aim to undermine people's trust in serious sources of information. Then, when doubts and misgivings beset the poor targets, they offer their alluringly simplistic and reassuringly clear ideas and ideology as a snug and secure haven, providing certainty and the peace of mind that comes from keeping the apparent moral high ground. The difference with the political variety is that the driving forces behind private confusion campaigns tend actually to believe the warped insights and simplistic theorettes they propagate; the political variety is generally more cynical.

Finally, we must understand that a confusion campaign is not the same thing as spreading disinformation. A disinformation campaign is an intentional, carefully directed attempt to foist counterfactual and misleading information on targets, from handpicked individuals to whole populations, with a view to impair the quality of their thinking and decision-making. Confusers merely try to disrupt people's confidence and capacity to distinguish the wheat from the chaff.

3. Never waste a good crisis

Panem et circenses, 'bread and games', were what made the Imperial Roman world go round, its emperors knew. If circumstances were bad and the plebs grew restive – which was often – order could be bought by plying them with food, entertainment and coins. But the emperors also took care that the recipients were in no doubt as to where these costly goodies came from, to garner their sympathy and support. In doing so, they epitomized the great tradition of incumbent and aspiring political bigwigs using the poor people's plight to strengthen their power base. What they did not realize was that it is possible to do so on the cheap, without putting in real effort yourself or seriously delving into your coffers. Here's how.

The latest in the series of military juntas that had been misgoverning Myanmar since 1962, turning it into one of the poorest and nastiest dictatorships in the world, had planned to hold a referendum on a new constitution on 10 May 2008. This constitution was touted as a step towards ending military rule by 2010, but many saw it as just a ruse to perpetuate the power and privileges of the military leaders. It had been eighteen years since there had been general elections in the country, when the junta had been utterly defeated by Aung San Suu Kyi's National League for Democracy. It had not accepted the results then, so why would it step down of its own accord now?

As fate would have it, Cyclone Nargis hit the city of Rangoon and the Irrawaddy Delta a mere week before the planned date of the referendum, killing 60,000 and leaving between 1.5 and 2 million Burmese destitute, some 3–4 per cent of the population. Despite the mayhem and general destruction the junta went as staunchly ahead as it had after the electoral disaster of 1990. Far from halting preparations, it only postponed the referendum in those regions that had been hit hardest, and by a mere fortnight. Unfazed, the State Peace and Development Council, as the junta called itself, looked on the calamity as an opportunity sent from heaven. When aeroplanes of the United Nations World Food Programme came pouring into Rangoon airport, relief workers were denied access to the country. Instead, the generals, among them junta chairman Than Shwe, began dispensing the food themselves in boxes that had their names written on them, making people believe the generals were personally doing their utmost for the afflicted. Their trickery worked like a charm, and the junta carried the referendum by a majority of almost 93 per cent of the vote. In a country where nobody had much to thank the regime for, it was an astounding success even allowing for considerable government pressure and fiddling.

During the COVID-19 crisis, President Donald Trump used a similarly deceptive ploy in the United States. In April 2020 the American Treasury Department began paying sums of up to $1,200 into the bank accounts of more than 80 million needy Americans. But those who had not provided their banking details were sent a paper cheque. Such government cheques had always been signed by some civil servant working at the treasury. But not this time. What with 2020 being an election year, Trump saw an excellent opportunity to bolster his personal popularity. In an unprecedented move he demanded that his name be put on the cheques instead, falsely suggesting that he was personally responsible for the dole-out. Protest that the distribution of tax monies to those in need ought not to be politicized in this way remained unheeded.

Such propagandistic piggybacking on people's misfortunes can even be pulled off internationally. There is an old and much-used mechanism of relatively affluent and powerful nations providing military, civilian and financial aid to less fortunate countries in return for political influence or economic privileges and favours. All nations with something to offer have engaged in such practices, from the Chinese building railways and mines in Africa and Cuba sending medical personnel to all four corners of the globe to the military and other aid the Soviet Union bestowed on its allies and satellites, and services rendered by American advisers and peace corps. With some exceptions, such assistance is loudly publicized, emphasizing the friendship between the nations involved and the commendable benevolence of the donor – aid and propaganda go hand in hand.

It took Vladimir Putin to develop a new, much cheaper variant of the idea, taking advantage of a crisis elsewhere. In this case, elsewhere meant the European Union, which he views as Russia's primary rival. When Italy was battling the COVID-19 virus, which had only just begun to rear its head in Russia, Putin loaded a convoy with assorted medical materials and sent it with much fanfare to Bergamo, one of the worst-hit towns in Italy. Later, similar stunts were pulled elsewhere in Eastern Europe, albeit on a smaller scale, since by then Russia was feeling the pressure of the virus much more keenly itself. Opinions differ as to the relevance and quality of the Russian president's contribution to world health, but it certainly bolstered Russia's image and Putin's popularity, primarily in Russia, but also among more or less pro-Russian Europeans.

In some sense, Putin's stunt was pre-dated by 25 years by the chain of events set in motion by the French general Philippe Morillon in Bosnia during the Balkan Wars of the 1990s. In March 1993, when the Bosnian Muslim town of Srebrenica was besieged by the Bosnian Serbs, Morillon, serving with the United Nations peace-keeping mission UNPROFOR, tried to drive a humanitarian convoy through wind and snow into the beleaguered enclave, but failed. The Bosnian Serb army would only let him and a few assorted aides from the UNHCR and Médecins Sans Frontières pass through to assess the situation in the town, which turned out to be dreadful. Once inside, the desperate thousands who had descended on the now hugely overcrowded town refused to let him leave. On the morning of 13 March Morillon saw no other way out than to pick up a bullhorn and announce from the balcony of the post office that from now on Srebrenica was under the protection of the United Nations and that he would stay there until all the injured could be evacuated. The UN was unpleasantly surprised, but found no way to wriggle out from under Morillon's assurances, so a Security Council resolution was duly passed declaring Srebrenica a safe haven. This case of involuntary propaganda, so to speak, at first greatly boosted the prestige of the UN, but three years later it damaged its reputation even more when the organization proved unwilling to or incapable of living up to its promises. Ratko Mladić's Bosnian Serb army overran Srebrenica and went on to murder 8,000 Bosnian Muslims, with UNPROFOR standing idly by. This shows how self-defeating this kind of publicity can be if it is shown up as being just hollow words.

4. Make them laugh

In his *Theory of Moral Sentiments* of 1759, Adam Smith, primarily known as the founding father of modern economic thinking, argued that the thing people crave most in life is what he called sympathy but we know as empathy. It is to feel valued and understood by, and safely connected with, others. Laughing together is a prominent means of expressing and reinforcing such mutually reassuring bonds, and this makes witticisms, jokes and ridicule extremely important instruments for uniting people behind your cause. Putting a rival, an opponent or black sheep wittily and humorously in their place will elicit the kind of merriment that strengthens the bond between jokers and comedians and their audience. Be careful not to overdo it, however, or your audience may take pity on your victim and start rooting for the underdog. Nobody likes a bully.

But this is not all. For empathic bonding to work, it must to some degree be mutual. This means that the audience must not only feel respect for the joker and show it by laughing, hooting or applauding, but also themselves feel respected by him. Because outside the class-room, the office and the pub, comedians usually don't know anyone in their audience personally, this feeling resides entirely within the audience. The thing that interferes most with the illusion of being respected by a wit is feeling stupid. So if others in the audience begin laughing at some witticism, the rest will join in willy-nilly, even if they don't get it. There's safety in numbers.

At propagandistic meetings and other public venues, then, all a speaker has to do to create maximum bonding is be sufficiently funny or scathing for some in the audience to get the point and start to laugh or applaud. This is also why talk shows always have a studio audience, which is carefully primed and prompted to laugh and applaud, thereby bolstering the prestige and popularity of hosts and guests alike.

5. *Audi et alteram partem*

Fairness in reporting, the journalism student Alli Enticott wrote in 2016, is a matter of 'reporting the truth accurately, exploring every angle and view available'. Who could disagree, except that we have established that 'the truth' is not an immutable rock waiting to be picked up by some reporter but a matter of consensus? Luckily, surprisingly little changes if we make do without the pretence of truth. Then, fair reporting becomes 'reporting accurately, exploring every angle and view available'. Fairness is not about truth but about observing and thinking as shrewdly as you can and using all the data you can find, identifying and presenting the facts as facts and opinions as opinions. In fair reporting, as in conducting serious polemics, cherry-picking – using only those titbits that fit your bias or bubble to build a case while ignoring relevant but less convenient points – is out of the question.

One important element of fairness in reporting is the principle grandiosely named *audi et alteram partem*, 'hearken to the other side as well.' The idea is that in any conflict there are at least two opposing parties, each out to thrash the other, and journalists should avoid becoming a weapon in the hands of any one of them. Instead they should offer a balanced picture like the one a spectator would see from the stands at the arena. So if some citizen accuses the town council of unjustly refusing him a permit, the council should have a chance to present its side of the story too. As a consequence, a journalist out to publish the scandal should minimally give the town hall a bell and ask for comment. It also means that in reporting, supporters of one side of an issue ought not to be systematically denied access to the media. That would amount to censoring them.

Propaganda, however, is not about fairness. It is about exerting as much influence as you can, and *audi et alteram partem* may help you do just that. Over the past decades the dangerously misguided idea of cultural relativism has gained an ever stronger foothold among serious media. As a consequence, the principle of *audi et alteram partem* has been given the equally mistaken new interpretation of bothsideism. From a safeguard against people and ideas being broadsided without ever getting a chance to fire a single shot themselves, it has come to be seen as a right to equal exposure for all concerned, regardless of their interest or expertise in the matter at hand, or of whether the subject is a matter of debatable opinion or of fact. Whereas bothsideism is sensible and fair in televised electoral debates, it is nonsensical and detrimental in large parts of the world beyond politics, especially in discussing plain facts. Facts are not a democracy. One simply cannot debate or vote on the toxicity of strychnine, the identity of two samples of DNA, the elasticity of granite or the efficacy of a vaccine. Nevertheless, many in the world of the media are nowadays convinced that in matters of health, for example, trained physicians and quacks or shamans must be treated on an equal footing; that sportspeople, singers and other celebrities, as well as agitators and lobbyists, should be heard on specialist subjects they haven't a clue about, as representatives of the *vox populi*, and, ironically, to make things more interesting for the average viewer or listener.

In practice, this 'right' is exercised both haphazardly and self-servingly, and here lies your chance, especially if you are a small or new player in the field. Protesting that you and your point of view on some matter have been under-represented by certain media may get you the opportunity to publish a think piece or get you an interview or a seat on a talk show. And if they won't budge, yelling about unfairly biased reporting may also garner a considerable amount of publicity, which will help to swell the ranks of your followers.

6. Hide your intentions

As a rule people don't much appreciate being led by the nose. In authoritarian societies, where there is no alternative, they will abide by the official lore, but they will betray and desert their masters as soon as they can safely do so. If oppression is not an option, you can make people do your bidding best by allowing them the illusion that they do so of their own accord. This is why most effective propaganda in the free world either isn't readily recognizable as such, or merely presents an alluring opportunity.

By and large commercial propaganda embraces the latter strategy. It typically consists of offers you would be a fool to pass up, often with a measure of bonding humour mixed in. People will generally choose your product over similar others because they like you and wish to associate themselves with you rather than because it is so different or much better, even if your product is more expensive. In fact, this strategy has been applied so ubiquitously for so many years now that seeing through it has become a kind of shared secret between provider and customer, enhancing its effectiveness rather than damaging it. Customers like being in the know, which is why contests for best commercial are popular, even though people are aware that they are no more than prey to the advertiser.

Political, religious and ethical issues cannot be peddled so easily. Selling them involves more than getting people to throw a bag of crisps into a shopping cart on a whim and half a memory. The idea is that people make such ideas their own, act on them and pass them on to others. There are two kinds of target here. One is the kind who can be influenced but doesn't care too much one way or the other, the other comprises people who seek a real and deep commitment.

The former group reacts best to blatantly emotional appeals: photos of and horror stories about abused animals, underfed children, drowning migrants and aborted foetuses. Or, as the case may be, footing of barbaric enemies and cartoons of pernicious cabals trying to overthrow civilized society. They will donate money, perhaps occasionally volunteer to collect money for the cause or go flyering. Maybe they'll even join the rank and file of a movement or, in extreme cases, a violent lynching mob, but that's it.

The other kind of target is easily frightened off but much more valuable once you've got them hooked. They are people with an intrinsic motivation and a real interest in the subject at hand. They consider themselves independent, critical thinkers who make their own decisions, thank you very much. They don't want to be told what to think or do. To make these people climb onto your bandwagon, you will do well to disguise your propaganda as ideologically sound, indisputably factual information or as reporting scientific progress.

Modern covert propaganda is not the dreaded subliminal brainwashing of the 1950s. Back then, it was thought that flashing messages in film footage, for instance, so briefly that people weren't aware they had seen anything other than the film itself, might prime and condition them to think and agree with whatever you had been signalling. There is actually no proof that this works at all.

7. Preach to the choir

Most people take preaching to the choir to be a waste of time and energy. As it does so often, however, reality begs to differ. It is one thing to convince people of the superior qualities of your idea, agenda or product and recruit them into your camp, but quite another to keep them there. Every silver lining implies a cloud, and left to their own devices people might all too easily begin to doubt their chosen allegiance once they run into the not-so-funny aspects of what you've offered them. They might begin to grumble, renege or even turn on you. And don't forget: the competition never sleeps, and promises equally glittering prizes.

Like socialism, communism had this figured out right from the beginning. They made a distinction between agitation and propaganda. By agitation, they meant activities aimed at rousing people from their stultifying misery or complacent numbness, making them aware of the oppressive systems they were sustaining, and ultimately impregnating them with the superior, invigorating values of communist lore. Agitation, so to speak, is cultivating unexplored or hostile territory, the way Christian missionaries used to spread the faith among the heathen. Propaganda in the communists' sense, on the other hand, came after that, its tasks being to keep the flame burning among the converts, to bolster their new convictions and reaffirm their loyalty to the cause. Although agitation and propaganda have different goals, their means and methods overlap to a considerable degree, and none of those has much to do with the inherent qualities of what is proposed.

When it comes to keeping the sheep in the fold, there are three approaches. The first is simply to keep on doing what you have been doing to recruit and enlarge your flock during the agitation phase. Basically, this amounts to explaining your position and extolling its virtues (and your own), while pointing out the practical deficiencies, fundamental flaws and despicable character of others. Political, religious and other moral propaganda will, like personal propaganda, lean towards blackening the competition – the vile capitalists, the dreary, authoritarian communists, the ignorant heathens destined for hell, the unclean kafir, the murderously selfish pro-choicers, that shit in accounts receivable whom nobody likes anyway. But not commercial propaganda. Aggressive comparative advertising may have its merits in prying loose some of the other's clientele, but keeping your existing client base intact requires a more congenial tone of voice.

The second approach is to try to keep your followers from learning about possibly more attractive alternatives altogether. This is a means accessible only to territorially or socially closed systems such as political and religious movements, including sects. Religions and sects have generally worked hard to suppress heresy and ban all contact with adherents of other faiths and atheists. The Roman Catholic Church had its Index to keep common believers and Church officials alike in the dark about dissident thinking; Islam still deploys its social control and its fatwas against the risk of any undesirable thoughts reaching the ummah. Until relatively recently it was unthinkable for a Protestant to buy from a Catholic grocer in most places where the two brushed shoulders. Intermarriage between members of different denominations within Christianity or between a Christian and someone subscribing to some other belief system was anathema. In Islam intermarriage still is. To a considerable degree, these tactics work, although they are not airtight.

Socio-political systems have a harder time of it. They need to isolate whole nations as completely from the rest of the world as possible. Like Maoist China and present-day North Korea, the Warsaw Pact world attempted to do so by literally fencing its population in, jamming radio and television broadcasts coming in from outside, meticulously confiscating any undesirable foreign news or literature at its borders and suppressing any domestically produced subversive information by means of the harshest and most massive system of censorship the world has ever seen. Despite all that effort, despite all the lives that were destroyed in the process, the Soviet regimes never succeeded in silencing the *samizdat*, 'clandestine press'. On the other hand, for a long time these regimes did succeed in making a considerable majority of their population believe that, although they might not inhabit earthly paradise, conditions were far worse elsewhere. As with religion, isolation and suppressing information do work, by and large.

Third and last, but far from least, you can keep your flock together by buying your sheep's loyalty. One way of doing this is by simply offering superior quality at acceptable cost. Relatively happy people with things to lose don't change allegiance all that easily – witness the surprising resilience of democracy. Clumsily inefficient as it may seem, it undeniably delivers better quality of life and more prosperity to a greater proportion of the population than any other system in existence. It is the same with impeccably designed, functionally superior products. If not outrageously priced or too far ahead of their time, they will attract and retain a steady, loyal client base for a long time.

In the absence of obvious superiority, buying and retaining people's loyalty is accomplished by tapping into their emotional needs. What people crave most, perhaps even more than love or sex, is security and shelter. They may quite like to be left alone at times, but without exception they abhor being lonely and feeling unwanted. People want to belong, to bask in the comfort of a group, hence the popularity of the club concept with commercial propaganda and classroom bullies.

Political and religious propaganda uses similar means. Apart from requiring visible signs of membership such as yarmulkes, crucifix pendants, beards and rosaries, or wearing orange and red if you were a sannyasin, religious groups and sects often impart so-called secret knowledge to their members, further increasing their sense of belonging and, since they have been sworn to secrecy, enhancing complicity and impeding apostasy. Political freebies range from simple items such as badges and pins to complete uniforms. Fairly unusual and somewhat comparable to a monk's breviary was *Máo Zhǔxí Yǔlù* (Quotations from Chairman Mao), better known as the Little Red Book of the Great Oarsman's thoughts. Needless to say, these and other political and religious 'freebies' – the Phrygian hat of the French Revolution, the red shirts of the Italian Garibaldists or the Italian fascists' black shirts of the 1920s – were seldom free. But their appeal is the same as that behind baseball cards, gold or black credit cards and Pokémon: first and foremost, they identify you as member of a group or organization, one of a particular 'us'.

In one way, political and religious propaganda differ deeply and perniciously from commercial efforts. Although the latter may inspire to mild (collecting baseball cards, badges or pins) or not-so-mild forms of mass hysteria (Pokémon Go, stealing other people's trainers or smartphones), such crazes are ephemeral. After a while, people divert their attention elsewhere and nobody remembers what all the hubbub was about. Religious and political movements, however, often try to make joining them a one-way street. Religions mostly do so by upping the price to be paid for apostasy. Whoever has the bloody nerve to leave the community will be excommunicated or, in Amish terms, 'shunned'. The apostate may, as in some Islamic circles, even be declared fair game and murdered.

Religions can do so because they tend to be geographically concentrated. In a uniformly orthodox environment the apostate has literally nowhere to go. This was also true of Nazi Germany from 1933 onwards, and in the Soviet empire and a sprinkling of other countries. What could be more suspicious, what could be better proof of being an anti-revolutionary subversive traitor than a Russian openly renouncing his or her membership of the Communist Party? However, such political monocultures are relatively rare. Followers of certain political ideals are usually more or less evenly distributed among a much larger, differently inclined population. For this and other reasons, political movements sometimes follow the example of criminal gangs by making their novices commit, by way of initiation, some act that makes it impossible for them to resign and return to their former life as if nothing had happened. Before Mussolini and Hitler came to power, once someone joined the former's *camicie nere*, 'Blackshirts', or the German SA and was seen in uniform or partaking in one of the brawls for which both the Italian thugs and Ernst Röhm's SA were notorious, that person had become complicit and there was no turning back.

8. Use the global intimacy of the Internet

Not twenty years after it was opened up to the general public in 1993, the Internet had become a powerful instrument for all types of propaganda: moral, commercial and even personal. Free email gave organizations and congregations of all kinds, as well as advocates of every cause imaginable, unprecedented powers to reach out to prospective sympathizers and keep in close touch with existing supporters. It also allowed new interest groups to organize and promote themselves at virtually no cost through mailing lists. As printed media began moving to the World Wide Web and new media platforms sprang up there, much of the advertising that is their lifeblood followed. Lastly, social media came along to bring the immediacy, spontaneity and urgency of real conversation. At the same time, they gave a whole new meaning to personal propaganda, in the nasty guises of naming and shaming, revenge porn, stalking, trolling and threats.

For propagandistic purposes the Internet offers a unique combination of advantages. On the one hand, it allows access to audiences of unlimited scale. On the other, it does so while preserving the illusion of personal and individual contact. Obviously, people are far more likely to lend a willing ear if they are treated as respected individuals, worthy of attention. The instruments to achieve this illusion rely on what is nowadays called 'Big Data', enormous quantities of tiny morsels of information about how people behave on, and sometimes also off, the Internet.

> ### The biggest flaw of the Internet: it's free
>
> The Internet is an unparalleled miracle of technological complexity and size, unique in the speed with which it has encapsulated the world and in the communicative, informative and commercial facilities it offers to everyone, anywhere. Its downsides are huge as well. Email gave birth to an ever growing deluge of spam, unsolicited commercial propaganda that people spend millions of hours just to rid themselves of every day. A growing part of it is criminal in nature, either phishing mails aimed at diddling your bank-account data and funds from you, or anonymous threats to hold your digital possessions to ransom unless you cough up in bitcoins. Another serious and persistent problem is rampant copyright infringement, robbing journalists, writers, photographers and media alike of their sources of income. The popular adage that information is free just doesn't cut it. Next to intelligence, talent and education it takes time, dedication and resources to dig out what's real from the bottomless morass of facts, opinions, propaganda, half-baked theories, nonsense, misunderstandings, lies and disinformation we all wade around in.
>
> A lot of this could have been avoided from the start had there been a practical, fully automatic system for micro-payments, quietly running in the background, so that email could have been priced at, say, a penny per copy and page views at perhaps even less. A penny won't matter to any ordinary emailer or web user. Spam and phishing mails, however, must be spouted by the hundreds of thousands to generate an effect, which would cost the perpetrators real money, probably deterring most of them. Also, half a penny per page view would have taken much of the sting out of copyright infringement by ensuring fair payment proportional to use.
>
> Bankers, however, abhorred the idea of having to process immense numbers of puny transactions, even though this entailed no more than some extra number-crunching by their tireless computers. They have actively and effectively sabotaged all attempts at getting micro-payment systems up and running. So, next time you find yourself wading through your spam-cluttered mailbox, or barred from reading an interesting article by a paywall forcing you to take out yet another subscription, you know whom to blame.

By and large, Big Data are used in two diametrically opposed ways. One starts off from demographic data about the socio-economic, cultural and ethnic characteristics of the population, culled from the Internet and, if possible, other sources, to identify where an organization's best prospective supporters live, who they are and what they want most urgently. In politics, such methods played an important part for the first time in the election campaign that carried Barack Obama into the White House in 2008. It gave campaigners a better idea of where to go canvassing and even what issues to raise. It has also become a major factor in how insurance companies determine fees, how banks assess the risk involved in loans and mortgages, and where and how companies and political organizations deploy their propaganda efforts. What intelligence services are up to in this respect is anybody's guess.

The other way to use Big Data starts off by gathering information about the personal behaviour of individuals, and inferring from this what they want, need or are susceptible to. Cookies that betray your wanderings on the Internet and thereby presumably your interests are the primary source of data, combined with purchasing histories that show what you have actually bought. This is one reason why so many online shops and other sites pressure you into opening an account with them, even if you don't intend to visit ever again.

This latter strategy is what enables the likes of Amazon to make largely reasonable suggestions for what else you might like when you select a book with them. Basically they just compare your choices to those of others who bought the same book. It is called a form of artificial intelligence, but don't hold your breath. By its nature it cannot think ahead. It can just extrapolate from choices you are now making or have made in the past. This is why you see so many advertisements for lawnmowers during the weeks right *after* you have bought one, when a lawnmower is in fact now the last thing you need.

There is a third way Big Data are being used: to follow and manipulate people in the real world. Its mainstays are licence plate registration and facial recognition, and location data drawn from smartphones. However, these are methods not of propaganda, but of surveillance and oppression.

9. Images are for stirring up emotions

There is an old and common belief that a picture is worth a thousand words. This is as deeply misguided as it is widespread, and extremely dangerous. Although it is true that the immediate impact of drawings, cartoons, photographs and films is much greater than that of the spoken or written word, their ability to inform is almost negligible.

The image is crystal clear, but what do you see?
a. Woman falls from window, to helpless husband's dismay;
b. Startled by burglar, panicking woman jumps from window;
c. Crazed black man throws innocent woman from window.

This is why paintings in a museum always have labels explaining what they are about, even if the text just reads 'Untitled'. It is also why photographs in the media always have captions, and why you can generally follow a television show reasonably well by just listening to the sound, but hardly, if at all, by looking at the screen with the sound off. Images need textual explanation. If you don't get any, chances are you haven't a clue as to what you are looking at.

Text, on the other hand, generally makes do without any pictures whatsoever. Some 250 years ago the pioneering novelist Laurence Sterne tried to integrate pictorial elements in his *The Life and Opinions of Tristram Shandy, Gentleman* (1759–67), but only one of these – the black page – survived. And it did so only as a figure of speech, not as something visual. Since then others – notably certain poets, the anonymous Japanese artist who created Umi-Umi in Chapter Eight and the Scottish novelist Alasdair Gray – have been turning their pages into graphic art. But they did not integrate images into the text, as if they were words or sentences. Instead, their pictorial efforts gave an extra visual interpretation to the text as a whole. The plight of Facebook is another indication of the great chasm between text and speech on one hand, and images on the other. In 2020 the company was made to fork out $52 million to provide psychiatric assistance to moderators who had developed PTSD just from watching and weeding out the pictorial filth that sloshes around Mark Zuckerberg's hang-out. Written literature certainly produces its fair share of revolting smut, but text editors or censors who have psychological trouble reading it are unheard of.

So why can images make your stomach turn so easily, but not text? The reason is that pictures affect us on a visceral level, while text and speech are first and foremost cerebral. Images have an immediate emotional effect on the psyche, but text and speech must first pass through the rationalist decoding filters of the human language faculty to discover their meaning and emotional overtones. These filters bring all the analytical power of structured, language-based thinking to processing incoming information. This would seem to have a dampening effect on their emotional impact. Moreover, any text we read or hear has first been put together by a speaker or writer using that very same analytical language machinery. Processing text is hence basically a matter of unpacking the interpretation that has already been coded in. Pictures lack such built-in interpretations; they are raw sensory impressions.

However, as a visual species that relies primarily on eyesight for survival, we intuitively bestow enormous credibility and weight on what we perceive 'with our own eyes'. While this made good sense in our distant past, when our primitive hunter-gatherer forebears spent their days looking for food while keeping an eye out for hungry hyenas and slithering snakes, its relevance diminished as life became more complex, as the notorious unreliability of eyewitnesses of complex or shocking events illustrates. Our powers of observation and retention of what we see just aren't all that sophisticated. Things get even worse when visual impressions are no longer the result of direct interaction with our physical environment, but occur out of context, as is the case with drawings and paintings, photos and film. Then textual explanation of a sort becomes indispensable.

Our overestimation of the credibility of visual input has enormous consequences. Warped portraits of political and religious luminaries have influenced the way people think about them at least since the days of Martin Luther. When the late nineteenth century brought the technology to trap reality on glass plates and later celluloid, it was widely believed that photos and films would put an end to poetic and artistic license, self-serving embellishment, misrepresentation and lies. Finally we would all be able to see with our own eyes what the world really looked like, and perceive what really went on. In fact, the new media were used to lie and cheat and feed people what has recently come to be called fake news right from the beginning. During the second Boer War, a mere five years after the Lumière brothers had shown the world's first ever film in Paris, newsreel cinema was used for propaganda purposes, to blacken and revile the enemy. In it, South African Boers were shown attacking a Red Cross tent where doctors were fighting for the life of a wounded soldier. What the audience was not made aware of was that the whole

This picture was taken from the Internet in 2020. With the text taken out, can you guess the message the maker wants to get across, beyond 'lots of unfriendly people'? When done, check the original on page 419.

thing was a hoax, filmed on Hampstead Heath in London with a crew of hired actors.

Ever since then, much iconic documentary photography and film has proved to have been either tampered with or staged, including the planting of the Stars and Stripes on Iwo Jima and the hoisting of the Soviet banner on the ruins of the Reichstag building in Berlin in 1945. Uniquely famous, although far from unique, are the Party big shots from Stalin's days who went missing from official Soviet photographs as they fell from grace. Even Robert Capa's world-famous 'Falling Soldier' photograph from the Spanish Civil War, officially entitled *Loyalist Militiaman at the Moment of Death, Cerro Muriano, September 5, 1936*, is thought not to have been made on the date Capa claimed, or in that location, and was possibly staged altogether. The only exception of note seems to have been the Vietnam War. It was the first war to be reported directly on television, and the American and South Vietnamese authorities left journalists uniquely free to shoot what and where they wanted, simply because they were slow to realize what enormous impact bringing the war directly into the homes of countless Americans and Europeans would have. After that, starting with the Gulf War of 1990, came so-called embedded journalism, which meant exclusive, carefully monitored and orchestrated access for approved journalists. It was not only strict proactive censorship; journalists were also fed partly bogus footage of, for instance, the famous precision strikes on targets in Iraq.

From then on, the possibilities of using pictures and film to deceive the people have skyrocketed. Thanks to the new digital platforms, changing the meaning of photographs and film footage or even completely inverting it, and so misleading people on a worldwide scale, requires little more than changing captions and a handful of mouse-clicks. One example is a film clip that appeared on YouTube in 2014, weeks after skirmishes between pro-Russian eastern Ukrainian insurgents and Ukrainian forces had flamed into an actual, vicious war. Its caption read 'Punitive Ukrainian National Guard Mission throwing dead bodies near Kramatorsk (Donetsk region) on 3 May 2014', suggesting that Ukrainian soldiers were defiling the corpses of pro-Russian compatriots they had murdered by way of reprisal. As it turned out later, the clip actually shows Russian soldiers throwing dead Dagenstani warriors into a heap. No doubt, however, the clip with the faulty caption is still out there somewhere (although, it

Two varieties of a rare, virtually self-explanatory pictorial message. Only the words 'Spanish' and 'Turkish' are necessary; explicitly mentioning Erdoğan is actually superfluous. It works because everybody knows the game and the true layout of the board. Notice, by the way, that both pictures still contain a lot of text.

would seem, not on YouTube), doing its poisonous work. Whether or not such frauds are exposed is essentially immaterial; the damage has already been done.

Of course, the limitations of pictorial evidence haven't gone entirely unnoticed. For instance, World Sailing, the leading authority on sailing races, will consider photographic and video evidence to settle disputes only if it satisfies a whole list of caveats and conditions – forget it if you used a telephoto lens, for example. But, generally speaking, visual imagery remains a treasure trove for all those who wish to misinform or enrage people. Don't think that only sinister politicians have images doctored or misleadingly captioned. There are lots of rancorous, delusional or merely mischievous amateurs out there. And the fact that we are all taken in by a tearful child's face or swollen hunger belly is not lost on even the most ethical of do-gooders.

So, as a consumer, never take any drawing, photograph or video and film footage at face value. Ask yourself every time: does the material actually show the situation or event it purports to show? What was the original context, who took it, who is now showing it and what is their interest in doing so? And, equally importantly: what are you not being shown? What was Photoshopped in or out or otherwise retouched? What ended up on the cutting-room floor, and why?

10. Law of Repetition

In May 1997 the BBC *Newsnight* interviewer Jeremy Paxman tried to force an unwilling Michael Howard, the former British home secretary, to reveal his intentions regarding the chairmanship of the Tory Party, by posing the same question no fewer than twelve times in a row. From a propagandistic point of view he did everything right, keeping it simple and hammering in the same message time and time again: you are not being upfront with the electorate. But Howard wouldn't budge and Paxman not only lost the skirmish but involuntarily raised some sympathy for the evasive politician. What went wrong?

Basically this: Paxman forgot that, although it may have considerable propagandistic value, a serious television interview is not a propaganda effort, and most viewers don't want to see it degrade into one. Nor did they appreciate the flashy, good-looking Paxman, whom they held in high esteem as a journalist, behaving like a propagandist, a suave classroom bully on his own turf terrorizing a somewhat nerdy-looking, squirming guest. It shows that Hitler had been wrong when, after his failed beer-hall putsch of 1923, he declared: 'Propaganda, propaganda, propaganda, all that matters is propaganda.'

In his wording, however, the future Führer had hit the nail on its proverbial head. Repetition or, in psychological terms, priming is the linchpin of effective propaganda, both in recruiting new followers and in keeping the flock motivated. For this reason commercial advertising is virtually never a one-off. Rather, it is a sustained barrage of one or two simple messages aired time and time again for weeks, months and sometimes years on end – which is precisely why many people find it so infuriating. Priming enhances the prominence of concepts and ideas in people's minds, which is why so many authoritarian regimes shower their underlings with impressively large images of the revered leader on every street corner, and many cultures constantly remind the people of their god: churches everywhere, daily calls to prayer, religious symbols in every classroom and home. Belief in the infallible superiority of gods, regimes and products needs constant stoking.

11. Law of Simplification and Disinformation

In his *Mein Kampf* (1925/7), Adolf Hitler set out the ground rules for successful political propaganda. It was essential, he asserted, to avoid abstract and complex ideas. Instead, one should concentrate on continually serving up just a handful of simple statements, set in stereotyped phrases without any regard for alternative views. Propaganda, he wrote, should engage in 'attracting the crowd, and not in educating those who are already educated'. In this he was diametrically opposed to his Marxist contemporaries, who considered propaganda a means to educate the masses, both before and after they had been converted to communism. In practice, however, both to some extent ended up carrying out the other's agenda. Hitler's minister of propaganda, Joseph Goebbels, was keenly aware of the necessity of continuous indoctrination to keep the fire burning among his Nazis,

Bet you didn't think of this one.

and the Soviets quickly learned the value of touting highly simplified ideas to keep their proletarians on the right track. Real, open discussion on any level would only invite criticism and new, unorthodox thinking, which is definitely not what any authoritarian regime wants.

Bar crude violence, controlling people means controlling their minds. This is done by limiting their access to extraneous information as much as possible, while feeding them whatever information is convenient, including all manner of expedient simplifications and lies. It is amazing how easily disinformation will be accepted and trusted, even by people who do not implicitly trust its source. A good example is the way Soviet Russia exploited the now legendary miner Alexey Stakhanov (1906–1977), who was credited with mining truly Herculean masses of coal. On 31 August 1935 the Soviet media spread the news that this coal miner from eastern Ukraine had single-handedly produced 102 tonnes of coal in one shift, fourteen times the quota. In September they let the world know that Stakhanov had that day beaten his own record by another 125 tonnes, totalling a staggering 227 tonnes of black coal. Since the Soviets were not known for running their mines like care homes, even doubling the quota would have been an astonishing feat for any man, and Stakhanov doubling his quota would have had him dig roughly the 'Sixteen Tons' the Kentucky-born singer-songwriter Merle Travis was to make into a famously back-breaking burden in 1946. It was all a hoax, of course. Stakhanov was credited with the labour of a whole crew of colleagues, and even then the results were greatly polished up. Anyone capable of putting two and two together should have seen through this highly improbable story immediately, yet nobody did. By 16 December Stakhanov had even ended up on the cover of *Time* magazine as an inspiration to all, and the Soviet Union had achieved a resounding double propaganda victory.

First, because the West had swallowed the story hook, line and sinker, the prestige of the Soviet Union got an important boost. Second, the Stakhanov hoax was used domestically as a justification for draconically upping the quota miners had to meet. Apart from much abuse, this actually yielded some positive effects in the long run, in the shape of better mining techniques and improved logistics. The success was big enough for the Kremlin to award Stakhanov all sorts of perks and promotions during the rest of his life, and appoint him Hero of Socialist Labour as late as 1970.

12. Perfume lingers, mud sticks and lies pay off

Why do people pay huge sums for aesthetically rather unremarkable Louis Vuitton handbags or ungainly trainers that give you sweaty feet? Why do they sometimes even resort to robbery and plunder to avail themselves of precisely these utterly unessential items? It is because they have been told time and time again how these things define you as a special, attractive and respected person. Not just by the firms making these things, but by their own peers and by people they look up to: celebrities, rappers and nowadays that strange breed called influencers. These icons of the high life, so to speak, are true miracles of marketing. First, you need a conspicuous design and ditto logo to ensure visibility. Then, the trick is to start as many positive rumours about the product as possible. If you do it right, these rumours will perpetuate themselves because the perfume of praise lingers: if people hear positive messages about a product often enough, they will start believing them and craving the article in question, especially once they become aware that others do so too.

The beauty is that gratification comes in three ways. First, there is the joy of owning something that 'everybody' seems to want to have. Second, flaunting your possession will mark you out as belonging to a class of owners that 'everybody' envies. Third, the inordinately high price preserves the illusion of exclusiveness and privilege.

The converse of perfume lingering is that mud sticks, which it does. One of the most effective ways to discredit an opponent is to start spreading negative rumours and stories about them. Horror stories are often planted this way, as rumours. If people hear such rumours a few times, they are prone to start believing that there must be some truth to them – that where there's smoke, there must be fire.

Mud-slinging is especially effective against individuals. Companies and institutions do not keel over all that easily and usually have the legal savvy and money to defend themselves. Also, organizations employ people to do their defending for them, and for those people it is all in a day's work. Accusations, however offensive or unfair, are no skin off their backs; on the contrary, fending off mud that is being slung at their paymasters is their *raison d'être*. This makes it very hard for anyone to dent any substantial organization. Individuals, on the other hand, have a much harder time of it. First, they are personally hit, regardless of whether an accusation is true or groundless. Their self-respect and personal reputation are immediately at risk, as are their relations with family and friends. Chances are that even if your accusations, true or not, come to nothing, you'll get your man and a couple of lives will be ruined or at least seriously damaged.

13. Demons divide and unite

Perhaps the most effective and most frequently used ploy for uniting a wavering constituency behind you is polarization. That way people who are not particularly attracted to you or to what you propose can be forced to choose between you and some other, much worse alternative – so they will get behind you.

The first thing you'll need is a demon. A good demon is presented as a despicable 'them' in sharp contrast with an inherently good and decent 'us'. Then you start further demonizing it by attributing all manner of undesirable properties and intentions to it. The beauty of this is that you can concentrate fully on the negative aspects of your demon, and you don't have to say much, if anything, about why 'we' are so much better. That simply goes without saying.

In some cases, such as when war has been declared on you, the demon is ready to hand: it's the enemy! A good enemy, meaning one that behaves badly, will do much of the work for you. You just need to feed people's indignation by pointing to the enemy's underhand, murderous behaviour. All fires need stoking, so in time, when morale begins to sag, you'll need to boost it with renewed demonization, possibly throwing in an atrocity story or two.

In the absence of war, the demon can be simply any and all people who do not fully underwrite your views. This is the way totalitarian regimes, moral and religious fanatics, social-justice warriors and believers in identity politics work: every dissenter is automatically denounced as morally, deeply, wrong, incapable of seeing what's right and true. They are a threat to unity, therefore any manifestation of 'them' is drowned and demonized in a sea of moral indignation. This is the way the Turkish president Recep Tayyip Erdoğan uses his erstwhile friend and companion Fethullah Gülen, and it is also how right-wing activists in general make use of the billionaire-turned-philanthropist George Soros. In the Third Reich, the Soviet Union, China, North Korea, Pol Pot's Kampuchea, Myanmar, Chile under Augusto Pinochet, Argentina during the years of Jorge Rafael Videla and Nicolás Maduro's Venezuela, to name but a few, the consequence was or is public humiliation, incarceration or death. In the modern Western democracies, social-justice warriors quite successfully resort to intimidation, boycotting and what they call 'de-platforming' their opponents, who are often framed as unenlightened 'deniers' or '-phobes'.

Lastly, there are circumstances in which no clear demon presents itself. This happens frequently when one is in need of a scapegoat to divert attention from one's own shortcomings and miscalculations, or from some other, more dangerous subject. Then a demon must be invented. A good example is Obamagate, a fictitious demon conjured up in 2020 by Donald Trump to divert attention from the failings of his inept administration. Obamagate consisted of nothing but loudly advertised suggestions of unspecified crimes supposedly committed by Trump's predecessor when he was in office. Arrests were to be expected in a matter of weeks! Although there was no substance to the allegations, they did the trick: Trump's supporters rallied behind their idol once more. What it failed to do, however, was to attract new supporters. In this respect, Trump fared better with his demonization of his opponent in 2016, Hillary Clinton. His constantly repeated 'lock her up', for reasons forever unclear, attracted many disgruntled Americans and certainly helped Trump to gain the White House that year.

Perhaps the most notorious and disastrous example of a trumped-up demon is what became known as the backstabbing myth, by means of which the German military and administrative elite washed their hands of the disgrace of losing the First World War, and unwittingly prepared the ground for the next. They claimed that Germany had in fact not lost fairly and squarely at all. On the contrary, its military had been very successful, as proven by the highly favourable peace terms exacted from the fledgling Soviet Russian regime at Brest-Litovsk in March 1918. Even in the West the German armies had not really been defeated on the battlefield. Instead, Germany had been stabbed in the back by the Allies' pernicious propaganda, which had undermined morale at home and so given left-wing extremists an opportunity to stage their November Revolution, which had brought a new defeatist cabinet and the Armistice. As time went by, this back-stabbing legend came to be used not only to set the Germans against their old enemies, but to 'prove' the existence of a Jewish-Bolshevik conspiracy against their nation. Between the backstabbing Allies to the West and the scheming Jews and communists inside and to the East, there was nowhere to turn to, no one for the Germans to trust but their own nationalist leaders. The legend was instrumental in Hitler's rise to power with the help of Reichskanzler Franz von Papen and Reichspräsident Paul von Hindenburg. In 2020 Trump, the losing contender for the American presidency, tried to revert his loss and destabilize the country by floating a closely similar myth, with 'the Democrats', who had purportedly 'stolen the elections', in the combined roles of the Allies and the Jewish–Bolshevik conspiracy.

Demons are not only effective in uniting people against a shared enemy; they can also be used to sow social and political discord. Once more the Nazis provide the archetypical example. Although they made quite an effort to spread their theories about a worldwide Jewish–Bolshevik conspiracy across Europe and the Americas, Goebbels's propaganda forces did not expect to recruit any nations into their camp. Their aim was to make sufficient converts in a country to create social unrest and political infighting over the matter, weakening that nation's resolve and drawing attention away from what the Reich was actually doing. In view of the divisive positions respected Americans such as Henry Ford and particularly Charles Lindbergh took up late in the interwar period, it worked quite well. In fact, the Nazi approach was an early form of today's fake news and disinformation factories. The idea was not so much to convince, but to confuse and generate mistrust.

14. Have a Holy Writ

Political, religious and certain other moral propaganda can profit enormously from a Holy Writ, a book or body of writings revealing the unassailable truths and tenets a movement is based on and clings to. It can function as a source of inspiration for missionary activities and as a yardstick in case of internal ideological disputes. Also, it affords members of a movement the means to flaunt their zeal and expertise, and gives them something to bicker about without having to look elsewhere for intellectual exercise – which would only invite unorthodoxy and heresy.

As a rule Holy Writs have no place in commercial propaganda, where the content of claims and assertions is irrelevant except that it be positive. Over the past few decades, however, companies subscribing to philosophies such as corporate social responsibility have begun to issue mission statements that come close. Here and there, 'green' and 'fair trade' ambitions have acquired almost religious overtones.

Outside the world of commerce, Holy Writs have proven themselves effective instruments of power and control for many centuries. Today the Bible and the Quran are the most prominent examples, but communism has Karl Marx's *Das Kapital* (1867–94), the Nazis touted Hitler's *Mein Kampf* and in Mao Zedong's day the whole of China brandished the Little Red Book. Joseph Smith began his Latter-day Saints movement in 1824 by publishing the *Book of Mormon*, his translation into English of what he claimed was a book of gold plates revealed to him by an angel. Likewise, the Scientology sect was founded on L. Ron Hubbard's book *Dianetics* of 1950. These are examples not only of religious and political but, at least in the latter two cases, of personal propaganda.

Revelational Holy Writs are also popular, in a negative sense, as proof of the other man's guilt and evil intentions, among conspiracy theorists. The classic example is the early twentieth-century *Protocols of the Elders of Zion*. It is a complicated hoax, largely concocted by the tsarist security service Ochrana on the basis of an older French anti-monarchist pamphlet, to blame Russian Jewry for the sorry state Russia was in during the Belle Époque and the ensuing social unrest. The Protocols were the fictitious minutes of equally fictitious secret meetings of Jewish foremen concocting schemes to take over the world. Although they were soon debunked, antisemitic groups from the Nazis all the way to Hamas have been promoting them and using them for indoctrinatory purposes ever since.

In a twisted way, the writings of the erstwhile diplomat Richard von Coudenhove-Kalergi (1894–1972) have become a Holy or, if you will, Unholy Writ as well. Kalergi – a Bohemian count with an Austrian father and a Japanese mother, who eventually ended up a Frenchman – strongly advocated the idea of European integration, to which end he founded the International Pan European Union in 1923 by publishing the manifesto *Pan-Europa*, in which he sketched his dream of a single European nation. Over time, quite a number of prominent Europeans and institutions became affiliated to the Pan European Union. This discreetly functioning international platform, together with Kalergi's colourfully international personal background, was a natural target for antisemites and ultra-right-wing nationalists. But it was only after the neo-Nazi Gerd Honsik published a rather misleading book about Kalergi and his ideas in 2005 that the 'Kalergi Plan' acquired real notoriety among Eurosceptic, antisemitic and nationalist-racist fringe groups in both Europe and the United States, as a genocidal ploy to replace the population of Europe by Asian and African immigrants. Although nobody actually reads Kalergi's writings, they count as the Devil's Cookbook in conspiratorial circles.

15. Keep it verbal

There are, broadly speaking, three ways in which to gain and maintain power over people. The first is by sheer violence. Second, one can count on loyalty and bonds of honour. The third is by gaining people's trust.

The first strategy is the law of the jungle, where mere strength rules. It is entirely possible to establish and maintain a position of power this way, but never for very long. One day, someone younger and capable of worse violence than you will come along, who will oust and replace you. Ruling by violence is also an inefficient strategy. Dead people don't serve anyone, while prisoners and forced labourers are an uneconomical and restive burden to any regime. This is nothing new; it is why Adam Smith pleaded against colonialism and slavery way back in the eighteenth century. Besides, relying on violent suppression implies that one can trust nobody. As a consequence most of the day must be devoted to reaffirming your strength, spotting and eliminating any signs of unrest or opposition, and setting sufficiently deterring examples. Such paranoia-ridden schemes are how most criminal and terrorist gangs operate.

Loyalty, oaths and honour underlay medieval feudal order in Europe. At its core were strong ethnic identities and a system of undisputed authority based on land ownership, entitlement and allegiance, so that everybody knew their place. Where oaths are the only insurance, one must be able to count on a person's word. Similar systems obtained among many peoples elsewhere, even in relatively egalitarian societies. There, authority depended to varying degrees on clan membership, bloodlines, age and merit.

In the static and relentlessly hierarchical feudal world, authority was not only undisputed but undisputable. Doubts about what's what and who's who might make the whole social structure come crashing down. This was the main reason that heresy and blasphemy were such a big deal then, worthy of being ruthlessly stamped out. Where loyalty is supreme, throwing orthodoxy to the wind is treason, the most dangerous and damning of social transgressions. It also meant that maintaining the social and political status quo necessitated a considerable amount of vigilance and violent repression.

The third power-management strategy is so-called soft power. It relies on winning the hearts and minds of people, making them believe in you and your ideas and support you of their own accord. Where a violent society is based on exploiting fear and a feudal one on exploiting awe, this third strategy exploits admiration and agreement, and its instrument is propaganda: you have to make your qualities, generosity and potential known.

Every organized community in history has in fact run on a mixture of all three driving forces: fear, awe and agreement. There have never been any purely unidimensional societies, although some came close. In criminal and terrorist gangs, for instance, brutality is the norm, as it was in the Khmer Rouge's Kampuchea, Stalin's Soviet Union and i.s.'s short-lived caliphate. But that held mainly for relations between elites and the rank and file. Among those who held power at any level, feudal elements such as personal loyalty and undisputable authority were more prominent, stoking even greater paranoia. In modern democracies, feudal values still obtain, especially within civil organizations such as political parties and businesses. Physical violence, however, has become the exclusive prerogative of the state, under the control of the law. Citizens will accept a certain level of violence and repression as necessary to ensure the untroubled existence and rights of the many. They trust the state implicitly to use its power wisely – until it doesn't.

In such societies soft power is paramount. Every leader depends on sufficient popular support, which, even if actual performance is blatantly below par, can largely be generated by propaganda. Such propaganda does include verbal violence. Intimidation and vilification are no strangers to democracies, nor are libel and slander. Like it or not, these can be effective weapons when it comes to scuttling an initiative, removing a rival or simply holding on to your seat. What it does not include, however, is what impatient nineteenth-century anarchists dubbed 'propaganda of the deed'. By this term, they meant political murder and terrorism: acts of physical violence against random civilians, with an aim to destabilizing political order. While it is true that political and religious violence can cause considerable shock and panic, their propaganda of the deed did not get the old anarchists anywhere. Or anyone else. In fact, ideologically inspired murder and terrorism have always been remarkably ineffectual when perpetrated against established, stable societies. People get hurt and die; there is a surge of grief and outrage. There might even be a form of retaliation, usually against people who had little to do with the crime committed, but eventually more or less everything goes back to normal, except for the instigators and perpetrators of the terrorist acts, who, if found, are ostracized. By and large, assassinations and acts of terrorism are bad for business. Instead of setting regimes and societies aquiver, they tend to trigger a rally-around-the-leader effect. Well-entrenched societies don't crumble easily.

The apparent exception is, of course, the assassination of Archduke Franz Ferdinand by Gavrilo Princip at Sarajevo on 28 June 1914, which triggered a rather stupid chain of events leading to one of the greatest tragedies of all time just a month later: the outbreak of the First World War. However, the ineptitude and irresponsibility with which the Central European political and military establishment handled events that summer suggests that they were a more likely cause of the disaster. Their bungling tipped the balance that had already become precarious on account of rampant nationalism and a widespread conviction that war was the very means to cleanse and reinvigorate a society that had become complacent and degenerate. Had it not been for Princip's 'lucky' shot, some other incident would probably have led to much the same result rather sooner than later.

A lie which is part a truth is ever the blackest of lies, . . .
a lie which is part a truth is a harder matter to fight.
Alfred Lord Tennyson, 'The Grandmother'

13
HOW TO WIN A WAR

War is a messy business at best, full of uncertainties, surprises, pitfalls and downturns. What's more, no two wars are ever the same. This is a lesson too many generals seem unable to grasp, hence the saying that the military is always planning for the last war. Nevertheless, one thing about wars never changes: their purpose. Anyone who goes to war aims to win. Whether they plan to do so by means of bombs and bullets or verbal warfare alone makes no difference.

The goal of every war, then, is perfectly clear. But it is not so clear what 'winning' actually means. It depends only rarely on the total destruction of the adversary, the small wars we wage on gnats at night being the obvious exception. Even vermin as obnoxious, destructive and threatening to our health as cockroaches, mice and rats generally do not have to be annihilated, if only because annihilation is more than we may hope to achieve. We'll settle for a certain balance of power, a stand-off that keeps 'their' intrusion on 'our' turf to an acceptable minimum.

The same generally holds when nations, tribes or organizations wage war on one another, even when one of the contestants demands unconditional surrender, as was the case in the Second World War. In the end, Germany and Japan were very badly damaged but they were neither dismantled nor annihilated. Instead, the Allies pulled their military fangs, but otherwise allowed and helped them to flourish once more as card-carrying members of the international community – in both cases with great success and to the benefit of all parties.

This is a very important point. Although there is truth in the old adage 'know thine enemy', knowing yourself is even more important when it comes to victory in war. Had the triumphant Allies of 1918 seen their harsh treatment of the German Reich for the petty vindictiveness that it actually was, they might have refrained from kindling all that resentment and revanchism that would spark another world war in 1939. It is even more important to know exactly what you want before any hostilities take place, and to weigh carefully the feasibility of your goals. This is in large part what Sun Tzu meant when he said that the successful general first wins and then goes to war.

When it comes to verbal warfare, there are two major kinds of conflict: rows and debates. Although rows are usually more spectacularly warlike, arguments, debates and discussions are far more interesting from the point of view of the strategist.

@#$%!

A ROW IS AN EMOTIONAL OUTBURST, driven by rage, perhaps the oldest emotion known to man and most animals alike. Rage, as we have seen, is an ugly but evolutionarily useful customer, a last line of defence, to be deployed when you find yourself cornered by a violent adversary determined to end your life. Had rage stuck to its original purpose, violently angry people would have been a much rarer sight. But in the course of evolution the range of conditions that may trigger rage broadened. It came to include interference with food, for example. Any animal that does not guard its catch jealously against all comers will ultimately starve to death. In that sense, appropriating someone else's food is tantamount to threatening their life. That is why you had better not come between loyal Fido and his bowl, or your easy-going, cuddly quadruped may suddenly turn into a vicious cur snapping at his master-turned-thief. It's not just dogs that react in this way; people respond equally violently. To appreciate this, just walk into a café and casually take a bite from a stranger's sandwich or a sip from their drink. You'll be lucky if the exchange doesn't come to blows.

With food, it is the 'imminent death' theme that triggers rage. Two other major triggers are frustration and stress, both of which tap into the 'no way out' aspect. Rampant rage often strikes in people who have mentally been manoeuvred into a corner. Tension starts building, and if they fail to find a way out of their predicament, they may at some point just snap. 'Going postal' is one American term for extreme cases of this kind of rage, coined around 1990 in reference to a remarkable spate of killing sprees perpetrated by employees of the United States Postal Service (USPS). The first took place in 1986 at the post office in Edmond, Oklahoma, when one Patrick Sherrill killed no fewer than fourteen of his colleagues and wounded another six before taking his own life. Having been reprimanded by two of his superiors the day before, he woke up on the morning of 20 August feeling mad as hell and unwilling to take it any more. He packed his two guns, drove to the office and wreaked havoc. Whatever we may think of Sherrill's heinous crime, for him to resort to such a hopeless act of wanton destruction there must have been festering much, much more inside him than just anger at being told off about his performance. And he was by no means the only one. Over the next ten years employees of the USPS alone killed another 26 people – colleagues, supervisors and bystanders – in similar workplace-related bloodbaths.

There is yet another element present in these atrocities, one that does not seem to derive from the central defensive function of rage. Going postal involves retribution. It is a way of getting back at your oppressors, of doing to 'them' what they did to you, of at least taking a few of them with you if you can't see any solution other than to end it all. It is rage degraded from a means of self-preservation into an instrument for inflicting damage on others, out of spite and that other great and ancient emotion: jealousy. Jealousy is what drives both the toddler who furiously tramples a toy to a pulp in kindergarten just because some other kid is allowed a chance to play with it, and the spurned spouse who kills his ex because 'If I can't have her, then nobody will.'

It would seem that these last two sources of rage are typically human. Animals are no strangers to behavioural effects of stress or frustration, but vengeance, spite and jealousy are hardly in evidence among them. Dogs may resent a newcomer in the household, such as a new baby, sometimes dangerously. They may react to attention being lavished on another member of the household by wriggling themselves into the centre of things, but such behaviour seems to be a normal part of their defending their position in the pack that we, people, mistake for a family with a dog. With the possible exception of chimpanzees and bonobos, harming others or their belongings out of spite or revenge seems by and large alien to animals. An explanation might be that the real motivation for taking revenge or hurting someone out of spite is not the detrimental effect it has on the object of one's displeasure, but the feeling of satisfaction those effects generate within them. For that, you have to be able to put yourself in the other one's shoes. You have to form an image in your own mind of what they experience and how they are affected by it. The ability to do so is what psychologists and ethologists call having a theory of mind, and it's beyond all animals, except, to a limited extent, chimps and bonobos.

Getting back at an obnoxious fellow human being is also the driving force behind road rage. As traffic grew, driving became evermore stressful. These days the smallest intrusion can trigger violent outbursts in drivers, even in otherwise well-behaved stiff-upper-lippians. Who has not been angrily honked at or given the finger in situations where they can't for the life of them figure out what it was they might have done to annoy someone? Who has never shouted 'Bloody idiot!' at their own windscreen? Somewhat less innocent is momentarily tapping the brakes just to show a driver behind you their place, or cutting in too closely in front of what you consider to be an offending party. Occasionally, people even try to run each other off the road and start a shouting match or worse on the hard shoulder.

The strange thing about road rage is that it typically occurs 'after the fact'. People fly off the handle not in the face of imminent danger, but immediately after the danger has passed. A clumsy move, a near miss or an insignificant fender-bender: those are the situations in which people truly fly off the handle. Their rage is cathartic, seeming to function as a way of burning off the frightful stress spike caused by the danger from which they have just escaped.

Far more than self-preservation, vengeful, jealous and cathartic rage makes rowing dangerously destructive. For one thing, what starts as a shouting match may easily derail into a real fight with irreversible consequences. Even worse, since temporary loss of control, restraint and fear is its essence, rage is all too often directed at someone who has little or nothing to do with what ignited it in the first place. All too often the victim is someone who just happens to be in the firing line at the wrong moment.

Much domestic fighting and domestic violence is like that. Anger from stress and frustration arising from problems away from the home is taken out on the partner, parent or child, who is always around (and through their unrelenting presence perhaps even a catalyst), while the real causes of one's frustration, human or otherwise,

Walking the dog

On 17 November 2015, just four days after the Bataclan theatre bloodbath in Paris, readers of the Dutch national newspaper *Het Parool* were shocked to read this letter from a fifty-something lawyer walking her dog late at night in a quiet residential area of Amsterdam:

Kill you all

As I'm walking my doggy past a car manoeuvring into a parking spot, I ask the driver to please turn down his (loudly booming) car stereo somewhat. 'There are children sleeping,' I add by way of explanation.

'You shut the fuck up, you white cunt with all your rules,' I'm told. Just for a second I'm convinced I must have misheard him, but it doesn't stop there: 'I.S. is going to kill you too – death to all whites! I.S. is coming to get you too, you antisocial shit, look me in the eye! I.S. is coming for you too, you white cunt!'

It has now been exactly three days since the terrorist attacks in Paris. I'm a strong believer in keeping things in perspective and certainly don't wish to allow myself to become fearful at all. So I and my tail-wagging doggy continue on our way. I notice a police motor-cyclist and wonder if I should warn him, but he's off too fast. I still hear the man yelling all sorts of abuse at me, I.S. remaining the prime ingredient. I keep talking to my dog in an attempt not to hear it and reach home. I decide not to start mulling things over. Instead, I sit down and begin writing this note.

MB, Amsterdam

cannot be touched. This is often why domestic rowing and domestic violence are so persistent: the true causes of the anger are never addressed or removed. What it amounts to is nothing but ineffectual bouts of cathartic hostility, resulting in feelings of guilt, shame and fear that only add to the pile of stress and frustration that triggered the outburst in the first place.

Of course, although rowing is as unpredictable and unsafe an instrument as a chainsaw in the hands of a child, there are times when a row may help to clear the air between people. Having it out with someone can be a way to express things that are too taboo, too shameful or just too ill-defined to lay on the table in a quiet, rational manner. A row may also serve to convince someone of the emotional importance of certain issues, since expressing deep-seated emotions is one of the few things language is poorly equipped to do. Emotions are much more effectively shown than described, and anger is a good way of stressing emotional urgency. However, don't expect too many concrete results. The positive effects of a row are as vague as the feelings you have been trying to get your opponent to tune into. If they realize that something means more to you than they thought or were willing to admit, that's an excellent outcome.

Instigating a row or giving the impression that you are about to do so is also an effective way of steering away from unwanted discussions. It is quite an effective avoidance strategy that plays on other people's diffidence and fear. Uncertain leaders often resort to bullying and intimidation in order to feign control and avoid having to tackle problems they are not up to solving, in the hope that their underlings will make them go away anyway. More often than not, authoritarianism is an impressive tumulus covering a deep, deep abyss of uncertainty and ineptitude. In this respect, there is little difference between the boardroom of a multinational and an ordinary drawing room. The mere threat of yet another explosion of vicious verbal abuse will set everybody on edge and make them try to placate mum, dad or the CEO in any way they know how.

With all that, there is still not much point in advising people that they had best avoid instigating a row. The very essence of rage is that it besets and overwhelms us when our brain and body decide that desperate measures are called for, putting all normal behavioural-management systems on hold. All we can do to keep ourselves from starting a row is to try and keep a sharp eye out for signs that we're close to 'losing it' and steer away, which isn't easy. Once things have gone from pudding to poop anyway, you are best to try and regain some sort of grip on yourself as quickly as possible to minimize the damage, then calm down as fast as is useful.

Yes, that's right: 'useful', not 'possible', for when the rage, with its complete loss of control, begins to abate, the row turns into an argument. It changes into a still heated, emotionally charged but no longer fully out-of-control dispute. A heart-rending experience, perhaps, but still a discussion in which more or less rational arguments begin to replace the earlier outbursts. This may well be the time when you have the fullest attention of your opponent, who is as impressed by what just happened as you are. And there is still enough hormonal drive left to force out what you could never say in normal circumstances. It would be a shame to waste such an opportunity.

@#$%!

OF COURSE, PEOPLE EXPERIENCE moments of rage and unchecked verbal aggression in isolation. Road rage can be like that, since quite often nobody out there notices what throes of exasperation you're in. Likewise, a worker alone in the office or workshop may take out her vexation on her computer or any other hapless utensil, and in desperation a solitary monk may start hurling abuse at the staunchly impassive heavens. But a real row requires a victim, who may be the actual cause of the rage or just an available easy target. In both cases, if you suddenly find yourself under attack from a seriously enraged other, you do have a choice about whether to engage in the row or not. In fact, you have three options.

The first is to respond in kind and set to with all you've got. It is by far the most spectacular option, but there is a real risk that it will cause things to come to blows, since this course of action will further enrage your opponent. It is definitely inadvisable to react in this way when you're dealing with a stranger, while in a domestic setting it may start the crockery flying. And you won't be helping. All-out rows of this kind typically end with two exhausted opponents and nothing cleared away or clarified; they are great in films but shoddy, useless affairs in real life.

A second way of dealing with a rage-driven verbal attack is to refuse to take up the gauntlet. Simply ignoring your assailant and walking away from the fracas often works well with strangers, since in the overwhelming majority of cases their real beef is not with you anyway. It is also appropriate when you are dealing with someone you know well but who truly hates your guts. Nobody can row against a tide of ill will. On the other hand, ignoring someone does not work well at all if it is somebody to whom you are close. They feel they have a right to be heard, and quite often their rage is induced precisely by the feeling that they have been denied that right for far too long – by you, by their boss, by the world . . . And now that they are finally speaking out, you refuse even to listen!

Perhaps the best way to counter an attack by an enraged relative, friend or partner is to accept the challenge, but without losing control yourself – which may be a lot to ask. Don't let feelings of outrage or fear get the better of you, and resist the temptation to let go. Yes, the attack on you is unfair, but remind yourself that either the attack is not really directed at you – you're just the lightning rod – or your opponent is desperately trying to make a point, which may be, but need not be, about you, but which he or she feels unable to make in any other way. So listen well, keep your wits about you and stand your ground against unfair personal attack as best you can. This is how you, as the victim, can help to turn an uncontrolled row into a much more useful argument. Here lies the potential for real gain; the argument stage is what brings the understanding, the release of unmanageable tension, and the catharsis.

Clearly, then, a row is not something that can be won. Rows are generally either misdirected outbursts of frustration and stress or desperate attempts at communication – or both. In either case, with rows among close associates the best outcome is some kind of clarification and mutual understanding of what is the matter with one of them or between them. That outcome must be mutually acknowledged to be effective, so kiss and make up! A row is *caused* by dissatisfaction, frustration, worrying and moping; it must not result in it.

Rows with strangers have no positive outcomes whatsoever and cannot be won either. There is nothing to be gained because there is nothing the enraged party has to ask of the victim, and the victim has nothing to give. Even the street thug who violently demands 'respect' does not really feel better and more secure if you defer to him. Your humouring him will only add to his need to be shown still more 'respect' by all and sundry, to add to the dunghill called street cred. However, rows between strangers can in a perverted sense be lost. This is where the audience comes in.

If two strangers become mixed up in a row, the outcome is usually a stand-off, with both parties retreating in the firm belief that the other party is wrong and an idiot. If all that has been exchanged are words, there is little harm done apart from the victim having had the fright of their life. But things change if there is an audience present that looks upon the incident as a joust and takes sides.

This happens often when one of a band of Saturday-night revellers gets into trouble with someone. If all goes well, the company will try to break up the row and take their mate with them, but, especially if drink and drugs are involved, chances are that they will cheer their comrade on instead, thus denying him or her the chance to bow out without losing face. The friends, or accidental bystanders as the case may be, play the traditional role of women in war: egging the combatants on by cheering and, if necessary, jeering and taunting them: 'C'mon Sally! Give the bitch a piece of your mind! You're not going to let'r get away with that, are you?' Such rows are senseless and always end badly for the fighters themselves; it is only the crowd that gets a cheap thrill out of them.

When all is said and done, there remains one thing that you must never do. Don't ever start or allow yourself to be drawn into a row with someone you do not truly respect. Remember that a row starts by relinquishing your self-control. In that enraged state you're not only far meaner, ruder and louder than usual, you're also far more outspoken and you don't care if you let your opponent know just how you feel about them. Chances are that even mild reservations about their qualities will come out as deep disdain so hurtful that it causes permanent damage and mistrust. Some things just cannot be unsaid. Some damage cannot be patched up.

@#$%!

ROWING IS, THANKFULLY, not the preferred mode of verbal communication, nor is it the most frequent. Under normal circumstances we engage either in discussions, debates and disputes – we'll use those terms indiscriminately here, since they are essentially the same kind of thing – or in what might be called normal conversation. If rowing serves to impress emotionally, debate serves to convince by rational means. Conversation is the kind of human communicative interaction that keeps the social machinery greased. It is also how we normally keep each other appraised of what is going on inside us and around us.

Conversation comprises things such as small talk, gossip, joking, storytelling and the exchange of information and advice. In writing, it includes personal letters and neutral business correspondence, most of the press and literary fiction. Much literature is unadulterated amusement. Fantasy, thrillers and whodunits are examples, but also the works of authors as diverse as P. G. Wodehouse, Tom Robbins, John Irving, Helen Fielding and Gabriel García Márquez, to name but a few. Of course, many ambitious novelists claim that they tell their stories to make a – usually deep – point, but what lessons there are to be learned from literature are rather general as a rule, vaguely moralistic and ethical. Novels tend to paint a picture of how life is or was at some point in history or in one or another class, social environment or phase in life. Often they are about coming to terms with yourself, family, the gods, loneliness and isolation, love and hatred – or failing to do so. Or they are about the meaning of life in general. But, for some mysterious reason, literature counts only as literature as long as any messages it sends remain implicit. As soon as the point of a story becomes even slightly obvious, a work is dubbed a social satire, a pamphlet, science fiction, a historical novel or any of a hundred other names that signify that we're not dealing with literature proper.

There is no clear dividing line between 'true' literature and those neighbouring genres. Nor is there a clean boundary separating fiction from non-fiction. Between the rarefied fiction of belles-lettres and the plodding austerity of an instruction booklet or the penal code stretches an immense realm populated by thoroughbreds and mongrels of every kind you can imagine, each catering in its own way for its own readership. Countless are the books in which actual history is used as a mere backdrop for a completely fictional story, from Margaret Mitchell's *Gone With the Wind* (1936) to Donna Tartt's *The Goldfinch* (2013). A popular ploy in educational books for children and adolescents is the exact reverse: using a fictional figure with whom children can easily identify to paint a more or less true picture of what life was like in another period or part of the world. John le Carré's later work balances between fiction and socio-political criticism, whereas Umberto Eco specialized in instruction in semiotics, philosophy, history and a lot more under the guise of entertaining fiction. Michel Houellebecq is a representative of the dystopic tradition of George Orwell, William Golding and Aldous Huxley: fiction as a serious socio-political warning. Different again is Julius Caesar's more than 2,000-year-old *De Bello Gallico* (About the War for Gaul), which is at once a pack of blatant propaganda riddled with lies and exaggeration, and surprisingly accurate historical documentation.

The work of socially and politically engaged authors, especially, shows how the boundaries between conversation and debate are equally fuzzy. They tell their stories with a clear ulterior motive; they are sending a message and try to convince people of the validity of their worries. Similar secondary aims, such as instruction in the ways and values of one's culture, also hide beneath the surface of countless at least partly fictional biographies, allegories and myths, up to and including collections such as the Bible and the Quran.

Although the different modes of verbal communication tend to blend like pigments in a watercolour, the basic division of labour is clear. Rows vent anger or allow people to break their own taboos, while conversations are for entertainment, contemplation, and informing and instructing one another. But debates and discussions exist to convince. In every debate there is a point to be pressed home, a decision to be made, an agreement to be reached or a conclusion to be drawn. Debates and discussions are sophisticated activities, drawing heavily on conscious thought and rational planning. They are serious games people play, games that can be won with the help of painstaking preparation, careful consideration of your opponent and usually a good deal of trickery.

@#$%!

A DEBATE OR DISCUSSION may be about any number of discordant views. Think, for instance, of the pandemonium that ensues when a school class is asked where to go on the annual outing or which charity the proceeds of the fair should go to this year. However, the actual number of opponents is of practical significance only; it takes just two to disagree. But that is not all. In every debate a third party is indispensable: the audience. In a debate, it functions as a jury, deciding who has won. No matter how utterly right you may be and how superior your arguments, if you fail to curry favour with the audience, you're lost. Good debaters are people who successfully make out that they know what they're on about, but who can also make the audience wish to be on their side. Debates, then, are about charisma, presentation and coming across as an attractive person just as much as they are about arguments and sound reasoning. That is one reason why winning a debate is not a simple yes-or-no matter.

Perhaps the most iconic venue for debate in today's world is the British House of Commons, where the audience are the factions, who send their champions into the arena on opposite sides of a central table and order is kept by the periwigged speaker. In reality, however, the Commons are a pretty bad example, because the debates there have become highly ritualized. The chances of anyone actually convincing members of other factions of anything are negligible, if only because the members are usually committed to the official views of their party, regardless of what arguments are brought forward.

A true debate is structured more along the lines of the games in the old Roman amphitheatres. There gladiators fought to the death before a frenzied crowd, which in the end cheered the winner but also determined the fate of the loser; if a man succeeded in generating sufficient sympathy by his conduct, he might live to fight another day. If that happened, both contestants won. A close modern variant is the televised election debate. The opponents are in the arena, facing the cameras, there is a referee to keep the debaters out of each other's hair, the audience are in the stands of their own homes and on their behalf groups of illuminati decide afterwards on- and off-screen who won and who lost – and how badly.

Elections themselves are like that, too. In February 1992 Bill Clinton, then no more than a somewhat overambitious governor of Arkansas, had been fighting an increasingly unsuccessful campaign for the Democratic nomination for the presidency. As expected, he lost the primary in New Hampshire to his rival, Paul Tsongas, on the eighteenth of that month, but the number of votes he did get looked so much like a classical thumbs up that in an interview that same night Clinton dared dub himself 'the Comeback Kid'. The rest is history: Clinton went on to win the nomination as well as two terms as president of the United States.

So, although in many elections the winner takes all, there is room for compromise and nuance even then, which shows that winning is a more complex notion than one might expect. The same complexity holds of the three essential roles in a debate as well. They are not always as explicitly represented as the amphitheatre model would suggest.

One role that is often dispensed with is that of the explicit referee. In a meeting, the kind of get-together where people gather around a table to discuss various subjects, convince one another, draw conclusions and make decisions, there is usually a designated chairperson, but a group of camping teenagers deciding what to do with the rest of their day can get along without one quite well. If necessary, one or another member of the group will momentarily step in to preserve or restore order and prevent the discussion from getting out of hand: 'Hey guys, let's hear Francis out first, shall we?' This happens even in a private discussion between two people. If one of them launches into what threatens to become a lengthy but not very relevant rant, for instance, the other may call him to order: 'All right, but really, that's not what this is about now, dear.'

Surprisingly, the last example shows that the audience's role is as fluid and transferable as that of the referee. For how else could there be debates and discussions with no one present but the two opponents? Such debates are highly frequent, as well. Take any couple. In the privacy of their own living room they try to convince each other about whether to buy this or that refrigerator, send their daughter to that posh, costly school or not, eat lox or lobster tonight, whose parents to spend Christmas Day with and a zillion other weighty matters. Even such debates are decided by an audience, for at some point one partner will step out of their role of opponent to assume that of audience and grant the other victory: 'OK, you're right, let's do it your way.' Remember how that feels? You've been there: you have to relinquish your position as opponent, step aside and assume the role of jury. It is a very conscious thing to do.

A fully fledged debate is even possible in the presence of only one opponent. That may sound crazy but it is true, provided there is a real audience. Imagine a speaker at a conference. She may occasionally be cheered, applauded or booed, but there is no real turn-taking. And yet, she is usually conducting a serious debate with some competing view or received wisdom on the subject at hand. Unopposed, the speaker herself switches to the role of adversary whenever necessary, which affords, by the way, great opportunities for manipulation and misrepresentation. Surprisingly, this doesn't guarantee that the speaker will win the debate. That is once more up to the audience, who will express their appreciation by polite applause, but far more directly later over drinks, where people attending will say things like: 'I thought she might be right there, I found her main point fairly convincing, don't you think?' or 'My God, did she really expect us to buy all that half-baked mumbo-jumbo? Does she even have a clue?'

The traditionally preferred means of communication for such one-sided debates is paper, of course. Libraries are full of books, and magazines and newspapers brim over with texts meant to convince the reader of one thing or another. Then, the fate of the writing debater is in the hands of readers, reviewers and writers of letters to the editor.

That leaves just one marginal kind of debate, which happens to be the only one you are certain to win. We are talking, of course, of the belated soliloquy. It is an internal debate that you conduct in the absence of both your opponents and your audience, giving you the opportunity to play both groups to your own advantage. The French call it *esprit d'escalier* – the genius that awaits you at the exit. It is the familiar experience of suddenly knowing exactly what brilliant things you should have said, once the opportunity to do so has passed.

@#$%!

IN AN IDEAL WORLD, winning a debate would be a consequence of being right and having the best arguments. In this world, having a strong case and being right may help, but make-believe and sleight of hand are at least as effective. All depends on winning the audience over. So, you have to do as lawyer Billy Flynn in the musical *Chicago* (1975) instructs, and 'Razzle Dazzle' them! Don't flatter yourself that you wouldn't stoop to using dodgy methods to win a debate or discussion. You do, we all do. But even if you insist that you don't, it is worthwhile to be able to spot the tricks the other party might use to trip you up. And they are many.

Broadly, instruments for forcing an argument to go your way are of two kinds. One group comprises psychological tricks directed at the opponent, the audience or both. The other is a collection of ways of misrepresenting the subject under debate. Both groups are traditionally thrown together under the heading 'fallacies', which strictly speaking applies only to the flawed arguments of the second group. Unsavoury as they may be, there is nothing fallacious about the psychological armoury in the first group.

First among the psychological devices is a host of cheap tricks playing on base sentiments and primitive emotions called PLAYING THE AUDIENCE – *argumentum ad populum* in Latin. The terms 'cheap', 'base' and 'primitive' in the previous sentence are an example. Just by casually throwing in those undesirable qualifications, I had you half-agree that tricks, sentiments and emotions are by no means the cornerstones of a decent discussion. Innocent-looking clichés such as 'more and more' and 'evermore' serve a similar purpose. In a statement such as 'More and more immigrants pour into Europe each day, and what does the government do about it?', that seemingly innocuous 'more and more' is enough to put everyone in worry mode: it suggests that things are bad and steadily getting worse. If you can get people to worry, you're halfway towards convincing them.

Terms such as 'naturally', 'evidently' and 'clearly' do a slightly different job. When someone casually sprinkles them in, there is a good chance that what they are stating is actually far from natural, evident or clear. But these jaunty qualifications are highly likely to prevent you from raising your hand in protest. They make you fear that doing so would show you up as ignorant, stupid or an uncooperative bore. In a meeting, it is not easy to speak up against something that is 'clearly' the case, especially when everybody else is nodding their approval.

Prodding psychological weak spots, such as the fear of not being in the know or of seeming out of touch, is a popular and effective way to hide a lack of real arguments. Beware of people who claim that certain objects, practices or ideas are 'a thing of the past', 'out of date' or 'anachronistic', 'no longer fit the demands of modern society' or – the latest variety – 'sooo last year'. What these people usually mean is that they lack a sound reason for disparaging the object of their disapprobation. Instead, it is to be rejected mainly because they wish it to be frowned upon. Such arguments are arguments of fashion, not merit.

Of course, much will become useless or irrelevant over time, but age is never the decisive factor. Better, more efficient alternatives elbow their way on to the scene instead, the way the electric train ousted steam traction and methods of modern medicine did away with bloodletting. But the 5,000-year-old art of writing is more widespread and more important than ever, and both the old-fashioned pencil and the paperclip still hold their own, as, in a different context, does the ancient combination of hammer and nail.

Compared to the above inconspicuously elegant ways of glossing over weak or unsound points without the audience noticing, two other popular methods, stonewalling and steamrollering, are heavy-handed artillery.

STONEWALLING is an implicit refusal to enter into a proper discussion of the subject at hand by ignoring questions or giving evasive answers. Or, better still, by simply substituting one's own message for a real answer. Politicians and functionaries are actually *taught* how to do this by professional media trainers. British home secretary Michael Howard, who, as we saw in Chapter Eleven, stolidly kept refusing to answer the question Jeremy Paxman equally stubbornly kept posing, is a cast-iron example of successful stonewalling.

STEAMROLLERING consists of drowning both your opponents and your audience in an avalanche of irrelevant side issues, obscure terminology and overly complex sentences. There is a beautiful example of its effects in Oliver Goldsmith's novel *The Vicar of Wakefield* (1766), when a visiting squire remorselessly trounces Moses, the vicar's gullible son, in a debate over the tithes and tricks of the Church, which the visitor claims are all 'confounded imposture'. 'Very well, Sir,' the squire grins to Moses:

'if you are for a cool argument upon that subject, I am ready to accept the challenge. And first, whether are you for managing it analogically, or dialogically?' 'I am for managing it rationally,' cried Moses, quite happy at being permitted to dispute. 'Good again,' cried the 'Squire, 'and firstly, of the first. I hope you'll not deny that whatever is is. If you don't grant me that, I can go no further.' – 'Why,' returned Moses, 'I think I may grant that, and make the best of it.' – 'I hope too,' returned the other, 'you'll grant that a part is less than the whole.' 'I grant that too,' cried Moses, 'it is but just and reasonable.' – 'I hope,' cried the 'Squire, 'you will not deny, that the three angles of a triangle are equal to two right ones.' – 'Nothing can be plainer,' returned t'other, and looked round with his usual importance. – 'Very well,' cried the 'Squire, speaking very quick, 'the premises being thus settled, I proceed to observe, that the concatenation of self existences, proceeding in a reciprocal duplicate ratio, naturally produce a problematical dialogism, which in some measure proves that the essence of spirituality may be referred to the second predicable' – 'Hold, hold,' cried the other, 'I deny that: Do you think I can thus tamely submit to such heterodox doctrines?' – 'What,' replied the 'Squire, as if in a passion, 'not submit! Answer me one plain question: Do you think Aristotle right when he says, that relatives are related?' 'Undoubtedly,' replied the other. – 'If so then,' cried the 'Squire, 'answer me directly to what I propose: Whether do you judge the analytical investigation of the first part of my enthymem deficient secundum quoad, or quoad minus, and give me your reasons: give me your reasons, I say, directly.' – 'I protest,' cried Moses, 'I don't rightly comprehend the force of your reasoning; but if it be reduced to one simple proposition, I fancy it may then have an answer.' – 'O sir,' cried the 'Squire, 'I am your most humble servant, I find you want me to furnish you with argument and intellects too. No, sir, there I protest you are too hard for me.' This effectually raised the laugh against poor Moses, who sat the only dismal figure in a groupe of merry faces: nor, did he offer a single syllable more during the whole entertainment.

Steamrollering is not the same as using jargon, although jargon may be put to excellent use in steamrollering. Jargon consists of the vocabulary, expressions, figures of speech and style particular to a profession or lifestyle. Jargon may be mysterious and impenetrable to outsiders, but within its group everything is crystal clear – and needs to be. Every Allied pilot in the Second World War knew exactly what 'bandits at three o'clock' signified, just as every s&m aficionado knows the difference between a 'sub', a 'dom' and a 'domme'. Steamrollering, to the contrary, is only about obfuscating things. And yes, it too is a popular strategy among politicians, but also among many who consider themselves specialists and professionals.

One particularly obnoxious variety of steamrollering is management speak, the mumbo jumbo full of suggestive but not quite definable notions that modern executives and officials and their spokespeople are so fond of, not just in their dealings with outsiders, but also among one another. This kind of steamrollering even gave rise to a game called Bullshit Bingo. Rules vary, but it is played by participants in a business meeting and always involves making a list of terms you hear there whose exact meanings you are not sure of, but wouldn't dare to ask about. It usually turns out that when notes are compared after the meeting, everybody has more or less the same list. The scary point of the game is, of course, that managers and executives appear to be eternally engaged in making decisions on the basis of discussions and analyses full of concepts and terms that none of those involved properly understands.

When Albert Einstein stated that if you cannot explain something in simple terms, you don't understand it yourself, he was referring to yet another world where steamrollering was de rigueur in his day and, to only a slightly lesser extent, still is: academia. Even today there are many scholars and scientists who believe earnestly that their subject is too holy, too deep or too technical to speak or write about plainly. First among these are those who speak of communication about science with the world at large as 'vulgarization' and frown upon 'popular science'. Strangely, the only people who would really stand to benefit from this kind of steamrollering in any way would be charlatans, researchers with something to hide, from lack of professional expertise to outright fraud. But most of its supporters are decent run-of-the-mill scholars and scientists, whereas many known fraudsters were gifted communicators. It might be their very mediocrity within the scientific community that makes academicians so eager to preserve the myth of academia as a world of excellence by hiding behind thick walls of obscure words. After all, being unassuming and transparent was easy for Einstein; he was an acknowledged, revered genius and he knew it. It might also be plain laziness and lack of interest. Whatever the cause, one effect is that much scientific literature is unnecessarily inaccessible, even some that is ostensibly directed at the general public. Another is that students the world over have to sit through lectures that are as incomprehensible as they are boring.

Opponents who won't let themselves be intimidated in this way can always be discredited by being tarnished, or by one of two special cases of this tactic, the look-who's-talking defence and whataboutism. TARNISHING pure and simple is a matter of levelling random accusations at an opponent. Traditionally, tarnishing is called the *argumentum ad hominem*: playing the man instead of the ball. Way back in the days of the Cold War, the very suggestion that somebody was a 'communist sympathizer' was enough, for most Americans, to render his opinions worthless and even dangerous. Many in Western Europe thought so too. During the early 1950s, when the American senator Joseph McCarthy and his House Un-American Activities Committee held sway in the United States, such suggestions put many people on his blacklist, out of business or even in jail. On the other side of the Iron Curtain, things were far worse than that. Accusations of being insufficiently loyal to the state might land you in Siberia, in Lubyanka prison or in front of a firing squad. Failing that, any sensible Soviet citizen would surely plug his ears as soon as you opened your mouth.

These days communist sympathies are no longer grounds for wholesale excommunication, but accusations of racism or child abuse are, at least in the West. Tarnishing need not always be this grim, however. A great way of discrediting an opponent is to make them look ridiculous. The fight for the American presidency in 1960

Anonymous anti-Nixon poster, distributed during the 1960 U.S. presidential election.

between Congressman John F. Kennedy – who eventually won – and incumbent vice-president Richard Nixon produced a classic example. Somewhere within Kennedy's Democratic Party machine an anonymous campaigner remembered that Nixon's parents had owned a petrol station, and designed a poster showing a smirking Nixon under the sarcastic heading 'Would YOU buy a used car from this man?' Of course, neither the way Nixon's parents earned their keep nor the legendary unreliability of second-hand-car salesmen had anything to do with the vice-president's qualities as a politician. And although Nixon would eventually be exposed as a fraud and a liar, that was still more than a decade in the future. But as always, mud sticks and people do believe that where there's smoke, there must be a fire.

More recently, anything the American real-estate tycoon, professional VIP and contestant for the Republican presidential nomination in 2016 Donald Trump said could be debunked by a simple: 'That's all very well, but just look at the man's HAIR!' It's true that Trump – a vain blonde who had been trying very hard to remain in the public eye for most of his life – did sport a highly unusual coiffure often likened to a hamster or marmoset, but it is also neither here nor there. Talk-show hosts and comedians love this kind of stratagem as an easy way to hurt their victim while boosting their own popularity as a humoristic bully.

Such silly jibes at your opponent can be fun, but as the Trump example proves, the effects are usually limited. They may sway a few doubters and strengthen the convictions of those already on your side, but that's about the size of it. Again, the wild accusations of Trump as president of the United States at anyone or anything that got in his way are a clear example. Much stronger and more dangerous are the effects of tarnishing when there seems to be a dark, unsettling connection between the accusation and its object, especially if the accusation is hard to deny. When in 2011 the American congressman Anthony Weiner inadvertently posted a link to a photograph of himself in underpants filled with an obviously enthusiastic John Thomas – or should we say weeny – on his public Twitter account, his political career went bust in a matter of minutes. By American standards Weiner was a dangerous left-winger, almost a socialist, which many consider immoral to begin with. He was also an ill-tempered loudmouth. And now, thanks to his own mistake, it transpired that this newly-wed husband and father had been exchanging racy text messages with about half a dozen women. This was just what his enemies had been waiting for: there you have it, the man has no morals whatsoever! Who would be so crazy as to vote for this monster? And yes, Weiner tried. And no, people didn't.

A downright gruesome result of tarnishing was the fate that befell Bijan Ebrahimi of Bristol, southwest England, in June 2013. Ebrahimi, a disabled refugee from Iran, was not an easy man to live with. He was a suspicious loner who fell out with his neighbours and had a long history of complaining to the police about being racially abused. Nobody liked him much, and Ebrahimi wanted to be rehoused elsewhere. So when he saw a neighbour playing with his children while swigging a can of beer, he started filming them as an example of the antisocial behaviour he claimed to be surrounded by. The neighbour, not quite sober, concluded that the obnoxious Iranian was filming not him but his children, hence: a paedophile! It came to a scuffle, and when at last the police came by they took not the aggressive neighbour with them to the nick to cool off, but the bruised Ebrahimi. The crowd took that as proof that the neighbour had been right: Ebrahimi was obviously a pervert and a paedophile. After two days of rising tension, during which Ebrahimi, now returned, repeatedly called in vain for the police to come and protect him, the neighbour went over to Ebrahimi's flat, beat the man senseless and then, with the help of another man, set fire to his body, killing him.

Ebrahimi may have been a quarrelsome pest, but that was all. A drunken neighbour's wild accusation that he was a paedophile, that twenty-first-century incarnation of the old-fashioned witch, was enough. Once again the mud stuck, initiating a spiral of mounting abhorrence and hatred that prepared the ground for bloody murder.

The LOOK-WHO'S-TALKING defence is a special case of tarnishing, where you accuse opponents of the very thing they are holding against you, or question their credibility by pointing out inconsistencies between what they preach and what they practise. It is the wife berating her husband about breaking it to his mother that they won't be spending Christmas with her, and him reacting: 'Why me? As if *you* ever would let *your* mother down like that.' Sometimes, the look-who's-talking defence can be bitter, as when one irritated person growls to another: 'Mind your language, please,' and gets back, 'No, *you* mind your words, idiot!' A particularly awkward incident of this kind took place in the Dutch parliament in 2011, when the populist leader Geert Wilders threw all protocol to the wind and snarled at the prime minister, 'Act your age, man!' The appalled PM could not but retort, 'No, *you* act your age, man!' and try to laugh off the matter.

The look-who's-talking defence is one more somewhat crude ploy to deflect the blows of an attacking opponent. Much harder to counter is WHATABOUTISM. Instead of going straight for your opponent, you belittle their point by setting it off against something similar but ostensibly much more serious. It is a classic among old-fashioned educators, who use it against whining children:

Sophie: Mum, can I have a sandwich? I'm so hungry!
Mum: Hungry? You're not hungry. The poor children in Africa are hungry. You're just spoiled.

Half a century ago Western European parents drove their children mad this way using their war experience: 'Hungry? Back in the war we were hungry! You just have an appetite.' The strong point of whataboutism is that both the opponent and his point are discredited: the opponent for his self-serving selective interest or indignation, the point for its insignificance in the greater scheme of things. The fallacy involved is that the validity of the alternative point does not change either the seriousness or the moral validity of the issue. For instance, when the Western world was shocked by the terrorist attacks in Paris in November 2015, some advocates of the Arab world were quick to point out:

> But what about the scores of victims of terrorism a city like Beirut is confronted with month after month? Why don't they ever get flowers, candles and a solemn march in their honour? Don't they count?

Of course they should count, and these advocates are right to remind us that they don't, or at least not as much as fellow Western Europeans. Painfully, out of sight really does mean out of mind – everywhere. But none of that has any bearing on the importance, the impact or the seriousness of what happened in Paris.

In the morning hours of 29 January 2016 Twitter threw up this particularly insidious gem, a contribution to the controversy about whether or not the statue of the great Victorian imperialist Cecil Rhodes that adorns the facade of Oxford's Oriel College should be torn down:

> I wonder what those who insist on the integrity of historical monuments in the case of Cecil #Rhodes feel about the #Parthenon marbles?

The idea is clear: those who want to keep Rhodes's statue intact are merely driven by ugly white-supremacist conservatism – keep Rhodes on the college, keep the Elgin Marbles in London. But this is a highly questionable, malicious insinuation. It is quite likely that there are defenders of Rhodes's statue who feel that for the same reason they don't want it tampered with the Marbles should be returned, namely to keep the historical record as intact as possible. Also, the analogy is totally false – which makes it a thoroughbred whataboutism. In the case of the Marbles, two nations fight over the right to care for them and proudly exhibit them, whereas the anti-Rhodesians are merely out for the obliteration of the image of a figure they hate, which is rather closer to the Victorian urge to put trousers on table legs lest the naked wood remind you of disturbing things. No stance on the Parthenon matter changes anything about the controversy involving Rhodes.

Of course, whataboutism won't help you to promote your own proposition. It is reasonable to expect anyone who makes a claim or advocates a position to defend it rationally and fairly. But if your claim is ill-founded or you just don't know, you might resort to a number of ways of DODGING THE BURDEN OF PROOF to save the day. One way of doing so is simply to refuse to give any arguments.

> Statler: Spaniards are not to be trusted, they are all swindlers.
> Waldorf: How do you know?Statler: It's evident, I'm amazed that you even ask!

Another good one would be: 'Wow, I can't believe how naive you are! What stone have you been living under all these years?' This might not only humble a somewhat hesitant opponent into submission, but make the audience choose the side of the savvier one, meaning *yours*. Another way to level an accusation while keeping your hands clean is this one:

> Politician: It is clear to me that identity theft is fast becoming a big problem in this country.
> Interviewer: So you agree with Mr Collingwood that strong legislation and more executive powers for the police are called for?
> Politician: Those are your words.

Or:

> Politician: I would merely like to point out that before the elections Mr Collingwood promised the electorate in so many words to lower income tax, and not only failed to live up to his promise but is now actually *raising* taxes.
> Interviewer: The question is, of course, whether voters will remember next time that Mr Collingwood cannot be trusted.
> Politician: I didn't say that, but people do well to keep their eyes peeled.

A popular and simple way to avoid having to prove anything at all is by enlisting the audience right from the start, like this:

> I don't have to tell you that Spaniards are swindlers, but . . .

or,

> We all know what socialists are likely to do when they get their hands on our money. So . . .

Sometimes it is more effective to turn the tables and dump the burden of proof into the hands of your opponent. Half a lifetime ago, a lawyer called Pim Lier caused quite a stir by claiming to be the illegitimate brother of Queen Juliana of the Netherlands. When proof was demanded, he simply said that he really was a royal bastard and if people did not believe him, it was up to them to prove him wrong. The royal family kept mum. The matter faded from the news without ever being resolved, so he had been at least partly successful.

One need not stop at trying to saddle the opponent with the burden of proof. It can be quite effective to positively discredit an opponent by accusing him of a caricature of the opposite of what you are claiming. Such fallacious reasoning is also known as the FALSE DILEMMA. Take, for example, the following short altercation that took place on Twitter in January 2016:

> Blackbird: Refugees should not be entitled to free medical care when nobody else is.
> Osprey: So you want poor, traumatized people to just rot away and die?

Judging from what is actually said, Blackbird's message is that it would be reasonable to expect refugees to contribute to the cost of their medical needs in the same way as the rest of us do, leaving the particulars open for debate. He certainly did not call for ruthless murder by neglect. But Osprey, trying to avoid a debate, suggests precisely that. First, he tacitly introduces two unwarranted presuppositions. One is that all refugees are penniless, the other that Blackbird would under no circumstances agree to medical attention for free. Thus, he accuses Blackbird of being an inhuman ogre whom no sane person would want to associate with.

Around 1980 a similar line of reasoning was popular concerning nuclear arms. Those who advocated trying to find ways to get rid of them were often accused of wanting the Soviets to overrun the Free World. Of course nobody – a few old-fashioned communist diehards excepted – wished that to happen. Most of the protesters just considered nuclear arms a bigger threat to humankind as a whole than Soviet aggression and thought the Bear in the East could and should be kept at bay by other means.

Perhaps the most popular stratagem for avoiding the burden of proof is invoking a FALSE AUTHORITY. But before we get into that, let it be absolutely clear that by itself there is nothing wrong with invoking authority. What child has not been at the losing end of debates like this:

> Sophie: Mum, can I have an ice cream?
> Mum: No.
> Sophie: Mu-um! Come on, Mum . . .
> Mum: No, Soph, now go and play with your brother.
> Sophie: But I want an ice cream, Mum, why can't I have an ice cream?
> Mum: BECAUSE I SAY SO!

A show of sheer, naked authority like this usually puts an end to the matter. Sophie may sulk for a minute or two, but that will be the end of it. Of course, there is power involved in such dealings. Sophie knows better than to persist, because she knows that her mother can make life very difficult for her. But power only partly explains why true authority works, and it's not even the most important part. Sophie's mother would have resorted to wielding mere power if she had threatened: 'Now shut up, or I'll tell your father!' Then Sophie would have backed down out of fear of her father's anger. Instead, by using 'Because I say so', her mother calls upon Sophie's respect for her and her wishes. The essence of real authority, then, is not power but respect. Just look at this little scene, so different from the earlier angry altercation about what to do about mother come Christmas:

> Connie: Oh, Walter, let's stay at home this Christmas! Just you and me?
> Walter: But what about Mother? You know she counts on us to come and stay with her.
> Connie: Please, darling, just this time. Tell her we'll be over again next year, we will.
> Walter: But she'll be devastated . . .
> Connie: Please, please, Walter . . . will you do it? Just for me?

Chances are that Walter will actually confront his mother, not from fear of what Connie might do to him, but out of respect for her and her wishes. 'Just for me' is equally as unreasonable an argument as 'because I say so', and in the right circumstances it can be equally as effective. Unlike this kind of soft-pawed pressure, a direct threat to make Walter's life any more difficult than she is making it already would get Connie nowhere.

In ordinary life, we rely on authorities all the time. We trust the plumber to fix the sink, the vicar to keep our relations with God properly greased, and manufacturers' instruction booklets to guide us when operating our cars, kitchen aids and computers. At school, children jump obediently through bizarre hoops such as filling in blanks intentionally created in inane texts, and spend a good part of their days answering questions they know their teacher already knows the answers to, all in the belief that the teacher knows what's good for them, and cares about them. We do as our doctors tell us; we let them fill our bodies with pills we haven't a clue about and even let them cut us open. But these kinds of authority are not unconditional. We do check whether the plumber is properly registered and certi-fied, trust the vicar because he has all the trimmings of his profession – rectory, church and the rest – and was introduced to the parish by the bishop. We entrust the teacher with our children because he is employed by a proper school.

More than three centuries ago the great British philosopher John Locke christened invoking authority in a discussion the *argumentum ad verecundiam*, the appeal to deference, and if the wisdom and expertise are real, it may be a perfectly valid argument. Things begin to go awry when we get to self-proclaimed diet-mongers, health and management gurus, life coaches and a thousand other pedlars of hope and salvation. Their credentials are a lot shakier. Although some mean well and may even be on the level, many are downright frauds. But there is clearly a lush and profitable market for them. Their following typically does not seem to be interested in finding out what their merchandise is based on, but rather just yearn for all the hope they can get. Here the argument runs along the lines of 'Trust me, I know what I'm talking about.' That may be true or not, who's to say?

This is where the appeals to respectable authority begin to make way for authoritarian intimidation. When that happens, Locke's *argumentum ad verecundiam* degenerates into a means to prevent an open discussion and compromise. The greatest example of this is of course the Word of God, or Allah and his prophet, or Yahweh, which cannot be questioned 'for I am the Lord, thy master'. All monotheistic gods and their representatives on Earth demand unquestioning obedience on no more grounds than their say-so – and, amazingly, they actually get it from a great many people. The family patriarch is another figure whose status may inflate to godlike proportions. How many love affairs have been terminated in tears on the basis of a simple 'Papa won't have it'? And Twitter once threw up this beauty: 'You shouldn't comment on this issue about which, from what you write, it is clear I know much more than you!'

Perhaps the most famous authority argument comes from the bitter controversy surrounding the Vietnam War in the late 1960s, one that was adopted subsequently by those who defended South African apartheid, and nowadays by certain black anti-racists: 'You cannot understand, let alone judge these things if you haven't been there yourself.' While it is always wise to take a close and critical look at the facts before drawing conclusions, this is a completely mistaken idea. First of all, actually going to Vietnam during the war mainly affected people's emotions. A direct confrontation with the chaotic squalor, the fear and horror of a war zone, in combination with – and this was what that 'you cannot judge' was about – the depraved cruelty of a faceless, omnipresent enemy, was bound to push even the staunchest pacifist towards viewing 'us' as the beleaguered well-meaning few and 'them' as subhuman barbarians, fit only for ruthless eradication. But it would hardly contribute to a careful and fair judgement of the merits of either side in the conflict. Worse, direct involvement will actually cloud your judgement. The worst position from which to follow a battle is right in the middle of it, where there is only smoke, din and death.

A special case of the authority argument is the LEMMINGS' LEAP. 'Da-ad? *Everybody* in my class has K-7s, so why can't I have them?' is the children's version. The idea is to blackmail your opponent into going along with you out of conformism. You have to be pretty self-confident to uphold your own views and principles when nobody agrees with them, and even more so when you are saddling the fruit of your loins with the consequences. For who wants himself, his child or, for that matter, his parent to be branded an oddball, an outcast, a freak? Adults often resort to the lemmings' leap, too, when they appeal to 'everybody agrees that' or 'who in their right mind could deny?' The subtext is that there is something wrong with you if you don't conform to what 'everybody' thinks.

Notice, by the way, that unlike what is usually claimed, the lemmings' leap has nothing to do with truth or falsehood. Nobody cares about objective truth; all a lemmings' leaper wants is to get their conformist way. From that perspective, 'everybody' is undeniably the perfect, unquestionable authority.

Perhaps the most dangerous psychological device to trip up your opponent is the TRICK QUESTION or LEADING QUESTION. A master at them is Gestapo Kommissar Escherich in Hans Fallada's Second World War novel *Jeder stirbt für sich allein* (Alone in Berlin; 1947). Escherich has finally cornered a suspect in his hunt for a man who for two years has been spreading postcards with anti-Nazi texts all over Berlin. The commissioner knows full well that this Enno Kluge, a malingering lazybones arrested in a doctor's waiting room, is the wrong guy, but Escherich desperately needs an arrest to keep his superiors happy.

> So he pulled the card from his pocket, laid it in front of Kluge and said casually: 'You are familiar with this card, Herr Kluge?'
> 'Yes', Enno Kluge began unthinkingly, but then he jumped and corrected himself: 'I meant no of course. I was made to read it out just now, the beginning I mean. Otherwise I don't know the card. So help me God, Herr Kommissar!'

See how it did not matter at all whether Kluge answered yes or no: 'yes' would brand him a seditious criminal, 'no' a liar and, by lying about being familiar with the card, a seditious criminal. So Escherich, playing good cop, goes on a bit about concentration camps and his ill-tempered colleague who would feed Kluge to the *Volksgerichtshof*, the 'people's court', 'after which your head will absolutely come off, Herr Kluge'. Then he says:

'No, I do not think you are the card-writer. But that it lay there in the corridor at the doctor's, while you were in that corridor suspiciously often, and your unrest, your attempt to escape . . . And us having reliable witnesses to all of it – no, Herr Kluge, it is best for you to tell me the truth now. I would not have you bring disaster on yourself.'

'The card must have been put through the letterbox from outside, Kommissar. I have nothing to do with it, honestly I don't, Herr Kommissar!'

'It cannot have come through the letterbox, on account of where it lay. And it had not been there five minutes before, the doctor's girl will swear to that. And meanwhile you were in the toilet. Or would you claim that someone else from the waiting room was in the bog?'

'No, I don't think so, Kommissar. No, absolutely not. Not if it's five minutes we're talking about. You see, I had been fancying a cigarette for quite a while so I watched if anyone went to the toilet.'

'Well, well now,' the commissioner said, looking very pleased. 'Now you say it yourself. Only you can have placed the card in the corridor, no one else.'

Kluge stared at him, eyes wide and utterly startled.

'So now that you have confessed to this . . .'

'I've confessed nothing, nothing! I only said that in those five minutes nobody was in the toilet before me!'

Kluge almost shouted this out.

'Aber Herr Kluge,' the commissioner said, shaking his head disapprovingly, 'surely you don't wish to go back on a confession just made, surely you are far too sensible for anything like that? I would have to add your retraction to the report, which would hardly make a favourable impression.'

Kluge looked at him in despair. 'But I haven't confessed to anything,' he muttered in a toneless voice.

'No doubt we will reach an agreement there,' Escherich said reassuringly. 'But first tell me who asked you to put that card there, please. Was it a close acquaintance, a friend? Or did someone accost you on the street and give you a few marks to do it?'

'Nothing! Nothing!' Kluge screamed once more. 'I never touched that card, I'd never seen it until your colleague gave it to me!'

'Now, Herr Kluge! You just admitted yourself that you put the card in the corridor . . .'

'I didn't admit anything. I never said that!'

'No,' said Escherich, passing a finger along his moustache to hide a smile.

Trick questions are not particular to sinister forces such as the old Nazi Gestapo. They are in the toolkit of the police and intelligence agencies the world over. They are the main reason why in every half-decent society police interviews must be taped or videoed. This is done not so much to prevent physical cruelty, but in order to be able to assess in hindsight whether a confession holds water or not. Surprisingly, with the help of trick questions and some browbeating it is not all that hard to put an innocent suspect into such a state of confusion that they start believing they must have done something after all and will confess to anything just to end the ordeal. In Britain, think of the Guildford Four, the Birmingham Six and the Maguire Seven. In the United States, think of the steady trickle of septuagenarians and octogenarians who spent most of their lives behind bars on the strength of a confession that eventually turns out to be completely bogus.

The lure of leading questions and trick question also turns interviewing young children into a minefield. Young children cannot keep facts from fantasy very well. As a consequence, a single slip-up such as 'Now show me where Uncle Harry touched you' will likely convince them that their uncle actually did something funny, regardless of whether anything untoward ever actually took place. Also, like most people in a pinch, children are pleasers, only too eager to curry favour with these friendly, interested grown-ups. So they'll do their best to help by saying what's right, which in their world is whatever these concerned grown-ups want to hear.

The environment where leading questions and trick questions flourish is also the natural habitat of PUTTING STICK ABOUT: winning an argument by means of threats and intimidation. In a sense, this *argumentum ad baculum*, the truncheon argument, is not a real debating technique. It is much better suited to the privacy of a quiet tête-à-tête than to being deployed in front of a real, impartial audience, although this does happen sometimes when a meeting is on the verge of turning into a brawl:

> Statler: Come on, Waldorf, it was clear that the committee saw things my way.
> Waldorf (turning purple): WHAT!? What did you say? Of all the ... Do you want me to tell everyone here how that went? Do you really want me to repeat to them what you said in there??
> Statler: Uh, now ... keep your hair on, Waldorf, I didn't mean to paint the wrong picture – it was just the impression I got, but well, if it matters that much to you ...

This is a dangerous move that is likely to backfire. For what if the audience demands that Waldorf make good on his threat, right then and there? Even if Statler shamelessly lied to 'the committee' and manipulated it, Waldorf's telling on him will reflect badly on both of them. This does not matter, of course, when only the opponents – and perhaps a few cronies – are present, or when the threatening party does not care about his positive reputation:

> Thug: See, this is a dangerous neighbourhood ... things can happen, but I can see to it that they don't.
> Publican: I don't know what you mean. I don't need anything from you.
> Thug: Of course, couldn't agree with you more ... but I think your family would agree with me. Two kids, isn't it? Thirteenish, no? The girl's a blonde? Lovely face on her too ...
> Publican (dejectedly): What is it you want from me?
> Thug: See? I knew we understood each other! Here's the deal ...

Finally, and quite unrelated, there is the NON SEQUITUR, baffling your opponent with a statement that has a resolute ring but is really neither here nor there. It does take some panache – or stupidity, as the case may be – but a good non sequitur (which is Latin for 'it does not follow') can be surprisingly effective, especially on banners carried at demonstrations and in advertising. In advertising slogans of the kind 'Feel free, have a Heineken' or 'Things go better with Coke' it is fully accepted and not even noticed by the public that the association between the positive sensation or effect and the product is 100 per cent spurious. A beautiful example from the world of politics is the young revolutionary who had a poster in his window that read 'THINK FOR YOURSELF, DON'T VOTE!' As a slogan it sounded nice and decisive, but how voting could be detrimental to one's political awareness – which is probably what he meant by thinking for oneself – remains a mystery.

@#$%!

SO FAR, EVERYTHING has been about manipulating opponents and audiences into agreeing that you are right. But instead of manipulating them, one might also manipulate the issue. That is, you can try to present your case in such a way that the audience, and perhaps even your opponent, will see things your way. More often than not this is tantamount to misrepresenting the issue to some extent. This happens inadvertently at least as often as it is done on purpose, simply because people fail to notice the bias, the flaws and the inconsistencies in their own reasoning. As a result, many a debate ends in consternation and fruitless bickering, with people talking at cross purposes without even realizing it. All much to the chagrin of the well-meaning debater, of course, not to mention the damage done to whatever greater good the debate was supposed to serve.

One cannot overestimate the importance of being able to spot and defuse such misrepresentations. Any fool can throw a spanner in the works by painting a flawed picture, but it takes intelligence, attention and care to set things straight and keep a discussion on track – and sometimes to turn the tables.

If tarnishing is priming the audience to dislike or mistrust your opponent, FRAMING is all about priming your audience to view the issue from a particular angle. None of us is able to avoid framing, simply because the things we talk about are things we care about or think important. It is only natural to present your case in the best possible light, just as a photographer crops and lights her subject as best she can, singling it out against the best possible backdrop. If the issue is something bad, you can paint it in shrill, clashing colours or dark, sombre tones. If you consider it desirable, you dress it up in the pleasantly soft and fluid hues of a watercolour. It is good to keep in mind that there is *always* a bias to anything you propose, attack or defend, or the subject would be too uninteresting to warrant your attention. That is what American right-wing opinion-makers such as Ann Coulter, Bernard Goldberg and their epigones, who consistently complain about those damned leftist mass media, fail to understand or knowingly exploit to frame their socio-political adversaries as insincere liars and conspirators.

Framing is the bread and butter of propaganda and the advertising industry. The trick with framing is to bend the truth while avoiding outright lies. Lies are dangerous, for if they are detected, chances are you are hung out to dry and watch your credibility go up in smoke. Instead, you artfully knit together your subject with properties unproven or unprovable, or with conclusions as yet unwarranted, so that these become inextricably interwoven with the subject of the debate. Often this takes no more than a carefully chosen term or two. Labelling the masses who went on the move from Africa, the Middle East and other unstable parts of the world in the wake of the failure of the Arab Spring 'refugees', 'migrants' or 'fortune-seekers' goes a long way when it comes to steering the debate about them in a particular direction.

One of the most blatant and successful instances of positive framing in history was the advertising campaign centred on the slogan 'More doctors smoke Camels than any other cigarette,' run by the R. J. Reynolds tobacco company throughout the 1940s. Of course, Reynolds could not really prove that their boast was true, although they did take the precaution to bolster it by going to medical conventions, giving out free packets of Camels to the participants and then polling them at the exit about what cigarettes they had in their pockets right then. But neither could anyone else prove that the claim was wrong. That way, the company had created a secure base from which to promote its real interest, the close association between cigarette-smoking and the trusted, reliable, health-orientated father-figure of the family GP. If he smoked (and smoked Camels!), what could be wrong with that? It was a very effective way of taking the wind out of the sails of those who at the time were voicing the first, slowly rising misgivings about links between smoking and diseases of the lungs.

Advertisement for Camel cigarettes, 1946, launched
by R. J. Reynolds Tobacco Company.

A particularly pernicious example of negative framing struck
the WikiLeaks founder Julian Assange in 2016. By February of that
year he had been cooped up in the cramped embassy of Ecuador
in London for 43 months. Assange was a much-wanted prey of the
United States government, who aimed to put him behind bars and
throw away the key for having put heaps of classified documents on
the Internet. A few of these, particularly some horrendous videos

such as 'Collateral Murder', which showed American military personnel casually picking off random Iraqi people from a helicopter, had caused a considerable stir in 2010. From then on the Americans, to make good on their loss of face, meant to catch Assange at all costs. The plot thickened when in Sweden two women went to the police with a rape story involving Assange. Although the whole thing sounded rather like a case of regrets on the rebound, the Swedish judiciary decided to haul Assange in for questioning and issued a European warrant for his arrest. Assange, who was in London at the time, feared that the whole thing was a set-up and that the Swedes, once they laid hands on him, would extradite him to the United States. So he fled to the Ecuadorian embassy, where he was granted political asylum, and so found his prison, for the British police made it clear that they would honour the warrant for his arrest the minute he stepped out onto the street. When in February 2016 a United Nations panel concluded that practically speaking Assange had been detained for more than three years without good reason, certain hostile Twitterati began adding insult to injury by referring to him as 'the accused rapist Assange'. While it is true that Assange has been accused of rape by these two women, there exists no such thing as an accused rapist. Just as 'motorist' refers to people actually driving a car from time to time, not to boys who wish to own a car one day, the term 'rapist' applies only to those whose guilt has been established. That's the whole point of having a trial. And so far Assange had not even been indicted.

Sometimes framing is reduced to mere name-calling. Remember how, during the Hundred Years War, Joan of Arc and her supporters came to refer to English soldiers as *les godams* – a nickname that in those religious times must have carried quite a load, somewhat like calling the unemployed leeches, women bitches or employees plebs today. Once you start hurling such abuse there won't be much room for discussion – but it can be a devastating put-down. However, this kind of blunt attack may backfire. Perhaps the most famous case of this took place in Brussels in the year 1566. Protestant nobles from what is now the Netherlands but were then dominions of his most Catholic Majesty Philip II, ruler of the all-powerful Spanish empire, came to petition their governess, Margaret of Parma, to stop the ruthless persecution of Protestantism by the Spanish Inquisition. Margaret's top adviser Charles de Berlaymont, after whom much later the seat of the European Commission would be named, sensed Margaret's fear on being confronted with several hundred noble malcontents and whispered: *N'ayez pas peur, Madame, ce ne sont que des gueux*, 'Never fear, ma'am, these men are but beggars.' In a strictly literal sense, Berlaymont was not wrong, since the nobles had indeed come to beg a favour. But the intended disparagement was not lost on the few *gueux* who overheard. When Margaret refused to curb the hounds of the Inquisition, the offended nobles adopted Berlaymont's scathing epithet as a *nom de guerre* and turned from supplicants into rebelling *geuzen*. The rest is history. Not half a century later Spanish power was dwindling quickly whereas the Netherlands had become the first federal republic of the Modern Age, fast on its way towards becoming a world power.

A special, extreme kind of framing is the STRAW MAN. The idea is first to erect a straw man by grossly exaggerating, oversimplifying or caricaturing whatever your opponent is proposing or defending, and then burn it to the ground. If you do it well, chances are that the audience will be convinced that you have well and truly trounced your opponent, whereas in fact you have carefully avoided addressing their real argument.

Letters to the editor abound with straw men, particularly those beginning along the lines of 'Mr Mashedpotato obviously wants the nation to . . .' What follows is usually a gross distortion of what the poor author, interviewee or politician actually proposed and a scorching though misdirected rebuttal – notice, by the way, the telltale 'obviously'. Comments in social media and below articles in online papers and magazines are like that too, only more rustic. The sad thing is that many of these commenters are completely serious. They have no idea that they have misunderstood and now misrepresent the argument and are therefore barking up the wrong tree. Such opponents are even harder to correct than malicious ones.

Ethics and religion are a real hotbed of bitter disagreement and discussion rife with straw men. When a university in the Netherlands decided not to provide their Muslim students with dedicated prayer rooms, the latter cried out that the university had forbidden them to fulfil their religious duties. And this in a country that holds religious freedom in high regard; bad university! Only, the university had done nothing of the kind. As a public institution, it had merely declined to make special arrangements with regard to what it considered to be a private matter, and took exception to the Muslim students' demand for separate rooms for men and women. Here, denial of constitutional freedom of religion was the straw man for what in a secular, human-rights-based society must count as an irregular, unreasonable and even unconstitutional demand. Another example is the way pro-life groups, particularly in the United States, are wont to portray abortion as 'a war on innocent life'. It is true that abortion is never pretty. But anyone can see that it has nothing to do with war, which is a planned and sustained wholesale assault on a people to gain power over them and make them do the assailant's bidding. There is no power or collective planning in abortion, only individual sadness and loss.

Whereas labelling abortion as a war merely distorts the issue, one may also try to replace the subject of a debate with a different, more convenient bone of contention. In 2016 the British prime minister David Cameron stated that in the matter of the referendum about the continued British membership of the European Union, his cabinet ministers were free to speak out and vote as they saw fit. Nigel Farage, a member of the European Parliament and a staunch campaigner for Britain leaving the union, was unpleasantly surprised when it became clear that the cabinet minister Nick Herbert, long thought to be a Eurosceptic, would vote for the United Kingdom to stay in. 'What I suspect,' Farage commented, 'is most senior politicians in the Conservative Party will put their careers before their conscience and back the prime minister's position.' Now there's a straw man that needs not even be lit; it will spontaneously combust. Henceforth, whatever reasons Herbert and his colleagues offered for not turning against their PM and the EU would be tainted with a distinct whiff of insincerity.

A close relative of the straw man is the FALSE ANALOGY. An analogy is a likeness between an unfamiliar or complex phenomenon and a more familiar or simple one, strong enough to talk about the former in terms of the latter, as when people talk about the structure of a company as if it were a family, with the CEO as the benign and wise paterfamilias and the workers as the youngest children. Analogies are extremely useful when the real subject is so abstract, so technical or so abstruse that non-specialists cannot be expected to grasp it. One particularly famous example is the solar-system analogy that the physicist Ernest Rutherford invented in the early years of the twentieth century to explain how atoms are structured. He portrayed the atom as a small, dense core of protons and neutrons. As the sun is surrounded by planets, this core was surrounded by electrons, each orbiting the core along a set path. To the layperson, it did not matter that electrons aren't in fact the solid balls the solar-system analogy suggested. It was better than nothing and close enough to offer real insight.

Although analogies are great for painting vivid, even insightful pictures of otherwise murky matters, they are hard to handle and can be outright dangerous. For one thing, a poorly chosen analogy, whether on purpose or by accident, can distort an issue beyond all recognition and lead to disastrous conclusions and decisions. In 1990, when the Internet was still in its fledgling years, the American lawyer Mike Godwin was struck by the gusto with which those participating in online discussions resorted to analogies, often bent or ridiculous ones involving Hitler, Nazis or the Holocaust, to blow the opposition right out of the water. It inspired him to formulate the now famous Godwin's Law: as an online discussion proceeds, it becomes evermore likely that some participant will drag Nazis, Hitler or the Holocaust in, regardless of the subject. The aptness of this observation was widely acknowledged, and people fallaciously began interpreting Godwin's Law as a ban on all such analogies: 'Don't mention the war,' as the unforgettable John Cleese character Basil Fawlty once said, or you're out!

Even pertinent analogies can become a source of confusion and misunderstanding. No analogy is perfect, simply because the subject and its analogue must be different – it does not help to explain something by comparing it to itself. So even an apt analogue shares only part of its properties, behaviour and implications with the subject. These likenesses are useful, but all other properties of the analogue should be kept out of the discussion. More often than not, however, people get carried away by an attractive, suggestive analogue, spuriously attributing all sorts of its properties and associations to the actual subject. By doing so they inevitably turn even the best analogies into false ones.

False analogies can cause damage on a vast scale. Towards the end of the twentieth century, for some reason the idea of Darwinian evolution became virtually everybody's pet analogy. With the waning of the memories of the atrocities of Nazism and Stalinism, social Darwinism returned to fashion. Something called evolutionary psychology appeared on the scene. Even market economics was redefined in terms of natural selection and survival of the fittest. But none of the self-styled gurus who preached this new evolutionary economic gospel took the trouble to acquaint themselves with what Darwin was really about, or they would have seen the gaping hole in their reasoning: natural selection is all about procreation and successive generations; evolutionary advantages spread in offspring only. But there are no generations in any meaningful sense in the world of companies and businesses. Although most of us have experienced what it's like to be 'fucked over' by a company, firms simply do not procreate. One can only guess at how many stupid, misguided policies were adopted and decisions made as a consequence.

Next to false analogies, there are FALSE GENERALIZATIONS. These are overly hasty conclusions about an entire group based on anecdotal evidence (the famous 'Smoking can't hurt, my granddad smoked like a chimney and he reached 94 in perfect health, then a bus got him'), too few data, too shallow knowledge or plain mistakes. They are the stuff that ethnic and racial prejudice is made of, as well as a good many conspiracy theories: Kenyans are great long-distance runners – look at Lornah and Edna Kiplagat; Spaniards are lazy, because they sleep in the afternoon; journalists tell us only what the elite wants us to believe – just look at them, cheek to jowl with their political puppet-masters at the White House Correspondents' Dinner. Similarly, the principle of equality creates its own false generalizations. 'I want more pocket money, because Alice gets more than me and I'm just as old as she is!' is a popular argument among teenagers, happily ignoring any differences that may exist between themselves and Alice, and their respective parents. 'What is sauce for the goose, is sauce for the gander' sounds reasonable and just to modern Western democratic ears, but it makes sense only if goose and gander are indeed equal, a condition that is often overlooked – and frequently on purpose.

From there, it is but a small step to the CAMEL'S NOSE argument, also known as the SLIPPERY SLOPE: as the Arabs used to say, once you allow a camel to put its nose into the tent, the rest of the beast will surely follow. An example is the teacher who is denied a new video projector for his classroom by the school board on the grounds that 'Next, they will all come clamouring for new projector and whatnot.'

Usually, camel's nose arguments come in the shape of warnings not to do something. The most famous camel's nose in history was perhaps the so-called Domino Theory, which underlay American foreign policy in the Far East from the end of the Second World War until roughly 1975. This theory said that if Vietnam were allowed to have a communist regime, all the other nations in the region – Cambodia, Thailand, Burma, the Philippines and ultimately Indonesia – would follow suit one by one. The theory proved to be wrong. Despite all the American efforts, 58,000 American casualties and immense suffering among the Vietnamese, the country did become communist in 1975. The only country to do something similar in its wake was innocent Cambodia, but only because the Americans had politically destabilized it so badly and had so maimed it by wholesale bombing that they virtually handed it to a communist fringe group, Pol Pot's murderous Khmer Rouge, on a silver platter. Ironically, it would be the Vietnamese armies that put a stop to the genocidal terror the Khmer Rouge unleashed on the Cambodian people upon seizing power.

While it is of course always wise to consider the consequences of one's actions or decisions, camel's nose arguments take things to the extreme. Like the Domino Theory, most of them are based on fear instead of cautious reasoning. And, just as importantly, they are mostly based on a flawed understanding of basic human psychology, the idea that if you give people half a chance to do something immoral or destructive, they'll take it. As in these examples:

One man one vote, you say? Should we allow penniless paupers the right to vote like responsible citizens? Fiddlesticks, Sir! God knows, they might be demanding the vote for women next, hawhawhaw!

If we were to legalize cocaine, soon the whole population would be sniffing their brains out.

If we were to legalize weed, they'd all be on heroin in a matter of weeks.

If you tell your children about sex and how it works, and give them access to prophylactics, they'll only start fornicating like rabbits and getting pregnant.

If we open the door to euthanasia, people will soon be planning granny's demise to fit conveniently between her cherished Christmas family dinner and New Year's Eve at the hipsters' club.

But that is typically not what people do or want. Despite their greed, lust and lack of self-control, the great majority is much too conventional to rock the boat. Where the vote is concerned, ideas about what was acceptable and desirable changed with time, so that when first all men and eventually women did get voting rights, these decisions only reflected contemporary norms. Also, in countries where the use of cannabis is least repressed, its use is relatively low. The same holds, by the way, for alcohol. The Anglo-Scandinavian idea of drinking until you drop is alien to the alcoholically much more relaxed Roman cultures, where taxes are much lower and regulations more relaxed. Furthermore, there has never been a shred of evidence to confirm the so-called stepping-stone theory, which predicts that smoking pot ultimately leads to shooting heroin. And in countries with a relatively open attitude to sex, such as the Netherlands, the age of defloration is somewhat higher and the number of teenage pregnancies and abortions dramatically lower than in tight-arsed nations such as the United States or Poland. On euthanasia the verdict is still out, but there is no reason to fear that people tend to take it any less seriously than they should.

Camel's noses also work in hindsight. When in 2016 it came out that many people at the BBC had long known that there was something definitely unsavoury about the media star Jimmy Savile, but never dared to report their misgivings to their bosses, one newspaper editor made the following comment:

> It makes you think about your own organization. About the little things, the small, slightly off-colour remarks that are tolerated because they come from a popular guy. For that's how it starts.

As before, that is not how it starts. Off-colour jokes and risqué remarks may not be everyone's cup of tea, but normal people do not turn into ruthless sex fiends like Savile on account of them.

The only good thing about the camel's nose is its potential for ridiculing policies and the people proposing them, and for this reason they're a godsend to commentators and comedians. Here's an example:

> In order to improve its service to the public, the Metropolitan Transport Authority has decided to do away with 5 per cent of all stops. They say fewer stops will boost both efficiency and punctuality, because less time will be lost on account of people boarding and getting off. Obviously, the MTA's idea of perfect service to the traveller would be to run its trains and buses empty from point of departure to final destination without ever stopping on the way.

> @#$%!

> Every nation, in every region, now has a decision to make. Either you are with us, or you are with the terrorists. From this day forward, any nation that continues to harbour or support terrorism will be regarded by the United States as a hostile regime.

The date was 20 September 2001, the venue the Capitol in Washington and the speaker George W. Bush, 43rd president of the United States. His address to the Joint Session of Congress and the world, just over a week after the destruction of the Twin Towers, sounded as firm and determined as it was hollow and inadequate. For one thing, rulers across the Arabian peninsula laughed their heads off and went on financing most of the mayhem disrupting the world as before, while remaining best of friends and close allies of Washington and the rest of the West. Second, Bush's simplistic dichotomy between friends and foes was logically flawed and, as a consequence, stupid. Thankfully, the world is far more complex than he made it seem. Of course not everybody who wasn't a sworn ally was America's enemy. By pretending they were, the American administration just denied the whole world the chance to mediate and thus help to defuse an extremely dangerous situation. We have all seen the direct consequences. The nasty cartoons that showed Taliban-ruled Afghanistan as one great hole after having been nuked into oblivion (in fact, none of the nineteen terrorists involved in the 9/11 attacks had close ties to the Taliban; they were al-Qaeda operatives. Fifteen were Saudi Arabians, two came from the Emirates and the remaining two from Lebanon and Egypt); the shameful tragedies of the extraordinary-rendition programme and Guantanamo Bay prison; the misguided and botched takeover of Iraq; the hopeless 'bringing democracy' to Afghanistan; and ultimately the I.S.-mediated chaos in most of the Middle East.

This wholesale political, military and moral destabilization is arguably the worst example in history of what a FALSE OPPOSITION may lead to. But it is far from unique. Countless generals have gone into battle crying 'Victory or Death', only to discover that much of their armies preferred staying alive to either option. And, contrary to their motto 'Live free or die', the inhabitants of the American state of New Hampshire have more willingly than most of their compatriots suffered the limitations of federal administration for more than two hundred years now.

Those New Hampshirites illustrate the heart of the matter. Pairs of notions such as friend and enemy or freedom and death are mutually exclusive, in the sense that someone cannot very well be your friend and your enemy at the same time and there is no freedom to act in death. But they are not binary oppositions. Binary oppositions are like the states of a light switch: if the light is not on it's off, and if it's not off it's on. If someone is not your enemy, however, that does not necessarily make him your friend. He might just be a vague acquaintance, or an admirer, a fan, a cautious neighbour, a distant relative or a nameless face in the crowd. Similarly, loss of freedom does not entail dying in any way.

As the case of the 43rd president shows, the damage caused by mistaking mutually exclusive categories for oppositions can be huge. Thankfully, things aren't always as bad as that. Sometimes the result is just silly. Yet these mistakes are very popular, as these well-known examples show:

Better red than dead.

Better dead than red.

Make love, not war.

What doesn't kill you makes you stronger.

False oppositions are by no means the only way in which debates and discussions derail because of people's limited grasp of the laws of logic. People routinely make all kinds of logical mistakes and, conversely, easily overlook other people's logical fallacies. As a consequence, they frequently get away with logically flawed reasoning, unless we keep a few things in mind.

Logic is all about implication, by which we mean the conditional relations between two states of affairs or events. For example:

If you are a boy, you will start growing a beard some time during puberty.

If you are human, you will die.

Both are simple truths, but they are of different kinds. Since the word 'beard' normally only refers to the kind of hairy outgrowth on a male human's face, the first example works both ways: if you grow a beard, we may safely assume that you are a man. The implication is symmetrical. On the other hand, while humans do invariably die, the fact that some organism dies obviously does not make it human. So this is a one-way implication only. Treating a one-way implication as if it were symmetrical is logical WRONG-WAY DRIVING, and people do it all the time. For instance, while it is true that eating bad food makes you feel sick, feeling sick does not entail that you have eaten bad food. Likewise, if you snore, your partner may have trouble sleeping. But if your partner can't sleep that does not necessarily mean that you snore. Nor does the fact that rich people tend to be tight-fisted mean that the parsimonious are rich.

Another fallacy with implications is the FORBIDDEN U-TURN. With symmetrical implications, the exact opposite of an implication is true as well. Thus, if you are not a boy, you won't be growing a beard in the future. But you can't safely reverse a one-way implication. If something is not human, that does not make it immortal. All creatures, from cows to cockroaches, die just as we do. Forbidden U-turns seem to be especially popular where physical and mental well-being is concerned:

Smoking will give you lung cancer, so if you don't smoke or stop smoking, you won't get lung cancer.

Drinking milk helps to develop a strong skeleton, so if you don't drink milk, your bones will go brittle.

Industrial junk food and soft drinks make you fat and ill, so munching natural foods and sipping fruit juices will make you thin and healthy.

Learning to play a musical instrument makes you smarter, so without a musical education you will end up stupid.

School is full of nerdy people, so if you want to be a cool person, drop out.

Ordinary people with poor taste buy at Ikea, so not buying there is a sign of refined taste and sophistication.

The exhaust fumes of internal-combustion engines are climate-killers, so we should all drive exhaust-free electric cars.

None of these statements is more than half true, if that. While musical training is indeed supposed to have a positive effect on the development of the frontal cortex, not learning to play an instrument does not have a bad influence. The intestines of most of the world's population cannot process milk after childhood, but these people have fine skeletons. Abstaining from smoking, or quitting, will certainly reduce the risk of developing lung cancer, but the disease has other causes as well. The remark about school is mere juvenile stupidity, as is the idea that shunning Ikea would put you in a better class. Fruit juices are as chock-full of sugar as any soft drink, and natural foods, whatever they may be, are not per se very healthy. Lastly, in the case of electric cars versus petrol vehicles, much depends on how and where the electricity is generated and what materials and methods are used to make and recycle their batteries.

The forbidden U-turn can also be used to construct a semblance of positive proof out of a lack of data, also called an ARGUMENTUM AD IGNORANTIAM. For example, athletes who pass one doping test after another say that their record proves they are 'clean'. However, the mere fact that it has not been established that they used forbidden substances does not prove the opposite: that they did *not* use such substances. Not logically and not in the real world. The legendary road-racing cyclist Lance Armstrong is living proof. When after an unparalleled career including seven consecutive victories in the world's biggest cycling event, the Tour de France, he was finally caught out in 2012, it turned out that he had been breaking every rule in the book from the beginning. His downfall was as spectacular as his earlier success. He was stripped of all his titles, proceedings were started to force him to pay back most of his prize money, and the Irish chairman of UCI, the international cyclists' union, even issued a 'fatwa' that Armstrong's name deserved to be forgotten in cycling.

Interestingly, the *argumentum ad ignorantiam* is actually the rule in the courtrooms of civilized nations. At first glance, criminal law seems to follow the rules of logic. If there is no proof or insufficient proof, people are not proclaimed innocent, but 'not guilty', suggesting a reservation of judgment. Logically, this is the right thing to do, because short of a rock-solid alibi it is hardly ever possible to prove that somebody did not do something. But there are both practical and ethical objections. From a practical point of view it is important that legal proceedings come to a definitive end at some point. There are limits to the amount of unrest caused by a trial that society can handle, and to the expenditure in terms of money and expertise. Ethically, it wouldn't do to leave a lifelong cloud of suspicion hanging over someone on account of an unsubstantiated accusation. There must be a clear acquittal, freeing them of all suspicion. This is achieved by two fundamental rules, the first of which is the presumption of innocence. It positively states that a person accused of some transgression is innocent until proven guilty, so that in criminal law, 'not guilty' actually does mean 'innocent'. The second pillar of justice is the principle of *ne bis in idem* or double jeopardy, which states that a person cannot be tried twice for the same fact. At the end of the path through trial and appeals, the verdict is final.

Perhaps the most likely to be misunderstood is the special kind of implication that links an effect to its cause. One thing everybody does realize is that effects always follow their causes. To give a simple example, your birth has been the direct effect of your father and mother having had a romp about nine months before (or having paid a visit to an IVF clinic). So the only way you could pre-date your parents' consorting would be by first being conceived, then travelling back in time to watch them do it. This, science tells us, is impossible for everyone except Doctor Who.

So any effect necessarily follows its cause, and every cause necessarily precedes its effects. But that's where it ends. By itself, the order in which events occur does not entail anything about the way they are related, or even if they have anything to do with each other at all. People may bonk away for years without any reproductive effect. And if a child is born, how come it is blonde when the parents are both dark-haired? The baby is still the result of a sperm and an ovum combining, but the man who contributed the former may not be the one who calls himself Dad, and the woman who produced the latter may have been an anonymous donor. Nowadays, it is not uncommon for fertilization to have come about without two people 'doing it' at all.

Although people have no trouble understanding these technical facts of life, their instincts tell them otherwise and they start committing logical traffic violations similar to wrong-way driving and forbidden U-turns. Few people can resist the occasional POST HOC, ERGO PROPTER HOC fallacy, a term that literally means 'after it, therefore because of it'. In plain English: if two events are part of the same story and one precedes the other, the former caused the latter. Here is an example:

> That fateful morning, Sam Hereford told his wife Joanna over breakfast that he wished to divorce her and would not be coming back tonight. Even though their marriage had never been a passionate one, Joanna had seen no signals that anything was seriously amiss between them. Devastated by the news, she sat motionless behind her cooling toast for what seemed an eternity, staring incredulously at Sam, before breaking down into helpless tears. Meanwhile, Sam stiffly rose, desperately keeping his mind focused on the ravishing twenty-two-year-old Ukrainian off the Internet who had promised to become his. The goddess whom he had booked an airplane ticket for and wired the money for a visa from his study last night, while his wife sat watching *EastEnders* downstairs. In an attempt to hide his embarrassment, he turned on his heels like a soldier and marched out of the house, picking up the overnighter he had prepared in the hallway. No, he must not think of Joanna

now, not look back at his sobbing wife of thirty years, the mother of his two children. He slung his bag into the boot of the Mondeo, got in, donned his safety belt and fired up the engine. As he pulled out of the drive and on to the road, there was a loud blaring sound and a shrieking of tyres. Sam looked up to the right just in time to see the huge red front of a truck slam into his car door.

For years, Joanna would say to her friends, her family and her psychiatrist that Sam's death was on her conscience. That if only she had not just sat there sobbing, if she had run after him, held him and clung to him and kissed away his anger and estrangement, if she could have detained him even for a second or two, he would not have died.

Joanna reacted in a way that was as human as it was faulty. Sam's breaking up his marriage when he did and his accident were just two unrelated events, each of which could have been caused by a million things – or none of them. Things would have been different if *any* of the events leading up to Sam's death had been different. The truck driver might have stopped for a cigarette and passed Sam's home later. Or he might have jumped a red light and been there half a minute earlier. What it boils down to is that apart from their temporal order, there is no relationship between events here.

Strangely, nobody seriously accepts that 'by not stopping for a cigarette, the truck driver caused Sam to die.' But Joanna's self-incrimination sounds only too plausible. As does, for instance: 'No sooner had Putin annexed the Crimea in March 2014 than oil prices began to fall from around $100 per barrel to a meagre $36 by the end of 2015.' The obvious suggestion is that Putin's imperialist adventurism caused the dramatic dwindling of the price of crude oil, and people are much inclined to go along with it – all the more so because incorporating the Crimea was a destabilizing geopolitical act that might indeed have had such an effect. In fact, the Russian president's machinations had little to do with the price of oil. The real cause was the shale oil from the United States that had begun flooding the markets, in combination with Saudi Arabia refusing to play its traditional role and stabilize the oil price by throttling its own production.

It is in fact not at all easy to determine the true cause of a given effect. Often, when there are many contributing factors, it is nigh impossible. It is hardly surprising, then, that philosophers and logicians have been at each other's throats for centuries about what the word 'cause' even meant, and how a cause differed from a mere implication. But for practical purposes, we can assume that causes are about how or why things came about, whereas implications are about what is logically true or not. So 'If you flip the switch, the lights go on' is about cause and effect, whereas 'If you're hungry, you should eat' is about the validity of the proposition 'you should eat'.

Many people think that an event counts as the cause of an effect if that effect would not have happened if the event had not occurred first. To give an example, pressing the on button causes your television to come on, because as long as you don't, the thing stays off. But even that is not as clear-cut as it seems. If the current happens to be off, pressing the on button won't make a difference. So we might as well say that it is the electric current or the electricity company providing it that causes the television to play. Or take winning the lottery. If you don't buy a ticket, you'll never win. But, as we have all experienced, if you do buy one, nothing happens most of the time anyway. So buying a ticket does not cause you to win; it is merely a necessary condition for winning, a step you must take in order to be able to play – and perhaps win.

The direct cause of someone winning the lottery is a notary drawing their number. Like buying a ticket, the draw is a necessary condition, for as long as the notary does not draw a number, nobody wins. But it is also a sufficient one. As soon as the notary does perform the draw, the player with the corresponding ticket wins and all others lose. That is what a cause is: a necessary *and* sufficient condition for some event to occur.

The lure of SPURIOUS CAUSATION is particularly visible in media reports on the results of medical and psychological research. Experiments usually establish associations between phenomena within a sample of subjects that the scientists hope is representative of the population at large or of a well-defined segment of it: youngsters, women, diabetics, Justin Bieber fans and so on. An example of such associations would be a tendency for high blood pressure to co-occur with a penchant for salty liquorice, an above-average frequency of sleeping problems among long-term users of antidepressants or a tendency towards smoking pot among teenagers from shrubby suburbs. The problem is that an association is just that.

They are not causal relations. They are not even hard-and-fast implications; for all the researchers know, there might be a third, unknown factor behind both the associated phenomena. A diabolic metabolic quirk, perhaps, which helps to raise blood pressure and causes a craving for salt – hence the liquorice. Not rarely, associations that researchers detect turn out to be accidental despite all the precautions taken to ensure a meaningful outcome. Samples may not be sufficiently representative of the group under scrutiny after all, some crucial assumption may prove wrong, there may have been procedural flaws, statistical errors – experimental science is difficult, painstaking work fraught with pitfalls.

All this argues for extreme caution when reporting results to the public at large. But neither university communications departments nor journalists – or ambitious researchers, for that matter – are very keen on downplaying their results with lots of modal verbs and maybes. That is how many a somewhat shaky association ends up as a sensational certainty in headlines such as 'Reheating Spinach May Kill You', 'Left-Handers Prone to Breast Cancer' or 'Cure for Alzheimer's in Sight'.

An equally alluring logical fallacy is ARGUMENTUM AD CONSE-QUENTIAM, which is simply to deny some obvious truth on account of its unwelcome wider implications. Feminists use it who refuse to accept that men are better at map-reading, because to do so would fly in the face of the equality of the sexes. It is a fallacy of politicians who don't want the ethnic background of criminals to be registered, for fear of stigmatizing a particular minority. Discussions with people who confuse what's real with what's desirable are never easy and seldom fruitful.

Lastly, there are CIRCULARITIES and BEGGING THE QUESTION. Although these two terms are often used indiscriminately, they refer to rather different things.

In the days of Aristotle, begging the question was a debating trick that consisted in trying to manipulate the opponent into conceding the very point you need to prove, thus establishing a DAMNING PREM-ISE. In other words, you ask them to give the show away before it has even begun. Of course, you cannot do so upfront; indirection is the name of the game. Suppose you want to advocate some far-reaching breach of privacy in order to battle terrorism, child pornography or any of a host of similar modern plagues. A good opening would be,

'I take it we can all agree that, first and foremost, we want our children to be safe from harm.' Who could disagree with that without losing much of the sympathy of the audience? The poison, of course, is in the words 'first and foremost'. From this moment on your opponent is vulnerable every step of the way to the lethal reproach that he's willing to sacrifice innocent children to his cause. And if he does honour the principle that child safety trumps everything, every breach of privacy is of course acceptable and he has lost the dispute.

Later, begging the question came to refer to circularities such as this well-known proof of the existence of God:

Aisha: God exists, for it says so in the Quran.
Thomas: But why is that proof?
Aisha: Because God himself dictated the Quran to the prophet.

This is indeed begging the question, since how could God have dictated anything if he did not exist? From there on, begging the question came to refer even to straight circularities such as this:

Thomas: I think Donna Tartt is the greatest writer of them all!
Aisha: Why is that?
Thomas: Because she writes better than anybody I've ever read!

A particularly painful case of circular reasoning is the failure of President Barack Obama to close Guantanamo Bay, that carbuncle on the face of America as a decent constitutional state. It had been erected as a kind of temporary judicial no-man's-land in the wake of the terrorist attacks of 11 September 2001, a kind of geographical 'state of emergency' where supposed terrorists could be detained, tried and punished without regard to the statutes and limitations of American law and the treaties the United States subscribes to. As it turned out, in most cases there were insufficient grounds to try the inmates for anything in particular, but for various reasons sending them back where they came from was not an option either. The logical thing would have been to transfer these people to regular prisons inside the United States and take it from there under the aegis of American law. But that was consistently blocked by the American Congress saying, 'We cannot allow these people on American soil, it's the law.' But it was a law that congress itself had passed specifically to keep them out. In short: we cannot let them in because we said we don't want to let them in. This is why first George W. Bush and then Obama after him had to beg other countries to relieve the United States of this embarrassment of its own creation by adopting a few prisoners each. Little wonder the rest of the world wasn't too keen on doing so. Although diplomatic mores prevented governments from saying so out loud, the general feeling was that the United States should clean up its own mess, which especially the American Republicans stubbornly kept refusing to do.

@#$%!

But what to do if nothing works? What if it dawns on you that you are definitely losing the battle, when all your sound arguments have failed to impress the audience and there isn't a trick in the book left to help you? Then it's time either to concede defeat and drown your sorrows in a bottle of wine or to take recourse to SCHOPENHAUER'S LAST RESORT. The advice of this nineteenth-century philosopher to debaters at their wits' end was to 'get personal, insulting and rude'. In other words, to play your opponent as if you're in the football cup finals and the referee is looking the other way. An all-out personal attack may save the day yet. It's a desperate ploy, and a dangerous one to boot, because it may backfire. A scorching 'Oh, come on, admit it, you old sod! You're out of touch, unable to read the signs of the times,' is just as likely to have the audience side with you against all stuffy old farts as it is to make them take pity on your opponent and boo you as a disrespectful lout.

Of course, hardball is a game that two can play, so you might find yourself at the other end of the stick: a winner faced with an opponent refusing to accept defeat. If that happens, Schopenhauer recommends that you don't obey what might be your first impulse: to pay your assailant back in kind. That way, the whole thing will degrade into a shouting match, perhaps even a true row, which – as we have seen – can only be lost. However, it is not wise to counter such an attack by refuting every rash accusation calmly and politely, either. Your attacker will only interpret your stolidly polite repartee as the aloofness of an arrogant winner, and become even more embittered. Worse, the audience might transfer its sympathy to the yapping underdog, which would defeat your purpose altogether. The best thing to do, therefore, is to deflect the blows of your opponent by calmly stating that what he says has no bearing on the issue at hand and stating once more what that issue is, a strategy not unlike walking away from a row with a stranger.

Debates tend to derail more often when opponents differ considerably in power, experience or level of education. Although the better-equipped party can usually win easily on the basis of rational argument, the opposition is likely to feel that they never had a chance to begin with, and refuse to accept defeat. Sometimes such lopsided debates are unavoidable, as when a mother has to convince her fifteen-year-old romantic hothead of a son that it is not a good idea for him to drop out of school and become a travel guide in Kathmandu. Or consider the hapless mayor called upon to make the community accept that the closing of the town library is unavoidable, or to defuse panicky rumours about a ring of child-abusers prowling the streets. But, apart from these, it is best to follow Aristotle's advice – politically incorrect by today's standards but nevertheless effective – and debate with equals only. People whom you know well enough to be sure that they will listen to reason, who are capable of conducting an orderly debate and who are confident enough to accept defeat. 'The rest', as Schopenhauer puts it, 'are best left to say whatever they want, for it is a human right to be a fool, and let's keep in mind Voltaire's "Peace is more valuable than truth", and the Arabic proverb "From the tree of keeping silent hang the fruits of peace."'

> Poor Hayduke: won all his arguments but lost his immortal soul.
> Edward Abbey, *The Monkey Wrench Gang* (1975)

EPILOGUE: THE TROUBLE WITH RATIONALITY

My own sex, I hope, will excuse me, if I treat them like rational creatures,
instead of flattering their fascinating graces, and viewing them as if they
were in a state of perpetual childhood, unable to stand alone.
Mary Wollstonecraft, *A Vindication of the Rights of Woman* (1792)

Much of this book has been about things that belong to the irrational. Things such as emotions and their effects, oaths, manipulation, magic, delusions and religion. However, from the onset of the Enlightenment, the dominant Western cultures have been taking an ever dimmer view of the irrational as backwards and unhealthy. Bit by bit the devoutly Christian naturalists of Newton's day began transforming themselves into modern scientists, recalibrating their mission accordingly. Slowly but inexorably they moved their focus from revealing the Great Plan of the Lord to explaining how the universe hung together and functioned per se, scrubbing religion from their fields along the way. François Antommarchi, Napoleon's physician during the fallen emperor's final years in St Helena, tells us how Bonaparte remembered receiving the magnum opus of Pierre-Simon Laplace, the 'Newton of France', from the author's hands. Tipped off by some science buff, Napoleon had chaffed the great scientist by asking how it was that the name of the Creator, which flowed from the pen of his eminent colleague Joseph-Louis Lagrange so profusely, never once occurred in Laplace's book. *C'est, me répondit-il*, Napoleon told Antommarchi, *que je n'ai pas eu besoin de cette hypothèse*, 'That, he told me, is because I did not need that hypothesis.' Opinions differ on whether Laplace had God himself in mind or merely His active intervention in the day-to-day running of the universe, but the point remains that here, for the first time, the bond between science and the irrational is explicitly and unequivocally severed. Scientists kept on believing or not – Darwin, for one, did, in a way – but God had no active place any more in the business of science. In time, their new attitude grew into what is nowadays called the scientific method, a set of strictly rational principles and protocols that, as far as we can tell, guarantee the most reliable, insightful and fruitful results.

As in science, so in manufacturing and even in philosophy and literature. Starting from the eighteenth century, manufacturing and the economy were transformed beyond recognition, first by the steamy technological innovations of the Industrial Revolution, then by pioneers of rationalization such as Henry Ford with his assembly line. Utilitarian philosophers like Jeremy Bentham developed rationalist views of society and social institutions, culminating in, among other things, the persistent ideal of the greatest happiness of the greatest number. In the process, the irrational came to represent our pre-Enlightenment, animal and inferior aspects. Rational thought, on the other hand, was and still is considered one of the essential qualities that set us apart from the animal world, and above it. To be rational came to mean to be truly human, a condition not even women could long aspire to, hence Mary Wollstonecraft's complaint above.

Ayn Rand, that rogue philosopher of the twentieth century, in her *Atlas Shrugged* (1957), went so far as to extoll strict rationality as the only source of true happiness:

> Happiness is not to be achieved at the command of emotional whims. Happiness is not the satisfaction of whatever irrational wishes you might blindly attempt to indulge. Happiness is a state of non-contradictory joy – a joy without penalty or guilt, a joy that does not clash with any of your values and does not work for your own destruction, not the joy of escaping from your mind, but of using your mind's fullest power, not the joy of faking reality, but of achieving values that are real, not the joy of a drunkard, but of a producer. Happiness is possible only to a rational man, the man who desires nothing but rational goals, seeks nothing but rational values and finds his joy in nothing but rational actions.

It is true that the importance of our knack for rational thought cannot be overrated. It has given us vastly superior capabilities for planning and for modelling and understanding the world we live in, and so afforded humanity its technological sophistication and material wealth. Without it, the Sumerians could not have cultivated the mudflats of Mesopotamia. Without it, the Greeks could not have built their temples and theatres, nor the Phoenicians their ships or the Romans their aqueducts, and so on, right up to the plastics, the airliners and the medical wonders of our time. Without it, the Chinese could never have developed the structures and managerial savvy that have somehow held together their vast but much beleaguered empire for thousands of years.

At the same time, however, rationality has been at the root of some of the greatest disasters in history. The Soviet experiment is a case in point. Its misguided reliance on rational planning and callous disregard for the quirks of the individual drove millions to their deaths and ruined the lives of countless more. The industrial murder machine of the Nazi regime was the fruit of relentlessly rational thinking based on spurious concepts such as *Blut und Boden* and historical destiny, combined with sophisticated planning. The overwhelming logic of the Nazi system perhaps explains why it was so difficult for Germans to go against it: one had to beat the logic before one could even begin to dismantle the ideas. And rational capitalism, which has brought mankind much material and immaterial progress, also dehumanized the existence of large parts of the workforce, reducing workers to a status less than that of slaves in times of abolitionism. In large parts of the world, this is still standard practice. Lastly, at this moment the Chinese regime is busily installing technology with which to realize that old utilitarian dream of Jeremy Bentham's, the panopticum, on a nationwide scale. China is on its way to becoming the ultimate surveillance state, where every citizen is a meticulously monitored, managed and manipulated cog in a wheel of an immense, strictly rational machinery that must pass for society. Others, Russia for one, but also certain African nations, seem to be eagerly following China's example.

How can it be that a mental instrument that is so powerful and has been so beneficial to mankind has been and still is the undoing of so many at the same time? The answer may well lie in one basic property of rational thinking: binary categorization. Making rational sense of the chaotic world around us begins by ordering it into binary opposites: large and small, high and low, hot and cold, weak and strong, black and white, good and bad, life and death. By the same token, inveterate dualists that we are, we divide the world into things rational and irrational, as if they were straight opposites. This is, in the extreme, Rand's position.

As far as the inanimate worlds of physics and chemistry are concerned, and even to understand the secrets of the lower levels of biological life, adopting a strict focus on rational, empirical research and logical theorizing, to the exclusion of all other considerations, was just what the doctor ordered. Profits for humanity from these fields of inquiry have been growing exponentially ever since. But what we generally call the animate world is a different matter. Somewhere on the way from DNA and proteins to active, sentient life, the starkly rational beauty of physics and chemistry is lost, giving way to the moist and messy biological reality of just-abouts and more-or-lesses that we are part of.

It begins with the lowly amoeba and other monocellular life. They, like the dung beetle, the majestic elephant and ourselves, are driven by the urge for self-preservation. This is not will, there is no intent, no wish. It is just nature and natural selection that have honed organisms into a form that includes a behavioural repertoire conducive to its continued existence and proliferation under current circumstances. We call this repertoire the will to live, nonetheless. And it is not rational. There is no logical reason for such a repertoire to exist, and no objective cause for it. If it were no longer there, species would simply disappear without even a shrug from Atlas. Nevertheless, it does exist and it is immensely important in mankind, which is – rationality being a human affair – our only point of reference.

In her *We Are All Completely Beside Ourselves* (2013), the novelist Karen Joy Fowler remembers how her father, an irritatingly pedantic college professor,

> didn't believe animals could think, not in the way he defined the term, but he wasn't much impressed with human thinking, either. He referred to the human brain as a clown car parked between our ears. Open the doors and the clowns pour out.
>
> The idea of our own rationality, he used to say, was convincing to us only because we so wished to be convinced. To any impartial observer, should such a thing exist, the sham was patent. Emotion and instinct were the basis of all our

decisions, our actions, everything we valued, the way we saw the world. Reason and rationality were a thin coat of paint on a ragged surface.

At first glance, it would seem that old man Fowler's position is the opposite of Rand's, giving pride of place to a ragtag and clownish irrationality. But in fact they think along exactly the same lines. The only difference is that Fowler lacks Rand's optimism, believing that her thoroughly rational happy man does not exist. What they share is the deep conviction that rationality and the irrational are opposites, the former positive, creative and essentially human, the latter whimsical, backwards and infinitely inferior. In doing so, they both miss the same essential point, which is that rationality and irrationality aren't opposites at all, just different components of our mental faculties.

@#$%!

RATIONAL THINKING IS the very aware, dispassionate and slow kind of reasoning that is indispensable for planning, whether it concerns our daily shopping, a trip abroad or an entire career. It allows us to compute sums, compose stories and essays, construct buildings, manufacture utensils and do all those other things that require step-by-step consideration along the lines of common or formal logic. It enables us to analyse the world and create an orderly picture of it, to explain the past and calculate the likely consequences of some future course of action. It is clearly linguistic and, as such, probably unique to our species. And it is what psychologists usually refer to as System Two.

Since rational thinking is strictly procedural, without intrinsic content or meaning, it can only operate in unison with a different kind of dealing with the world, one that does provide meaning. This is the irrational, instinctive and even visceral kind of thinking that is characteristic of what psychologists call System One. It does not depend on consciousness or language, is lightning-fast but not very flexible and does not analyse much. It comprises, among other things, our innate and acquired physical skills and just responds to current circumstances, driven by internal urges, emotions and direct sensory experience. This is the kind of coping we share with the animal kingdom. In this respect there is no principled difference between us, an ape and an eel.

What we call our wits is the more or less effective combination of both rational and irrational thought, as situations require. A general planning a campaign with the help of maps and situation reports must first and foremost rely on rational thinking, but a soldier under fire or in hand-to-hand combat had better first trust his instincts. Rational analysis will not let him dodge a bullet or twist away from a bayonet thrust in time. Depending on the situation in which we find ourselves, the relative prominence of either system may vary. Keeping your cool is to let rational thought control your thinking just enough to curb the irrational but perfectly understandable urge to panic and flee from trying and possibly dangerous conditions, or to overreact aggressively and smash everything up. It is what keeps the surgeon operating on horribly mauled bodies, what makes a parent clean up after a violently sick child and not scold it, and what keeps you on your chair during an unnerving exam or job interview.

While rationality thus adds structure and discipline to everyday behaviour, your irrational self provides meaning and purpose. Will, wants and urges are all part of the irrational, as are a whole host of deeply felt emotions, including love, family bonds and a measure of regard for human life in general. Cannibalism, murder and serious mistreatment are not things people actively engage in easily. It takes a measure of dehumanization of the other – by branding them the enemy or a lesser kind of person, or reducing them to a blip on a screen – to make most of us cross that particular threshold.

Normal social behaviour is the product of rational procedures applied to situations in the light of irrational pressures. When rational thought is directed to those irrational pressures themselves, ethics emerges, an attempt to derive an intuitively satisfying and fairly coherent set of explicit values and principles from emotions and instinctive truths. As rationalizations of inherently irrational entities, those values and principles remain irrational themselves, hence the endless rational clashes and incompatibilities between particular values.

Our deepest feelings, wants, emotions and instinctive truths are part of our biological constitution and therefore universal. At their core are the so-called Five Freedoms: freedom from hunger and thirst; freedom from discomforts, such as lack of shelter; freedom from pain, injury and disease; freedom from fear and distress; and freedom to express oneself. Curiously, these Five Freedoms were formulated only in the 1970s by the British Farm Animal Welfare Council, in an attempt to define animal, not human, welfare. Nevertheless, nobody can deny that the council succinctly summarized the essential prerequisites for a satisfactory and rewarding human life for ourselves and our nearest and dearest. What is not universal, however, is who else we consider worthy of them or, for that matter, of any derived or additional freedoms and rights. Some, these days, have no qualms granting them all to parts or all of the animal kingdom. Others will not even extend them to people of different nations or races, to anyone who does not adhere to their own creed, or to women.

This is, finally, why – notwithstanding the apparent lack of a universally shared set of ethical values – those who preach cultural relativism are fundamentally in the wrong. There does in fact exist a set of fundamental, natural and undeniably universal values. They are the values that are part and parcel of being human. The dispute is not about those values but about inclusion. It is about us and them, U and non-U, self-aggrandisement and little else. It is, therefore, a sad irony that these days the notion of inclusion has become inextricably tied up with cultural relativism.

@#$%!

IT IS NOT ALWAYS EASY to recognize rational and irrational thought and behaviour for what it is. One example is the freezing response in animals. I once saw a frog being caught on the lawn by a cat. Already between the cat's drooling fangs but still unharmed, the frog decided on a desperate all-or-nothing strategy: it went completely limp and pretended to be dead. Confused by this unexpected turn of events, the cat dropped its suddenly unresponsive prey on to the grass and began ogling it from different angles, sniffing at it and pawing it now and again. The frog didn't budge. After a few minutes the cat lost interest and slunk off to better hunting grounds. No sooner was it out of sight than the frog sprang to life and hobbled off to the safety of the undergrowth. It looked like a cleverly rational ploy, a Ulyssian ruse based on the frog's realization that cats don't hunt carrion. But was it? Or did I just witness an instinctive reflex in both animals?

First of all, it is unclear how a frog might rationally know a cat's views on carrion – irrationally, it might 'know' by natural selection. Second, the dependence of rational thinking on natural language, which is clearly unique to the human species, pleads compellingly against either frogs or cats possessing it. And third, think of the unbelievable stress a rational, fully conscious freezing strategy would expose the frog to. It is true that there have been people who came away alive from mass executions by pretending to be dead. But this always happens when the individual is not at the centre of attention but blends in among many real corpses. Now picture yourself in the frog's position, fully aware of the mortal danger of the fangs under the nose nudging you, feeling lethal claws pawing you and cruel eyes scrutinizing you for the merest hint of a twitch. How long do you think you might force yourself to keep limp and unresponsive? How long might you suppress the fatal urge to make a run for it? Your best chance would be to be in shock so deeply that your rational powers shut down. So, far from a demonstration of calculated cool, freezing is most likely an instinctive, irrational response.

A different mix-up of rationality and irrationality concerns criminal justice and mercy. Usually, meting out justice according to the law is considered rational behaviour, whereas showing mercy is seen as an emotional, sometimes even irresponsibly sentimental response of the kind and weak-hearted. In fact, neither is true. Criminal proceedings basically serve three goals: the perpetrator must atone, the victim must be compensated and others tempted to commit a crime at any point in the future must be deterred. There is very little that's rational about these three goals. Prison, the usual form of atonement, does keep a culprit off the streets for a while but otherwise has little to recommend it, either morally or educationally. What remains is deeply irrational: a grim form of *Schadenfreude* derived from making the culprit suffer, to the emotional satisfaction of victims and society as a whole. It's tit for tat, an eye for an eye, payback. But from a rational point of view, watching a criminal suffer does not compensate for anything. Finally, scientific research has shown that criminal justice deters neither the career villain nor the habitual hoodlums and halfwits that fill most of our prisons. All told, justice as meted out in our criminal courts is far from rational. It is a somewhat ineffectual procedure kept in place by fear, our sense of fairness, the need for revenge and lack of a better idea.

Forgiveness, on the other hand, is a rational brake on desires for retribution and the spiral of violence they may set in motion. We might want to tear those who wrong us limb from limb, but instead

Rational thinking and human language

Another widespread frame is the supposed contrast between science- and arts-orientated people, or STEM people and non-STEM people. This opposition broadly reflects that between System Two and System One, or between a propensity for rational reasoning versus a primary focus on emotional values and feelings. Although the idea is not entirely wrong, it fosters counterproductive polarization between people, regrettably inflating a relative difference to a fundamentally unbridgeable rift. As a consequence STEM people tend to underestimate and downplay the importance of emotional and moral considerations, while non-STEM people assume a negative attitude towards what they see as a cold, emotionally and culturally impoverished world of formality and technology.

At the root of this regrettable mutual enmity is a misappreciation of the role of the human language faculty, which comprises the common core of all the languages ever spoken (and to be spoken) in the world. Traditionally the study of language and languages is grouped with the humanities, in accordance with its culturally prominent functions literature, poetry and song. In reality, however, human language is the source and vehicle of rational thought itself. Literally all instruments of rational thought – common and formal logic, mathematics and all computer languages – are derived from natural human language. For example, operators such as $+$, $:$, $=$ and $\sum$ are the verbs of mathematics, relating terms such as 3, π and x, its nouns. All these so-called formal languages are greatly impoverished natural languages. All the flourishes and flexibility are stripped away, as is as much ambiguity as possible, so that only the strictly logical core of grammar is retained. Literary and poetic language, on the other hand, makes the most of the subtlety and ambiguity that natural languages allow, so that no subject is out of bounds. If people of either orientation would realize that they ultimately use the same instruments, albeit to vastly different ends, they might not find each other's worlds so impenetrable and hostile. Learning someone else's language can be daunting, but it's not impossible.

we muster some understanding of their motives and circumstances, consider the consequences of vengeance and satisfy ourselves with less than our due. Showing mercy is not weakness, it is a privilege of the strong, a rational, calculated way of putting conflicts to bed and coming to terms with the irrevocable. It is the partly successful way in which Nelson Mandela tried to defuse the pent-up rage about the apartheid era in South Africa. It is how Paul Kagame restored a semblance of unity to the traumatized nation of Rwanda after the genocidal slaughter of 1994.

Surprisingly, even beliefs in the supernatural and religions spring from a solidly rational fount. This may seem strange, considering the obvious absurdity of the global menagerie of elves, naiads, fairies, gnomes, goblins, spirits, imps, sprites, ghosts, saints, deities and monotheistic gods. But really, all these were invented to answer early rational concerns about what is behind the endless variety of unfathomable phenomena people have found themselves confronted with since the beginning of time. Questions such as what causes that creaking in the dark, what is that light out there on the swamp? What causes thunder to roll, who sparks lightning? Whence comes the wind? Why does it rain, or not? Why do I dream and what do dreams mean? Why do people get ill? What caused my child to die? What happens to 'me' when the body I own and inhabit dies? Why are we here? Lacking the means and methods to find out the true causes and answers, people everywhere arrived at variations on Aristotle's theme in his *Metaphysics*: 'There must be an immortal, unchanging being, ultimately responsible for all wholeness and orderliness in the sensible world.' This idea of an 'unmoved mover' equally easily paves the way for the idea of an omnipotent supreme being as for the concept of fundamental laws of nature. God and his colleagues great and small are rationalizations in the face of a lack of knowledge, mysteries explained as enigmas.

Failure to see the importance of irrational considerations has also led to glaringly mistaken concepts such as *homo economicus*. Epitomized by Gordon Gekko in the film *Wall Street* (1987), he is an abstract, Ayn Randian actor in the marketplace, a thoroughbred consumer driven solely by the idea of maximizing his profits. This unidimensional grab-all has dominated economic theory for more than half a century, in spite of the fact that everybody knows from their own experience that on average people are not like that at all. Of course people generally want to earn more than they do and not squander their assets lightly, but the true *homo economicus*, if it exists, is a pathological anomaly, perhaps to be found only among the consummate misers on the boards of banks and hedge funds.

Normal people, be they rich or poor, aren't driven by rational calculation alone – in this, old Fowler was right. They want to *feel* wealthy, worthy and comfortable rather than *be* rich. Many apply themselves as volunteers and do each other good turns without expecting much in return beyond friendship and a smile. They bend over backwards to provide a good future for their children. They donate to the unlikeliest causes. They buy expensive clothes, not because these are warmer or better tailored or exclusive, but because of the logo on them, to blend in with the right crowd. They throw money away in bars and restaurants and on needless trips to nowhere in particular. They blow fortunes on pornography, on lotteries, on shoes, on drugs. They buy themselves a boat, knowing full well that they are acquiring a hole in the water they will keep throwing money into and use only a handful of times a year. And even when they select a new fridge from the hundreds of makes and models on offer with meticulously rational care, they tend to end up with three almost perfect, almost identical candidates. Then they revert to irrationality for their final decision: 'I'll have the one with the blue stripe.'

So, on the whole, many of the things we do aren't even half rational. Unfortunately, this also applies to our dark side. Beginning in the UK, Italy, Belgium and the Netherlands in April 2020, people started burning 5G telecom towers like latter-day Luddites, despite millennia of civilization, because of rumours that 5G communications technology was fuelling the COVID-19 pandemic that was then newly raging. For decades Islamic terrorists have been going around wreaking havoc in the sick, misanthropic belief that all who don't fully share their beliefs must be subdued or perish. In these and many other cases – and this is the sorry state humanity is in – fear is the driving force. Fear of some evil conspiracy trying to harm 'the people' in the 5G case, fear of missing out on a privileged place in a supposed heaven accessible only to 'martyrs' among radical Muslims.

All these mistakes and delusions stem from a failure to understand that rationality and irrationality aren't opposites at all. It is a tenacious failure, a clear case of cognitive dissonance: even though you know an idea is wrong, you cannot shake it. But it is also understandable. Rationality is very much bound up with consciousness, self-awareness and language, the three cerebral faculties that fuel the dualism in us. These are responsible for the deep-seated certainty that an individual is not a seamlessly integrated whole. We strongly feel that we don't coincide with our bodies, but that we own and inhabit them. We prefer to say that our bodies ache to saying 'I ache'

– except in 'I ache for you', where it is the soul that is in pain. It is this dualism that convinces many that they, meaning their souls, will shuffle off the mortal coil they inhabit when they die, creating the need for a god exploiting a heaven to house the homeless souls. It is so strong that the idea of separating a person, in the form of their brain, from a worn-out or malfunctioning body and having it survive on some cybernetic substrate has become a popular theme in science fiction. We think of ourselves as orderly, abstractly rational, cerebral beings, locked up inside the almost perfect opposite: a moist and messy, hormonal, emotional and eventually animal body.

The consequences of such thinking are dire. With our unparalleled mental powers we have created a highly complex and often confusing world for ourselves to live in. Managing it to our advantage requires maintaining a careful balance between rational and instinctive thinking. If we lose our heads, throwing rationality to the wind, unchecked emotions and instincts take over and panic and fanaticism ensue, spawning oppression and witch-hunts. If, on the other hand, we let ourselves get carried away by the austere beauty of rational reasoning – which can be flawed to boot – methods and solutions will be adopted that are socially and humanly unacceptable. History is rife with terrible examples of both, so let us try to keep a clear head and a warm heart. If we do, we can make the world a better place and keep our warfare verbal.

> He remembered having said to his uncle (with a solemn dogmatism
> better befitting a much younger man): 'Surely it is possible to love
> with the head as well as the heart.' Mr Delagardie had replied,
> somewhat drily: 'No doubt; so long as you do not end
> by thinking with your entrails instead of your brain.'
> Dorothy L. Sayers, *Busman's Honeymoon* (1937)

REFERENCES

One: Verbal Bloody Warfare

1 I. J. Semper, 'The King's English', *English Journal*, XVIII/4 (1929),
 pp. 307–12, cited in Ashley Montagu, *The Anatomy of Swearing*,
 Rapp & Whiting (1967).
2 Thomas Hobbes, *Leviathan* [1651], www.gutenberg.org (2009), Part I,
 Chapter 13.
3 'Les peuples sur qui nous régnons, ne pouvant pénétrer le fond des
 choses, règlent d'ordinaire leur jugement sur ce qu'ils voient au
 dehors, et c'est le plus souvent sur les préséances et les rangs qu'ils
 mesurent leur respect et leur obéissance.' Quoted on Wikipedia,
 'Étiquette à la cour de France', https://fr.wikipedia.org, accessed
 7 October 2021

Two: Fire and Brimstone

1 For more on the difference between animal communications systems
 and human language, see Rik Smits, 'Animal Languages Don't Exist',
 www.academia.edu, 2019.

Three: I Put a Spell on You

1 Quoted in James G. Frazer, *The Golden Bough: A Study in Magic and
 Religion* [1890] (Macmillan, 1976), 3.2.
2 Derek Parker and Julia Parker, *The Power of Magic*, Mitchell Beazley
 (1992), p. 52.
3 Quoted in Melissa Mohr, *Holy Sh*t: A Brief History of Swearing*, Oxford
 University Press (2013), p. 45.
4 Quoted in Ashley Montagu, *The Anatomy of Swearing*, Rapp & Whiting,
 (1967), p. 47.

Four: The Queen's Cunt

1 See 'Grab Them By the Pussy Donald Trump', www.youtube.com,
 21 January 2017.
2 See Rik Smits, *Dawn: The Origins of Language and the Modern Human
 Mind*, Transaction Books (2016), Chapter 7.
3 Both examples, and the medieval examples that follow, are taken from

Melissa Mohr, *Holy Sh*t: A Brief History of Swearing*, Oxford University Press (2013), which offers a wealth of other examples.

Five: Taking Them Down a Peg or Two

1 Laurence French, 'Racial and Ethnic Slurs: Regional Awareness and Variations', *Maledicta*, IV/1 (1980), pp. 117–26.

Seven: Infuxation and Other Miracles of Language

1 G. Legman, 'A Word for It!', *Maledicta*, I/1 (1977), pp. 9–18.
2 Victor A. Friedman, 'Turco-Slavica', *Maledicta*, I/2 (1977), pp. 185–8.

Ten: The Politics of Swearing

1 Cited in Ashley Montagu, *The Anatomy of Swearing*, Rapp & Whiting (1967).
2 Lawrence Evelyn Jones, *Anatomy of a Georgian Afternoon*, St Martin's Press (1958), p. 234.
3 See Nicole Wheeler, 'Publication Bias Is Shaping Our Perceptions of AI: Is the Media's Reluctance to Admit AI's Weaknesses Putting Us at Risk?', www.towardsdatascience.com, 1 August 2019, and reference cited there.
4 Quoted in Michael Herz and Peter Molnar, eds, *The Content and Context of Hate Speech: Rethinking Regulation and Responses*, Cambridge University Press (2012).
5 Article 11: 'La libre communication des pensées et des opinions est un des droits les plus précieux de l'Homme: tout Citoyen peut donc parler, écrire, imprimer librement, sauf à répondre de l'abus de cette liberté dans les cas déterminés par la Loi.'

Eleven: The Names of the Lord, the State and the Insecure

1 'Als God zich opnieuw in de Levende Stof gevangen geeft, zal Hij als ezel terugkeren, hoogstens in staat een paar lettergrepen te formuleren, miskend en verguisd en geranseld, maar ik zal Hem begrijpen en meteen met Hem naar bed gaan, maar ik doe zwachtels om Zijn hoefjes, dat ik niet te veel schrammen krijg als Hij spartelt bij het klaarkomen.'
2 'En God Zelf zou bij mij langs komen in de gedaante van een eenjarige, muisgrijze ezel en voor de deur staan en aanbellen en zeggen: "Gerard, dat boek van je – weet je dat ik bij sommige stukken gehuild heb?" "Mijn Heer en mijn God! Geloofd weze Uw Naam tot in alle Eeuwigheid! Ik houd zo verschrikkelijk veel van U", zou ik proberen te zeggen, maar halverwege zou ik al in janken uitbarsten, en Hem beginnen te kussen en naar binnen trekken, en na een geweldige klauterpartij om de trap naar het slaapkamertje op te komen, zou ik Hem drie keer achter elkaar langdurig in Zijn Geheime Opening bezitten, en daarna een present-eksemplaar geven, niet gebrocheerd, maar gebonden – niet dat gierige en benauwde – met de opdracht: "Voor De Oneindige. Zonder Woorden."'
3 Quoted from a letter by Rushdie to Grant.
4 Quoted in Paul Cliteur and Tom Herrenberg, *The Fall and Rise of Blasphemy Law*, Leiden University Press (2016), p. 137.

5 Please forgive the slightly flawed quotation, which should read 'check out' instead. However, near the beginning of the song, the hotel's hostess promises 'plenty of room . . . any time of year'.

6 'Democratie is niet voor bange mensen.'

7 Quoted in Toby Green, *A Fistful of Shells: West Africa from the Slave Trade to the Age of Revolution*, Allen Lane (2019).

8 'Nous chercherons à nous tenir dans un juste milieu, également éloigné des excès du pouvoir populaire et des abus du pouvoir royal.' Answer to questions from the city of Gaillac, January 1831.

9 Azadeh Moaveni, 'ISIS Women and Enforcers in Syria Recount Collaboration, Anguish and Escape', *New York Times*, 21 November 2015.

Twelve: The Fifteen Laws of Propaganda

1 *Paris Match*, 'Charlie Hebdo porte plainte après de nouvelles menaces de mort', 12 August 2016, www.parismatch.com.

2 For more on the tenuous relation between us and the 'real' world we live in, see Rik Smits, *Dawn: The Origins of the Modern Human Mind*, Transaction Books (2016), Chapter 3.

3 John le Carré, *The Pigeon Tunnel*, Penguin (2016), Chapter 27.

4 Quoted in Marcel H. van Herpen, *Putin's Propaganda Machine: Soft Power and Russian Foreign Policy*, Rowman and Littlefield (2016), p. 68.

5 Ibid.

BIBLIOGRAPHY

(Author names marked by * are pseudonyms)

A. P. and G. M., 'Malas Palabras: Talking Dirty in Cuban Spanish', *Maledicta*, i/1 (1977), pp. 19–22

Aarons, Z. A., 'Notes on a Case of *Maladie des tics*', *Psychological Quarterly*, xxvii/2 (1958), pp. 194–204

Abbey, Edward, *The Monkey Wrench Gang*, Avon Books (1975)

Abraham, R. D., 'Playing the Dozens', *Journal of American Folklore*, lxxv/297 (1962), pp. 209–20

Agyekum, Kofi, 'Menstruation as Verbal Taboo among the Akan of Ghana', *Journal of Anthropological Research*, lviii (2002), pp. 367–87

——, 'Ntam Reminiscential Oath Taboo in Akan', *Language in Society*, xxxiii/3 (2004), pp. 317–42

Alexander, Bob, 'Male and Female Restroom Graffiti', *Maledicta*, ii/1–2 (1978), pp. 42–59

Alford, Richard D., and William J. O'Donnell, 'Linguistic Scale: Cussing and Euphemisms', *Maledicta*, vii (1983), pp. 155–63

Algeo, John, 'Xenophobic Ethnica', *Maledicta*, i/2 (1977), pp. 133–40

Allan, Keith, and Kate Burridge, *Forbidden Words: Taboo and the Censoring of Language*, Cambridge University Press (2006)

Allen, Irving L., 'Acrimonious Acronyms for Ethnic Groups', *Maledicta*, v/1–2 (1981), pp. 95–102

——, 'You Are What You Eat: Dietary Stereotypes and Ethnic Epithets', *Maledicta*, vii (1983), pp. 21–30

Aman, Reinhold, 'Bavarian Terms of Abuse Derived from Common Names', *Maledicta*, vii (1983), pp. 212–17

——, 'Clean Up Your Fexing Language! Or, How to Swear Violently without Offending Anyone', *Maledicta*, iv/1 (1980), pp. 5–14

——, 'Dingbatted *Maledicta* – Symbolic Euphemisms', *Maledicta*, iii/2 (1979), pp. 208–11

——, 'Doctors, Hospitals, and Operations: A Glossary of Ironic and Insulting German Terms', *Maledicta*, vi/1–2 (1982), pp. 180–88

——, 'Gimp, Pimp, Simp and Wimp: Political Pejoration Past and Present', *Maledicta*, viii (1985), pp. 81–90

——, 'Is George Bush a Wimp? Or, Name-Calling Made Easy', *Maledicta*, ix (1986), pp. 23–34

——, 'James Watt's *Cripple*', *Maledicta*, viii (1985), pp. 193–6

——, 'Kakologia', *Maledicta*, vi/1–2 (1982), pp. 290–314

—, 'Kakologia: A Chronicle of Nasty Riddles and Naughty Wordplays', *Maledicta*, VII (1983), pp. 275–305

—, 'Kakologia: A Chronicle of Nasty Riddles and Naughty Wordplays', *Maledicta*, VIII (1985), pp. 203–30

—, 'Linguistic and Blasphemous Aspects of Bavarian Micturition and American Toilet Names', *Maledicta*, XII (1996), pp. 147–51

—, 'Medieval Maledicta', *Maledicta*, XII (1996), p. 28

—, 'Menomini Maledicta: A Glossary of Terms of Deprecation, Sexuality, Body Parts and Functions, and Related Matters', *Maledicta*, V/1–2 (1981), pp. 177–90

—, '*New Improved Dreck!* Interlingual Taboo in Personal Names, Brand Names, and Language Learning', *Maledicta*, III/2 (1979), pp. 145–52

—, 'Offensive Words in Dictionaries III: *Sodomy, Bestiality, Buggery, Bugger, Pederasty*', *Maledicta*, IX (1986), pp. 227–46

—, 'Offensive Words in Dictionaries IV: Ethnic, Racial, Religious, and Sexual Slurs in an American and an Australian Dictionary', *Maledicta*, X (1989), pp. 126–35

—, 'On Spoonerisms', *Maledicta*, VII (1983), pp. 34–7

—, 'A Taxonomy of the Provenance of Metaphorical Terms of Abuse', *Maledicta*, I/2 (1977), pp. 317–22

—, '"They Are a Hairy, Cruel, Savage Nation": Ethnic Slurs Anno 1774', *Maledicta*, V/1–2 (1981), pp. 273–83

—, 'What Is This Crime that Dare Not Speak Its Name? Legal, Religious and Journalistic Aspects of *Sodomy*', *Maledicta*, IX (1986), pp. 247–68

Ambler, Eric, *Judgment on Deltchev*, Hodder and Stoughton (1951)

Andersson, Lars-Gunnar, and Peter Trudgill, *Bad Language*, Penguin (1990)

Andrews, Edna, 'Cultural Sensitivity and Political Correctness: The Linguistic Problem of Naming', *American Speech*, LXXI/4 (1998), pp. 389–404

Antommarchi, F., *Mémoires du docteur F. Antommarchi, ou les derniers momens de Napoléon*, vol. I, Barrois L'Ainé (1825)

Appignanesi, Lisa, 'Liberté, égalité and fraternité: PC and the French', in *The War of the Words*, ed. Sarah Dunant, Virago (1994)

Arbeitman, Yoël, 'Look Ma, What's Become of the Sacred Tongues', *Maledicta*, IV/1 (1980), pp. 71–88

Aristotle, *The Complete Works of Aristotle: The Revised Oxford Translation*, ed. Jonathan Barnes, Bollingen Series 71, Princeton University Press (1984)

Ashley, Leonard R. N., 'The Cockney's Horn Book: The Sexual Side of Rhyming Slang', *Maledicta*, II/1–2 (1978), pp. 115–20

—, '*Kinks and Queens*: Linguistic and Cultural Aspects of the Terminology for *Gays*', *Maledicta*, III/2 (1979), pp. 215–56

Aufderheide, P., ed., *Beyond PC: Toward a Politics of Understanding*, Graywolf Press (1992)

Austin, J. L., *How to Do Things with Words*, Harvard University Press (1962)

Avdikos, Evangelos, '"May the Devil Take Your Head and Brain": The Curses of Karpathos, Greece, Social Counterstructures, and the Management of Social Relations', *Journal of American Folklore*, CXXIV/492 (2011), pp. 88–117

Averna, Giuliano, 'Italian and Venetian Profanity', *Maledicta*, I/1 (1977), pp. 63–4

—, and Salemi, Joseph, 'Italian Blasphemies', *Maledicta*, VI/1–2 (1982), pp. 63–70

Ayoub, Millicent R., and Stephen A. Barnett, 'Ritualized Verbal Insult in White
    High School Culture', *Journal of American Folklore*, LXXVIII/310 (1965),
    pp. 337–44
Bach, K., and R. Harnish, *Linguistic Communication and Speech Acts*, MIT Press
    (1979)
Bailey, Lee A., 'More on Women's – and Men's – Expletives', *Anthropological
    Linguistics*, XVIII/9 (1976), pp. 438–49
Baird, Lorrayne Y., 'OED Cock 20: The Limits of Lexicography of Slang',
    Maledicta, V/1–2 (1981), pp. 213–25
Baker, C. Edwin, 'Hate Speech', in *The Content and Context of Hate Speech:
    Rethinking Regulation and Responses*, ed. Michael Herz and Peter Molnar,
    Cambridge University Press (2012)
Baker, Donald C., 'An Unpublished Seventeenth-Century Epitaph and a Byronic
    Query', *Maledicta*, IV/2 (1980), p. 180
Bardis, Panos D., 'A Glossary of Homosexuality', *Maledicta*, IV/1 (1980),
    pp. 59–63
Barker, Mark, *The Writings on the Wall: A Collection of Good Old British Graffiti*,
    John Clare Books (1979)
Barrick, Mac E., 'Celebrity Sick Jokes', *Maledicta*, VI/1–2 (1982), pp. 57–62
Barton, Richard O., 'Medical *Maledicta* from San Francisco', *Maledicta*, X (1989),
    pp. 31–5
Baxter, Leslie A., and William W. Wilmot, 'Taboo Topics in Close Relationships',
    Journal of Social and Personal Relationships, II/3 (1985), pp. 253–69
Belnap, Allison G., 'Defamation of Religions: A Vague and Overbroad Theory
    that Threatens Basic Human Rights', *BYU Law Review*, DCXXXV (2010),
    pp. 635–86
Bernard, H. Russell, 'Otomi Obscene Humor', *Journal of American Folklore*,
    LXXXVIII/350 (1975), pp. 383–92
Binet, Laurence, *MSF and Srebrenica, 1993–2003*, Médecins sans Frontières (2015)
Blythe, Ronald, *The Age of Illusion: England in the Twenties and Thirties,
    1919–1940*, Faber & Faber (1963)
Bolinger, Dwight, 'Truth Is a Linguistic Question', *Language*, IL/3 (1973),
    pp. 539–50
Boon, Ton den, 'Waar komt de uitspraak "niet voor bange mensen" vandaan?',
    Trouw, 4 March 2017, www.trouw.nl
Boulton, James T., ed, *The Letters of D. H. Lawrence*, vol. I: *1901–13*, Cambridge
    University Press (2002)
Bowers, Jeffrey S., Christopher W. Pleydell-Pearce and Anne Castles, 'Swearing,
    Euphemisms, and Linguistic Relativity', *PLOS ONE*, VI/7 (2011)
Bright, W., 'Toward a Typology of Verbal Abuse: Naming Dead Kin in
    Northwestern California', *Maledicta*, III/2 (1979), pp. 177–81
Britt, Brian M., 'Curses Left and Right: Hate Speech and Biblical Tradition',
    Journal of the American Academy of Religion, LXXVIII/3 (2010),
    pp. 633–61
Britten, Matthew, 'Don't Get the Wrong End of the Stick: Lifting the Lid
    on Roman Toilet Behaviour', *Reinvention: An International Journal of
    Undergraduate Research*, VII/1 (2017), p. 1
Brodersen, K., and A. Kropp, *Fluchtafeln: Neue Funde und neue Deutungen zum
    antiken Schadenzauber*, Verlag Antike (2004)

Bronner, Simon J., 'Who Says?: A Further Investigation of Ritual Insults among White American Adolescents', *Midwestern Journal of Language and Folklore*, IV/2 (1978), pp. 53–69

Brophy, J., and E. Partridge, *Songs and Slang of the British Soldier: 1914–1918*, E. Partridge Limited, at the Scholartis Press (1930)

Brown, Kate E., and Howard I. Kushner, 'Eruptive Voices: Coprolalia, Malediction, and the Poetics of Cursing', *New Literary History*, XXXII/3 (2001), pp. 537–62

Brown, Penelope, and Stephen C. Levinson, *Politeness: Some Universals in Language Usage*, Cambridge University Press (1978)

Buckser, Andrew, 'Before Your Very Eyes: Illness, Agency, and the Management of Tourette Syndrome', *Medical Anthropology Quarterly*, XXII/2 (2008), pp. 167–92

Byron, George G. B., and Thomas Moore, *Life, Letters, and Journals of Lord Byron*, John Murray (1839)

Cawqua, Urson*, 'Two Etymons and a Query: *Gay – Fairies – Camping*', *Maledicta*, VI/1–2 (1982), pp. 224–30

Chappell, Charles, 'The Sanitized Ending of William Faulkner's *The Wild Palms*; or, Fifty Years of No Shit', *Maledicta*, XI (1995), pp. 49–58

Charles, Donald*, 'Peter Metre', *Maledicta*, V/1–2 (1981), pp. 45–6

Christopher, Richard*, 'Ethiopian Jokes', *Maledicta*, VIII (1985), pp. 37–42

——, 'Poonerisms', *Maledicta*, VII (1983), pp. 31–3

Cliteur, Paul, and Tom Herrenberg, *The Fall and Rise of Blasphemy Law*, Leiden University Press (2016)

Closson, David L., 'The Onomastics of the Rabble', *Maledicta*, I/2 (1977), pp. 215–33

Cohen, Gerald L., and Ernest Germano, '*In a Pig's Eye* and Related Expressions', *Maledicta*, IV/1 (1980), pp. 65–70

Cole, P., and J. Morgan, eds, *Syntax and Semantics*, vol. III: *Speech Acts*, Cambridge University Press (1975)

Collins, Terence, 'Self-Image through Imagery: Black Arts Poets and the Politics of Excrement', *Maledicta*, III/1 (1979), pp. 71–84

Colombo, John Robert, 'Canadian Slurs, Ethnic and Other', *Maledicta*, III/2 (1979), pp. 182–4

Conlin, Jonathan, *Adam Smith*, Reaktion Books (2016)

Conrad, Joseph, *Heart of Darkness* [1899], Everyman (1993)

Coombs, Orde M., ed., *We Speak as Liberators: Young Black Poets*, Dodd Mead (1970)

Cooper, Janet R. M., et al., 'Nursing Students' Perceptions of Bullying Behaviours by Classmates', *Issues in Educational Research*, XIX/3 (2009), pp. 212–26

Coulter, Ann, *Slander: Liberal Lies about the American Right*, Three Rivers Press (2002)

Cragg, Dan, 'Viet-Speak', *Maledicta*, VI/1–2 (1982), pp. 249–61

Crist, Clifford Mortimer, 'Lethal Limericks', *Maledicta*, IV/2 (1980), pp. 161–6

Crozier, Alan, 'Beyond the Metaphor: Cursing in Ulster', *Maledicta*, X (1989), pp. 115–25

Crystal, David, *The Cambridge Encyclopedia of Language*, Cambridge University Press (1987)

Cubberly, Norman, 'Your Mother Has Yaws: Verbal Abuse at Ulithi', *Maledicta*,
VIII (1985), pp. 154–60

Dacey, A., *The Future of Blasphemy: Speaking of the Sacred in an Age of Human
Rights*, Continuum (2012)

Darou, Wes G., 'Personality and Verbal Abuse', *Maledicta*, VII (1983), pp. 178–86

Deffenbacher, Jerry L., et al., 'The Driving Anger Expression Inventory:
A Measure of How People Express Their Anger on the Road', *Behaviour
Research and Therapy*, XL/6 (2002), pp. 717–37

Demakopoulos, Steve A., 'A Greek Gay Is a Greek Gay Is a Greek Gay . . .',
Maledicta, VI/1–2 (1982), pp. 45–51

Dictionaries of the Scots Language, www.dsl.ac.uk (accessed 6 August 2021)

Dingemanse, M., 'Redrawing the Margins of Language: Lessons from Research
on Ideophones', *Glossa*, III/1 (2018), pp. 1–30

Dorinson, Joseph, 'The Gold-Dust Twins of Marginal Humor: Blacks and Jews',
Maledicta, VIII (1985), pp. 163–92

Dunant, Sarah, ed., *The War of the Words*, Virago (1994)

Dundes, Alan, J. W. Leach and B. Özkök, 'The Strategy of Turkish Boys' Verbal
Duelling Rhymes', in John J. Gumpertz and Dell Hymes, eds, *Directions in
Sociolinguistics: The Ethnography of Communication*, Holt, Rinehart and
Winston (1972)

Edwards, Mark U. Jr, *Printing, Propaganda, and Martin Luther*, University
of California Press (1994)

Ehrenreich, Barbara, *Dancing in the Streets: A History of Collective Joy*,
Metropolitan Books (2006)

Eidinow, E., *Oracles, Curses, and Risk among the Ancient Greeks*, Oxford University
Press (2007)

Eisiminger, Sterling, 'A Continuation of a Glossary of Ethnic Slurs in American
English', *Maledicta*, IX (1988), pp. 51–61

——, 'A Glossary of Ethnic Slurs in American English', *Maledicta*, III/2 (1979),
pp. 153–74

Elias, Norbert, Über *den Prozess der Zivilisation: Soziogenetische und
psychogenetische Untersuchungen* [1939], Suhrkamp Verlag (1976)

'Elite Maledicta', *Maledicta*, VIII (1985), pp. 249–56

Ellis, John M., *Literature Lost: Social Agendas and the Corruption of the
Humanities*, Yale University Press (1997)

Enticott, Alli, 'What Do Fairness and Balance Mean in the Journalistic Context?',
www.allienticott.wordpress.com, 12 October 2016

Falassi, Alessandro, 'A Note on Two Tuscan Curses: *Dio Faust* and *Dio Mottarello*',
Maledicta, II/1–2 (1978), pp. 175–6

Fallada, Hans, *Jeder stirbt für sich allein* [1947], Aufbau Verlag (2011)

Feinberg, Leonard, 'The Great American *Shimpfmeister*: Hundred Years of
H. L. Mencken', *Maledicta*, IV/1 (1980), pp. 15–21

Feinsilver, Alexander, 'A Talmudic Curse', *Maledicta*, V/1–2 (1981), p. 270

Feldman, Harry, '*Kapekape*: Contexts of Malediction in Tonga', *Maledicta*, V/1–2
(1981), pp. 143–50

Fine, Gary Alan, 'Recurring Political Satire', *Maledicta*, VI/1–2 (1982),
pp. 71–4

——, 'Rude Words, Insults and Narration in Preadolescent Obscene Talk',
Maledicta, V/1–2 (1981), pp. 51–68

Fleming, Margaret, 'Analysis of a Four-Letter Word', *Maledicta*, I/2 (1977), pp. 173–84

Fog, Rasmus, 'Mozart's Bizarre Verbal Behavior: A Case of Tourette Syndrome?', *Maledicta*, XI (1995), pp. 59–62

Foss, Gwen, 'Domino's Pizza Jargon', *Maledicta*, XII (1996), pp. 5–24

Fowler, Karen Joy, *We Are All Completely Beside Ourselves*, Putnam (2013)

Fraser, Bruce, 'An Account of Innuendo', in Harnish 2001

——, 'Meta-Graffiti', *Maledicta*, IV/2 (1980), pp. 258–60

Frazer, James G., *The Golden Bough: A Study in Magic and Religion* [1890], Macmillan (1976)

Freedman, M. H., and E. M. Freedman, eds, *Group Defamation and Freedom of Speech: The Relationship between Language and Violence*, Greenwood Press (1995)

Freeman, Derek, *Margaret Mead and Samoa: The Making and Unmaking of an Anthropological Myth*, Harvard University Press (1983)

French, Laurence, 'Racial and Ethnic Slurs: Regional Awareness and Variations', *Maledicta*, IV/1 (1980), pp. 117–26

Friedman, Victor A., 'Macedonian Toponomastics: Popular Etymologies and Etymological Popularities', *Maledicta*, I/1 (1977), pp. 41–2

——, 'Turco-Slavica', *Maledicta*, I/2 (1977), pp. 185–8

Fussell, P., *Class: A Guide through the American Status System*, Summit (1983)

Gage, William W., ed., *Language in Its Social Setting*, Anthropological Society of Washington (1974)

Gager, J. G., and C. F. Cooper, *Curse Tablets and Binding Spells from the Ancient World*, Oxford University Press (1999)

Geltrich-Ludgate, Brigitta, 'Teenage Jokesters and Riddlers: A Profile in Parody', *Maledicta*, VII (1983), pp. 85–98

Gil, David, 'Wool and Eggs', *Maledicta*, IV/1 (1980), pp. 97–8

Giordano, M., *La parola efficace: Maledizioni, giuramenti e benedizioni nelle Grecia arcaica*, Istituti Editoriali e Poligrafici Internazionali (1999)

Goldberg, Bernard, *Bias: A CBS Insider Exposes How the Media Distort the News*, Regnery Publishing (2002)

Gray, Alasdair, *Lanark*, Canongate (1969)

Green, Toby, *A Fistful of Shells: West Africa from the Slave Trade to the Age of Revolution*, Allen Lane (2019)

Greenawalt, K., *Freedom to Offend Fighting Words: Individuals, Communities, and Liberties of Speech*, Princeton University Press (1995)

Greene, Graham, *Stamboul Train*, William Heinemann (1932)

Gregersen, Edgar A., 'A Note on English Sexual Cursing', *Maledicta*, I/2 (1977), pp. 261–8

Grice, H. P., 'Logic and Conversation' [1967], in *Syntax and Semantics*, vol. III: *Speech Acts*, ed. P. Cole and J. Morgan, Cambridge University Press (1975)

Gumpertz, John J., and Dell Hymes, eds, *Directions in Sociolinguistics: The Ethnography of Communication*, Holt, Rinehart and Winston (1972)

Haas, Mary R., 'Interlingual Word Taboos', *American Anthropologist*, New Series, LIII/3 (1951), pp. 338–44

Haiman, F. S., *Speech and Law in a Free Society*, University of Chicago Press (1970)

Hamans, Camiel, 'Between Abi and Propjes: Some Remarks about Clipping in
     English, German, Dutch and Swedish', SKASE *Journal of Theoretical Linguistics*,
     XV/2 (2018), pp. 24–59
Harnish, Robert, ed., *Perspectives on Semantics, Pragmatics and Discourse:
     A Festschrift for Ferenc Kiefer*, John Benjamins (2001)
Harris, Catherine L., Ayşe Ayçiçeği and Jean Berko Gleason, 'Taboo Words and
     Reprimands Elicit Greater Autonomic Reactivity in a First Language Than
     in a Second Language', *Applied Psycholinguistics*, XXIV/4 (2003), pp. 561–79
Head, Tom, 'History of Television Censorship', www.thoughtco.com, updated
     23 March 2019
Herpen, Marcel H. van, *Putin's Propaganda Machine: Soft Power and Russian
     Foreign Policy*, Rowman and Littlefield (2016)
Herz, Michael, and Peter Molnar, eds, *The Content and Context of Hate Speech:
     Rethinking Regulation and Responses*, Cambridge University Press (2012)
Heynick, Frank, 'Verbal Aggression in Dutch Sleeptalking', *Maledicta*, V/1–2
     (1981), pp. 285–97
Hobbes, Thomas, *Leviathan* [1651], www.gutenberg.org (2009)
Hooke, Robert, 'These to My Much Esteemed Friend, Mr Isaack Newton, at His
     Chambers in Trinity College in Cambridge' (letter), www.newtonproject.
     ox.ac.uk (1675)
Hooker, John, *Working across Cultures*, Stanford University Press (2003)
Huang, Shu-min, and D. M. Warren, 'Chinese Values as Depicted in Mandarin
     Terms of Abuse', *Maledicta*, V/1–2 (1981), pp. 105–22
Hughes, G., *Swearing: A Social History of Foul Language, Oaths and Profanity
     in English*, Blackwell (1991)
Huizinga, J., *Homo ludens*, Tjeenk Willink (1938)
Hurbon, Laënnec, *Voodoo, Truth and Fantasy*, Thames & Hudson (1995)
Huston, Nancy, 'Blasphemy in "Nouvelle France" Yesterday and Today', *Maledicta*,
     V/1–2 (1981), pp. 163–9
Huxley, Aldous, *Antic Hay*, Penguin (1948)
——, *The Devils of Loudun*, Chatto & Windus (1952)
Hymes, Dell, *Language in Culture and Society*, Harper and Row (1964)
Jackson, Bruce, 'White Dozens and Bad Sociology', *Journal of American Folklore*,
     LXXIX/312 (1966), pp. 374–7
James, Charles J., '*Heute bleibt die Klowand kalt*: Advertising, Rhymed Couplets,
     and Graffiti in German', *Maledicta*, V/1–2 (1981), pp. 298–300
Janssen, Jac. J, 'The Smaller Dâkhla Stela (Ashmolean Museum No. 1894. 107 b)',
     Journal of Egyptian Archaeology, LIV/1 (1968), pp. 165–72
Jaworski, A., 'A Note on Sexism and Insulting with Examples from Polish',
     Maledicta, VIII (1985), pp. 91–4
Jay, Timothy B., 'Doing Research with Dirty Words', *Maledicta*, I/2 (1977),
     pp. 234–56
——, *Why We Curse: A Neuro-Psycho-Social Theory of Speech*, John Benjamins (2000)
Johnson, Falk S., 'Ruined *Lady*', *Maledicta*, VII (1983), pp. 129–38
Jowett, G. S., and V. O'Donnell, *Propaganda and Persuasion*, 5th edn, Sage
     Publications (2012)
Kahneman, Daniel, *Thinking Fast and Slow*, Penguin (2011)
Karlen, Arno, 'Cherry, Fuzz, and Spiders on the Ceiling: Patterns in Slang',
     Maledicta, VI/1–2 (1982), pp. 165–8

Kauffman, Charles A., 'A Survey of Russian Obscenities and Invective Usage', *Maledicta*, IV/2 (1981), pp. 261–89

Kaye, Barbara K., and Barry S. Sapolsky, 'Taboo or Not Taboo? That Is the Question: Offensive Language on Prime-Time Broadcast and Cable Programming', *Journal of Broadcasting and Electronic Media*, LIII/1 (2009), pp. 22–37

Kehl, D. G., 'Roman Hands Gave Us the Verbal Finger: Graffiti and Literary Form', *Maledicta*, I/2 (1977), pp. 283–92

Keker, J. W., and W. L. Want, 'Offensive Speech and the FCC', *Yale Law Review*, LXXIX/7 (1970), pp. 1343–68

Kennedy, Randall, *Nigger: The Strange Career of a Troublesome Word*, Vintage Books (2003)

Kerr, David S., *Caricature and French Political Culture 1830–1848: Charles Philipon and the Illustrated Press*, Clarendon Press (2000)

King, Tabitha, 'Dump on Vulgarity', *Maledicta*, X (1989), pp. 5–13

Knightly, Phillip, *The First Casualty*, André Deutsch (1975)

Knowlton, Edgar C. Jr, '*Carajo* and Hispanic Congeners in Borrow, Byron, Ford, and Scott', *Maledicta*, IV/1 (1980), pp. 99–107

Koontz, Dean, *Cold Fire*, Putnam (1991)

Kord, Susanne, *Murderesses in German Writing, 1720–1860*, Cambridge University Press (2009)

Kunene, D. P., 'Notes on Hlonepha among Southern Sotha', *African Studies (Johannesburg)*, XVII/3 (1958), pp. 159–83

Kushner, Howard I., 'Medical Fictions: The Case of the Cursing Marquise and the (Re)Construction of Gilles de la Tourette's Syndrome', *Bulletin of the History of Medicine*, LXIX/2 (1995), pp. 224–54

Labov, William, 'The Art of Sounding and Signifying', in *Language in Its Social Setting*, ed. William W. Gage, Anthropological Society of Washington (1974)

Lakoff, Robin, *Talking Power: The Politics of Language*, Basic Books (1990)

Langerak, Annelie, 'Critici van de Thaise monarchie "verdwenen na uitlevering"', *De Telegraaf*, 10 May 2019

Langworth, Richard M., 'Democracy Is the Worst Form of Government . . .', www.richardlangworth.com, 26 June 2009

Lederer, Richard, 'A Guide to Political Mudslinging', *Maledicta*, VI/1–2 (1982), pp. 33–5

Legman, G., *No Laughing Matter: Rationale of the Dirty Joke. Second Series*, Bell (1975)

——, 'A Word for It!', *Maledicta*, I/1 (1977), pp. 9–18

Locke, John, *An Essay Concerning Human Understanding* [1690], ed. Peter H. Nidditch, Oxford University Press (1975)

Luckerhof, Casper, 'Iraanse "Angelina" de cel in voor instagram-grep', *De Volkskrant*, 8 October 2019

Luther, Martin, *On the Jews and Their Lies* [1543], Christian Nationalist Crusade (1948)

McCarthy, John J., 'Prosodic Structure and Expletive Infixation', *Language*, LVIII/3 (1982), pp. 574–90

McEnery, T., *Swearing in English: Bad Language, Purity and Power from 1586 to the Present*, Routledge (2005)

Macintyre, Ben, *The Spy and the Traitor*, Penguin (2018)

McMillan, James B., 'Infixing and Interposing in English', *American Speech*, LV/3 (1980), pp. 163–83

McPhee, Nancy, *The Complete Book of Insults*, Book Club Associates (1982)

Maher, John Peter, 'Go West, Young Man: Bulgarian Necessities', *Maledicta*, VII (1983), pp. 187–8

——, 'Thomas Crapper's WC and *Crapping Ken*: A Back-Formation and a Circumlocution', *Maledicta*, IX (1987), pp. 85–8

Mann, Charles C., *1491: New Revelations of the Americas before Columbus*, Alfred A. Knopf (2005)

——, *1493: Uncovering the New World Columbus Created*, Alfred A. Knopf (2011)

Margalith, Sanford H., 'The Peckerwood Poets: A Tribute', *Maledicta*, X (1989), pp. 137–43

Marlin, Randal, *Propaganda and the Ethics of Persuasion*, Broadview Press (2002)

Mazar, Nina, On Amir and Dan Ariely, 'The Dishonesty of Honest People: A Theory of Self-Concept Maintenance', *Journal of Marketing Research*, XLV/6 (2008), pp. 633–44

Mead, Margaret, *Coming of Age in Samoa*, William Morrow (1930)

Mengers, Douglas, 'The View from the Heights: The Language of Claiming Space in San Diego', www.academia.edu (2013)

Merry, Bruce, 'What Are Graffiti For? Folk Epigraphy and Anonymous Rhetoric', *Maledicta*, VI/1–2 (1982), pp. 101–16

Milton, John, *Areopagitica: A Speech of Mr John Milton for the Liberty of Unlicenc'd Printing, to the Parlament of England*, London (1644)

Moaveni, Azadeh, 'Escape from ISIS', www.thetimes.co.uk, 5 December 2015

Mohr, Melissa, *Holy Sh*t: A Brief History of Swearing*, Oxford University Press (2013)

——, 'The Modern History of Swearing: Where All the Dirtiest Words Come From', www.salon.com, 11 May 2013

Moller, Herbert, 'Wet Dreams and the Ejaculate', *Maledicta*, IV/2 (1981), pp. 249–51

Monnot, Michel, 'Puns in Advertising: Ambiguity as Verbal Aggression', *Maledicta*, VI/1–2 (1982), pp. 7–20

Montagu, Ashley, *The Anatomy of Swearing*, Rapp & Whiting (1967)

Morrison, James F., 'Fallout from Chernobyl: Radioactive and Irreverent Polish Humor', *Maledicta*, IX (1988), pp. 67–70

Mpang, Mukanar, and Joseph G. Foster, 'Verbal Aggression in Dinga', *Maledicta*, VIII (1985), pp. 107–16

Mulcahy, F. David, and Beverly Koniar, 'Argentinian Verbal Aggression', *Maledicta*, VI/1–2 (1982), pp. 265–89

Multatuli (Eduard Douwes Dekker), *Ideeën van Multatuli, vierde bundel, met een nawoord van J. J. Oversteegen* [1872], Querido (1986)

Murray, Stephen O., 'Ritual and Personal Insults in Stigmatized Subcultures: Gay – Black – Jew', *Maledicta*, VII (1983), pp. 189–211

Murray, Thomas E., 'Swearing as a Function of Gender in the Language of Midwestern American Students: Who Does It More, What Do They Say, When and Where Do They Do It, and Why Do They Do It?', *Maledicta*, XI (1995), pp. 139–52

Newall, Venetia, 'The Moving Spray Can: A Collection of Some Contemporary English Graffiti', *Maledicta*, IX (1988), pp. 39–47

Newton, Isaac, 'Letter to Robert Hooke, 5 February 1676', www.newtonproject. ox.ac.uk

Nežmah, Bernard, 'The Consequences of Yugoslav Wars on the Occurrence of Swearwords in the Mass Media', *Maledicta*, XII (1996), pp. 115–18

Nierenberg, Jess, 'Proverbs in Graffiti: Taunting Traditional Wisdom', *Maledicta*, VII (1983), pp. 41–58

Nilsen, Don L. F., 'SIGMA EPSILON XI: Sex in the Typical University Classroom', *Maledicta*, V/1–2 (1981), pp. 79–91

Noland, Soraya, and D. M. Warren, 'Iranian Values as Depicted in Farsi Terms of Abuse, Curses, Threats, and Exclamations', *Maledicta*, V/1–2 (1981), pp. 229–41

Nuessel, Frank, 'Ageist Language', *Maledicta*, VIII (1985), pp. 17–28

O Broin, Fiach, 'Some Examples of the Historical Insult Grievous in Contemporary Ireland', *Maledicta*, III/1 (1979), pp. 26–8

Ogier, James M., 'Sex and Violence in the Indo-European Languages', *Maledicta*, XII (1996), pp. 85–90

Ọládèjì, Níjì, 'The Language and Style of Malevolence: A Language Analysis of Yoruba *Èébú*', *Maledicta*, XII (1996), pp. 121–30

Onomasticon, Melanchthon*, 'Don't Call a Fruiterer a Fruiter (Unless He Is One)', *Maledicta*, IV/1 (1980), pp. 89–90

Oppenheimer, Joel, 'The Poetry of Porking', *Maledicta*, IX (1987), pp. 94–104

O'Reilly, Bill, and Martin Dugard, *Killing Kennedy: The End of Camelot*, Henry Holt (2012)

Packard, Vance, *The Hidden Persuaders*, D. McKay (1957)

Parekh, Bhikhu, 'Is There a Case for Banning Hate Speech?', in *The Content and Context of Hate Speech: Rethinking Regulation and Responses*, ed. Michael Herz and Peter Molnar, Cambridge University Press (2012)

Parker, Derek, and Julia Parker, *The Power of Magic*, Mitchell Beazley (1992)

Parkinson, Dilworth B., 'Egyptian Arabic Abuse', *Maledicta*, X (1989), pp. 145–61

Parris, Matthew, *Scorn, with Added Vitriol*, Hamish-Hamilton (1995)

Pattison, Mark, *Milton* [1879], Cambridge University Press (2011)

Perry, Ruth, 'A Short History of the Term Politically Correct', in *Beyond PC: Toward a Politics of Understanding*, ed. P. Aufderheide, Graywolf Press (1992)

Petropoulos, Elias, and Gershon Legman, 'Πυγμή-Φαλλός: Fist – Phallus', *Maledicta*, III/1 (1979), pp. 103–7

——, *Songs of the Greek Underworld: The Rebetika Tradition*, Saqi Books (2000)

Philippe, Robert St Vincent*, 'A Philologist's Prayer', *Maledicta*, I/1 (1977), p. 62

di Pietro, Robert J., 'On the Defamation of Italian Americans', *Maledicta*, VII (1983), pp. 75–84

Pinker, Steven, *The Language Instinct*, W. Morrow (1994)

——, *The Stuff of Thought: Language as a Window into Human Nature*, Viking (2007)

Preston, Dennis R., 'Lusty Language Learning: Confessions on Acquiring Polish', *Maledicta*, VI/1–2 (1982), pp. 117–20

Preston, Mike, 'A Sympathetic Response to Your Editor's Tribulations', *Maledicta*, I/2 (1977)

Pruitt, William R., 'Understanding Genocide Denial Legislation: A Comparative Analysis', *International Journal of Criminal Justice Sciences*, XII/2 (2017), pp. 270–84

Pullum, G. K., *The Great Eskimo Vocabulary Hoax and Other Irreverent Essays on the Study of Language*, University of Chicago Press (1991)
The Racial Slur Database, www.rsdb.org, accessed 6 August 2021
Radtke, Edgar, '*Prostituta* in Modern Italian: 1. Suffixation and the Semantic Field', *Maledicta*, I/2 (1977), pp. 201–10
Raeithel, Gert, 'Karl Marx, Maledictor', *Maledicta*, VI/1–2 (1982), pp. 29–32
Rand, Ayn, *Atlas Shrugged*, Random House (1957)
Raskin, Victor, 'The Semantics of Abuse in the *Chastushka*: Women's Bawdy', *Maledicta*, V/1–2 (1981), pp. 301–17
Razvratnikov, Boris Sukitch*, 'Elementary Georgian Obscenity', *Maledicta*, x (1989), pp. 37–42
——, 'Elementary Russian Obscenity', *Maledicta*, III/2 (1979), pp. 197–204
——, 'On Christian–Moslem Relations in the Balkans', *Maledicta*, I/1 (1977), p. 68
Reve, G. K. van het, *Vier pleidooien*, Athenaeum – Polak & Van Gennep (1972)
Rice, Ronald E., and Charles K. Atkin, *Public Communication Campaigns*, 4th edn, Sage Publications (2015)
Rowland, Beryl, 'Goats and Monkeys! A Guide to Beastly Invective', *Maledicta*, IV/2 (1981), pp. 203–12
Russ, Daniel, 'The Run Up to the Spanish American War Was Repeated in the Run Up to Iraq II', www.civilianmilitaryintelligencegroup.com (2013)
Salemi, Joseph S., 'Catullus XXXIII', *Maledicta*, x (1989), pp. 189–90
——, 'Catullus XLII', *Maledicta*, V/1–2 (1981), pp. 93–4
——, 'Catullus XCVII', *Maledicta*, III/2 (1979), pp. 259–60
Salleveldt, Henk, 'Dutch Soldiers' Latrinalia', *Maledicta*, XII (1996), pp. 49–84
Salmons, Joe, and Monica Macaulay, 'Offensive Rock Band Names: A Linguistic Testimony', *Maledicta*, x (1989), pp. 81–99
Sanders, M. S., 'Viewpoints: What Is the Significance of Crude Language during Sexual Relations?', *Medical Aspects of Human Sexuality*, III (1969), pp. 8–14
Saporta, Sol, 'Linguistic Taboos, Code-Words and Women's Use of Sexist Language: A Double Bind', *Maledicta*, x (1989), pp. 163–6
——, *Society, Language and the University: From Lenny Bruce to Noam Chomsky*, Vantage Press (1994)
Schenkel, Mark, 'Zwarte Magie jaagt Congolese kinderen de oorlog in', *De Volkskrant*, 4 August 2018
Schmid, Rudi, 'The Taxonomy of Benediction and Malediction', *Maledicta*, x (1989), pp. 240–42
Schulz, Amelia Susman, 'Swiss Swearwords: Epithets in the Alps', *Maledicta*, III/2 (1979), pp. 261–74
Searle, John, *Speech Acts: An Essay in the Philosophy of Language*, Cambridge University Press (1969)
Selth, Jeff, '*Caveat Viator*: Notes on Australian English for the Wary Traveller', *Maledicta*, VI/1–2 (1982), pp. 37–44
Semmel, B., *Imperialism and Social Reform: English Social-Imperial Thought 1895–1914*, Allen & Unwin (1960)
Semper, I. J., 'The King's English', *English Journal*, XVIII/4 (1929), pp. 307–12
Shipley, Joseph T., 'The Origin of Our Strongest Taboo-Word', *Maledicta*, I/1 (1977), pp. 23–9
Shuy, Roger W., *Creating Language Crimes*, Oxford University Press (2005)
——, *The Language of Confession, Interrogation and Deception*, Sage Publications (1998)

Sisman, Adam, *John le Carré: The Biography*, Bloomsbury (2015)

Sitwell, Edith, *Aspects of Modern Poetry*, Duckworth (1969)

Smits, Rik, 'Animal Languages Don't Exist', www.academia.edu (2019)

——, *Dawn: The Origins of Language and the Modern Human Mind*, Transaction Books (2016)

Solt, John, 'Japanese Sexual Maledicta', *Maledicta*, VI/1–2 (1982), pp. 75–81

Sprachman, Paul, 'Private Parts and Persian Insult Poetry', *Maledicta*, VI/1–2 (1982), pp. 238–48

Steiner, Roger J., 'Putting Obscene Words into the Dictionary', *Maledicta*, IV/1 (1980), pp. 23–37

Sterne, Laurence, *The Life and Opinions of Tristram Shandy* [1759–67], Penguin (1967)

Stubbe, Hannes, 'Dialectics of Brazilian Negro Proverbs', *Maledicta*, VIII (1985), pp. 59–68

Sumner, W. G., *Folkways: A Study of the Sociological Importance of Usages, Manners, Customs, Mores, and Morals*, Ginn & Co. (1906)

Swartz, Marc J., '*God Curse You, and the Curse Is that You Be What You Already Are!*: Swahili Culture, Power, and Badtalk', *Maledicta*, X (1989), pp. 209–30

Taylor, Philip M., *Munitions of the Mind: A History of Propaganda from the Ancient World to the Present Era*, Manchester University Press (1995)

Ter Laan, K., and C. Keijsper, *Multatuli Encyclopedie*, Sdu Uitgevers (1995)

Teruggi, Mario E., 'Potentiation of a Spanish Insult', *Maledicta*, V/1–2 (1981), pp. 77–8

Tse, Sou-Mee, and Tao-Lin Yu*, 'Semantic Functions of the Allegedly Obscene Particles "X" in Cantonese', *Maledicta*, IV/1 (1980), pp. 45–51

Ture, Sue*, 'Milwaukee Medical Maledicta', *Maledicta*, VIII (1985), pp. 117–18

——, 'More Milwaukee Medical Maledicta', *Maledicta*, X (1989), p. 36

Unknown, 'Union Dogs', *Maledicta*, IV/1 (1980), p. 44

Urdang, Laurence, 'You Have Only Your Asterisk', *Maledicta*, III (1979), pp. 205–7

Van Lancker, D., and J. L. Cummings, 'Expletives: Neurolinguistic and Neurobehavioral Perspectives on Swearing', *Brain Research Reviews*, XXXI/1 (1999), pp. 83–104

Van Veen, P.A.F., *Etymologisch woordenboek: De herkomst van onze woorden*, Van Dale Lexicografie (1989)

Vartija, Devin, *The Colour of Equality: Racial Classification and Natural Equality in Enlightenment Encyclopaedias*, diss., Utrecht University (2018)

'Verd*%#mme Rusland verbiedt vloeken', NRC *Handelsblad*, 6 May 2014

Verschuere, Bruno, et al., 'Registered Replication Report on Mazar, Amir, and Ariely (2008)', *Advances in Methods and Practices in Psychological Science*, I/3 (2018), pp. 299–317

Vinyoles, Joan J., 'Catalan Blasphemies', *Maledicta*, VII (1983), pp. 99–107

Von Clausewitz, C., *Vom Kriege* [1832], Nikol (2008)

'Vrancks 2018, no. 39', VRT *Television* (2018)

Warren, Dennis M., and Owusu Brempong, 'Attacking Deviations from the Norm: Poetic Insults in Bono (Ghana)', *Maledicta*, I/2 (1977), pp. 141–66

——, Tijani Abioye-Salami and Mary S. Warren, 'Yoruba Terms Denoting Individual and Social Shortcomings', *Maledicta*, III/1 (1979), pp. 39–54

Watson, A., 'Curses, Oaths, Ordeals and Trials of Animals', *Edinburgh Law Review*, I/4 (1997), pp. 420–36

Waugh, Evelyn, *Decline and Fall*, Chapman & Hall (1928)

Wescott, Roger W., 'Phonesthesis and Scatology: A Brief Résumé of Phonesthetic Devices Occurring in Obscene English Expressions', *Maledicta*, I/1 (1977), p. 65

Wesseling, H. L., *Verdeel en Heers: De deling van Afrika, 1880–1914*, Bert Bakker (1991)

Wheeler, Nicole, 'Publication Bias Is Shaping Our Perceptions of AI: Is the Media's Reluctance to Admit AI's Weaknesses Putting Us at Risk?', www.towardsdatascience.com, 1 August 2019

Wind, Robert, 'Martial XI.99', *Maledicta*, X (1989), pp. 191–2

Withuis, Jolande, 'Alleen al aan zijn woorden herken je de vijand', NRC *Handelsblad*, 7 September 2019

Yankah, Kwese, 'From Loose Abuse to Poetic Couplets: The Case of the Fante Tone Riddle', *Maledicta*, VII (1983), pp. 167–77

Želvys, Vladimir Ilyich, 'A First Look at Armenian *Maledicta*', *Maledicta*, X (1989), pp. 245–6

Zerhusen, Robert, *Detective Columbo as Theologian*, Alliance of Confessing Evangelicals (n.d.)

Zwicky, Arnold M., et al., *Studies Out in Left Field: Defamatory Essays Presented to James D. McCawley on His 33rd or 34th Birthday*, Linguistic Research (1971)

ACKNOWLEDGEMENTS

No work of substance is achieved alone. So here is my thanks to all those who, one way or another, helped me along the way, in particular Mela Beinema, Ben Haring, Jan-Albert Hootsen, Olaf Kaper, Liesbeth Koenen, who sadly passed away in 2020, László Máracz, Gerjan van Schaaik, Haldor Stefansson, Hugo Strötbaum, Giota Tsotsou and Jaap Jan de Vries. And of course Uncle Mal, the late Reinhold Aman, supreme *Schimpfer* without whose tireless efforts on his journal *Maledicta* this book could never have been written.

PHOTO ACKNOWLEDGEMENTS

The author and publishers wish to express their thanks to the below sources of illustrative material and/or permission to reproduce it. Every effort has been made to contact copyright holders; should there be any we have been unable to reach or to whom inaccurate acknowledgements have been made please contact the publishers, and full adjustments will be made to any subsequent printings. Some locations of artworks are also given below, in the interest of brevity:

Belfast Media Group: p. 151; © Bestie 2022/www.bestie-art.co.uk: p. 259; Das Bundesarchiv, Koblenz (Bild 183-J05235): p. 13; from *Le Charivari*, III/17 (17 January 1834), photo Bibliothèque nationale de France, Paris: p. 362; Cornell University Library, Division of Rare and Manuscript Collections, Ithaca, NY: p. 214 (*right*); © Ben Garrison/GrrrGraphics.com: p. 376; courtesy Dani Gove: p. 417 (*right*); Granger Historical Picture Archive/Alamy Stock Photo: p. 447; Herzog Anton Ulrich-Museum, Braunschweig: p. 214 (*left*); after Jac J. Janssen, 'The Smaller Dâkhla Stela (Ashmolean Museum No. 1894. 107 b)', *Journal of Egyptian Archaeology*, LIV/1 (August 1968): p. 49; John Frost Newspapers/Alamy Stock Photo: p. 374; Musée du Louvre, Paris: p. 365 (*far right*); Musée d'Orsay, Paris: p. 93; Museo Chiaramonti, Musei Vaticani, Vatican City: p. 365 (*centre, bottom right*); Palacio de Liria, Madrid: p. 365 (*centre, top right*); Rik Smits: pp. 27, 202 (photos StudioPortoSabbia/CafePress/Shirtcity); Science History Images/Alamy Stock Photo: p. 20; from the collection of Stanford Research into the Impact of Tobacco Advertising (SRITA)/tobacco.stanford.edu: p. 462; © Peter Vey: p. 97; Walker Art Gallery, Liverpool: p. 365 (*far left*); after Henri Wild, *Le Tombeau de Ti*, fasc. 2: *La Chapelle*, part 1 (Cairo, 1953): p. 176; from Richard Wünsch, *Sethianische Verfluchungstafeln aus Rom* (Leipzig, 1898), photo Bibliothèque nationale de France, Paris: p. 88.

Obankston, the copyright holder of the image on p. 76, and Ronhjones, the copyright holder of the image on p. 194 (bottom), have published them online under conditions imposed by a Creative Commons Attribution-ShareAlike 3.0 Unported License. premier.gov.ru, the copyright holder of the images on p. 295, has published it online under conditions imposed by a Creative Commons Attribution 4.0 International License. Readers are free to: share — copy and redistribute the material in any medium or format; adapt — remix, transform, and build upon the material for any purpose, even commercially. Under the following terms: attribution — You must give appropriate credit, provide a link to the license, and indicate if changes were made. You may do so in any reasonable manner, but not in any way that suggests the licensor endorses you or your use; share alike — If you remix, transform, or build upon the material, you must distribute your contributions under the same license as the original.

GENERAL INDEX

Page numbers in *italics* indicate illustrations

adultery 129, 301

advertising 153, 392–3, 405, 407, 418, 460–62

aggression 27, 34, 182, 354, 435

allegiance 42–3, 137, 408

allegory 330, 359

alphabet *see* script

anger 26–8, 98, 176, 195–6, 204, 226, 382, 432–4

animal signals, conventionalized *37*, *38–9*, 193

anonymity 154–5, 356, 411

anthropomorphization 58, 60

anti-authoritarian 189, 360

aphasia 40–41

apostasy 137–8, 409

appropriation 136, 218, 279, 351, 430

arousal 27–8, 30, 103, 109, 382

arts 57, 490

Aryan(s) 75, 143–4

atrocity story 389

audience 158, 219, 260, 403, 436, 439–43, 451–2, 459–60, 464

authoritarianism 143, 171, 307, 340–44, 346, 349, 352, 355, 357–8, 364, 420, 434

authorities 63, 286, 311–12, 322, 339, 346, 361, *365*

authority 70, 106, 256, 286, 296, 299, 307, 327, 339, 343, 352–3, 360, 426–7, 453–6

backstabbing myth 423–4

BBC 14–15, 196, 313-4, 325, 331, 388, 418, 469

bias 316, 321, 324, 330, 344, 386, 399, 405, 460–61

Bible 43, 66, 79, 108, 141, 301, 348

Big Data 10, 319–20, 410–12

blasphemy 13, 116, 334–72, 427

blessing, Russian 132, 203

bloody 11, 16–18, 28, 119–20, 132, 198, 205–8, 211, 310

book-burning 336–7

Book of Mormon 77, 425

bowdlerization 306, 312–13, 329, 351

brain/brains 31–3, 36, 40–41, 60, 159, 200, 256–8, 260, 317–18, 381, 434

brainwashing, subliminal 406

Buddhism 68, 145, 339, *365*

bugger 123–4

bully(ing) 155, 304, 309, 359–60, 364, 392–3, 448

camaraderie 99–100

cancel culture 314, 354

cannibal(ism) 55, 140, 146, 487

caricature 359, 361, *362*, 452, 464

Carthartic Swearing Hypothesis 39, 41

causal relations 53–4, 57, 191, 320, 366, 432–3, 436, 474–9, 485, 491

cause 54, 191, 320, 474–7

censorship 9, 12, 153, 155, 234, 307–34, 361–3, 408, 416

Charles Bonnet syndrome 59–60

Charlie 150

Charlie Hebdo 10, 13, 363, 376

charms 64

China 24, 71, 106–7, 140–41, 154, 310–11, 330, 333, 347, 425, 484

Christian(ity) 47, 62, 64, 77–8, 85, 307, 338, 396, 408

cipher *see* code
Civil Rights Act 1964 351
civil rights/liberties 241, 315, 331,
    351
civil servant/service 13, 114, 146, 307,
    364, 401
civil war
    American 134, 136, 215, 275
    English 19, 136
    Russian 243
    Spanish 416
civilians 100
civility 27, 94, 115–16, 290–91, 474
civilization process 115–17, 492
class (distinctions) 14–16, 22, 24,
    109–10, 113–17, 121, 135, 148, 184,
    187, 197, 350, 353, 397, 473
cleansing, historical/cultural 306,
    327, 329, 428
cockney 16, 111, 195
cockney rhyming slang 111, 113
code 35, 72–3, 414
code of conduct 14, 23, 100, 116, 302,
    314, 391
cognitive dissonance 352, 396, 492
coincidence 52, 54
Comanche 148
communication
    animal 34–6, 38, 157, 256
    human 34, 100, 109–10, 157–8,
    161–5, 436–7, 445–6
    ministry of 331–3
Communism 12, 407, 419, 425
complicity 103, 344, 392–3, 409–10
compliment 132, 179, 183, 186, 196,
    217–8, 293
computer 188
confessing 51, 164, 457–8
confirmation bias 395–6
confirmation bias 395–6
conspiracy (theories) 53, 168, 302,
    380, 389, 424–5, 467
conversation 22, 94, 156–9, 161–2,
    166–7, 259–61, 410, 437–8
copyright 310–11
court 24, 116, 189, 286, 311, 342, 358
court of law 42–4, 65, 111, 137, 248,
    327–8, 335, 338, 354, 370, 371,
    457, 474, 489

cultural relativism 345–6, 352, 383,
    385–6, 404, 488
curse/cursing 31, 46–9, *49*, 65, 86–7,
    88, 89–90, 98, 174–7, 199,
    203–6, 286, 304–5
    Russian 132, 203

damn 186
danse-lwa 59
debate 311, 322, 351, 404, 437–44,
    460–61, 481
decorum 23, 176, 255
defamation 341, 369–71
deference 20, 22, 108, 454
defixio *see* spell; binding
delight 28, 258
demonization 306, 328, 422–4
de-platforming 9, 307, 327, 329,
    353–4, 423
desemanticization 186–7
Devil 66, 104
dialect 110, 126, 204, 308
diplomacy 23, 153, 345
discrimination 138, 142, 150, 250
disinformation 10, 156, 170, 399–400,
    411, 417, 424
doctor 67, 95, 97, 99, 307, 382
dominance 115, 130–31, 134, 138, 144,
    279, 352, 360, 375
Domino Theory 468
downgrading 187–90
dozens, the 278
drive 19, 30, 434
dualism 492–3
dupe 182

educators 376–7
effluvia, bodily 22, 116, 181–2
elation 31, 68, 98
embarrassment 22, 100, 102–3, 260,
    304
emoji 166
emotion 11, 27–33, *37*, 39–41, 118, 158,
    192, 256, 393–4, 412–14, 430–31,
    433–4, 442, 482–3, 489–90, 493
Enigma 73
Enlightenment 50, 139, 141, 311,
    347–9, 482–3
Eskimo 148

INDEX OF NAMES

Page numbers in *italics* indicate illustrations

INDEX OF LANGUAGES

Page numbers in *italics* refer to illustrations